Excel 3 for Windows™ Bible

Excel 3 for Windows™ Bible
James G. Meade

A Division of Macmillan Computer Publishing
11711 North College, Carmel, Indiana 46032 USA

In memory of a mentor,
Ben Faneuil,
and
to Jack and Mary
and
to Sam and Eleanor

©1992 by SAMS

All rights reserved. No part of this book shall be reproduced, stored in a retrieval system, or transmitted by any means, electronic, mechanical, photocopying, recording, or otherwise, without written permission from the publisher. No patent liability is assumed with respect to the use of the information contained herein. Although every precaution has been taken in the preparation of this book, the publisher and author assume no responsibility for errors or omissions. Neither is any liability assumed for damages resulting from the use of the information contained herein. For information, address SAMS, 11711 N. College Ave., Carmel, IN 46032.

International Standard Book Number: 0-672-30092-3
Library of Congress Catalog Card Number: 91-66563

94 93 92 91   8 7 6 5 4 3 2 1

Interpretation of the printing code: the rightmost number of the first series of numbers is the year of the book's printing; the rightmost number of the second series of numbers is the number of the book's printing. For example, a printing code of 91-1 shows that the first printing of the book occurred in 1991.

Screen reproductions in this book were created by means of the program Collage Plus from Inner Media, Inc., Hollis, NH.

Printed in the United States of America

Publisher
Richard K. Swadley

Associate Publisher
Marie Butler-Knight

Managing Editor
Marjorie Hopper

Acquisitions/Development Editor
Mary-Terese Cagnina

Manuscript Editor
Linda Hawkins

Editorial Assistant
Tracy Kaufman

Cover Designer
Tim Amrhein

Designers
Scott Cook and Michele Laseau

Indexer
Johnna VanHoose

Production Team
Beth Baker, Jeff Baker, Michelle Cleary, Scott Boucher, Brook Farling, Sandy Grieshop, Audra Hershman, Betty Kish, Phil Kitchel, Bob LaRoche, Laurie Lee, Anne Owen, Juli Pavey, Howard Peirce, Kevin Spear, Lisa Wilson, Phil Worthington

Special thanks to C. Herbert Feltner and David Knispel for ensuring the technical accuracy of this book.

For to live is to function. That is all there is in living.

— *Oliver Wendell Holmes, Jr.*
Radio address on his ninetieth birthday [March 8, 1931]

Overview

1 Basic Techniques

1. Basic Excel 3.0 Features, *3*
2. Basic Worksheet Operations, *23*
3. Basic File Operations, *47*
4. Basic Macros, *57*
5. Basic Database Operations, *63*
6. Basic Charts, *73*
7. Printing, *95*

2 Advanced Techniques

8. Formulas and Functions, *109*
9. Advanced Worksheet Management, *117*
10. Advanced Database Management, *153*
11. Advanced Macros and Application Customization, *167*
12. Drawing with Graphic Objects, *201*
13. Advanced Charting, *219*
14. Analyzing, Calculating, and Using Solver, *255*
15. Using Q+E, *279*

3 Complete Reference

A. Installing Microsoft Excel for Windows, *905*
B. Keyboard and Function-Key Shortcuts, *909*

Table of Contents

I BASIC TECHNIQUES

1 BASIC EXCEL 3.0 FEATURES, 3

The Keyboard and the Mouse, 3
    Mouse Pointer Shapes, 6
    Keyboard Shortcuts with Ctrl and Alt Keys, 7
    Keyboard Shortcuts with Function Keys, 8
Menus, 8
    The Control Menu, 8
    The Menu Bar, 9
    Full Menus or Short Menus, 9
Commands, 9
    Choosing Commands, 9
    Undoing Commands, 10
    Repeating Commands, 11
    Cancelling Commands, 11
Dialog Boxes, 11
Windows, 13
    The Menus and Windows, 14
    Windows and the Mouse, 16
Help, 18
    Starting Help, 18
    Navigating in Help, 19
    Returning to Your Document, 20
    Lotus 1-2-3 Help, 21

2 BASIC WORKSHEET OPERATIONS, 23

Starting Excel, 23
    Starting Excel Under Windows with a Mouse, 23
    Starting Excel Under Windows with the Keyboard, 24
    Starting Excel Directly from DOS, 25
    Starting Excel Under OS/2, 26
The Excel Worksheet, 26
    Moving the Active Cell Around the Worksheet, 28
    Moving Around the Worksheet Without Moving the Active Cell, 29

Entering Data, 29
    Entering Text, 31
    Entering Numbers, 31
        Entering Dates and Times, 32
Formatting, 32
Formulas, 35
    Entering Formulas, 35
    Using the Point Mode, 36
Functions, 37
    Entering Functions, 37
The Toolbar, 38
    The Style Box, 39
    Outline Buttons, 39
    Auto-Sum Button, 40
    Bold and Italic Buttons, 41
    Alignment Buttons, 41
    Line, Rectangle, Oval, and Arc Tools, 42
    Selection Tool, 44
    Chart Tool, 44
    Text Box Tool, 44
    Button Tool, 45
    Camera Tool, 45

3   BASIC FILE OPERATIONS, 47

The File Menu, 47
    Save and Save As, 47
        File Formatting Options, 50
    Open, New, and Close, 53
        Open, 53
        New, 54
        Close, 55
    Delete, 55

4   BASIC MACROS, 57

Recording a Macro, 57
Running a Macro, 59
The Macro Sheet, 60

5 BASIC DATABASE OPERATIONS, 63

Creating a Database, 64
Using Data Form with Your Database, 65
   Field Values and Field Names, 66
   Moving Between Records and Between Fields, 66
   The Command Buttons, 67
      New, 67
      Delete, 67
      Restore, 67
      Find Prev, 67
      Find Next, 68
      Criteria, 68
Sorting Your Database, 69

6 BASIC CHARTS, 73

The Parts of a Chart, 73
   Data, 73
   Menu Bar, 74
   Data Marker, 74
   Data Series, 75
   Category, 75
   X-Axis and Y-Axis, 75
   Scale, 76
   Tick Marks, 76
   Legend, 76
Creating a New Chart, 76
   Creating an Embedded Chart, 77
   Creating a Chart as a Separate Document, 78
   Configuring Data on the Chart, 79
Moving and Resizing a Chart, 81
Basic Chart File Operations, 83
   Opening a Chart Saved as a Separate Document, 83
   Opening an Embedded Chart, 84
   Saving a Chart Created as a Separate Document, 84
   Saving an Embedded Chart, 85
   Closing a Chart, 85
   Deleting a Chart, 85
   Printing a Chart, 86
Choosing and Customizing Chart Types, 86
   The Gallery Menu, 86

Chart Types, 87
    Area Charts, 87
    Bar Charts, 88
    Column Charts, 89
    Line Charts, 89
    Pie Charts, 90
    Scatter Charts, 92
Legends, 92

7 PRINTING, 95

Printer Setup, 95
    Installing a New Printer, 97
Page Setup, 98
Print Preview, 101
Print, 103
    Printing in Sections, 104
        Multiple Selections, 105

II ADVANCED TECHNIQUES

8 FORMULAS AND FUNCTIONS, 109

Arithmetic Formulas, 109
    Using Cell References in Formulas, 110
Formula Operators, 110
    Arithmetic Operators, 111
    Text Operator, 111
    Comparison Operators, 112
    Reference Operators, 112
Excel Functions, 113
Troubleshooting, 115
Further Information on Functions, 116

9 ADVANCED WORKSHEET MANAGEMENT, 117

Workspace Customization, 117
Worksheet Calculations, 122
    Calculation with Displayed Values, 123
    Saving Without Calculating, 124
Importing from Other Applications, 124

Importing with the Clipboard, 124
Importing with the File Open Command, 125
Linking, 127
Linking Among Microsoft Excel Worksheets, 127
Saving Linked Worksheets, 129
Data Consolidation, 130
Consolidating Data from Lotus 1-2-3 Files, 133
Creating a Workgroup, 134
Workgroup Editing, 137
Outlining, 139
Creating the Outline, 139
Working with the Outline, 142
Clearing an Outline, 145
File Protection, 145
Protecting Documents on the Disk, 146
Creating a Read-Only Document, 148
Protecting Open Documents, 148
Running Excel on a Network, 150
Opening a Document on a Network, 151

10 ADVANCED DATABASE MANAGEMENT, 153

Creating and Setting Up a Criteria Range, 153
Computed and Comparison Criteria, 155
Using OR Logic in a Criteria Range, 156
Placing a Criteria Range in Another Worksheet, 157
Finding Records, 158
Extracting Records, 160
Extracting Records from Another Worksheet Database, 161
Editing, Adding, and Deleting Records, 162
Using Functions with a Database, 164
Q+E, 166

11 ADVANCED MACROS AND APPLICATION CUSTOMIZATION, 167

Macro Sheets, 167
Entries on the Macro Sheet, 168
Adding an Additional Macro to a Macro Sheet, 169
Macro Buttons, 170
Editing Macros, 172
Functions Available in Macro Sheets, 172
Using Cell References, 173

Using Macro Functions, 174
Testing and Debugging Macros, 176
    Using Step and Evaluate, 176
        The Step Function, 178
    Displaying Values, 178
    Macro Debugging, 179
Customizing Dialog Boxes with the Dialog Editor, 182
    Using the Dialog Editor, 183
    Placing a Dialog Box in a Macro Sheet, 187
    Using a Dialog Box in a Macro, 190
    Creating a Customized Dialog Box for a Database, 192
Running Macros Automatically and Add-in Macros, 193
    Running Macros Automatically, 194
    Add-in Macros, 194
Customizing Commands, Menus, and Menu Bars, 195
    Customizing Commands, 195
    Customizing a New Menu, 197
    Customizing a New Menu Bar, 198
    Customizing Help, 198

12 DRAWING WITH GRAPHIC OBJECTS, 201

Drawing Shapes with Special Attributes, 201
    Using the Ctrl Key for Exact Positioning, 202
    Using the Shift Key to Draw Exact Shapes, 202
    Using Ctrl and Shift Together to Combine Attributes, 203
Selecting Graphic Objects, 204
    Selecting Multiple Objects, 204
    Selecting All Objects, 204
Moving and Sizing Graphic Objects, 205
    Moving Objects, 205
    Resizing Objects, 206
    Detaching Objects from the Worksheet Cells, 206
    Locking a Graphic Object, 207
Formatting Graphic Objects, 208
    Borders, 209
    Fill, 210
        Arc Border, 210
        Arc Fill, 210
    Arrowheads on Lines, 211
Copy, Cut and Paste, Delete, 212
Layered Objects, 214
Grouped Objects, 215
Drawing on Embedded Charts, 216

13 ADVANCED CHARTING, 219

Chart Plotting, 219
   How Excel Plots Chart Data, 219
     Controlling Chart Plotting, 222
        Using Paste Special to Control Plotting, 222
Selecting Parts of a Chart, 224
Plotting Multiple Selections, 225
3-D Charts, 225
   Formatting 3-D Charts, 229
Combination: Main and Overlay Charts, 231
   Formatting Main and Overlay Charts, 232
Adding to, Editing, and Deleting Existing Chart Data Series, 234
   Adding Additional Chart Data, 234
   Adding Series from Another Chart, 235
   Using the Series Formula to Create and Edit Data Series, 236
      Creating and Editing with the Edit Series Command, 239
      Creating and Editing with the Formula Bar, 239
   Deleting Data Series, 241
   Direct Adjustment of Data Markers, 242
Customizing a Chart, 243
   Adding Objects to a Chart, 243
Formatting, 244
   Patterns Command Options, 246
   Font Command Options, 247
   Text Command Options, 247
   Scale Command Options, 248
   Legend Command Options, 249
Changing Your Default Chart Format, 249
   Reverting to the Default Chart Type, 250
Using Pictures as Data Markers, 250
Linking Chart Text to a Worksheet Cell, 251
Using Move and Size, 253

14 ANALYZING, CALCULATING, AND USING SOLVER, 255

Using the Series Command, 255
Working with Array Formulas, 258
   Creating an Array Formula, 258
   Single-Output Array Formulas, 259
   Selecting and Editing Array Formulas, 259
   Using Constants in Array Formulas, 260
   Common Array Functions, 261

Goal Seeking, 261
Iteration, 263
Using What-if Analysis in Tables, 264
    Making a One-Input Table, 264
    Making a Two-Input Table, 266
    Editing a Table, 268
Using Solver, 269
    Using the Solver Parameters Dialog Box, 269
        Starting Solver, 270
        Setting the Problem, 270
    Using the Solver Dialog Box and Printing Reports, 272
    Imposing Constraints in a Problem and the Reset Button, 273
    Using the Options Button, 275
        Saving and Reusing Solver Problems, 276
    Using Solver with Macros, 277

15 USING Q+E, 279

Installing Q+E, 280
Starting Q+E and Opening Files, 281
Joining Database Files, 284
Moving, Selecting, Zooming, and Searching, 285
    Moving, 286
    Selecting, 286
    Zooming a Field, 287
    Searching for Fields and Records, 287
Querying and Extracting, 288
    Sorting Records, 288
    Selecting Records, 288
    Formatting, 290
    Adding Computed Columns and Totals, 292
SQL Statements, 294
    Editing an SQL, 296
    Opening a Query Window with SQL, 297
Saving, 298
    Saving as a Query, 299
    Saving as a Database, 299
    Saving as Mailing Labels, 299
Querying and Editing, 300
    Using Form, 301
Creating New Databases, 302
    Editing a Database Definition, 304

Copying and Linking Q+E Data to Other Applications, 305
   Linking Excel to Q+E with an SQL Statement, 307
   Common Errors in Linking, 308
Directly Accessing Databases from Excel, 308
   Setting Up Excel, 308
   Accessing an External Database, 309
      Using Options When Opening Files, 310
   Extracting Fields and Records, 312
      Pasting Fieldnames, 312
      Extracting Records, 313
      Deleting the Data, 314
   Using SQL to Edit and Extract, 314
   Additional Macro Functions, 315
      DB.EXTRACT() and DB.EXTRACT?(), 315
      DB.GET.DATABASE(), 316
      DB.LOGON(), 317
      DB.PASTE.FIELDNAMES(), 317
      DB.SET.DATABASE(), 317
      DB.SQL.QUERY(), 318
Accessing Q+E Menu Commands Through Excel, 318
   Functions Used with the Execute Function, 319

III COMPLETE REFERENCE

A INSTALLING MICROSOFT EXCEL FOR WINDOWS, 905

Hardware Requirements, 905
Copying Your Source Disks, 906
Installing Excel, 906

B KEYBOARD AND FUNCTION-KEY SHORTCUTS, 909

Keyboard Shortcuts with the Ctrl and Alt Keys, 909
Shortcuts with the Function Keys, 912

INDEX, 915

Contents by Feature

A

Array Formulas
    Creating an Array Formula, 258
    Common Array Functions, 261
    Selecting and Editing Array Formulas, 259-260
    Single-Output Array Formulas, 259
    Using Constants in Array Formulas, 260-261

B

Buttons
    Alignment Buttons, 41
    Auto-Sum Button, 40
    Bold and Italic Buttons, 41
    Command Buttons, 67
        Criteria, 67-68
        Delete, 67
        Find Next, 68
        Find Prev, 67
        New, 67
        Restore, 67
    Macro Buttons, 170-171
    Reset Button, 273-275
    Options Button, 275-276
    Outline Buttons, 39
Button Tool, 45

C

Camera Tool, 45
Charts, 73
    Adding to, Editing, and Deleting Existing Chart Data Series, 241-242
        Adding Additional Chart Data, 224-225
        Adding Series from Another Chart, 231-232
        Deleting Data Series, 241-242
        Direct Adjustment of Data Markers, 242
        Using the Series Formula to Create and Edit Data Series, 236-239
            Creating and Editing with the Edit Series Command, 239
            Creating and Editing with the Formula Bar, 239-241

Basic Chart File Operations, 73
    Closing a Chart, 85
    Deleting a Chart, 85-86
    Opening a Chart Saved as a Separate Document, 84
    Opening an Embedded Chart, 85
    Printing a Chart, 86
    Saving a Chart Created as a Separate Document, 84
    Saving an Embedded Chart
Changing Your Default Chart Format, 249-250
    Reverting to the Default Chart Type, 249-250
Choosing and Customizing Chart Types, 86, 242, 249-250
    The Gallery Menu, 86-87
Combination: Main and Overlay Charts, 231-234, 617
    Formatting Main and Overlay Charts, 657-659
Creating a New Chart, 44
    Configuring Data on the Chart, 79
    Creating a Chart as a Separate Document, 84
    Creating an Embedded Chart, 77-78, 84
Customizing a Chart, 86, 242, 249-250
    Adding Objects to a Chart, 243-245
Formatting a Chart, 229-230
    Font Command Options, 247
    Legend Command Options, 249
    Patterns Command Options, 208
    Scale Command Options, 248-249
    Text Command Options, 247
Legends, 76, 92, 243, 249, 357-358
Linking Chart Text to a Worksheet Cell, 251-252
Moving and Resizing a Chart, 81-82
Parts of the Chart
    Category, 75
    Data, 74, 75, 79
    Data Marker, 74
    Data Series, 75
    Legend, 76
    Menu Bar, 74
    Scale, 75-76
    Tick Marks, 76, 247
    X-Axis and Y-Axis, 75-76
Plotting Charts, 219-222
    Controlling Chart Plotting, 222-224
        Using Paste Special to Control Plotting, 222-224
    How Excel Plots Chart Data, 219-222

Plotting Multiple Selections, 225
Selecting Parts of a Chart, 224-225
3-D Charts, 225-230, 468-469, 669, 679-680
    Formatting 3-D Charts, 229-230
Types of Charts, 73
    Area Charts, 87-88, 680
    Bar Charts, 88, 681
    Column Charts, 89, 681
    Line Charts, 89-90, 681
    Pie Charts, 90-91, 682
    Scatter Charts, 82, 92, 682
Using Move and Size, 81-82
Using Pictures as Data Markers, 250-252

Commands
    Cancelling Commands, 11
    Choosing Commands, 9
    Customizing Commands, 195-197
    Repeating Commands, 11, 631
    Series Command, 255-257
    Undoing Commands, 804

Customizing
    Commands, 195-197
    Help, 198-199
    New Menu, 197-198
    New Menu Bar, 197-198

D

Database
    Creating a Database, 64-65
    Creating and Setting Up a Criteria Range, 153-155
        Computed and Comparison Criteria, 154-156
        Placing a Criteria Range in Another Worksheet, 157-158
        Using OR Logic in a Criteria Range, 156
    Editing, Adding and Deleting Records, 300
    Extracting Records, 160-162
        Extracting Records from Another Worksheet Database, 160-162
    Finding Records, 158-159
    Q+E, 299
    Sorting Your Database, 69-72
    Using Data Form with Your Database, 65-69
        Command Buttons, 67
            Criteria, 67-68
            Delete, 67

     Find Next, 68
     Find Prev, 67
     New, 67
     Restore, 67
   Field Values and Field Names, 64-66
    Moving Between Records and Between Fields, 66, 286
  Using Functions with a Database, 164-166
Dialog Boxes, 11-13
  Customizing Dialog Boxes with the Dialog Editor, 182, 192-193
   Creating a Customized Dialog Box for a Database, 192-193
   Placing a Dialog Box in a Macro Sheet, 187-190
   Using a Dialog Box in a Macro, 190-192
   Using the Dialog Editor, 182-185
Drawing with Graphic Objects, 204
  Copy, Cut and Paste, Delete, 212-213
  Drawing on Embedded Charts, 216
  Drawing Shapes with Special Attributes, 201
   Using the Ctrl Key for Exact Positioning, 202
   Using the Ctrl Key and Shift Key to Combine Attributes, 203
   Using the Shift Key to Draw Exact Shapes, 201
  Formatting Graphic Objects, 208-209
   Arrow Heads on Lines, 211-212
   Borders, 209-210
    Arc Border, 210
   Fill, 210-211
    Arc Fill, 210-211
  Grouped Objects, 215-216
  Layered Objects, 214-215
  Moving and Sizing Graphic Objects, 205
   Detaching Objects from Worksheet Cells, 206
   Locking a Graphic Object, 207-208
   Moving Objects, 205
   Resizing Objects, 206
  Selecting Graphic Objects, 204
   Selecting All Objects, 204
   Selecting Multiple Objects, 204

E

Entering Data, 29
  Entering Dates and Times, 32
  Entering Numbers, 31
  Entering Text, 31

F

File Menu, 47
    Close File, 55
    Delete File, 55
    New File, 54-55
    Open File, 53-54
    Save and Save As, 47-49
        File Formatting Options, 50
Formatting, 32-34
    File Formatting Options, 50
Formulas, 35
    Array Formulas, 258
    Basic Formulas and Functions, 109-116
        Arithmetic Formulas, 109-110
            Using Cell References in Formulas, 110
    Entering Formulas, 31
    Formula Operators, 110
        Arithmetic Operators, 110
        Comparison Operators, 68, 110-112
        Reference Operators, 110
        Text Operator, 110-111
    Using the Point Mode, 36-37
Functions, 37
    Entering Functions, 37
    Excel Functions, 113-115
    Further Information on Functions, 113-115
    Troubleshooting, 115

G

Goal Seeking, 261-263, 527

H

Help
    Lotus 1-2-3 Help, 21-22
    Navigating in Help, 19-20
    Returning to Your Document, 18-19
    Starting Help, 18-19

I

Importing
    Importing with the Clipboard, 125
    Importing with the File Open Command, 125
Installing
    New Printer, 97
    Q+E, 280
Iteration, 263

J

Joining Database Files, 301

K

Keyboard
    Keyboard and Mouse, 7
    Keyboard Shortcuts, 7
        with Function Keys, 8
        with Ctrl and Alt Keys, 7

L

Linking
    Common Errors in Linking, 308
        Linking Excel to Q+E with an SQL Statement, 307, 308
    Copying and Linking Q+E Data to Other Applications, 305-307
    Linking Among Microsoft Excel Worksheets, 127-128
        Saving Linked Worksheets, 127-128
    Linking Chart Text to a Worksheet Cell, 251-252
    Linking Q+E Data to Other Applications, 305-307

M

Macros
    Add-in Macros, 179, 193-195
    Automatic Macros, 193-195
    Editing Macros, 172
        Macro Functions, 174-176
        Using Macro Functions, 174-176
        Using References, 173-174
    Macro Sheet, 167-169
        Adding an Additional Macro to a Macro Sheet, 169-170
        Entries on the Macro Sheet, 167-168

　　　　　　Macro Buttons, 170-171
　　　　　Recording a Macro, 57-59, 167-169, 715-716
　　　　　Running a Macro, 59-60, 717-718, 683
　　　　　Running Macros Automatically and Add-in Macros, 193-195, 179
　　　　　　　Add-in Macros, 179
　　　　　　　Running Macros Automatically, 193-194
　　　　　Testing and Debugging Macros, 176-181
　　　　　　　Displaying Values, 178-179
　　　　　　　Macro Debugging, 176, 179-181
　　　　　　　Using Step and Evaluate, 176-178
　　　　　　　　　The Step Function, 178
Menus
　　　　Menu, Bar, 9, 74, 728-729
　　　　Menu Bar, New, 197-199
　　　　Menu, Control, 8, 14
　　　　Menu, Full or Short, 9, 689
　　　　Menu, New, 197-199
　　　　Menus and Windows, 15, 119
Mouse
　　　　Pointer Shapes, 6-7

N

Network, Running Excel on a Network, 151
　　　　Opening a Document on a Network, 150-151
New Menu, 197-199
New Menu Bar, 197-199

O

Outlining
　　　　Creating the Outline, 39, 139-144, 677
　　　　Clearing an Outline, 145
　　　　Working with an Outline, 139-144

P

Printing, 103-104
　　　　Page Setup, 104
　　　　Printer Setup, 95
　　　　　　Installing a New Printer, 97
　　　　Printing in Sections, 104-105
　　　　Printing Multiple Selections, 104-105
　　　　Print Preview, 101

Q

Q+E, 279
    Accessing Q+E Menu Commands Through Excel, 318-319
        Functions Used with the Execute Function, 319
    Copying and Linking Q+E Data to Other Applications, 305-307
        Common Errors in Linking, 305-307
        Linking Excel to Q+E with an SQL Statement, 307-308
    Creating New Databases (with Q+E), 299
        Editing a Database Definition, 304
    Directly Accessing Databases from Excel, 308-311
        Accessing an External Database, 309-310
            Using Options When Opening Files, 299
        Additional Macro Functions, 315-318
            DB.EXTRACT and DB.EXTRACT(?), 315
            DB.GET.DATABASE, 316
            DB.LOGON, 317
            DB.PASTE.FIELDNAMES, 317
            DB.SET.DATABASE, 317, 318
            DB.SQL.QUERY, 318
        Extracting Field Names and Records, 312
            Deleting the Data, 314
            Extracting Records, 312
            Pasting Fieldnames, 312, 317
        Setting Up Excel, 318-319
        Using SQL to Edit and Extract, 296-297
    Installing Q+E, 280
    Joining Database Files, 281-283
    Linking Q+E Data to Other Applications, 305-307
        Common Errors in Linking, 308
        Linking Excel to Q+E with an SQL Statement, 305-307
    Moving, Selecting, Zooming, and Searching Q+E, 287
        Moving Q+E, 287
        Searching for Fields and Records, 287-288
        Selecting Q+E, 295
        Zooming a Field, 295
    Querying and Editing, 287
        Using Form, 288
    Querying and Extracting, 302
        Adding Computed Columns and Totals, 292-294
        Formatting, 290-292
        Selecting Records, 288-290
        Sorting Records, 288

Saving, 298-300
   Saving as a Database, 299
   Saving as Mailing Labels, 299-300
   Saving as a Query, 298
SQL Statements, 294-295
   Editing an SQL, 296-297
   Opening a Query Window with SQL, 297
Starting Q+E and Opening Files, 281-283

R

Recording a Macro, 57-59, 167-169, 715-716
Running Excel on a Network, 151
Running a Macro, 193-194
   Running Macros Automatically and Add-in Macros, 193-194
      Add-in Macros, 179, 193-195
      Running Macros Automatically, 193-194

S

Series Command, 255-257
Solver
   Iteration, 263
   Using Solver, 269-272, 528-529
      Imposing Constraints in a Problem and the Reset Button, 273-275
      Using Solver with Macros, 277-278
      Using the Options Button, 275-276
         Saving and Reusing Solver Problems, 276-277
      Using the Solver Parameters Dialog Box, 272-273, 528
         Starting Solver, 270
         Setting the Problem, 276-277
      Using the Solver Parameters Dialog Box and Printing Reports, 269-272
   Using the Series Command, 255-257
Starting Excel, 24-26
   Directly from DOS, 25
   Under OS/2, 26
   Under Windows with the Keyboard, 24
   Under Windows with the Mouse, 23-24

T

Tables
   What-if Analysis in Tables, 264
   Editing a Table, 268-269

        Making a One-Output Table, 264-266, 851-852
        Making a Two-Output Table, 264, 266-268, 852
Toolbar, 39
    Alignment Buttons, 41
    Auto-Sum Button, 40
    Bold and Italic Buttons, 41
    Button Tool, 45
    Camera Tool, 45
    Chart Tool, 44, 77
    Line, Rectangle, Oval, and Arc Tools, 92, 203
    Outline Buttons, 39
    Selection Tool, 44
    Style Box, 39
    Text Box Tool, 44

W

What-if Analysis in Tables, 264
    Editing a Table, 268-269
    Making a One-Output Table, 264-266, 851-852
    Making a Two-Output Table, 264, 266-268, 852
Windows
    And Menus, 8
    And Mouse, 3
Worksheet
    Calculations, Worksheet, 123-124
        Calculation with Displayed Values, 123-124
            Saving without Calculating, 124
    Creating Read-Only Documents, 147-148
            Protecting Open Documents, 148, 207
    Creating a Workgroup, 692
            Workgroup Editing, 137
    Data Consolidation, 130-133
            Consolidating Data from Lotus 1-2-3 Files, 130-133
        File Protection, 145-146
            Protecting Documents on the Disk, 145-146
    Importing
        Importing with the Clipboard, 125
        Importing with the File Open Command, 125
    Linking
        Linking Among Microsoft Excel Worksheets, 127-129
        Saving Linked Worksheets, 47-49
    Moving Around the Worksheet without Moving the Active Cell, 29

Moving the Active Cell Around the Worksheet, 29
Outlining
    Creating the Outline, 39, 139-144, 677
    Clearing an Outline, 145
    Working with an Outline, 139-144
Running Excel on a Network, 151
    Opening a Document on a Network, 150-151
Workspace Customization, 117-122

X–Z

X-Axis, 75-76, 360-361
Y-Axis, 75-76, 360-361
Zooming, 287

Introduction

Microsoft Excel in itself—before it became Excel for Windows—was already an amazingly powerful yet surprisingly easy-to-use spreadsheet program. Microsoft Windows in itself—without Excel running under it—was likewise an astonishingly powerful program that was also remarkably easy to use.

Combine the two and you have much more than either Excel by itself or Windows by itself. In terms of power, Excel 3 for Windows has seemingly endless capabilities—from standard worksheets and graphics and macros to such attractive features as importing Lotus 1-2-3 spreadsheets just as if they were Excel spreadsheets, charting at the click of a button, outlining in a spreadsheet as in a word processor, and custom macros and advanced functions.

In terms of ease of use, you can choose all the Excel for Windows capabilities with a click of the mouse and implement them by filling in straightforward dialog boxes. Even advanced features are readily accessible—if not downright easy—if you just proceed through them step by step.

Because Excel is so powerful, you could spend months or even years with a book like this getting to know all that it can do. On the other hand, because it is *so* easy to use, you could begin to use it quite well without reading any support materials at all—by just working your way through the tutorials and the menus. The best choice, of course, is to do something in between the extremes of reading all about the program or reading nothing. This book, on the one hand, attempts to make this easy-to-use software even easier, simply by helping you recognize and put to use the Excel tools and shortcuts. On the other hand, it can be your steadfast companion and guide as you delve into the power of Excel for Windows over the weeks and months ahead.

Aimed at intermediate to advanced Excel users, this "bible," as its name implies, is ambitious—consisting of three main parts. If one of the parts does not meet your needs, another one should. If you are new to Excel and just want to get going, Part 1, "Basic Techniques," gets you off to a good start.

If you know the basics already and want to move into advanced capabilities, you should find what you need in Part 2—"Advanced Techniques."

And if you are not looking for detailed instruction but rather for comprehensive reference information, turn to Part 3 —"Complete Reference."

Part 1, Basic Techniques

If you have been using Excel for some time, you may be able to skip over some of the chapters in Part 1. However, because almost no one is likely to be familiar with all the capabilities in such a powerful product, even advanced users will find helpful material in this beginning section.

Among the topics covered are the following:

- Starting Excel and using the menus, windows, the mouse, and Help.
- Understanding formulas and functions, and using the powerful Toolbar (new with Excel 3 for Windows).
- Performing such File operations as Open, Close, New, Save, Delete, and Save As.
- Recording and running macros, and understanding the macro sheet.
- Creating a database and sorting records in the database.
- Creating and using basic charts.
- Setting up the printer, using Print Preview, and printing in Excel.
- Getting started with Excel formulas and functions.

It is not likely that you will read all of the chapters in sequence; indeed, you don't need to in order to benefit from them. Eventually, though, you ought to become familiar with all the basic Excel capabilities by reading every chapter in Part 1.

Part 2, Advanced Techniques

Excel is remarkable—above all—for its power. When you have this kind of power at your fingertips, it is almost a crime not to use it. In Part 2, you find out about advanced capabilities and learn how to use them step-by-step.

Among the topics covered are these:

- Linking worksheets, importing from other applications, and outlining.
- Advanced database management, including extracting records and using functions with a database.
- Charting, including customizing and formatting a chart.
- Using Excel Solver.
- Using Q&E.

Turn to these advanced chapters after you know the basics and are looking for shortcuts and increased power with Excel.

Part 3, Complete Reference

The Complete Reference is an alphabetical listing of commands, functions, and related topics. It describes each Excel 3 for Windows command, tells you the sequence of menu commands to invoke it, provides examples, shows the actual steps to put it to use, and provides numerous tips, notes, and cautions. In addition, the Complete Reference is structured so that you can look up a function and immediately see what information is required to use it. General topics and features are also explained throughout.

Trademark Acknowledgments

All terms mentioned in this book that are known to be trademarks or service marks are listed below. In addition, terms suspected of being trademarks or service marks have been appropriately capitalized. SAMS cannot attest to the accuracy of this information. Use of a term in this book should not be regarded as affecting the validity of any trademark or service mark.

Lotus and 1-2-3 are registered trademarks of Lotus Development Corporation.

Microsoft, PowerPoint, and Multiplan are registered trademarks and Toolbar and Windows are trademarks of Microsoft Corporation.

Acknowledgments

I remember taking comfort once at a sign I saw in the library at Harvard University. Knowledge, it said, was not necessarily what you knew. It was knowing where to look for what you needed. In preparing this bible, I have been most fortunate in knowing where to look for what I needed.

This book has been in all respects a team effort. In many respects, I am not even the leader of the team. That distinction goes to SAMS acquisitions editor Mary-Terese Cozzola Cagnina, to whom I am deeply indebted for her vision in conceiving the project, for her gentle but firm guidance throughout, and for her overall sense of timing, which seemed to me just about perfect.

I would like to thank Scott Flanders, President of Macmillan Computer Publishing, for the opportunity to do the project. I am also indebted to manuscript editor Linda Hawkins, to the technical reviewers, to the production people, and to any others at SAMS who have participated in the project.

As for those who have helped in the actual writing, I am once again indebted to my associate Phil Magnier, who has helped me with several previous books. A spreadsheet expert, accountant, graphics expert, and writer, he is the reason that the first two sections of the book are what they are. What Phil did for the first two sections, Anne McCollum did for the reference section. A mathematician, programmer, and teacher, she went lovingly through the functions and, as far as I know, exceeded all previous efforts in explaining them.

Others who contributed to the reference section were programmer and Excel wizard Jackson Jarvis, software tutor and trainer Ellen Finkelstein, and "The Software Instructor" Kerry Bell. Michael Baxter, who has been implementing real

Excel applications as long as there has been an Excel to implement, offered guidance and troubleshooting along the way. I would also like to thank Kirk Neff for his last-minute heroics.

Above all, I want to thank my family—Nina, Molly, Ben, and Josh. And I want to thank the players on my Iowa State Bank Little League team for not knowing or caring what I did when I was not with them and for forcing me into the rites of spring in spite of myself.

PART ONE

BASIC TECHNIQUES

CHAPTER 1

BASIC EXCEL 3.0 FEATURES

This chapter reviews the basic features of Excel 3.0. Many of these features are also Windows 3.0 features. That is, the menus, the commands, the techniques for using the mouse and keyboard, the techniques for working with multiple documents, and much else in Excel 3.0 are the same as they are in Windows 3.0 and in other Windows 3.0 programs. If you already know how to use Windows 3.0, then you can work your way through a good bit of Excel without having to relearn many of these basics.

Nevertheless, even if you already know Windows 3.0, you may want to see how the familiar interface works to handle the needs of this particular spreadsheet. This chapter describes features that apply specifically to Excel. Though you may already know how to use the Windows Help files, for instance, you'll learn about a Help file unique to Excel—Help for Lotus 1-2-3 users. You will also find tips and techniques on using the program more efficiently. And while you may know how to use the keyboard instead of the mouse, you may not know the keyboard shortcuts designed specifically for Excel.

The Keyboard and the Mouse

The mouse is as essential to the graphical user interface as the menus, icons, and various buttons on the Toolbar and elsewhere on the screen. The advantage of a graphical user interface is that you can use the mouse to simply point at what you want to use, without having to know any keyboard combinations or commands.

4 Basic Techniques

 Tip: It is generally easier to select commands with the mouse when you are learning the program because you can read the menus and "point" to what you want. Once you know the program, however, the keyboard is often faster than the mouse because you can press key combinations without taking the time to move the pointer or open and read menus and submenus.

Table 1.1 summarizes operations you can do with either the keyboard or the mouse.

Table 1.1 *Operations done with either the keyboard or the mouse.*

Operation	Keyboard	Mouse
Manipulate windows	Control menu	Maximize and minimize buttons, click and drag with the mouse
Choose commands; select options from dialog boxes	To choose from menu bar, hold down Alt and press underlined letter. To choose from submenu, press underlined letter.	Point to command and click.
Move in a worksheet or chart; select cells or objects	Use the arrow keys ("movement keys") on the keypad. Hold down Shift and press movement keys to select multiple cells or objects.	Move the mouse pointer and click. Click and drag through multiple cells, or hold down Ctrl key and click on multiple cells or objects.
Work with charts	Use the arrow keys. See Chapter 6, "Basic Charts."	Click on the item to select. See Chapter 6, "Basic Charts."

Note: Some operations can only be done with the mouse. You must use the mouse to choose certain buttons from the Toolbar or to size, move, and select graphic objects on the worksheet or macro sheet.

For example, suppose you want to select the Delete command from the Excel Edit menu. To select the command with the mouse, follow these steps:

1. Click on the name of the menu in the menu bar, Edit.

   The menu containing the list of Edit commands appears, as shown in Figure 1.1.

2. Move the pointer to the command you want (Delete) and click.

Tip: Instead of clicking on the menu bar, moving the pointer, and then clicking on the command, you can click on the menu bar, drag the pointer to the command you want, and release it.

If the command has an ellipsis (...) after it, the command has a dialog box where you can supply further information for the command. See the section on dialog boxes later in this chapter. Once you have completed the dialog box, Excel carries out the command.

To choose the Delete command from the Edit menu with the keyboard, follow these steps:

1. Hold down the Alt key and press the underlined letter in the menu—the *E* in Edit.

   The menu opens.

2. This time, without holding down the Alt key, press the underlined letter in the command you want—*D* for the Delete command.

   If there is a dialog box, you see that box. Otherwise, Excel implements the command.

6 Basic Techniques

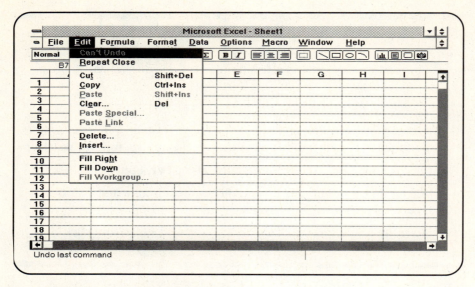

Figure 1.1   *The Edit menu in a worksheet.*

Mouse Pointer Shapes

The shape of the mouse pointer confirms that you have positioned the mouse properly or otherwise gives you information about the mouse. The shape of the mouse pointer changes depending on where you have it on the screen, as summarized here:

Shape of Mouse	*Action of Mouse*	*Location on Screen*
Basic arrow	Point and select	Menus, scroll bars, graphic objects, chart window
German cross	Click for selecting cell; drag for selecting range	Inside worksheet
Plus sign	Drag cross hairs to draw object	Inside worksheet after selection of tool from Toolbar
I-bar insertion cursor	Click into location where text is to be edited, inserted, selected	In formula bar, in text box inside dialog box

Shape of Mouse	Action of Mouse	Location on Screen
Cross with vertical arrowheads	Drag for adjusting row heights	Along borders between row headings
Cross with horizontal arrowheads	Drag for adjusting column widths	Along borders between column headings
Two white arrows: first one vertical, second one horizontal	Drag for vertical or horizontal window sizing	Along window border
Two white arrows, oblique position	Drag for simultaneous vertical and horizontal window sizing	Along corners of window borders
Horizontal arrowheads, crossed with two vertical bars	Drag to split box and divide worksheet into vertical panes	Vertical split box
Vertical arrowheads, crossed with two horizontal bars	When working with split box, drag to move box and divide worksheet into horizontal panes	Horizontal split box
4-pointed ninja throwing star	When working with horizontal and vertical split boxes together, drag to move boxes and divide worksheet window into both vertical and horizontal panes	Appears during Control Split command in upper-left corner of screen
Magnifying glass	Click to "magnify" page for easier reading	On sample page while previewing pages prior to printing

Keyboard Shortcuts with Ctrl and Alt Keys

Overall, using the keyboard can be faster than the mouse simply because you save the time that it takes to move the cursor through the menus with the mouse. In Excel, the keyboard can save considerably more time as well, because Excel has a number of keyboard shortcuts that allow you to implement commands without using the menus at all. You can also use shortcut keys to edit, move, and select documents more quickly than you can with the mouse or with standard keyboard procedures.

Combining certain keys with the Ctrl or Alt key is one type of keyboard shortcut. Sometimes key combinations substitute for menu commands. The combination Ctrl-=, for instance, is a shortcut for Options Calculate Now. For some keyboard shortcuts, there is no menu equivalent. In a chart, for example, arrow keys allow you to move through items or between classes of items. See Appendix B for a list of the shortcuts you can take using the Ctrl and Alt keys.

Keyboard Shortcuts with Function Keys

For bypassing the menus altogether (as opposed to using the keyboard to move through menus quickly), you can use function-key shortcuts. For instance, instead of clicking on the Help menu with the mouse or pressing Alt-H to open the Help menu, you can press F1. See Appendix B for a summary of the function-key shortcuts.

Menus

In Windows 3.0, commands for any program appear in menus that are located across the top of the screen. Figure 1.2, for instance, shows the menus you see in an Excel worksheet.

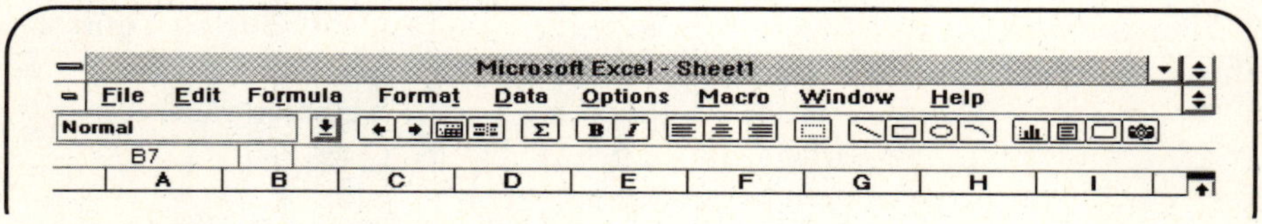

Figure 1.2   Excel worksheet menus.

The menus change depending on the document you are in. You see different menus when you are using Help, for instance, than when you are in a worksheet. Each of the three types of Excel documents—the worksheet, the macro sheet, and the chart form—has its own menu. A Control menu appears on the menu bar for each of the Excel document types.

The Control Menu

In the upper-left corner of every Windows document is a small box called the *Control menu* with commands that allow you to restore the application window to its former size, move the window using the keyboard, change the size of the window with the keyboard, maximize or minimize the window, and perform a number of other operations you are likely to find useful as you work in Windows 3.0. Below the Control menu for the application is a Control menu for the document you are using. See "Windows" later in this chapter for a full discussion of the Control menu.

The Menu Bar

The menu bar, which stretches across the top of the screen, shows the menus available. Choose a menu from the menu bar; then choose a command from the menu itself. You can choose commands from the menu bar using either the mouse or the keyboard.

Full Menus or Short Menus

You have a choice of working with either full menus or short menus. Full menus have all the commands that are on the short menus plus commands for advanced tasks. The default setting is Full Menus.

Tip: You may prefer to work with short menus while learning the system. Because you are likely to use the basic commands, not the advanced ones, the short menus may be less confusing.

To change from full to short menus, follow these steps:

1. Select the <u>O</u>ptions menu from the menu bar.
2. Choose Short <u>M</u>enus.

Commands

Issuing commands is at the heart of all your activity in the spreadsheet. Everything else you do—manipulating windows, using menus, using the mouse or the keyboard—is essentially to help you accomplish that basic activity.

Choosing Commands

To operate in a spreadsheet, you issue commands like Print and Define Name and Data Sort. In Excel, those commands appear on menus.

To choose a command, first select the menu that contains the command; then select the command itself. You can use either the keyboard or the mouse to choose commands, as explained earlier. Figure 1.1, for instance, shows the Edit menu in a worksheet window.

When a menu command has an ellipsis (...) after it, the menu item has an accompanying dialog box where you choose additional options or make other choices.

In Excel you can also choose some commands not listed on the menus by pressing the Shift key and the underlined letter in a command on the menu. Table 1.2 lists the commands you can choose with the Shift key.

Table 1.2   Shift key commands.

Menu Command	Command with Shift Key
File Menu, Close	File Menu, Close All
Edit Menu, Copy	Edit Menu, Copy Picture
Edit Menu, Fill Right	Edit Menu, Fill Left
Edit Menu, Fill Down	Edit Menu, Fill Up
Edit Menu, Paste	Edit Menu, Paste Picture
Edit Menu, Paste Link	Edit Menu, Paste Picture Link
Options Menu, Calculate Now	Options Calculate Document

Undoing Commands

Immediately after you complete some Excel commands, you have the option of undoing the command. You can undo only the last command you completed. That is, once you perform another command, you can no longer undo the previous one. Follow these steps to undo a command:

1. Select Edit from the menu bar.
2. Select Undo.

If the undo choice appears dimmed on the menu and says Can't Undo, Undo is not available for this situation.

 Tip: There are three commands you cannot undo—File Delete, Data Delete, and Data Extract. Therefore, use extra caution when applying those commands.

After you select Undo, the command on the menu changes to Redo. You can choose Redo (u) and the name of the operation that was undone from the menu or press Alt-Backspace to select the command. As with Undo, Redo is available only until you use another command.

Repeating Commands

You can repeat any command that it makes sense to repeat. For instance, if you choose Edit Clear Formulas to clear the formulas from one cell, you may want to move to another cell and repeat the command. If you format one cell in a particular way, you may want to move to another cell and repeat the formatting command. You cannot repeat commands that it would not make sense to repeat, such as Edit Clear All. (When you have cleared all once, there is nothing left to clear.) When Repeat is not available, the phrase `Can't Repeat` appears dimmed on the Edit menu.

To repeat a command using the menus, execute a repeatable command, move to the next appropriate location, and follow these steps:

1. Select the Edit menu.
2. Choose Repeat.

    For a shortcut using the keyboard, press Alt-Enter.

    You can also cancel commands or, in other words, decide not to implement them in the first place, as explained in the next section.

Cancelling Commands

There are two ways to cancel a command you have selected on the menu but have not yet implemented:

- When a command is highlighted on a menu, click anywhere outside the menu. The menu closes.
- Using the keyboard, press Esc to close the menu and cancel the command.

Dialog Boxes

Sometimes a command on a menu has an ellipsis (...) after it, which indicates that there is a dialog box for that item. As you can see in Figure 1.3, for instance, almost all the commands on the File menu have dialog boxes with them.

12 Basic Techniques

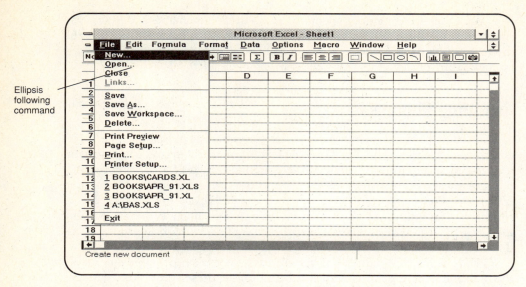

Figure 1.3 *File menu, with most commands followed by an ellipsis.*

Familiar to Windows users, dialog boxes allow you to specify additional options for a menu command. The boxes appear in a variety of forms depending on the options available. Sometimes you simply review additional information or give confirmation. At other times, you put in text or numbers or change settings for the command.

The dialog box for Format Font displays most of the dialog box elements, as shown in Figure 1.4.

Table 1.3 lists the various features of dialog boxes and describes what they do.

Table 1.3 *Dialog box features.*

Feature	Function
List box	Lists suitable choices for the command. Scroll through the list with arrow keys or mouse, or press the first letter of a selection when the list box is active.
Text box	Type in text or numbers to carry out the command. (If the box is attached to a list box, you can select from the list instead of typing in the information.)

Feature	Function
Drop-down list	Like a list box, but only the first item is displayed. To display the other items, click the arrow or press Alt-down arrow with the list active.
Option button	You can choose only one option in a group at a time. Click on the button to select or deselect it. A black dot indicates that the option is selected.
Check box	Unlike option boxes, check boxes allow multiple options to be selected at once. Click on a box to select or deselect it.
Command button	A rectangular button with a command name on it. If it is the default, it appears with a bold border. Excel will implement it if you choose OK.

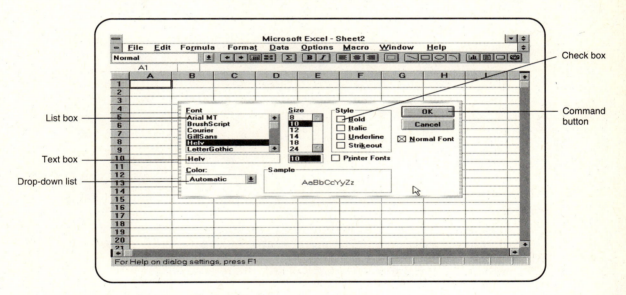

Figure 1.4 Sample dialog box.

Windows

Since "windows" appears in the very name of the application—Windows 3.0—we might expect the windowing capability in Excel to have much to do with the power of Excel. In fact, Windows does lend much power to this spreadsheet program. Thanks to Windows, you can readily work with multiple documents at once within Excel and with multiple applications in addition to Excel.

In Windows 3.0 there are two types of windows—application windows and document windows. Figure 1.5 shows the application window and the document window for an Excel worksheet.

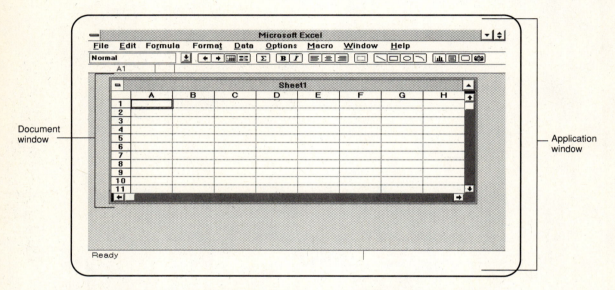

Figure 1.5 *Application window and document window for an Excel worksheet.*

The *application* window shows the menu bar at the top and is the workspace for any Windows application—Excel, PowerPoint, Word, etc. The *document* window contains the individual documents for the application. In the case of Excel, these are the worksheets, charts, and macro sheets you are working with.

You can work with Windows with either the keyboard or the mouse.

The Menus and Windows

Two menus on the Excel menu bar particularly apply to working with Windows—the Control menu, shown in Figure 1.6, and the Window menu, shown in Figure 1.7.

From the Control menu, you can resize, move, and restore the document. You can also close it.

1 — Basic Excel 3.0 Features

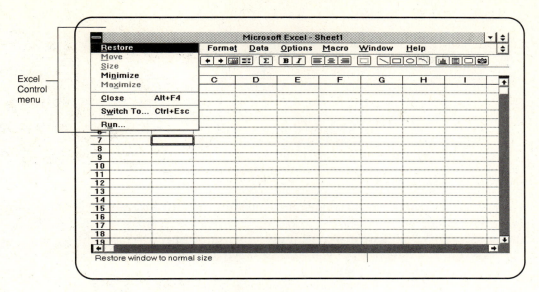

Figure 1.6 *The Excel Control menu.*

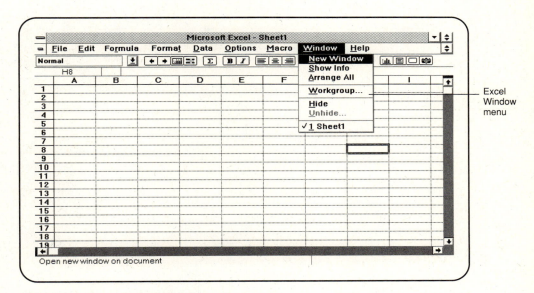

Figure 1.7 *The Excel Window menu.*

16 Basic Techniques

 Tip: To close any Excel document quickly, double-click on the Control menu.

With the Window menu, you can switch from one document window to another and also perform such operations as hiding a window and selecting a workgroup.

Windows and the Mouse

You can work with the Control and Windows menus using either the keyboard or the mouse. Though the keyboard can be faster than the mouse in some cases, the mouse adds a dimension that is not available in a spreadsheet that uses only the keyboard: You can often point at what you want and click, without having to remember keystroke combinations.

Figure 1.8 shows a blank Excel document window with callouts pointing to the parts of the window you manipulate with the mouse. Table 1.4 summarizes the window operations you can perform with the mouse.

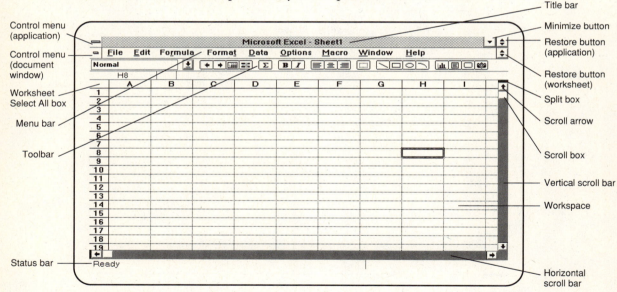

Figure 1.8   *Excel document window.*

Table 1.4 Manipulating windows with the mouse.

Feature	Function
Control menu (application)	Displays Control menu for application, with commands for changing the size of the application window, and so on
Title bar (application)	Displays the name of the application
Menu bar	Displays the names of the menus for the application
Toolbar	Displays buttons for using specific tools, such as outlining, adding, drawing, and selecting. See Chapter 2, "Basic Worksheet Operations."
Workspace	Main work area in the application, which may contain multiple document windows
Minimize button	Shrinks window to an icon
Restore button	Restores window to its previous size (before the last time you minimized or maximized it)
Control menu (document)	Displays the control menu for the document, allowing you to change the size of the document window, and so on
Title bar (document)	Displays the name of the document in the current window
Worksheet Select All box	Selects the entire worksheet (all cells)
Maximize button	Expands window to maximum size (appears as an option whenever the window is *not* maximized)
Scroll arrows	If you click on them, they move you through the worksheet one row or column at a time.
Scroll boxes	Drag them to scroll through the document. Click above or below them to move one screen at a time.
Scroll bars	Contain scroll arrows and boxes. Use to move through the document.
Split boxes	Drag with a mouse to divide a worksheet into panes

Help

To save yourself a good deal of time later on as you use Excel, you might find it worthwhile to learn how to use Excel's fine Help system. If you don't know how to use a command or option or simply want to brush up on some of its finer points, you can have Excel provide *context sensitive help*—which relates specifically to the action you're performing. Or you can go to the general Help index and choose a topic.

Starting Help

There are several ways to access Help. One is to choose it from the menu bar. (The Help menu is the last item on the menu bar.) To do this:

Mouse: Click on the Help menu and choose Index.

Keyboard: Press F1.

The first Help screen, shown in Figure 1.9, appears.

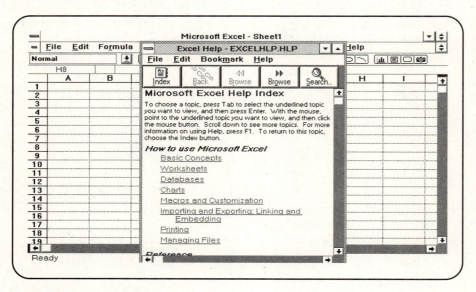

Figure 1.9 Initial Help screen.

Accessing Help in this way is ideal when you don't know exactly what information you need. However, when you want help on a specific command you are using and don't want to take the time to search for the command with the Index, follow these steps to use Excel's context-sensitive help:

1. Press Shift-F1.

   The mouse pointer turns into a question mark.

2. Move to the command you want to choose.

   Mouse: Move the mouse pointer, and click on the command you want on the menu.

   Keyboard: Choose the command by holding down Alt and pressing the underlined letter on the main menu and then pressing the underlined letter (without Alt) on the submenu.

Navigating in Help

There are several ways to navigate within Help once you are there. If you have not used context-sensitive help to begin with, you may want to use Search to move to the topic you want. Follow these steps:

1. Choose the Search button from the top of the menu.
2. In the Search dialog box, type in the topic for which you want Help. If Help does not have the exact topic, it matches your topic as closely as it can in the alphabetic listing.

You can also navigate with the other buttons at the top of the Help screen. Table 1.5 summarizes the buttons for navigating in Help.

As you read through Help, you will notice two additional ways to navigate through the help files: *jump terms* and *defined terms.* Jump terms are underlined with a solid line. Defined terms are underlined with a dotted line.

To use a jump term, do the following:

Mouse: Click on the term you want.

Keyboard: Press Tab until you reach the jump term. Press Enter.

When you choose a jump term, Help goes immediately ("jumps") to the Help on that term.

Use this procedure to choose a defined term:

Mouse: Move the pointer to the term. Hold down the left mouse button.

Keyboard: Press Tab until you reach the defined term. Hold down the Enter key.

The definition remains on the screen as long as you hold down the mouse button or Enter key.

20 Basic Techniques

Table 1.5 *Help navigation buttons.*

Button	Use to
Index (Alt-I)	Display the Help Index
Back (Alt-B)	Move back one topic at a time until you move all the way back to the Help Index
Browse << (Alt-R)	Move back one topic at a time in a series of topics
Browse >> (Alt-O)	Move forward one topic at a time in a series of related topics
Search (Alt-S)	Search through the complete list of key words for the application

Returning to Your Document

Help is actually a separate Windows application. Therefore, you can have it running in one window while you have your worksheet or another Excel application running in another. To move from one window to another, simply click on the window you want to use—Help, the Excel application, or another Windows application in another window.

You can also apply the Control menu commands—maximize, minimize, size, and so on—to the Help window, as explained in the section entitled "The Control Menu."

 Tip: You can keep Help available on the screen while you are applying the Help instructions in your document. To do that, use Windows' resizing techniques to put Help in one rectangle on the screen and the application in another rectangle right next to it, as shown in Figure 1.10. To resize with the mouse, drag the sides or corners of the window. To resize with the menus, use the Control menu.

You exit from Help the same way you exit from other Windows applications (see Chapter 5, "Basic Database Operations"): Choose File Exit.

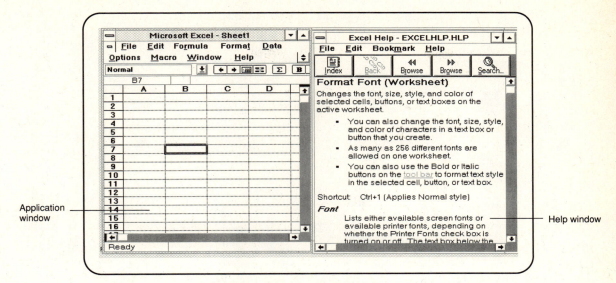

Figure 1.10 *An application window and a Help window side by side on the same screen.*

Lotus 1-2-3 Help

To make it easier for established 1-2-3 users to use Excel, Microsoft provides Lotus 1-2-3 Help, which readily tells you the Excel equivalent for any 1-2-3 command.

Follow these steps to use Lotus 1-2-3 Help:

1. From Excel choose Help.

2. From the Help menu, choose Lotus 1-2-3.

   The Lotus 1-2-3 Help dialog box appears, as shown in Figure 1.11. Instructions in the middle of the dialog box tell you how to use the box.

   First, choose either to have Help offer instructions for performing the Excel equivalent of a 1-2-3 command or to see a demo of the 1-2-3 command being implemented in Excel.

3. In the Help Options box on the dialog box, choose either Instructions or Demo. (The default is Demo.)

4. From the column labeled Menu, select one of the commands.

5. Press Enter.

22   Basic Techniques

Depending on what choice you made in step 3, Help either runs the demo or gives you instructions on performing the equivalent of any 1-2-3 command.

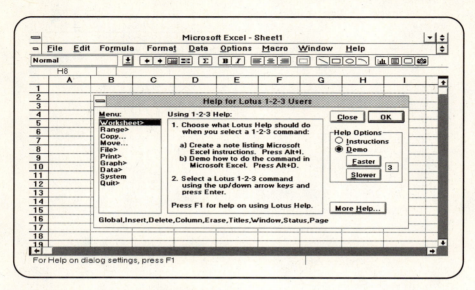

Figure 1.11   *The Lotus 1-2-3 Help dialog box.*

There is also help for Multiplan users, though it is not nearly so elaborate as that for 1-2-3. To use it, follow these steps:

1. From the Help menu, choose Multiplan.

   A dialog box appears.

2. In the dialog box, type the Multiplan command sequence.

Help tells you the equivalent Excel sequence or, if there is no exact equivalent, the closest similar task.

2
CHAPTER

Basic worksheet operations

This chapter explains basic worksheet features and functions, including what a cell is, how to move around a worksheet, how to enter text, how to format cells for numbers, the use of the formula bar, and the difference between formulas and functions.

Starting Excel

Microsoft Excel must be installed before you can start using it. Refer to Appendix A of this book to learn how to install Excel. The Install program creates a group icon in the Program Manager window in Windows. You can start Excel under Windows using your mouse or your keyboard, at the DOS prompt, or under OS/2.

Starting Excel Under Windows with a Mouse

Follow these steps to start Excel with your mouse:

1. Type **Win** at the DOS prompt to enter Windows if you are not already there.

2. Double-click on the Excel group icon.

The Excel window opens, showing up to four icons. (All four icons will be displayed if you installed all the options available.) Your screen should now look like Figure 2.1.

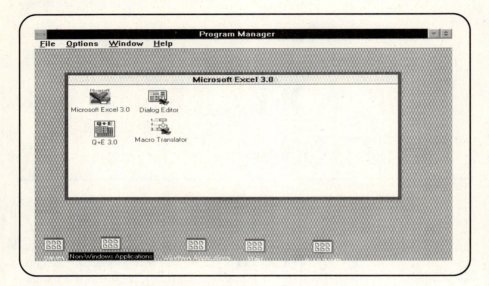

Figure 2.1 *The four options available in the Excel group window.*

3. Double-click on the Microsoft Excel 3.0 icon.

   Excel comes up in its own window and automatically opens a new worksheet for you to work on. Your screen should now look like the one shown in Figure 2.2.

Starting Excel Under Windows with the Keyboard

Follow these steps to start Excel using the keyboard:

1. Type **Win** at the DOS prompt to enter Windows if you are not already there.

2. Press Alt-W to access the Window option in the Windows menu bar.

   The Window menu drops down.

3. Press the number corresponding to Microsoft Excel 3.0 (the number to the left of the line that reads `Microsoft Excel 3.0`). This number will vary according to how many applications you have installed in Windows.

The Excel window opens, showing up to four icons. (All four icons will be displayed if you installed all the options available.) Your screen should now look like Figure 2.1. The icon labeled `Microsoft Excel 3.0` is highlighted (indicated by the blue background around the label). Use the left and right arrow keys to highlight the different icons when necessary.

4. Press Enter to start Excel.

Excel comes up in its own window and automatically opens a new worksheet for you to work on. Your screen should now look like the one shown in Figure 2.2.

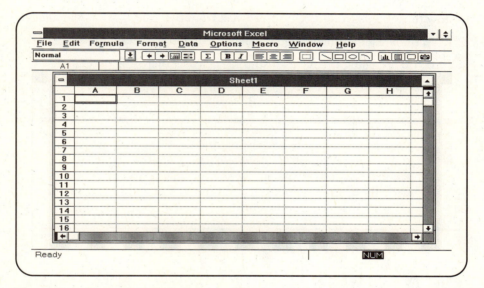

Figure 2.2 *The initial Excel screen.*

Starting Excel Directly from DOS

It's not necessary to launch Windows before you start Excel. Follow these steps to access Excel directly from the DOS prompt:

1. Access the Excel drive and directory using the CD\ command.
2. Type **Excel** and press Enter.

   This command invokes both Windows and Excel.

Tip: If a worksheet, macro sheet, or chart already exists and you know its name, you can specify it when starting Excel. Just type `Excel`, then a space, then the name of the existing sheet or chart. Excel opens with that document on screen instead of a new worksheet.

Starting Excel Under OS/2

Follow these steps to start Microsoft Excel from the Presentation Manager:

1. In the Presentation Manager, open the group that contains Excel.

2. If you are using the mouse, double-click the Microsoft Excel icon. If you are using the keyboard, press the arrow keys to select the Microsoft Excel icon, and then press Enter.

Tip: You can specify an existing document to open when starting Excel simply by double-clicking on one of the icons labeled `Worksheet`, `Macro Sheet`, or `Chart`. You can start Excel with all the documents you had open when you saved a particular workspace by double-clicking on the Workspace icon.

The Excel Worksheet

When you first launch Excel, the program automatically opens and displays a new worksheet called *Sheet1*. The worksheet, or spreadsheet, is your main workspace for entering, analyzing, and manipulating your data. Figure 2.3 shows the initial Excel display.

The worksheet is displayed in its own window called the *document window*. The name of the worksheet, *Sheet1* until you rename it, is displayed along the top of the document window in the area called the *title bar*. The worksheet is contained within the *application window*, which displays `Microsoft Excel` along its own title bar.

Excel divides each worksheet into rectangles called *cells*, which are formed by the intersection of the *rows* and *columns*. The rows are numbered down the left border, from 1 to a maximum of 16,384. The columns are identified across the top border by letters A through Z, then continuing with AA, AB, up to IV, the 256th column. Excel locates each cell by reference to the intersection of its row and column—called the *cell address*. Cell A1, for instance, is the cell in the upper left of the worksheet. The cell to its right is B1, while the cell below it is A2.

A group of cells selected together is called a *range*. If the cells are beside one another, you can use a shorthand way of referencing them (Excel uses it automatically), separating the first cell address and the last cell address with a colon. A1:F1, for instance, includes cells A1, B1, C1, D1, E1, and F1. A1:F4, for example, includes all cells on the first four rows as far right as F.

In a new worksheet, A1 is automatically made the *active cell*, as demonstrated by the heavy border around it. When a cell is the active cell, anything that you type will be entered in it. The address of the active cell appears on the left side of the applications window just above the worksheet window. This row of the applications window is called the *formula bar*.

Along the bottom of the applications window is the *status bar*, which displays information on what is happening in the worksheet. When you first open the worksheet, the status bar reads Ready, meaning that Excel is waiting for you to type in data.

You have two choices when you move around your worksheet—to move the active cell or to display another area of the worksheet without changing the active cell.

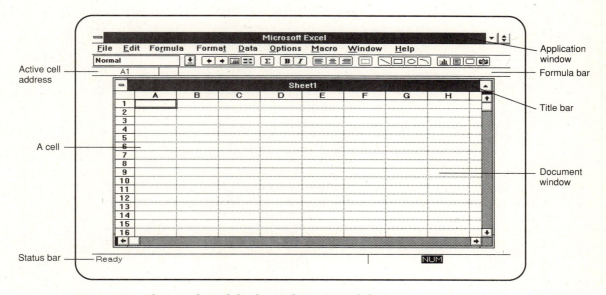

Figure 2.3 *The initial Excel display with a new worksheet.*

Moving the Active Cell Around the Worksheet

You can use several keys to move around the worksheet. The most basic are the arrow keys. Pressing an arrow key takes you one cell in the direction indicated on the key. To go to B1 from A1, for instance, you would press the right arrow key.

The Page Up and Page Down keys move the active cell up and down one worksheet page. If you press Page Down with A1 as the active cell, the cell in the first row below the window display becomes the active cell. Pressing Ctrl at the same time as Page Up or Page Down moves the active cell a page across or back rather than up or down.

Use the Scroll Lock key to take advantage of a quick way to move the active cell in a worksheet window. Press Home or End with Scroll Lock on and the active cell moves to the cell in the upper left or lower right respectively. Please note that turning on Scroll Lock causes the Page Up and Page Down keys to work differently, as explained in the next section. Table 2.1 summarizes the keystrokes for the movements.

Table 2.1   Moving the active cell.

If You Press	The Active Cell Moves
Any arrow key	One cell in the same direction
Page Up	Up one screen
Page Down	Down one screen
Ctrl-Page Up	Left one screen
Ctrl-Page Down	Right one screen
Home	To the first cell along the same row
End	To the last nonblank cell along the same row
Ctrl-right or left arrow keys	To the next nonblank cell to the right or left along the same row. If no nonblank cell exists, it moves to the last (IV) or first (A) column in this row.
Ctrl-up or down arrow keys	To the next nonblank cell up or down in the same column. If no nonblank cell exists, it moves to the last (16384) or first (1) row in this column.
Home with Scroll Lock on	To the extreme upper left of the screen
End with Scroll Lock on	To the extreme lower right of the screen

If You Press	The Active Cell Moves
Ctrl-Home with Scroll Lock on	To the first cell in the worksheet
Ctrl-End with Scroll Lock on	To the last nonblank cell in the worksheet

Moving Around the Worksheet Without Moving the Active Cell

It's not necessary to move the active cell to see the rest of the worksheet. You can use the horizontal or vertical scroll bars to display any section of the worksheet. Clicking on a scroll bar arrow moves the worksheet display one row or column in the chosen direction. Clicking on one side of either the horizontal or vertical scroll block moves the worksheet display one screen horizontally or vertically.

If you prefer using the keyboard, you can turn on Scroll Lock and then use the arrow keys to scroll one row or column, the Page Up and Page Down keys to scroll up and down one screen (or window), and the Ctrl and Page Up or the Ctrl and Page Down keys to scroll left or right one screen. Table 2.2 summarizes this information.

Table 2.2   Scrolling using the keyboard.

With Scroll Lock on, Press	And the Screen Display Scrolls
Any arrow key	One row or column up, down, or across
Page Up	One screen up
Page Down	One screen down
Ctrl-Page Up	One screen to the left
Ctrl-Page Down	One screen to the right

Entering Data

You can enter text, numbers, scientific notation, functions, and formulas in Excel worksheet cells. Anything you type is entered in the active cell. Follow these simple steps to enter data:

1. Select or move to the cell where you want to enter the data.

   The status bar along the bottom of the worksheet reads Ready.

2. Type the text, number, or formula.

   As soon as you begin typing, you are in Edit mode, which means that whatever you type appears immediately in the formula bar. Two buttons—one with an *x,* the other with a check mark—appear on the formula bar. The word Enter appears in the status bar as you type, indicating that pressing Enter will put the typed data into the cell. Figure 2.4 shows what the screen would look like if you typed the word "Sales" in cell C3.

3. Accept what you've typed by pressing Enter, one of the arrow keys, or Tab. You can also click on the check mark in the formula bar. The cell you typed in remains the active cell if you used Enter or the check mark.

Press Esc or click on the button with the *x* in the formula bar to wipe out what you've written if the cell remains the active cell. You can also use the Backspace and Delete keys to delete individual characters.

To edit a cell after accepting it, follow a similar procedure. First select it; then either click on the entry in the formula bar or press F2 on the keyboard. This brings up the I cursor in the formula bar. Make your changes after moving the cursor with either the arrow keys or the mouse pointer and accept them according to step 3.

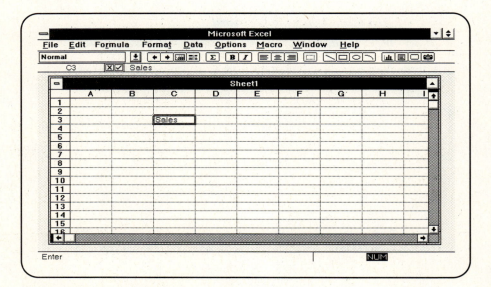

Figure 2.4 *The Excel screen after entering text.*

2 — Basic Worksheet Operations 31

Entering Text

You can enter any keyboard character as text, even numbers. When you want to enter numbers as text, type an equal sign and enclose the number in double quotes: `="123"`, for example. This is not necessary when you include any letters with the number. For example, Excel recognizes an entry like 400 W. Hempstead Avenue as text because it contains letters.

> **Note:** Check Formulas in the Display dialog box (available through Display in Options) to see formulas on the worksheet—for example, `="123"`. Uncheck the Formulas option to see the result of a formula—123 in this example. Also, when Formulas is unchecked and the cell is active, the formula is displayed in the formula bar and the outcome or result of the formula is displayed in the cell.

Excel will accept as many as 255 characters in one cell. If the text is too long for the current width of the column, Excel allows it to overlap the cell to the right when the next cell is empty. If the next cell is not empty, Excel displays as much text as it can and conceals the rest although it keeps all the characters as part of the cell contents.

Entering Numbers

Excel recognizes numbers in several different formats: as integers, as decimals, in scientific notation (for example, 2.34E+5), as dollars, as percentages, and as times and dates.

An integer is a whole number like 25, as distinct from a number with a decimal point like 333.12. Dollars and percentages are indicated by the $ and % symbols together with the number: $1003 and 47%, for example.

The maximum number of digits that can be displayed in a number cell is 15, although Excel stores the number as you enter it. For example, enter the number 1 sixteen times in one cell and it is displayed as `1.11E+15`. But any calculations involving this cell will calculate correctly. Sometimes the number is too long for even this scientific notation. Excel then displays the number symbol, #. In this case you should widen the column to correctly display the notation, for example, `1.67E+06`.

Use the minus sign or parentheses to identify negative values. If you like, include commas to separate thousands (as in $242,000); however, commas are not necessary.

Entering Dates and Times

If a number is entered using the date and time formatting, Excel recognizes the entry as a date or a time. You can then add and subtract dates in your worksheet. Use the slash (/) and hyphen (-) on the keyboard with dates and the colon (:) with time.

Table 2.3 shows the complete list of date and time formats that Excel recognizes, and includes examples of each, where *d* stands for day, *m* for month, and *y* for year.

Table 2.3 Date and time formats acceptable in Excel.

Date/Time Format	Example
m/d/yy	5/6/52
d-mmm-yy	6-MAY-52
d-mmm	6-MAY
mmm-yy	MAY-52
h:m AM/PM	6:30 AM
h:mm:ss AM/PM	6:30:35 AM
h:mm	18:30
h:mm:ss	23:03:46
m/d/yy h:mm	5/6/52 22:45

Excel does not accept nonsense dates, even if they are entered in an acceptable format. For example, 32-Feb-89 is not recognized as a date. The program stores each date as a number, with the 1st of January 1900 counted as 1 and the 31st of December 2078 counted as 65380. Any date outside this range is not recognized as a date.

Formatting

Formatting refers to the way you set up a cell to receive, interpret, and display data. At a more superficial level, it can mean choosing a font like Helvetica or Times Roman, a color, or a point size. In other words, you can set up a cell to display its contents in a more suitable way. For instance, text is often displayed prominently in bold letters when it acts as a heading for data that you want to draw attention to.

2 — Basic Worksheet Operations

Formatting can affect the cell contents in a more fundamental way also. The preceding section of this chapter discussed how Excel recognizes numbers entered in a cell as dates. The formatting of the entry—4/12/72, for example—tells Excel that these numbers represent a date.

It is also possible to format a cell before you enter anything. Excel can automatically add dollar signs, decimal points and zeros, and percentages when you enter numbers. For example, if a cell is formatted as d-mmm-yy (representing days, months, and years), you can simply enter 19120 and Excel will display it as a date, 6-May-52.

Follow these steps to format cells:

1. Select the cells to format.

2. Open the Format menu and choose Number.

   Figure 2.5 shows the Format Number dialog box.

   Table 2.4 explains the formatting symbols in the dialog box. The default choice, General, indicates that numeric values will display exactly as they are entered.

3. Scroll down to see the full range of number formatting options.

4. Click on your choice to apply it to the selected cells and then choose OK.

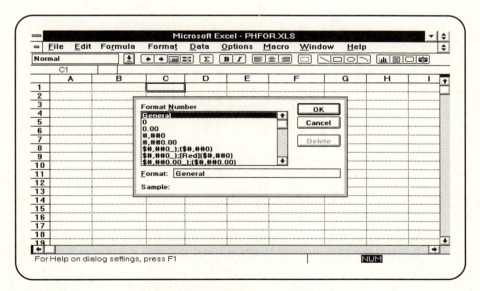

Figure 2.5 *Formatting options in the Format Number dialog box.*

Table 2.4 Formatting symbols in the Format Number dialog box.

Formatting Symbol	Application
# and 0	These formatting symbols place digits in the positions you indicate. 0 adds zeros; when used alone, it rounds to the nearest whole number. Examples: .7 typed in a cell formatted with 0.00 appears as 0.70; 9.7 typed in a cell formatted with 0 appears as 10. Examples of use of # appear below.
.	The period or decimal point symbol adds the decimal point when it's not entered. Example: use #,##0.00 and 77 displays as 77.00.
,	The comma is useful with large numbers. Example: use #,##0 and 9999 displays as 9,999.
$	Adds a dollar sign. Example: use $#,##0 and 99 displays as $99.
%	Adds the percentage symbol, and the number typed in the cell is multiplied by 100. Tip: type decimal points in the cell, not fractions (not 2/4, for example). Examples: use 0% and .25 displays as 25%; use 0% and 8 displays as 800%.
E	This is the scientific format. The menu choice is 0.00E+00. Examples: type 7 in a cell and you get 7.00E+00.; type .4 and you get 4.00E-01; type 6666 and you get 6.67E+03.
y m d h s AM/PM	Use these with date formatting. They stand for year, month, day, hour, and second. Example: use h:mm AM/PM and 7 displays as 7:00 AM.

 Note: By default, Excel stores and calculates numbers to a precision of 15 digits. If you don't need this kind of precision, check the Precision as Displayed option in the Calculation dialog box in Options and the numbers will be used to the precision of the digits on display in the cell.

Formulas

Formulas are inserted in cells like other data entries. They produce new values from the values and operators you specify. The values you specify can be constants, like the number 65, and/or cell references, like B21.

The operators can add, multiply, subtract, divide, and give the exponent of a number (for example, 5 to the power of 2 is 25). Table 2.5 shows the operators that are used in formulas.

Table 2.5   The operators used in formulas.

Operators	Description
+	Addition
*	Multiplication
–	Subtraction
/	Division
^	Exponentiation

Entering Formulas

All formulas must begin with the equal sign (=). Suppose you had a series of data like that shown in Figure 2.6.

Two fields in the example, $ per hour and Hours, multiply together to give another field called Salary. You can use a formula to perform this calculation.

Follow these steps to enter a formula:

1. Select the cell that will contain the formula.

    In the example shown in Figure 2.6, the cell is E9.

2. Type an equal sign, =, followed by the value or reference—in this case, **C9**.

3. Type the operator and any other values or cell references you want included in the formula.

    In the example, you complete your formula by adding ***D9**. The formula bar now reads =C9*D9.

4. Press Enter or click on the check mark. Excel performs the calculation.

In this case E9 now displays 400, the result of multiplying 10 and 40 together. Though the cell displays the result, the formula bar still displays the formula with values, cell references, and operators, because the actual numeric value of the cell comes from the formula. The number may change if values included in the formula change.

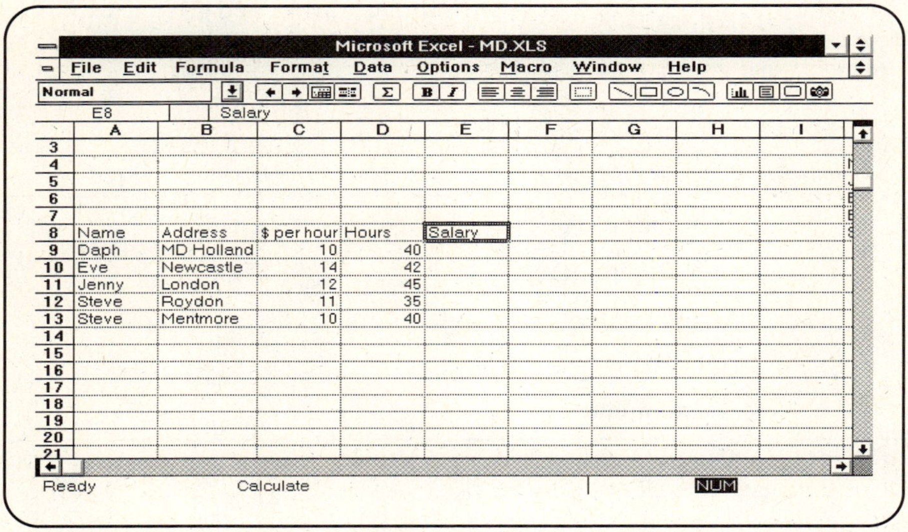

Figure 2.6   *A worksheet with cell values.*

Using the Point Mode

It's easy to make a mistake when entering a formula by accidentally specifying an incorrect cell address. Excel helps you avoid this by providing a feature called *Point mode*. Follow these steps to use Point mode:

1. Select the cell to receive the formula and type =.

    To continue with the example shown in Figure 2.6, select E10.

2. Click on the first cell to use in the formula.

    In the example, this is C10. The cell address appears in the formula bar.

3. Type the operator.

    In this case, type *, the multiplication sign.

4. Click on the second cell to use in the formula.

    In the example, this is D10.

5. Press Enter or click on the check mark and the formula is correctly entered with the result displayed in the formula cell.

 Tip: You can build formulas on top of formulas. For instance in the example, you could have another column titled *Bonus* and use it to add a fixed dollar amount like $25 to the Salary result.

Functions

The term *function* as used in Excel refers to built-in formulas that come with the program. You can access them at any time through the Formula menu. Using functions saves you the time and trouble of creating formulas yourself.

Entering Functions

You might have a row of numbers that you want to add together. You could type a formula in a cell that specifies each cell address and puts the addition sign in between each of them. An easier way is to use the SUM function. Follow these steps to use a function:

1. Select the cell to receive the function.
2. Choose Paste Function from the Formula menu.

    Excel displays the dialog box shown in Figure 2.7.

    The full list of functions, starting with ABS(), can be seen if you scroll through the scroll bar box. You can also access a function by typing in the first letter (S for SUM(), for example), which takes you to that section of the alphabetically listed functions.

3. Select the function to use and choose OK.

    The function is displayed in the formula bar, with the first argument (or component) of the formula highlighted.

4. Type in the first value or cell address in the function.

    For example if you used SUM, your formula now reads =SUM(number1,number2,...) with number1 highlighted. If you type in a cell address or value, it replaces number1. Now put in the second cell address or value to replace number2.

5. Separate your inserted values or cell addresses with a comma. Do not use any spaces.

An example of an inserted function is =SUM(B12,C12,D12,E12). You can also insert in a range format using a colon. For example, =SUM(B12:E12) is the same as =SUM(B12,C12,D12,E12).

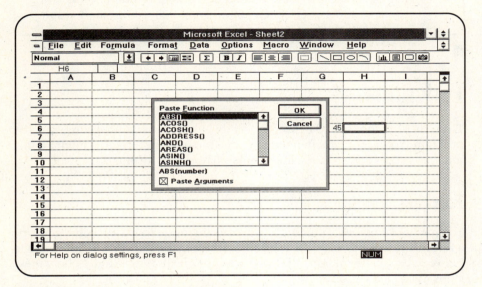

Figure 2.7 *The Paste Function dialog box.*

 Tip: If you know the format of the function, you can type it in the cell directly without accessing the Paste <u>F</u>unction command and pasting it in.

The Toolbar

Excel provides many important features in the Toolbar. Some, like the style box, provide quick ways to perform functions you can also perform through the menus; others, like the camera tool, are only available through the Toolbar. Figure 2.8 identifies the buttons and tools on the bar. You must use the mouse to access all tools and buttons.

2 — Basic Worksheet Operations 39

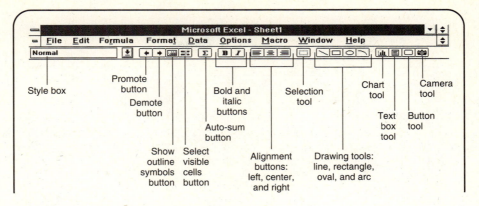

Figure 2.8   *The Toolbar buttons and tools.*

The Style Box

The style box provides a quick way to apply certain styles of formatting to selected cells. Follow these steps to use this tool:

1. Select the cell or cells you want to apply the style to.
2. Click on the down arrow to the right of the style box.

   The menu drops down showing four options: Comma, Currency, Normal, and Percent.

3. Click on an option.

Comma, Currency, and Percent apply only to numbers. Any cells with text that have these style options are treated as normal text. Figure 2.9 shows examples of Comma, Currency, and Percent. In each case the same number was inserted into the formatted cell—1000.

Outline Buttons

The four buttons to the right of the style box relate to manipulating outlines in your worksheet. The outline buttons are especially useful when a worksheet naturally divides into levels. For instance, a worksheet with sales figures might be organized into daily, weekly, and monthly sales results. Using the outline buttons, you could display only cells pertaining to daily, weekly, or monthly sales. Excel's outlining feature is explained in Chapter 9, "Advanced Worksheet Management."

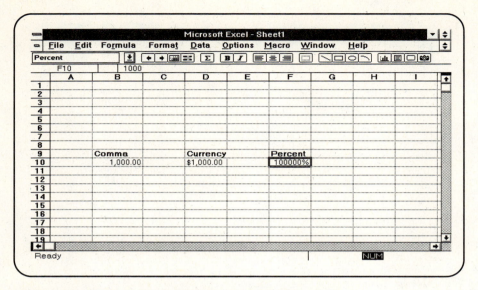

Figure 2.9 *Cells with different styles chosen from the style box.*

Auto-Sum Button

The auto-sum button inserts the SUM function in the active cell. When inserted, the SUM function looks for numbers in the cells directly above the active cell and, if it finds any, puts the cell addresses into the function automatically. If it doesn't find any numbers above the active cell, it looks for numbers in the cells to the left of the active cell. Follow these steps to use the auto-sum button:

1. Select the cell to receive the SUM function. In the example shown in Figure 2.10, the cell is I22. Cells F22 to H22 need to be added together to give the quarterly totals.

2. Click on the auto-sum button.

    In this case auto-sum finds no numbers in the cells above, so it selects the cells to the left and displays what it selected with the marquee. The marquee stops at F22 because there is a space before this cell address, at E22.

3. Press Enter or click on the check box. The function, with cell references, is inserted.

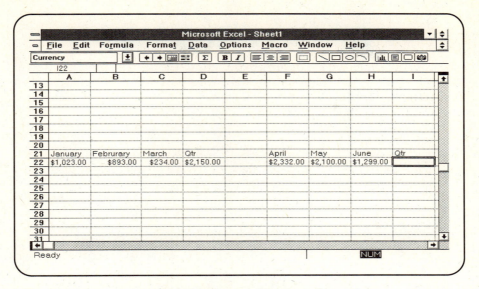

Figure 2.10 *A situation where the auto-sum button can be used.*

Bold and Italic Buttons

The bold and italic buttons speed up the procedure for making the selected cell contents display in bold and italic styles, which can also be achieved using the Font command in Format. Follow these steps to use the buttons:

1. Select the cells that you want to appear in bold or italic.

2. Click on the bold or italic button.

    Cells can be displayed in bold and italic simultaneously.

The buttons are displayed in black when bold or bold italic has been applied to the active cell. Figure 2.11 shows cells with bold, bold italic, and italic applied. The names of the months are both bold and italic, while "Qtr" is just bold and "YEAR 1991" is just italic. To turn off the bold or italic in a cell, select the cell and click on the button again.

Alignment Buttons

The three alignment buttons place the data in a cell to the left, the center, or the right—depending on which you choose. In Excel, the default alignment for text is to the left and for numbers to the right. Follow these steps to change the alignment of cells:

1. Select the cell(s) to be aligned.
2. Click on the desired alignment button.

The button to the left of the three aligns to the left, the center button to the center, and the right button to the right. Figure 2.12 shows text that has been aligned to the center.

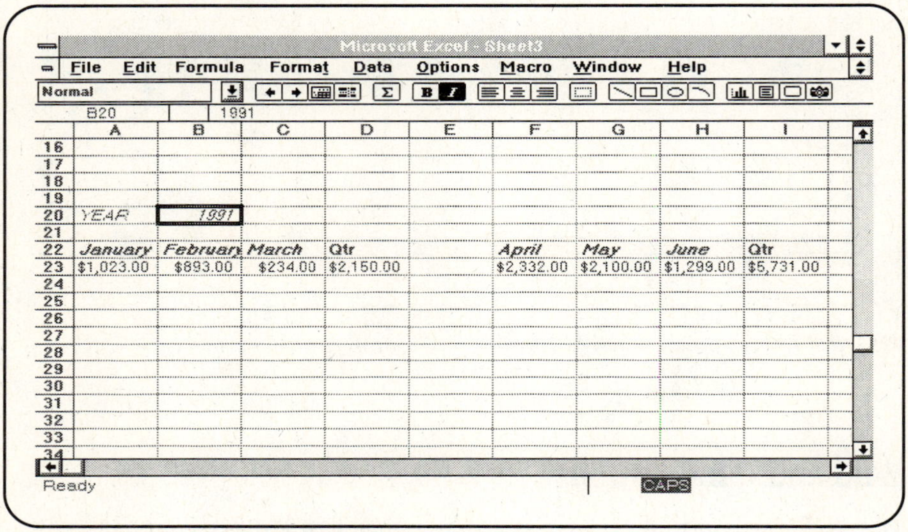

Figure 2.11 *Bold and italic styles.*

Line, Rectangle, Oval, and Arc Tools

These are the Excel drawing tools. Select a tool and Excel allows you to draw the shape shown in the button: a line, a rectangle, an oval, or an arc. Follow these steps to use the drawing tools:

1. Click on the tool you want to use. The mouse pointer takes on a cross-hatch design.
2. Place the pointer on the worksheet where you want the shape to begin.
3. Press the mouse button and drag the pointer in the direction you want the shape to go.

    The drawn object is not permanent until you release the mouse button. Move the mouse around and the drawing moves also.

4. Release the mouse button when the shape is correctly drawn.

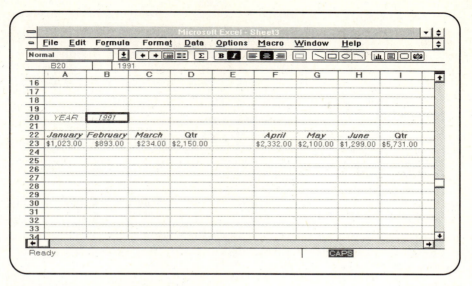

Figure 2.12   *Text aligned to the center.*

Figure 2.13 shows examples of drawings using the four shapes.

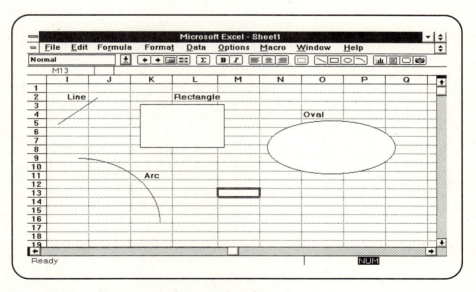

Figure 2.13   *A line, a rectangle, an oval, and an arc.*

> **Tip:** To draw shapes to specific restrictions, hold down the Shift key while drawing an object. Lines will then be drawn only vertically, horizontally, or at a 45-degree angle. Ovals will be drawn as perfectly round circles, rectangles as perfect squares, and arcs as perfect quarter circles.

Selection Tool

Use the selection tool to select objects on your screen. Objects include drawings, pictures taken by the camera tool, and text boxes created by the text box tool. Another way to select an object is to click on it. The selection tool is quicker to use when you have many objects near each other on the worksheet area. Follow these steps to use it:

1. Select the selection tool by clicking on it.
2. Place the mouse pointer above and to the left of the area containing the objects to be selected.
3. Press the mouse button and drag the pointer toward the objects.

   A rectangle with broken lines is drawn in the path of the dragging pointer.
4. Enclose the objects with the rectangle and release the mouse button.

   All objects inside the rectangle (which disappears when you release the mouse button) are now selected.

Chart Tool

The chart tool creates a chart from whatever cells are selected. Chapter 6, "Basic Charts," and Chapter 13, "Advanced Charting," have further information about this tool.

Text Box Tool

Creating text boxes of any size provides an alternative to typing text in individual cells. The advantage is that you can make the box as big as you need to fit the text. Follow these steps to create a text box:

1. Select the text box tool by clicking on it.
2. Place the mouse pointer at the starting position of the text box on the worksheet.
3. Press the mouse button and drag the pointer in the direction you want to draw the box.

   The box is not permanent until you release the mouse button. Move the mouse around and the box moves also.
4. Release the mouse button when the box is drawn as desired.

The line cursor appears in the text box when it is drawn and you can immediately type in your text.

Button Tool

The button tool enables you to place a button shape on a worksheet and to link it with a macro so that the macro is invoked when you click the button. Macros are explained in Chapter 4, "Basic Macros," and Chapter 11, "Advanced Macros and Application Customization."

Camera Tool

With the camera tool you can take a "photo" of any area of the worksheet and paste it elsewhere on the worksheet, on another Excel document, or in another application. Here are the steps:

1. Select the cells to "photograph."

   Any graphic objects on top of the cells will also be photographed; the camera tool *doesn't* work if a graphic object is selected.
2. Click on the camera tool.
3. Click on a cell in the worksheet that you want to paste to.

   This cell becomes the upper-left corner of the picture. The resulting picture can be resized as you like. To copy it to another application, just choose Copy from Edit, go to the application (Microsoft Word, for example), and paste it.

3 CHAPTER

Basic File Operations

You are probably familiar with such operations as save and delete from other applications and probably even other Windows applications. Saving, deleting, and otherwise working with files is not difficult. But if you do not save a worksheet properly, you may lose the work you put into it. And if you delete the wrong file, you may lose material that you wanted to retain. Excel's basic File operations can save you time and trouble by allowing you to do such things as save an original of a worksheet while creating a fresh copy to experiment with.

The File Menu

Each worksheet, macro sheet, and chart in Excel becomes a file when you save it. The File menu option under the word File in the upper left of the Excel screen allows you to access your files. This menu is the means for opening, closing, deleting, and performing other operations on your files as well as saving the one on the screen. In this section you learn how to use the most common functions in the File menu, which is shown in Figure 3.1.

Save and Save As

When you start Excel, a worksheet automatically appears on screen. This worksheet is not a file on your disk, however, until you save it. Follow these steps to save a file:

1. Choose Save from the File menu. Excel displays a dialog box, as shown in Figure 3.2.

48 Basic Techniques

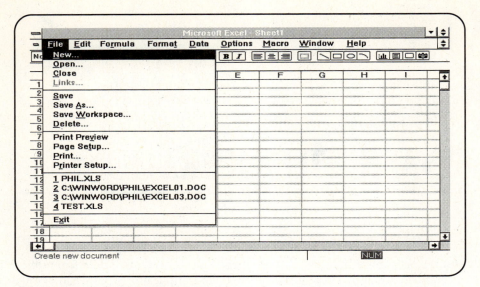

Figure 3.1   *The File menu in Excel.*

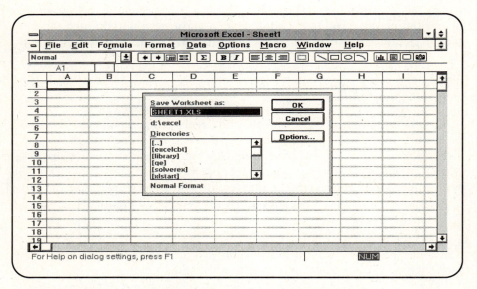

Figure 3.2   *The Save Worksheet As dialog box from the File option.*

Excel provides a default file name in the Save Worksheet As box. You can keep this name or type a new file name here to save the file. The normal DOS file name rules apply: You can use up to eight characters before the period separator and up to three after.

3 — Basic File Operations

Excel gives all of its worksheet files the .XLS extension, unless you specify otherwise. Macro sheet files have an .XLM extension, and chart files have an .XLC extension. Using these standard extensions will help you later when you identify Excel worksheets, macro sheets, and charts and want to differentiate them from other files you may have in the same directory (such as Lotus 1-2-3 .WK1 files).

2. Type up to eight characters to name the worksheet. For example, type **Test**.

   Below the name and after the current directory, you see the title `Directories`. The current directory should say something like `C:\Excel`. Any file that you save goes into the directory displayed in the dialog box.

   Change the current directories the same way as in all Windows applications. That is, move up to a higher level (for example, from the \Excel subdirectory back up to C:) by clicking twice on the [..] line in the directory box. To move into a lower subdirectory, click twice on the line showing the subdirectory name in the directory box.

3. Click on the box containing OK to save the file to disk.

   The menu box disappears.

> **Tip:** As a way to organize your "desktop," create subdirectories called XLS, XLM, and XLC within the Excel directory and save all your worksheet, macro sheet, and chart files respectively to those subdirectories.

Once you have saved the new worksheet, the designated name—Test.XLS, for example—replaces the default title, Sheet1, Sheet2, etc., at the very top of the screen.

If you had used the Save As command in the preceding steps instead of Save, it would have worked exactly the same. Save As always asks for a name. Save, on the other hand, only asks for a name the first time you save a new worksheet. After that, it automatically saves to the file on disk with the same name as that displayed at the top of the screen.

> **Tip:** Use Save As when you want to create a new worksheet similar to one already on file. Just open the existing worksheet and, as soon as it comes on screen, use the Save As option to rename the worksheet and save it to disk. Then change the worksheet as necessary. That way you keep the two worksheets on file separately.

File Formatting Options

Sometimes when you need to transfer data to other applications, you need to save a file in the format of that application. You can save your file in a different format using the Save As command, which brings up the same dialog box shown in Figure 3.2. Follow these steps to save your file in a different format:

1. Choose Save As from the File menu.

2. Choose Options.

   Excel displays a new dialog box.

3. Click on the arrow to the right of the Format box displaying Normal.

   The scroll box containing the full list of formatting options drops down, as shown in Figure 3.3. Table 3.1 describes all of these formatting options and when to use them.

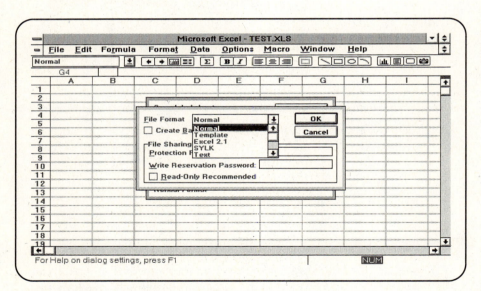

Figure 3.3 *The formatting options in Save As under File.*

Table 3.1 *The File Format options when saving.*

Option	Use
Normal	The default formatting. Use for all Excel work and for when you are linking worksheets.
Template	Saving a file that has titles or cell formatting or functions added as a template means that you can use it as a prototype when you create new files. The default extension is .XLT.
Excel 2.1	For transferring files to Microsoft Excel version 2.1 for Windows. This file formatting is also accepted by Microsoft Excel version 2.2 for OS/2. Graphic objects such as buttons, text boxes, and embedded charts do not transfer. Neither do cell border styles or outline formatting, though cell formatting is retained. The default extension is .XLS.
SYLK	Stands for symbolic linking. Use it to transfer to Macintosh version 1.5 (or earlier) applications like Multiplan or Excel. The default extension is .SLK.
Text	For transferring values to word processors. All formatting is lost. Different columns on the worksheet are separated by tabs with rows separated into paragraphs (Enters or carriage returns). When a cell contains a tab or a comma, the cell value gets double quotes around it on transfer. The default extension is .TXT.
CSV	Stands for comma separated values and is identical to the Text option, except that in the transfer, commas separate the different columns, not tabs. The default extension is .CSV.
WKS	For transferring data to Lotus 1-2-3 Release 1 or Lotus Symphony. The default extension is .WKS.
WK1	For transferring to Lotus 1-2-3 Release 2.01 and 2.2. The default extension is .WK1.
WK3	For transferring to Lotus 1-2-3 Release 3. The default extension is .WK3.
DIF	Stands for data interchange format. Use it to transfer to VisiCalc. The default extension is .DIF.

continued

Table 3.1 *continued*

Option	Use
DBF 2	For transferring a worksheet database to dBASE II. The default extension is .DBF.
DBF 3	For transferring a worksheet database to dBASE III. The default extension is .DBF.
DBF 4	For transferring a worksheet database to dBASE IV. The default extension is .DBF.
Text (Macintosh)	For transferring to a Macintosh applications
Text (OS/2 or DOS)	For transferring to an OS/2 or DOS application.
CSV (Macintosh)	For transferring to a Macintosh application.
CSV (OS/2 or DOS)	For transferring to an OS/2 or DOS application.

4. Choose a formatting option.

   The Options dialog box has certain other options you can choose to use:

   - *Create Backup File* automatically renames the old version of the file on disk with a .BAK extension every time you save the file. If you use it, you always have two versions on disk: one representing the most recent save and the other the previously saved version.

   - *Read-Only Recommended* displays a message recommending that the file be opened in read-only mode when the file is opened. You can ignore the message when you open the file. Excel does not display the message if the read-only option in the Open file dialog box is already on.

   - *Protection Password* allows you to insert a set of characters that users must type when they want to access the file.

   - *Write Reservation Password* allows users to access the file, but they must type in the password if they want to make changes and then save the file to disk.

5. Choose any option and press OK to save the file.

Open, New, and Close

Like all Windows applications, Excel allows you to have multiple files open at the same time. You cannot, however, have two copies of the same file open at the same time (unless one of the two is untitled.)

Open

Excel automatically opens a worksheet for you when you invoke Excel. Often, however, you need to open an existing worksheet. To do so, follow these steps:

1. Choose Open from the File menu.

    Excel displays the dialog box shown in Figure 3.4.

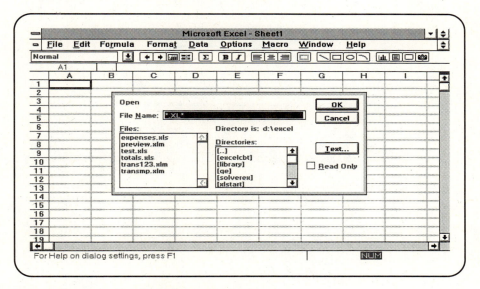

Figure 3.4   The Open dialog box under File.

The Open dialog box functions much like the Save and Save As dialog boxes. The directory is the one you specified the last time you used any of the File options (Save, etc.), C:\Excel, for example. The Files box on the left displays the *.xl* files in this directory.

The two asterisks in this file description are wild cards. This means that they can stand for any other character or characters (see Chapter 5, "Basic Database Operations," for a full explanation). So *.xl*, for example, finds all files with x and l immediately following the separator.

54 Basic Techniques

2. Choose the file to open.

    If you wish to view the file without making any changes, choose the Read Only option.

3. If you want to open a text file, choose the Text button option and make another set of choices.

    Excel displays the dialog box shown in Figure 3.5.

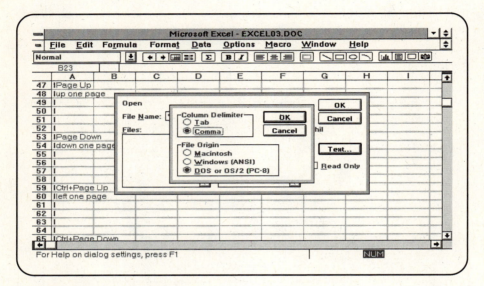

Figure 3.5 *The Text dialog box.*

Choose between Tab or Comma to determine whether Excel should use tabs or commas to divide the text between cells. Choose among Macintosh, Windows (ANSI), and DOS or OS/2 (PC-8), depending on which of the three produced the file.

4. Choose OK to exit the Text dialog box and OK again to close the dialog box and bring up the file chosen in step 2.

    The file opens and displays on your screen.

New

The steps for opening a new file and closing an active one are simple. Follow these steps to create a new worksheet, chart, or macro sheet:

1. Choose New from the File menu.

Excel displays a dialog box asking whether you want to open a new worksheet, chart, or macro sheet.

2. Choose among worksheet, chart, and macro sheet, and then choose OK.

Close

When you use the Close option in File, you close the active worksheet. Follow these steps:

1. Choose File.
2. When the File menu is displayed, choose Close.

If you have made changes since you last saved the file, Excel prompts whether you want to save the changes (for example, `Save changes in 'Sheet 1'?`). You have three options: Yes, No, or Cancel. Choose one of the first two and the file closes.

Delete

Excel gives you the opportunity to delete a file within the application rather than having to go to File Manager or DOS. Follow these simple steps:

1. Choose Delete from the File menu.

   Excel displays a dialog box showing available files and directories. Note that you cannot delete any files that are currently open.

2. Choose the directory containing the file to delete and choose the file.
3. Choose OK.

   With another dialog box, Excel asks you to confirm that you want to delete the file.

4. Choose Yes to continue the deletion, or No to cancel the deletion.

In addition to the topics discussed in this chapter, there are other choices on the File menu, such as Links and Save Workspace. You will learn about these advanced commands in Chapter 9, "Advanced Worksheet Management."

4
CHAPTER

Basic macros

Macros are sets of instructions that you can invoke with a single keystroke after you have created them. You use them mainly to make repetitive tasks easier and quicker—inserting a set of headings on a worksheet, for example, or moving columns. There are two basic types of Excel macros—*command* macros and *custom function* macros. Command macros, which are featured in this chapter, automate repetitive tasks. Chapter 11, "Advanced Macros and Application Customization," discusses the second, more sophisticated kind of macro—custom function macros, which enable you to customize special calculations and create your own menus and dialog boxes.

The following sections discuss the process of recording a command macro, running it after you have recorded it, and using the macro sheet to store it.

Recording a Macro

Before creating a macro, you should have a clear idea of what you want to record. Otherwise, you may end up putting unnecessary steps into your macro. Or you may find that you have to go back and create the macro all over again once you have figured out what you really want to do.

Figure 4.1 shows a set of titles on a worksheet. Suppose, for example, you wanted to create a macro to insert this set of titles in a worksheet without having to type it in every time. Not only would a macro do this quicker and easier, it would also lead to standardization between different worksheets, which would have exactly the same titles in the same positions. Preplanning here, as in most macros, involves deciding where to start on the worksheet—the positioning of the column and row headings—with particular regard to where the user will input values under these titles, and the formatting of the titles. In the example, the sales figures would be inputted in cells B18 to G18.

58 Basic Techniques

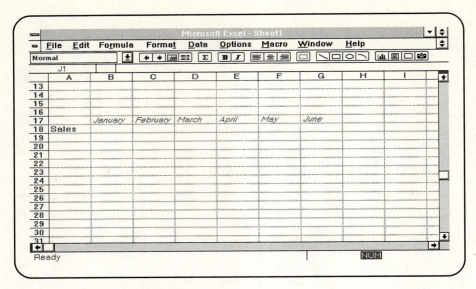

Figure 4.1 Titles on a worksheet.

Follow these steps to create a macro:

1. Choose Re**c**ord from the **M**acro menu.

   Excel displays the dialog box shown in Figure 4.2.

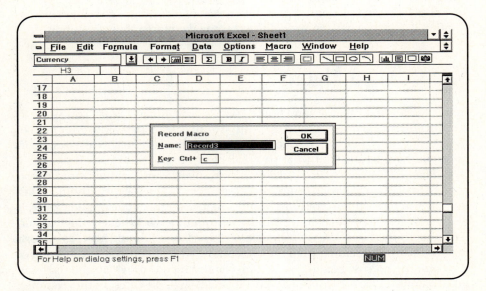

Figure 4.2 The Macro Record dialog box.

In this dialog box, you must provide Excel with two pieces of information: the name of the macro and the key combination you will use to invoke it. Excel supplies you with default names and key combinations, which you can accept or change. You may prefer to formulate names and key combinations that remind you of what the macro does. When choosing a key combination, you must always use Ctrl in conjunction with a letter. You actually have a total of 52 possible keys from which to select a macro name because Excel distinguishes between capital and lowercase letters.

2. Accept the default name and key, or type in a new name and/or key.

   The box disappears and Excel returns you to the worksheet.

3. Execute all the individual steps you want the macro to perform.

   In the example in Figure 4.1, you would type the headings in the different columns, *January, February,* etc., in italics and the word *Sales* in bold; then you would format the columns (the empty cells underneath January, February, etc.) in the currency format.

4. When you have completed the steps, choose Stop Recorder from the Macro menu.

   You have now recorded the macro, and you can instruct Excel to repeat the keystrokes for you automatically at any time simply by running the macro.

Running a Macro

After you create a macro, you can run it in two ways: through the Run option or by pressing the key combination you selected when you recorded the macro. Follow these steps to access a macro using the menu system:

1. Choose Run from the Macro menu.

   Excel displays the dialog box shown in Figure 4.3.

   This dialog box displays the macros present in every macro sheet that is open. (Macro sheets are discussed in the next section.) Only when a macro sheet is open can you access its macros. In Figure 4.3, for instance, two macro sheets are open: Macro3 and WCCLIENT. Both contain two or more macros with each displayed individually.

2. Click on the macro you want to run; the full reference name appears in the reference box. Or, you can type in the full reference name yourself, dividing the sheet and macro names by an exclamation mark: Macro3!Record3, for example.

3. Choose OK to run the macro.

60 Basic Techniques

Chapter 11 demonstrates how you can use the Step option to perform one instruction of the macro at a time.

To the left of the macro name, the Run dialog box displays the key letter that in combination with Ctrl invokes the macro. Press Ctrl and this letter at the same time to run the macro.

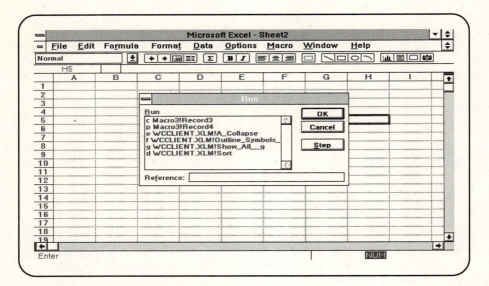

Figure 4.3   *The Run dialog box.*

The Macro Sheet

Excel stores macros in *macro sheets.* You can access macros only when the macro sheet that contains them is open. Any macro sheet that is open is displayed in the Window menu.

When you create a macro, Excel automatically inserts it into a macro sheet. In our example, the macro created, Record3, is inserted into the Macro3 macro sheet. You can see what the macro sheet looks like by choosing it from the Window menu. Figure 4.4 shows the Record3 macro.

A macro sheet looks like a worksheet, although the columns are a little wider. You can perform worksheet operations like cutting, pasting, and column widening in the macro sheet also. Excel inserts each macro into a separate column. In Figure 4.4 the name of the macro, Record3, together with the key that invokes it, c, appears in the first line. Each line after that contains one instruction, one step of the macro. In the example, the first line selects the cell in row 18, column 1 (R18C1); the instruction in the second line inserts the text *Sales;* and so on.

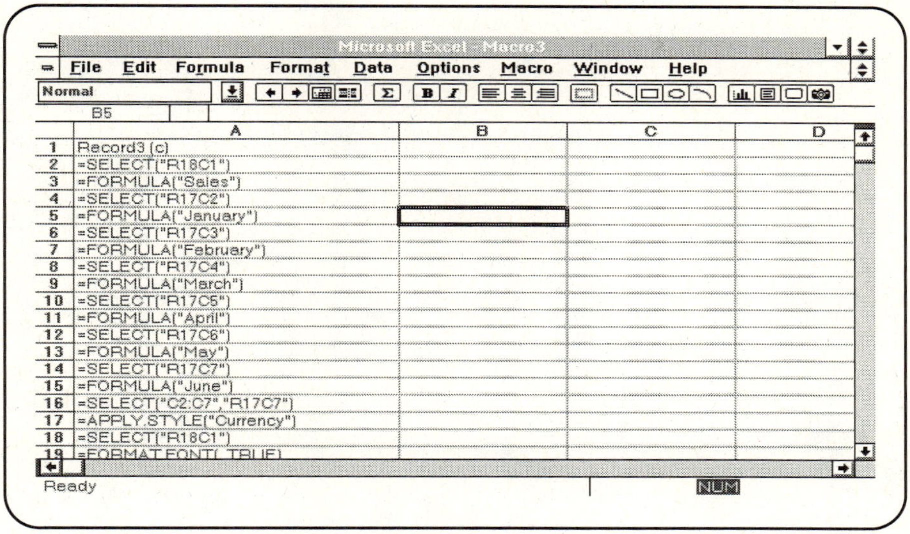

Figure 4.4 *A macro sheet.*

Notice that in this example the cell references are absolute; that is, the macro always inserts the text *Sales* into the cell in row 18, column 1, and so on. Absolute cell references is the default. Before (or even during) the recording of a macro, you can make the cell references relative (to the active cell) by choosing Relative Record from the Macro menu. To change back to absolute references, choose Absolute Record from the Macro menu.

You can alter macro instructions directly on the macro sheet. You could add brackets around each cell reference, R[18]C[1], for example, to make them relative instead of absolute. Chapter 11, "Advanced Macros and Application Customization," discusses this in detail.

The basic steps for creating and running macros are simple, but their uses can be quite sophisticated. When you create the simplest macro, you are actually custom programming Excel for your individual needs and saving yourself or other users a good deal of time and trouble. In Chapter 11, you can apply the basic steps taught in this chapter to more advanced uses.

CHAPTER 5

BASIC DATABASE OPERATIONS

Excel operations are divided into three main categories: spreadsheet, graphics, and database. A *database* stores information, often in the form of text but also including numbers and formulas, so that the information can be accessed and changed quickly. Databases are divided into records to make them easier to manage. An example of a database is a collection of information about employees in a business, with each record comprising one employee. Each record consists of fields—for example, the employee's name, address, salary, etc. Figure 5.1 shows an example of a database in Excel.

Many programs, such as dBASE and Paradox, exist solely to handle and create databases. When you use one of these programs, each database is contained in a separate file. But with Excel you can set aside an area of your worksheet and use it as a database while using other areas in the same worksheet for number-crunching functions and graphics.

A database can be as big as an entire spreadsheet, and you can have only one database on a spreadsheet at a time. However, you can redefine another area of the worksheet as the database and switch the defined database area when you want.

Defining an area of your spreadsheet as a database gives you access to several invaluable operations. The two most important are finding data and sorting data. You can also extract data and place it in another part of the spreadsheet, perform calculations, and print database records to suit your needs.

64 Basic Techniques

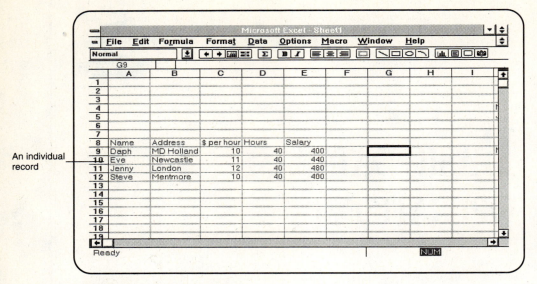

Figure 5.1 *A sample database.*

Creating a Database

Before you can use the database options, you must create and define your database. You define an area of your spreadsheet as a database using the Set Database option in the Data menu. Each row (after the first row) in the range selected and defined is a record. Follow these steps to create and define a database in Excel:

1. On the first row of the area you intend to use as your database, type in the names of the fields in your database—one field name per cell. In the example shown in Figure 5.1, this is the eighth row of the spreadsheet, reading Name, Address, etc.

   This first row of the database range must contain all the names of the fields in the database records. Field names must be text.

2. On each row after the first row, type the *field values* for each record, one record per row.

   A field value is the data contained in each field—a name, for instance, or the dollar amount payable per hour to an employee. You don't have to enter a value for each field in each record; it's all right to leave a blank.

5 — Basic Database Operations   65

In the example, the Salary field value is a formula: =C9*D9 for the first line, =C10*D10 for the second, etc., meaning Hours multiplied by $ per hour.

3. Select the range or area of the database, starting at the first row containing the field names and including each record. In the example, select the range A8:E13 so that you can easily add another record later.

   Do this even if the worksheet is used exclusively as a database.

4. Choose Set Database from the Data menu.

   Your database is now defined. Each row in your database is a record. You can add, delete, or change the records and fields in your database at any time in the future.

 Tip: It's good practice to include one blank row underneath the last record as part of the database. Then, when you want to add a record directly in the worksheet, you can select this blank row, add a new row with Insert from the Edit menu, and type in the new record above the blank. Because Excel knows the blank row is part of the database, you don't have to redefine the database.

Using Data Form with Your Database

Excel offers two basic ways to manipulate the data in your database—either directly through your worksheet or through the Form option in Data. For beginners, the Form option is usually easier to use.

With Form you can find records, move between them, use your own criteria to select only certain records, add records, delete records, and alter records. You must have the database defined before you can use Form. If you don't, Excel sends this message to the screen: `Database range is not defined`. When you have created and defined your database, choose Form from the Data menu. The dialog box shown in Figure 5.2 appears.

With the Data Form dialog box, you can view one record at a time and perform various operations on the fields in the record. The following sections explain each function and feature of the dialog box.

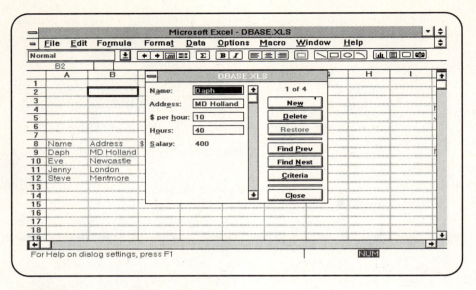

Figure 5.2 *The Form dialog box in Data.*

Field Values and Field Names

Along the left side of the dialog box, you see the *field names* of your database, In Figure 5.2 these are Name, Address, $ per hour, Hours, and Salary. Further right are the actual *field values* of this particular record: Daph, MD Holland, 10, 40, and 400.

Most of the field values are contained in *text boxes*. Any number and text entered directly in a field is displayed in a text box. A field value that has no text box around it is a computed field: the Salary field value, for instance, in Figure 5.2. A *computed field value* is derived from a formula or function.

Any field value contained in a text box can be altered directly. Just click on the value with the mouse pointer and retype a value. In the example, you can change the Salary field value by changing either $ per hour or Hours (because Salary is $ per hour multiplied by Hours), but you cannot change it directly.

Moving Between Records and Between Fields

To the right of the field values is the *scroll bar,* which enables you to move between records. Click on the up arrow to move back through the records; click on the down arrow to move forward.

Above the command buttons on the far right is the *Record number indicator*. This tells you the number position of the record on display and the total number of records: 1 of 4 in Figure 5.2.

You can move between fields in a record using the mouse or the keyboard: Just click on a field to get to that field using the mouse. To move to the next field using the keyboard, press Tab; to move to the previous field, press Shift + Tab.

The Command Buttons

With the command buttons on the far right of the dialog box, you can perform a variety of functions to manipulate the database. Their functions and usage are summarized in the following sections.

New

If you choose New, the field values go blank and the indicator in the upper right of the dialog box changes to New Record. To insert a new record in your database, just fill in the fields as required (you can leave some fields blank if necessary); then choose either New or Close and Excel inserts the record in your database.

Delete

When you choose Delete, Excel deletes the current record on display. Before the deletion, Excel asks for confirmation saying Displayed record will be deleted permanently. Choose OK to delete. Afterwards, the record is gone and cannot be restored (not even through the Restore button).

Restore

Choose Restore when you want to go back to the original field values after making changes. You can only use it before you go to another record. You can't use Restore after deleting a record.

Find Prev

When used with the Criteria button, Find Prev finds and displays the previous record that matches the criteria you set up. Used on its own without any criteria setup, it displays the previous record in the database.

Find Next

When used with the <u>C</u>riteria button, Find <u>N</u>ext finds and displays the next record that matches the criteria you set up. Used on its own without any criteria setup, it displays the next record in the database.

Criteria

Choose the <u>C</u>riteria button to specify criteria when you want to find and display only certain records in your database. The following steps illustrate how to use Criteria:

1. With the Form dialog box on-screen, choose <u>C</u>riteria.

   All text boxes on the screen go blank. Note that a computed field does have a text box in Criteria. You can set a *comparison criterion* in one or more of the text boxes to select only certain records of your choice.

2. Type the comparison criteria in the blank text boxes. You can use the six *comparison operators* in Table 5.1. For example, you might type `>420` in the Salary field to find only those records with salaries greater than that value.

   In addition to operators you can use characters, meaning anything that can be typed with your keyboard. This includes *wild-card characters* that can be used to represent unknown characters. The wild-card characters are ? and *. Use the question mark (?) to find one character in the same position as the question mark. For instance, `?e` in the Address field in the example would find the Newcastle and Mentmore records. The asterix (*) finds one or more characters in the same position. For example `Mr.*` in the Name field would find all records with the prefix *Mr.*

   Figure 5.3 shows an example of a set of criteria. Notice that the Criteria button is now called `Form` and the title `Criteria` appears on the upper right of the dialog box. Use the Form button to return to the regular form features—that is, to exit Criteria.

   The next step is to display a record.

3. Choose Find <u>P</u>rev or Find <u>N</u>ext to display the first record in either direction that matches your criteria.

   When Excel finds a matching record, it displays it. You can choose the Find Prev and Find Next options as many times as you like. Excel beeps when it runs out of records to display in any one direction.
   With Criteria in Form, you can use only comparison criteria; you cannot use computed criteria. See Chapter 10, "Advanced Database Management," for information on using computed criteria with a database.

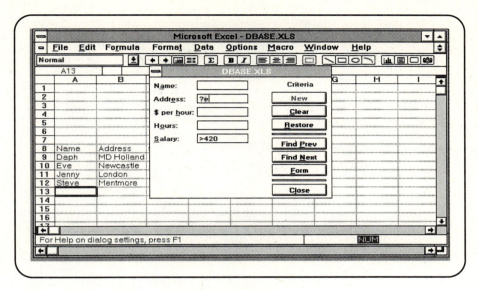

Figure 5.3   *The Criteria screen in the Form dialog box.*

Table 5.1   *Comparison operators.*

Operator	Description
=	Equal to
>	Greater than
<	Less than
>=	Greater than or equal to
<=	Less than or equal to
<>	Not equal to

Sorting Your Database

With the Sort command in Data, you can arrange either the rows or the columns in your database in ascending or descending order using the field(s) of your choice. If you sort by *rows*, the records in your database are sorted. If you sort by *columns*, the field names and values in your database are sorted. Rows is the default. Follow these steps to use Sort:

1. Select the range of the database that you want sorted.

   If you're sorting by rows, which is usually the case, you should not include the first row of your database in the selection. This is the row with the field names. If you do include it, chances are it will change position. If you want to sort by columns, you should include the first row; otherwise, field values will not correspond to field names after the sort.

2. Choose Sort from the Data menu.

   Excel displays the dialog box shown in Figure 5.4.

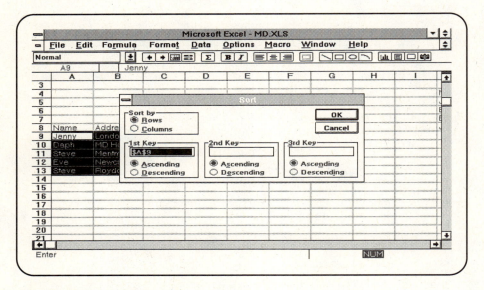

Figure 5.4 *The Sort dialog box.*

3. Choose Rows or Columns in the Sort by option in the upper-left corner of the dialog box.

   Specify the *sort keys* using absolute cell references, such as $A$9. This tells Excel the field to sort by. When you choose Rows, $A$10 and $A$11 refer to the same field since they are in the same column, that is, they are under the same field name.

   In other words, choose Rows and $A$9, and Excel sorts the rows by name in alphabetical order. Choose columns and $A$9 (or $B$9 or $C$9), and Excel sorts the columns by what is in the ninth row—in ascending order you would end up with row 9 reading (in this example) `10, 40, 400, Daph, MD Holland`.

Sort allows you to use up to three different keys in one sort. Excel first sorts using the sort key specified in 1st Key. Then, if other keys are specified, additional sorts are performed using these keys. 2nd and 3rd sort keys come into play when Excel finds duplicate fields in the 1st sort key field. If, for example, you sorted by name and Excel found three O'Callaghans, it would then look to the 2nd sort key—specifying Zip code, for example, to sort these three records. If you don't specify a 2nd sort key, then, in the same example, after putting the three records together, Excel leaves their order as it found them.

4. Specify the 1st Key using an absolute cell reference.

   Excel allows you to sort in *ascending* or *descending* order by each sort key. When you choose ascending, Excel puts numbers first, then text, then logical values (anything that produces TRUE or FALSE), then error values (where a formula in a cell produces a nonsense value). With descending order this is reversed. Blank cells always come last in both ascending and descending order.

5. Choose Ascending or Descending for the 1st sort key.

6. Specify the 2nd and 3rd sort keys if needed, choosing the Ascending or Descending option in each case.

7. Choose OK to begin the sort.

   Figure 5.5 shows an example of a database sorted in ascending order using $A$9 (referring to Name) as the 1st sort key, with $B$9 (Address) as the 2nd sort key, this time in descending order.

Tip: Even though there are only three sort keys in the Sort dialog box, you are not limited to three sort keys. To use other keys, you simply perform other sorts. For example, suppose you wanted to use all five fields as keys in the database shown in Figure 5.5 with Name as the first, Address as the second, Salary as the third, $ per hour as the fourth, and Hours as the fifth. You would need to perform two sorts in this case. In the first, specify the least important keys: $ per hour as 1st Key and Hours as 2nd Key. In the second sort, specify Name as 1st Key, Address as 2nd Key, and Salary as 3rd Key. The second sort is more important than the first since it's more recent.

72 Basic Techniques

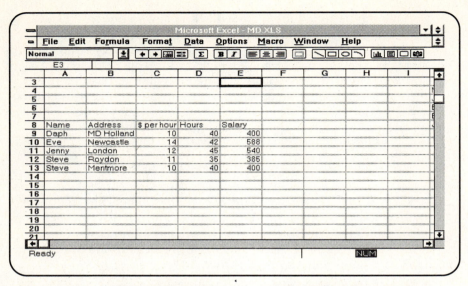

Figure 5.5 *A sorted database using Name as the 1st key in ascending order and Address as the 2nd key in descending order.*

6 CHAPTER

Basic Charts

When you are ready to display the data on a worksheet, you may leave the numbers and text arranged in cells or choose a more graphical arrangement, such as a chart. Well-designed charts interpret and clarify your information, making it easier to understand and remember. Excel allows you 11 different chart types—six basic, one combination, and four 3-D—each of which you can customize for your own purposes.

An Excel chart can be embedded in a worksheet, or it can reside in its own file. Each chart type has a different set of standard features. This chapter takes you through the basic chart operations in Excel.

The Parts of a Chart

Excel uses specific terms to identify the various features and parts of a chart. This section covers these terms in detail. Figure 6.1 shows the basic elements of a (two-dimensional) chart, in this case a chart embedded in a worksheet.

Data

Chart data means all the data in your worksheet that you use to create a particular chart. Data consists of names, dates, and/or numbers. There is an active link between a chart and the data from which it was created: Whenever you make changes in the data, the chart immediately changes accordingly.

Chart data has dimensions. For instance, it can be four cells wide by three cells deep. The dimensions of your chart data determine what the resulting chart will look like. Generally, the values along the longest side of the highlighted data on your worksheet appear as categories along the x-axis.

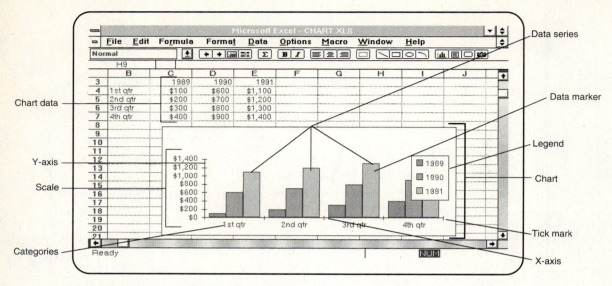

Figure 6.1 *The basic elements of a chart.*

Menu Bar

The chart *menu bar* appears whenever you open a chart, whether it is an embedded chart or one saved as a separate document (see "Opening an Embedded Chart" later in this chapter). Figure 6.4 is basically the same as Figure 6.2, except that in Figure 6.2 the chart is open and the chart menu bar appears instead of the worksheet menu bar.

The chart menu bar contains menus options—like Gallery and Chart—that are not contained in the worksheet menu bar, and vice versa. And even when the menu names remain the same, the menu items can be completely different, as in the case of the Format menu. The chart menu bar contains the following options: File, Edit, Gallery, Chart, Format, Macro, Windows, Help.

Data Marker

A *data marker* represents a single value from the data on the chart. The form of a data marker depends on the chart type you use: in a column chart it will be a column, in a pie chart a wedge, and in a scatter chart a little square.

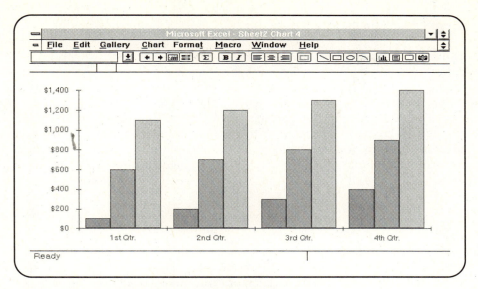

Figure 6.2   *An opened chart with the chart menu bar.*

Data Series

A *data series* is a series of related data markers. *Related* in this case means that the data values that each data marker represents come from the same row or column in the chart data. There can be one or more series in each chart. All the data markers in a data series have the same color and/or pattern so that the relationship is obvious.

Category

A *category* is a cluster or grouping of data series. There can be just one category or several. By default the values from the longest side of the chart data become categories. In the case of chart data on a worksheet whose sides have equal length, the side which contains names or dates provides the categories. Categories consist preferably of names or dates, although numbers can be categories.

X-Axis and Y-Axis

The two axes (three in a three-dimensional chart) are the lines that set the scaling for the data references on the chart. Usually the *x-axis* contains the categories of your chart data and the *y-axis* contains the data values. Bar charts reverse this.

Scale

The *scale* is the numbering system along the axes. The range of the scale is determined by the highest value in the chart data, excluding those values which are used as categories and/or in the legend (if the first cell is empty). By default the scale starts at 0 where the x-axis and the y-axis meet.

The range of the scale depends partially on the height of the chart. For instance, if a chart with chart data up to 1400 has room for only three gradations, the scale shows the following range: 0, 1000, 2000. If the same chart is stretched, the scale shows more gradations, but a shorter range; that is, 0, 100, 200, going up to 1300, 1400.

Tick Marks

A *tick mark* is a little line intersecting and perpendicular to the x-axis or y-axis. Tick marks show the division between two categories on the category axis (usually the x-axis) and the location of a gradation of scale along the data axis (usually the y-axis). Tick marks help the viewer of a chart to determine the precise value of a particular data marker.

Legend

A *legend* is a box inside a chart that names and illustrates data series by showing the colors or patterns of all data series next to their names.

Creating a New Chart

When creating a new chart, you have two options. You can either embed the chart inside your worksheet, or you can create a chart as a separate but linked document. An embedded chart can help clarify data in a direct way because when you change data on the worksheet, you immediately see the change appear in the chart. On the other hand, the embedded chart takes up space on your worksheet. A separate but linked chart also changes when data is changed, but you must open that document file to see it.

 Tip: So that they'll be easy to read on the worksheet, make your embedded charts at least five columns wide and eight to nine rows deep.

Creating an Embedded Chart

An embedded chart appears on the worksheet along with the data, so you can refer to it readily.

Follow these steps to create an embedded chart:

1. Highlight all the data you want to use in the chart.

    Figure 6.3 shows an example of highlighted data in a worksheet.

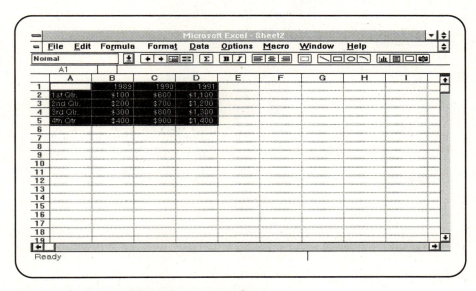

Figure 6.3 *Data highlighted to create a chart.*

   Toward the end of the Tool bar (fourth from the right) is an icon that looks like a stylized column chart. This is the chart tool.

2. Click on the chart tool.

    The data you highlighted is surrounded by a "running marquee" highlight, and your pointer takes on the shape of a thin cross.

3. Position your pointer where you want your new chart to appear. Hold down the mouse button and drag.

    You find yourself drawing a rectangle. If you want a square chart, hold down the Shift key while you drag. If you want the borders of your chart to coincide with the cell gridlines, hold down the Control key while you drag.

4. When the rectangle has the shape and size you want, release the mouse button.

Excel makes a chart from the data you previously highlighted. Figure 6.4 shows the result in the example.

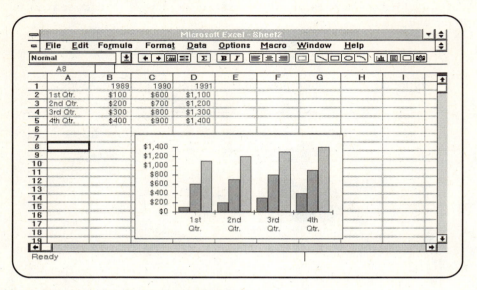

Figure 6.4 *An embedded chart in a worksheet.*

 Tip: Avoid selecting empty cells. If you select empty cells (other than the cell in the upper left), Excel treats them as data, and strange holes might appear in your chart.

Creating a Chart as a Separate Document

Although there are advantages to the embedded chart, creating the chart as a separate document also has its uses. It does not take up space on the worksheet. And it exists as a separate file, which means it can be manipulated easily. Another consideration is that if the embedded chart displays close to the chart data, the screen must be redrawn every time you change a value in the data (unless calculation is set at manual in the Calculation command under Options).

Follow these steps to create a chart as a separate document:

1. Highlight all the data you want to chart.

2. Choose New from the File menu.

The dialog box with three options—Worksheet, Chart and Macro Sheet—appears.

3. Choose Chart and OK.

A chart window called *Chart* appears, followed by a number. Excel automatically plots your data in a chart, using the default column chart format.

 Tip: As an alternative to choosing commands through the File menu when creating a chart, press either F11 or Alt-F1 and a new chart will be created in a separate window.

Configuring Data on the Chart

When Excel is unsure as to how to interpret the data you selected, it prompts you with a dialog box, either the First Row Contains or the First Column Contains dialog box. Figure 6.5 shows the First Column Contains dialog box.

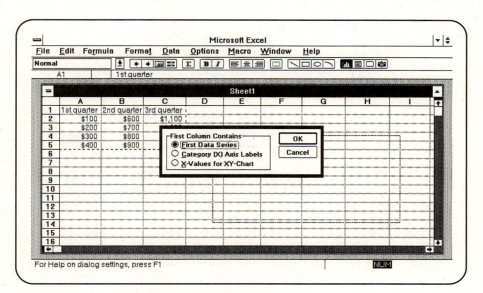

Figure 6.5 *The First Column Contains dialog box.*

You see the First Row Contains dialog box, for instance, when the title names in your range of data are on the shortest side or your data contains no titles. If your data is deeper than it is wide, the First Column Contains dialog box appears. If the data is wider than it is deep, the First Row Contains dialog box appears. Both dialog boxes give you the same three options:

- First Data Series
- Category (X) Axis Labels
- X-Values for XY-Chart

With these options it is possible to end up with three different configurations from the same data selection.

As mentioned, a *data series* is a group of related values, for instance, the rainfall in Iowa in July, August, and September. Choose the First Data Series option when you want the data in the first row or column (depending on whether the dialog box is called First Row Contains or First Column Contains) to be the first series of values on the x-axis, the horizontal axis.

Suppose your data is in a square, as in Figure 6.6. Choosing the chart tool will bring up the First Row Contains dialog box. Accept the default option First Data Series, and you get a chart in which the first data series (in Figure 6.6 the black data markers) consists of values from the first row.

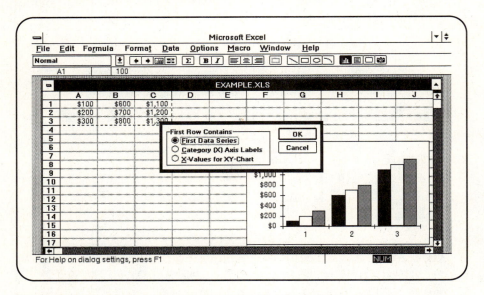

Figure 6.6 *The black data markers representing the first data series.*

Note that in the example in Figure 6.6, your categories along the horizontal or x-axis are simply named 1, 2, 3, etc., in the absence of chart titles that can serve as categories.

Choose the Category (X) Axis Labels option when you want the data in the first row or column to be the categories on the x-axis, the horizontal axis. Choosing this option with the same block of data in Figure 6.6 results in a chart (Figure 6.7) in which the values of the first row become category labels to the rows beneath them.

In this particular example, choosing Category is meaningless. You would use it when the first row or column contains headings—usually text (July, August, Sept, for example, or A, B, C). But it illustrates that Excel does what it's told—you make the choice.

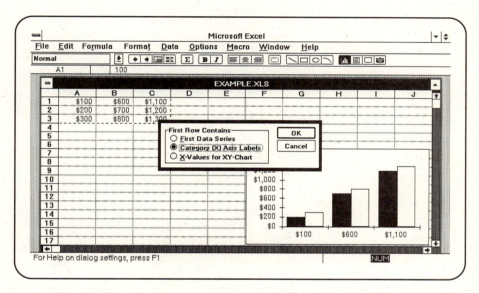

Figure 6.7 *The first-row values as categories with the Category (X) Axis Labels option.*

Choose the X-Values for XY-Chart option when you want the data in the first row or column (depending on whether the dialog box is called First Row Contains or First Column Contains) to be on the x-axis and the other rows or columns on the y-axis. This option always produces a scatter chart, even if the preferred chart format is another type of chart, say a column chart. Figure 6.8 shows the result in the example when you choose this option.

Moving and Resizing a Chart

Once you have created an embedded chart, you may decide that its location or dimensions, or both, are not ideal.

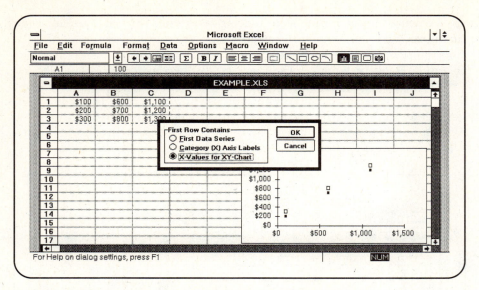

Figure 6.8   A scatter chart from the X-Values for XY-Chart option.

Follow these steps to move an embedded chart:

1. Click on the chart to select it.

   Along its sides, eight black squares appear to show the chart has been selected.

2. Place the mouse pointer on the selected chart and hold down the mouse button.

3. While holding down the mouse button, drag the chart where you want it.

4. Release the mouse button.

When you use long category names, you might need to enlarge your newly created chart to straighten out scrunched-up category names, as in Figure 6.9.

Follow these steps to resize an embedded chart:

1. Select the chart.

2. Place your pointer over one of the little black squares, the resizing handles.

   Your pointer becomes a thin cross.

3. Press down the mouse button and drag.

4. When the chart has the shape you want, release the mouse button.

6 — Basic Charts 83

When your chart is not embedded but is in a separate chart window, you can move and resize it using the normal Windows techniques.

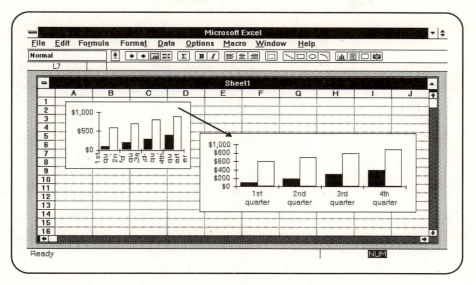

Figure 6.9 *Resizing can improve the readability of an embedded chart.*

Basic Chart File Operations

Earlier, the section "Creating a Chart as a Separate Document" showed you how to use the New option in the File menu to create a new chart. This section discusses how to open, close, save, delete, and print charts. The steps will be familiar if you know how to perform similar commands with worksheets.

Opening a Chart Saved as a Separate Document

To open a chart saved as a separate document, follow these steps:

1. Choose Open from the File menu.
2. Go to the directory in which you saved the chart.

 Note: Charts have the extension .xlc; worksheets, the extension .xls; and macros, the extension .xlm.

3. Select the chart you want and choose OK.

   If the worksheet linked to this chart is already open, Excel automatically updates the chart from the worksheet data. If the worksheet is not open, Excel displays this prompt: `Update references to unopened documents?`

4. Choose Yes to update the chart, No not to update.

 Tip: If you recently used the chart you want to open, check the bottom section of the File menu first: It contains a list of the last four documents you opened.

Opening an Embedded Chart

To open an embedded chart, follow these steps:

1. Move your pointer over the embedded chart you want to open and click on it to select it.
2. Double-click on the selected chart to open it.

   The chart will open into a separate window (the same size as the chart on the worksheet), which you can minimize or maximize like any other window. If you look at the top of the chart window, you will see your chart now also has a name, consisting of the name of the worksheet the chart belongs to, followed by *Chart* and a number. This name shows up in the Window menu.

Saving a Chart Created as a Separate Document

You can save a chart created as a separate document like any other document. With the chart window activated, perform the following steps. To activate a chart that is already open, choose the chart name from the Window menu.

1. Choose Save from the File menu.
2. Choose the directory in which you want to save the chart.
3. Type in a name of no more than eight letters for your chart.

   Unless you specify otherwise, Excel gives charts the extension .XLC.

4. Choose OK.

   The chart retains its links with the data from which it was originally created. In other words, if you change the data in your worksheet, the data in the chart will automatically change also.

Saving an Embedded Chart

It is not necessary to save an embedded chart under its own name because any changes are automatically saved every time you save your worksheet. But if you want to (because you want to print the chart separately, for instance), you can. Once you've opened the embedded chart, the procedure is the same as for saving a chart created as a separate document.

When you save an embedded chart under its own name, a copy of the chart is saved in a separate document. This procedure will break all links between the saved chart and its original in the worksheet, and also with the data from which the chart was created.

In other words, if you make any changes in a formerly embedded chart now saved under its own name, the changes will not show up in the original embedded chart still in the worksheet. And any changes made in the worksheet will not appear in the separately saved chart. You can avoid the second situation by selecting the same data again and creating a new chart as a separate document.

Closing a Chart

You close all open charts, whether embedded or not, in the same way:

1. Choose Close from the File menu.

Because all open charts (including embedded ones) are in a window, you can also close them using the Control button located in the upper left of each window. Click on the button and then choose Close from the menu that appears, or simply double-click.

An embedded chart automatically closes when you close the worksheet.

Deleting a Chart

To delete an embedded chart, follow these steps:

1. Select the embedded chart.
2. Press either the Backspace or the Delete key.

If you have second thoughts, go to the Edit menu before you do anything else and choose Undo Clear.

To delete a chart saved as a separate document, follow these steps:

1. Choose Delete from the File menu.

Excel displays the Delete dialog box.

2. Locate the chart, select it, and choose OK.

   Excel asks you to confirm the deletion.

3. After making sure that you are deleting the right chart, choose Yes to delete or No to cancel the deletion.

Printing a Chart

Any chart, including an embedded chart, can be printed on its own:

1. Open the chart or activate its window.
2. Choose Print from the File menu.

   Excel displays the Print dialog box.

3. Choose the required options from this box or accept the defaults.

   With the Copies option, you can tell Excel how many charts to print. If the chart is more than one page, you can print All pages or specify the starting page in From and the ending page in To. See Chapter 7 for information on the Draft Quality and Print Preview options.

Choosing and Customizing Chart Types

Once you have created your chart, you can format it to interpret your data most appropriately. You might change the type of chart you use. Excel uses the column chart by default, but there are six basic types of charts, each with different options, giving you a total of 39 basic possibilities (not counting the combinations and 3-D charts), which are discussed in Chapter 13, "Advanced Charting."

The Gallery Menu

You change the chart type using the Gallery menu. When you open a chart or activate its window, the Gallery and Chart menus replace the Formula, Data, and Options menus of the worksheet menu bar.

The Gallery menu (shown in Figure 6.10) displays six two-dimensional charts (the basic charts), the Combination option with which you can combine them, and four 3-D charts. The Combination and 3-D charts are discussed in Chapter 13.

Opening an embedded chart activates the chart menu bar. The Gallery menu lets you change the chart type. Follow these steps to change a chart type:

1. Open the chart you want to change or activate its window.

2. Choose the new chart type from the Gallery menu.

   A dialog box appears, showing the different options available for each chart type. Figure 6.11, for example, shows the options for the area chart type.

3. Select one of these options and choose OK to put your change into effect.

   If you change your mind about the chart type you want, click on Next or Previous. Excel displays the dialog boxes for all the other chart types in the sequence in which they are listed in the Gallery menu.

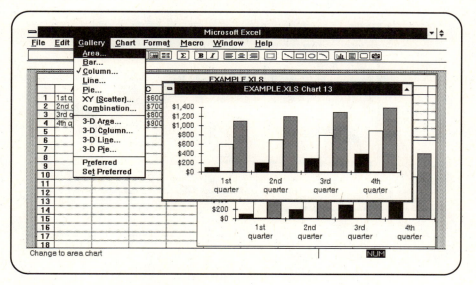

Figure 6.10   *The Gallery menu.*

Chart Types

Excel has six basic, two-dimensional chart types, each having five to eight suboptions.

Area Charts

Area charts are useful for showing the parts as a proportion of the whole, often over a time period on the horizontal axis. Use them to emphasize the broad trends of your data over a period of time.

Option 1 in Figure 6.11 is a standard area chart. Option 2 is a 100-percent area chart; it allows the viewer to compare at a glance the values of the different data series.

Options 3, 4 and 5 are variations on the standard area chart. Option 3 gives you droplines that emphasize the borders of your categories. Option 4 uses both droplines and scale lines that help the viewer determine the value and place of a particular point in the chart. Option 5 incorporates the legend in the chart, instead of in a separate box.

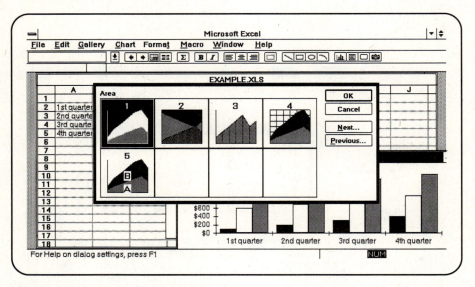

Figure 6.11 *The area chart options.*

Bar Charts

With bar charts the time flow is not as emphasized as it is in column or area charts. Use them to compare data at a certain point in time.

Option 1 in Figure 6.12 is the standard bar chart. Option 2 adds up the individual data markers of each data series, allowing you to place emphasis on comparing the data series rather than individual values. Option 3 is a segmented bar chart, meaning that you can display data markers from a category as parts of the same bar, emphasizing relative rather than individual values. Option 4 lets you suggest depth by overlapping the data markers from the highest one on top.

Option 5 is a 100-percent segmented bar chart; use it to give an overview of the whole. Option 6 adds droplines to the standard bar chart to make it easier for the viewer to determine the value of each data marker. And option 7 displays the value of each data marker next to it. While this feature saves your viewer the trouble of having to figure out the values, it can make a chart crowded.

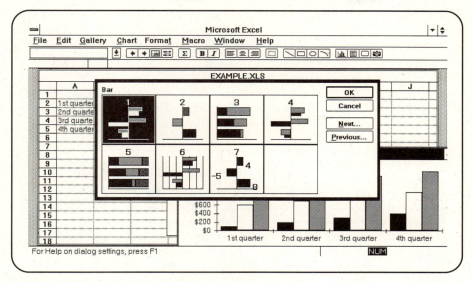

Figure 6.12 *The bar chart options.*

Column Charts

Column charts emphasize the change of the parts over a time period. Use them to suggest the passage of time.

Option 1 in Figure 6.13 is the standard, default column chart. Option 2 displays the total value of each data series. Option 3 is a segmented column chart; by displaying the data markers of a category as parts of the same column, you emphasize their relative values to each other. Option 4 lets you suggest depth by overlapping the data markers starting with the last on top.

Option 5 is a 100-percent segmented column chart, which gives an overview of the whole. Option 6 adds scale lines to the standard column chart to make it easier for the viewer to determine the value of each data marker. Option 7 displays the value of each data marker next to it. Option 8 lets you remove the spaces that separate the categories in the other options.

Line Charts

Line charts, like column charts, emphasize change over a time period, concentrating on the trend rather than on the actual numbers.

In Option 1 in Figure 6.14, the data markers make it easier for your viewer to determine the value of your individual data, while Option 2 emphasizes the trend in your data almost exclusively. Option 3 is the opposite of Option 2, emphasizing individual values. The disadvantage here is that the chart can easily become confusing.

Option 4 is basically Option 1 with scale lines added to make it easier for the viewer to determine the value of a data marker. Option 5 adds droplines to Option 4. Option 6 uses a logarithmic scale with scale lines. Option 7 is a hi-lo chart, used to emphasize the contrast between two values in a particular period of time. Option 8 was designed specifically for stock quotes. One data marker can show the high, the low, and the close value of a stock.

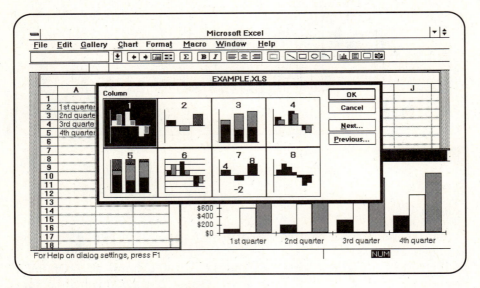

Figure 6.13   *The column chart options.*

Pie Charts

Pie charts always show just one series of data. If your chart data contains more than one data series, the resulting pie chart will display the first data series. This is the best chart to show the proportion of parts to the whole. No time measure is given.

Option 1 in Figure 6.15 is the standard pie chart, each wedge being a data marker. Option 2 displays the category names next to the data markers, which are all the same color. With Option 3 you can draw attention to the first value of the data series by having it "explode." Option 4 is a completely exploded pie chart. Option 5 displays, like Option 2, the category names next to the data markers, but now each wedge has its own color and/or pattern. Option 6 shows the viewer at a glance the percentage each wedge occupies in the whole of the data series.

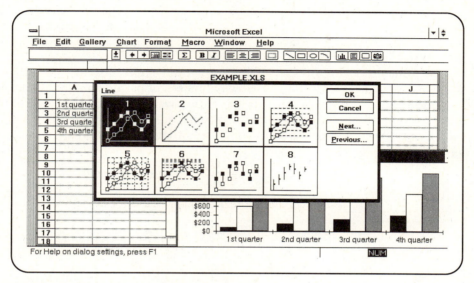

Figure 6.14 *The line chart options.*

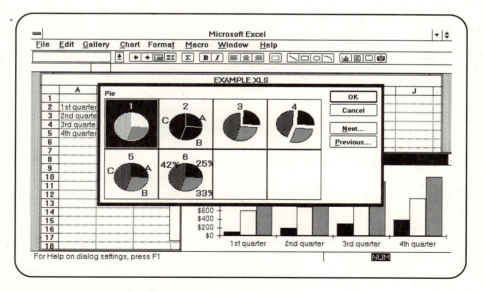

Figure 6.15 *The pie chart options.*

Scatter Charts

Scatter charts are different from all the others in that you don't see labels along either axes, just numbers. In other words there are no categories. Use them to show the relationship between two or more series or values. Where data markers are scattered, there is low correlation; where they are clustered, there is high correlation. Scatter charts are especially useful if you have a lot of data and are not sure whether there is a significant relationship.

Option 1 in Figure 6.16 lets you draw your own conclusions. Option 2 connects the data series with lines showing intersections and parallel trends. Option 3 adds a grid to Option 1 to help the viewer determine the value of individual data markers. Option 4 allows you to use a logarithmic scale along the y-axis, and with Option 5 you can have logarithmic scales along both axes.

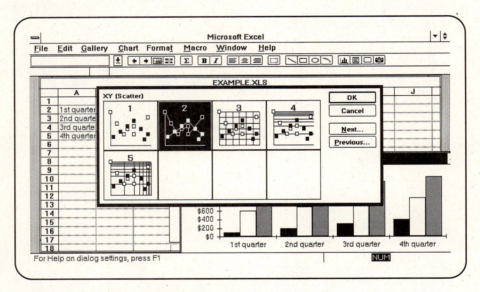

Figure 6.16 *The scatter chart options.*

Legends

When you make a chart, Excel automatically distinguishes your data series by different colors and/or patterns. The viewer, however, won't know what each data series stands for, unless you add a legend.

To make a chart with a legend like the one in Figure 6.17, follow these steps:

1. Open the chart or activate its window.
2. Choose Add Legend from the Chart menu.

   A box appears identifying the colors that go with each of the data series.
3. Enlarge your chart if necessary to make room for the legend.

   When the first cell of the worksheet data is not empty, the default names that Excel uses in the legend box are rather bland: Series 1, Series 2, etc. If you leave the first cell empty, Excel will use the names you have entered in the rows or columns.

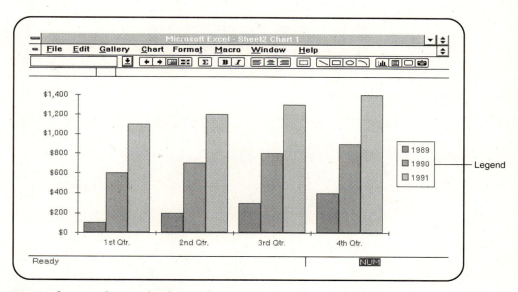

Figure 6.17 A chart with a legend.

CHAPTER 7

PRINTING

The four commands discussed in this chapter are available through the File menu: Printer Setup, Page Setup, Print Preview, and Print. All except Print Preview are directly involved in producing printed output. You don't have to leave Excel to set up your printer—for example, to change from a dot-matrix printer to a laser printer or to change from draft mode printing to letter-quality printing. Excel also lets you define the look of the page by including or excluding headers and footers, for instance, or by putting in column headings and gridlines. After you've chosen your setup specifications, you can preview the printed output to make sure it looks the way you want it to. Then you can print your document.

Printer Setup

Printer Setup allows you to choose which printer to print to and also the various settings to use, such as paper width and height, graphics resolution, and horizontal or vertical orientation. Follow these steps to use this command:

1. Choose Printer Setup from the File menu.

    Excel displays a list of the installed printer drivers similar to the one in Figure 7.1. This list varies according to what you installed when you first installed Excel. See the next section, "Installing a New Printer," to learn how to add a new printer to the list.

2. Choose one of the printers listed to select it as the printer to use.

    Sometimes you need to change the basic settings on the printer.

96 Basic Techniques

3. Choose the Setup button to change the settings.

   Excel displays a dialog box similar to that shown in Figure 7.2.

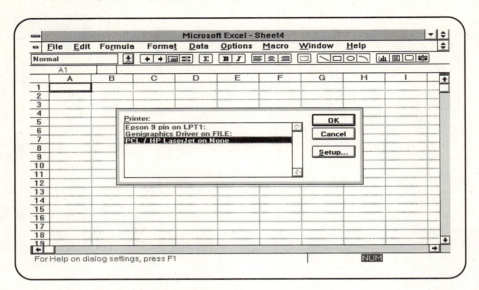

Figure 7.1 *A list of printer drivers from Printer Setup.*

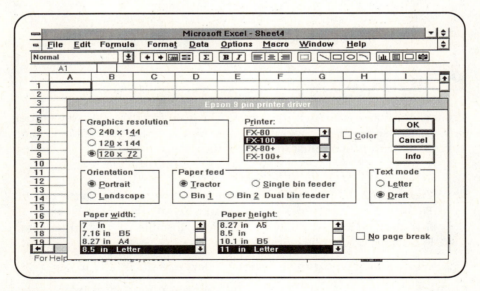

Figure 7.2 *A Printer Setup dialog box.*

7 — Printing

The options presented in this box vary according to which printer is currently selected. Many of the options are self-explanatory: Paper **w**idth and Paper **h**eight, for instance, where you specify the size of the paper being used. Under P**r**inter, you specify the subtype of the printer selected—FX-80, FX-100, etc., in the example shown in Figure 7.2. The two options available under Text Mode, L**e**tter and **D**raft, refer to the quality of the printed output. Letter mode is higher quality but takes longer to print out; the faster draft mode can be useful for producing a quick first draft of your output.

Graphics Resolution applies only to graphics—not to text and characters. The higher the numbers here (for example, 240x1**4**4 versus 12**0**x144), the higher the quality of the printing and the slower the printing. The default setting for Orientation is **P**ortrait, where the characters and graphics are upright when the paper is held with the longer side in a vertical position. In **L**andscape the characters and graphics are upright when the paper is held with the longer side in a horizontal position.

Memory specifies the amount of memory in your printer with a default of 512K. **C**opies specifies the default number of copies for each page printed. These latter two are not shown for all printers.

With all these options, you can accept the default settings. If in doubt, it's best to leave the settings as they are.

4. Choose OK to return to the list of printers; then choose OK again to accept your changes and return to the worksheet.

Installing a New Printer

You don't need to exit Excel to install a new printer driver. Just follow these steps:

1. Choose R**u**n from the Control menu box in the upper left of your screen.

2. Choose Control **P**anel.

   This is the Control Panel option found in the Program Manager.

3. Double-click on the Printers icon or choose **P**rinters from the **S**ettings menu.

4. Choose **A**dd Printer from the Printers dialog box.

5. Select a printer from the **L**ist of Printers scroll box.

6. Choose **I**nstall.

98 Basic Techniques

Excel prompts you to insert a disk containing the printer driver into a floppy disk drive. This is usually the Microsoft Windows Setup disk #5, but if you have a later upgraded or updated version of the printer driver, you should use it.

7. Insert the disk and select OK; your list of installed printers is updated.

   You can configure (tell it which port to use) the new printer using the Configure option in the same dialog box.

8. Choose OK to exit the dialog box and return to the Control Panel.

9. Close the Control Panel.

Page Setup

The Page Setup command enables you to determine the look of the printed output. You can decide whether to include headers and footers, how big to make the margins, whether to include gridlines and column headings, and whether to use some of the other options described in Table 7.1. Remember that these settings are saved with the individual document.

1. Choose Page Setup from the File menu.

   Excel displays the dialog box shown in Figure 7.3.

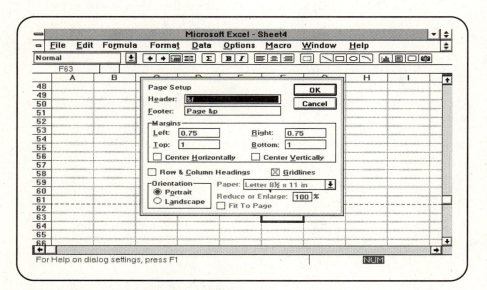

Figure 7.3 The Page Setup dialog box.

Depending on what printer is selected, various options are displayed in gray, meaning that they cannot be changed. When you're in a chart, an additional option called *Size* allows you to specify how the chart will be printed. Table 7.1 explains the various options in this dialog box.

Table 7.1   *What the options in the Page Setup dialog box mean.*

Option	Usage
Header and Footer	What you specify here is printed at the top (header) and bottom (footer) of each page. Regardless of what you specify at Margins, headers always print .5" from the top and footers .5" from the bottom of the page; both print .75" from the side. It's not mandatory to print anything. Table 7.2 provides further information on headers and footers.
Margins	Margins enables you to set the amount of space between the outside edge of the paper and the print area on Left, Right, Top, and Bottom. Since the headers and footers are always printed in the same place, you should allow room for them by making Top and Bottom greater than .5" and Left and Right greater than .75".
Center	You can center the printed output Horizontally or Vertically on the page.
Row & Column headings	Choose this option to print the row and column headings. This option does not apply to charts.
Gridlines	Choose this option (it's on by default) to print the vertical and horizontal gridlines. This option does not apply to charts. Screen gridlines are turned off using the Display command from Options only.
Orientation	Portrait prints vertically and Landscape prints horizontally relative to the long side of the paper.

continued

Table 7.1   continued

Option	Usage
Paper	Sets the paper size, for example, letter or legal. Access and choose the available options using the scroll box.
Re_d_uce or Enlarge	The printed output can be reduced or enlarged according to the percentage you type here.
F_i_t to Page	When a document is too big for one page, you can use this option to reduce it so that it fits.
Size	This option is available with a chart only. S_c_reen Size reproduces the screen chart size. Fi_t_ to Page prints as large as possible in the screen height-to-width ratio. F_u_ll Page always fills the entire page regardless of ratios.

2. Choose the options you want and then choose OK to exit.

You can print headers and footers in a variety of formats, including bold and italics. Use the ampersand (&) character with other specific characters to tell Excel how to print. Each individual code sets up the formatting for the characters that follow it. For example, *&CSoccer Results&R&D* prints the text *Soccer Results* as center aligned (&C) and then prints the current date (&D) as right aligned (&R). Table 7.2 summarizes the codes.

Table 7.2   Header and Footer codes.

Code	Effect
&L, &C, &R	Left align, center, and right align
&B, &I, &U, &S	Bold, italic, underline, and strikethrough
&D, &T	Print current date, current time
&F	Print the name of the document
&P, &P–a number, &P+a number	Print the page number, the page number minus another number, and the page number plus another number. For example, *&P+2* starts the page numbering at 3 instead of 1.

Code	Effect
&N	This prints the total number of pages in a document. It can be used with &P, as in *Page &P of &N*, which prints Page 1 of 12, for example.
&"fontname", &nn	Set up your font and type size with these two codes, where *nn* stands for a number. For example, *&"Times"&12* uses the Times font in 12-point size.
&&	Prints a single ampersand.

Print Preview

The main purpose of Print Preview is to enable you to view the document page by page exactly as it will print out. However, you can also perform a variety of other functions with this command, including changing the margin settings directly on the page (as distinct from changing them with new number settings), changing the column widths, and changing the page settings.

1. Choose Print Preview from the File menu.

    The page is displayed as shown in Figure 7.4. The page is not displayed if the worksheet has no entries!

    When you place the mouse pointer on the page in Print Preview, the cursor changes to a magnifying-glass shape. You can use this to see any part of the page in close-up.

2. Click on a section of the page, and the screen zooms in on that section.

    The command buttons are displayed across the top of the screen under the title bar. You can use the Zoom button as an alternative to clicking on the page. Click on the button and then use the scroll bars to view the part of the screen you wish to see. To return to the full page view, click on the page or choose Zoom again.

    The Setup button brings up the Page Setup dialog box, which was discussed earlier. You can use it to change any of the options available in that box. Print brings up the Print dialog box by which you send output to the printer. Next and Previous display the next and previous pages of the document on display.

    Margins is useful for setting the exact amount of empty space around your printed output.

102 Basic Techniques

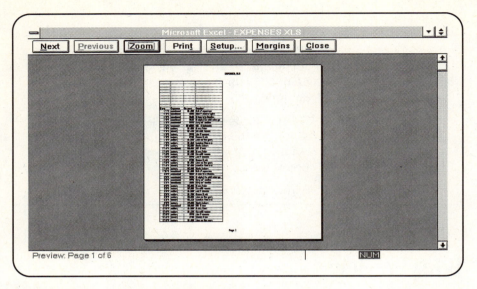

Figure 7.4 *An example page shown in Print Preview.*

3. Choose <u>M</u>argins.

   Excel displays the margin and column settings, as shown in Figure 7.5.

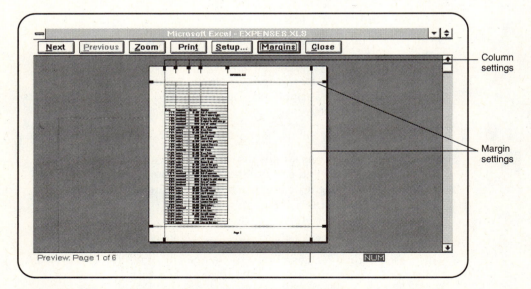

Figure 7.5 *The Print Preview screen with margin and column settings shown.*

If necessary, use the magnifying tool or Zoom to see a portion of the page in close-up when examining margins. When the mouse pointer is positioned on a margin line or a column line, its shape changes to a dark cross with arrowheads on either the vertical or the horizontal axis (depending on which way the margin or column can be moved). You can then move the margins or columns directly, as shown in step 4.

4. Press the mouse button when the cross shape appears over the margin or column lines and drag the mouse to change the position of the line.

   Note that when you change a column width by this method, the actual worksheet or macro sheet changes also. Choose Margins again to remove the margin and column lines from view.

5. Choose Close to return to the main screen.

Print

Once you've set your printer settings and your page settings and have previewed each page, you can use the Print command to print out your chart, macro sheet, or worksheet. You can specify whether to print the whole document, a range of pages, a multiple selection of cells, draft mode, or other options. Follow these steps to print your document:

1. Choose Print from the File menu.

   Excel displays the dialog box shown in Figure 7.6.

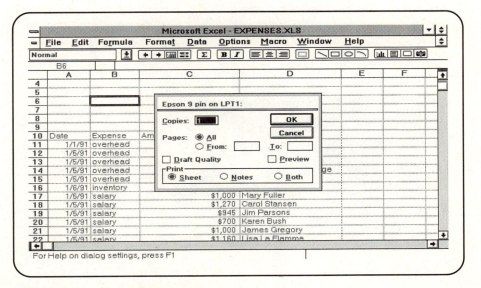

Figure 7.6 *The Print dialog box.*

104 Basic Techniques

At <u>C</u>opies, type in the number of copies you want of each page in the document or accept the default of 1.

You don't have to print out all the pages in a document every time. The default is <u>A</u>ll, meaning all pages will be printed, but you can specify a range by entering a starting page in <u>F</u>rom and an ending page in <u>T</u>o. Choose <u>D</u>raft Quality when you want a quick printout and you don't mind a lower print quality. When you choose <u>P</u>review and afterwards OK to print, Excel displays the first page in the preview window, which was discussed earlier.

Finally, with worksheets and macro sheets, you can print just the <u>S</u>heet, just the <u>N</u>otes, or <u>B</u>oth.

2. Choose OK to begin printing.

Printing in Sections

The Print dialog box allows you to print as little as one page of a document, but you can further refine the amount to be printed by creating a *print area*. A print area can be as small as one cell, and it can also encompass a *multiple selection* of cells. A multiple selection is a collection of selected cells in different areas of the worksheet. Follow these steps to create a print area:

1. Select the cells to print.

   Figure 7.7 shows an example of a print area.

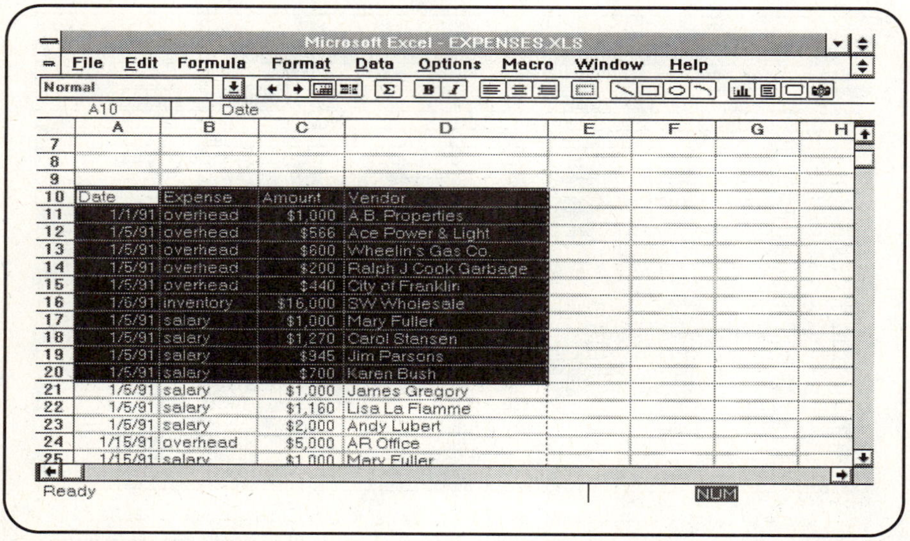

Figure 7.7 A print area.

2. Choose Set Print Area from the Options menu.

   Only one print area can be set per worksheet. Excel keeps this selection as the print area until you remove the print area (by selecting the entire worksheet and choosing Remove Print Area), or until you set another selection as the print area.

3. Choose Print from the File menu.

   Each separate area of selected cells (if there is more than one) is printed on a separate page.

Multiple Selections

Multiple selections are useful not only for print jobs but for many other commands in Excel where you want to work on certain cells and leave out others.

To make a multiple selection:

1. Select the first group of cells in the usual way.
2. Hold down the Ctrl key and select another group of cells.

   The first group remains selected.
3. Select as many additional groups of cells as you like using the same technique.

   Print in the usual way. Figure 7.8 shows a multiple selection.

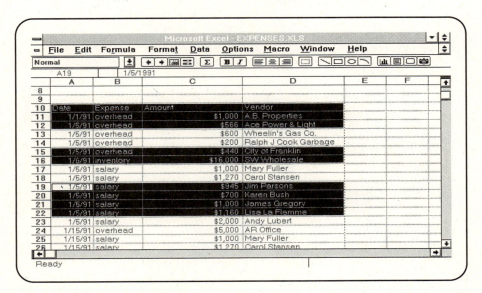

Figure 7.8 *A multiple selection.*

PART
TWO

ADVANCED TECHNIQUES

8
CHAPTER

FORMULAS AND FUNCTIONS

One of the great advantages of using spreadsheets is the ability to use *formulas* in individual cells. Formulas enable you to manipulate, analyze, and draw conclusions about information on your spreadsheet. With a formula, you can do any arithmetic operation—addition, subtraction, division, multiplication—you can join text, and you can compare values.

Functions are formulas that Excel builds in because Microsoft feels it is easier to have them "on tap." Their use is explained in the section "Excel Functions."

Chapter 2, "Basic Worksheet Operations," introduced you to formulas and functions. This chapter elaborates on what you learned there, particularly in regard to the use of operators. It also tells you about the trouble you may run into while using formulas and directs you to their advanced use in subsequent chapters.

Arithmetic Formulas

The simplest formula you can create is an arithmetic equation. If you were to type an arithmetic equation without the answer and then move the equal sign from the end of the equation to the beginning, you would have an Excel formula.

For example, if you wanted to add together the amounts on several checks that you had written, you would write the amounts with a plus sign between them like this: 120.98+11+7.64+1.25 =. Changing the position of the equal sign would make the formula a valid Excel formula: = 120.98+11+7.64+1.25.

Figure 8.1 shows this situation on the screen.

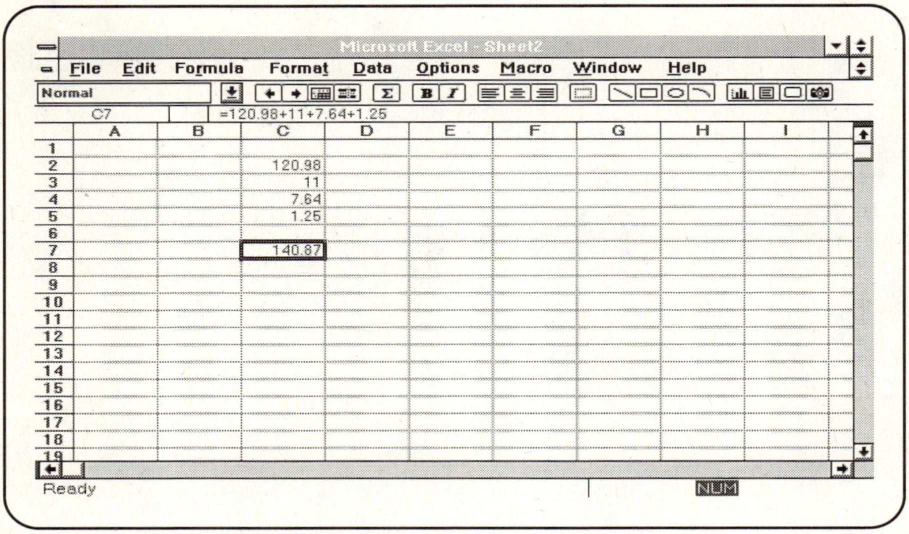

Figure 8.1 *An arithmetic formula summing a range of cells.*

Using Cell References in Formulas

Rather than taking the time to type in each value yourself, you can use a cell address to reference a value. For instance, in the example shown in Figure 8.1, enter all your check amounts in cells C2 through C5. Then in cell C7 type this formula: **= C2 + C3 + C4 + C5**. After you press Enter, Excel will display the same answer in cell C7 as it would if you had typed the arithmetic formula.

Now that your checks are listed one in each cell, you can type the check descriptions in the first column, in cells A2 through A5. Label your calculated sum in cell C7 by typing the word **Total** in cell A7. One of the advantages of such a layout is that you have a complete picture of each expenditure and the total expenditures. Figure 8.2 shows the new formula using the cell referencing method.

Formula Operators

Operators specify the actions to be performed on values in formulas. They are the equivalent of verbs in sentences, whereas values are the equivalent of nouns.

Excel uses four different kinds of operators: *arithmetic, text, comparison,* and *cell referencing*. They are discussed in the following sections.

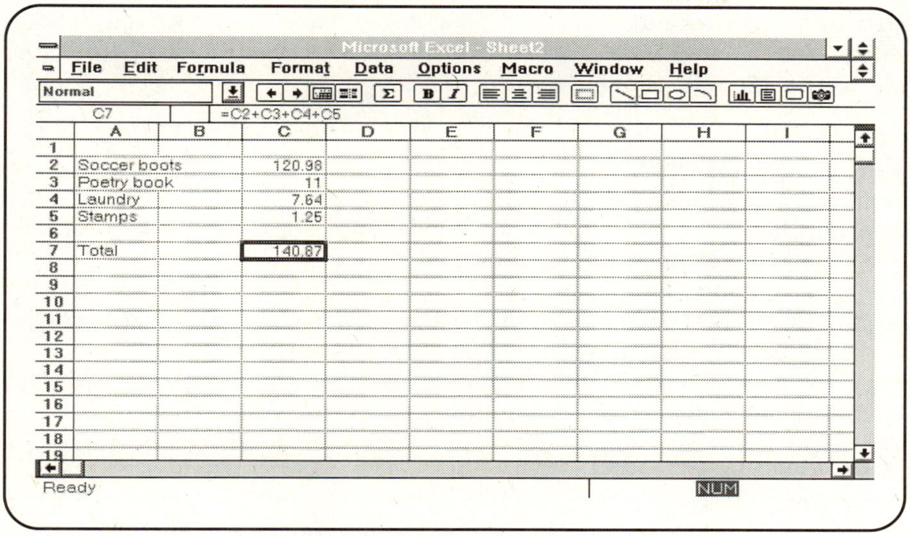

Figure 8.2   An arithmetic formula using cell references.

Arithmetic Operators

Excel has six different types of arithmetic operators: addition (+), multiplication (*), subtraction (–), division (/), exponentiation (^), and percentage (%).

For example, the formula =3^3*2 multiplies 3 by itself 3 times (27) and then multiplies by 2, producing 54. Also, =23*9% gives 2.07. Using % is the same as multiplying by the percentage amount (9 here) and dividing by 100.

Text Operator

The single text operator, &, joins text values together. For example, the formula ="Profits for"&C5 where C5 contains the text "1988/89" produces Profits for 1988/89. If a cell reference contains a formula, the value produced by that formula is used. For example, if C5 is SUM(C1:C4) and a formula reads ="Profits="&C5, the result would be Profits=, followed by the value produced by C5.

Comparison Operators

Excel has six comparison operator possibilities: =, >, <, >=, <=, <>. After comparison, the formula returns TRUE or FALSE. For example, if a cell contains the formula =A4>4 and A4 contains 3, then the formula returns FALSE; if A4 contains 6, then the formula returns TRUE.

Reference Operators

The three kinds of cell reference operators— colon (:), space, and comma (,)— combine two cell references into one reference.

For example, E4:E7 stands for E4, E5, E6, and E7. You could use the comma reference operator in this example also. So the two formulas, =SUM(E4,E5,E6,E7) and =SUM(E4:E7), give the same result.

The space reference operator combines cell references by what cells they have in common. If they have nothing in common, the formula returns #NULL!. Figure 8.3 shows an example of a formula that uses the space operator.

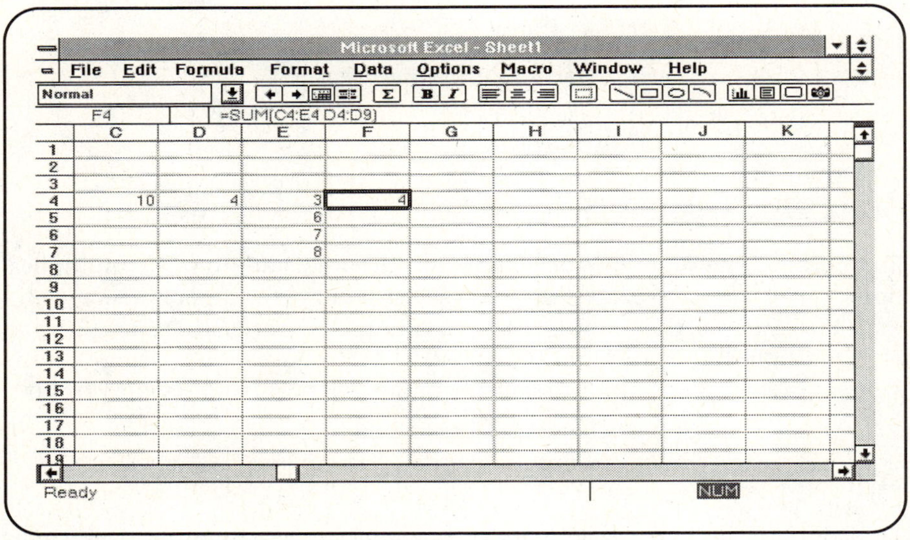

Figure 8.3 *A formula that uses a space in cell referencing.*

The formula (in cell F4) is =SUM(C4:E4 D4:D9). The single space lies between E4 and D4. Excel looks at the two cell ranges and sees that they have only one cell, D4, in common. This is the only cell used in the computation.

Excel Functions

Creating formulas in Excel is a convenient way to perform simple calculations, like displaying and summing a few checks. But what if you had 200 checks that you wanted to include in one total? Using an Excel function instead of a formula would save you time and trouble. With one Excel function you could add up 200 checks or more, using just a few keyboard characters. There is no upper limit on the number of values you may put in a function.

A *function* is a formula that is built into Excel. It takes values that you supply, performs operations on them, and gives a result—a new value.

For the example begun in Figure 8.2, in which you're adding numbers, use the Excel function called *SUM*. This function is a simple formula that is already defined in your copy of Excel. Use it and all other functions by choosing it and then specifying the values to be operated on in the function.

Replace the formula used in cell C7 with the SUM function, as shown in the following steps. You've already entered the information about the checks, including the descriptions and amounts. First, you must choose the function to use. The easiest way to do this is to paste a function from the Formula menu.

1. Make the cell to receive the function the active cell.

    Here it is cell C7, where you want the total of all the checks to appear.

2. Choose Pas*t*e Function from the F*o*rmula menu.

    The Paste Function dialog box appears, as shown in Figure 8.4.

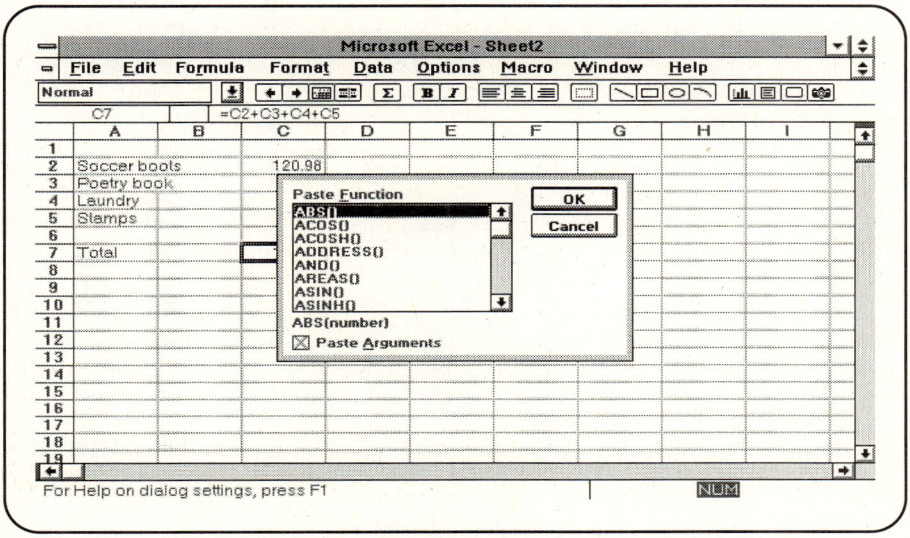

Figure 8.4 *The Paste Function dialog box.*

3. Pick your function from the scroll box.

   You can do this by scrolling down the Paste Function menu until the SUM function, displayed as SUM(), appears in this example. Or you can press **S** to quickly get to the functions beginning with the letter *S* and then continue from there.

4. Decide whether you want to choose the Paste Arguments option.

   Arguments are the values and information you supply to the function for Excel to compute or execute. If you choose the Paste Arguments option, it displays descriptions of what the arguments should be. For example, the SUM function appears as SUM(number1,number2,...), meaning that you enter the numbers (or cell references of the numbers) you want to add up in the positions currently occupied by *number1, number2,* etc., separated by commas. If you don't use this option, you see only SUM().

   Above the Paste Arguments option in the dialog box, Excel always displays the function with the argument descriptions (regardless of whether Paste Arguments is chosen or not). It's recommended that you paste the arguments because syntax errors are easily made and having descriptions of what to enter can help you avoid them.

   For the example choose Paste Arguments.

5. Choose OK.

   The function is then displayed in the cell and the formula bar. Here SUM(number1,number2,...) appears with number1 highlighted. You could enter each number or cell reference individually, but it's easier to indicate a cell range, where you specify the beginning and ending cells and Excel works out the remaining cells. Chapters 1 and 2 discussed this concept.

6. Delete all information inside the parentheses when you want to type in a cell range.

7. Type the cell address range using a colon to separate the addresses.

   In this case, type **C2:C5**. In the formula bar you see: =SUM(C2:C5).

   As another example, if you had 200 checks in column C starting at cell C2 and ending at column C202, you would type **=Sum(C2:C202)** to sum all 200 checks.

8. Accept the function by pressing Enter or clicking the check mark in the formula bar.

   Figure 8.5 shows the result of this example.

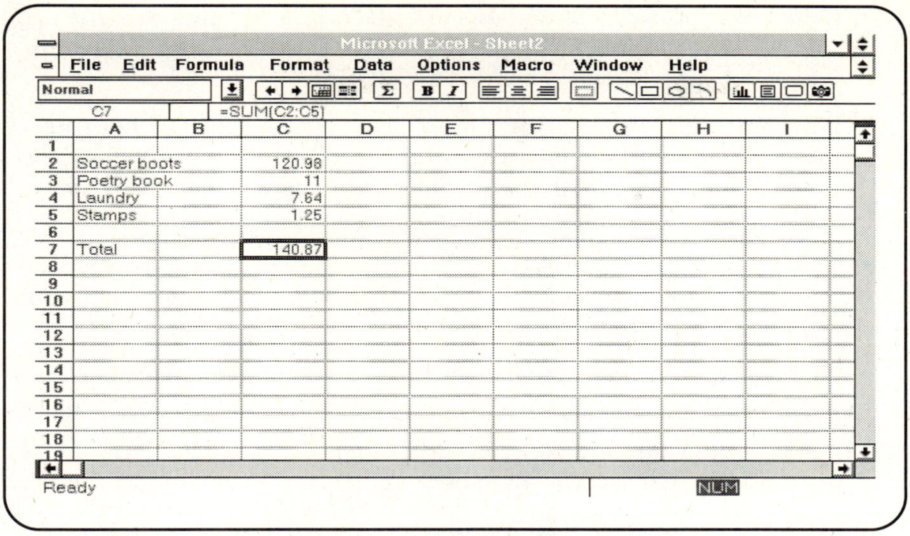

Figure 8.5 *A pasted function.*

All functions can also be typed directly into the formula bar. This can be faster, but with more complex functions it is easy to make mistakes in syntax. You should end up with exactly the same characters in the formula bar either way: an equal sign, the function name, and arguments separated by commas (or cell ranges) enclosed in parentheses.

You may not always have a column of values to sum. If you have several separate cells, columns, or rows, you can refer to each of them separately in your formula. All you do is separate the different cell addresses, columns, and rows with a comma between each address. A formula using the SUM function might look like this: =SUM(C2,D6:D9,B3,A5:E5).

Troubleshooting

Sometimes the function may not return the answer you expect. Here are some possible errors:

- If a message box appears with the message ! error in formula, then look at the values inside your parentheses. Check that each cell address is written correctly (the column letter followed by the row number) and that a colon appears between each range of addresses (no other punctuation mark can be used).

- If the error message #NAME? appears, make sure that there are no spaces in the formula name or between the formula name and parentheses. You are using a name that Excel can't recognize.

- If the answer is smaller than it should be, check to see whether you have the correct cell addresses. If you use a cell address that does not have a number in it, then the Excel function assumes that you want to use the number zero for that information.

- When a formula returns #DIV/0!, it means that you are trying to divide by zero, a mathematical impossibility. The best advice is to check your cell references.

- $N/A means that no value is available. You are referencing cells that contain no values.

- If #NULL! appears, you are referencing two cell areas that don't intersect. See the section "Reference Operators" earlier in this chapter.

- #NUM! means that there is a problem with a number. You might be using a negative number where only positive numbers are relevant, or a formula might be unable to find a result.

- #REF! means that you are referencing a cell that isn't valid. You may have deleted the cell.

Further Information on Functions

Three chapters in Part 2, "Advanced Techniques," give more information about the use of functions.

Chapter 14, "Analyzing, Calculating, and Using Solver," has a section on array formulas. Sometimes you find yourself inserting an identical formula in many cells with no difference between them except the cell references. Array formulas can save you time and computer memory in these circumstances.

Chapter 11, "Advanced Macros and Application Customization," discusses the use of functions in macro sheets. Functions can be broken down into two types: *worksheet* functions and *macro* functions. Worksheet functions—for example, ABS()—can be used on both worksheets and macro sheets. Macro functions—for example, SELECT()—are only available in macro sheets.

Chapter 15, "Using Q+E," discusses functions that can be used (through macros) to manipulate the Q+E application.

CHAPTER 9

Advanced Worksheet Management

There are a number of ways to manage worksheets to make them work even more efficiently for you. In this chapter, you'll find out how to customize the workspace by hiding windows, turning on and off features such as scroll bars, and working with a group of documents as a single workspace. You'll learn how to link Excel worksheets with each other, with other Excel documents, and with documents from other applications.

You'll find out how to consolidate data from different ranges so that you can work with it as one set of data and how to import data from other applications (including other spreadsheets, such as Lotus 1-2-3).

Excel's powerful outliner, which allows you to expand and collapse views of a spreadsheet so that you view only as much as you want to at one time, is also described.

As you work with multiple files, you may want to set up protection so that you do not inadvertently write over data. Protection is particularly important if you are running Excel on a network.

Workspace Customization

The "workspace" is the area Excel uses to display the documents you have open — one worksheet or multiple worksheets, charts, and macro sheets. The workspace is whatever you are working with at one time. As you work, you may find that you tend to use certain documents together, such as a sales report for the region, a sales report for the district, sales reports for certain individuals, graphs of sales results, and perhaps a balance sheet that shows the effects of sales on the bottom line. Customizing your workspace helps you to perform your tasks more effectively.

You can customize the workspace by:

- Hiding windows or documents in your workspace.

- Turning on or off certain features, such as the scroll bars.

- Setting options to apply to all the open documents in the workspace, such as whether the documents should have absolute or relative reference.

You can save the group of documents in the workspace as a single workspace and then later recall the documents all together, simply by recalling the workspace.

You may want to hide a window in the workspace to prevent yourself or someone else from making unintentional changes to the document in that window. When you hide a document, it does not appear in the listing of documents when you choose Window from the menu bar. It does remain "linked" to any documents you have linked it with (this concept is explained in a later section, "Linking"), and macros in the hidden window remain available.

Tip: To keep a document in the workspace for later use without having it clutter your list of documents under Window, use Window Hide.

Follow these steps to hide a document:

1. Be sure you are using full menus.

2. Click on the document you want to hide to make it the active document.

3. From the Window menu, choose Hide.

Figure 9.1 shows the Window menu.

As soon as you choose Hide, the document disappears. It remains a fully functional part of the workspace but is invisible on the screen and on the Window menu.

To "unhide" the document (make it visible again), follow these steps:

1. From the Window menu, choose Unhide. (Again, you must be using full menus.) The Unhide dialog box appears (Figure 9.2), listing all the hidden documents.

2. Choose the worksheet you want to make visible.

If you have assigned a password to the document, Excel asks for the password and then makes the document visible again.

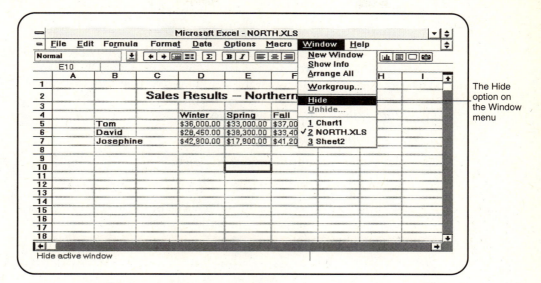

Figure 9.1   The Window menu.

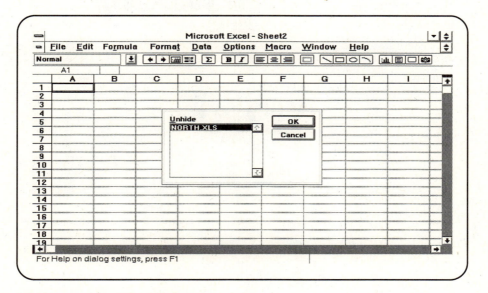

Figure 9.2   The Unhide dialog box.

120 Advanced Techniques

 Tip: If you have made all the documents invisible, the Unhide command moves to the File menu. You can find it there.

Just as you can hide entire documents within the workspace, you can decide to hide parts of the workspace itself. If you are not using the horizontal scroll bars, for instance, you may want to hide them. That way you can see another row of cells at the bottom of your worksheet.

To customize the workspace, use Options Workspace. Follow these steps:

1. Make certain you are using full menus.

2. From the Options menu, choose Workspace.

   You see the Workspace dialog box, shown in Figure 9.3.

3. To customize your workspace, turn the check boxes in the dialog box on or off. Table 9.1 summarizes the choices you can make in the Workspace dialog box.

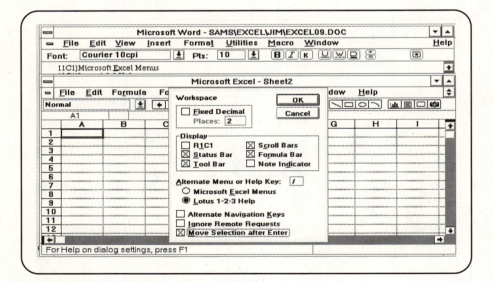

Figure 9.3 *The Workspace dialog box.*

Table 9.1   The Workspace dialog box options.

Option	Effect
Fixed Decimal	Elect to have a fixed number of decimal places (without having to type them in).
Places	If Fixed Decimal is turned on, specify the number of decimal places.
R1C1	Changes to the rows and columns style of referencing from A1 style.
Status Bar	Displays or hides the status bar.
Tool Bar	Displays or hides the tool bar.
Scroll Bars	Display or hide the scroll bars.
Formula Bar	Displays or hides the formula bar.
Note Indicator	If active, displays a small dot in the top right corner of a cell with a note attached.
Alternate Menu or Help Key	Specify a key (such as backslash) to activate the menu bar.
Microsoft Excel Menus	Display Microsoft Excel menus when you press the Alternate Menu key.
Lotus 1-2-3 Help	Display Help for Lotus 1-2-3 users when you press the Help key.
Alternate Navigation Keys	Provides alternate keystrokes for navigating in the spreadsheet, entering formulas and labels, and doing other actions.
Ignore Remote Requests	Causes Excel to ignore or not ignore requests from other applications.
Move Selection after Enter	If checked, means that Excel automatically moves the active cell down one row when you enter a formula or value into a cell.

Once you have set up a number of documents in the workspace and customized it to suit your purposes, you can save the workspace and retrieve it later. Follow these steps to save the workspace:

1. Using full menus, choose File Save Workspace.

2. In the Save Workspace dialog box, type a name for the workspace. (Unless you specify a different extension, Excel uses .XLW.)

3. Choose OK.

   You have saved your workspace and can reuse it.

 Caution: The workspace you save is not the actual files but just a list of the files. You must save the files individually as well. Be sure to save changes in them before closing the workspace. Simply saving the workspace does not, in itself, save the files.

Worksheet Calculations

Since worksheets calculate automatically, you can use a worksheet in basic ways without having to worry about calculation. You don't even have to choose "Total," as you might on a cash register. Excel works out calculations based on values and formulas you have entered. However, you can change how Excel calculates to suit your own purposes.

Unless you specify otherwise, a worksheet recalculates each time you change the value in one of the cells. Particularly for large, complex worksheets, calculation can take some time. To speed up Excel's response time, you can set it to calculate only on request. Manual calculation can save you time when you are working with charts or tables, too. When you change values that affect the charts, Excel redraws open charts on the active worksheet or charts linked to it.

Follow these steps to calculate manually:

1. Choose Calculation from the Options menu.

   The Calculation dialog box, shown in Figure 9.4, appears.

2. Click on the Manual option.

 Tip: You can also choose Automatic Except Tables. With that option, Microsoft automatically calculates everything except tables each time you change a value in one of the cells.

3. To begin manual calculation, choose Options Calculate Now.

9 — Advanced Worksheet Management 123

When you choose Options Calculate Now, Excel recalculates all open worksheets, macros sheets (including data tables), and charts.

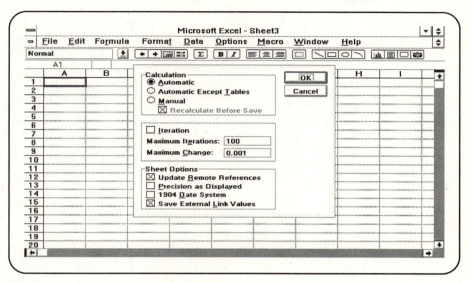

Figure 9.4   *The Calculation dialog box.*

You can choose to calculate only the active worksheet (along with charts on the worksheet or charts linked to it) instead of all open worksheet, macro sheets, and charts.

Follow these steps:

1. Hold down Shift and choose Options.

2. Choose Calculate Document.

Calculation with Displayed Values

Unless you specify otherwise, Excel calculates with stored full values (15 digits) instead of displayed values. The choice you make can change displayed values, though. If you display numbers rounded to two decimal places, for instance, then a calculation based on displayed values might differ from full values. (If you add .253 and .253, the full value is .506, which would display as .51. The rounded value, though, would be .50.)

Follow these steps to use displayed values instead of full values:

1. Choose Calculation from the Options menu. The Calculation dialog box appears.

124 Advanced Techniques

2. Click on the Precision as Displayed check box.

3. Choose OK.

4. After Excel asks for confirmation, choose OK again.

Choosing Precision as Displayed affects only the active worksheet, not other open worksheets. It does not affect numbers you have formatted in the General number format, which it always calculates with full precision.

 Tip: Be careful about using Precision as Displayed with large worksheets. Calculation is slower because Excel has to round numbers as it calculates.

Saving Without Calculating

Unless you specify otherwise, Excel automatically calculates a worksheet when you save it even though you are using manual calculation. For a large worksheet, however, you may not want to wait for Excel to do the calculation. Follow these steps to save without calculating:

1. Choose Options Calculation.

2. Choose Manual.

3. Turn off the Recalculate Before Save check box.

Excel will not recalculate the worksheet before saving.

Importing from Other Applications

There are two main ways to import data and pictures from other applications into Excel—with the clipboard and with the File Open command.

Importing with the Clipboard

Importing with the clipboard is like using the clipboard for any other operation. You cut or copy information into the clipboard and then paste it into the sheet you are working on. Follow these steps to import data from another application into Excel:

1. Make active the document you want to copy from another application.

9— Advanced Worksheet Management

2. Using procedures from that application, cut or copy the data. In doing so, you place the data on the clipboard.
3. Make the Excel sheet the active document.
4. Select the cells where you want to paste the data from the clipboard.
5. Choose Edit Paste.

 Tip: To paste a picture of the data rather than the data itself, hold down the Shift key when you choose Edit. Then choose Paste Picture.

Table 9.2 summarizes the clipboard formats you can import into Excel.

Table 9.2   Clipboard formats that can be imported into Excel.

Format	Identifier
Microsoft Excel file format	BIFF
Text (tab delimited)	TEXT
Text (formatted)	RTF (only from Microsoft Excel)
Comma-separated values	CSV
Symbolic link format	SYLK
Lotus 1-2-3 Release 2.0	WK1
Data interchange	DIF
Picture	METAFILEPICT
Bitmap	BITMAP (only from Microsoft Excel)
Embedded Object	NATIVE

Importing with the File Open Command

Importing with the File Open command is not much different from opening an Excel worksheet. For the formats it recognizes, Excel does the importing automatically.

Follow these steps to import a file with the File Open command:

1. Choose File Open.

126 Advanced Techniques

You see the Open dialog box, as shown in Figure 9.5.

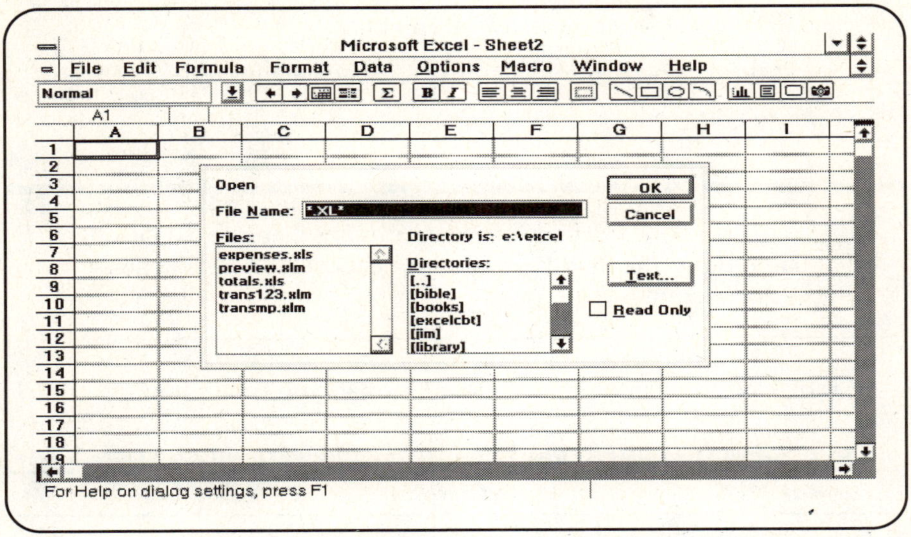

Figure 9.5 *The Open dialog box, for importing files.*

2. Choose the directory for the files you want to import.
3. For file name, type ***.***.

> **Tip:** If you know the directory and name of the file you want to import, you can just type them in directly.

4. Choose OK.

    You see a list of files in the specified directory.

5. From the Files box, select the document you want to import.
6. Choose OK.

    Table 9.3 lists the file formats you can import into Excel.

Table 9.3 *File formats that can be imported into Excel.*

Format	Document Type
CSV	Comma-separated values
DBF 2	dBASE II
DBF 3	dBASE III
DBF 4	dBASE IV
DIF	Data interchange format (VisiCalc)
Normal	Standard Microsoft Excel format
SYLK	Symbolic link (Microsoft Multiplan)
Text	ANSI text for Windows, ASCII text for OS/2, text for Macintosh
WK1	Lotus 1-2-3 Release 2
WKS	Lotus 1-2-3 Release 1 and Lotus Symphony
WK3	Lotus 1-2-3 Release 3
Excel 2.x	Microsoft Excel version 2.x

Linking

Whenever you create an external reference in a worksheet—that is, create a formula or define a name that refers to a cell, cell range, or name from another worksheet—you "link" those two worksheets. You can link one or more Excel worksheets, one or more Excel macro sheets, or a worksheet and a chart. You can also create a link between an Excel worksheet or chart and a document in another application. This type of linking uses *dynamic data exchange (DDE)* and enables you to keep data in multiple related documents current with each other.

Linking Among Microsoft Excel Worksheets

To link two (or more) Microsoft Excel worksheets, create a formula in one document that contains an external reference to a value in the other. An external reference formula has the following syntax:

=sheet1.xls!$B$2

128 Advanced Techniques

The first part of the formula (before the exclamation point) gives the name of the worksheet that contains the cell being referred to. The second part of the formula (after the exclamation point) contains the actual cell, range, or named range in the linked worksheet. You can type in the actual syntax, but you do not have to. You can call up the two documents simultaneously and point with the mouse to set up the link. Figure 9.6 shows two worksheets, side by side, with one linked to the other by an external reference.

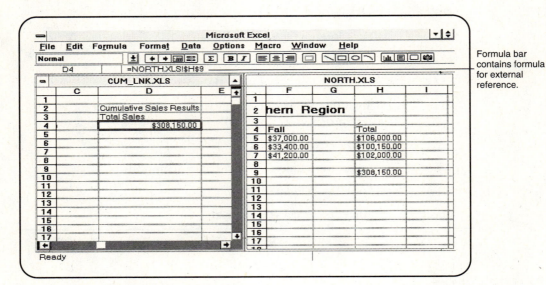

Figure 9.6 Two linked worksheets.

Follow these steps to link two Microsoft Excel documents:

1. Open the "dependent" worksheet, the worksheet that will depend upon a "supporting" worksheet for certain information.

2. Open the window containing the supporting document (the document containing the information you want.)

 Tip: Use Window Arrange All to have Excel display the worksheets in the workspace at the same time.

3. In the supporting document, select the cell or cell range to which you want to refer.

4. Choose Edit Copy.

9 — Advanced Worksheet Management   129

You see the marquee around the selected range.

5. Click on the dependent worksheet to make it active.
6. Select the cell (or, for a range, the upper-left corner of the range) that will contain the external reference.
7. Choose Edit Paste Link to establish the link.

Excel links the two worksheets with an external reference formula.

Saving Linked Worksheets

As a general practice, you should save the supporting documents (the documents with the information used in the linked document) before saving the dependent document (the one linked to the supporting documents). That way you can be certain that the document names you use in your external references are the current names. If you change the name of a supporting document, be sure that the dependent document is open when you do so. Then the external reference in the supporting document will be updated. Excel does not allow you to save a dependent document that has a reference to an unnamed document. It displays a message and asks you to name the supporting document.

Follow these steps to save linked worksheets:

1. Make the supporting document window the active window.
2. Choose File Save (or File Save As for unnamed documents).
3. Repeat steps one and two for any additional supporting documents.
4. Make the dependent document the active window.
5. Choose File Save.

> **Tip:** If possible, save linked documents in the same directory so that it's easy for you to find the documents and work with them later. If you move the worksheets to new directories, for instance, you can keep the link intact by moving all the linked documents to the new directory.

You do not have to save linked documents into the same directory. If you link to documents in other directories, though, be particularly careful to save the supporting documents before the dependent documents. If you use the File Manager to move documents to other directories, you may destroy the links. If you do, you can restore the link with the File Links command.

Data Consolidation

Consolidating large or small amounts of data that reside in different cells or ranges of cells into one range can be quite useful for seeing combined results from a number of different places on the worksheet. The Consolidate option in Data allows you to perform 11 different functions, like SUM and AVERAGE, on data in different ranges painlessly. The cell ranges can be in the same worksheet, or they can be in separate worksheets. You can perform a one-time consolidation, or you can create a *dynamic data exchange,* using the linking option to make the consolidation an ongoing process. The command consolidates only numbers, not text or formulas (although you can transfer the text in title names). Number formats (but not text formats) do get inserted into the destination area.

It's not necessary to open the worksheets containing the source areas (the areas to be consolidated), though you might find it easier to do so, since otherwise you must remember the cell ranges or the cell ranges' names. The worksheets do need to be saved on disk before data from them can be consolidated with other data.

Follow these steps to consolidate data:

1. If you are using separate worksheets, make the destination worksheet (the worksheet to consolidate to) the active worksheet.

2. Select the destination area that will contain the consolidated data.

    If you select a single cell, Excel inserts the consolidated data down and to the right. Select a row or a column and the data is inserted down or to the right respectively. Select a range of cells and Excel inserts as much as can fit into the area—displaying a message if the area is not big enough.

    If you define a range as Consolidate_Area, Excel always uses that range as the destination range in a consolidation.

3. Choose Consolidate from the Data menu.

    The Consolidate dialog box appears, as shown in Figure 9.7.

    In the example, the two windows on the right contain the source areas displaying rainfall over four months in separate locations. Suppose you want to sum the amounts into the destination area in the window on the left.

4. Choose your function from the dialog box.

    The 11 functions available are AVERAGE, COUNT, COUNTA, MAX, MIN, PRODUCT, STDEV, STDEVP, SUM, VAR, and VARP. SUM is the default. See Part 3 for information on each available function.

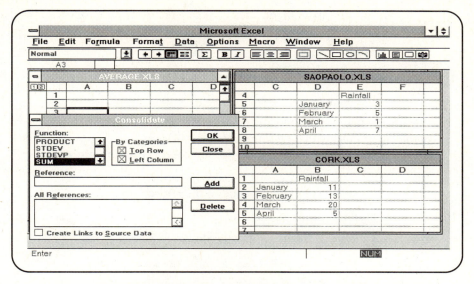

Figure 9.7 *The Consolidate dialog box with the three open worksheets arranged in different windows.*

If you want to transfer titles (also known as categories) either in rows or in columns, you can use the Top Row or Left Column options or both. In the example, the top row has `Rainfall` as a title, while the left column has `January`, `February`, etc., as titles. Only text in those cell positions of the designated source areas will be transferred.

5. Check Top Row and/or Left Column if you want to consolidate by category (title).

   In the example both options are chosen.

6. Now you must specify where the data is coming from. Specify the first range to consolidate from in the Reference box.

   You can specify the range in two ways: by typing in the reference or by actually going to the other worksheet and selecting the cell range. When the cursor is in the Reference box in the Consolidate dialog box, Excel allows you to select the cell ranges on each sheet directly. If you choose Arrange All from Window before choosing the Consolidate command, worksheet windows display as in Figure 9.7, making things easier. But even with the Consolidate dialog box on screen, you can change between worksheet windows, selecting as you go. The dialog box remains on screen.

   In the example, the data is coming from two worksheets, both open and arranged on the screen. SaoPaolo.xls!$D$4:$E$8 is the reference

132 Advanced Techniques

name for the first worksheet. This is the worksheet name followed by an exclamation mark and the cell range.

7. Choose the <u>A</u>dd button in the dialog box.

   The reference is added to the All References box in the dialog box.

8. Repeat steps 6 and 7 for each range of cells to consolidate.

   The alternative to specifying ranges in the Reference box is to use names defined through <u>D</u>efine Names in the Fo<u>r</u>mula menu. This way is safer since it's easy to make a mistake when specifying cell ranges.

9. Select the Create Links to <u>S</u>ource Data option if you want Excel to update the numbers as they change in the source ranges.

10. Choose OK.

    Figure 9.8 shows the total rainfall for the areas selected.

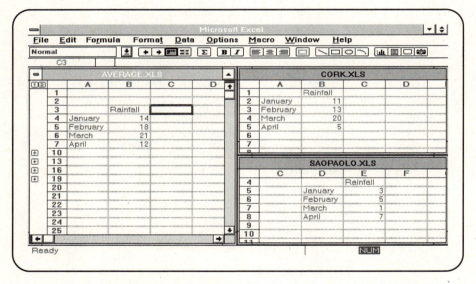

Figure 9.8   *A consolidated set of figures.*

 Tip: You can use wild-card characters, asterisks, and question marks in the Reference box. For example with a series of files named Rain1.xls, Rain2.xls, Rain3.xls, etc., you could specify Rain?.xls!Total in the Reference box and Excel would consolidate all of them.

9 — Advanced Worksheet Management   133

It's also possible to consolidate *without* transferring titles. Simply uncheck Top Row and Left Column and choose only the data to consolidate, not the titles, in the worksheets. For example, in Figure 9.9, the column Average was produced by typing *Average* and consolidating $E$5:$E$8 from Saopaolo.xls and $B$2:$B$5 from Cork.xls, using the AVERAGE function.

In some situations, you may need to delete references no longer needed—where one consolidation is already completed, for instance, or where you made a mistake. Just select the reference in All References and choose Delete to do this.

You can edit, add, and delete references at any stage after the first consolidation.

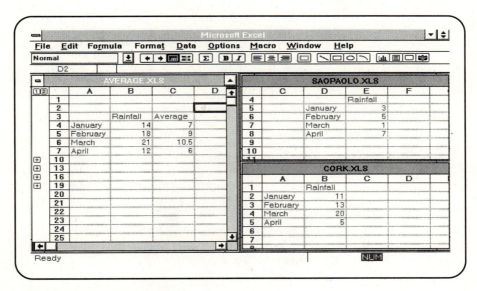

Figure 9.9 *Consolidated data.*

Consolidating Data from Lotus 1-2-3 Files

You can also consolidate data from Lotus 1-2-3 files. Like the Excel files, they don't have to be open to be consolidated, and you can even create links to 1-2-3 files when you consolidate.

Creating a Workgroup

If you are working with a group of closely related documents, you may want to create a workgroup out of them. The advantage of a workgroup is that changes you make to one document appear in all the documents in the group. This goes beyond dynamic data exchange to affect all aspects of the documents. You can change the formatting, enter and edit data, and change display options. For example, if you have a series of documents with the title in the same location, you can change the formatting of the title from 12-point bold to 14-point bold in one document and be certain that you have made the change uniformly in all the other documents.

To create a workgroup, follow these steps (you must use full menus):

1. Use File Open to open the worksheets you want to have in the workgroup. (You can have other worksheets open as well and not include them in the workgroup.)

2. Be sure that the active worksheet is the one in which you want to make the changes that will affect all worksheets in the group.

3. Choose Window Workgroup.

The Select Workgroup dialog box appears, as shown in Figure 9.10.

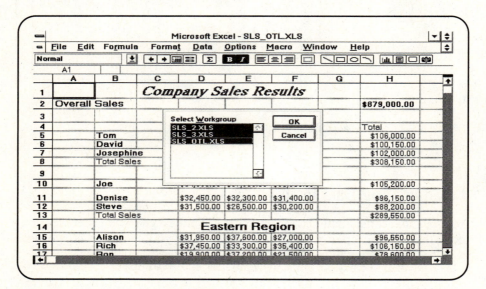

Figure 9.10 *The Select Workgroup dialog box.*

4. Select the documents you want to have in the workgroup. (To select multiple documents in an Excel dialog box, hold down the Shift key and click on the document names with the mouse. With the keyboard, hold down Ctrl and press the up arrow or down arrow to move to the worksheet you want to choose. Press the space bar to select it.)

5. Click on OK.

If you click on the Window menu, you will see "Workgroup" listed along with the names of worksheets or macro sheets. (You cannot put a chart in a workgroup.)

Once you have set up the workgroup, you can choose to see all the documents in the workgroup at once. (Even though you know a change in the top document is supposed to affect all the others, you may want to watch all the documents to make sure you are getting the result you want.)

To see the documents all at once, use a command similar to the Window Arrange All command. Once you have set up a workgroup, you see the Window Arrange Workgroup command. Follow these steps:

1. Choose Window.

2. Choose Arrange Workgroup.

Excel arranges all the documents in the workgroup and displays them on the workspace. It does not display documents that are open but not in the workgroup.

Figure 9.11 shows a workgroup after Excel has arranged it in the workspace.

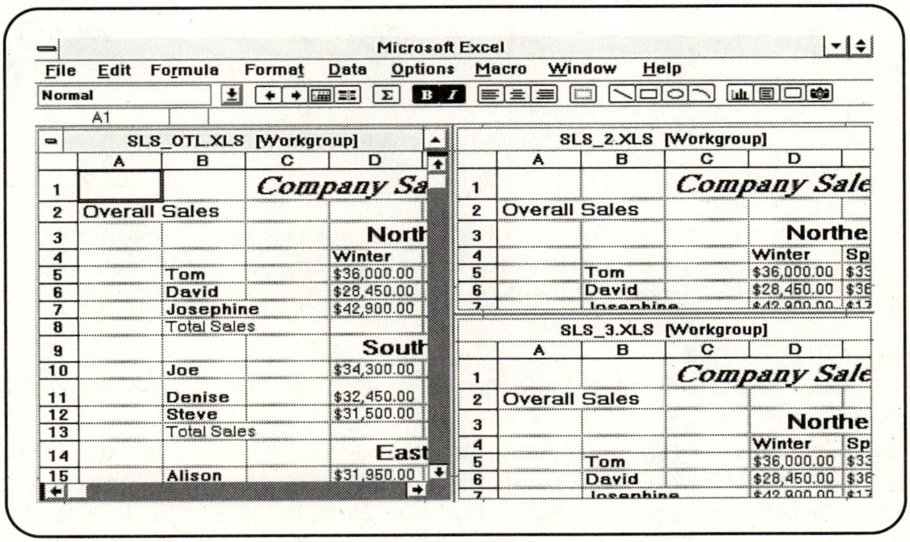

Figure 9.11 *A workgroup arranged in the workspace.*

You can change a workgroup once you have set it up. Follow these steps to delete or add a document:

1. Choose Window Workgroup.

   You see a list of all open macro sheets and worksheets (except hidden ones), including those presently in the workgroup.

2. To add a document not currently in the list or to delete one that is:

   Mouse: Hold down Shift and click on the name of the document.

   Keyboard: Hold down Ctrl, and press the up or down arrows to move to the document you want to add or delete. Press space bar.

3. Choose OK.

You can also enter data directly into the workgroup. What you enter into the active sheet goes into the other sheets in the same location as in the active sheet. Follow these steps:

1. In the active sheet, move the selection box to the cell or range where you want to enter the data.

2. Type in the data.

   In the active sheet you see the data in the formula bar and in the active cell.

3. Click on the enter box or press Enter.

To delete the data instead of entering it, press Esc or choose Cancel.

You can also copy the contents, the formatting or both from a location in one sheet in the group to the same location in the other sheets in the group. Follow these steps:

1. In the active worksheet, select the cells to copy.

2. From the Edit menu, choose Fill Workgroup.

   You see the Fill Workgroup dialog box. Choose All to copy contents, formatting, and formulas. Choose Formulas to copy only formulas. Choose Formats to copy only formats.

3. Choose OK.

Excel copies the selected cells to the same cell location in the other worksheets in the group.

To stop working with a workgroup, choose a worksheet that is not in the workgroup by clicking it, choosing on it from the Window menu, or pressing Ctrl-F6. The term [Workgroup] disappears from the title bar. To use the workgroup again, you have to create it again from the Window menu.

Workgroup Editing

Not all Excel commands apply to workgroups. Table 9.4 lists all the commands that do and describes their effects.

Table 9.4   Excel commands for workgroups.

Command	Effect in a Workgroup
Data Series	Enters the data series into all sheets in the workgroup. (If the starting values are different in each sheet, the data series will be different as well.)
Edit Clear	Clears the selected cells — for all sheets in the workgroup
Edit Delete	Deletes the selected cells, for all sheets in the workgroup
Edit Fill Down	Fills the selected cells down or up, for all sheets in the workgroup
Edit Fill Right	Fills the selected cells right or left, for all sheets in the workgroup
Edit Fill Workgroup	Copies the selection in the active sheet to all other sheets in the workgroup
Edit Insert	Inserts the selected cells into all sheets in the workgroup
File Close	Closes all sheets in the workgroup, one by one
File Page Setup	Applies all page setup settings to all sheets in the workgroup
File Print	Prints all sheets in the workgroup, one by one
File Save	Saves all sheets in the workgroup, one by one
File Save Workspace	Saves the workgroup (all sheets) as a workspace file
Format Alignment	Aligns the data for the same cells in all sheets in the workgroup
Format Border	Applies borders for the same cells in all sheets in the workgroup

continued

Table 9.4   continued

Command	Effect in a Workgroup
Format Cell Protection	Applies cell protection for the same cells in all sheets in the workgroup
Format Column Width	Changes column width for the same cells in all sheets in the workgroup
Format Font	Changes the font for the same cells in all sheets in the workgroup
Format Number	Applies a built-in or custom number format for the same cells in all sheets in the workgroup. (If you delete the custom format, Excel deletes it from all sheets in the workgroup with the format.)
Format Patterns	Applies cell patterns and shading for the same cells in all sheets in the workgroup
Format Row Height	Changes height for the same rows in all sheets in the workgroup
Format Style	Applies a style for the same cells in all sheets in the workgroup
Formula Goto	Selects the named area or reference for the sheet where you are entering data
Formula Paste Function	Pastes a function for the same formula in all sheets in the workgroup
Formula Show Active Cell	Displays the active cell into which you are entering and editing data
Macro Relative/Absolute Record	Changes the macro setting for all sheets in the workgroup
Macro Record	Records a macro for all sheets in the workgroup
Macro Run	Runs a macro for all sheets in the workgroup
Macro Start Recorder	Available only if you used Macro Set Recorder on a single macro sheet before creating the workgroup. (Do not include the macro sheet in the workgroup, or changes you make will write over entries in the sheet.)

Command	Effect in a Workgroup
Options Calculate Now	Calculates the formulas for all formulas in all sheets in the workgroup
Options Short Menus	Displays short menus for all sheets in the workgroup
Options Workspace	Applies settings for all sheets in the workgroup
Window Arrange Workgroup	Arranges on the workspace the windows of the sheets in the workgroup
Window Workgroup	Creates workgroup out of designated worksheets and macro sheets

Outlining

As you saw earlier in this chapter, in the section entitled "Linking," you can simplify your view in any one worksheet by presenting only certain information in the worksheet and then creating a link to another worksheet that contains additional detailed information that you would prefer not to show on your initial worksheet. One worksheet might contain corporate sales information, for instance. A linked worksheet might contain regional sales information. Another linked worksheet might have district sales information.

There is another, often more convenient, way to get various views of your information: the outlining feature. If you are working with information that has numerous levels—such as sales results by region and district or by quarter and year—outlining can allow you to see one, two, three, or up to eight levels of the information at one time.

Creating the Outline

There are two ways to create an outline: You can have Excel create it for you, or you can create it yourself manually. You can create the outline either in a new worksheet or in an existing worksheet. To create the outline, you must have all references in the worksheet pointing consistently in one direction, such as up in rows or left in columns.

Follow these steps to create an outline:

1. Select the range you want to outline. If you select a single cell, Excel treats that the same as if you had selected the entire worksheet.

140 Advanced Techniques

2. Choose Formula Outline.

The Outline dialog box, shown in Figure 9.12, appears.

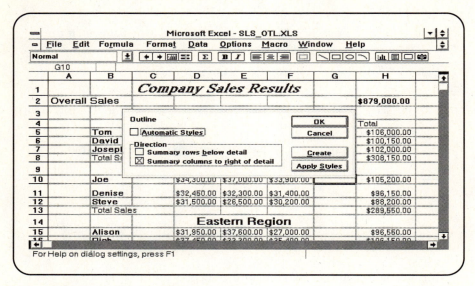

Figure 9.12 *The Outline dialog box.*

3. Choose Create.

Excel creates the outline, and you see the outline symbols in the worksheet, as shown in Figure 9.13.

 Tip: To create an outline manually without having Excel outline the entire worksheet, choose the Demote button from the Toolbar.

Table 9.5 summarizes the tools you can use in working with an outline.

9 — Advanced Worksheet Management **141**

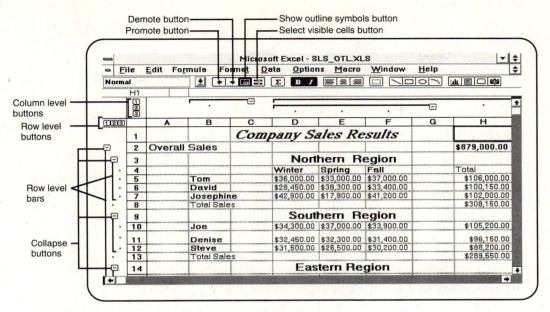

Figure 9.13   *A worksheet with outline symbols.*

Table 9.5   *Outlining tools.*

Tool	Use
Promote button	Raises the selected columns or rows to a higher level
Demote button	Raises the selected columns or rows to a lower level
Select visible cells button	Selects all the cells that are visible in an outline range
Show outline symbols button	Displays or hides the outline symbols
Expand button	Indicates that there are collapsed levels. Click to display the collapsed levels.
Collapse button	Indicates that lower levels are displayed. Click to collapse the levels.

continued

142 Advanced Techniques

Table 9.5   continued

Tool	Use
Row and column level buttons	Indicates the number of levels in an outline. Click on a certain level (such as 2) to display the information for that level and the levels above it.
Row and column level bars	The bars indicate that you have displayed all the rows or columns for that level. To collapse the levels beneath the bar, click on the bar or the collapse button at the end of the bar.

Working with the Outline

When you work with the outline, you essentially promote or demote rows or columns in the outline to make the worksheet display the information you want. You can promote or demote individual rows or columns, or you can collapse or expand entire levels.

Figures 9.14, 9.15, and 9.16, for instance, show three views of the same worksheet. Figure 9.14 shows all three levels in the outline, providing complete sales information for a company. Figure 9.15 shows just two levels, providing information on regional sales totals and overall sales only. Figure 9.16 shows overall sales only.

You can promote or demote individual rows or columns, or you can expand or collapse entire levels of the outline at once. Follow these steps to promote or demote an individual row or column:

1. Select the entire row or column you want to promote or demote. (If you do not select an entire row or column, a dialog box asks whether you want to demote rows or columns.)

2. **Mouse:** Click on the Demote button in the Toolbar. The row or column moves down a level in the outline — for instance, from level one to level two.

   Keyboard: Press Alt-Shift-right arrow.

To expand or collapse entire levels of the outline, follow these steps with the mouse:

1. To collapse the level, click on either the collapse button or the level bar for the data you want to collapse. To expand a level with an Expand button next to it (a button with a plus sign on it), click on the Expand button for that level.

Figure 9.14 *An outline with no levels collapsed.*

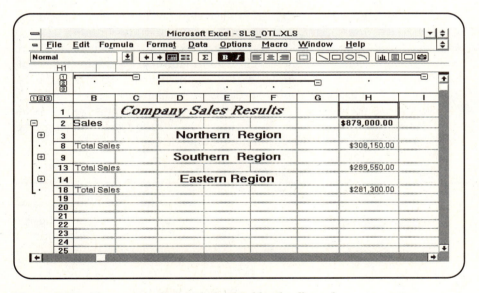

Figure 9.15 *The same outline with the third level collapsed.*

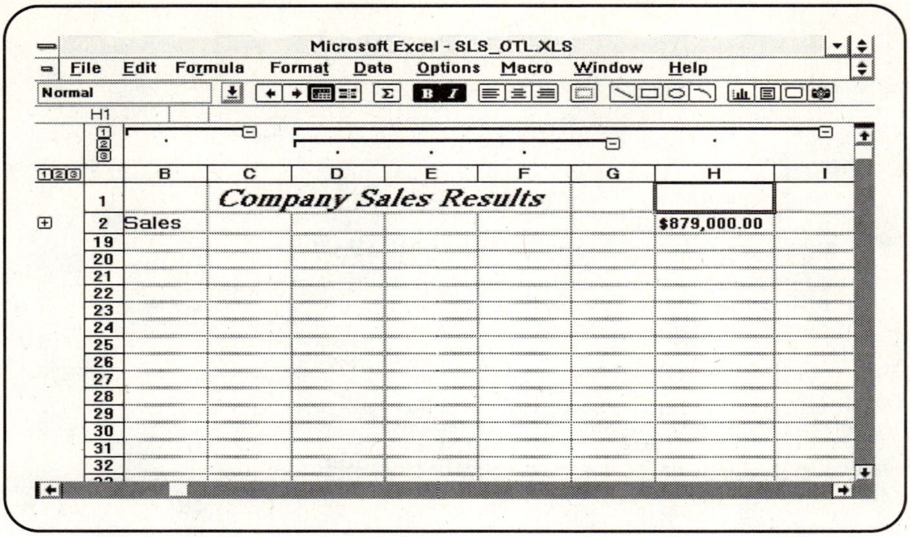

144 Advanced Techniques

[Screenshot of Microsoft Excel - SLS_OTL.XLS showing an outline with second and third levels collapsed. The worksheet displays "Company Sales Results" in row 1 and "Sales" with value "$879,000.00" in row 2, followed by rows 19-32.]

Figure 9.16 *The same outline with the second and third levels collapsed.*

You can work with the data in other ways, too. For one thing, you can adjust the ways you see the data. If you are familiar with outlining in word processors like Microsoft Word, you are accustomed to seeing subordinate information appear below higher levels of information. In a worksheet, though, the subordinate information can appear below, above, to the right, or to the left of higher levels. It can also appear vertically or horizontally.

To change the way you see the outline, use the Formula Outline command. When you choose Formula Outline, you see the Outline dialog box. Table 9.6 summarizes the choices in the Outline dialog box.

Table 9.6 *Choices in the Outline dialog box.*

Option	Effect
Automatic Styles	Have Excel apply built-in cell styles to the summary rows and columns of the outline when you promote or demote them
Direction—Summary rows below detail	If activated, places summary rows in the outline below detail rows
Direction—Summary columns to right of detail	If activated, places summary columns in the outline to the right of detail columns
Create	Automatically assigns outline levels based on the formulas in the worksheet. (If you have checked Automatic Styles, Excel applies built-in cells styles as well.)

Option	Effect
Apply Styles	Applies styles for row and column levels to the selected outline if it does not currently have them
OK	Accept setting for Automatic Styles and Direction you choose when you create the outline manually

Once you have hidden certain levels of the worksheet, you can work with the displayed levels just as if they were a single worksheet. You can select just the visible cells, format them, copy them, use the chart tool or the File New command to chart them, or use the Edit Paste Special or Edit Paste Link command on them.

Clearing an Outline

If you don't plan to work with the outline for some time, you may not want the outline symbols and tools at the top and left of the outline. Follow this step to clear the symbols:

1. Click on the Show Outline Symbols button in the Toolbar. (The button is a "toggle switch.") You can use it to display the symbols when they are hidden or to hide them when they are displayed.

Clearing the symbols but keeping the outline is one thing. Sometimes, however, you may want to eliminate the outlining you created for a worksheet altogether. Follow these steps to clear the outlining:

1. Select the outline.
2. **Mouse:** Click on the Promote button in the Toolbar until you have moved all rows and columns to outline level one.

    Keyboard: Press Alt-Shift-left arrow until you have moved all rows and columns to level one.

File Protection

Most of the time, if you are a single user, you do not have to protect your documents or windows. Unless you have a good reason to protect them, it is a good idea not to; because if you assign a password, you may forget it later and have trouble getting into your own document.

146 Advanced Techniques

At times, though, you may need to protect documents. If you are working with multiple users on a network, as explained in the section "Running Excel on a Network," then you may well want to protect certain documents from being accidentally opened or changed. Even if you are not on a network, you may want to protect documents if multiple users have access to them and the documents contain confidential or sensitive information.

You can protect documents in two ways: You can protect them on the disk. That is, you can prevent people from opening them or from saving them. Or you can protect documents that are already open by locking certain cells, which prevents people from changing them, or by hiding cells, which prevents people from reading the cells at all.

Protecting Documents on the Disk

When you assign a password to a document, anyone who wants to open it has to enter the password. Also, anyone who wants to use the document as a linked document has to use the password.

Follow these steps to assign a password to a document:

1. Open the document, or make it the active document.

2. Choose File and Save As.

3. Click on the Options button.

You see the Options dialog box, shown in Figure 9.17.

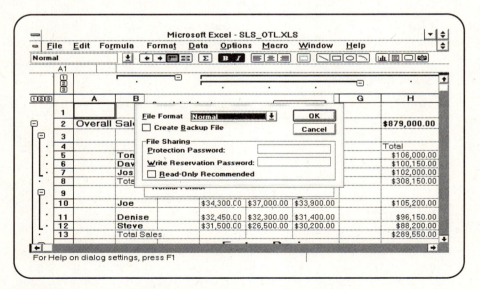

Figure 9.17 *The Options dialog box.*

4. Type a password in the Protection Password box.

   The password can be up to 16 characters long and can have any combination of letters, numbers, and symbols. The passwords are case-sensitive.

   As you type the password, you see an asterisk in the Protection Password box for each character that you type.

5. Choose OK.

   You see a dialog box asking you to retype the password to confirm it.

6. Type the password again.

7. Choose OK.

   The Password Confirmation dialog box closes, and you return to the File Save As dialog box.

8. Choose OK.

   If you have previously stored the document with the same name, Excel asks if you want to replace the existing document with the new one (the document with the password).

9. Choose OK.

You have now protected the document. To open it in the future, you must type in the password.

You can also protect the document in a less extreme way—by allowing read-only access to the document so that the document cannot be changed. That is, you allow other people access to the document, but they cannot change it.

> **Tip:** If someone does make changes to a document with read-only protection, he can save the document under a new name simply by choosing Save As in the File menu and choosing a new name.

Follow these steps to restrict a document to read-only access:

1. Open the document, or make it the active document.

2. Choose File and Save As.

3. Click on the Options button.

   You see the Options dialog box, shown in Figure 9.17.

4. Type a password in the Write Reservation Password box (instead of the Protection Password box as in the previous series of steps).

5. Choose OK.

   You see a dialog box asking you to retype the password to confirm it.

6. Type the password again.

7. Choose OK.

   The Password Confirmation dialog box closes, and you return to the File Save As dialog box.

8. Choose OK.

Once you have saved a document with a write reservation password, you cannot save another file with the same name to replace the protected document.

 Tip: You can remove the password once you have created it. Delete the password from the Protection Password box or from the Write Reservation Password box.

Creating a Read-Only Document

Read-only protection is less strict than password protection because users do not have to know the password to use the document. They can read the document, but they cannot change it. Whereas only one person at a time can have access to a document with write permission, multiple users can have access to a read-only document. On a network you may want to set up documents as read-only, as explained in the section "Running Excel on a Network."

Read-Only Recommended is one of the choices in the File Save As dialog box if you click on the Options button. To create a read-only document, click on the Read-Only Recommended box when in the File Save As dialog box.

Protecting Open Documents

You do not have to protect an entire document. You can leave the document unprotected but choose to protect certain cells, graphic objects, or windows within the document.

Follow these steps to protect worksheet cells:

1. Select the cells you want to protect.

2. Choose Forma**t** Cell Protect**i**on.

   You see the Cell Protection dialog box, shown in Figure 9.18.

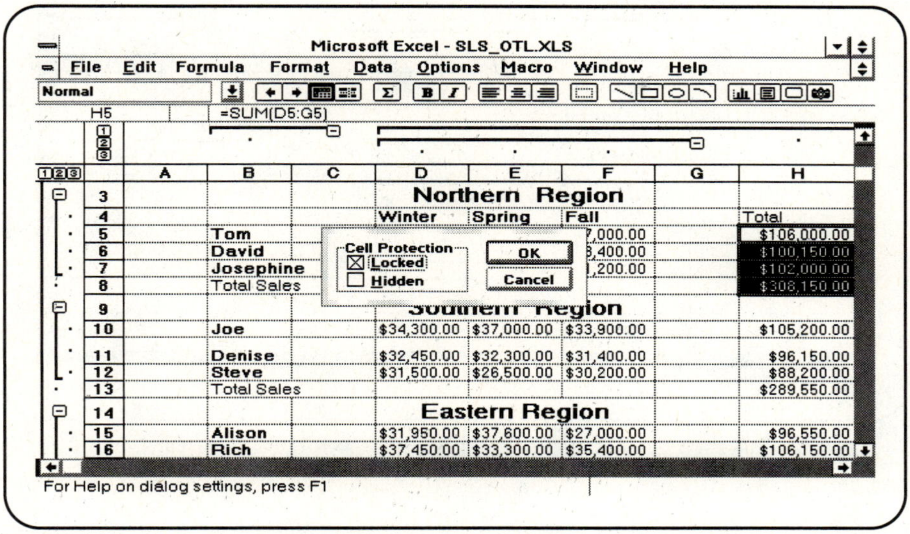

Figure 9.18   The Cell Protection dialog box.

You can choose either Locked or Hidden protection. If you choose Locked, no one can change the contents of the cell. If you choose Hidden, the cell's formula is not displayed in the formula bar when the cell is selected. Only the result of the formula is displayed.

Protecting graphic objects is similar to protecting cells. First, select the graphic objects you want to protect; then choose Forma**t** Object Protect**i**on. In the dialog box, you have only one choice—Locked. You can choose to have the object locked or not. If you choose to lock the object, no one can select, move, size, or format it.

To have protection take effect for worksheet cells and graphic objects, you must set the protection for the document. You use the same steps to set protection for windows in the active document. Follow these steps to set document protection:

1. Choose **O**ptions **P**rotect Document. (For a chart, choose **C**hart **P**rotect Document.)

   You see the Protect Document dialog box, shown in Figure 9.19.

150 Advanced Techniques

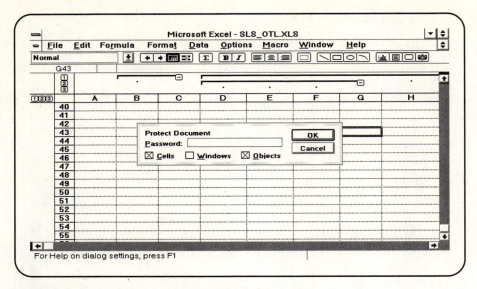

Figure 9.19 *The Protect Document dialog box.*

You can protect cells, windows, or objects. Click on whichever options you want to protect. That is, click on Cells to protect the cells in a worksheet or macro sheet that you have set up to be protected. Click on Objects to protect graphic objects set up for protection. Click on Windows to prevent anyone from changing the size or position of the active window.

In the Password box in the Protect Document dialog box, you can type in a password. Then, if anyone wants to turn off the document protection, he must first type in the password.

Tip: To turn off document protection, choose Options Unprotect Document. (For charts, choose Chart Unprotect Document.) If you have entered a password in the Protect Document dialog box, you have to know the password before you can unprotect the document.

Running Excel on a Network

Once you have Excel set up on a network, multiple users can use the same documents and print them out. For details on setting up and running your network itself, refer to the documentation for the network.

9 — Advanced Worksheet Management **151**

To install Excel on a network instead of on an individual computer, type the name of the network directory when Excel asks you during installation for the name of the directory where you want to install the program.

To start Excel on the network, switch to the directory on the network containing Excel. Then start Excel in the usual way.

Running Excel properly on a network is largely a matter of setting proper protections for the documents, as explained in the previous section. That is, be certain that you assign passwords as appropriate and allow users either read or read/write access.

In any case, only one person at a time can have write access. On a network, if someone attempts to open a document to which he has read/write access while someone else with read/write access is using it, the second user will have only read access to the document.

Opening a Document on a Network

When you open a document on a network, you can have any of the protections explained in the previous section—password protection, read-only access, read-write access. You can also link your own document to a shared document on the network. See "Linking" earlier in this chapter for information on setting up and using such links.

Opening a document on the network is the same as opening a document on your own PC. Follow these steps:

1. From the File menu, choose Open.

2. In the Open dialog box, type the full path name for the document you want to open.

If you do not understand the path names for your network, refer to the documentation for the network.

10
CHAPTER

Advanced Database Management

Chapter 5, "Basic Database Operations," explained how to add, delete, edit, and find records in your database using the data form (available through the Form option in Data). This chapter shows you how to perform these operations directly on the database. You will also learn how to set criteria and extract ranges on the worksheet itself. You can then use extract ranges to copy records from the database meeting the criteria in the criteria range.

The following sections begin by demonstrating how to set up a criteria range on a worksheet. Setting up a criteria range enables you to find records directly on the database through the worksheet, extract (copy) records to another part of the worksheet, and delete records.

Creating and Setting Up a Criteria Range

Chapter 5 showed you how to search for records using criteria specified in the data form. You can also perform this search using criteria specified directly on the worksheet, using what is called a *criteria range*. This method has certain advantages over the data form: One, you can delete many records at once rather than one at a time. Two, you can extract or copy records meeting certain criteria to another part of the worksheet. And third, you can set up more complex criteria in a criteria range.

A database must be set up and defined in Excel before you can create and use a set of criteria. To use a set of criteria directly on the worksheet, you have to specify the criteria in a range of cells that is apart from the database. The range can be on another worksheet, but it must be separate from the database range.

154 Advanced Techniques

It's important to remember that the two methods of setting criteria—using the data form and setting up a criteria range—are separate. Criteria set in the data form do not affect record selections made through the worksheet criteria and vice versa.

Follow these steps to set up a criteria range:

1. Type in the criteria name or names in the first row of the criteria range.

   When you use comparison criteria, you must use the field names of the database, though you need not include all of them. If you use computed criteria, the criteria names can be anything except the database field names. (Comparison and computed criteria are discussed in the following section.)

2. Select the range containing the criteria names and also the blank cells in the row directly underneath.

Figure 10.1 shows an example of a selected criteria range (A1:E2) with the database below it. You insert your criteria in the row of blank cells underneath the names.

> **Tip:** It's usually a good idea to place a criteria range above the database range because then you can extend the database range (that is, add more records underneath the field names) without overwriting the criteria.

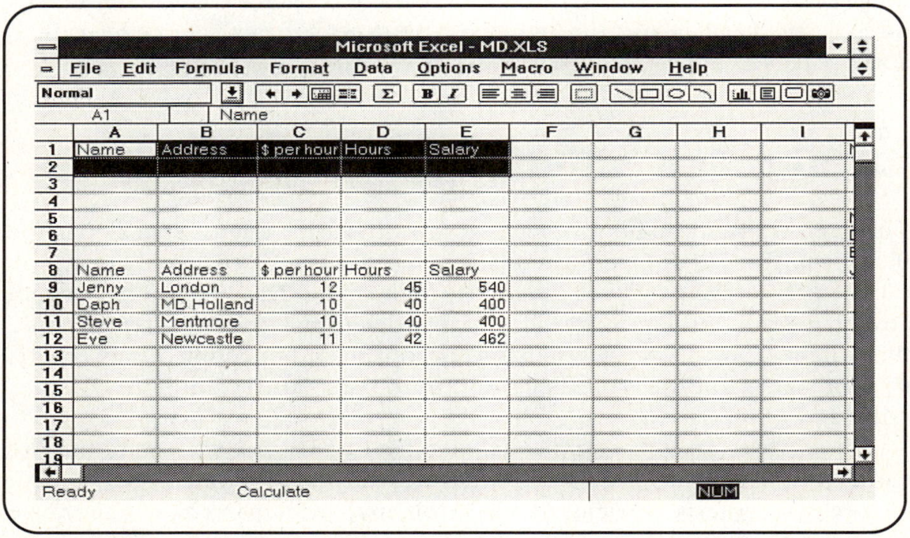

Figure 10.1   A line of criteria names with a blank row underneath.

Computed and Comparison Criteria

There are two kinds of criteria: *comparison criteria* and *computed criteria*. With comparison criteria, you compare the values in one or more fields in your database with other criteria values. The three types of comparison criteria that can be used when setting up a criteria range are the same as those that can be used in data form (discussed in Chapter 5). They are characters (either text, number, data, or logical value); quantities; and wild-card characters (?, *, and ~).

With computed criteria, you use a formula that incorporates at least one field in your database. Excel calculates this formula for each record in the database and selects the record if the result meets the criterion—that is, returns TRUE—or if the number produced by the formula is not zero. If the result is FALSE, zero, a text value, or an error value, the record is not selected. Most of the time the result is TRUE or FALSE.

Figure 10.2 shows an example having both a comparison and a computed criteria.

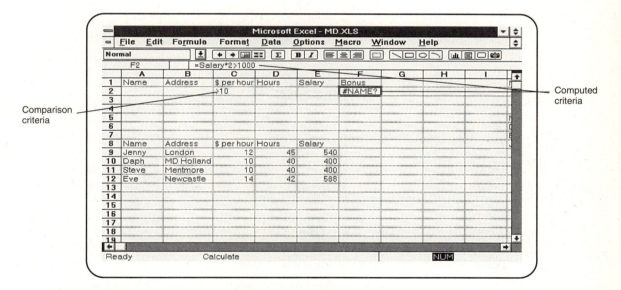

Figure 10.2 Comparison and computed criteria in a criteria range.

The >10 in the $ per hour field is a comparison criterion. The formula Salary*2>1000 (using a field name of Bonus) is a computed criterion. It measures whether someone's salary multiplied by 2 is greater than $1000, in which case the employee is entitled to a bonus. Notice the new name, Bonus; you can't use a database field name to name a computed criterion.

In the example, you would need to redefine the criteria range because you added the Bonus criterion.

If you don't define a field name (Salary here) before using it in a computed criterion, the formula returns the error value, #NAME? However, it works just as well when you use Find or Extract to search for records. For neatness, you can define the name in Define Name in the Formula menu.

You can use text when setting up a criterion. If you need to make an exact match of text, put the text plus an equal sign in quotes. For example, if you want to find John but not Johnson, enter `="=John"`.

When you want to match and find every record in the database, don't put anything in the blank row under the criteria names.

> **Tip:** Don't use the space bar to clear the data in a cell that is part of a criteria range. If you do, Find looks for the space character for that field (see "Finding Records" later in this chapter).

The usage of criteria just described is called *AND logic,* in which you apply two or more criteria that work in conjunction in a record search. Criteria using *OR logic* are discussed in the next section.

Using OR Logic in a Criteria Range

One advantage of setting up a criteria range as distinct from using criteria in the data form is the increased complexity possible when specifying criteria. Using computed instead of comparison criteria, for instance, provides more options.

Another way to give a criteria range increased complexity is to use OR logic. Data form criteria use only AND logic. For instance, using the example in Figure 10.2, you could find records with an hourly wage greater than $10 AND a Bonus value greater than $1000. An example of an OR logic search is finding records that meet those two criteria OR records that have the address Mentmore, as shown in Figure 10.3.

Follow these steps to use OR logic with a criteria range:

1. Type in the criteria name or names in the first row of the criteria range. Type in the first set of criteria in the row underneath.

   If the names and criteria (as in our example) are already typed, you can skip this step.

2. In the row underneath the first set of criteria, type in a new set.

   In the example in Figure 10.3, `Mentmore` was typed in the Address field.

   Next, you need to define the new criteria range for Excel.

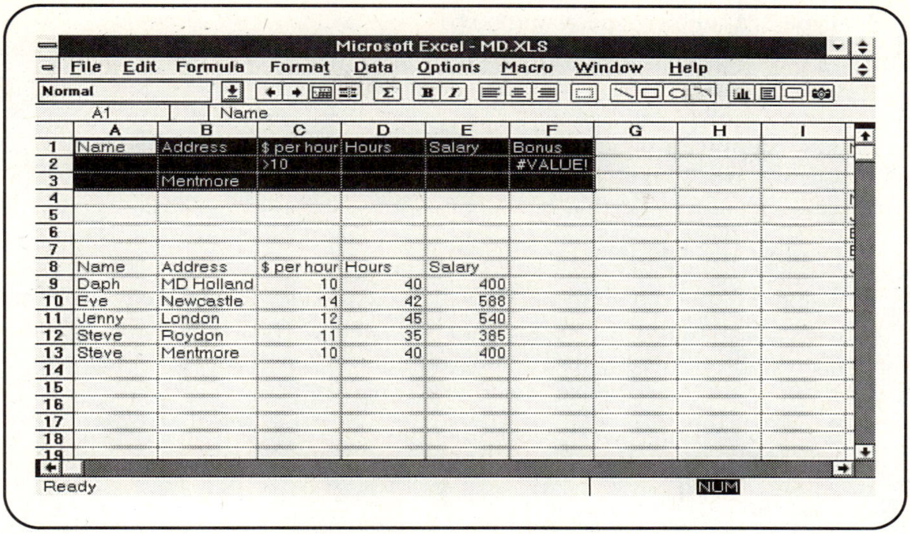

10 — Advanced Database Management   **157**

[spreadsheet screenshot showing Microsoft Excel - MD.XLS with criteria range A1:F3 and database starting at row 8]

Figure 10.3 *Two rows in a criteria range using OR logic.*

3. Select the range containing the criteria names and the rows of criteria, the range A1:F3 in the example.

>   **Tip:** If you find yourself changing your criteria range frequently, say by inserting and removing rows, you may find it useful to draw a border around the current range using the Border command in Format. This will remind you of the current criteria being used.

The next section shows you how to place your criteria range on another worksheet.

Placing a Criteria Range in Another Worksheet

Placing the criteria range in a different worksheet from the database leaves extra space on the database worksheet. Follow these steps to use this option:

1. Open the other worksheet and enter the criteria names and the row(s) of criteria.

2. Go to the database worksheet and choose Define Name from the Formula menu.

3. Type **Criteria** in the Name box.

4. In <u>R</u>efers to, enter the external file name, an exclamation mark, and the cell range.

   For example, if the criteria were in Crit.xls with a cell range of A1 to C2, you would type **Crit.xls!$A$1:$C$2**. Use the point method of cell selection to do this easily.

5. Choose Add and then OK.

Use the <u>F</u>ind command (as shown in the next section) exactly the same way when the criteria are in another worksheet. One important point to remember is that the worksheet containing the criteria must be in memory—that is, open—in order to use the criteria range.

Now that the criteria are set up, you can begin to select records.

Finding Records

The Find option is the most direct way to search for records when the database and criteria ranges are set up and defined. It actually pinpoints and selects the records, one by one, in the database. Follow these steps to find a record:

1. Choose <u>F</u>ind in the <u>D</u>ata menu, using the criteria range shown in Figure 10.2.

   The first record in the database that matches the criteria will be selected, as occurs in the example shown in Figure 10.4.

   If the active cell is not inside the database range, Find selects the first record that matches the criteria. As in the example, if the active cell is in the database, Find selects the first record below the active cell.

   Press Shift before you choose Find to reverse this order—that is, to go backwards through the database.

   Notice that the horizontal and vertical scroll bars have diagonal lines, indicating that you are "in" Find. Also, the row containing the database names becomes the top row in your window, and as long as you remain within Find, you won't be able to go above this row.

   In the example, the first record found is the Eve record.

2. Now press the down-arrow key to find the next record that matches the criteria.

   In the example, this is the Jenny record. Use the up-arrow key to move backwards in the database. You can also use the scroll bar and the Page Up and Page Down keys to find records when you have already chosen Find.

10 — Advanced Database Management **159**

When you choose the Find command the Find title in the drop down Data menu changes to `Exit Find`. Find remains active until you exit.

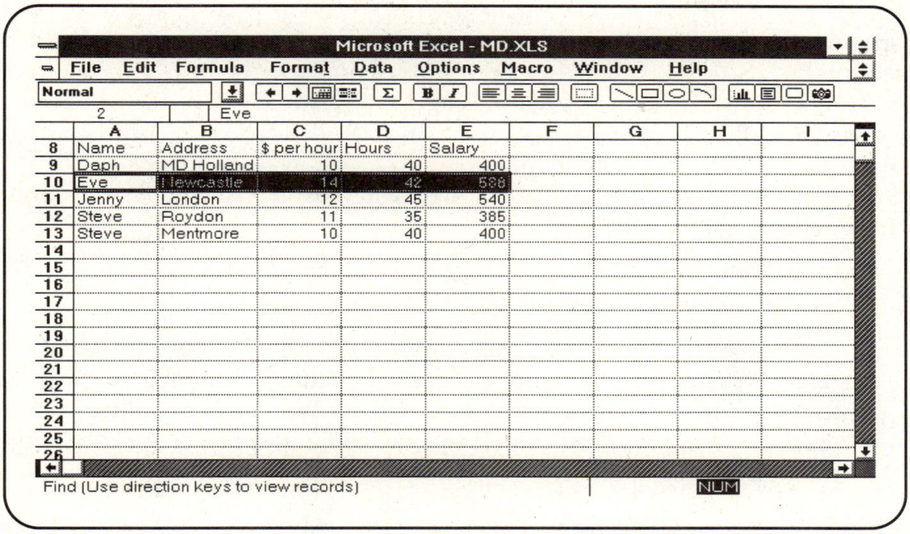

Figure 10.4 *Using the Find command to search the database.*

3. When you've finished searching the database, choose Exit Find from the Data menu.

Pressing Esc, changing a cell value, or selecting a cell outside the database also exits you from Find.

Tip: As an alternative to using Find from the Data menu, you can use Find in the Formula menu. It can be more straightforward, and you don't need to set up a criteria range to use it.

Tip: If you have trouble using Find, make sure that your database and criteria ranges are set up correctly. An easy way to do this is to choose Goto from the Formula menu and then choose database and criteria in turn. Excel highlights the ranges defined, and you can easily check them.

Extracting Records

Sometimes you need to do more than just find records in a database. The Extract option gives you the opportunity to go one step further—it not only finds records but also copies them to a specified area on the worksheet. For example, you might want to list employees who worked overtime (more than 40 hours, for instance) for a certain week. As with Find, the database and criteria ranges must already be set up and defined.

To name and define an extract range, you must use the field names from the database. Follow these steps:

1. Type in the field names or copy them from the database names. Use one or as many field names as you like.

   The number of blank rows that you include in the defined extract range determines how many records can be extracted. Include three, for example, and a maximum of three records will be copied from the database. However, you can set up and define just one row containing the field names and Excel will extract *all* records that meet the criteria.

> **Tip:** If you extract from your database using just the field names (no blank rows), take care to keep the column(s) beneath the extract names free. The reason is that all data in the columns—right down to the bottom of the worksheet—is wiped out even if the cells are not actually written into. In other words, in contrast with the criteria range, it's best not to place the extract range above the database records.

   You do not have to define the range with the Set Extract option to use Extract. You can just select the cells containing the field names (step 1) and choose E<u>x</u>tract, and the records meeting the criteria will copy into the rows underneath. However, if you want to limit the number of records extracted (by the number of blank rows you include in the definition) or if you want to use the Goto command to find the Extract range easily, you should continue with the following steps to define the extract range.

2. Select the range containing the field names and, if you want to limit the records extracted, any number of blank rows underneath. Then choose Set E<u>x</u>tract from the <u>D</u>ata menu.

   You are now set up to extract records.

10 — Advanced Database Management   161

3. Choose Extract from the Data menu.

   If you didn't define your range (step 2), you must select the cell(s) containing the extract names. If you did define the extract range, the selected cell or cells are irrelevant.

   Figure 10.5 shows an example of extracted records (Eve, Jenny, and Steve) with just one field name, Name. Cell A17 contains the extract field name.

   If any of the fields in the extracted records derive from formula fields in the database, only the current number is copied, not the formula.

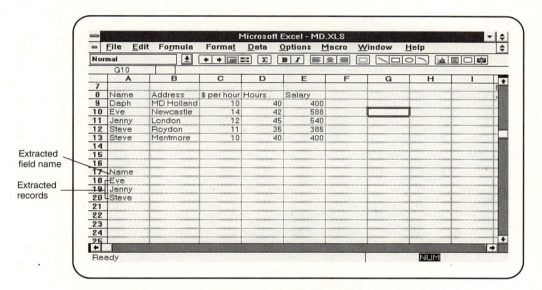

Figure 10.5   *Three extracted records showing the Name field.*

Extracting Records from Another Worksheet Database

Placing your extracted records on the same worksheet as the database can be difficult when the database is large. A way around this is to place the records in another worksheet with just a few simple steps to set it up. This feature can also be very useful for creating reports with certain specified records. Follow these steps:

1. Open up the worksheet or macro sheet to copy/extract to.

2. Choose Define Name from the Formula menu.

   The Define Name dialog box comes on screen, as shown in Figure 10.6.

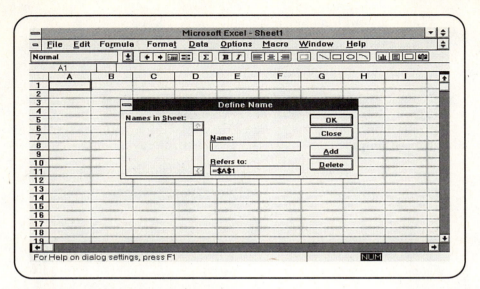

Figure 10.6 *The Define Name dialog box.*

3. In the Name field of the dialog box, type **Database**.

4. In the Refers to field, type an equal sign; then type the name of the worksheet containing the database to extract from, then an exclamation mark, then the word **Database** (assuming the database is defined in the other worksheet) or the absolute cell range in the worksheet to extract from.

   In the example we've been using, you would type **=MD.XLS!Database** or **=MD.XLS!$A$8:$E$13**.

5. Set up and define a criteria range and set up (and define if you choose) an extract range.

6. Choose Extract from the Data menu.

Please note that the worksheet to extract from must be on disk (already saved to disk), not just in memory.

Editing, Adding, and Deleting Records

Editing, adding, and deleting records can be done with the data form or directly on the worksheet. Chapter 5 discussed how to perform these operations through the data form. This section discusses the alternative.

10 — Advanced Database Management

Editing a field in a database is identical to editing any other cell in a worksheet. The cell is selected and the changes are made in the formula bar. Delete the cell's contents, using the Delete key or by choosing Clear from the Edit menu.

When making many identical changes in a database, you can use the Replace command in the Formula menu to make life easier. Just supply the text or value to change and the text or value to change to and perform the changes individually or for the whole database.

When adding a record to the database, you first need to add a new row with the Insert command from the Edit menu. You can add the row between existing records, and afterwards enter the field data into the individual cells on that row. If you included a blank row at the bottom when you defined the database, you can insert a new row and record there. If you did not include a blank line, Excel does not recognize new data inserted after the last database record as part of the database.

Use the Delete command in the Data menu with great caution! You cannot undo what you delete through the Edit menu (as you can many other Excel commands), and Excel does not display the records before they are deleted. As a precaution, you can save the worksheet to disk before performing the Delete. Also, checking what the criteria setup actually selects with the Find option is another way to ensure that you don't delete the wrong records. If you want to delete just one record, you might find the data form easier and safer.

To use the Delete command, you must already have defined both the database and the criteria ranges. The Delete command in the Data menu then deletes those records that match the criteria range. Follow these steps:

1. Choose Delete from the Data menu.

   You see a message: `Matching records will be deleted permanently.`

2. Choose OK to continue.

Excel deletes any records found that meet the criteria and moves the remaining records up to fill the gaps. No other cells in the worksheet outside the database are changed or moved.

Tip: If you feel nervous about deleting records and need to delete quite a few, sort them first. Insert a new column and, as you go through each record, mark the ones to delete with a number or letter—for example, the letter *a*—and leave the others blank. Then sort the whole database using this new column; the records to delete are placed at the top of the database after the sort. Delete them after checking again to make sure that you are deleting the correct records.

Using Functions with a Database

Excel provides 12 functions that are designed to work specifically, but not exclusively, with databases. Functions are ready-made formulas that Excel provides to save you the time and trouble of entering the formulas yourself. Chapter 8, "Formulas and Functions," Chapter 11, "Advanced Macros and Application Customization," and Chapter 15, "Using Q+E," give detailed information on using functions.

When used with databases, functions can find and perform calculations on the fields in the records. Follow these steps to use a database function:

1. Select the cell in which to place the function.

    For an example, continue with the database used earlier in this chapter. Type **Highest Salary** in the G8 cell and then make G9 the active cell.

2. Choose Pas<u>t</u>e Function from the Fo<u>r</u>mula menu.

3. Select a function in the Paste Function scroll box.

    To get to the database functions quickly, type **d**. For the example, use the DMAX( ) function.

4. Choose OK.

    The function appears in the cell and the formula bar. Each database function has three arguments: the range of cells (the database), the field, and the criteria, which must be filled in to use the function.

    If you have a database and criteria range set up and defined, you may simply use the words *database* and *criteria* for the first and third arguments. If not, you can still use the function, but you must enter the cell ranges in each case. The layout of the ranges must be the same as the layouts you would use for databases and criteria ranges—names on the first row, etc.

    With the field argument, you can enter the cell address of the field name; or if the field name is defined (with Define Name in the Formula menu), you may simply enter the name. When using a defined name, don't put quotes around it.

    In the example, the entry is DMAX(Database,$E$8,Criteria).

5. Enter the arguments and accept the result.

    Figure 10.7 shows the result in the example. Here the criteria find all records because the row below the criteria names is blank. The maximum salary of any record in the database is displayed in the function cell: $588.

10 — Advanced Database Management

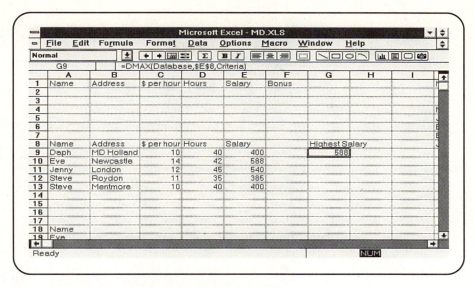

Figure 10.7 *A pasted database function.*

Table 10.1 lists the 12 database functions.

Table 10.1 *The 12 database functions.*

Function	Usage
DAVERAGE	Calculates the average of a set of numbers
DCOUNT	Calculates the number of times a number or range occurs
DCOUNTA	Calculates the number of times a certain text entry occurs
DGET	Finds and extracts a specific value. Be careful to set up the criteria so that only one record is found with this function.
DMAX	Finds and extracts the maximum of a set of values
DMIN	Finds and extracts the minimum of a set of values
DPRODUCT	Multiplies a set of numbers together
DSTDEV	Calculates the standard deviation of a sample range of numbers
DSTDEVP	Calculates the standard deviation of a whole population

continued

166 Advanced Techniques

Table 10.1 continued

Function	Usage
DSUM	Adds numbers
DVAR	Calculates the variance of a sample range of numbers
DVARP	Calculates the variance of a whole population

Tip: With large databases that contain many formulas and functions, you may find yourself waiting for Excel to recalculate after you make an entry. One way to avoid this is to turn off the automatic calculation function. Do this by choosing Calculation from the Options menu and changing from Automatic to either Automatic Except Tables or Manual in the dialog box. Then when you want to recalculate at any time, choose Calculate Now from Options. See Chapter 9, "Advanced Worksheet Management," for more information.

Q+E

If you use large databases, you might run out of space on a worksheet. Worksheet databases only contain as much information as your computer memory can hold. Q+E, Query and Editing, a database program, can be an alternative in these situations. With Q+E you can create large dBASE files on disk and then use Excel to extract only those records that you need at any one time. Of course, you can also perform the usual adding, deleting, and editing of records. And you can use Q+E to link worksheets to dBASE files so that updating changed information takes place automatically. This type of linking is called *Dynamic Data Exchange* (DDE). See Chapter 15, "Using Q+E," for more information on DDE.

11
CHAPTER

Advanced Macros and Application Customization

Chapter 4, "Basic Macros," took you through the steps required to record and run a macro, and showed you how to view the macro in the macro sheet. This chapter discusses more advanced aspects of macros—in particular, editing them in the macro sheet—but also fundamentals like using cells in different ways on a macro sheet, adding multiple macros to a single macro sheet, and creating macro buttons on your worksheet. One section describes steps to take when a macro doesn't work properly.

The latter half of the chapter deals with customization—of dialog boxes, of date forms, of commands and menus, and of help. All of these customizations are done through macros.

Macro Sheets

As you know, you can create three kinds of documents with Excel: worksheets, charts, and macro sheets. All macros are recorded in *macro sheets*. When you start recording a macro with Record from the Macro menu, Excel automatically opens a new macro sheet and records the commands in this sheet. From then on, this macro and all other macros recorded in this macro sheet become available when the macro sheet is open.

The File menu options, relating to opening, closing, saving, and printing a document, work with macro sheets the same way as they do with worksheets. So even if you are not aware that Excel opened a new macro sheet when you recorded a macro, you are prompted to save the macro sheet when you close your worksheet. If you don't save the macro sheet at this stage, the macro is lost forever.

Entries on the Macro Sheet

Figure 11.1 shows a simple macro in column A of the macro sheet. It was created using Record from Macro and then edited. In column B are text entries explaining what each macro entry does. It's a good idea to document your macros if you have any intention of saving them for use in the future. Since Excel ignores any text entries in macro sheets, entering a comment in a cell does not interfere with the running of the macro.

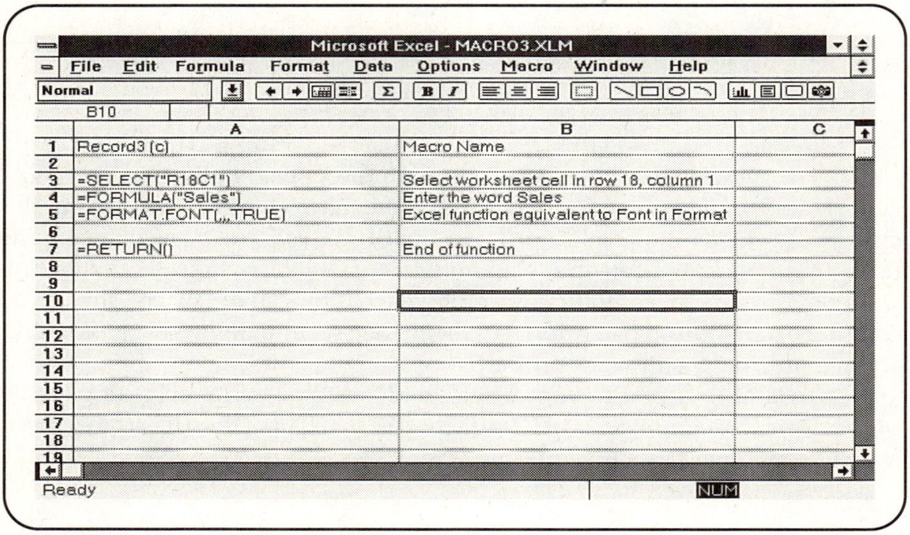

	A	B
1	Record3 (c)	Macro Name
2		
3	=SELECT("R18C1")	Select worksheet cell in row 18, column 1
4	=FORMULA("Sales")	Enter the word Sales
5	=FORMAT.FONT(,,,TRUE)	Excel function equivalent to Font in Format
6		
7	=RETURN()	End of function

Figure 11.1   A macro in a macro sheet.

As indicated in the comments in column B, the first line of the macro is the macro name, Record3. The shortcut key, c here, appears in parentheses beside the name. This is the format that Excel uses when a macro is recorded. Below the name is a blank line, which was inserted using the Insert command in Edit. Excel ignores blank lines in macro sheets just as it ignores text entries.

The next three cells contain the macro commands, the lines that actually perform the actions when you invoke the macro. Notice that all three begin with an equal (=) sign, indicating that they are formulas. All three are available through the Paste Function command in Formula. =SELECT selects the cell(s) of your choice; =FORMULA enters characters in the cell; =FORMAT.FONT formats the characters to your specifications.

Each macro ends with =RETURN() or =HALT(), complete with the equal sign. Excel gets confused if neither is present and usually cannot finish the macro successfully.

Adding an Additional Macro to a Macro Sheet

Macro sheets can contain many macros. Save similar macros together in one macro sheet and when you open the sheet, all macros become available. You can add an additional macro through the Record command in Macro or by typing the macro directly into the macro sheet.

To use Record to add to an existing macro sheet, you first need to tell Excel where the new macro starts. Follow these steps:

1. Enter the name of the new macro in the first cell of the area that will contain the new macro.

2. Select the cell range on the macro sheet for the new macro.

   This can be a single cell containing the name of the macro entered in step 1, in which case Excel starts at this cell and inserts the macro from this cell down in the same column. It can also be a range of cells. In the example in Figure 11.1, A9 would be a good cell to choose.

3. Choose Set Recorder from Macro.

4. Activate the worksheet to record the macro.

5. Choose Start Recorder from Macro.

   Start Recorder does not work unless a macro range has already been defined.

6. Perform the actions to record.

   Excel knows to insert the formulas in the cells beneath the inserted name on the macro sheet.

7. Choose Stop Recorder from Macro when you are finished.

Go back to the macro sheet to view the new macro on the macro sheet; it is still not available for use from the worksheet. Confirm this by choosing Run from the Macro menu; you see that the macro is not yet in the list of available macros. You must activate the new macro by naming it and assigning a shortcut key.

Activate a new macro as follows:

1. Select the cell in the macro sheet that contains the new macro name.
2. Choose **D**efine Name from the Fo**r**mula menu.

    Excel displays the dialog box shown in Figure 11.2. The specified name appears in the Name box.

3. Choose **C**ommand in the Macro box.

    This tells Excel you are naming a macro.

4. Choose and enter a **K**ey—a single character to be used with the Ctrl key to invoke the macro.

5. Choose OK.

You may now invoke the macro in the worksheet, either through Run in the Macro menu or through the shortcut key.

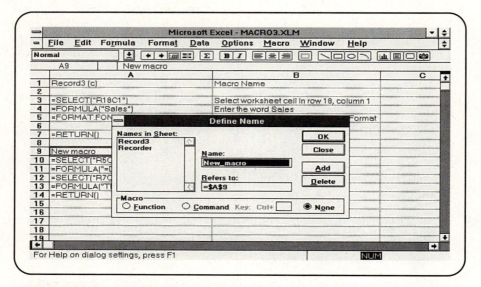

Figure 11.2 *The Define Name dialog box.*

Macro Buttons

One interesting and useful feature of macros is that Excel allows you to link a macro to a "button" on a worksheet. Then to invoke the macro, you can just click on the button. Using this facility saves you time and trouble, especially for macros you use frequently.

11 — Advanced Macros and Application Customization 171

Follow these steps to create a macro button:

1. Select the macro button tool in the Toolbar. This is the button second from the right, to the left of the camera button.

   The mouse pointer takes the shape of a cross.

2. Position and draw the button on the worksheet.

   When you do this, the Assign to Object dialog box appears, as shown in Figure 11.3. This dialog box contains a scroll box with available macros.

3. Select one of the macros to attach the button to, or alternatively type the reference in the Reference box.

4. Choose OK.

You can then invoke the macro by clicking on the button. The button can be resized like any other drawn object. However, selecting it is more difficult than selecting other drawn objects because you can't just click on it as usual without invoking the macro. Use either the object selection box in the Toolbar, or press Ctrl before clicking on the button.

When the button is selected, click on it again. The line cursor appears, and you can change the name or the formatting of the text in the button.

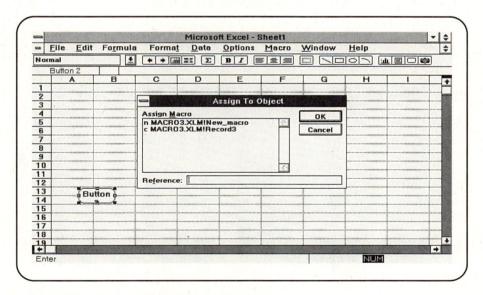

Figure 11.3 *The Assign to Object dialog box.*

Excel also allows you to link a macro with any other drawn object. The procedure is the same:

1. Select the object.
2. Choose Assign to Object from Macro.

    Excel again displays the Assign to Object dialog box shown in Figure 11.3.

3. Choose a macro and OK.

You can also reassign a macro button through the same steps: Just pick a different macro before choosing OK.

Editing Macros

The best reason for editing your own macros is the fantastic power you get by doing it properly. Editing macros gives you options that aren't available when you simply record a macro. For instance, when you edit, you can use a macro command that prompts for and receives input from the user. Your edited macro can even proceed down a path that varies, depending on what information the user inputs. This particular feature is called *branching,* where a value determines which macro commands are executed. Another macro feature available only through editing is *looping,* where certain actions, designated by the macro commands, are repeated until a required condition is met. Also, you can run (or invoke) other macros from within a macro.

When editing macros, use the Edit cutting and pasting, inserting and deleting commands in the same way you would use them on a worksheet.

Functions Available in Macro Sheets

Use the many functions available in Excel to access the full possibilities of editing in macro sheets. The best way to access Excel's macros is through the Paste Function command in Formula. Using this command, rather than typing in the formula directly, lessens your chances of making syntactical errors.

Many of the functions available in macro sheets are also available in worksheets, such as ABS(); however, many, like INPUT(), are not. It's useful to break down macro functions into related groups:

Command functions are equivalent to worksheet menu commands: DATA.DELETE() is equivalent to Delete from the Data menu, and FILL.DOWN() is equivalent to Fill Down in Edit, for example.

Action-equivalent functions perform actions on the worksheet: SELECT(), for instance, selects specified cells; FORMULA() inserts values.

Value-returning functions return a value after performing an operation: LAST.ERROR() and ACTIVE.CELL() are both useful examples of this type.

Control functions work to internally regulate macro operations. For instance, IF() and ELSE() work the branching operations mentioned in the preceding section, and WHILE() is used for looping.

Customizing functions regulate the appearance of menus and dialog boxes on the screen and are used to customize commands, options, and formats to your own requirements. Examples of customizing functions are ADD.BAR() and RENAME.COMMAND().

Part 3, "Complete Reference," discusses the available macro functions individually, giving examples of how to use them. The following sections specify how to reference cells within macros and present an example of a macro that employs several useful functions.

Using Cell References

With macros, as with worksheets, you can use either the A1 style of referencing or the R1C1 style. However, there is an added complication because macro sheet cells, as well as worksheet cells, can be referenced in functions in macros—in control functions, for instance.

Tip: If you are referencing both macro and worksheet cells in a macro, be careful when using relative cell referencing—Excel can get confused as to which sheet you are referring to.

Table 11.1 summarizes how to use references so that Excel knows how to distinguish between them.

Table 11.1 Using references in a macro function.

A1 Style	R1C1 Style	Usage
$A$1	R1C1	Absolute reference to the specified cell in the same macro sheet as the macro
A1	R[1]C[1]	Relative reference to the specified cell in the same macro sheet as the macro
!$A$1	!R1C1	Absolute reference to the specified cell in the active sheet—whether a worksheet or macro sheet. The active sheet is the sheet from which you are running the macro.

continued

174 Advanced Techniques

Table 11.1   continued

A1 Style	R1C1 Style	Usage
!A1	!R[1]C[1]	Relative reference to the specified cell in the active sheet—whether a worksheet or a macro sheet
filename!$A$1	filename!R1C1	Absolute reference to the specified cell in the specified (filename) sheet
filename!A1	filename!R[1]C[1]	Relative reference to the specified cell in the specified (filename) sheet

When specifying a reference to the active sheet in a function, you can insert it as text (see the next paragraph) or as a straight reference. One important consideration is which style is selected as the workspace default. You can change the style by choosing Workspace from Options and checking or unchecking R1C1.

You can reference the active sheet as text, for example, =SELECT("R2C3"). Text references must always be in R1C1 style and the exclamation point (!) can be omitted.

When you don't use text when referencing the active sheet, you must include the exclamation point, and the style used (R1C1 or A1) must be the style currently used in your workspace.

When you reference cells in a macro sheet, the reference style must also be the current workspace style.

 Tip: Use the R1C1 style of referencing if you have any intention of writing complex macros—it makes the macros easier to understand.

Using Macro Functions

The best way to learn how to write and edit macros is to practice. Be sure to practice on sheets that are not important to you! This section discusses an example of a macro that, though short, uses several excellent functions.

Figure 11.4 shows the macro called "Date of Birth." It was created directly in the macro sheet by typing in the name, defining the macro to Excel (using Define Name from the Formula menu as shown in the section "Adding an Additional Macro to a Macro Sheet"), then pasting the functions onto the sheet, and typing in the arguments.

11 — Advanced Macros and Application Customization

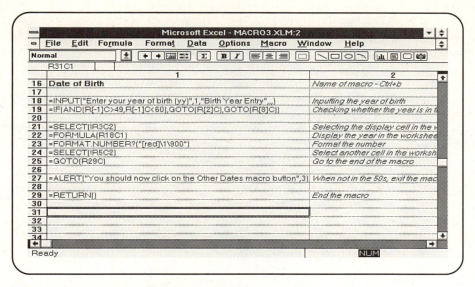

Figure 11.4 *A macro called "Date of Birth".*

The blank lines were added to make the macro easier to read. Each line in the macro is discussed in the following paragraphs.

=INPUT("Enter your year of birth (yy)",1,"Birth Year Entry",,,) prompts the user with a dialog box titled Birth Year Entry and the prompt Enter your year of birth (yy). The second argument, 1, tells Excel that the input will be a number.

=IF(AND(R[-1]C>49,R[-1]C<60),GOTO(R[2]C),GOTO(R[8]C)) evaluates what was entered in the INPUT function and branches along two different routes in the macro, depending on the evaluation. Translated into English, the function picks up what was inputted one row up from this one in the same column (R[–1]C) and subjects the value to two tests: Was the number greater than 49 and was the number less than 60? If both of these tests return TRUE, then the first GOTO comes into operation, which sends the branch two rows down (R[2]C). If either one is FALSE, then the second GOTO comes into play and branches eight rows down (R[8]C).

Notice that you reference the value returned by INPUT by the macro cell that contains it.

=SELECT(!R3C2) and =SELECT(!R5C2) select the cells in row 3, column 2 and row 5, column 2 of the active worksheet respectively. The first SELECT shows where the macro branches when a year in the 1950's has been entered.

=FORMULA(R18C1) inserts the value contained in the macro cell in row 18, column 1, which contains the INPUT function, into the active cell of the worksheet.

=FORMAT.NUMBER?("[red]\1\900") formats the active cell to the argument specification. In this case the argument specifies the color red, and the addition of two numbers, 19, to complete the year.

The ? preceding the parenthesis is a useful addition to macros because it prompts the user with the actual dialog box he or she would get with the menu equivalent: Number from the Format menu in this case. The arguments display as the chosen options, but the user can override these options.

=GOTO(R29C) sends the macro branch to a cell in row 29 of the same column in the macro sheet, to the end of the macro in this case. This GOTO is utilized in order to avoid the ALERT() function.

=ALERT("You should now click on the Other Dates macro button",3): The macro branches here when the number entered was not in the 1950's. ALERT displays a dialog box that displays the text message and gives advice.

Adding comments explaining your macros, as done in column 2 of Figure 11.4, is a very good idea in most cases.

Testing and Debugging Macros

It's easy to make mistakes when creating macros. Excel supplies several features that enable you to rectify mistakes when they happen. The most important consideration is pinpointing which line and argument is causing the problem. Several methods for doing this are outlined in the following sections.

Using Step and Evaluate

Step breaks up the performance of a macro into separate lines. Evaluate goes one stage further by breaking the performance down into operators within a function. Using these options makes errors in the macro easy to spot and, in the case of branching, ascertains whether the proper lines are being accessed.

Follow these steps:

1. Choose Run from Macro.

   Figure 11.5 shows the Run dialog box.

2. Select the macro to run from the Run scroll box.

3. Choose Step.

   Excel then displays the Single Step dialog box shown in Figure 11.6.

   The macro or worksheet cell currently active is displayed after Cell: with the formula being evaluated displayed after Formula:. In the example shown in Figure 11.6, the cell is the first cell of the macro, the name cell.

11 — Advanced Macros and Application Customization

You have four options in this box. Step performs each line of the macro separately and then waits for you to choose it again to continue with the next line. (Step even displays the blank lines.) Evaluate breaks the steps down further into operators. Halt stops the running of the macro. Continue restarts the macro running normally.

Try running the Date of Birth macro with Step. When you come to the IF function after inputting a year, switch to Evaluate. If you entered a year in the 1950's (don't enter the *19*), the input is evaluated and displayed by Excel as follows:

IF(AND(TRUE,TRUE),GOTO(R[2]C),GOTO(R[8]C))

In other words, the number entered registers as TRUE for both conditions. Choose Evaluate again and Excel displays:

IF(GOTO(R21C1),GOTO(R[8]C))

telling you the absolute cell reference, the first, it will branch to. Choose Evaluate again and the formula displayed is =SELECT(!R3C2), the contents of cell R21C1.

4. Choose the various buttons in Single Step as you need to.

The keyboard alternative to Evaluate is Shift-Enter; you must be in the Single Step dialog box to use it.

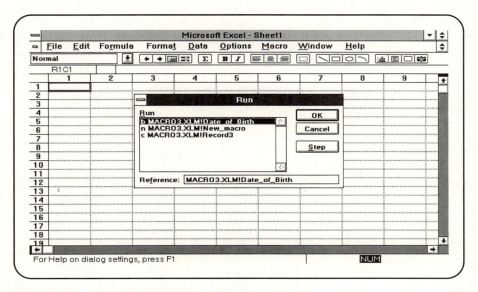

Figure 11.5 *The Run dialog box.*

178 Advanced Techniques

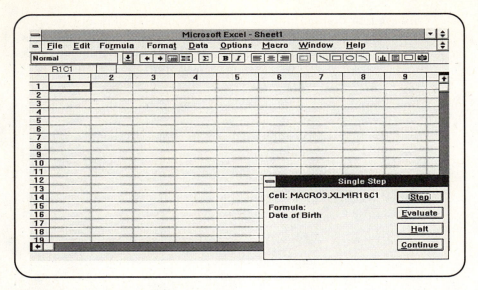

Figure 11.6 *The Single Step dialog box.*

 Tip: You can press Esc at any time to interrupt the running of a macro. Excel displays a dialog box with Halt, Step, Continue, and Goto buttons. The first three work as just described. Choose Goto and you go to the cell where the macro stopped.

The Step Function

It's possible to insert a function into your macro to bypass having to bring up and choose Step from the Run dialog box. Insert an empty cell in your macro right above where you want the stepping to begin. This can be at any point in the macro. Then enter **=STEP()** in the empty cell. When you run the macro, Excel displays the Single Step dialog box when it encounters this function.

Displaying Values

Another way to evaluate the functioning of your macros is to change the display from formulas to values. After you run a macro, each function then displays either TRUE or FALSE unless the function returns an actual value as distinct from a logical. Any function line that has been used in the running of the macro should display TRUE. If it's FALSE, then something is wrong except where the macro has branched around this line. (As you saw, when a macro branches around a macro line, the function in that line is not used.) Before the macro is run, all functions display as FALSE.

For example, in the Date of Birth macro, if you change to values and then run the macro and enter 52, each line in the macro sheet displays TRUE except the INPUT line, which displays 52, and the ALERT line, which has not been accessed.

To change to displaying values, choose Display from the Options menu and uncheck Formulas.

To redisplay formulas, go into Display again and check Formulas.

Macro Debugging

Using the debugging feature takes the evaluation of macros one step further. Specifically, using the debugger, you can stop the macro where you specify and have Excel display specific values, which helps you decide where the problem is.

Before you can use the debugger, you must open it. The debugger is contained in the Debug.Xla file in the Library subdirectory. It's an add-in macro, meaning that it doesn't display as a macro sheet but rather adds various options to the menus.

Follow these preliminary steps to make use of the debugger:

1. Open debug.xla in the Library subdirectory.

2. Go to the macro sheet to be tested.

3. Choose Debug from the Macro menu.

   The macro sheet menu options change, as shown in Figure 11.7.

Many of the commands in the new menus are equivalent to commands in the normal menus, as outlined below:

Display: Formulas/Values switches between displaying formulas and values on the macro sheet. Arrange All is the same as Arrange All in the normal Window menu. Show Info is the same as Show Info in Window.

Formula: Goto and Find are the same as the normal Goto and Find in Formula. Hidden Names looks at the values of hidden notes. Note adds, edits, and deletes cell notes.

Other commands are discussed later.

The main way to use debug is to specify debug points in certain cells. There are two kinds of debug points: *tracepoints* stop the running of the macro at the designated cell and put it in single step mode; *breakpoints* stop the macro as well but also display the values of a group of cells and names you specifically asked for.

180 Advanced Techniques

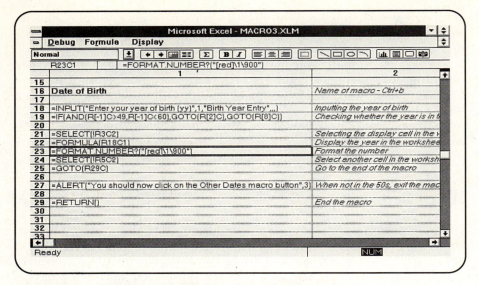

Figure 11.7 *The macro sheet screen with the debug options.*

To set a debug point:

1. Select the cell before the point you want to stop.

2. Choose either Set Breakpoint or Set Tracepoint from Debug.

   With a breakpoint, you can also type a message that displays when the break comes in the running of the macro. Type a message like **This is the breakpoint** in the Alert String box of the Set Breakpoint dialog box if you want this.

   Remove a debug point by choosing Erase Debug Point from Debug.

3. Choose Breakpoint Output from Debug if you chose Set Breakpoint in step 2.

   With the Breakpoint Output dialog box, you tell Excel which variable values to display at this stage. Without doing this, setting a breakpoint is pointless.

   Now type in the variables in Variable and choose Add to add them to the Variables to Output scroll box. Delete any you no longer need by selecting the variable and choosing Delete.

   As an example, you could choose the cell containing the IF() function in Date of Birth as a breakpoint and then designate R18C1 and R19C1 as the variable values to output to the screen.

   Run a macro with debug as follows:

11 — Advanced Macros and Application Customization

1. Choose Arrange All from Display to get the worksheet window on screen.
2. Make the worksheet the active sheet.
3. Choose Run Macro from Debug.
4. Choose the macro to run in the normal way.

    When Excel reaches the debug point, it stops. With a tracepoint, it changes to single step mode, discussed earlier. With a breakpoint, it displays a dialog box showing the alert message and the values you specified.

    Figure 11.8 shows an example of a Breakpoint dialog box.

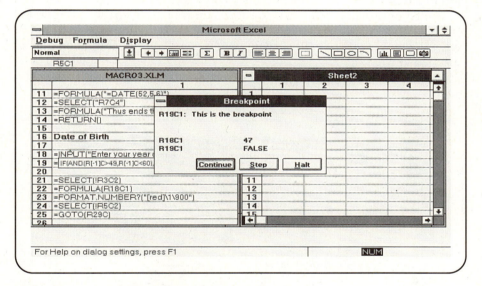

Figure 11.8 A Breakpoint dialog box.

In the example, 47 has been entered by the user at the input stage. The variables outputted are the cell results at the Input and If stages: 47 and FALSE in this example.

5. Choose Continue, Step, or Halt from this box.

For other debugging, choose Select Errors from Formula to select all cells in the macro with formulas that evaluate to errors.

Choose Select Debug Points from Formula to select all the macro cells with debug points.

Choose Exit Debug from Debug to return to the normal menus for the macro sheet.

Customizing Dialog Boxes with the Dialog Editor

The Dialog Editor is a separate software program that Microsoft provides free of charge with Excel. Use it to design new dialog boxes for inputting values. The customized dialog box can then be used in two ways: It can be accessed from a macro and have its inputted values processed by that macro, or it can be used as a data form with a worksheet database. Customizing dialog boxes can be very useful for inexperienced computer spreadsheet users. But you can also use them to standardize operations (like inputting sales values daily, for example) and to eliminate unnecessary options.

All the normal features of dialog boxes are available with the Dialog Editor: buttons, options, scroll box lists, OK buttons, Cancel buttons, Group boxes, and so forth. The size of individual items as well as the whole dialog box can be changed at will.

Figure 11.9 shows an example of a dialog box created with the Dialog Editor.

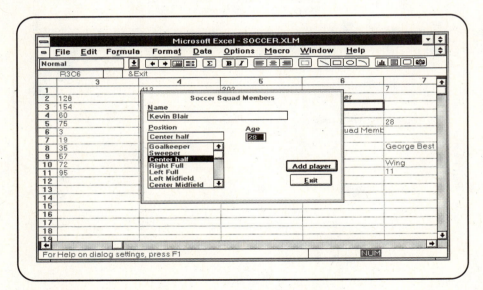

Figure 11.9 *A sample dialog box created with the Dialog Editor.*

This dialog box inputs three items of information about a squad of soccer players: the name, the position, and the age of each player. In the lower right, the OK button is renamed Add player and the Cancel button is renamed Exit. The scroll box is linked to the Position input box so that any position title selected in the scroll box list appears in the Position box.

Using the Dialog Editor

Because the Dialog Editor is a separate application from Excel, you need to invoke it before you can use it. The Dialog Editor is displayed as a separate icon in the Excel group of icons.

Perform this step to invoke the Dialog Editor: Double-click on the Dialog Editor icon in Program Manager. Alternatively, you can choose Run from the Excel Control Box and choose Dialog Editor there.

When you use the Run method, the current directory must be the main Excel directory. You can change the current directory through Open in File if necessary.

Figure 11.10 shows the initial Dialog Editor screen. The framed rectangle in the center of the screen is the empty dialog box set up for your use. Resize the dialog box in the usual Windows way by placing the mouse pointer on the border and dragging.

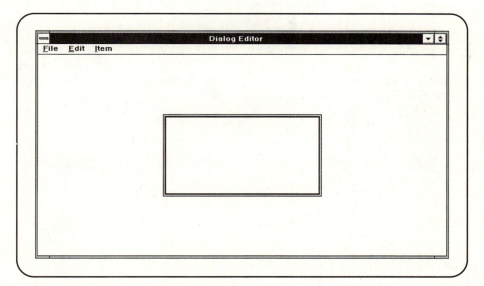

Figure 11.10 *The Dialog Editor screen.*

Choose the items that you want to insert in the dialog box from the Item menu.

Consider the dialog box shown in Figure 11.9; it is used by a soccer coach to list his squad and relevant information. In the example, the titles—Soccer Squad Members, Name, Position, and Age—were created with the Text command in Item. The input boxes underneath Name, Position, and Age were created with Edit Box. Just the command and the object appear. The scroll box was created with List Box and is linked to the preceding edit box, so it had to

184   Advanced Techniques

be created immediately afterwards. The next section, "Placing a Dialog Box in a Macro Sheet," explains how to display a list of available choices in this scroll box.

Resize and move the titles boxes, input boxes, and scroll boxes in the usual Windows way.

Each Item menu command, except Text and Group Box, has several different subtypes of items, amounting to a total of 22 available items. A complete explanation of each is given in Table 11.2.

The Group Box command is for visually grouping options that naturally go together, like Bold, Italic, and Underline in a dialog box for changing text. To use a group box, choose Group Box from Item and add your individual items (usually Option from Button).

Deselect the group box to add more items to the dialog box outside the group box. If you want to add an item from another part of the dialog box to the group box, you have to cut it, select the group box, and then paste it.

Most of the Edit commands work the same way as in other Windows applications, including Excel. Duplicate creates a copy of the currently selected item and places it underneath the item.

Info in the Edit menu is very useful for getting information on the selected item, including the dialog box as a whole. Bring up the information box by choosing Info after selecting the item or by double-clicking on the item. Figure 11.11 shows the information box for the edit box (inputting integers only) that goes with Age in the example.

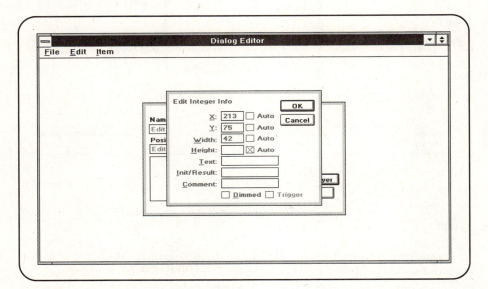

Figure 11.11   *The Info box.*

X and Y determine the position of the item, that is, the x and y coordinates. With X, Y, Width, and Height, you can check the Auto box or use your own measurements.

Text in this example is blank. It shows the title of the particular item. Any title text you enter for the item shown in Figure 11.11—an edit box—does not appear in the actual dialog box in the Dialog Editor. It's just a way of identifying the item. With other items, like text boxes, the title text *does* appear in the customized dialog box. Nevertheless, it is recommended that you do give a title to each item in the Dialog Editor—for identification purposes in the macro sheet. The following section, "Placing a Dialog Box in a Macro Sheet," explains this further.

Another feature of Text is that you can use it to add underlining to characters in the displayed dialog box so that the user can combine that character with Ctrl in the usual way to access the corresponding edit box. For example, in the Age text box, as shown in Figure 11.9, the *g* is underlined in the dialog box. This is achieved by typing an ampersand (&) before the *g* in the relevant Info box.

Init/Result makes more sense when you know how macros combine with the Dialog Editor to display dialog boxes. At this stage, all you need to know is that anything you enter here will display initially in the dialog box; that is, it is the default display for this item.

Use Comment for your own purposes, like specifying whether this was an original item, any special features it has, and so forth.

When Trigger is checked, the dialog box stays on screen—instead of disappearing—when the user chooses the trigger button. For instance, you could make an OK button (renamed to `Add Player` in this example) a trigger button; then when a user fills in the options in the dialog box and adds a player, the dialog box stays on screen afterwards. Check Dimmed to show the user that an item is not available at this particular time.

The File menu has no Save command because you can't save to disk from the Dialog Editor. Any dialog box you create in the Dialog Editor has to be transferred to a macro sheet or a worksheet in order to use it. Use the New command to wipe out the dialog box on screen and start afresh.

Table 11.2 Descriptions of each item in a dialog box.

No.	Type of Item	What It Does
1,3	OK button, default	Closes the dialog box, puts the inputted and not default values into the Init/Result column cells, and goes to the next macro command. Default means the button is initially selected. Created with Button in Item in the Dialog Editor.

continued

Table 11.2 continued

No.	Type of Item	What It Does
2, 4	Cancel button, default and not default	Closes the dialog box and goes to the next macro command. Default means the button is initially selected. Created with Button in Item.
5	Text box	Displays text for labeling and information purposes. Created with Text in Item.
6 7 8 9 10	Text edit box Integer edit box Number edit box Formula edit box Reference edit box	Edit boxes are the boxes through which the user inputs. Each edit box accepts only the specified type of input. Created with Edit Box in Item.
11 12	Option group button Option button	An option group button is created automatically when you create an option button. The group button must always come in the row before the option buttons. The group button text column can label the buttons. You can specify the selected option button in the Init/Result column of the group button by typing a number: 1 for the first option, 2 for the second, etc., in terms of rows down from the group button. Type #N/A if you want no button specified. Created with Button in Item.
13	Check Box button	Put TRUE in the Init/Result column to specify on; FALSE to specify off; #N/A to specify neither. Created by Button in Item.
14	Group box	This has no effect other than to visually group items together in your dialog box. Created by Group Box in Item.
15	List box, Standard	Displays a list in a scroll box. The list must be referred to in R1C1 style (or by a defined name) in the text column, column 6, of the item row. Created by List Box in Item.

No.	Type of Item	What It Does
16	Linked list box	Similar to standard except that it has a text edit box above it and when something is selected in the list box, it automatically appears in the edit box. Specify the default selection in the Init/Result column. Created by List Box in Item.
17	Icon	Three icons are available. When the text column has 1, users must make a choice; when 2, information is presented; when 3, an error has occurred. Created by Icon in Item.
18	Linked file list box	These three items are created together. Their order should not be altered—19 after 18, 20 after 19; though, as explained below, you can have a text box between 19 and 20. 18 lists files in a directory and must follow a text edit box that specifies the filenames to appear. 19 lists drives and directories. Create a text box (type 5 item) after it and it displays the current drive and directory and updates it as it changes. 20 displays the name of the current directory. It doesn't update it after the dialog box comes on screen. Created by List Box in Item.
19	Linked drive and directory list box	
20	Directory text	
21	Dropdown list box	These are the same as standard list box except the list drops down when invoked. Column 5, the height column, specifies the height of the list. The combination box must have a text edit box preceding it. Created by List Box in Item.
22	Dropdown combination edit/list box	

Placing a Dialog Box in a Macro Sheet

When the dialog box looks right in the Dialog Editor, it's time to transfer it to a macro sheet.

188 Advanced Techniques

 Note: Remember that a box can be edited in the future at any time, either on the macro sheet itself or by going back to the Editor.

Follow these steps:

1. Choose Select Dialog from Edit.

   This selects the whole dialog box.

2. Choose Copy from Edit.

3. Go to the macro sheet you want to copy to and select a cell.

   This cell becomes the upper-left corner of the pasted dialog box.

4. Choose Paste from Edit.

   Excel pastes the dialog box definition onto the macro sheet, coded as a series of numbers. The soccer squad example is shown in Figure 11.12.

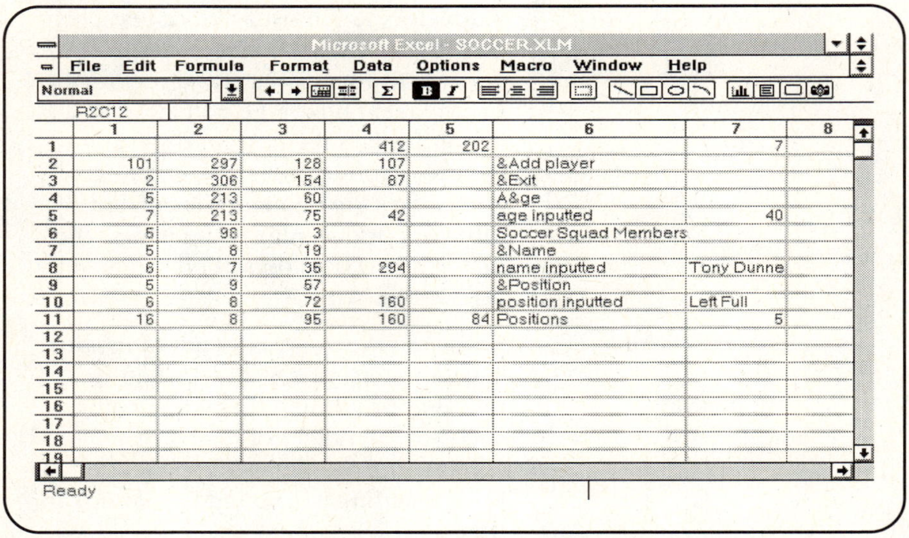

Figure 11.12   A dialog box definition pasted into a macro sheet.

5. While the dialog box is still selected on the macro sheet, choose Define Name from Formula and give a name to the dialog box definition.

You need to do this in order to reference the dialog box from a macro.

All dialog boxes take up seven columns in a macro sheet. The more items you have in the box, the more rows you have in the definition. Each column contains specific information about your dialog box items that Excel needs to have to display the dialog box:

Column 1 contains the item number, referring to a type. Each item has a separate line. In the example, for instance, the third row has the item number 2, which means it is a Cancel button (see Table 11.2).

Columns 2 and 3 tell Excel the position of the item in the box, specifically the x and y positions of the item's upper-left corner in points. When these cells and those in columns 4 and 5 are blank, then Excel uses automatic numbering.

Columns 4 and 5 tell Excel the width and height of the item in screen units.

Column 6 displays what you entered or accepted in the Text box of the Info dialog box, discussed in the preceding section, "Using the Dialog Editor." For instance, the Cancel button is called `Exit` in the example and putting an ampersand before the *E* tells Excel to accept this character with Ctrl to choose this button. In row five, the words `age inputted` tell you that this row has the definition for the edit box that inputs age. This text serves no other purpose than to tell you that this is the input row.

Column 7 is the equivalent of Init/Result in the Info box. It displays the initial value you wish to display in the dialog box for this item and, after the user inputs, holds the inputted value.

A few things are noteworthy about dialog box definitions. First, you can edit cell entries directly on the macro sheet in the normal Excel ways. This includes moving whole rows. Since Excel looks for specific information in specific columns, don't move columns. Until you are very sure of what's involved, it's recommended that you stick to changing the cells in rows 6 and 7 for all examples.

Another important thing to note is that the order of rows can be vital. In the example, for instance, the age inputted, name inputted, and position inputted rows (all edit box rows) follow immediately after their text box equivalents: Age, Name, and Position. And row 11 contains a type 16 item, meaning a scroll list box that is linked to an edit box—the Position text box in this case—so it follows immediately after the edit box.

The word `Positions` in row 11 is a defined name referring to a range of cells that contain possible positions in a soccer game. These positions appear in the scroll box in the dialog box. For more information, refer to item 16 in Table 11.2.

Tip: To make an edit box the selected box when the dialog box first comes on screen, type the row number of the edit box minus one in the first row of the Init/Result column. In the example, the number 7 in the Init/Result column refers to row eight, the row that defines the name inputting edit box.

If you create items through the Dialog Editor in the right order, the syntax and row positioning are automatically correct. It's possible to create them directly on the macro sheet, in which case you must be careful about the positions of rows or the dialog box won't work.

If you want to edit a dialog box through the Dialog Editor and the macro sheet box definition is different from that showing in the Editor, the definition needs to be pasted back into the Editor. Select the definition in the macro sheet, copy it into the clipboard, go to the Editor, and choose <u>P</u>aste from the <u>E</u>dit menu. Then make your changes and select, copy, and paste back to the macro sheet. When pasting, make sure the defined name covers the cell range. Any items inserted or deleted mean the number of rows change.

Note: In the example in Figure 11.12, the item number in column 1, row 2 is 101 instead of 1. This is because the item is a trigger (see "Using the Dialog Editor"), which adds 100. Also, any item that is dimmed has 200 added.

Using a Dialog Box in a Macro

Once the dialog box definition is pasted onto the macro sheet, the next step is to call it up with a macro. Use the straightforward Dialog.Box function to do this. When the inputs are made by the user, your macro needs to find them in the Init/Results column and then use them for whatever purpose.

Figure 11.13 shows an example of what can be done with inputs from a dialog box. It shows a database on a worksheet that contains information about a squad of soccer players.

The custom-created dialog box shown in Figure 11.9 supplies the information to the database, one player or one line at a time. The macro button on the worksheet called Add a player starts the macro.

Figure 11.14 shows the macro that invokes the dialog box and subsequently places the inputs in the database. When the macro has done that, it displays the dialog box again so that the user can perform as many inputs as he likes at one time.

11 — Advanced Macros and Application Customization

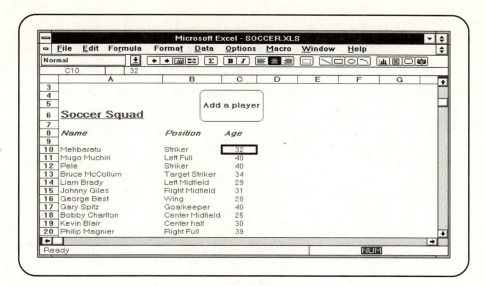

Figure 11.13 *A database on an Excel worksheet.*

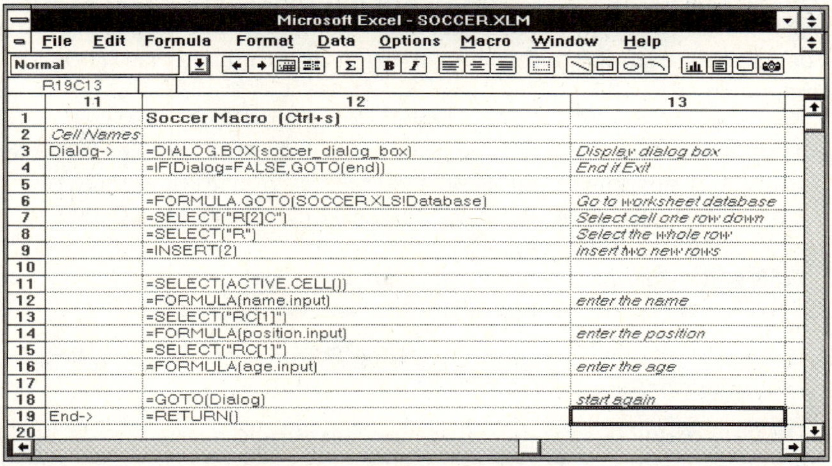

Figure 11.14 *A macro that invokes a dialog box.*

A couple of observations can be made about this macro. First, for clarity, defined names are used instead of cell references as much as possible. For example, the cell with the Return function is called "End," and the cell with the Dialog.Box function is called "start." All input references (name.input, position.input, age.input) are names for cells in the Init/Result column of the dialog box definition.

Also notable is that the macro loops back to the start through the =GOTO(Dialog) line until the user specifically chooses the Exit button.

Tip: Transferring the inputted values from the macro sheet to the database was done on separate lines in the macro—using SELECT and FORMULA functions—to make the macro easier to follow. Using the OFFSET function instead of SELECT is faster and simpler when you understand it. For example, using =FORMULA(name.input,OFFSET(ACTIVE.CELL(),0,0)) is simpler than using =SELECT(ACTIVE.CELL()) and =FORMULA(name.input).

Creating a Customized Dialog Box for a Database

Besides using a customized dialog box in a macro, you can customize the data form dialog box for inputting values into a worksheet database. For each field in your database, you enter a text box and an edit box. The steps to create the new data form are similar to those for creating a customized dialog box for use in a macro.

Figure 11.15 shows a standard data form dialog box.

Any customization can only be done to the left of the scroll bar. The scroll bar and the buttons to its right, New, Delete, etc., remain the same.

Unfortunately, the only types of items you can create for a data form box are text boxes and edit boxes.

Follow these steps to customize a data form. Define your database range on the worksheet before you perform these steps.

1. Create the dialog box using the Dialog Editor as shown in "Using the Dialog Editor."

   Do *not* create OK or Cancel buttons. You should create an edit box, and presumably a text box to go with it, for every field in your database.

2. Type the corresponding field name in the Init/Result box of each edit box.

   You access this Init/Result box through Info in the Edit menu.

3. Select the dialog box, copy it into the clipboard, and go to the worksheet containing the database.

11 — Advanced Macros and Application Customization   193

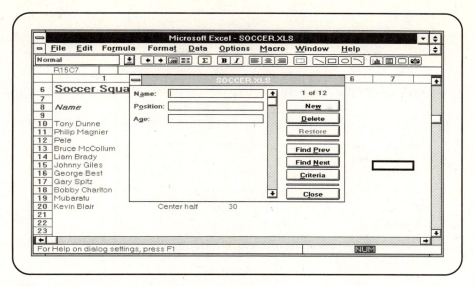

Figure 11.15 *A standard data form dialog box.*

4. Select a cell and choose Paste from Edit.

   Be sure to select a cell that isn't close to any important data in the worksheet so that nothing is overwritten in the paste. The definition is pasted onto the worksheet. Don't de-select it.

5. Choose Define Name from Formula.

6. Type `data_form` as the name and choose OK.

   Now use the Form command in Data in the normal way.

Running Macros Automatically and Add-in Macros

To save time and trouble, you can perform a few steps to have Excel run a macro automatically each time you open or close a document. The only time this does not work is when the document that specified the opening of the macro was itself opened by a macro. In that case you can use the Run macro function.

Any macro or custom function created can become an add-in macro. Once invoked, these macros or functions then seem to be part of Excel. Add-in macros are different from other macros in that the macro sheet is hidden and cannot be unhidden. And macros in the add-in macro sheet don't appear in the Run dialog box in Macro. What does happen is that custom functions, the macros in the macro sheet, appear in the Paste Function dialog box like ordinary functions.

Running Macros Automatically

Follow these steps to run a macro automatically when you open a document:

1. Make the document active and choose Define Name from Formula.

2. Type a name to identify the macro you want to run, starting with Auto_Open.

   You could use Auto_Open_soccer, for instance, to identify the soccer squad macro used in previous sections of this chapter.

3. Type the macro name or reference in the Refers To box.

   This must follow normal Excel syntax: for example,
   `=Soccer.xlm!soccer_macro`.

4. Choose OK and save the document.

   The next time you open the document, the macro will run.
   To run a macro automatically when a document closes, follow the exact same steps using Auto_Close instead of Auto_Open.

 Tip: To prevent the automatic running of a macro when you open or close the document, hold down Shift as you choose the OK button in the Open or Close dialog box.

Add-in Macros

To use the macros and custom functions on a macro sheet as an add-in macro, the macro sheet must first be saved as an add-in macro. Follow these steps to save as an add-in macro:

1. From the macro sheet that you want to save as an add-in, choose Save As from the File menu.

   You could, if you like, save the file under a new name, allowing you to use the old macro sheet as normal.

2. Choose Options from the dialog box.

3. Choose Add-In from the File Format dropdown scroll box.

4. Choose OK and OK to exit.

Excel automatically attaches the .xla extension to an add-in macro.

Having saved the macro as an add-in, just open it like any file to use it. Add-in macros stay open even if you close all the documents currently open.

 Tip: To open an add-in macro sheet as an ordinary macro, hold down Shift as you choose OK when opening it.

All add-in macros placed in the Xlstart subdirectory open automatically when you start Excel.

Customizing Commands, Menus, and Menu Bars

One of the most powerful features of Excel is being able to customize your commands, your menus, and even your menu bars through the various functions Excel supplies for use in macros. One reason you might want to customize is to make life simpler and more straightforward for users.

Designing an application like this to your own specifications is fun, but you should think about what you want the results to be before plunging in. Be clear as to what you want the final menus and commands to look like. And give some thought as to how the macros to run this new design will combine together. With a more complicated design, you might want to draw a flow chart to make it clearer. Be consistent in naming macros and cells in macro sheets so that—at a glance—it is obvious they work together.

Customizing Commands

Customizing commands covers adding your own commands to menus, renaming commands, dimming commands so that they are not available, adding or removing check marks, and completely removing commands from menus.

The functions (available only on macro sheets) to make these changes are ADD.COMMAND(), RENAME.COMMAND(), ENABLE.COMMAND(), CHECK.COMMAND(), and DELETE.COMMAND(). (Part 3 of this book, "Complete Reference," gives specific instructions and examples concerning how to use these and all other functions discussed in this section.) ADD.MENU() is another useful function in this context; it returns the number of the menu.

You can change and delete Excel's built-in commands also. If for some reason you want to delete Exit in File, make certain there is another way to quit Excel! You can restore deleted Excel commands with ADD.COMMAND( )—just use the command name in the command_ref argument.

When you add a command to a menu, Excel needs to find the relevant information in a very specific way on your macro sheet in an area called the *command table*. Figure 11.16 shows an example of how a command table looks on a macro sheet.

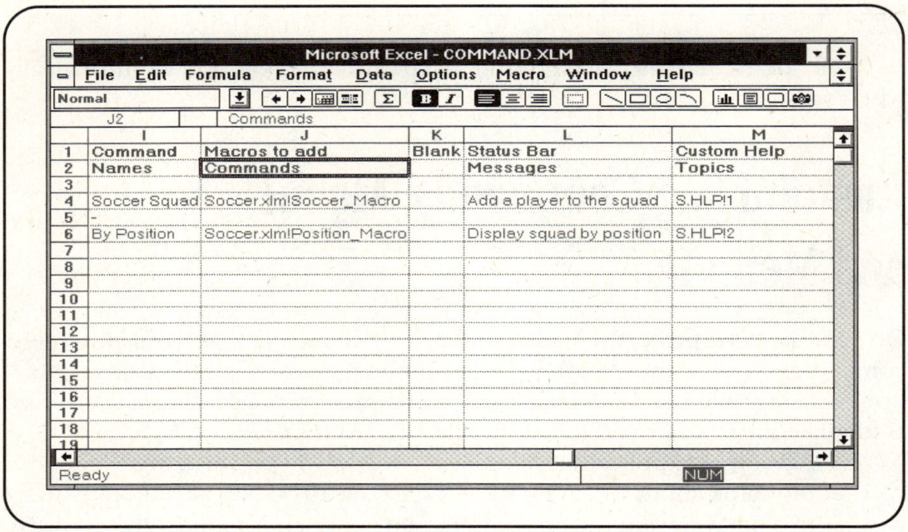

Figure 11.16   A command table in a macro sheet.

Each command table must have five columns. Each line in the table covers one menu command. When you refer to a line in a command table from a macro, you can use row and column referencing or you can define a name for each line. In Figure 11.16, the column titles have been put in for clarity—they are not actually part of the command table.

The *Command Names column* contains the actual title the new command has in the menu. Use an ampersand to designate an access key. Use two ampersands in succession (&&) when you want to use the ampersand character in the command. If you are inserting a series of commands in one menu, you can designate a line separator (like the one between Form and Find in Data) by typing a hyphen in this column and leaving the rest of the columns blank.

11 — Advanced Macros and Application Customization

In *Macros to add Commands,* specify the macro that contains the function to add the command. You can use names or R1C1 referencing as text.

The *Blank column* is needed for historical reasons that have to do with previous versions of Excel. In the Macintosh version of Excel, this column can specify a shortcut key.

Using the *Status Bar Messages column* is optional. Any text you type here is displayed in the status bar when the command is highlighted.

Using the *Custom Help Topics column* is also optional. If you want the user to have help available, specify a help file and topic number here. A later section, "Customizing Help," explains this further.

Customizing a New Menu

You can add, delete, rename, and disable your own custom menus or Excel menus. The functions you use are ADD.MENU(), DELETE.MENU(), RENAME.COMMAND(), and ENABLE.COMMAND(). With the latter two, use 0 in the command argument to specify a new menu.

You can use the GET.BAR() function to find the number of the active menu bar. This ranges from 1 to 6 since you can have full or short menus, even though there are only four menu bars. Here is how the menu bars are numbered in Excel:

Numbers 1 and 5 (full and short menus) are the Worksheet menu bar: File, Edit, Formula, Format, Data, Options, Macro, Window, and Help.

Numbers 2 and 6 (full and short menus) are the Chart menu bar: File, Edit, Gallery, Chart, Format, Macro, Window, and Help.

Number 3 is the Null menu bar: File and Help.

Number 4 is the Info Window menu bar: File, Info, Macro, Window, and Help.

Excel needs what is called a *menu table* in the macro sheet to refer to when adding menus. This is very similar to the *command table* discussed in "Customizing Commands." The first line contains the menu name in the Menu and Command Names column with the rest of the columns in that row blank.

Figure 11.17 shows an example of a menu table.

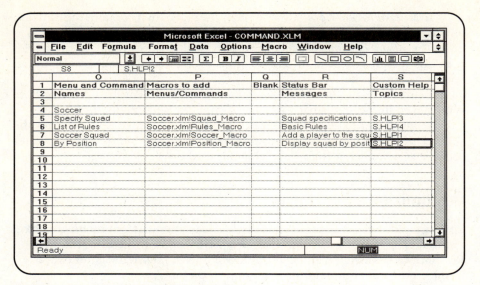

Figure 11.17 *A menu table in a macro sheet.*

Customizing a New Menu Bar

One step beyond creating commands and menus is creating an entire menu bar. Use the ADD.BAR() function to actually create the menu bar and the ADD.MENU() function to add menus to the empty menu bar. After this, you can display the menu bar using the SHOW.BAR() function. Each menu bar is identified by a bar number. Delete custom menu bars (not Excel menu bars) with DELETE.BAR().

Customizing Help

You can create Help for customized dialog boxes, customized commands and menus, and also for messages displayed when running a macro. To create this Help, you need special software—the custom Help conversion program, which is available free of charge from Microsoft.

 Note: Excel version 3.0 uses software for creating Help that is not compatible with previous versions. You cannot use the old Help text files.

11 — Advanced Macros and Application Customization

To create a Help file, follow these steps: First, create a plain text file, through Excel or Word, for example. Each file contains numbered topics, referred to in the command and menu tables.

Each topic in the Help file is identified with an asterisk, a number, and an optional comment—for example, `*1 Soccer Squad`—followed by the Help text. An example of Help text:

```
When you want to add a player to your squad, choose this
command to bring up the dialog box with all relevant
information to enter.
```

When the file is complete and saved, it needs to be converted using this syntax at the DOS prompt: `helpconv <filename>`. Afterwards, specify the file and topic in the command or menu table as shown in "Customizing Commands" and "Customizing a New Menu."

CHAPTER 12

Drawing with Graphic Objects

In this book, graphic objects include anything drawn with the four drawing tools—line, rectangle, oval, and arc—found on the Toolbar. But the term also covers any picture or photo created by the camera tool, any text box created by the text box tool, any button created by the macro button tool, and any embedded chart.

Chapter 2, "Basic Worksheet Operations," introduced you to the drawing tools available in the Toolbar and demonstrated the simple steps required to draw these shapes. This chapter discusses more advanced topics, such as drawing these shapes with special attributes, selecting multiple graphic objects, and moving and resizing objects. It also teaches you how to format, copy, paste, delete, layer, and group objects, and how to draw on embedded charts.

With all drawing tools, including the text box tool, the macro button tool, and the camera tool, the mouse pointer changes to a thin-line cross shape after you select the tool. Excel does this to orient you.

Drawing Shapes with Special Attributes

Excel provides various keys for positioning and drawing shapes to exact specifications. The following sections demonstrate how to use the Ctrl and Shift keys, both individually and combined, to produce special effects like starting and ending exactly at cell borders and drawing perfect circles and squares.

Using the Ctrl Key for Exact Positioning

Use the Ctrl key to draw lines that start and end on cell gridlines. Press the Ctrl key before you start drawing, and your line will begin at the intersection of a row and column gridline. Press the Ctrl key (unless you are already holding it down) before you release the mouse button, and the line will end exactly at an intersection.

Use the Ctrl key when you want the borders of rectangles and ovals and the ends of arcs to coincide with the cell borders. Press the Ctrl key (and keep it down) before you start drawing, and the beginning of the drawn object will be placed at a cell border. Similarly, to place the end of the object on a cell border, press the Ctrl key before you release the mouse button.

Figure 12.1 shows examples of drawn objects hugging the cell borders.

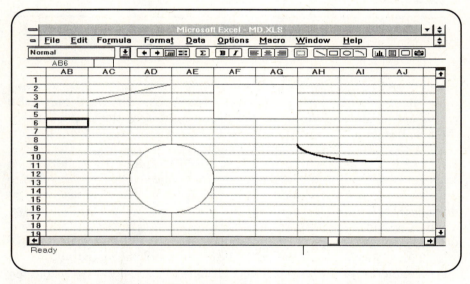

Figure 12.1 *Objects drawn along cell borders and intersections using Ctrl.*

Using the Shift Key to Draw Exact Shapes

If you hold down the Shift key while you drag, Excel will restrict the angle of a line to 45-degree increments.

When you want to draw a *perfect square,* hold down the Shift key while you drag with the rectangle tool. To draw a *perfect circle,* hold down Shift while you drag with the oval tool. When you want to draw a *quarter of a circle,* hold down Shift while you drag with the arc tool. In all three cases, be sure to hold down Shift until after you have finished dragging and have released the mouse button.

Using Ctrl and Shift Together to Combine Attributes

Using the Ctrl and Shift keys together when using the drawing tools combines the attributes that you get when using them separately.

If you use the Ctrl and Shift keys with the line tool while dragging, you get a line drawn at some multiple of 45 degrees whose ends coincide with the gridline intersections.

Use them with the rectangle tool, and you get a square whose edges are lined up with the cell borders.

Use them with the oval tool, and you get a circle that touches the cell borders.

Use them with the arc tool, and you get a quarter circle that starts and ends at the cell borders.

Table 12.1 summarizes the key strokes to use when drawing objects.

Table 12.1 Using Ctrl and Shift with the drawing tools.

Drawing Tool	With Ctrl	With Shift	With Ctrl + Shift
Line	The line begins/ends at the intersection of rows and columns.	The line is drawn at some multiple of 45 degrees.	The line is drawn at 45 degrees and starts/ends at intersections.
Rectangle	The rectangle borders coincide with cell borders.	You draw a square.	You draw a square touching the cell borders.
Oval	Oval borders coincide with cell borders.	You draw a circle.	You draw a circle touching the cell borders.
Arc	The arc starts/ends at the intersection of rows. and columns.	You draw a quarter circle.	You draw a quarter circle starting/ending at intersection points.

Selecting Graphic Objects

You should always try to coordinate the different features in your worksheet to create an overall effect. The proper placement, size, and formatting of graphic objects is important and sometimes requires you to select objects as a group.

Select any individual object by clicking on it.

Selecting Multiple Objects

When you want to select more than one object at the same time, you have two options: Use either the Shift key or the multiple selection tool. Chapter 2 described the simple steps for using the selection tool—select it and draw a rectangle around the objects to select. You can also use the Shift key for multiple selection, which gives you more flexibility in what individual objects to include in the selection.

To select multiple objects with the Shift key, follow these steps:

1. Press the Shift key.
2. Click on all objects you want to select, one by one, while holding down the Shift key.

When you want to deselect one object from a multiple selection, hold down Shift while you click on the object.

Selecting All Objects

When you want to select all objects in a worksheet, follow these three steps:

1. Choose Select Special from the Formula menu.

   Excel displays the dialog box shown in Figure 12.2.

2. Choose Objects, which is located in the lower right of the box.
3. Choose OK.

All objects on the entire worksheet will be selected. When you want to deselect a particular object, hold down the Shift key while you click on the object.

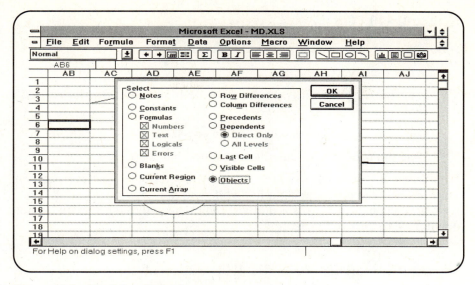

Figure 12.2 *The Select dialog box.*

Moving and Sizing Graphic Objects

After drawing a graphic object, you may want to move it around on the worksheet or make it larger or smaller. The following sections discuss how to use the mouse to move and resize objects.

Moving Objects

When you want to move an object, follow these steps:

1. Select the object.
2. Press the mouse button while the pointer is above the object.
3. Drag the object to its new position.

When you want the object to move only in a horizontal or vertical position, hold down the Shift key while you drag.

When you want to line up the object with the cell borders, hold down the Ctrl key while you drag.

Resizing Objects

Follow these steps to resize an object:

1. Select the object.

2. Place the mouse pointer on one of the sizing handles (the little black squares).

    The pointer takes the shape of a thin cross.

3. Drag the handle until the object has the right shape.

    When you want the rectangle or oval you are resizing to keep the same dimensions, hold down the Shift key while you drag.
    When you want the resized object to line up with the cell borders, hold down the Ctrl key while you drag.

Detaching Objects from the Worksheet Cells

One important thing to remember is that, by default, drawn objects and text boxes (though not camera pictures, charts, and buttons) are attached to the worksheet cells. Consequently, if you widen the columns or rows, the objects will also widen. If you want to keep an object exactly where it is regardless of cell widening, follow these steps:

1. Select the object to detach.

2. Choose Object Placement from the Format menu.

    Excel displays the dialog box shown in Figure 12.3.

    The Move and Size with Cells option is the default, meaning that the objects align with the cells underneath and change size when the cells move. Move but Don't Size means that the objects remain the same size when they move with the cells. Don't Move or Size means that the objects stay where they are regardless of cell alteration.

3. Choose Don't Move or Size to detach the selected object.

    Excel now treats the object as separate from the worksheet.

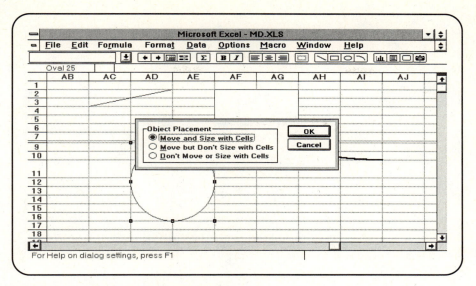

Figure 12.3 The Object Placement dialog box.

Locking a Graphic Object

All graphic objects can be locked so that they can't be selected, moved, resized, or formatted. This option is useful when you want to protect documents that took a lot of time to set up.

Excel confuses the situation somewhat by seeming to automatically set the lock for each drawn object to on. You can check this by selecting an object and choosing Object Protection from the Format menu. The dialog box shows the one option, Locked, set to on. In fact, the object is not really locked until you follow these steps:

1. Choose Protect Document from the Options menu.

    Excel displays the dialog box shown in Figure 12.4.

2. Choose the Objects option.

3. Type a password, if you want, in the Password box.

    Each character that you type appears as an asterisk in the box so that another person can't see what you're typing.

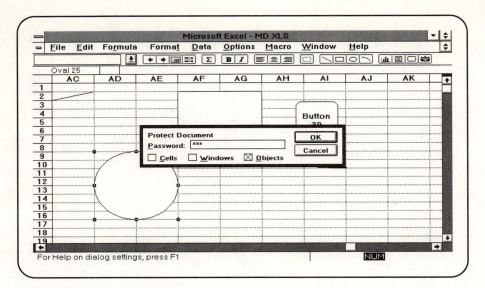

Figure 12.4 The Protect Document dialog box.

4. Choose OK.

   Excel prompts you to confirm the password.

5. Type in the password again if prompted.

   Excel returns you to the worksheet.

As its name implies, the Protect Document command applies globally. All objects that had the Locked option on are now protected, meaning that you can't change them in any way. You can't even select them. Only previously unlocked objects remain accessible.

You unlock objects before following the preceding steps by selecting them, choosing Object Protection from the Format menu, and then setting Locked to off.

Reverse the global locking by choosing Unprotect Document from the Options menu, supplying the password if necessary.

Formatting Graphic Objects

When you use the default settings, objects can look a bit thin and insubstantial. You can reformat their appearance using the Patterns command from the Format menu. The basic process is the same for all objects, but the dialog boxes differ depending on what kind of object you select.

Buttons can't be reformatted using the Patterns command (only text in a button can be formatted). Lines and arcs are discussed separately later in this chapter. For all other graphic objects—rectangles, ovals, pictures, text boxes, and embedded charts—follow these steps:

1. Select the graphic object.
2. Choose Patterns from the Format menu. Alternatively, double-click on the graphic object (and omit step 1 above).

A dialog box appears, divided into two sections—Border and Fill—as shown in Figure 12.5. Note that in both cases the "Automatic" option is checked.

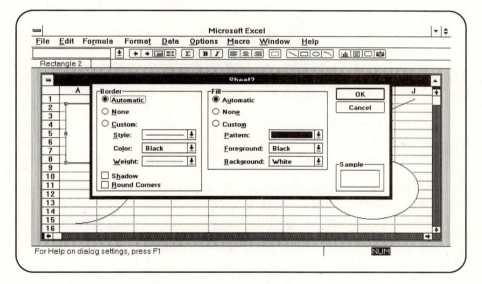

Figure 12.5 *The Patterns dialog box for a graphic object.*

The Shadow option gives your object a shadow along the bottom right. The Round Corners option, which is unavailable with a picture or an oval, rounds the corners of an object.

The Sample box, in the lower right-hand corner of the dialog box, gives you an idea of what your choice will look like on the worksheet. The border and fill options are discussed in the following sections.

Borders

A border is the line around a rectangle or oval. When you don't want a border but only a colored shape, for instance, check None. Checking None without giving the object a color through Fill makes the object invisible. Try it. When you want to modify the automatic border, choose Custom. With the Custom option you can modify three aspects of your border: its style, its color, and its weight. To see the possibilities for each option, click on the down arrow to its right. A drop-down box appears.

Style lets you choose between an uninterrupted border, four kinds of interrupted borders, and three kinds of patterns.

Color gives you the choice of 16 colors.

Weight regulates the lightness or darkness of a border. You have four possibilities: light, medium, dark, and double thickness.

Fill

The Automatic fill setting is for opaque: nothing underneath, including cell grids, is visible. When you do want the cell grid to be visible, check None.

When you want to create your own fill patterning, check Custom. With Custom you can choose from 18 patterns. You can further modify the fill with the 16 colors contained in Foreground and Background.

When you don't want a pattern, check the black rectangle in the Pattern drop box. Then use the Foreground drop box to select a color; you don't need the Background box.

When you do use a pattern, you can change the color combination with the Foreground and Background boxes. For instance, if you choose a pattern of dots and set the foreground to white and the background to black, you'll get white dots against black, and vice versa.

The Sample box, in the lower right-hand corner of the Patterns dialog box, gives you an idea of what your choice will look like.

Arc Border

Automatic is the default border for arcs. When you don't want a border, only a fill, it's smart to choose a fill before you choose None for Border; otherwise, your arc becomes invisible. Customizing style, color, and weight works the same as for other graphic objects.

Arc Fill

Strange as it may sound, you can fill an arc. An arc is one quarter of an oval, and that's how Excel treats the arc, as an oval from which three quarters are missing (see Figure 12.6).

For an arc, the default fill is None. Choose Automatic and the inside of the arc becomes opaque, meaning that the cell grid and anything else underneath is invisible.

When you want a pattern or a color, choose Custom. With Custom you can choose from 18 patterns, which you can further modify with the 16 colors contained in Foreground and Background.

Figure 12.6 shows examples of differently formatted arcs.

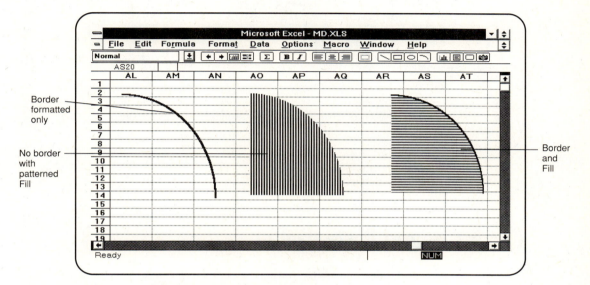

Figure 12.6 *Differently formatted arcs.*

Arrowheads on Lines

Figure 12.7 shows the Patterns dialog box for a line. Use the Line option on the left in the same way as the Border option for other graphic objects, as discussed previously. The Arrow Head option gives your line an arrow pointing in the direction you drew it. Style gives you a choice between no arrow, an open arrowhead, and a filled arrowhead. Width and Length let you decide how thick and how deep, respectively, you want your arrowhead to be.

The Sample box below the Arrow Head box gives you an idea of what your choice will look like.

212 Advanced Techniques

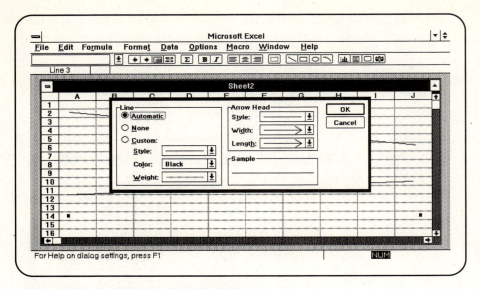

Figure 12.7   *The Patterns dialog box for a line.*

Copy, Cut and Paste, Delete

Copying, pasting, and deleting graphic objects are similar to performing these functions with cell values. Copying and pasting is especially useful if you want multiple objects of exactly the same size.

Follow these steps to copy or cut and paste:

1. Select the object.

2. Choose either Copy or Cut (Keyboard: Ctrl-Insert and Shift-Delete, respectively) from the Edit menu.

3. Place your mouse pointer where you want to paste your selection, and click to highlight the cell.

4. Choose Paste (Keyboard: Shift-Insert) from the Edit menu.

The object reappears in the same relation to the surrounding cells as the original. When you do not select a destination cell, the object is pasted in the same place as the original. If you copy the original, you will have two identical images on top of each other. You can then drag the top object to another place if you want to.

When you cut or copy a graphic object, Excel notes its position in relation to a rectangle of cells that surround it (see the highlighted area around each object in Figure 12.8). The copied object always positions itself in relation to the upper-left-corner cell.

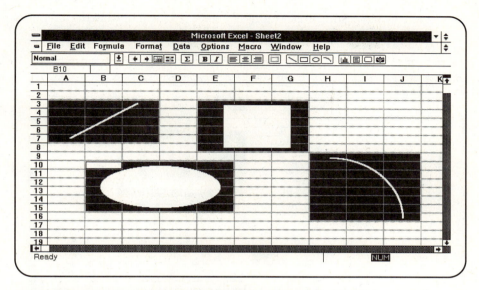

Figure 12.8   Graphic objects relative to their underlying cells.

When you highlight a cell as your paste destination, it becomes the new upper-left corner of the rectangle underlying your object.

 Tip: When you use the Multiple Selection tool, Excel counts all the cells you selected with the tool as belonging to the rectangle underlying the objects, no matter how wide your margins were. When you want to avoid this, use the Shift key for multiple selections instead of the selection tool.

Follow these steps to delete a graphic object:

1. Select the object.
2. Press the Backspace or Delete key.

If you have second thoughts about deleting the object, go to the Edit menu before you do anything else and choose Undo Clear.

Layered Objects

You can make interesting illustrations in your worksheet by drawing a series of simple, filled rectangles and ovals and layering them, as in Figure 12.9.

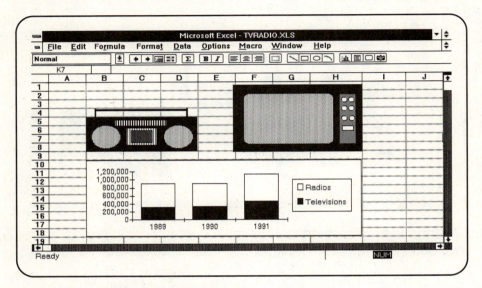

Figure 12.9   Patterned rectangles and ovals.

Control the sequence of your layered objects with the Bring to Front and Send to Back commands. For instance, suppose that you have a circle over which you draw a larger rectangle. Unless the rectangle is transparent, it will completely obscure the circle. You can easily remedy this situation (see Figure 12.10). Follow these steps:

1. Select the object on top.
2. From the Format menu, choose Send to Back.

You cannot select objects you cannot see, but when an object is partially visible, you can select it and choose Bring to Front. For example, the line behind the arc in Figure 12.10 can be selected and brought to the front.

> **Tip:** You cannot paste one object on top of another when your destination cell is covered by the latter. This is because you cannot select a cell you cannot see. In this case you have to paste somewhere near your destination and then drag your object to its intended place.

12 — Drawing with Graphic Objects 215

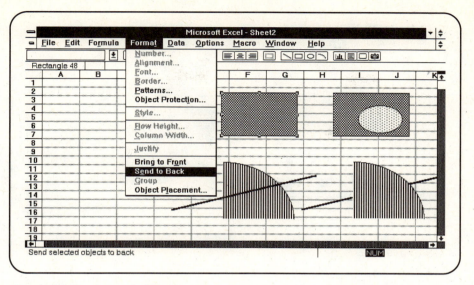

Figure 12.10   *Layered objects.*

Grouped Objects

When you have a series of objects that you want to keep together—for instance, the rectangles and ovals that make up the television and radio in Figure 12.9—you can group them. Grouped objects are like one object: when you resize the group, they are all resized; when you move the group, they all move. Group objects when it's important that their positioning relative to each other remains the same, as in the television figure or when you have a design for a worksheet using graphic objects.

1. Select all the objects you want to group.
2. From the Format menu, choose Group.

The selections around individual objects disappear and are replaced by one selection around the whole grouped object (see Figure 12.11).

216 Advanced Techniques

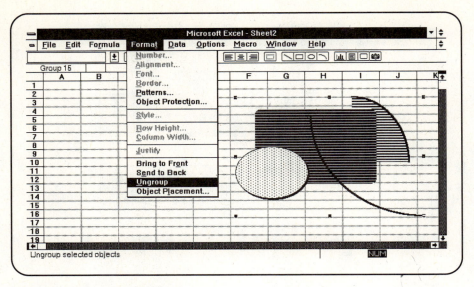

Figure 12.11 *Grouped objects.*

When you want to ungroup a grouped object, follow these steps:

1. Select the grouped object.
2. Choose Ungroup from the Format menu.

The selection around the grouped object will be replaced by selections around the individual objects.

Drawing on Embedded Charts

You can use the drawing tools to add graphics to an embedded chart but not to an opened chart whose window is activated. A drawing can be useful, for instance, when you want to draw attention to a particular value in your chart data (see Figure 12.12).

Embedded charts resemble graphic objects in many ways: An arrow over an embedded chart is like an arrow on top of an ordinary rectangle, for instance. You can use the Bring to Front and Send to Back commands (see "Layered Objects") with the embedded chart with the arrow.

However, when you open an embedded chart, the objects you've drawn on it will not appear in the chart window.

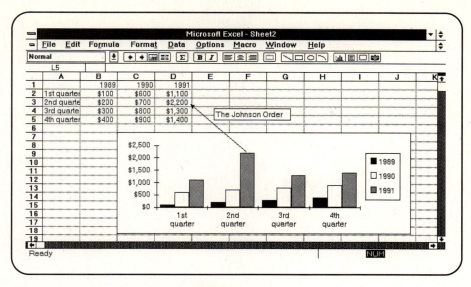

Figure 12.12 *Drawing on embedded charts.*

13
CHAPTER

Advanced Charting

Once a chart is drawn, the permutations available for adding, manipulating, and formatting the chart to your own specifications are unlimited. This chapter guides you through the commands and options available. It also discusses how the dimensions of the chart data on the worksheet affect the look of the chart and how data series can be added to, edited, and deleted from already existing charts.

Chart Plotting

Excel follows consistent rules when charting data. By understanding these rules, you can easily make adjustments to produce the chart you want. Excel helps by presenting dialog boxes when it first encounters an unusual plotting situation.

How Excel Plots Chart Data

The dimensions of the chart data you select play an important role in how Excel plots the resulting chart. Usually, the chart data on your worksheet will be in the form of a rectangle, meaning that one side of your chart is longer than the other or that it contains more rows than columns or vice versa. In Figure 13.1, for instance, the chart data is arranged in columns four cells high but in rows only three cells wide.

When the longest side of your data contains names or dates, you have what can be called the *ideal chart data* and the result will be a chart similar to Figure 13.1. The names on the longest side of your chart data are used as categories, plotted along the x-axis.

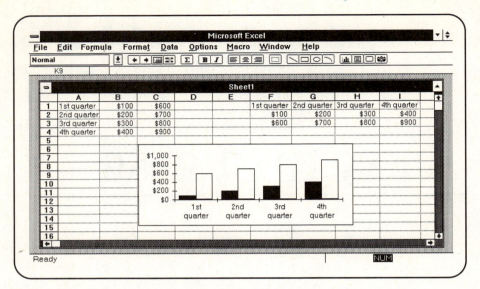

Figure 13.1 *Two sets of ideal chart data resulting in the same chart.*

When you create a chart, Excel looks at the first row or column on the longest side of your chart data to find names or dates it can use as categories. If you have no names or dates at all in your chart data, a dialog box will appear, asking you for further instructions (see the First Row or First Column Contains dialog box in Chapter 6, "Basic Charts").

Anytime Excel is confused, it prompts you with the First Row/Column Contains dialog box: for instance, if the title names in your chart are on the shortest side with one title in the first cell (the upper-left cell). If your data has names on the shortest side, as in Figure 13.2, you see the First Row/Column Contains dialog box as if you had no names or dates in your chart data.

In this example, there is a name in the upper-left cell. When plotting a chart, Excel does evaluate the contents of the first cell, but it is the contents of the second cell of the longest side that determine what the resulting chart looks like. In this case, Excel noticed a title on the longest side and therefore expected a name in the second cell as well. When the second cell turned out to contain only a number, Excel got confused and displayed a dialog box to ask you for further instructions.

Figure 13.3 gives a further demonstration of the importance of the second cell in plotting a chart, showing a chart of data that has a name only in the second cell.

Just one title name, if placed in the second cell on the longest side, promotes the contents of a whole row or column to the status of categories.

13 — Advanced Charting 221

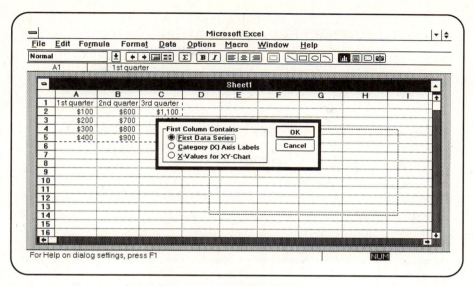

Figure 13.2   Plotting data with names on the shortest side.

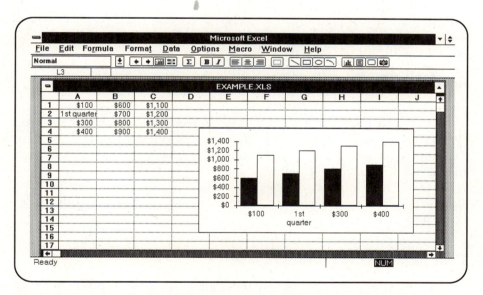

Figure 13.3   Even silly data with a name in the second cell on the longest side is plotted without a query from Excel.

The message from all of this is: Be aware of the rules when you plot data in a worksheet for a chart. These rules are summarized below:

- The cell in the upper left is not crucial when you make a chart. Its contents are evaluated; but if, in light of the contents of the second cell of the longest side, they do not make sense to Excel, the first cell is simply ignored.

- The second cell on the longest side is the crucial cell when you make a chart. If it contains a name or a date, the values of its row or column will automatically become categories in your chart.

- The contents of the third, fourth, etc., cells on the longest side are unimportant when you make a chart. Excel will assume their contents to be similar to the second cell, and treat them the same way as the contents of the second cell.

 Tip: For your own convenience, try to put category names in your data along the longest side and noncategory names on the shortest side.

Controlling Chart Plotting

Often you may need to override the assumptions that Excel makes about how your data is represented in a chart—what becomes categories and so forth. When the First Row/Column Contains dialog box is not presented, there are two ways to dictate your wishes to Excel: through the Paste Special command in Edit and through the Edit Series command in Chart. The use of Paste Special is discussed in the next section. See "Creating and Editing with the Edit Series Command" later in this chapter for information on using the Edit Series command.

Using Paste Special to Control Plotting

When you want to control your own categories and data series rather than accept the Excel choices, use the Paste Special option when creating the chart. Here are the steps:

1. Select the chart data on the worksheet.

2. Choose Copy from the Edit menu.

3. Choose New from the File menu and Chart from the resulting dialog box and then choose OK.

   Excel displays a blank chart window since it registers the fact that you copied the data into memory.

4. Choose Paste Special from the Edit menu.

   Excel displays the dialog box shown in Figure 13.4.

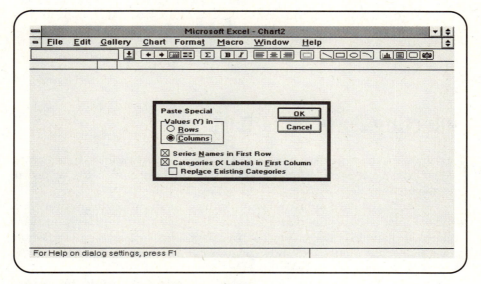

Figure 13.4 *The Paste Special dialog box.*

The logic behind the options in this box is similar to that of the First Row/Column Contains dialog box discussed in Chapter 6.

The first set of options, titled Values (Y) in, changes the names of the next two sets of options (see the following two paragraphs) according to the choice taken, Rows or Columns. Rows takes data series from the rows and categories from column headings. Columns takes data series from the columns and categories from the row headings.

Choose Rows and the next option down is displayed as Series Names in First Column. Check this and the cell contents of the first row in each column become the name of the data series. Choose Columns and this option displays as Series Names in First Row. Check this and the first column cell in each row becomes the name of the data series. Turn this option off and the cell contents of the first row or column become data points in the series.

Choose <u>R</u>ows and the third option is displayed as `Categories (X Labels) in First Row`. Check this and the first row cell contents in each column become categories. Choose <u>C</u>olumns and this option displays as `Categories (X Labels) in First Column`. Check this and the first column contents become categories. Again, if you turn this option off, the contents become data points.

The Repl<u>a</u>ce Existing Categories option pastes new categories into the chart. Use this when a chart already exists and you want to change the categories. Highlight the new categories in the worksheet, copy into memory, open the chart, choose Paste Special, and check this option to achieve this.

5. Choose your options and then OK.

Selecting Parts of a Chart

Part or all of a chart needs to be selected to perform operations like formatting and editing. Excel provides three ways of selecting: the mouse, the keyboard, and the menus.

Selecting with the mouse is like selecting with the mouse in any other part of Excel: Just click on the item to select. The item then appears with black squares, or handles. Click on any part of a data series in a chart and the whole series is selected. Figure 13.5 shows an example of a selected data series — the third series in each category in this case.

You can also select one data marker in a series by pressing the Ctrl key before you click.

Using the mouse pointer can be tricky with complicated charts, so sometimes you'll want to use the keyboard. Use any of the arrow keys to select things from the keyboard. The up (to reverse order, the down) arrow key selects classes of items like the chart and whole series. The right (to go forward) and left (to reverse) arrow keys select classes and individual items like data markers.

The whole chart and the plot area can be selected from the Chart menu. Choose Select <u>C</u>hart to select everything in the chart. Choose Select Plot <u>A</u>rea to select the area inside and including the axes.

The name of any item selected displays on the left side of the formula bar. The origin of any series is also displayed in the formula bar when a series is selected (see Figure 13.5). The worksheet title and cell locations of the chart data series are inside the parentheses.

Click outside the chart or press Esc to deselect anything.

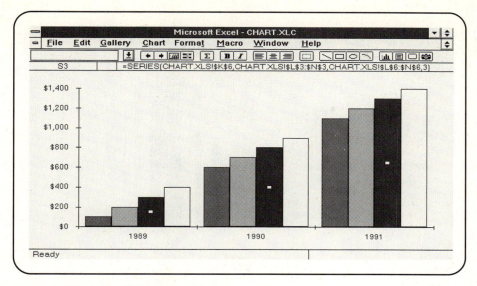

Figure 13.5 *A selected data series.*

Plotting Multiple Selections

Multiple selections can be defined as a chart. A *multiple selection* is a collection of ranges of selected cells that have unselected cells in between. You select them by pressing Ctrl each time you select a group of cells.

You might want to use this feature when the chart data on your worksheet has blank rows or columns that you want to leave out, or when you want to make a chart of a collapsed outline without including the invisible rows and columns, or when you want to plot only part of the data in a row or column.

The data you select should be able to form a rectangle if brought together. If this isn't true, then Excel examines the upper-left cell of the first range of cells. If this cell does not contain text or a date, then Excel doesn't look in the multiple selection for category or series names. If this cell does contain text or a date, then Excel looks at all the selected cells and tries to make category and series names.

3-D Charts

3-D charts are not as complicated as they may sound. Most of the time, choosing one of the four 3-D options in the Gallery menu—3-D Area, 3-D Column, 3-D Line, and 3-D Pie—just means adding depth to the data markers.

Figure 13.6 for instance shows a 3-D representation of the chart shown in Figure 13.5.

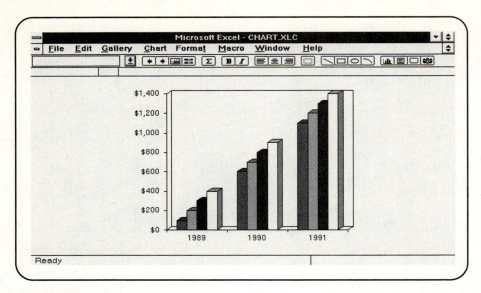

Figure 13.6 *A 3-D chart.*

This chart is the result of choosing 3-D Column from the Gallery menu, then choosing the first option of the seven subtypes of columns, and choosing OK.

The first four types in the 3-D Column dialog box, the first four in the 3-D Area dialog box, and all the types in the 3-D Pie box give this depth effect to your charts.

But you can also achieve an additional effect, producing a multicategory 3-D chart, with other types available in the 3-D Gallery options. All the 3-D Line types, the bottom three in the 3-D Column dialog box, and the bottom three in the 3-D Area dialog box give this effect.

Basically what happens is that Excel gives the categories an axis of their own. Figure 13.7 shows the result of choosing type 6 in the 3-D Column dialog box.

In the example in Figure 13.7, the categories, 1st qtr, 2nd qtr, 3rd qtr, and 4th qtr, now have an axis of their own. In many cases, using 3-D can more vividly illuminate the data. The values in the chart obviously remain the same since they come from the same chart data, but the changes from the two angles of looking at the information (years and quarters here) are more clearly delineated.

Figure 13.8 shows the full range of types available with the 3-D Column option. The other 3-D chart dialog boxes are similar. Next and Previous display the next dialog box and the last dialog box respectively on the Gallery menu, 3-D Line and 3-D Area, in this case. Use them as a shortcut to get to the other chart options.

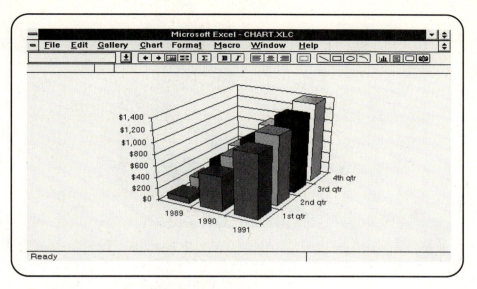

Figure 13.7 *A multicategory 3-D chart.*

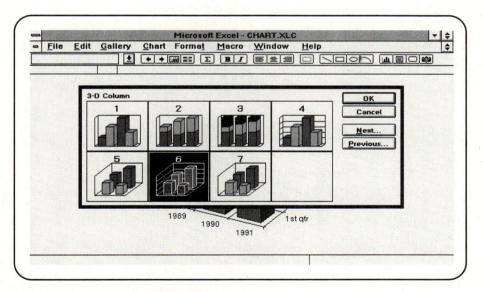

Figure 13.8 *The 3-D Column dialog box.*

Figures 13.9, 13.10, and 13.11 show examples of 3-D Area, 3-D Line, and 3-D Pie respectively, using the same chart data used in the previous figures.

228 Advanced Techniques

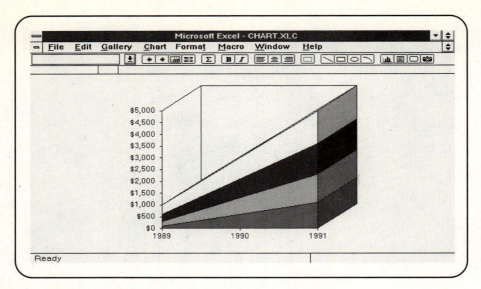

Figure 13.9 *A 3-D Area chart.*

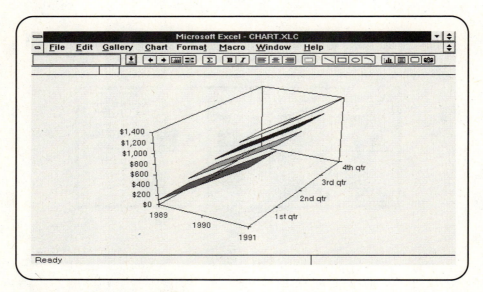

Figure 13.10 *A 3-D Line chart.*

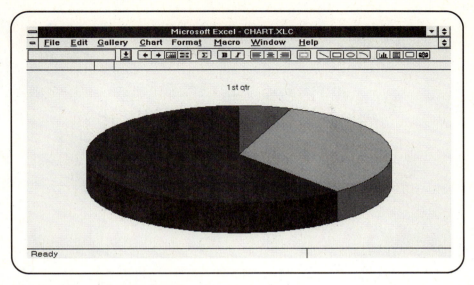

Figure 13.11 *A 3-D Pie chart.*

Formatting 3-D Charts

The 3-D View command in the Format menu gives you power to alter perspective and rotation angles in a three-dimensional chart to a degree that would have been a distant dream on personal computers a decade ago. The formatting possibilities are limitless.

Follow these steps to use 3-D View:

1. From your 3-D chart, choose 3-D View from the Format menu.

    Excel displays the dialog box shown in Figure 13.12.

    Each option in this box controls the angle of view of the chart. In the center of the box is a representation of the 3-D chart. As you change the various options, you can choose the Apply button to see the effect of your changes on this representation without exiting the dialog box.

    If you make too many changes to remember, choose the Default button and the option numbers revert to the Excel defaults.

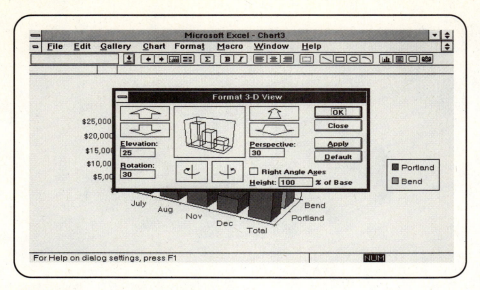

Figure 13.12   The 3-D View dialog box.

Elevation controls the height from which you view the chart in degrees. In all charts, except pie charts, the range to enter goes from −90 to 90. 90, for instance, shows the chart from straight overhead. With pie charts the range is from 10 to 80. Two large arrowheads in boxes above this option increase and decrease this number as an alternative to entering a number directly and choosing Apply.

The Perspective number (range of 0 to 100) is the result of dividing the front width of the chart by the back width of the chart. The greater the resulting number, the more the chart "stretches back into the distance." 0 means no perspective. The two large arrowheads over this option provide an alternative to entering a number.

The Rotation number (range 0 to 360) gives the angle in degrees of the whole chart around the vertical or z-axis. 180, for instance, gives the back view of the chart; 0 the front. The boxes with looped arrows provide an alternative to entering the number in the box.

Right Angle Axes puts the axes at right angles and cancels out the Perspective option (that option actually disappears from screen when you check the Axes box).

The percentage you enter at Height % of Base measures the height of the vertical (or z) axis as a percentage of the x-axis (or the width of the chart). The range is from 5 to 500. 100 makes the height and width equal; 500 makes the height (including the walls) five times greater than the width.

2. Change the options and choose OK to apply the changes to your chart.

Combination: Main and Overlay Charts

The Combination option in the Gallery menu is the final kind of chart available in Excel. Chapter 6, "Basic Charts," and the preceding section on 3-D charts discussed all the other types of charts. Combination combines two different kinds of charts—column with line, for example—in the same chart window. It's useful for comparing different data series in a very direct way to show contrasts and correlations.

Figure 13.13 shows a combination chart derived from our ongoing example. Create this chart in three steps:

1. Choose Combination from the Gallery menu.

2. Choose a chart type or format from the dialog box.

   Use type 1 in the example.

3. Choose OK.

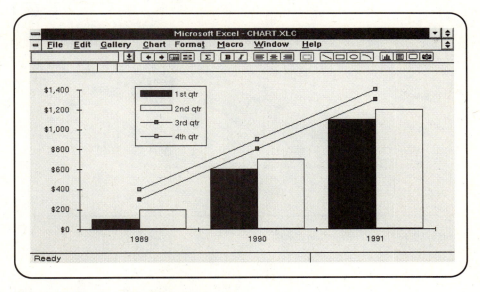

Figure 13.13 *A combination chart.*

You can't use 3-D in combination charts.

The example shown in Figure 13.13, though a poor example of the usefulness of combinations, does show how Excel divides up the data series by default when you choose Combination from the Gallery menu. The data series are divided between the *main chart,* the columns in this case, and the *overlay chart,* the lines in this case. With an even number of data series in a chart, Excel places the first half in the main chart and the second half in the overlay chart (as in the example). With an odd number of series, it puts the additional one in the main chart.

If your noncombination chart is already customized (with formatting options discussed in the following sections) and you want to retain the formats, follow this step:

1. Choose Add Overlay from the Chart menu.

You can then customize the overlay chart if you wish, as discussed in the next section. Figure 13.14 shows an example of how an overlay chart can be used for comparison. This chart has four new data series derived from projected sales for the first four quarters of each year. Placing these as overlays on top of the actual sales gives a quick comparison.

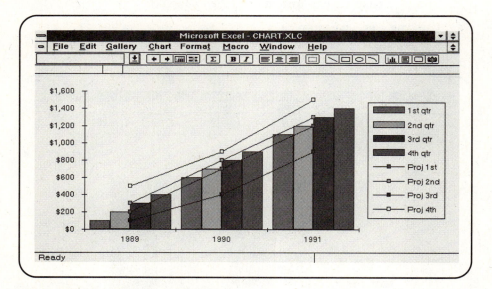

Figure 13.14   *A combination chart.*

Formatting Main and Overlay Charts

The appearance of both main and overlay charts can be customized to suit your own preferences. This section discusses the steps and the options available. Even when a chart is not a combination chart, you use the same steps to format the chart—Excel calls it the main chart even when there is no overlay.

To format a main or an overlay chart, follow these steps:

1. Choose <u>M</u>ain Chart or <u>O</u>verlay from the Forma<u>t</u> menu.

   Excel displays a similar dialog box in both cases. Figure 13.15 shows the Main Chart dialog box.

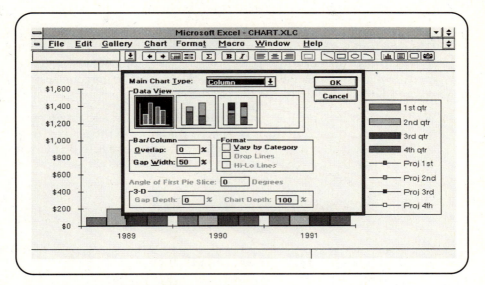

Figure 13.15   *The Main Chart dialog box.*

The only difference between the Main and Overlay dialog boxes is the bottom option. In the Main, it's a 3-D option; in the Overlay, it's an option called *Series Distribution,* as explained later in this section.

For main charts the default type is column; for overlays it's line. Change the type through the Chart Type scroll bar. Within Type you get what Excel calls the Data <u>V</u>iew, the subtypes. In Figure 13.15, for instance, there are three different views to choose from.

With Bar and Column types, you have two options that are unavailable with other types. <u>O</u>verlap allows you to overlap data series by a designated percentage. 100% means that you have perfect stacking because the series are on top of one another. A negative percentage puts space between the series. Gap <u>W</u>idth puts space between categories or clusters of data series. The number must be between 0 and 500; the higher the number, the greater the space.

You can play with three Format options, some of which will be unavailable depending on the chart type. <u>V</u>ary by Category (unavailable with Area) applies when you have only one data series. Check it and it gives different colors to the markers in the same series. <u>D</u>rop Lines (available with Line and Area only) draws vertical lines to the highest value in each group of data. H̲i-Lo Lines (available with Line only) draws lines from the highest to the lowest value in each group of data.

Angl̲e of First Pie Slice is available with Pie only. The number (default 0) represents the angle (in degrees) in a clockwise direction of a side of a pie slice with the vertical axis. Use it to rotate your pie as you wish.

With main charts you get two 3-D options when a 3-D chart is chosen. G̲ap Depth allows you to regulate the distance between data markers by specifying a marker width percentage. C̲hart Depth allows you to regulate the depth relative to the width; the higher the percentage entered (20 to 2000 only), the deeper the chart.

With overlay charts, the 3-D options are replaced by *Series Distribution*. You can accept A̲utomatic or specify a number in the F̲irst Overlay Series box. This number tells Excel the first data series to be plotted in the overlay chart. Each subsequent data series (those with a higher number) also goes into the overlay.

2. Choose your options and then OK.

Adding to, Editing, and Deleting Existing Chart Data Series

Even after a chart exists you can make as many changes as you like (besides the more obvious formatting changes) to make it look better. You can add new series and categories, edit those already in existence, and delete them when necessary. The following sections take you through these operations.

Adding Additional Chart Data

Earlier in this chapter, the section on chart plotting showed you how to use Paste Special to dictate the appearance of your chart to Excel. The steps for adding chart data are similar.

Say you wanted to add a data series totaling the sales figures for the years, at the line beginning `Total` after `4th qtr` in Figure 13.16.

1. Select the worksheet data to add to the chart.

    In the example, these are the cells containing `Total`, `$1,000`, `$3,000`, and `$5,000`.

2. Choose C̲opy from the E̲dit menu.

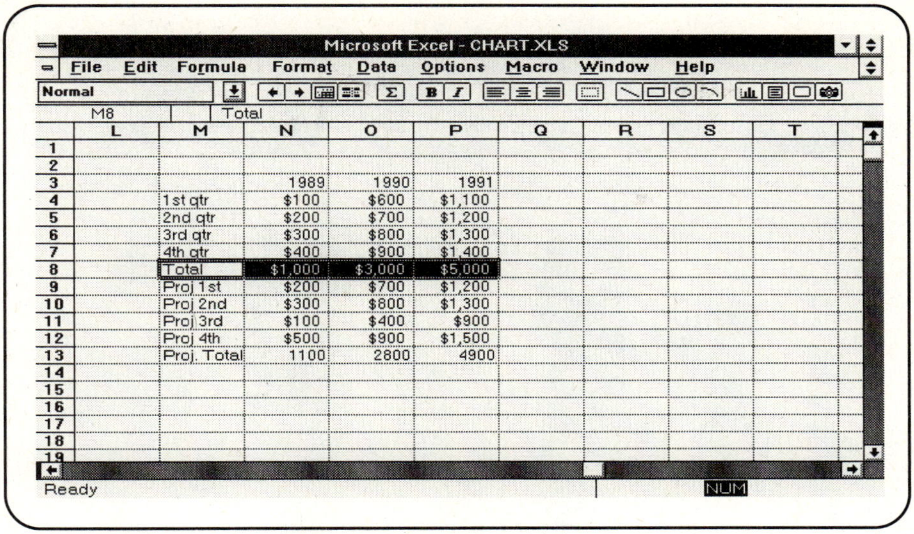

Figure 13.16 *A new data series in chart data.*

3. Activate the chart window.

   At this stage, you have the choice of using Paste and accepting Excel's plotting, or using Paste Special and controlling the plotting yourself. An earlier section, "Using Paste Special to Control Plotting," discussed how to use the Paste Special dialog box.

4. Choose either Paste or Paste Special from the Edit menu.

   If you choose Paste Special, you need to specify the options from the dialog box and then choose OK.

   Note that when adding series to an existing chart, you cannot use multiple selections. Data series that are not beside one another must be added separately.

Adding Series from Another Chart

As well as adding worksheet data series to an existing chart, you can also add directly from another chart. Figure 13.17 shows an example of two charts.

Say you wanted to add the chart in the left window, Chart 8, to the other chart, Chart 6. Follow these steps:

1. With both charts open, activate the chart window that you want to copy from.

Advanced Techniques

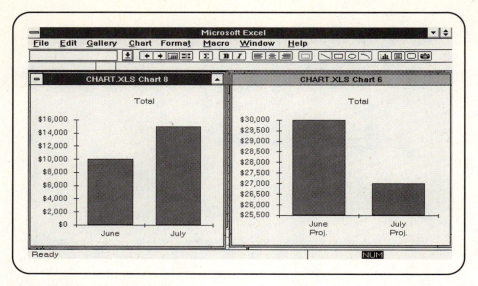

Figure 13.17   *Two charts.*

2. Select the whole chart using the mouse, keyboard, or menus.

3. Choose Copy from the Edit menu.

4. Go to the other chart (the chart you want to add to).

5. Choose Paste or Paste Special from the Edit menu.

Use Paste to accept what Excel does automatically. Paste Special in this case does not give the same dialog box shown when you add from a worksheet. It has three options: All, Formats, and Formulas. All gives the same result as Paste would. Formats copies only the formatting of the other chart, not the series. Formulas copies only the series, not the formatting.

Figure 13.18 shows the result in the example. Notice that the titles on the horizontal axis, June and July, are transferred with the data.

Using the Series Formula to Create and Edit Data Series

You may have noticed that when you select a data series in a chart, a formula beginning =SERIES appears in the formula bar. The arguments in this formula can be manipulated, either directly or through the Edit Series command in the Chart menu, to create and edit data series.

Figure 13.19 shows a series formula.

13 — Advanced Charting 237

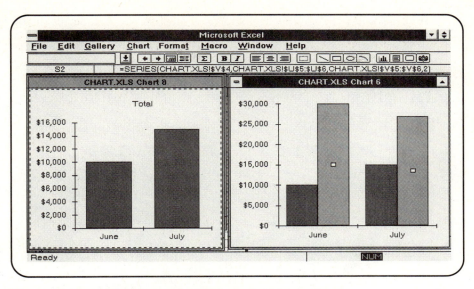

Figure 13.18 *Adding data series from one chart to another.*

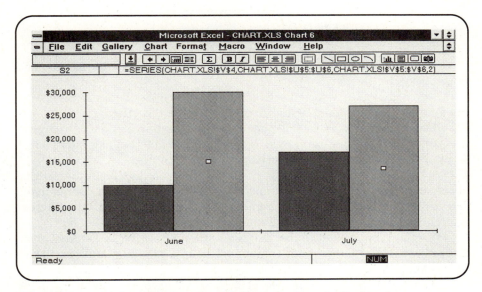

Figure 13.19 *A selected data series with the series formula displayed.*

This formula can be broken down into several parts: the function title, the series name argument, the category names argument, the values argument, and the plot order argument.

238   Advanced Techniques

The easiest way to see this breakdown is through the Edit Series dialog box, shown in Figure 13.20.

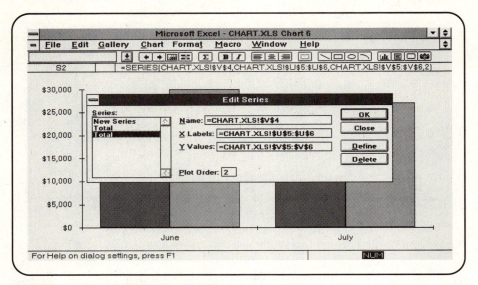

Figure 13.20 *The Edit Series dialog box.*

=Series defines the set of characters as a formula or function to Excel and must always be present.

The name of the selected series is highlighted in the Series scroll box on the left, Total here, listed beside all other series in this chart.

Excel puts the worksheet file name and cell location of the series name of this series in the Name box. Here it is =Chart.xls!$V$4. This can also be straight text but is usually an external absolute reference.

X Labels, equivalent to category names argument, is usually an external absolute reference, but it can be simply text within quotes. The first series in the category determines the category names used. If the other series have different references, it does not change the category names.

Y Values, equivalent to the values argument, must be an external absolute reference and corresponds to the y values in a 2-D chart and the z values in a 3-D chart.

The Plot Order determines the order in which Excel plots the series in the chart. Change the number here and the plot orders of the other data series automatically change as well. The order of the series in the Series box in this dialog box reflects the plot order. (New Series doesn't count.)

Tip: If there is a chance that the chart data could move on your worksheet, you can use names—not cell references—in the Series formula. Use Define Name in the Formula menu to do this.

Creating and Editing with the Edit Series Command

As you saw in the preceding section, the Edit Series command breaks down the Series function into its component parts. Editing and creating series in a chart can therefore be most easily done using this command. The steps for creating or editing through this option are similar, as shown below.

Please note that you can start with a blank chart by selecting a blank cell on the worksheet, then choosing New from the File menu, and Chart and OK from the dialog box.

1. If you want to edit, select the data series to edit in the chart. To add or create a series, start at step 2.

2. Choose Edit Series from the Chart menu.

    The Edit Series dialog box is shown in Figure 13.20. If you selected a data series, it is highlighted in the Series box; otherwise, New Series, the first entry, is highlighted. New Series, as the name implies, is used to create a new series in the chart.

3. Fill in or change the Name, X Labels, Y Values, and Plot Order boxes.

    The first three always start with the = sign.

4. To remain in the dialog box after entering or editing, choose Define and then start on the next data series.

5. Choose OK when finished.

    You can enter up to 255 series.

Creating and Editing with the Formula Bar

Editing a series function through the formula bar is the most direct way of making your changes. Follow the correct syntax of enclosing each argument—the series name, the category names, the values, and the plot order—within parentheses and separating each from the other with a comma.

If you don't need to enter an argument (if there are no categories, for instance), just leave the space between the commas blank.

240 Advanced Techniques

You can also enter a series formula by selecting the arguments on the worksheet and letting Excel insert them on the formula bar, as shown in the following steps. You can create a series in a blank chart window by selecting a blank cell on a worksheet and creating a new chart.

1. From the chart window, click on the formula bar and type **=series(**.

   Now each argument must be entered in turn. It's usually easier to arrange the chart and worksheet windows on the same screen so that you can move back and forth between them easily. Figure 13.21 shows an example of what the screen would look like at this stage with the worksheet on the right and the blank chart on the left.

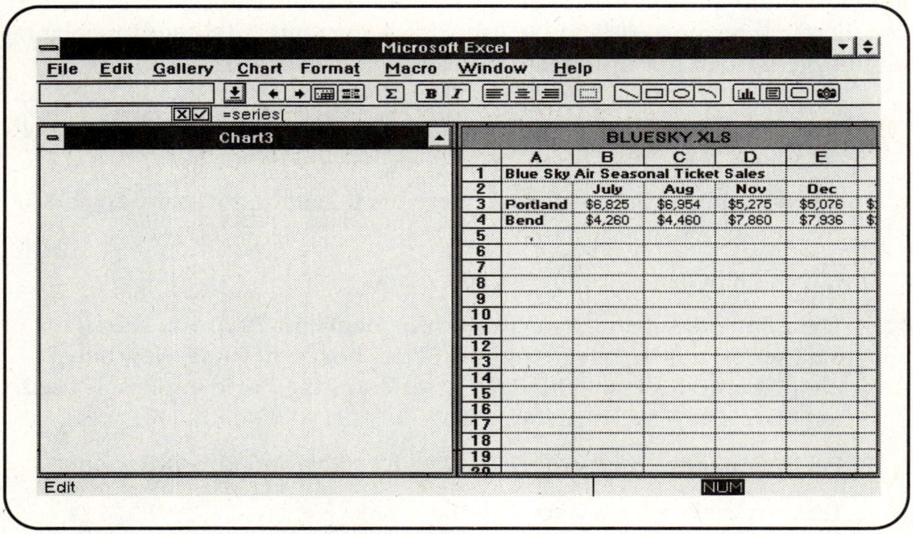

Figure 13.21 *Entering a series via the formula bar.*

2. Select the name of the first data series on the worksheet.

   In the example, this is cell A3, `Portland`. The worksheet name and cell reference appear in the formula bar.

3. Type a comma.

4. Select the category name cells on the worksheet and when they appear on the formula bar, type a comma after them.

   Here the category names are B2:F2.

5. Select the cell range for the values in this series and follow it on the formula bar with a comma.

   Here the range is B3:F3.

6. Type the plot order number of the series, starting with 1 for the first series, and type a closing parenthesis.

Here, use 1. In the example, your formula ends up looking like =series(Bluesky.xls!$A$3,Bluesky.xls!$B$2:$F$2,Bluesky.xls!$B$3:$F$3,1).

7. Accept the formula by pressing Enter.

Excel draws the series in a chart. You may add other series formulas as you wish. In the example, for instance, you could add the other series in the same way and end up with =series(Bluesky.xls!$A$4,,Bluesky.xls!$B$4:$F$4,2). Note that the category names are omitted in this second series. Since Excel takes the category names from the first series, it doesn't matter whether or not you enter them here.

Figure 13.22 shows an example of a two-series chart entered by this method of creating series.

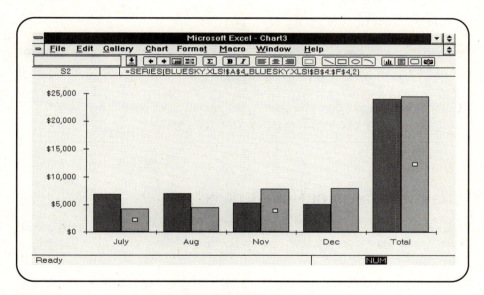

Figure 13.22   *Data series entered through the formula bar.*

Deleting Data Series

There are three separate ways to delete data series from a chart: through the Clear command in Edit, through the Edit Series command in Chart, and through the formula bar.

Follow these steps to delete through either of the menu commands:

1. Select the data series to delete.
2. Choose either Cl<u>e</u>ar from the <u>E</u>dit menu or Edit <u>S</u>eries from the <u>C</u>hart menu.
3. From the Clear dialog box, choose the Series option; from the Edit Series dialog box, choose the D<u>e</u>lete button.
4. Choose OK to exit.

Follow these steps to delete a data series through the formula bar:

1. Select the data series to delete.

   The data series formula appears in the formula bar.
2. Press Backspace.
3. Press Enter or click on the enter box.

Caution: Take care when deleting the first series in a category because that is where Excel gets the category names. If the new first series (after you delete) has no category reference, the category names will disappear on the chart.

Direct Adjustment of Data Markers

With certain kinds of charts, Excel allows you to adjust the values directly on the chart. These chart types are line, bar, and column charts, all in 2-D only. Follow these steps:

1. Select an individual data marker (not a whole series) by holding down the Ctrl key and selecting the marker.

   With all three chart types, one black rectangle appears on the data marker.
2. Drag this handle to increase or decrease the value.

   When you change a marker value like this, the corresponding value in the worksheet changes also.

Customizing a Chart

Formatting includes a host of commands and options that enable you to customize the appearance of your chart to your own requirements. "Formatting Main and Overlay Charts" and "Formatting 3-D Charts" discussed some customizing options. Other chart formatting and customizing can be broken down into two main areas: adding objects, such as arrow pointers, titles, and gridlines, to the chart; and changing the appearance of items in your chart, such as text fonts, scales of axes, and color. This section outlines the many tools available in any chart window for adding objects.

Adding Objects to a Chart

You can add (and subsequently delete if necessary) explanatory text, arrows, a legend, axes (Excel puts these in by default), and gridlines to charts. Table 13.1 gives a simple summary of which command adds or deletes which object.

Table 13.1   Adding objects to a chart.

Chart Menu Command	Object Added or Deleted
Attach Text	A box containing explanatory text
Add Arrow	A pointer arrow to draw attention to an item on a chart
Add Legend	A legend box containing data series identification
Axes	X-, y-, or z-axis in main charts; x- or y-axis in overlay charts
Gridlines	Major or minor gridlines. Gridlines work in conjunction with major and minor units of measure on your chart on both the horizontal and vertical axes. In other words they are lines on the chart from the tick mark units. Using them guides the eye to the unit that best measures the various data points and positions on the chart.

Two of these objects, the arrow and the legend, are added by simply choosing the command from the Chart menu while the chart window is active. Add Legend changes to Delete Legend when you use it. You can add only one legend box but as many arrows as you like to a chart. To delete an arrow, select it and the menu command then reads Delete Arrow.

244 Advanced Techniques

The other three options that add or delete text, axes, and gridlines display dialog boxes when chosen from the menu. When you add a check mark to any of the options, like Chart Title in Attach Text To, the object corresponding to that option is added when you exit the dialog box by choosing OK.

Most of the options in the dialog boxes—like Value (Y) Axis and Category (X) Axis—refer to axes (including overlay axes) and will be known to you from previous sections in this book. When in doubt, press the F1 key while the dialog box is on screen for an explanation of each term.

With the Attach Text To dialog box, when you want to attach the data marker value or other explanatory text to a marker, you check the Series and Data Point option and then specify both the Series Number and the Point Number in separate boxes.

All text in a chart can be changed and formatted to your own specifications, as demonstrated in the following section.

Tip: The easiest way to delete text is to select the object with the text and delete it through the formula bar. If a text box remains, you can get rid of it through the Patterns command.

Tip: Use Attach Text to add space to charts when you want. For instance, add text to the value axis, then delete the Y that appears, and press the space bar to move the chart right. Use the title and category text boxes similarly to move the chart down and up respectively.

Figure 13.23 shows a chart with added objects, including a chart title with an arrow pointing to it, a data marker with a value, a legend box, and major gridlines from both the x- and y-axes.

Formatting

This section discusses the formatting options Patterns, Font, Text, Scale, and Legend. Use them to customize the appearance of your chart, such as the scaling of your axes, the text font and size in any part of the chart, the patterning of the walls or floor in a 3-D chart, etc.

13 — Advanced Charting 245

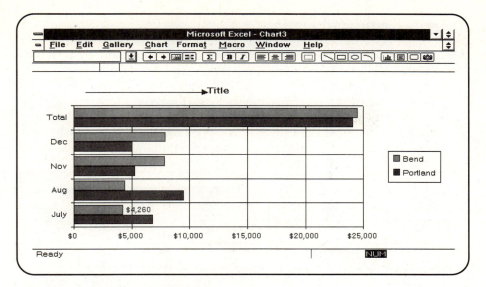

Figure 13.23   *Objects on a chart.*

The steps to use these commands are the same in all cases:

1. Select the chart item to format.

   This can be the whole chart. If nothing is selected, none of these options is available.

2. Choose the command from the Format menu.

3. Select and change the options in the dialog box.

4. Press OK when finished.

Many of these command dialog boxes connect with each other through buttons. For example, the Text dialog box has a Patterns button. Choose it and Excel takes you to the Patterns dialog box.

 Tip: The number formatting in the first data value in the first data series on the worksheet determines the number formatting on the value axis on the chart. Format this one cell on the worksheet (using Number in Format) and the whole axis changes.

Patterns Command Options

With Patterns you can change the appearance of borders and areas, legend boxes, data markers, 3-D walls and floors, tick marks, labels, gridlines, arrows, and text borders. Excel displays options to change the axis format and Tick Mark Type when you select an axis; otherwise, it displays options to change the border and area.

Figure 13.24 shows the Patterns dialog box options displayed when you choose an axis. Different options are displayed according to what is selected.

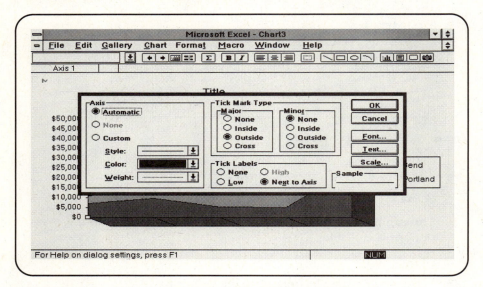

Figure 13.24 *The Patterns dialog box when an axis is selected.*

Automatic gives the Excel default formatting for borders and axes. Choose None when you don't want a border. You can't delete an axis through this command, only through Axes in the Chart menu, so the None option is unavailable when an axis is selected.

Custom, under either Border or Axis, has three components: Style lets you choose between an uninterrupted line for your border or axes, four kinds of interrupted lines, and three kinds of patterns. Color gives you the choice of 16 colors. Weight regulates the lightness or darkness of a line. You have four possibilities: light, medium, and dark, and double thickness.

When the Area options show (depending on what is selected in the chart), you can choose the Excel defaults (Automatic and None), or use the Custom options. The term *area* in this context refers to that part of the chart outside the x- and y-axes. In Custom you can choose from 18 Patterns. You can modify the area with the 16 colors contained in Foreground and Background. When you don't want a pattern, check the black rectangle in the Pattern drop box. Then use the Foreground drop box to select a color: you don't need the Background box. When you do use a pattern, you can change the color combination with the Foreground and Background boxes. For instance, if you choose a pattern of dots and set the foreground to white and the background to black, you get white dots against black, and vice versa.

The Tick Mark Type options are divided into Major and Minor, meaning the major and minor units of measure on the axis. Both Major and Minor have four options: None, Inside, Outside, and Cross. Inside and Outside mean the tick marks are moved to the inside and outside of the axis respectively; Cross means they stride the line.

Tick Labels, meaning the scaling numbers, show by default. If you want them "switched off," choose None. High, Low, and Next to Axis dictate the position of the labels.

Invert if Negative reverses the foreground and background colors of a series when the values are negative.

The Shadow option gives your object a shadow along the bottom right.

The Sample box in the lower right-hand corner of the Patterns dialog box gives you an idea of what your choice will look like.

 Tip: Double-click on a chart item to quickly go to the Patterns dialog box.

Font Command Options

Font governs the look of all text and characters on a chart, including the tick mark labels and legend text. Choose the preferred font, point size, test style, and text color from the Font, Size, Style (Bold, Italic, Underline, and Strikeout), and Color options in the Font dialog box.

Check Printer Fonts when you want a display of the fonts supported by your printer, as distinct from a display of fonts supported by your screen.

Under Background options, Automatic gives the Excel defaults for the background behind text; Transparent leaves the area behind text transparent; and White Out removes patterns but leaves the background color behind text.

Text Command Options

The Text command defines the orientation of the selected text. Besides Automatic, the dialog box allows you to choose among four orientations: horizontal and three varieties of vertical orientation.

Figure 13.25 shows the Text options.

248   Advanced Techniques

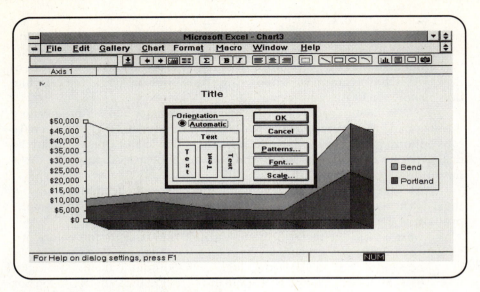

Figure 13.25   *The Text dialog box options.*

Scale Command Options

Scale, which is only available when an axis is selected on a chart, governs the positioning, the order, and the scale of tick marks and axes.

Different options appear depending on which axis is selected. The explanations in the following paragraphs group similar options from different dialog boxes together. With either 2-D or 3-D charts, the term *category axis* refers to the x-axis. With 2-D charts, the term *value axis* refers to the y-axis; with 3-D, the value axis is the z-axis. The term *series axis* refers to the y-axis in a 3-D chart.

Figure 13.26 shows the Scale dialog box when a y-axis is selected.

Enter a number in Value (Y) Axis Crosses at Category Number to dictate beside which category the y-axis is positioned. Check Value (Y) Axis Crosses Between Categories to place the y-axis between, as distinct from beside, categories. Check Value (Y) Axis Crosses at Maximum Category to place the y-axis at the maximum, not minimum, value. This option overrides Value (Y) Axis Crosses Between Categories.

Check Category (X) Axis Crosses at Maximum Value to place the x-axis at the maximum, not the minimum, value on the y-axis (this will be at the top of the chart, instead of at the bottom, in most cases). Category (X) Axis Crosses at allows you to position the x-axis to intersect the y at the value you choose.

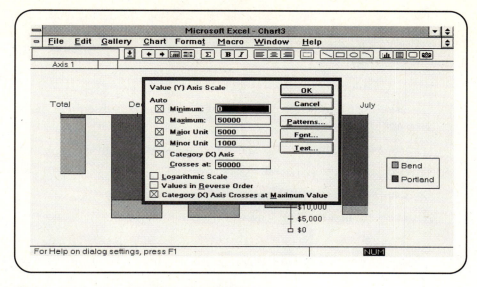

Figure 13.26 *The Scale dialog box for a value axis.*

Categories in Reverse Order and Values in Reverse Order reverse the default order of the categories or the values on the x- and y-axes respectively.

Check Logarithmic Scale to direct Excel to use a log scale on values.

Enter numbers at Minimum and Maximum to tell Excel the smallest and largest data values to appear. Enter numbers at Major Unit and Minor Unit to tell Excel the increments to use in major and minor tick marks.

Legend Command Options

Only available when the legend box is selected, the options in this Legend dialog box dictate the position of the box relative to the rest of the chart: Bottom, Corner, Top, Right, and Left.

Changing Your Default Chart Format

Customizing charts can take time. Once you have produced a chart that meets your requirements, Excel allows you to make this the default chart type, meaning that any more charts you create will automatically have this type and formatting. You can only have one default. Follow this step, once the chart is active:

1. Choose Set Preferred from the Gallery menu.

The active chart, including its formatting, becomes the default chart type, but only as long as you *don't* exit Excel.

You can change the default chart type *even before you create a chart* by following these steps:

1. Select a blank cell in the worksheet.

2. Choose New from the File menu and Chart from the subsequent dialog box, and then choose OK.

3. Choose a chart type from the Gallery menu.

4. Choose Set Preferred from the Gallery menu.

5. Choose Close from the File menu without saving the chart.

   Any chart created from now on will have this chart type.

Reverting to the Default Chart Type

Excel provides an easy way to return to the default chart type (no matter how much formatting you have done)—through the Preferred command. This command can work in conjunction with the Set Preferred command or not. If you have already reset the default chart with Set Preferred and then used different formatting and/or chart types, Preferred restores your default. If you have not used Set Preferred, Preferred restores the Excel default, the column chart.

With your chart window active, choose Preferred from the Gallery menu.

Using Pictures as Data Markers

With the line, bar, and column chart types, Excel allows you to replace data markers with pictures imported from other applications. When the pictures have been imported, you can format the markers with special options.

Follow these steps to use a picture as a data marker:

1. From the application containing the picture, select the picture and copy it into memory (the clipboard).

2. Activate the Excel chart to copy to.

3. Select the individual data marker or series to paste into.

4. Choose Paste from the Edit menu.

Figure 13.27 shows an example of data markers imported from another application, Microsoft PowerPoint, in this case.

Figure 13.27 *Data markers replaced with imported pictures.*

There are special formatting options available with imported pictures. Follow these steps to format the data marker pictures:

1. Select the individual data marker or the series.
2. Choose Patterns from the Format menu.

   Excel displays the dialog box shown in Figure 13.28.
   Stretch is on by default. Use it to stretch or shrink markers. Stack and Stack and Scale can be useful for more exactly representing the data value in a picture data marker. In Figure 13.28, the tiger data marker has Stack on, and the butterfly has Stack and Scale on.

Picture data markers can be deleted at any time:

1. Select the individual data marker or the series to delete.
2. Choose Clear from the Edit menu.
3. Check the Formats option.
4. Choose OK.

Linking Chart Text to a Worksheet Cell

Links between charts and worksheets can be initiated from either window. This section shows you the simple steps necessary to initiate from the chart.

252 Advanced Techniques

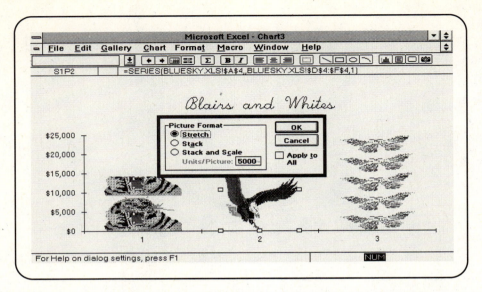

Figure 13.28 *A picture data marker with stacked and stacked and scaled options.*

Follow these steps:

1. Select the text in the text box on the chart.

2. Type an equal sign in the formula bar.

   Any text in the text box disappears.

3. Activate the worksheet window and select the cell to link to.

   The cell reference appears in the formula bar.

4. Accept the formula bar entry by pressing Enter or clicking the enter box.

   Any text in the cell appears in the chart.

This linking can be used with the space-making tip mentioned in "Adding Objects to a Chart" to create large comment text blocks that will be updated automatically in both charts and worksheets.

 Tip: You can have text in charts that only appears when certain conditions are met in the worksheet. For example, if a sales figure implies that a bonus is due, the text box can display words to that effect. You do this by making a text box in a chart refer to a worksheet cell that contains an IF() function. When the conditions in the IF function are met, the cell and the chart display the text.

Using Move and Size

The Move command in Format applies to arrows and legends only. The Size command applies to arrows only. Arrows and legends can easily be moved by selecting and dragging them in the usual way with the mouse pointer. Arrows have handles at both ends, so the direction the arrow is pointing can easily be reversed by dragging one end only.

To use either Mo*v*e or Si*z*e, select the arrow or legend, choose the command from the Forma*t* menu, and use the mouse to move or size.

14
CHAPTER

Analyzing, Calculating, and Using Solver

Excel provides a host of ways in which you can analyze and calculate data on your worksheet, ranging from simple to very complex. This chapter discusses all the main methods. Some, like the Series command in Data, save you time in entering data. Other methods, like building tables relating formulas to different inputs and outputs through the Table command in Data, and especially the Solver application, can do things that manually would not be feasible because of the complexity and time involved.

Using the Series Command

The Series command in Data can save you time when you want to enter dates and numbers that increase or decrease in a constant manner in adjacent cells. You might, for instance, have date headings that start at January 1, 1991, and increase by one month each time in a series of cells. Or you might have a series of numbers that grow at a constant rate from cell to cell.

Follow these steps to let Excel calculate and enter your series:

1. Enter the starting value in the first cell.

   In the example, 1/1/91 is entered as a date heading that will be increased by one month each heading.

2. Select the range of empty cells that will contain the series.

   This range can be along either a row or a column.

3. From the Data menu, choose Series.

   Excel displays the dialog box shown in Figure 14.1.

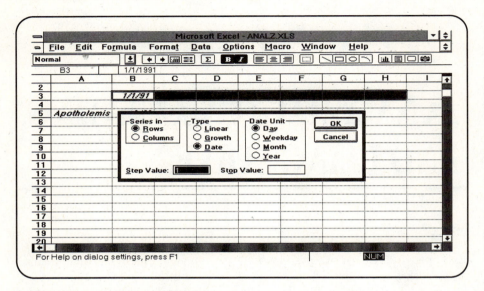

Figure 14.1   The Series dialog box.

4. Choose whether to put the series in Rows or Columns, or accept the default.

   Excel automatically selects one based on whether the cells you highlighted are in rows or columns.

   Next, choose from three types of series. *Linear* increases or decreases each number in the series by a constant amount (which you specify at Step Value): 10, 9, 8, 7, 6, for example, or 100, 110, 120, 130, 140, etc.

   Growth multiplies each number in the series by a constant amount specified at Step Value.

   Date can increase the starting date by a specified amount in terms of days, weekdays, months, or years.

5. Choose a type: Linear, Growth, or Date.

   In the example shown in Figure 14.1, Excel has selected Date because it recognizes the starting number as a date.

6. If you chose or accepted Date as the series type, choose now to increase by Day, Weekday, Month, or Year.

Day is the default. If you chose Year with the starting date of 1/1/91, and a Step Value of 1, the series becomes 1/1/91, 1/1/92, 1/1/93, etc. Choosing Weekday is particularly useful because Excel decides which days to leave out (all dates falling on Saturdays and Sundays). In this example, the series is 1/1/91, 1/2/91, 1/3/91, 1/4/91, 1/7/91. After the 4th, Excel skips two dates because they fall on a weekend.

7. Choose the amount to change by in Step Value.

   Use a negative number if you want to get a declining series with a Linear type.

8. If there is an upper (or lower) limit to your series, specify it at Stop Value.

9. Choose OK.

Figure 14.2 shows two series built with the Series command. The top is a date series increased by one month each cell. The bottom is a linear series multiplied each time by a factor of four. Use Growth or Step Value to step times four.

 Tip: You can fill in several series at a time when the series are all of the same type and use the same increment. Select the entire range (you can even use multiple selections), making sure that the starting values are the first cell in each row or column. Then proceed as shown in the preceding steps.

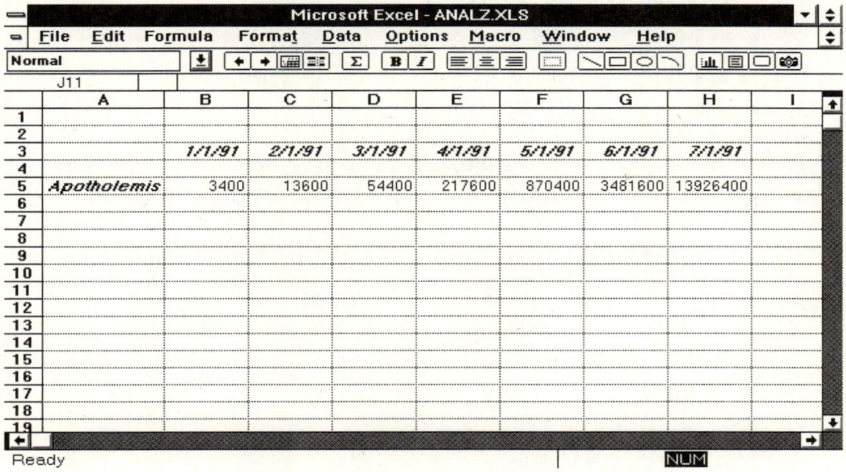

Figure 14.2 Two series built with the Series command.

Working with Array Formulas

An *array* is a group of values, cell references, or formulas collected together. A range of cells, for instance, is a type of array. Using array formulas can be a great time-saver. With an ordinary formula, you have several inputs (arguments) that combine to give one output (one result). Array formulas can produce as many results as you like, and use as many inputs as you like. Their main use is to reduce the amount of time you spend entering identical formulas.

Figure 14.3 shows an example of an array formula. The row titled Ratio shows a formula—{=$B$5:$H$5/$B$7:$H$7}—that applies to *all* selected cells on that row, that is, B9 through H9. Even though this is the case, each cell displays a different result. B9, for instance, shows the result of dividing B5 by B7. Excel knows to include in the argument calculations only those cells relevant to each formula cell.

The braces {} tell Excel that this is an array formula. Always let Excel enter these braces when dealing with arrays referencing cells, as shown in the next section.

Creating an Array Formula

Build an array formula as follows:

1. Select the cell or range of cells to take the formula.

   In the example, this is B9 to H9.

2. Enter the formula in the formula bar by using Pas<u>t</u>e Function from Fo<u>r</u>mula or by typing it yourself.

   In the example, you would type an equal sign first, then select B5:H5 (or simply type it in), type a division sign, and select or type B7:H7.

3. Press Ctrl-Shift-Enter.

   This tells Excel that you want to create an array formula. Excel then enters the braces in the formula and calculates and displays the cell results.

 Tip: If you press Shift-Enter only, Excel enters an ordinary formula in the active cell (not in all the selected cells). If you press Ctrl-Enter only, Excel enters an ordinary formula in all the selected cells.

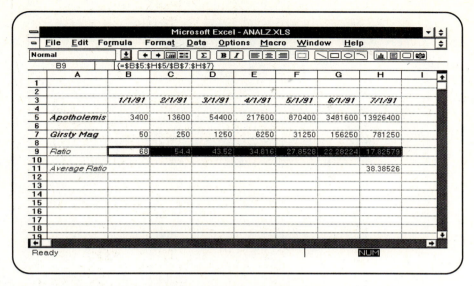

Figure 14.3 *A highlighted array range showing the array formula in the formula bar.*

Single-Output Array Formulas

One step beyond the kind of array formula used in the example in Figure 14.3 is when the result goes into one cell; that is, you have one output, even though an array formula is used. Figure 14.4 shows this kind of array formula in the H11 cell; it calculates and displays the average ratio of the top row of insects, Apotholemis, to the bottom row, Girsty Mag.

Notice that the formula {=AVERAGE(B5:H5/B7:H7)} does not use the Ratio row results. This formula was created by pasting the AVERAGE function into B11, selecting the cell ranges, and typing a divisor between them.

This kind of array not only saves you time and trouble but also saves computer memory and space.

Selecting and Editing Array Formulas

When array formulas go into more than one cell (that is, produce more than one output), the rules for editing them differ from ordinary editing in Excel. You can't change the contents, clear or move, or delete individual cells in an array range. Neither can you insert cells into an array range.

With some editing, you can just select one cell in the range and all the array changes, but often you need to select the entire array to edit. Follow these steps to select all the cells in an array:

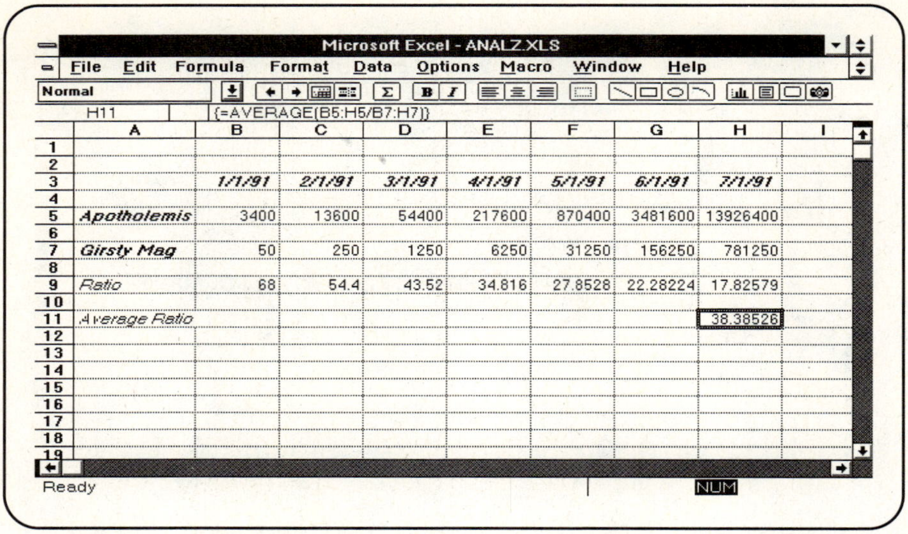

260 Advanced Techniques

Figure 14.4 An array formula with single output.

1. Select any individual cell in the range.

2. Choose Select Special from Formula.

3. Choose the Current Array option in the Select dialog box and then OK.

   You can bypass steps 2 and 3 by pressing Ctrl-/.
   When you click in the formula bar to edit, the braces disappear. Don't forget to use Ctrl-Shift-Enter when the editing is finished.
   Sometimes you might want to convert the array range to constants, that is, get rid of the formulas. For instance, you might want to insert or delete cells. Follow these steps to convert an array range to constants:

1. Select the array range.

2. Choose Copy from the Edit menu.

3. Choose Paste Special from Edit.

4. Select Values option in the Paste dialog box and OK.

Using Constants in Array Formulas

As with ordinary formulas, you can use constants as well as cell references in array formulas. One important thing to remember is that with constants you must enter the braces yourself.

Constants in arrays are referred to in terms of rows and values: A 1-by-4 array means one row and four values. A 4-by-1 array means four rows and one value on each row. Excel needs to know this layout when you specify constants in formulas. Separate values in one row by commas; separate rows by semicolons. For example, {34,35,36;37,38,39} is an array holding constants on two rows with three values on each row.

Contrast this with how you specify cell references in array formulas. For instance, you can't use {A3,A4,A5}; you have to use {A3:A5}.

As an example, the Average Ratio cell in Figure 14.4 would end up, as shown below, in a constant array formula:

{=AVERAGE({3400,13600,54400,217600,870400,3481600,13926400}/{50,250,1250,6250,31250,156250,781250})}

You type the two sets of braces inside the formula yourself. The braces around the whole formula are added when you end with Ctrl-Shift-Enter.

Common Array Functions

The following list includes functions that always input or output arrays and some that are commonly used with arrays. Those functions marked with an asterisk always input or output arrays.

APPLY.NAMES	COLUMN	COLUMNS
CONSOLIDATE	FILES	*FORMULA.ARRAY
GET.DOCUMENT	GET.WINDOW	*GROWTH
*HLOOKUP	*INDEX	*LINEST
*LOGEST	*LOOKUP	MATCH
*MDETERM	*MINVERSE	*MMULT
NAMES	ROW	ROWS
*SUMPRODUCT	*TRANSPOSE	*TREND
*VLOOKUP	WINDOWS	WORKGROUP

Goal Seeking

Goal seeking reverses the usual order of calculating formulas: You start by specifying the result and ask Excel to supply one of the inputs or values to get that result. For example, you could desire profits of $3000 for the month of May, and if you knew your overheads, you could use Excel's goal seeking command to calculate the sales necessary to generate the required profit.

Follow these steps to use goal seeking:

1. Select the cell containing the formula to produce the desired result.
2. Choose Goal Seek from Formula.

   Excel displays the dialog box shown in Figure 14.5.

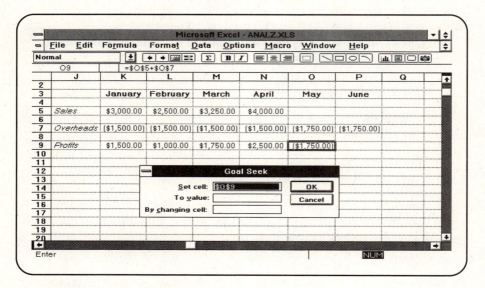

Figure 14.5 *The Goal Seek dialog box.*

The active cell displays in Set cell.

3. Type the desired result for the active cell in To value.

   In the example, this would be $3000.

4. Type the input cell reference in By Changing Cell, the cell that will show the necessary input value to produce the result.

   Here it is cell $O$5.

5. Choose OK.

   Excel then displays another dialog box showing the state of the goal seeking. You can let the calculation continue as normal by doing nothing, or you can stop it to see the steps involved, as shown in step 6.

6. Choose Pause to stop the calculating.
7. Choose Step to see the calculation after each iteration, or choose Continue to let Excel continue as normal.

In the example shown, it takes 17 iterations to arrive at the result, $4,750. (See the next section for an explanation of iterations.)

Iteration

An *iteration* is one round of calculation in a situation where Excel repeats the calculation numerous times to arrive at a result. Sometimes formulas refer to each other, which means that the formula that depends on another's result should be calculated after it. A further complication can be where two formulas are mutually dependent—they *both* contain a reference to the other—meaning that the result they produce will differ according to the result of the other. This is called a *circular reference*. To resolve a situation like this, Excel uses iteration, where a formula repeatedly recalculates until a condition is met.

In Excel, the condition to be met is where the iterations have gone around a specified maximum number of times (default 100) or where the calculations have produced a change that is below a specified change amount (default 0.001).

For example, to continue with the example shown in Figure 14.5, suppose your firm has established that sales for June depend on two factors—the sales for May plus 50%, together with a certain percentage of the overheads for June (the percentage spent on promotion). The overheads for June in turn depend on a fixed amount plus a percentage of the June sales, since greater sales mean more overheads, like overtime hours, etc.

The formula for June sales is =May_Sales*1.5–(overheads/10), while the formula for June overheads is =–1500–(Sales/20). "May_Sales" and "Sales" are the cells O5 and P5 defined as names.

Unless iteration is turned on, Excel will display a box that says `Cannot resolve circular reference`.

Follow these steps to turn iteration on:

1. Choose Calculation from Options.

    Excel displays the dialog box shown in Figure 14.6.

2. Check the Iteration box.

3. Specify the Maximum Iterations and the Maximum Change or accept the defaults.

    The more iterations and the smaller the number in Maximum Change, the longer the calculation takes. Also, the smaller the number in Maximum Change, the more accurate your answer is.

4. Choose OK.

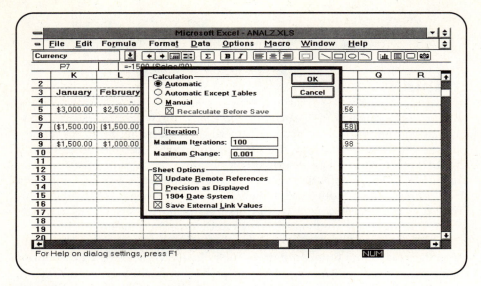

Figure 14.6 *The Calculation dialog box.*

Using What-if Analysis in Tables

What-if analysis involves changing certain values in formulas and seeing how this affects the results obtained. Excel provides an easy way to do this through the creation of a *data table*—a range of cells that display the new results. The alternative would be to change values manually one by one.

Excel has two different kinds of data tables. A *one-input table* takes different values for one variable and displays the effect on one or more formulas. A *two-input table* takes different values for two variables and displays the effect on one formula.

Making a One-Input Table

In a one-input table, you substitute different inputs or values for one variable and see the effect on one or more formulas. A common usage here, for example, is determining how interest rate changes affect your payments of a loan—finding out exactly how much the payments go up as the interest rate changes.

In order to use the Table command in Data that creates the table, you must have the table skeleton set up properly. Figure 14.7 shows the proper setup before the table is filled in by Excel.

14 — Analyzing, Calculating, and Using Solver 265

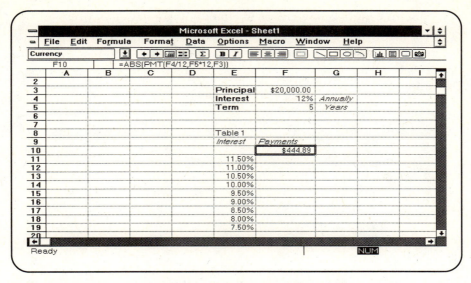

Figure 14.7 *Values set up in order to use the Table command.*

In this example, the table ranges from E10 to F19.

In each one-input table, the top-left corner must be a blank, with the formula to substitute into, directly to its right. The variables to substitute go underneath the blank cell, and after you invoke the command, the results go directly to their right.

It is also possible, though not very common, to put the substitute values in a row along the top of the table. The blank cell still goes in the upper left with the formula directly underneath. Excel then inserts the results on the same row as the formula.

In this example, the formula reads =ABS(PMT(F4/12,F5*12,F3)). This converts the time period from years to months and also refers to the cells that contain the principle, the interest, and the term of the loan.

Follow these steps to fill in the table:

1. Select the cell range containing the blank cell, the formula, the values to substitute, and the cells to display the results.

   In the example, you select E10:F19.

2. Choose Table from Data.

   The Table dialog box has only two options: Row Input Cell and Column Input Cell. Use Column with the normal table shape, where the values and results display in columns (as in the example). Use Row with the alternative, where the values and results display along rows.

3. Enter the input cell reference in either Row Input Cell or Column Input Cell and then choose OK.

In the example, the input cell is F4, the cell containing the current interest rate. This is the input value that changes. Excel fills in the table, as shown in Figure 14.8.

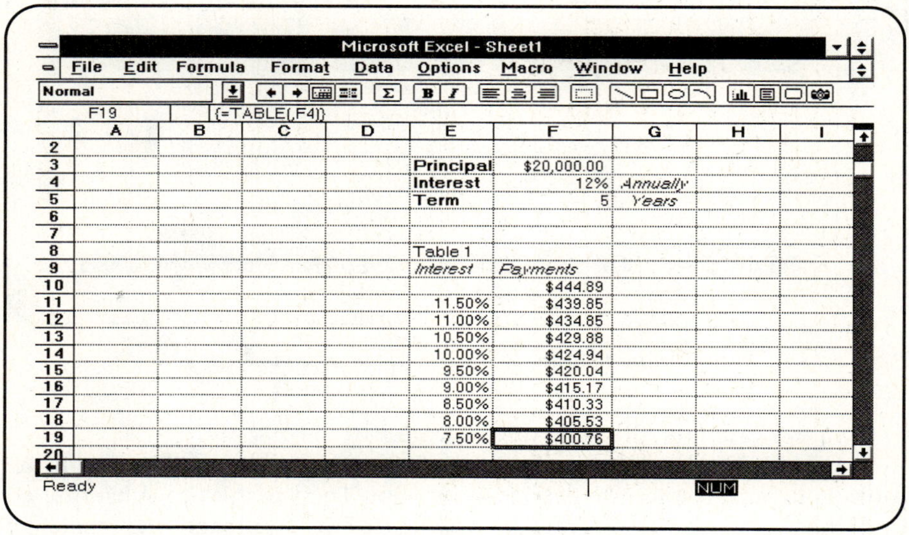

Figure 14.8 *A filled-in table.*

You can easily add more formulas to the same table to make use of the same substitute values. A new formula goes to the right of the existing one (or underneath if the table is in row format); then the whole new table is selected—from the blank cell in the upper left to the last cell that will contain the result in the new column. You then choose the Table command and indicate the input cell reference, and the new results are filled in. Figure 14.9 shows an example.

This example uses a very similar formula: =ABS(PMT($F$4/12,72,$F$3)). The cell reference to the term of the loan is replaced by a constant, 72, representing the total months. In this example, select E10:G19 before choosing Table.

Making a Two-Input Table

With a two-input table you have two inputs, or substitute values, and one formula. The setup on the worksheet is similar to the one-input table. This time the formula itself goes in the upper-left corner of the table and the input values go along the top row and the leftmost column.

Figure 14.10 shows a two-input table (with the results already filled in). The active cell, J9, shows the formula—in this case the same formula that was used in Table 1. To the right of this are the input values, different years of the term here. Below it are the other input values, the different interest rates.

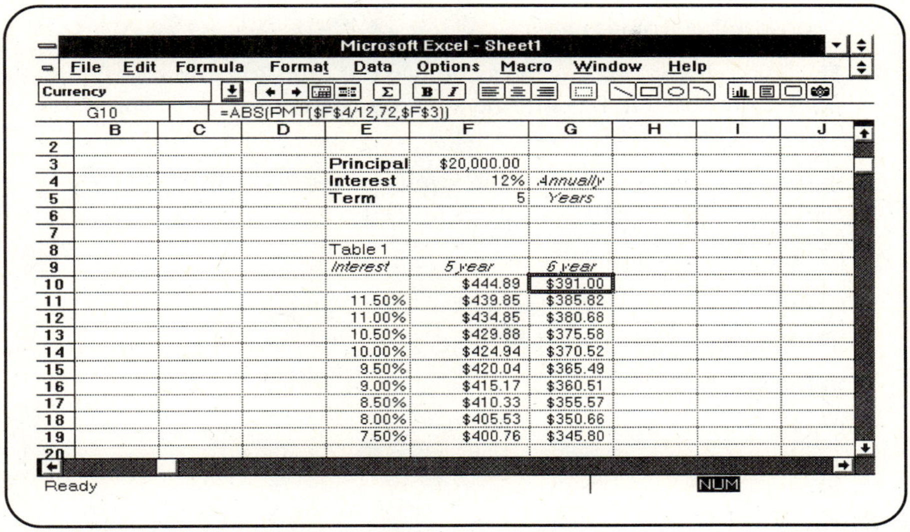

Figure 14.9 *A single-input table using two formulas.*

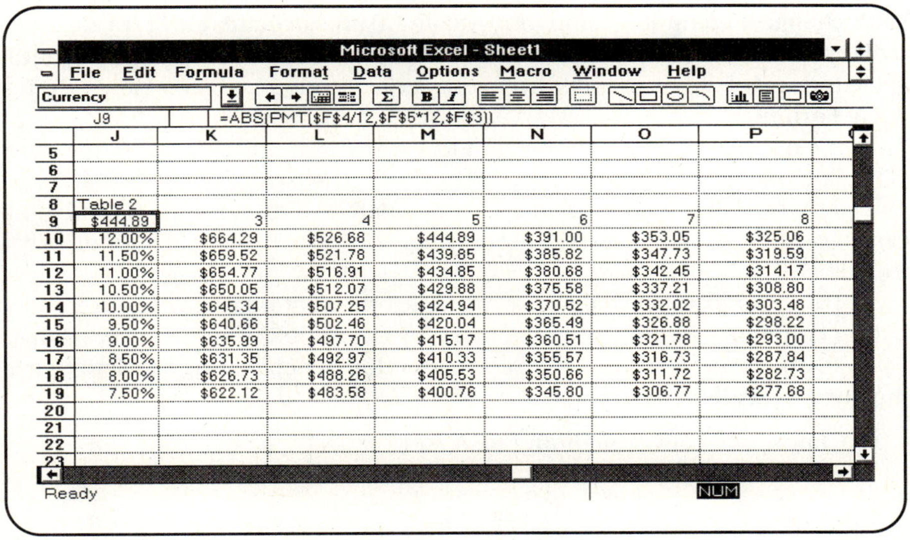

Figure 14.10 *A filled-in two-input table.*

Follow these steps to fill in a two-input table:

1. Select the whole table, from the formula in the upper left to the cell in the last column, last row.

    In the example, this is J9:P19.

2. Choose Table from Data.

    The Table dialog box has the same two options: Row Input Cell and Column Input Cell. By entering a reference in both boxes, you tell Excel that this is a two-input table.

3. In the Row Input Cell, enter the input cell reference that will be replaced by the top row of values in the table.

    In the example, this is F5 (see Figure 14.9).

4. In the Column Input Cell, enter the input cell reference that will be replaced by the leftmost column of values in the table.

    In the example, this is F4.

5. Choose OK and Excel fills the table.

Editing a Table

Excel regards a table as an array. For instance, if you select a result cell in a two-input table, the formula bar shows something like {=TABLE(D4,D5)}. You can't change a result in a table individually. To recalculate, move, or delete a table, you must select the entire table. To select the table, follow the steps for selecting array formulas, as shown in the earlier section "Selecting and Editing Array Formulas."

It's not necessary to go through this if you want to change a substitute value, or values, or even the formula(s) used. Just select the cell, make the change, accept the change, and Excel recalculates the table. This recalculation can take time, especially in a two-input table. The left of the formula bar displays the stage of the calculation.

You can add additional values to a table by entering them in adjacent rows and/or columns and redefining the table (by choosing Table from Data again).

You can change the results to constant values when editing restrictions get in your way. Follow these steps:

1. Choose the cells containing the result values (not the formula(s) or substitute values).

2. Choose Copy from Edit.

3. Choose Paste Special from Edit and select the Values option.

4. Choose OK.

> **Tip:** The HLOOKUP, VLOOKUP, and LOOKUP functions are useful for finding pieces of information previously entered in a table called a *lookup table*. For example, if you give a standard bonus to employees who perform well, you could use one of these functions to access the lookup table with the exact bonus.

Using Solver

The Solver software takes what-if analysis to a level of complexity beyond Excel tables. Using Solver, you can involve several formulas in what-if questions; you can set several conditions, or constraints, which must be met to arrive at a result; and you can work backwards from a result.

An example is the forecasting of net profits for a financial period. Many factors, quantified in formulas, can go into making the result, like the time of year, the amount of advertising, and the overheads, which can often depend on the volume of sales, etc. Solver can deal with a situation as complex as this where one-input and two-input tables could not.

An example of constraints imposed on the calculation in this case might be telling Solver that advertising can only rise to a certain level, even if Solver (with the values and information given it) calculates that profits can be much greater with more money spent on advertising.

If you accepted the defaults when you installed Excel, then Solver is automatically installed on your hard drive. Find out for certain by looking for the Solver command in the Formula menu (with full menus on). If it isn't installed, you must have unchecked the Solver option during installation. See Appendix A for installation information.

Using the Solver Parameters Dialog Box

Microsoft provides several excellent examples of worksheets that can use Solver to answer complex questions. They are contained in the Solverex subdirectory of the main Excel directory. The one used in Figure 14.11 as an example is Sample.xls. It's a worksheet set up in the usual way—Solver needs no special setup to work. Open the Solver.xls file in the normal manner.

To see how the cells interact, start in the Q1 (representing quarter 1) column at B2 and work down. Seasonality quantifies how sales fall and rise depending on the time of year. B4 to B7 measure and calculate gross profits from sales minus the cost of the products. Notice that B4, Units Sold, incorporates Seasonality and Advertising in its formula. B9 to B12 calculate Total Costs. Note that Corp Overhead is directly dependent on Sales Revenue.

270 Advanced Techniques

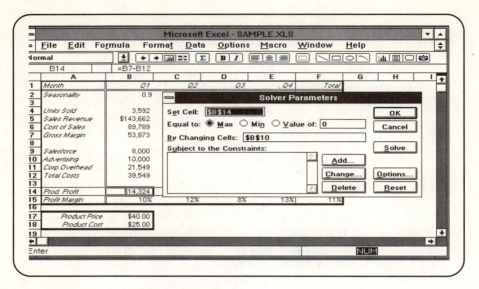

Figure 14.11 The Solver.xls worksheet.

A set of interlinked formulas such as this is tailor-made for use with the Solver application.

Starting Solver

Solver works in conjunction with an add-in macro. The first time you invoke the Solver command, Excel needs to bring the software into memory.

To start Solver, choose Solver from the Formula menu. Excel then loads Solver, which can take a minute or longer. It takes time because the macro is so big. Afterwards, it displays the Solver Parameters dialog box, where you set up your problem to resolve. The next time you invoke Solver, the dialog box comes up more quickly.

Setting the Problem

Figure 14.12 shows the Solver Parameters dialog box obtained by choosing the Solver command from Formula.

The bottom part of the dialog box deals with setting constraints, specifically Subject to the Constraints, Add, Change, and Delete.

The first three options set the problem for Solver to resolve: At Set Cell you specify the cell that contains the goal to reach. The goal can be specified (in Equal to:) as a number or in terms of a maximum or minimum amount. Net profit (Prod Profit in the example), for instance, would be a common cell reference here.

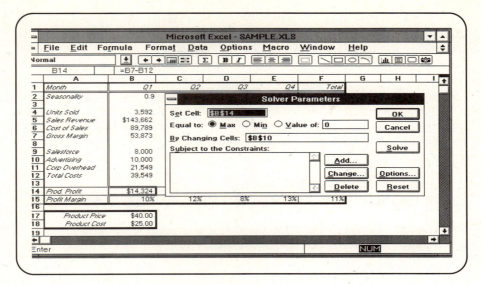

Figure 14.12 *The Solver Parameters dialog box.*

The next line in the dialog box, Equal to:, goes with Set Cell, and spells out whether you want Solver to make the Set Cell reference a maximum figure (Max), a minimum figure (Min), or a value, specified in the box next to Value of. You would usually want to maximize profit, for instance, or perhaps reach a certain specific profit goal for a time period. Min would tend to be used more with costs, for example.

The By Changing Cells option is where you specify the cells that Solver can change in order to best reach the goal or, in other words, solve the problem posed in the first two lines of the dialog box. So here you reference a cell or a cell range.

The cells specified in Set Cell and By Changing Cells must be related through formulas; otherwise, the exercise is pointless.

Filling in these first three lines allows Solver to work on quite complex problems, even without setting constraints.

To continue with the Solver.xls worksheet example, you could use B14, containing Prod Profit, aiming for a Max value, and relate it to the Advertising cell, B10. In other words, you could see how high profits would go if more money were spent on advertising.

To start Solver working on the problem, choose the Solve button in the dialog box.

As it processes, Solver displays messages in the status bar. First, it displays Setting Up Problem, then Activating Solver Application. When and if Solver finds a solution, it displays the Solver dialog box, discussed in the next section.

At this time the relevant cells in the worksheet have already been changed to display the solution. In the example, Solver found that if you increase advertising to $17,094, profits increase to $15,093. This is visible in column B in Figure 14.13. You could rerun this problem in a different form by using F14, total profit for the year, in Set Cell, and B10:E10 in the By Changing Cells box. This result would be that Solver calculates that you could make profits of $79,705 if you spent $89,544 over the year. Interestingly, the advertising budgets now differ in each quarter—the higher the Seasonality factor, the more you should spend on advertising, according to Solver. Try running this problem to see the results.

Using the Solver Dialog Box and Printing Reports

When Solver finishes working on a problem, it displays the Solver dialog box for further instructions, as shown in Figure 14.13.

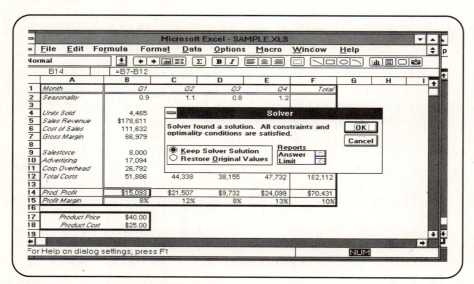

Figure 14.13 *The Solver dialog box.*

First, it tells you whether a solution was found or not. Solver now wants you to specify whether to keep the Solver solution on the worksheet, or to restore the original values before you set the problem.

1. Choose either **K**eep Solver Solution or Restore **O**riginal Values.

    For the example, restore the original values.

In addition, you can tell Solver to generate *reports* based on the solution. You can generate the Answer report and/or the Limit report. Both give information on the target cell (specified in Set Cell in the Solver Parameters dialog box) and the adjustable cells (specified in By Changing Cells). Answer also lists the constraints (discussed in the next section), while Limit specifies lower and upper limits and target results that go with them. A lower limit is the smallest value that an adjustable cell can take while holding all other adjustable cells fixed and still satisfying the constraints. An upper limit is the equivalent greatest value. And with each upper and lower limit, Solver specifies the target result that goes with it.

Create these reports by clicking on Answer or Limit with the mouse pointer. Hold the Shift key down to choose both. Solver actually creates these reports on new worksheets. You can access them through the window menu, and save and print them like normal worksheets.

2. Choose a report or not and then choose OK.

Imposing Constraints in a Problem and the Reset Button

Constraints are conditions that Solver has to meet to find a solution. Usually they will result in a different answer. For example, you could rerun the example in Figure 14.11 and 14.12 and set a constraint on the advertising budget.

1. Choose Sol<u>v</u>er from Fo<u>r</u>mula.

    Notice that the cells filled in previously, Set Cell, Equal to, and By Changing Cells, retain their values. Solver does this to make life a little easier. Choose <u>R</u>eset when you want a blank dialog box. Change the Set Cell reference to $F$14, total Prod Profit for the year.

2. Choose <u>A</u>dd to add a constraint.

    Solver displays the Add Constraint dialog box, which is shown in Figure 14.14.

3. Enter the cell to constrain in Cell <u>R</u>eference.

    Here use F10, the total advertising budget for the year. To the right of Cell Reference is a drop-down scroll box containing just three options: <=, =, and >=.

4. Choose one of the three options in this operator scroll box.

    Here choose <=.

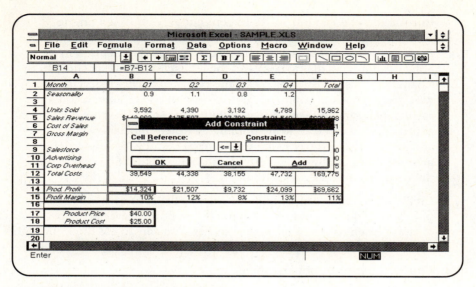

Figure 14.14 *The Add Constraint dialog box.*

5. Enter a value or a cell reference in Constraint.

    Use $40,000, the original advertising budget.

    You can use several different formats for constraints. Here the format is $F$10 <= 40000. You could, for example, use a cell reference, $F$9 say, the total budget for the Salesforce, as in $F$10 <= $F$9. Or you could add or subtract cells and/or values in the Constraint box, as in $F$10 <= $F$9 + 10000.

    You can also use cell ranges in either the Cell Reference or Constraint boxes. $C$13:$C$17 >= 0, for instance, means that the values in all these cells must be greater than or equal to 0. And $C$13:$C$17 >= $D$13:$D$17 means $C$13 must be greater than or equal to $D$13, $C$14 must be greater than or equal to $D$14, etc.

    To add further constraints at this stage, you would choose Add in this dialog box and the Cell Reference and Constraint boxes would go blank.

6. Choose OK to return to the Solver Parameters dialog box.

    The constraints imposed now appear in the Subject to the Constraints box. Use Change to make any alteration needed after selecting the constraint to change. Solver will display this constraint in the Add Constraint dialog box.

    Use the Delete button to delete a selected constraint.

7. Choose Solve to start Solver on this problem.

In this example, Solver calculates that you can increase your profits by spending your present advertising budget differently—specifically spending more in the quarters with high seasonality factors.

Using the Options Button

When you save a worksheet after using the Solver, the parameters of the last problem posed are saved with the file. It is also possible to save other problems previously set up, using the Options button in the Solver Parameters dialog box. The Options button can also be used to control the number of iterations used and to set other controls on how Solver works.

To access the Options dialog box, follow these steps:

1. Choose Solver from Formula.
2. Choose Options.

The Solver Options dialog box appears, as shown in Figure 14.15.

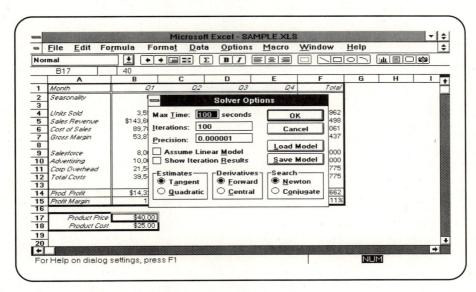

Figure 14.15 *The Solver Options dialog box.*

The options in this box are explained in the following paragraphs. If you are unsure what they mean, you are strongly advised to accept the defaults.

Calculating a solution can take Solver some time. You can set a maximum on the number of seconds spent in the Max Time box. Another limiting factor is the number of iterations you allow. The higher the number you enter in Iterations, the longer the calculation may continue.

276 Advanced Techniques

The Precision value must be between 0 and 1. The lower the value, the higher the precision Solver goes to (and usually the longer the calculations take).

The Assume Linear Model option can save a lot of time in the problem-solving process if the problem is a linear programming one. Check this option to turn it on.

The Show Iteration Results box, when checked, stops Solver after each significant change in the problem so that you can see the intermediate results.

The Estimates, Derivatives, and Search boxes each offer two options to choose from. They refer to technical approaches taken by Solver at various stages of problem solving. Unless you have an advanced mathematical background, you are advised to leave these options as they are!

Saving and Reusing Solver Problems

Some problems take a while to work out and set up in the Solver Parameters dialog box. Solver gives you the opportunity to store these for future use when you save a worksheet. Remember that the problem currently on view in the Solver Parameters dialog box is automatically saved with the worksheet.

Follow these steps to store a problem:

1. Choose Solver from Formula and enter the problem and constraints in the usual way.

2. Instead of (or after) choosing Solve, choose OK.

3. Select a blank range of cells on the worksheet to receive and store the coded problem. Select one cell for each constraint plus one cell each for every cell referred to in the Set Cell and By Changing Cells boxes.

   It's better to choose too many rather than too few cells—Solver just ignores the extra ones.

4. Choose Solver from Formula.

5. Choose Options.

6. Choose Save Model.

The range selected on the worksheet is filled with formulas that Solver can reinterpret to reload the problem when needed. Figure 14.16 shows a range of cells, K1 to P1, that holds a problem about maximizing profit by tinkering with advertising to an upper limit of $40,000. The formula bar shows the formula for the K1 cell referring to the maximization of the profit cell. Make each additional cell the active cell to see the other formulas.

To reload the formula:

1. Select the range of cells with formulas.

2. Choose Solver from Formula.

3. Choose Options.

4. Choose Load Model.

The problem is redisplayed in the Solver Parameters dialog box. Figure 14.16 shows a reloaded formula with the range on the worksheet that contains the stored problem.

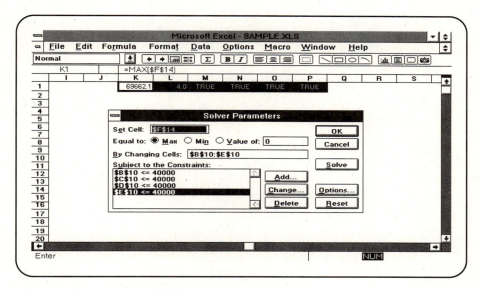

Figure 14.16 *A reloaded problem.*

Obviously, you have to remember which ranges of cell formulas contain the different problems when you store more than one. Examining the formulas stored in each cell can give you a clue.

Using Solver with Macros

Like most other things connected with Excel, the Solver can be manipulated with macros through functions that Excel provides. The functions are straight equivalents of the commands and options in the Solver dialog boxes. The SOLVER.OK function, for instance, accesses the Solver Parameters dialog box, and its arguments supply the values for Set Cell, Equal to, and By Changing Cells.

The 10 functions available with Solver are discussed in detail in Part 3, "Complete Reference": SOLVER.ADD, SOLVER.CHANGE, SOLVER.DELETE, SOLVER.FINISH AND SOLVER.FINISH?, SOLVER.LOAD, SOLVER.OK, SOLVER.OPTIONS, SOLVER.RESET, SOLVER.SAVE, and SOLVER.SOLVE.

Chapter 11, "Advanced Macros and Application Customization," discusses how to set up and use macros. They can be as complex or as simple as you make them. For example, you could have a three-line macro that invokes Solver and supplies the problem (through SOLVER.OK), that chooses the Solve button (through SOLVER.SOLVE), and that ends with a =Return() formula. See Sample.xlm in the Solverex directory for a complex example of using macros to manipulate Solver.

15
CHAPTER

USING Q+E

Q+E is a database application (separate from the Excel software) that has advantages over the database system in Excel. Excel databases are contained in worksheets and are limited by how much information can reside in memory. Q+E databases can be as big as you like, and because Excel can link to Q+E, information can pass back and forth between the two. Q+E can also serve as a link between Excel and other database systems like dBASE, text files, Oracle, SQL Server, and OS/2 Extended Edition. Q+E can also access these files without reference to Excel.

The letters *Q+E* stand for *querying and editing* or *querying and extracting,* depending on whether you took a certain option when you installed Excel and Q+E. If you did not install Q+E when you installed Excel, see the first section of this chapter, "Installing Q+E."

When Q+E is used in its querying and editing capacity, it can create new database files and edit existing ones. These capabilities are in addition to the sorting, selecting, formatting, and printing commands that go with the querying and extracting version of Q+E. People who need to protect their database files against changes by unauthorized people may use the querying and extracting version of Q+E.

There are many different ways of using Q+E. Its most common use is as a supplementary technique of accessing, presenting, editing, and linking to existing databases. It's important to remember that Q+E works differently with different database systems. The earlier sections of this chapter cover activities common to all systems in Q+E. Later sections describe how Q+E interacts with different database systems—with the primary focus on Excel.

280 Advanced Techniques

 Tip: An understanding of database operations (see Chapter 5, "Basic Database Operations," and Chapter 10, "Advanced Database Management") will help you to follow this chapter more easily.

Installing Q+E

If the Q+E icon appears in your Windows Program Manager window, then Q+E is installed. If not, then you can install it using these steps:

1. Insert the Microsoft Excel for Windows Setup disk into the A: drive.

2. Choose <u>R</u>un from the <u>F</u>ile menu in Program Manager.

3. Type `A:\Setup` and choose OK.

   Setup prompts you for the Excel directory, giving `C:\Excel` as a default.

4. Type the Excel directory or accept the default and choose Continue.

   The next screen shows the list of Excel options to install, including Microsoft Excel itself and, at the end, Q+E. Each option has a check mark.

5. Uncheck all options except Q+E.

6. Choose the Select Drivers button beside the Q+E option.

   Setup displays the screen shown in Figure 15.1. The top of the screen reads `Select Database Driver(s)`. A *driver* is software that needs to be installed to enable Q+E to interact with the various applications. The four choices are Excel Files; SQL Server; dBASE II, III, or IV; and Text (ASCII) Files.

7. Select the database drivers you want Setup to install.

   Below the drivers box are two other options. If you check the first, Install Q+E for Query and Extract Only, the version of Q+E installed will only read records, not create or edit them. Check the other option, Start Q+E with Microsoft Excel, and Q+E will start up automatically when you launch Excel.

8. Check either or both of these options if you want to.

   Below these, Setup specifies the space needed, to a maximum of 1,104K. Below that a Help scroll box gives information on the options.

When you return to the main Setup screen, press Enter and Setup installs Q+E.

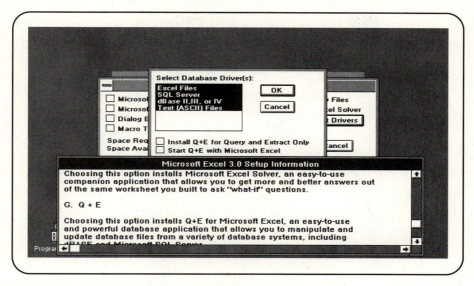

Figure 15.1 *The Select Drives screen in Q+E Setup.*

Starting Q+E and Opening Files

Q+E has a separate icon because it is run by software that is separate from Excel. In fact Q+E has no more in common with Excel than it has with dBASE or Oracle.

Start Q+E the way you start all other Windows applications: double-click on the icon or select the icon with the arrow keys and press Enter. When you invoke Q+E initially, only one menu option appears: File.

Other commands display in the File menu after a file is opened. Open a file as follows:

1. Choose Open from the File menu.

   Q+E displays the dialog box shown in Figure 15.2 with the list of Source options displayed.

   The Source option tells Q+E what kind of application produced the document you want to open. The Source list depends on what database drivers you installed when you installed Q+E. The full list of four is dBASEFile, ExcelFile, QueryFile, TextFile. An *ExcelFile* is a database contained in an Excel worksheet. A *QueryFile* is a file produced by Q+E, not an ordinary database file but a file referring to other database(s), as will be explained later in this chapter. *TextFiles* are produced mainly by word processors.

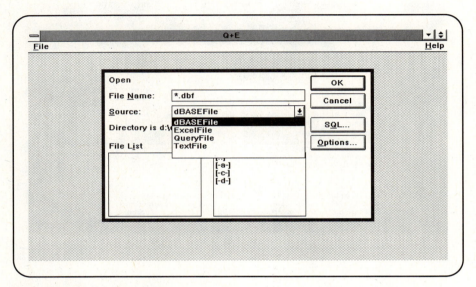

Figure 15.2 *The Open dialog box.*

2. Choose a Source file type.

   If you created a database in an Excel worksheet, you could open that now. Or if you have dBASE files on your disk drive (Microsoft supplies four in the \Excel\qe directory), you could specify that source type.

   When you choose a source, Q+E automatically specifies an extension in the File Name box. For dBASE files, this is .dbf; for Excel files, .xls; for query files, .qef; for text files, .csv.

3. When the Options button is available, choose it if you need to.

   Depending on what source you choose, the Options button may or may not be available. A later section, "Using Options when Opening Files," discusses what the options mean for files that are not Excel files.

   Press the Options button with an Excel source, and a dialog box presents you with three options. The first is Number of Records to Scan. The number you enter in this box determines how many records in the database Q+E examines to make out what data types are held in each column. Enter 0 and Q+E looks at all the database records (this can take time!). The default is 25.

Check Guess Data Types when you want Q+E to guess what data types are held in each column; the default is on (checked). Be warned: If you uncheck this, Q+E assumes all data types are character types.

Check Set Default to make your current choices the future defaults.

Choose OK to exit Options.

4. From the Open dialog box, choose the file and directory in the usual Windows manner and choose OK when the correct file is selected.

Q+E opens the file and displays it in what is called a *query window*. Figure 15.3 shows an Excel file open in a query window.

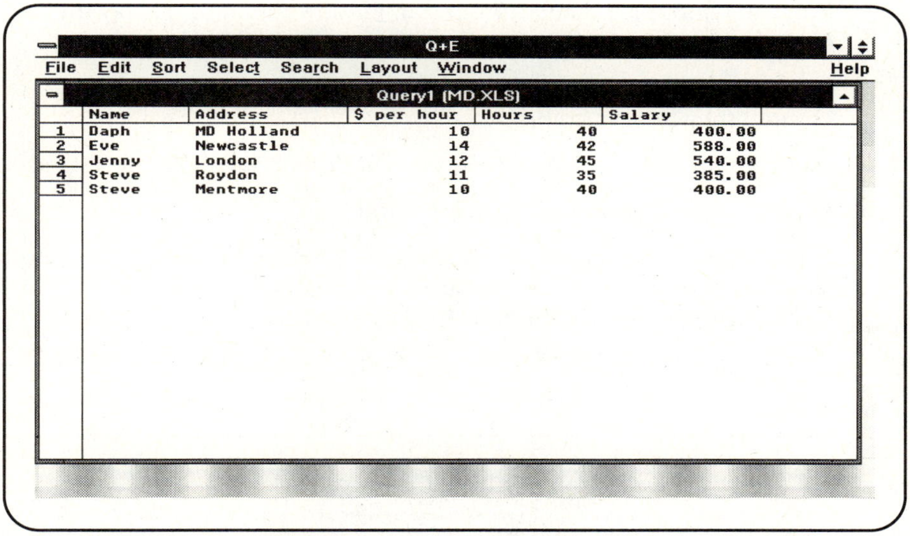

```
                            Q+E
File  Edit  Sort  Select  Search  Layout  Window                    Help
                        Query1 (MD.XLS)
    Name      Address       $ per hour   Hours      Salary
 1  Daph      MD Holland         10        40        400.00
 2  Eve       Newcastle          14        42        588.00
 3  Jenny     London             12        45        540.00
 4  Steve     Roydon             11        35        385.00
 5  Steve     Mentmore           10        40        400.00
```

Figure 15.3 *An open database file in a query window.*

Notice that the full list of menus is now displayed: File, Edit, Sort, Select, Search, Layout, Window, and Help. Q+E menus differ according to the Source application and whether the file is read-only. For instance, Allow Editing does not appear when your version of Q+E is read-only (query and extract).

Q+E works differently in many other ways, depending on what kind of source is used. With SQL Server, OS/2, and Oracle files (or more accurately tables), you log on using Logon in File to display them initially and Logoff to close. You create new databases with the Define in File command as discussed later in this chapter in "Creating New Databases."

Joining Database Files

One excellent feature of Q+E is the ease with which you can merge different databases. You can join as many as you like, though only two files are amalgamated in each individual join. Of the two files, one is the *source* file (fields and records are taken from this file), and one is the *destination* file (the fields are taken to this file). To join files, the files must have fields in one column in common: names, for instance, or locations.

Follow these steps to join files:

1. Open both the database files to join.

   You can choose Arrange All from the Window menu to display the two files on the screen at once.

2. Choose one field in both the source and destination files in the column they have in common.

   The column names (that is, field names) do not have to be the same.

3. Make the destination file the active window.

   Figure 15.4 shows two open database files before they are joined. Both these files come with Q+E and are located in the \qe directory. Dept.dbf is the destination file. The common column/field is the department number field, called Dept in Emp.dbf and Dept_id in Dept.dbf.

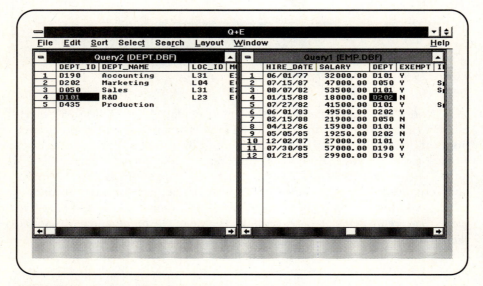

Figure 15.4 *An example of databases before joining.*

4. Choose Join or Outer Join from the Select menu.

Join is more selective than Outer Join. Join does not select any records that do not have matching fields in the chosen column. Outer Join selects and displays all records in the destination window whether there is a match or not.

Figure 15.5 shows the example after the two databases were joined.

Notice that the title of the query, Query2(DEPT.DBF, EMP.DBF) reflects the join that was made, with the destination file listed first.

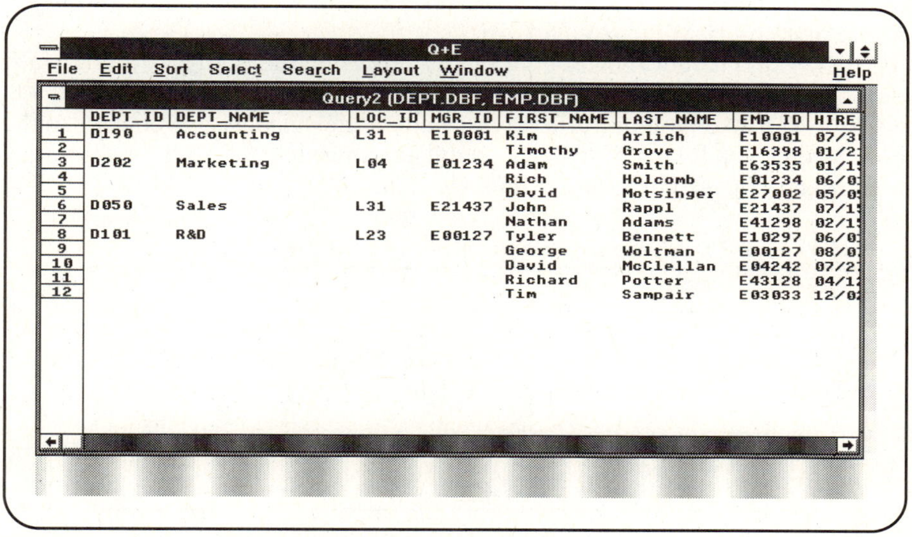

```
                                    Q+E
File  Edit  Sort  Select  Search  Layout  Window                    Help
                          Query2 (DEPT.DBF, EMP.DBF)
      DEPT_ID  DEPT_NAME      LOC_ID   MGR_ID   FIRST_NAME  LAST_NAME   EMP_ID   HIRE
 1    D190     Accounting     L31      E10001   Kim         Arlich      E10001   07/3
 2                                              Timothy     Grove       E16398   01/2
 3    D202     Marketing      L04      E01234   Adam        Smith       E63535   01/1
 4                                              Rich        Holcomb     E01234   06/0
 5                                              David       Motsinger   E27002   05/0
 6    D050     Sales          L31      E21437   John        Rappl       E21437   07/1
 7                                              Nathan      Adams       E41298   02/1
 8    D101     R&D            L23      E00127   Tyler       Bennett     E10297   06/0
 9                                              George      Woltman     E00127   08/0
10                                              David       McClellan   E04242   07/2
11                                              Richard     Potter      E43128   04/1
12                                              Tim         Sampair     E03033   12/0
```

Figure 15.5 *A query window showing two joined databases.*

This kind of join is called a *one-to-many relationship* because one dept in the destination file has several matching records in the source file. Q+E recognizes this by not repeating the department number with each record in the amalgamated window. An example of a *one-to-one* relationship, where each field is matched only once, is joining Loc.dbf and Dept.dbf from the dBASE files that came with the software, using Dept.dbf as the destination.

After joining two files, you can add as many as you like to create a *multiple* join. You could, for example, join Loc.dbf to Dept.dbf and then join Emp.dbf to the result.

Moving, Selecting, Zooming, and Searching

Once the fields and records are displayed in the query window, you need to know some basic maneuvering and manipulation techniques, which are discussed in the following four sections.

Moving

Using a mouse to move to different fields in a query window is identical to using a mouse in an Excel worksheet. Using the keyboard to move around in a Q+E file is similar in most respects to moving around in an Excel worksheet.

The Page Up and Page Down keys, for instance, move the screen up and down. Ctrl with Page Up moves the screen left, while Ctrl with Page Down moves the screen to the right. Up arrow and down arrow move one row (equivalent to a record) up and down respectively. Home and End move you to the first and last fields in a record.

Two keys that don't work the same are the left and right arrow keys; they don't move you from field to field. Use Tab to move to the next field in Q+E. Pressing Tab takes you to the following field in the database—even if it's in the next record. Use Shift-Tab to move to the previous field. Table 15.1 shows the keystrokes in Q+E that differ from those in Excel.

Table 15.1 Q+E keystrokes for moving from field to field.

Press	To Move to
Tab	The next field
Shift-Tab	The previous field
Ctrl-Home	The first record
Ctrl-End	The last record

Selecting

Selecting fields with the mouse works identically in Excel and Q+E. Selecting with the keyboard in Q+E works differently.

Though the left and right arrow keys do not move you from field to field in Q+E, they do have an effect. Press either one and the selected field is unselected, while the cursor is placed to the left or right of the start or end character. You can then edit as you like (after choosing Allow Editing from the Edit menu; see "Querying and Editing" later in the chapter). To select characters in a field, press Shift and either the right or left arrow key at this stage.

The left and right arrow keys can also be used with the function key F8 to select a range of fields through the keyboard. Here are the steps:

1. Select the first field in the range.

2. Press F8.

3. Use any of the arrow keys to select the range.

4. Press F8 when finished.

   If you want to select multiple ranges, continue as follows after selecting the first range.

5. Press Shift-F8 to keep the current range selected.

6. Using the arrow keys, move to the first field in the other range.

   If you use the mouse pointer, the current selection is lost; use Ctrl as in Excel when using the mouse.

7. Repeat steps 1 to 4 to select the new range. Repeat steps 5 to 7 to select more ranges.

   Table 15.2 shows other selection possibilities with the keyboard.

Table 15.2   Selecting with the keyboard.

Press	To Select
Shift-Spacebar	A record
Ctrl-Spacebar	A column
Shift-Ctrl-Spacebar	A whole window

Zooming a Field

You can edit a field using the left and right arrow keys, as shown in the preceding section. An alternative is to use the zoom window, which "blows up" the field and displays it in a separate window.

To access the zoom facility, double-click on the field that you want to view or edit. Or if you prefer to use the keyboard, select the field; then choose Zoom Field from the Edit menu.

Q+E displays the field in its own window. To return to Q+E, close the window in the normal ways: either choose Close from the Control menu, or double-click on the Control menu.

Searching for Fields and Records

By default, when you're doing a search, Q+E looks for a specified set of characters only in the column of the selected field. Widen this search by selecting a field in as many columns as you want searched. Follow these simple steps to use the Search menu options:

1. Choose Find in the Search menu.

2. Type the characters you want to search for in the dialog box.

3. Choose OK.

   Q+E finds and selects the next field with the character(s). Notice that when more than one column is searched, the search proceeds across and then down, record by record.

4. Choose Find <u>N</u>ext to go forward with the search or Find <u>P</u>revious to go backwards.

   The other command in the Search menu is Goto, used to find whole records. Choose <u>G</u>oto, type the record number in the dialog box, and press OK. Q+E highlights the first field in that record.

Querying and Extracting

Most people tend to use Q+E not to maintain database files (creating new ones and editing existing ones) but to display, extract records from, and analyze existing databases to tease more information out of them. The join commands discussed previously is one way of doing this. This section discusses other methods—like sorting and selecting records, formatting, and adding totals.

Sorting Records

The sort commands are very straightforward and easy to use. Follow these steps:

1. Select any field in the column to sort by.

2. Choose <u>A</u>scending or <u>D</u>escending in the <u>S</u>ort menu.

   All records are sorted by the chosen column. You can undo the sort by choosing <u>R</u>eset Sort afterwards.

   Perform multiple-column sorts by doing two or more sorts. Use the more important column in the first sort. Figure 15.6 shows an example of a multiple sort on the query window that was displayed in Figure 15.5. First, the records were sorted in ascending order on the Dept_ID column and then sorted in ascending order on the Emp_ID column.

Selecting Records

Selecting records that meet certain conditions through Q+E is similar to the process in other databases. You can specify as many conditions as you like and you can also use wild card characters. For example, you could specify that you want to select only those records with department ID's greater than D100 in the query window displayed in Figure 15.6.

15 — Using Q+E

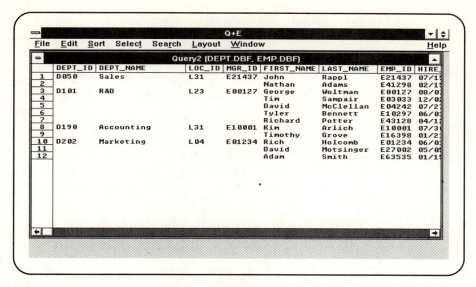

Figure 15.6 *A multiple sort.*

Follow these steps to select records meeting certain conditions:

1. Select a field in the column that will set the selection condition.

   The selection commands in Select do not appear unless a field is selected.

2. Choose Add Condition from the Select menu.

   Q+E displays the Add Condition dialog box.

   The field name you choose is displayed at the top after Column:. The first six operators work the same way as in other database software: Equal, Not Equal, Less Than, Less or Equal, Greater Than, Greater or Equal. Select the default (Equal), for instance, and all records with fields the same as the characters specified in Value are chosen and displayed.

   The Like and Not Like operators work with wild card characters. The wild cards used depend on what you set up in the Open statement (see "Starting Q+E and Opening Files" earlier in this chapter) or the Options command in Layout; see other formatting options in the next section. For MS-DOS, the characters are * and ?, where the asterisk stands for many or no characters and the question mark stands for one character. For SQL, the % and _ characters perform the same functions.

3. Choose an operator.

4. Type a value.

For example, use Greater Than and D100 in the Value box. Case Sensitive, when on, treats upper- and lowercase characters differently.

5. Check or uncheck Case Sensitive and choose OK.

Q+E displays only those records that meet the conditions. If at this stage you want to add more conditions, just go through the same procedure again. Q+E recognizes that this is another condition and adds two more choices in the Add Condition box: And and Or. Check And and the selection conditions are more stringent—all records chosen must meet both selection conditions. Check Or and a record that meets either condition is displayed.

For example, choose the Emp_ID column, And, Not Like, and type **E0*** in the Value box. Figure 15.7 shows the result in the example. Only records with Dept_ID greater than D100 and Emp_ID not equal to E0* are displayed.

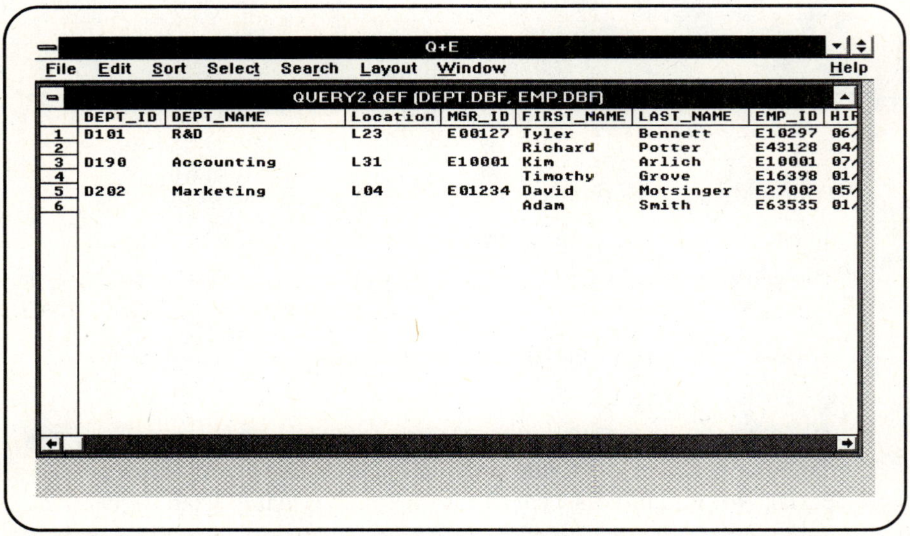

Figure 15.7 Selected records.

Formatting

The Layout menu contains most of the formatting commands. Use these commands to alter the appearance and size of characters, change the width and headings of columns, move and remove columns, and hide duplicate rows.

Choose Font from the Layout menu to access the Font dialog box. You can change Size, Typeface (Bold, Italic, Underline, and Strikeout), and the Font itself through this box. If checked, the Set Default option applies any newly chosen options in this box to all future query windows.

Change column width using the mouse or the menu. The mouse technique is the same one used with Excel: Place the pointer over the line to the right of the column heading, where it changes to a dark cross shape; then drag in the required direction. Choose Column Width from Layout to specify a number for the width. Check Default Width in the dialog box to revert to the default width.

Change a column name or heading as follows:

1. Choose Define Column from the Layout menu.

2. Type in the new name in the Heading box and choose OK.

The other options in the Define Column dialog box—Expression, Fields, and Add—are discussed later.

Follow these steps to move a column:

1. Select a field in the column.

2. Choose Move Column from Layout.

3. Position the column as follows: With the mouse, simply click on the new position. With the keyboard, move to a column beside the new position; then use the left or right arrows to place the column to the left or right.

To remove a column, select a field in it, and choose Remove Column from Layout.

Q+E automatically displays all fields from a database in separate columns. As shown above, you can remove any of these. To restore columns, perform the following steps:

1. Choose Define Column from Layout.

   Q+E displays the dialog box shown in Figure 15.8.

   Every field from the database, even if removed, is displayed in the Fields scroll box. When you have a query window on display that is a join of two or more databases, the field names are prefixed by the database names. For instance, in the example, the Loc_ID field is called `Dept.Loc_ID` because it originated in the Dept.dbf file.

2. Choose the field corresponding to the column you want to restore.

   The field name appears in the Expression box. If you want a different column heading, type in a new one now. The use of Expression is discussed in the next section.

3. Choose Add.

   Q+E returns you to the window.

4. Place the new column, following step 3 of the instructions for moving a column, which were described earlier.

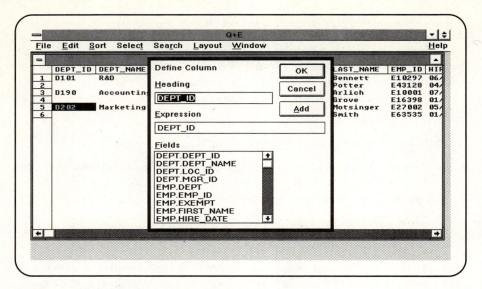

Figure 15.8 *The Define Column dialog box.*

With Excel databases you can change data types through the Define Field command in Layout. After selecting a field in the column, choose the command and then choose from one of the types.

The Options command gives other formatting options. Choose Options from Layout to display the Options dialog box.

Set the maximum column width in the Character, Number, and Date options. The Like options, DOS and SQL, refer to the wild card character types mentioned in the preceding section, "Selecting Records." Check the option you prefer. Finally, check Use Thousands Separator when you want Q+E to insert a comma to indicate thousands in numeric fields.

When accessing data from SQL Server, Oracle, and OS/2 Extended Edition, Q+E presents an option not available with other database sources like dBASE. Choose Distinct from the Select menu to hide rows, that is, records, in your data that are duplicates. Choose it again to reverse the procedure.

Adding Computed Columns and Totals

Because Q+E works with the source database applications (dBASE, etc.) in evaluating computations, you can use whatever calculations and formulas, combined together as expressions, they use when you are in Q+E.

All database systems let you use the addition (+), subtraction (-), multiplication (*), and division (/) operators.

Q+E allows you to add a new column to display computed columns. To do so, follow these steps:

1. Choose Define Column from Layout.
2. Type the name of the computed column in Heading.
3. Type the calculation in Expression.

   The expression can be any combination of operators and fields allowed by the underlying database: two fields added together, for instance, or a field multiplied by a number. Expressions are used in SQL statements also. See the next section, "SQL Statements."

4. Choose Add.
5. Place the new column in the usual way.

   Add Totals to your columns as follows:

1. Select a field in the column to total.
2. Choose Totals from Layout.

   Q+E displays the dialog box shown in Figure 15.9.

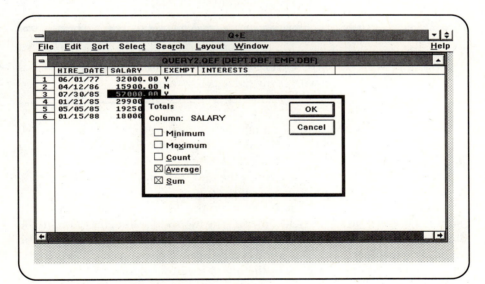

Figure 15.9 *The Totals dialog box.*

3. Check any or all of the five options and Q+E will display them underneath the column in question.

   Minimum and Maximum give the minimum and maximum field in the column; Count gives the number of fields; Average gives the average; and Sum gives the sum of all fields in the selected column.

294 Advanced Techniques

To remove any totals in the future, uncheck the options in the Totals dialog box.

4. Choose OK.

Column totals change as the records on display change—new records are added, for example.

Sometimes you might want to show only totals without any records. To do this, choose <u>O</u>nly Show Totals from <u>L</u>ayout. Choose it again to redisplay the records.

SQL Statements

SQL stands for *Structured Query Language,* a standard programming language used in databases. Every change you make in Q+E—selecting, sorting, joining, formatting, etc.—is recorded by Q+E in the SQL language. You can edit these changes, recorded in a statement, directly and you can even write them from scratch, as shown in the next section, "Editing an SQL."

 Note: It is important to distinguish between the SQL language and Microsoft SQL Server, which is a database system. The SQL language works with many database systems.

Q+E provides you with two methods for viewing these SQL statements. Choose <u>S</u>how Info from the <u>W</u>indow menu to see full information about your query; an example is shown in Figure 15.10.

The SQL statement is displayed at the end, after information concerning the source application, any joins, sorting, etc.

Another way to view SQLs, as well as editing the statements directly, is to choose SQL Query from the Select menu. The identical statement found in the Show Info window appears in a separate scroll box, but this time it can be edited. You can also access this scroll box by double-clicking on the box to the left of the first column heading in the query window. Figure 15.11 shows an SQL scroll box.

Each statement is divided into *clauses,* which correspond to the menu commands you executed. Some of the clauses in the statement may not be visible. Scroll down to see them. A clause can be thought of as a sentence, while a statement is a whole paragraph or more. Every time you execute a command in Q+E, a clause is added.

Figure 15.10 *The Show Info window.*

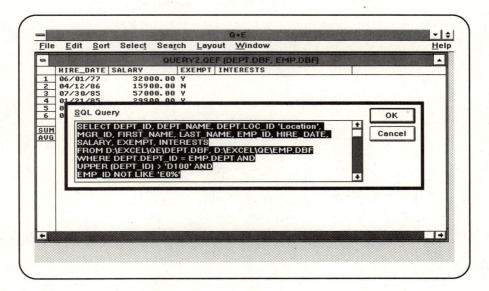

Figure 15.11 *An SQL scroll box.*

Every SQL statement includes at least two clauses: the *Select* and the *From*. The former specifies fields displayed; the latter names the database file. Other common clauses start with *Where* (generated by selecting records), *Order* (from sorting records), and *Compute* (from adding totals). In each case, the clause corresponds to a menu command.

Table 15.3 links each clause to the corresponding menu command.

Table 15.3 SQL clauses and Q+E menu commands.

SQL Clause	Equivalent Q+E Command	From Menu
Select	Open	File
	Add Condition	Select
	Reset Conditions	Select
	Join	Select
	Outer Join	Select
	Define Column	Layout
	Move Column	Layout
	Remove Column	Layout
From	Open	File
	Join	Select
	Outer Join	Select
	Use Index (OS/2)	File
Where	Add Condition	Select
	Reset Conditions	Select
Order By	Ascending	Sort
	Descending	Sort
	Reset Sort	Sort
Compute	Totals	Layout
Options	Only Show Totals	Layout
Distinct	Distinct (OS/2)	Select

Any column you add through a computation, defined by an expression, becomes part of the Select clause since this lists all columns/fields. For instance, if you added a special field to compute vacation money as a percentage (1%) of total salary, it would show in Select in this example as `Emp.Salary*0.1 'Vacation'`, where `Vacation` is the new column name.

Editing an SQL

Using the SQL scroll box, you can change clauses in SQL statements. You can add or delete fields from the display, for instance, by adding or deleting the field name in the Select clause in the statement. Or you can alter the Where clause to change the selection conditions.

In some cases you can make changes that would not be possible through the menus. For instance, if you wanted to select only employees who had been hired within the last 90 days from a file and the date of hiring was contained in Hire_Date, then you could insert a clause:

```
Where Date()-Hire_Date<=90.
```

The `Date()` argument gives today's date; it can only be used when the source application supports it.

To edit an SQL statement, bring up the scroll box by choosing SQL Query from the Select menu, make your changes, and choose OK when completed. Q+E changes the display when you return to the query window.

Be sure to follow the correct syntax when editing and remember that SQL can differ between source applications. For example, the From clause in an Excel source file always shows the data types, as in:

```
FROM C:\EXCEL\LIBRARY\MD.XLS (CHAR(9), CHAR(14), MONEY,
INTEGER, FLOAT)
```

where `char`, `money`, `integer`, and `float` stand for data types, and the numbers in parentheses stand for column widths.

Opening a Query Window with SQL

If you feel confident or adventurous, you can bypass most Q+E menu commands and type in the SQL clauses yourself. The only proviso is that the source database support the clauses used. Follow these steps to start the process; then add as many clauses as you like:

1. Choose Open from the File menu in Q+E.
2. Choose the SQL button.
3. Enter the Select and From statement.

An example is Select Loc_ID From dBASEFile|C:\Excel\QE\Loc.dbf. This displays one field from one of the database files supplied by Microsoft.

Alternatively, you could choose the file and the source in the Open dialog box before you choose the SQL button and Q+E would insert the From statement itself.

Specifying the source application in the SQL statement overrides whatever source is chosen in the Open dialog box. The syntax for the different sources are given in Table 15.4.

Table 15.4 Syntax for From clause with different sources.

Source	From Clause Syntax
dBASE	dBASEFile|
Text file	TextFile|
OS/2 SQL Server	SQLServer|
Oracle	Oracle|
OS/2 Extended Edition	EEDataMgr|
Microsoft Excel worksheet	ExcelFile|

Saving

You can save Q+E files in many different ways, just as you can open them in many ways. This section deals with saving as a query file, as a new database file, and as mailing labels.

The basic steps are similar for all three types of saving:

1. From the query window to save, choose Save As from the File menu.

   The Save As dialog box appears.

2. From the dialog box, pick the type of file to save as in the Destination scroll box—like QueryFile, MailingLabels, etc.

   Q+E gives the correct extension in the File Name box.

3. Type the file name in File Name.

4. Where available, check or leave unchecked the Use Headings for Field Names box.

   This option is available with some databases. When unchecked, it takes the title of expressions, not the actual field name/column heading, when an expression is used in the Select statement. See the previous section "SQL Statements" for background information on this.

5. Choose the Options button when available.

6. Choose OK to exit.

Saving as a Query

When you take the QueryFile option in the Save As dialog box, you are basically saving the SQL statement. This records the file(s) used, the field(s) displayed, and the menu commands executed. In other words, you are not saving each record in the query window. If the source database documents change after you save as a query and you open this query file again, Q+E displays the new situation.

Saving as a Database

Any of the database options save the records shown in the query window. Remember two things about these database options: one, column totals are not saved; and two, computed columns are saved as ordinary columns, that is, the numbers, using the current numbers.

Saving as Mailing Labels

The Mailing Labels option can be very useful for formatting query fields so that they print out neatly. The fields to print in the label must be selected in the window first, before you choose Save As. Any label can have up to 128 lines.

It is possible to put two field names next to each other on a label line, but they have to be together in the query window. Move the columns, if necessary, so they are beside one another. Select other fields to print by using the multiple-selection techniques discussed elsewhere in this book.

Q+E records the order in which you select the fields and whether you use multiple selection or not and displays the fields accordingly. For example, if you wanted to put two fields on the first line, a third on the second, and a fourth on the third line, you should select the first two in the query window, select the third, and then the fourth.

After selecting, choose Save As from File.

Use the Options button in Save As to edit the fields in the label. Figure 15.12 shows the Options dialog box for a label, accessed through Save As.

First, choose New when you are going to change the labeling.

The Label Definition scroll box shows the fields as they appear on each line (three lines in the example) on the label. In Figure 15.12, the top line has two fields. Q+E automatically separates them with a space, represented in the box by the blank space enclosed in single quotes. You can include any character in the label by enclosing it in single quotes and using the plus sign (+) to link it with the fields. For example, you could add + ' in warehouse' to the second line after Loc_Id, and this would be printed every time. Add, delete, or move fields as necessary.

Lines Between dictates how many blank lines should appear between lines.

*Column Start Position*s dictates where to print the labels on the page, in batches of up to four. At 1 indicate which column to print the first, fourth, etc., label. At 2, indicate which column to print the second, fifth, etc., label. And so on for 3 and 4. Most labeling pages use four across.

File Character Set applies to .Lab files (the default extension for label files in Q+E). ANSI and IBM PC are similar, but ANSI is better for international characters.

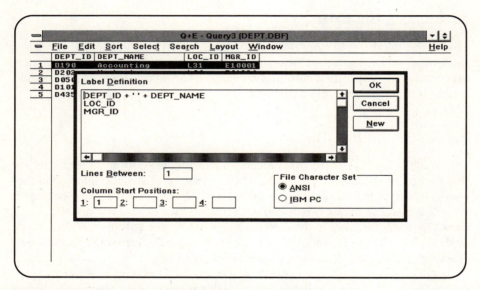

Figure 15.12 *The Options dialog box for mailing labels.*

Querying and Editing

This section is relevant only if you chose the Query and Edit version of Q+E when you installed (see "Installing Q+E" at the beginning of the chapter). With the Query and Edit version of Q+E, you can add, delete, and edit records in databases.

Q+E works differently from other databases when it performs these operations, because when you open a file in Q+E (a dBASE file, for instance) and make any changes, the record in the database file changes as soon as you make the change in Q+E. You *don't* have to save to register the change. As easy as this seems, it is also dangerous when misused, especially since some of the changes can't be undone.

Perform one step before editing:

1. Choose Allow Editing from the Edit menu.

A check mark appears beside Allow Editing when it's on. If you choose Distinct from Select, editing is disallowed.

Other restrictions on maintaining a database apply when two or more databases have been joined: You can't add or delete records, though you can do straight edits on field values.

You can *edit* a field directly or through the Zoom window. Undo an edit (when this is possible) by choosing Undo Edit from Edit or pressing Esc. Q+E allows you to change several fields at once by selecting them, choosing Update All from the Edit menu, entering a new value in Value, and choosing OK.

Copying, cutting, and *pasting* work the same way as in other applications. However, if the area selected to paste into is too small, Q+E truncates the data. In addition, if the data type you are pasting into (character, number, date) differs from that copied or cut, then Q+E may not be able to paste. Paste Append is useful in that the record copied is always inserted at the end of a query window, in the last row, when you choose it. Copy Special is discussed later in "Copying and Linking Q+E Data to other Applications."

You can *add* records by choosing Add Record or Form from Edit. With Add Record, Q+E displays the Form dialog box with blank field boxes. So it's the same as choosing Form and then choosing the New button, as described in the following section.

To *delete* a record, select a field in the record and choose Delete Records from Edit. With this command, you can undo the delete afterwards.

 Tip: Q+E does not always resort and reselect records or update computed columns as changes are made. To see the result of changes, choose Query Now from the Select menu.

Using Form

Like the database option in Excel, Q+E has a form to make maintaining records easier. Use it as follows:

1. Select a field in a record, or double-click on the record number.

    Q+E displays the dialog box shown in Figure 15.13.

2. Choose one of the buttons on right to perform the maintenance.

    Use the New button to *add* records. Fill in the blank fields after choosing it.

Use Du<u>p</u> to *duplicate* the record currently on display.

Use <u>D</u>elete to *delete* the record on display. Be warned that with this option, you cannot undo the delete; whereas with the Delete Records command in Edit, you can.

Use <u>R</u>estore to *undo* any changes made to the fields on display. This option can't be used to undelete a record.

Choose E<u>x</u>it when you're done.

You can customize the Form dialog box using the F<u>o</u>rm Setup command from the <u>E</u>dit menu. If you choose the command, three options for which you can specify a maximum value are presented. The value in <u>N</u>umber of Columns determines the maximum number of columns displayed across the dialog box. (Columns here does not refer to columns in the query window.) The value in <u>F</u>ields per Column determines the maximum number of fields under each of these columns. The Field <u>W</u>idth value determines the maximum width of characters in the edit boxes.

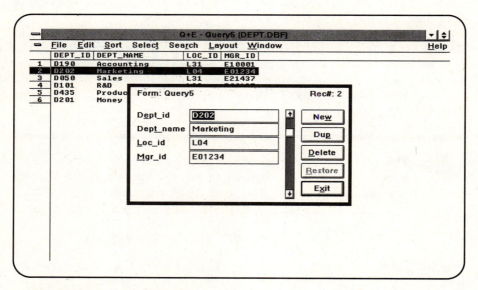

Figure 15.13 *The Form dialog box.*

Creating New Databases

When you create a new database in Q+E, the first step is to define the file and the fields. After that, you can open this new file and insert records and edit, etc., in the usual way. Follow these steps to create a file:

1. Choose <u>D</u>efine from the <u>F</u>ile menu.

   Q+E displays a dialog box almost identical to the Open box with a list of files and directories and the File Name and Source boxes. The difference is that this box has two extra buttons: New and Delete. Delete is used to delete databases.

2. Specify the name, source, and directory for the file.

3. Choose Ne<u>w</u>.

   Q+E displays the define window, an example of which is shown in Figure 15.14.

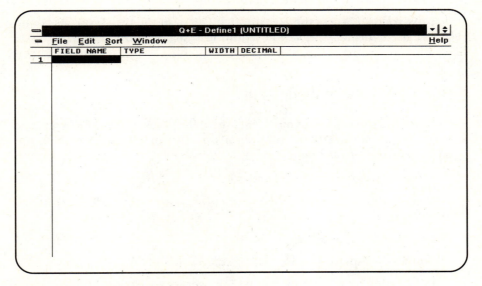

Figure 15.14 *A define window.*

In this window, you define the fields in your file, one field on each row. The values you need or want to enter vary according to what kind of database you are defining. But Q+E always needs three pieces of information on each field: the name entered under Field_Name, the type, and the width.

The order of the rows determines the order of the columns in the query window.

4. Enter a field name in the first column and press Tab, or use the mouse pointer to move to the next column.

   Q+E displays a list of data types to choose from: character, numeric, etc.

5. Enter a type by typing the first letter or clicking on the type in the displayed list.

6. Enter a column width.

    The decimal field is only relevant if the field is a number. Enter a number corresponding to the number of decimal places when necessary.

7. Enter other field information; then proceed to the next row to enter other fields.

8. After entering all fields, choose Save from File.

9. Choose Close from File to exit the define window.

    Now you can access the file, through Open, in the usual way. As yet no records exist in the file. Choose Allow Editing from Edit and add as many as you like with Add Record or Form from the Edit menu.

Editing a Database Definition

Q+E gives you the option of modifying the definitions of files after you have created them. You can edit field definitions and add or delete fields. First, you need to get back into the define window.

1. Choose Define from the File menu.

    The existing file is displayed with its normal extension, .dbf for dBASE and so on.

2. Choose the file and OK.

    The file is displayed in the define window.

3. Edit a value by selecting it and typing over it.

    Use the Cut, Copy, and Paste commands in the usual way.

4. Add a field by selecting a value in a row, choosing Add After or Add Before from Edit, and entering the new values in the row.

    Add After and Add Before insert blank rows, after or before the selected row value.

5. Delete a field by selecting a value in the row and choosing Delete Fields from Edit.

    Be careful when you are deleting. All the values in that column in the database are deleted. However, you can choose Undo from Edit immediately afterwards if you make a mistake.

6. Choose Save from File to save your changes.

    You can print out your definition by choosing Print from File while you are in the define window.

Copying and Linking Q+E Data to Other Applications

Q+E can copy and link data values to other Windows and OS/2 applications. This includes Excel and Microsoft Word for Windows. The basic steps are simple copy and paste with other options also available for more complicated linkups.

Follow these steps to copy or link:

1. From Q+E select the values to copy or link.

2. Choose Copy or Copy Special from Edit.

    Copy does a straight copy to the clipboard or memory buffer. The Copy Special dialog box is shown in Figure 15.15.

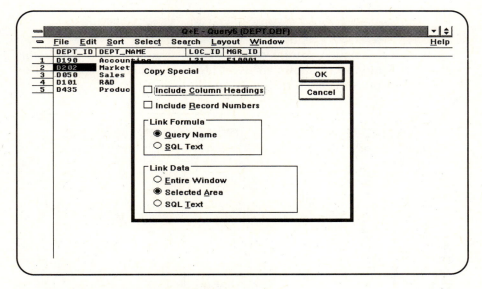

Figure 15.15   *The Copy Special dialog box.*

3. If you choose Copy Special in step 2, check the options you want and choose OK.

    Check Include Column Headings and Q+E copies the headings as well as the data.

    Check Include Record Numbers and Q+E copies the record numbers.

306 Advanced Techniques

When you link Excel to Q+E, a formula, visible in the Excel formula bar, provides the linking information. If you are linking, check one of the options under Link Formula to determine how the Q+E window linked to is identified: Query Name shows the query window name in the formula bar; SQL Text shows the query Select statement (see the earlier section "SQL Statements") in the formula bar.

Link Data specifies what data to copy to the clipboard. Entire Window copies everything in the query window; Selected Area copies whatever is selected; SQL Text copies the Select statement, not the records, to the clipboard.

The chosen Link Data option ultimately determines what goes into the Excel cells. The chosen Link Formula option determines what appears in the formula bar when a link is made.

4. Go to the Excel worksheet and select an area large enough to contain the data.
5. Choose Paste or Paste Link from the Edit menu.

The link command ensures continuous updating between Q+E and the application. Figure 15.16 shows an Excel file with pasted linked data. The formula bar displays the linking formula.

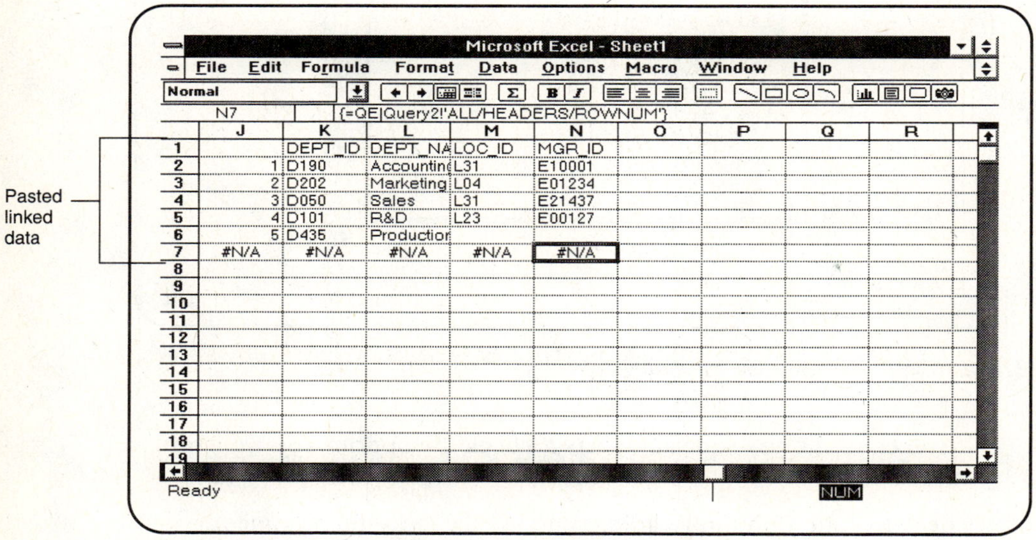

Figure 15.16   Excel file with pasted linked data.

The cells showing #N/A are selected cells that were not used in the paste; that is, the selected area was too large. The linking formula appears in the formula bar even though one of these #N/A cells is selected.

The formula breaks down as follows:

QE stands for Q+E, the application linked to, always followed by |. Query2 is the Q+E file name, followed by !. ALL, HEADERS, and ROWNUM mean that all the Q+E file was copied together with the column headers and row numbers.

Linking Excel to Q+E with an SQL Statement

The steps in the preceding section showed how to link Excel or Word to Q+E. The discussion of Copy Special mentioned that you can link directly to the Select statement in Q+E as opposed to specifying the query name. Doing this can give you more flexibility in what you display in the Excel worksheet.

If you had chosen SQL Text in Link Formula in step 3 in the preceding section, you would have ended up with the Excel worksheet shown in Figure 15.17.

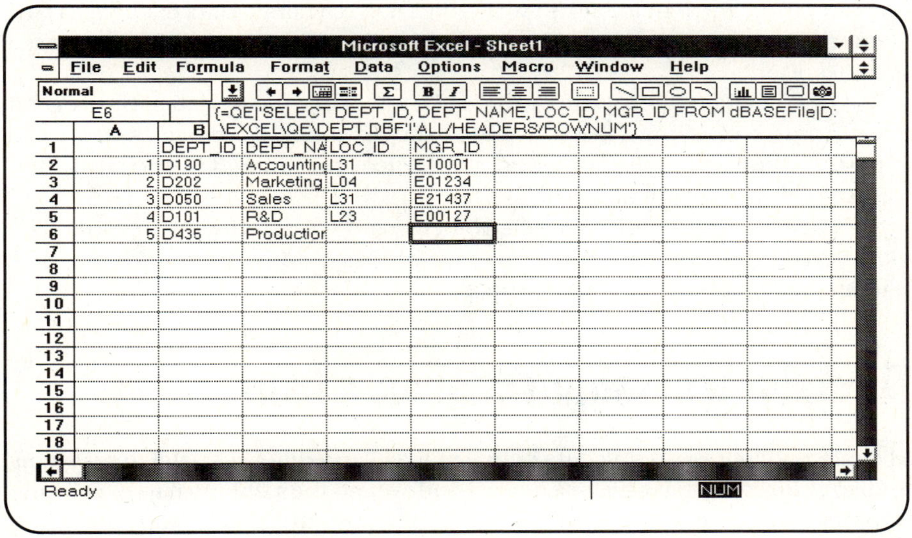

Figure 15.17   Excel linked to a Q+E Select statement.

In the formula bar, the Select statement has replaced the query file name.

You can edit this formula in the normal Excel way. You could, for instance, delete a field or add Where clauses, etc. See the earlier section "SQL Statements" for more information on clauses. When you have finished editing, press Ctrl-Shift-Enter.

Q+E creates a new query window when you edit a Select statement.

You can also initiate the whole procedure from Excel—that is, create a link—by simply typing in the formula from scratch in the formula bar. Follow these steps:

1. Select the Excel cells to paste and link to.
2. Type the linking formula in the formula bar.
3. Press Ctrl-Shift-Enter.

The database values are then pasted into Excel.

Common Errors in Linking

Sometimes the linking doesn't work. Various characters appear in the Excel cells when this is the case.

When you see #N/A in a cell, you have selected too large a paste area. This does not invalidate the link.

When you see #NULL, you have a memory problem. Close other applications and try again. If that doesn't work, the DDE (Dynamic Data Exchange) 64K memory limit has been exceeded. Try pasting fewer records or use area specification.

Q+E needs to be running for Excel to perform the updates. If you get a query from Excel asking if Q+E should be started and reply yes, and still no data is pasted, then Excel couldn't find the Qe.exe program. Try specifying the Qe.exe path in the Autoexec.bat file.

When you see #NAME? in a cell, something is wrong with the formula. The file referred to might not exist, the path given could be wrong, or the SQL statement might have incorrect syntax.

Directly Accessing Databases from Excel

As explained, Q+E can link data between Excel and different database systems by displaying a database file in a query window and then linking it to Excel. One step beyond this is using Q+E software to bypass the actual query windows while accessing other database system files directly in Excel. This accessing includes extracting, linking, and deleting records and fields.

Setting Up Excel

Before you can access other databases from Excel, you must modify the Data menu. You do this with a file called *Qe.xla*, an add-in macro that comes with your Excel and Q+E installation package. Refer to Chapter 11, "Advanced Macros and Application Customization," for more information on add-in macros.

Follow these steps:

1. From Excel, choose Open from File.

    You need to find and select the Qe.xla. Unless you moved it, it should be in the Xlstart\Qemacro subdirectory of the Excel directory, along with the file Qestart.xla.

2. Select Qe.xla in the Files box and choose OK.

    Excel then loads the macro and, as a result, three new options appear in the Data menu: Paste Fieldnames, SQL Query, and Activate Q+E. In addition, other Data menu options like Set Database offer new options.

> **Tip:** If you want Excel to start automatically with the additional Data menu commands, you can copy or move the files in Qemacro up a level to Xlstart. If you move (or copy) Qestart.xla up to Xlstart to display the commands on entry into Excel, Excel actually loads Qe.xla when you first access a Data menu command. Take the automation one step further by copying or moving Qe.xla up to Xlstart, and Excel not only displays the additional commands but loads Qe.xla when you start it. Excel takes longer to load when you make these moves. And be warned: Excel looks in the Qemacro directory for macro functions (see "Additional Macro Functions"), so it's better to copy the file rather than move it.

Accessing an External Database

Even though the menu has changed, the Data menu commands basically work the same after you have set up the external database as the worksheet database. Please note that you can change to an internal worksheet database at any time.

Follow these steps to access an external database file:

1. Choose Set Database from Data.

    Excel prompts you with the Set Database dialog box, showing two options: Current Selection and External Database.

2. Choose External Database and OK.

    Excel displays the dialog box shown in Figure 15.18.

310 Advanced Techniques

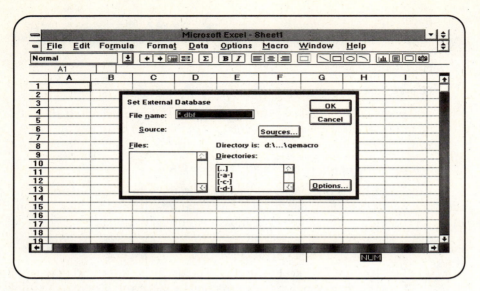

Figure 15.18 *The initial Set External Database dialog box.*

This is where you choose the external database system file. Use File name, Files, and Directories to select the correct file.

Use Source for dBASE, Text, and Excel files. Use Sources for database system files that need to be logged onto: Oracle, SQL Server, and OS/2.

The next section deals with the Options button commands.

3. Select your file and Options, if relevant, and choose OK.

   Excel displays the Set database dialog box, showing the name and location of your chosen file, with two buttons: Change and Add.

   At this stage, you can join another database file to the one already open by choosing Add and opening another file.

   Use the Change button, now or later, to change the choice of external database.

4. Choose Change or Add if you need to use them. If you do, you eventually return to this dialog box. Choose OK to exit.

Using Options When Opening Files

The Options button appears when you choose either dBASE or text files. The two sets of options available with these two kinds of files are discussed together below.

With both dBASE and text files, check Use Q+E Defaults to let the Q+E software make your choices. When this is on, no other option is available in the dialog boxes.

File Character Set in both dBASE and text files determines what character set is used to store data. ANSI (American National Standards Institute) and IBM PC are similar, though ANSI has more support for international characters. DBASE by default uses IBM PC; Excel by default uses ANSI. If you are using Q+E exclusively to create and maintain database files, use ANSI.

SQL Compatibility, a dBASE option, determines the type of SQL used in building Select statements: either ANSI or dBASE IV. The latter is the default.

Figure 15.19 shows the Options dialog box for text files when opening them from Excel.

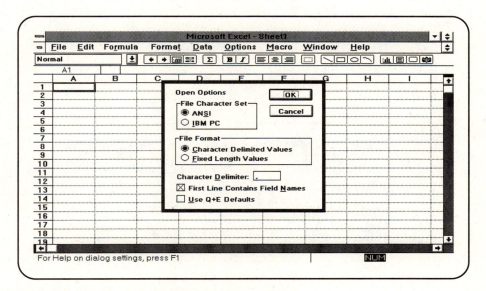

Figure 15.19   *The Options dialog box for text files.*

File Format determines how a text file is read. Check Character Delimited Values if the text file has character-separated values. Check Fixed Length Values if the values are of fixed length.

When you check Character Delimited Values, you need to specify the type of character in Character Delimiter. Usually it's a comma or a Tab; type **TAB** if the latter is the delimiter.

Check First Line Contains Field Names if the first line of the text file serves as column headings.

Extracting Fields and Records

Once an external file is designated in Excel, you can proceed to extract fields and records to view and edit. The first step in doing this is to specify and paste field names.

Pasting Fieldnames

1. Select the worksheet cell to start pasting the field names to.
2. Choose Paste Fieldnames from the Data menu.

    Excel displays the field names from the chosen file in a scroll box, shown in Figure 15.20. Four buttons are displayed on the right.

    Paste pastes the selected field names. Paste All pastes all the field names in the external file. Order Fields, when chosen, extends the dialog box to its full length, as shown in Figure 15.20. It should be used when you want to re-order the field names, or to add or remove field names.

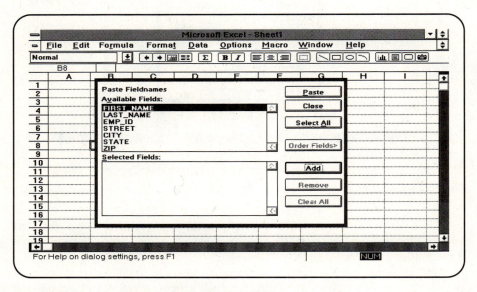

Figure 15.20 *The full Paste Fieldnames dialog box.*

When the full Paste Fieldnames dialog box is shown after choosing Order All, the Paste All button changes to Select All. Choose Select All to select all field names.

Choose <u>A</u>dd to display any selected field name in the lower scroll box. You can order the display of field names by selecting and adding them in your own order. Select a field name in the lower scroll box, and choose <u>R</u>emove to remove it from display (or to reorder it by adding it again). Choose <u>C</u>lear All to clear the lower scroll box.

When the full Paste Fieldnames dialog box is displayed, Excel pastes the lower scroll box contents, not the upper.

3. Make your choices of field names, and order them if you need to.

4. Choose <u>P</u>aste to paste them onto the worksheet.

5. Choose Close to exit the dialog box.

Extracting Records

Once the field names are pasted into Excel, you can proceed to extract the records. Normal Excel database commands and procedures apply in doing this. You can set criteria to select only those records you want by defining a criteria range through Set Criteria from Data, and you can define an extract range through Set Extract from Data. Both of these steps are optional. If you don't have a criteria range, Excel extracts all the records.

Follow these steps to extract a record:

1. If you don't have an extract range defined, select the field names.

   You can also select the field names plus the cells underneath. In that case, Excel only pastes into the selected area. Excel extracts and pastes only into those field names chosen.

2. Choose <u>E</u>xtract from <u>D</u>ata.

3. Choose OK when asked whether you want to extract only unique records.

   Excel and the Q+E software search the external database file, which can take some time. After records are found, a small dialog box tells you how many and prompts `Linked or Unlinked`, meaning you can link directly to the external database.

4. Check <u>L</u>inked or <u>U</u>nlinked.

   At this stage, you can use the <u>S</u>ave As button in this dialog box to save the fields and records selected to a text file.

5. Choose <u>P</u>aste to paste the records.

   The normal Excel database functions and analytical procedures can now be used on your data.

Deleting the Data

You can delete data in the external file directly through a menu command in Excel. This is true even when you choose the unlinked option when extracting. All the data selected is deleted in the external file. The data is not deleted in Excel. Use normal procedures—the Delete key—to delete this data.

> **Caution:** Be careful when using the Data Delete command. You can't undo. *All* the data extracted, not just the selected cell(s), is deleted in the external file.

To delete data in an external file, follow these steps:

1. Select a cell that contains the extracted data.
2. Choose <u>D</u>elete from <u>D</u>ata.

Using SQL to Edit and Extract

One of the commands added when you set up Excel by adding in Qe.xla is SQL Query. As you extract records using the menu commands, the SQL statement gets built up and can be viewed and edited through this command. You can also build the statement from scratch if you feel brave enough.

1. Choose SQL <u>Q</u>uery from <u>D</u>ata.

    Figure 15.21 shows an example of a query window with a statement.

    You can edit the statement (for example, deleting a field or adding a Where clause) directly in this window. To the right of the window are these buttons:

    <u>R</u>un executes the statement from scratch and pastes any selected records at the active cell on the worksheet.

    <u>N</u>ew clears the current statement. If the statement has not been saved, you can choose to save it or not.

    <u>O</u>pen opens any text or query (.qef) file and displays the SQL statement.

    <u>S</u>ave enables you to save the SQL statement to a query (.qef) file.

2. Choose your option.
3. Choose Close to exit.

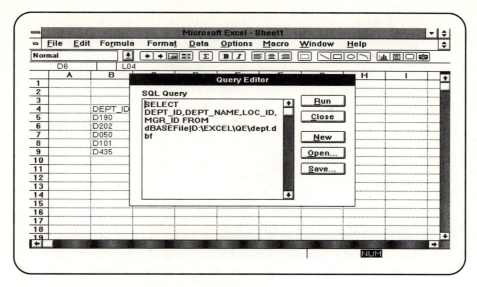

Figure 15.21 *The SQL query window in Excel.*

Additional Macro Functions

When Qe.xla is added to a worksheet, 10 additional macro functions appear, most of which relate directly to the new menu commands and options. Chapter 11, "Advanced Macros and Application Customization," discusses how to use macro functions. The following sections outline what each new function does.

The macro functions appear in the Paste Function scroll box in Formula only when a macro sheet is open and active.

With all the functions that are equivalents of menu commands (that is, all except DB.GET.DATABASE), you get a ? alternative function, as in DB.EXTRACT?( ). When you run this ? alternative, the appropriate dialog boxes are displayed when the macro is run, prompting you for selections.

DB.EXTRACT() and DB.EXTRACT?()

This command is equivalent to the Extract command in the Data menu. It extracts the fields and records that meet the selection criteria. With DB.EXTRACT?( ) you don't supply the arguments—the user enters them directly through the dialog box. With DB.EXTRACT( ), you *do* supply the arguments. Use the following syntax:

DB.EXTRACT(*unique,destination,filename,linked*); DB.EXTRACT?( )

unique applies only to SQLServer, Oracle, and EEDataMgr sources. If it's TRUE, Excel extracts unique records only; if it's FALSE, Excel extracts all records meeting the criteria.

destination is a number from 1 to 3 specifying where the extracted records go. The default 1 pastes the selected range. 2 extracts to a file named *filename*. 3 does 1 and 2 together.

filename is the file extracted to when you use 2 or 3 in *destination*. The default is "QE mm/dd/yy hh:mm:ss."

linked is a logical: if TRUE, then the extracted data is linked to the source; if FALSE, it is not linked.

DB.GET.DATABASE( )

No menu command equivalent exists for this macro function. Use it to get information about the database you are using. Use the following syntax:

DB.GET.DATABASE(*info_type*)

info_type is a number from 1 to 8. Each number refers to a different type of information, as the following explains:

Number	Information Returned
1	Returns 1 if the internal database range is active. Returns 2 if external database is active
2	Returns the name of the source
3	Returns the locations of the external files or tables connected to Q+E
4	Returns the names of the external files or tables connected to Q+E
5	Returns schema name in Open dialog box (e.g., directory or owner)
6	Returns file name in Open dialog box (e.g., file or table)
7	Returns the names of sources logged onto
8	Returns the names of sources that can be logged onto

DB.LOGON()

This macro function is equivalent to an option in the menu command Set External Database in Data. It comes into play when you choose the Sources button and enter information in the Source Connections dialog box. Use it to log onto a source from which you want to extract data.

Use the following syntax:

DB.LOGON(*source,database,username,password*); DB.LOGON?()

source specifies the source.

database specifies the file to read.

username is your log in user name.

password is your password.

DB.PASTE.FIELDNAMES()

Use this macro function to paste fieldnames in Data. It inserts *all* fieldnames from a specified database. Use the following syntax:

DB.PASTE.FIELDNAMES (*filename*); DB.PASTE.FIELDNAMES?().

fieldname is the name of the file to get the fieldnames from. You can use more than one file name, as in {"dept.dbf","emp.dbf"}.

> **Note:** Use FORMULA or FORMULA.ARRAY functions to insert selected fieldnames.

DB.SET.DATABASE()

This function is equivalent to the Set Database command in the Data menu. It sets up the external database. Use the following syntax:

DB.SET.DATABASE(*internal,source,filename*); DB.SET.DATABASE?()

internal is a logical: if TRUE, the internal database is active; if FALSE, the external database is active.

source is the external database source.

filename is the file to access. You can use more than one file name, as in {"dept.dbf","emp.dbf"}.

DB.SQL.QUERY()

This macro function is equivalent to SQL Query in Data. It executes an SQL query and transfers it to Excel. Use the following syntax:

DB.SQL.QUERY(*type,query,destination,filename,linked*);
DB.SQL.QUERY?()

type is a number from 1 to 3:

Number	Command
1	Executes previous query
2	Executes *query* argument when it is a text string
3	Executes *query* argument when it is a file name

query here is related to *type* as explained above. With type 1, there is no argument here. With type 2, *query* is a text string up to 256 characters specifying an SQL query. With type 3, *query* is the name of a file containing a valid SQL query.

destination is a number from 1 to 3 specifying where the extracted records go. The default 1 pastes the selected range. 2 extracts to a file named *filename*. 3 does 1 and 2 together.

filename is the file extracted to when you use 2 or 3 in destination. The default is "QE mm/dd/yy hh:mm:ss."

linked is a logical: if TRUE, then the extracted data is linked to the source; if FALSE, it is not linked.

Accessing Q+E Menu Commands Through Excel

"Directly Accessing Databases from Excel" showed how to bypass a Q+E query window (using macro functions if you wish) to access other database files. This section puts the Q+E query windows back in the picture by showing how you can start Q+E, send and receive information from Q+E, and access the Q+E menu commands through a compatible application's macro sheet.

Q+E's ability to link up with other database operations is powerful. Its commands can be accessed from any application with Dynamic Data Exchange (DDE) capabilities. Any database system, including Excel, that has DDE can perform similar feats.

When Excel uses DDE to communicate with Q+E, the messages fall into four different areas. First, you open a channel through the Initiate function. Then you send or request data through the Request or Poke functions. You execute Q+E commands through the Execute function. And finally, you close the channel through the Terminate function.

Suppose that you want to find a name in a query data window and then print the entire contents of the query window in letter quality. This macro performs the task:

```
CHAN=INITIATE("QE",Query1)
NAME=REQUEST(CHAN,"R10C12")
=EXECUTE(CHAN,"[PRINT(1,FALSE)]")
=TERMINATE(CHAN)
```

Query1 is the query window name. R10C12 is the row and column number containing a name, which is placed in the variable NAME in the second line.

Chapter 11, "Advanced Macros and Application Customization," and Part 3, "Complete Reference," have further information on using macro sheets in general and macro functions that interact with Q+E in particular.

Functions Used with the Execute Function

The EXECUTE function is used in conjunction with a host of other functions to access the Q+E menus. All of these are outlined in Part 3, "Complete Reference." Only two arguments need to be specified with EXECUTE: the number of the channel and the function (and its own arguments) used with EXECUTE.

For example, you can use FETCH, which pastes data into another application, with EXECUTE:

```
=Execute(chan,"[Fetch('Excel','Sheet2','R5C3:R32C4','ALL')]").
```

Please note that opening a channel on the System topic means that you link to the Q+E application as a whole instead of a query window. When you do this, you can use many query windows on one channel.

See "Q+E Functions" in Part 3, "Complete Reference," for a full list and explanation of the functions used with EXECUTE to access Q+E from an Excel macro sheet.

PART THREE

COMPLETE REFERENCE

INTRODUCTION TO THE COMPLETE REFERENCE

In the previous two sections of this book, you have read about subjects in an order that is logical for learning Excel for Windows. Each chapter builds on information and experience gained in previous chapters. In the Complete Reference, however, information is organized for those who know what they are looking for. Information and advice on commands, operations, and other topics are broken into entries, which are organized in alphabetical order. Here you can find information on the commands and functions in Excel for Windows, and on many related matters, as long as you have some idea of what you are looking for.

Structure of the Reference Section

Below is an outline of the headings contained in the Complete Reference. This should help you to better find and understand the wealth of information provided there. Not all headings appear in each listing, only those that are appropriate. Furthermore, the headings have slightly different meanings depending on the type of listing. A description, for instance, can mean something different for a macro than it does for a File Print command.

Name

First of all, each entry is alphabetized based on the name of the command, function, or topic. A *command name* is considered the menu name followed by the name of the menu choice. For example, to learn how to open a new file, look under "File New." If you are uncertain about what menu a command is in, check the program or look it up in the index. To find more information about a named topic—a function, for example—simply look up the name of the function. When necessary, "See Also" notes redirect you within the Complete Reference.

Syntax

For function entries, the syntax appears next. The arguments required for each function are in parentheses—for example, ABS(*number*)—so that at a glance you can see the information you need to enter to use the function.

Description

Descriptive paragraphs follow the name of a command or topic, and "Description" precedes the description of a function. Often, the name of the entry itself does not reveal enough about the nature and functionality of the command or topic. Sometimes, the description can be the most vital aspect of the listing, especially when the entry covers a topic, like a function or macro, rather than a command or operation.

In function entries, this section includes an explanation of the arguments required for the function as seen under "Syntax."

Keystrokes

For commands, "Keystrokes" consists of the sequence of menu commands for both keyboard and mouse. Using the keyboard, choose from the main menu by pressing Alt plus the underlined letter in the menu and then, once the menu is showing, choose from the submenu by pressing just the underlined letter. With the mouse, just click on the command that you want.

Examples

Often it is useful to see how to use a command or function in a real situation. The "Examples" section helps to make the abstract concrete with instances of how the entry can be put to use. You may understand the Gallery Preferred command in charting, for instance, but may not have a feel for when to use it. The example gives you that extra understanding.

Steps

Once you understand the entry, know its syntax, and see how to use it, you may be ready to put it to use. To do so, except in the case of functions, you carry out a series of specific steps. The steps in this reference are designed so that you can see the sequence of steps you follow to choose the command from the menu and put it into effect.

Boxed Notes

In most cases, you will learn all you need to know about a entry by reading through the description, any steps listed, and any examples used. In other cases, though, additional information can be extremely helpful. There are three types of boxed notes used in the Complete Reference:

Note: *Notes* reveal additional information that helps you apply the information to practical situations.

Caution: *Cautions* warn you about errors or possible pitfalls that may come up.

Tip: *Tips* are handy pointers for using the entry effectively.

A

A1.R1C1 *(see* Macro Functions That Perform Actions*)*

ABS( ) *(see also* Function, SIGN*)*

Syntax

ABS(*number*)

Description

ABS is a function that returns the "absolute value" or positive value of the given number. Absolute value is a standard mathematical operation that makes any number positive whether it was originally positive or negative.

The information required for function ABS:

number is any number or a cell address, formula, or function that yields a number.

 Note: ABS can be used to avoid errors when only positive results are desired (see "Examples"). ABS is also useful when calculating differences where the larger of two values is not known.

Examples

Formula	Returns
=ABS(2)	2
=ABS(–2)	2
=SQRT(ABS(–9))	3

Absolute Reference

(*see also* **Relative Reference**)

An *absolute reference* (as distinct from a *relative reference*) is a means of referring to cells in a worksheet in a way that locates the cell regardless of where the active cell is. To distinguish absolute references in Excel, you put dollar signs before row and column references: $A$2, for example, as distinct from A2.

Example

Suppose that you have a formula in D5: =SUM(D2:D4). This is a relative reference. Copy the formula to cell F5 and the formula changes to =SUM(F2:F4). The cell referencing changes because the location of the formula cell has changed. Now change the formula in D5 to =SUM($D$2:$D$4) and copy it to F5. It is now an absolute reference. In F5 the formula remains the same, referring to $D$2:$D$4.

Changing a Cell Reference from Relative to Absolute

1. Make the cell containing the cell reference the active cell.   The cell reference appears in the formula bar.
2. Add a dollar sign ($) before each row and column reference.   The new cell reference appears in the formula bar.

> **Tip:** You can combine relative and absolute references in a single cell reference. For example, $B3 will always refer to column B wherever you copy a formula with that cell reference, but the row reference will change.

ABSREF *(see Macro Functions—Value Returning)*

ACOS( ) *(see also Function, ASIN, COS, PI, SIN)*

Syntax

ACOS(*number*)

Description

ACOS is a function that returns in radians (–PI/2 to PI/2) the arccosine of the given number. The arccosine is the inverse of cosine. The arccosine of a number is the angle which has a cosine that is the given number. For example, because the cosine of PI/3 is .5000, the inverse cosine or arccosine of .5000 is PI/3.

The information required for function ACOS:

number is a number between –1 and 1.

 Tip: To convert to degrees, multiply by 180/PI( ).

Examples

Formula	Returns
=ACOS(1)	0
=ACOS(–1)	3.1415 (PI)
=ACOS(0)	1.5707 (PI/2)

ACOSH( ) *(see also Function, COS, COSH, ASINH)*

Syntax

ACOSH(*number*)

Description

ACOSH is a function that returns the inverse hyperbolic cosine of the given number. The inverse hyperbolic cosine is a standard trigonometric function.

The information required for function ACOSH:

number is any number.

Examples

Formula	Returns
=ACOSH(1)	0
=ACOSH(2.509178)	1.5708
=ACOSH(11.59195)	3.1514

ACTIVATE

(*see* Macro Functions That Perform Actions)

ACTIVATE.NEXT

(*see* Macro Functions That Perform Actions)

ACTIVATE.PREV

(*see* Macro Functions That Perform Actions)

ACTIVE.CELL

(*see* Macro Functions—Value Returning)

ADD.ARROW

(*see* Macro Functions That Perform Chart Commands)

ADD.BAR (*see* Macro Functions—Customizing)

ADD.COMMAND

(*see* Macro Functions—Customizing)

ADD.MENU (*see* Macro Functions—Customizing)

ADD.OVERLAY

(*see* Macro Functions That Perform Chart Commands)

ADDRESS( )

(*see also* Function, ACTIVE.CELL, SELECTION, COLUMN, ROW, OFFSET)

Syntax

ADDRESS(*row_num,column_num,abs_num,a1,sheet_text*)

Description

ADDRESS is a function that returns a cell address in text form.
The information required for function ADDRESS:

row_num is the row number of the cell address returned by function ADDRESS.

column_num is the column number of the cell address returned by function ADDRESS.

abs_num is a number that specifies absolute or relative addressing for the column or row:

If abs_num Is	Reference the Row as	Reference the Column as
1	An absolute reference	An absolute reference
2	An absolute reference	A relative reference
3	A relative reference	An absolute reference
4	A relative reference	A relative reference

a1 is either TRUE or FALSE, or it can be omitted. If a1 is TRUE, then the cell address that ADDRESS returns is in A1-style reference. If a1 is FALSE, then the cell address that ADDRESS returns is in R1C1-style reference. If a1 is omitted, then the cell address that ADDRESS returns is in A1-style reference. For information on changing styles to A1-style or R1C1-style references, see the "Options—Workspace" listing.

sheet_text is the name in quotation marks of the worksheet or macro sheet that is used as an external reference. If sheet_text is omitted, no sheet name is used.

Examples

Formula	Returns
=ADDRESS(1,5,4)	E1
=ADDRESS(3,2)	$B$3
=ADDRESS(2,3,1,FALSE)	R2C3

ALERT (*see* Macro Functions—Customizing)

Alignment (see also Justify)

The Alignment feature aligns text horizontally at the left, center, or right boundaries or vertically at the top, center, or bottom boundaries. It rotates horizontal text 90 degrees in either direction, wraps text that is too wide for a single cell so that multiple lines are displayed in the cell, and fills a cell with repeating characters.

Keystrokes

For Buttons and Text Boxes

Keyboard	Mouse
Select button or text box to align.	Select button or text box to align.
Forma**t**	Forma**t**
Text	**T**ext or use Toolbar Alignment buttons

Note: Automatic Size shrinks the button or text box to fit the text. To select a button with a macro attached to it, hold down Ctrl while clicking on the button.

Tip: Change the alignment of multiple buttons and text boxes at one time by using the selection tool in the Toolbar or by holding down Shift while clicking on the desired objects.

For Cells

Keyboard	Mouse
Select cell to align.	Select cell to align.
Forma**t**	Forma**t**
Alignment	**A**lignment or use Toolbar Alignment buttons

334 ALIGNMENT

Alignment Option	*Effect on Cell*
Center	Text is displayed in middle of cell.
General	Text is left aligned, numbers are right aligned, logicals are centered.
Fill	Repeats text until cell is full.
Left	Text is displayed at left boundary of cell.
Right	Text is displayed at right boundary of cell.
Wrap Text	Displays text on multiple lines in a single cell.

Note: Only Center, Fill, Left, and Right are supported for export and import.

Caution: Wrap Text does not work with Fill. Alignment has no effect when Options, Display, Formulas is turned on.

For Charts

Keyboard	*Mouse*
Select text on chart.	Select text on chart.
Forma**t**	Forma**t**
Text	**T**ext or use Toolbar Alignment buttons

Note: Automatic Text returns attached text to the original default text that Excel created. Automatic Size shrinks the text area around the text to fit the text.

ALIGNMENT

(*see* Macro Functions That Perform Format Commands)

AND( ) *(see also* Function, OR, NOT)

Syntax

AND(*logical1,logical2,...*)

Description

AND is a function that returns TRUE if all the logical values that are given to AND are true. But if one or more of the logical values are FALSE, it returns FALSE. The information required for function AND:

logical1,logical2,... are the logical values TRUE or FALSE, or expressions that are TRUE or FALSE.

Values that are not logical are handled in various ways:

Type of Value	AND Returns
None of the logical1,logical2,... values is a logical value	#VALUE! (error message)
Cell address where the cell is empty or contains text	The same result as if there were no cells that contained nothing or text
An error message in a cell	The error message
0 in the list of values for the function	FALSE
Numerical values not equal to 0 in the list of values for the function	TRUE

Examples

Formula	Returns
=AND(FALSE,TRUE)	FALSE
=AND(TRUE,TRUE)	TRUE
=AND(TRUE,2+2=10)	FALSE
=AND("s"="s",2+2=4)	TRUE

Annuity Functions

Syntax

Annuity Function(rate, nper, pmt, pv, type)

Description

The annuity functions are the following worksheet functions: FV, IPMT, NPER, PMT, PPMT, PV, RATE. The annuity functions return information about an annuity, a series of constant cash payments that you make over a continuous period of time. These functions calculate information about annuities, such as loans and mortgages.

A short description of each annuity function follows. See individual listings of each function for more information. *FV* returns the future value of an investment. *IPMT* returns the interest payment for an investment period. *NPER* returns the number of payments for an investment. *PMT* returns the periodic total payment for an investment. *PPMT* returns the payment on an investment for a defined period. *PV* returns the present value of an investment. *RATE* returns the interest rate of an investment on a per period basis.

Functions PV, FV, and some of the other annuity functions use the following formulas:

If rate is not 0: $pv * (1 + rate)^{nper} + pmt(1 + rate * type) * (((1+rate)^{nper} - 1)/rate) + fv = 0$

If rate equals 0: $(pv + pmt) * (nper + fv) = 0$

Use the same unit of measure for specifying rate and nper. For example, if your payments on a loan are monthly, then rate should be the interest in one month (for example, the annual interest rate divided by 12) and nper should be the number of months in the loan or 12 times the number of years for the loan. If the payments are yearly, then rate is the annual interest rate and nper is the number of years in the loan.

If you have monthly payments on a three-year loan with an interest of 10%, use 10%/12 for rate and 3 * 12 for nper. If the loan has yearly payments rather than monthly, then for this three-year loan, nper is equal to 3 and rate is 10%, the annual interest rate of the loan.

In annuity functions, a negative number represents cash that you pay out and a positive number represents cash that you receive. For example, $500 that you paid to the bank would be –500 on your records, but +500 on the bank's records.

The information required for the annuity functions (all of the following values are numbers):

rate is the interest rate per period. For example, if you have monthly payments on a loan with a 14% interest rate per year, then 14%/12 per month is the interest rate you use in the annuity function.

per is a number in the range of 1 to nper. *per* is the specific period for which you are requesting interest.

nper is the total number of payment periods in an annuity.

pmt is the payment made each period and does not change over the life of the annuity. (Usually pmt includes principal and interest but no other fees or taxes.)

pv is the present value or total lump-sum amount that a series of future payments is worth now, in the present.

fv is the future value or cash balance that you want to achieve after the last payment is made. If fv is not included, the function assumes that fv is 0. (For example, a loan has a future value of 0.)

type is 0 or 1, indicating when payments are due, as shown below.

If type Is	Payments Are Due
0 or not included	At the end of the period
1	At the beginning of the period

Examples *(see individual listings for each function)*

Suppose that you are looking into buying an annuity that costs $57,000 and pays $600 at the beginning of every month for 10 years. The money paid out of the annuity has an annual rate of 8.25%. (This rate reflects inflation and other factors that decrease the value of the dollar in the future. This rate allows adjustment for the fact that one dollar will buy less in the future than it does today.) In this example, we have the current cost and all the information needed for the present value function, PV. After calculating the present value, we can compare the present value with the present cost of the annuity.

Putting the rate and nper in the same units as the monthly payments, we have a monthly rate of 8.25%/12 and 12 * 10 monthly periods in the 10-year annuity. The formula for this annuity, =PV(8.25%/12,12*10,600,0,1), returns −57,464.10. The amount returned is negative because this is the amount that you would have to pay now in order to receive the future benefits of the annuity. The annuity is a good investment since it costs only $57,000. $57,000 is $464.10 less than its present value or current worth of $57,464.10.

APP.ACTIVATE

(*see* Macro Functions That Perform Actions)

APP.MAXIMIZE

(*see* Macro Functions That Perform Control Commands)

APP.MINIMIZE

(*see* Macro Functions That Perform Control Commands)

APP.MOVE

(*see* Macro Functions That Perform Control Commands)

APP.RESTORE

(*see* Macro Functions That Perform Control Commands)

APP.SIZE

(*see* Macro Functions That Perform Control Commands)

APPLY.NAMES

(*see* Macro Functions That Perform Formula Commands)

APPLY.STYLE

(*see* Macro Functions That Perform Format Commands)

AREAS( )

(*see also* Function, ADDRESS, COLUMN, ROW, COLUMNS, ROWS, CELL, INDEX)

Syntax

AREAS(*reference*)

Description

AREAS is a function that returns the number of areas in reference. One area is a group of contiguous cells: for example, a column, C1:C5; a row, A3:F3; a group of cells, A3:F5; or a single cell. AREAS( ) counts each group of cells and returns the number of groups.

The information required for function AREAS:

reference is a set of cell addresses and/or a range of cell addresses.

 Note: If you have more than one area, remember to enclose the areas in a second set of parentheses inside the parentheses for the function.

Examples

Formula	Returns
=AREAS(B2)	1
=AREAS(D2:D5,A2)	2
=AREAS(C2:D3)	1
=AREAS(B1,C2:D9,D5)	3
=AREAS(G1:G4,W3:W6,E2:E3)	3

Advanced Example: You may want to limit the number of selected areas in a macro to one selected area. To do this, you can use SELECTION() to indicate the area(s) selected and use the following formula to check if there is more than one area selected. If there is more than one area selected, you can have nested inside your macro a macro called Selection_Error that processes the error (that is, prints out an error message and ends the macro). Sample formula: =IF(AREAS(SELECTION())>1,GOTO(Selection_Error)).

ARGUMENT (*see* Macro Functions—Control)

ARRANGE.ALL

(*see* Macro Functions That Perform Window Commands)

Array

An *array* is a type of value, an expression of information in a defined, precise form. An array can be a constant array, a value in a single cell, or several values in a range of cells.

Whenever you see a request for an array, you can use a single value or you can use a reference or name that spans a single cell or a range of cells. You can also use a formula that returns an array. If you use an array formula, make sure that you press Ctrl, Shift, and Enter whenever entering a formula that returns an array. (For information on what a reference is, see "References.")

A *constant array* is a list of values enclosed in curly braces where the values are separated by commas between values in the different columns and by semicolons between the list of values in different rows. When listing values in a constant array, begin listing them from the upper-left corner and the top row. After listing the values in the top row with commas between each value, type a semicolon; then list the values in the second row. Repeat this process for all other rows in the array. For example, an array whose top row contained 1, 2, 3 and whose second row contained 4, 5, 6 would be represented in a constant array as {1, 2, 3; 4, 5, 6}.

There are many types of arrays. A *text array*, such as {"First", "Second", "Third"}, contains text values. A *numeric array*, such as {0, 1, 2}, contains numbers. An array of no specific type, such as {"abc", TRUE, 45.1}, contains different types of values.

An array is one of six types of values: numbers, text, logical values, references, arrays, and error values. For more information about values in general and a summary of these other five types of values, see "Values."

Syntax

An array is a list of values either in a cell or cells, or in a constant array.

You can specify an array by naming a cell address, a range of cell addresses, or a constant array. The format of a constant array is a list of values enclosed in curly braces where the values are separated by commas between values in the different columns and by semicolons between the list of values in different rows: {value_R1C1,value_R1C2,...;value_R2C1,value_R2C2,...}.

Examples

A constant array: {"Sun",1;"Mon",2;"Tue",3;"Wed",4;"Thur",5;"Fri",6;"Sat",7}. An array in a range of cells: J5:L7. An array in a single cell: F4.

ASIN( ) *(see also* Function, ACOS, SIN, COS, PI*)*

Syntax

ASIN(*number*)

Description

ASIN is a function that returns in radians (–PI/2 to PI/2) the arcsine of the given number. The arcsine is the inverse of the sine. The arcsine of a number is the angle which has a sine that is the given number. For example, since the sine of PI/3 is .8660, the inverse sine or arcsine of .8660 is PI/3.

The information required for function ASIN:

number is a number between –1 and 1.

 Tip: To convert results to degrees, multiply by 180/PI( ).

Examples

Formula	Returns
=ASIN(1)	1.5707 (PI/2)
=ASIN(–1)	– 1.5707
=ASIN(0)	0

ASINH( )

(*see also* Function, COS, SINH, ACOSH, ASINH)

Syntax

ASINH(*number*)

Description

ASINH is a function that returns the inverse hyperbolic sine of the given number. The inverse hyperbolic sine is a standard trigonometric function.

The information required for function ASINH:

number is any number.

Examples

Formula	Returns
=ASINH(0)	0
=ASINH(2.301299)	1.5708
=ASINH(11.54874)	3.1415

ASSIGN.TO.OBJECT

(*see* Macro Functions That Perform Macro Commands)

ATAN( )

(*see also* **Function, ATAN2, ACOS, ASIN, TAN, PI, COS, SIN**)

Syntax

ATAN(*number*)

Description

ATAN is a function that returns in radians (–PI/2 to PI/2) the arctangent of the given number. The arctangent is the inverse of the tangent. The arctangent of a number is the angle which has a tangent that is the given number. For example, since the tangent of PI/3 is 1.732, the inverse tangent or arctangent of 1.732 is PI/3.

The information required for function ATAN:

number is a number between –1 and 1.

Tip: To convert the result to degrees, multiply by 180/PI( ).

Examples

Formula	*Returns*
=ATAN(1)	.7853 (PI/4)
=ATAN(–1)	– .7853 (–PI/4)
=ATAN(0)	0

ATAN2( )

(*see also* **Function, ATAN, ACOS, ASIN, TAN, PI, COS, SIN**)

Syntax

ATAN2(*x_num,y_num*)

Description

ATAN2 is a function that returns in radians (–PI/2 to PI/2) the arctangent or the angle that the specified x_num and y_num coordinates create with the origin and the x-axis. ATAN2 returns the arctangent by calculating the angle created by the x-axis and the line from the (x_num,y_num) point to the origin (0,0). For example, the angle created by the x-axis and the line through the point (0,0) and the point (2,3.464) has a tangent of 3.464/2 = 1.732. The inverse tangent or arctangent of 1.732 is PI/3. Hence, ATAN2(2,3.464) returns PI/3.

The information required for function ATAN2:

x_num and *y_num* can be a real number, cell address, formula, or function with a numerical value.

x_num is the x coordinate of the point.

y_num is the y coordinate of the point.

 Tip: To convert to degrees, multiply by 180/PI( ).

Examples

Formula	Returns
=ATAN2(1,1)	0.7853 (PI/4)
=ATAN2(1,–1)	–0.7853 (–PI/4)
=ATAN2(0,0)	#DIV/0! (error message)
=ATAN2(1,–1)	–2.356 (–3*PI/4)

ATANH( )

(*see also* Function, TANH, TAN, ACOSH, ASINH)

Syntax

ATANH(*number*)

Description

ATANH is a function that returns the inverse hyperbolic tangent of the given number. The inverse hyperbolic tangent is a standard trigonometric function.
The information required for function ATANH:

number is a number between, but not including, −1 and 1.

Examples

Formula	Returns
=ATANH(0)	0
=ATANH(0.91715)	1.5708
=ATANH(0.99627)	3.1415

ATTACH.TEXT

(*see* Macro Functions That Perform Chart Commands)

AVERAGE( )

(*see also* Function, SUM, COUNT, COUNTA, DAVERAGE, MEDIAN)

Syntax

AVERAGE(*number1,number2,...*)

Description

AVERAGE is a function that returns the average of the list of values given to the function (the average of number1,number2,...). In statistics this average is known as the arithmetic mean. The function AVERAGE adds all the numbers and divides by the number of numbers that are given to the function.

> **Note:** AVERAGE is useful for calculating an average of students' grades, average monthly profits, or any kind of average.

The information required for function AVERAGE:

number1,number2,... are numbers or cell address(es) that contain numbers. Each number or cell address must be separated from the others by a comma. The AVERAGE function takes up to 14 elements: number1,number2,...,number14.

> **Note:** Nonnumeric values, such as text and logic values, are sometimes converted to numeric values, sometimes ignored, and sometimes cause errors. If a value that was given to the function is not used in the calculations of the average, then it is completely left out of all parts of the calculations of the function AVERAGE.

A function, such as AVERAGE, that requires numeric values:

- Converts a value to a numeric value if the value is typed directly into the list of values for the function and is one of the following:

    a logical value

    a number that is in text form

- Does not convert a value to a numeric value if the value is a cell address in the list of values for the function, where the addressed cell:

    is empty

    contains text

    contains a logical value

- Returns an error if the list of values for the function contains a cell address and the addressed cell has an error value in it.
- Returns the #VALUES! error if there is text in the list of values for the function.

> **Note:** The numerical value 0 in a cell which is addressed in the list of values for the function AVERAGE is included in the calculations of average.

Tip: If you have turned off the display of zero values (in the Display dialog box under the Options menu), then you could be calculating an average with zero values that aren't visible in your worksheet. In order to avoid calculating an average based on invisible zero values, turn on the display of zero values for the areas where you use the AVERAGE function.

Examples

	Formula	*Cell(s) Contain*	*Formula Returns*
a)	=AVERAGE(5,7,9)		7
b)	=AVERAGE("4",–3,5)		2
c)	=AVERAGE(19,TRUE)		10
d)	=AVERAGE(19,FALSE)		9.5
e)	=AVERAGE(10,C4,"6")	FALSE	8
f)	=AVERAGE(C4:C7)	6, empty cell, 5, 4	5

Here is an example to help you become familiar with the automatic conversions that take place. If cells C3:C8 contained 10, 15, TRUE, "900", an empty cell, "letters", then the formula =AVERAGE(C3:C8,"5",9,TRUE) would return 8. In this example, "5" and TRUE are converted to numbers 5 and 1 respectively, since they are typed directly into the list of values for the function. 9 is also included since it is a number and needs no conversion. The values that are not directly typed into the list of values for the function are the values in the cell addresses C3:C8, that is, the logical value TRUE, the text numbers "900", and the text "letters". These are not included in the calculations of the average. Hence, 5, 9, 1, 10, and 15 are included in the average of these numbers: $(5 + 9 + 1 + 10 + 15)/5 = 40/5 = 8$.

Let's look at how an unusual error message can be returned. If cells C2:C4 contain 35,25,#NUM!, then the formula =AVERAGE(C2:C4) returns #NUM!.

AXES

(see **Macro Functions That Perform Chart Commands)**

B–C

BEEP (*see* Macro Functions That Perform Actions)

Border (*see also* Patterns)

The Border feature draws border lines around spreadsheet cells for improved visual appearance.

Keystrokes

Keyboard	Mouse
Select cells to add borders to.	Select cells to add borders to.
Format	Format
Border	Border

Border Option	Effect on Cell
Bottom	Draws border on the bottom of selected cells
Color	Sets color of border line
Left	Draws border on left side of selected cells
Outline	Draws border around selected cells
Right	Draws border on right side of selected cells
Style	Determines border line type and thickness
Shade	Applies default shading to currently selected group of cells
Top	Draws border on top of selected cells

Note: To modify borders around graphic objects, chart data markers, or chart text, use Forma**t** **P**atterns.

 Caution: If the border between two cells is specified differently by both cells, only one border will be displayed.

 Tip: Hide gridlines on the display by choosing **O**ptions, **D**isplay, and then **G**ridlines. Hide gridlines on printed output by choosing **F**ile, Page Se**t**up, and then **G**ridlines.

BORDER

(see Macro Functions That Perform Format Commands)

BREAK *(see Macro Functions—Control)*

BRING.TO.FRONT

(see Macro Functions That Perform Format Commands)

CALCULATE.DOCUMENT

(see Macro Functions That Perform Options Commands)

CALCULATE.NOW

(*see* Macro Functions That Perform Chart Commands)

CALCULATE.NOW

(*see* Macro Functions That Perform Options Commands)

CALCULATION

(*see* Macro Functions That Perform Options Commands)

CALL (*see* Macro Functions—Customizing)

CALLER (*see* Macro Functions—Value Returning)

CANCEL.COPY

(*see* Macro Functions That Perform Actions)

CANCEL.KEY

(*see* Macro Functions—Customizing)

CELL( ) *(see also* Function, GET.CELL*)*

Syntax

CELL(*info_type,reference*)

Description

CELL is a function that returns information about the contents, formatting, or location of the upper-left cell in *reference*.

CELL returns a code that represents the type of formatting that is used in a cell. This code is as follows:

If the Cell Format Is	*Then CELL Returns*
General	G
0	F0
#,##0	,0
0.00	F2
#,##0.00	,2
$#,##0_);($#,##0)	C0
$#,##0_);[RED]($#,##0)	C0–
$#,##0.00_);($#,##0.00)	C2
$#,##0.00_);[RED]($#,##0.00)	C2–
0%	P0
0.00%	P2
0.00E+00	S2
# ?/? or # ??/??	G
m/d/yy or m/d/yy h:mm	D4
d-mmm-yy	D1
d-mmm	D2
mmm-yy	D3
h:mm AM/PM	D7
h:mm:ss AM/PM	D6
h:mm	D9
h:mm:ss	D8

CELL () 353

 Note: The GET.CELL macro function provides a greater variety of options.

The information required for function CELL:

info_type is a text value that specifies what type of information you want to know about the cell specified by *reference*.

reference is a cell address, a single range of cell addresses, or a name that refers to either a cell address or a single range of cell addresses.

 Note: If *reference* is not included, then *reference* is assumed to be the cell where the cursor is.

 Note: If *reference* is a name that refers to more than one array, then CELL returns the error #VALUE!.

Options for info_type

If info_type Is	CELL Returns
"width"	The column width of the cell(s) (referred to by *reference*) rounded off to an integer. Each unit of column width is equal to the width of one character in the currently selected font.
"row"	The row number of the cell referred to by reference
"col"	The column number of the cell referred to by reference
"protect"	0 if the cell is not locked (or not protected); 1 if the cell is locked (or protected)
"address"	The text form of the cell address of the first cell in reference
"contents"	The contents of the upper-left cell in reference.
"format"	The text value that corresponds to the number formatting of the cell in reference. "–" appears at the end of the text value if the cell is formatted with color for negative values. "()" appears at the end of the text value if the cell is formatted with parentheses for positive or all values.

"prefix"	The text value that corresponds to the "label prefix" of the cell. See Table 1.
"color"	1 if the cell is formatted with color for negative values; 0 otherwise.
If info_type Is	**CELL Returns**
"filename"	In text format, the filename (including the entire path for the file) of the file in which reference is located. CELL("filename",ref) returns empty text (an empty cell) if the file has not yet been saved.
"parentheses"	1 if the cell is formatted for parentheses for positive or all values; 0 otherwise
"type"	The text value that corresponds to the type of value in the cell as indicated in Table 2.

Table 1   Text values corresponding to the cell alignment.

Using the info_type of "prefix", CELL Returns	To Indicate That the Cell Contains
A single quotation mark (')	Left-aligned text
A double quotation mark (")	Right-aligned text
A caret (^)	Centered text
A backslash (\)	Fill-aligned text
Empty text (nothing)	Anything other than the above

Table 2   Text values corresponding to the type of text in the cell.

Using the info_type of "type", Cell Returns	To Indicate That the Cell
"b" for blank	Is empty
"l" for label	Contains a text constant
"v" for value	Contains anything other than the above

Examples

If cell C4 contains "Monthly Budget", then the formula =CELL("contents",C4:F6) returns "Monthly Budget".

If cell B5 contains $59,042.70, then the formula =CELL("format",B5) returns C2 (assuming that you have not formatted cell B5 for color).

CELL.PROTECTION

(*see* Macro Functions That Perform Format Commands)

CHANGE.LINK

(*see* Macro Functions That Perform File Commands)

CHAR() (*see also* CODE)

Syntax

CHAR(*number*)

Description

CHAR is a function that returns the character in the character set for your computer that corresponds to the number you gave the function. Different operating environments can have different character sets. The Macintosh has its own character set, as does the OS/2 operating system and the windows environment on the DOS operating system (which uses ANSI code). The character or symbol that is returned for a particular number is based on the computer environment in which you are working.

The information required for function CHAR:

number is a number between 1 and 255.

Examples

Formula	Returns
=CHAR(77)	M
=CHAR(60)	<

The table of numeric codes and their corresponding characters (shown in the figure) could be used to encode or decode a special, private message. Instead of writing alphabetic letters and punctuation, use the numerical equivalent. When reading a message, look up the numeric values and write down their character equivalent. For decoding a message, you can use an Excel spreadsheet to translate the message into characters.

Chart Add Arrow

(see also Chart Attach Text, Chart Add Legend)

The Chart Add Arrow command adds an arrow to your chart that you can resize and reposition to make something clearer, for instance, to link a text box with some object.

Keystrokes

Keyboard	*Mouse*
Chart	Chart
Add Arrow	Add Arrow

Example

Suppose that you previously used the Overlay Value (Y)Axis option in Attach Text to add to the chart a text box referring to an overlay line. Choose Add Arrow and reposition the arrow so that it points from the box to the actual overlay line in question. This adds emphasis and clarity to your chart.

 Adding an Arrow to a Chart

1. Choose Add Arrow from Chart. — Excel adds an arrow to the chart. It is always the same length and always in the same position. The arrow remains selected.

2. Click and hold on the arrowhead end of the arrow and move it to the object you want to point to by dragging it with the mouse pointer.

3. Click and hold on the other end of the arrow and drag it where you need it. — If done properly, adding arrows can greatly enhance your charts.

Chart Add Legend

Use the Chart Add Legend command to provide identifying labels in a chart box that distinguish your data series by the use of different colors and/or patterns. Any chart with a lot of data series and markers will benefit from an explanatory legend box.

Keystrokes

Keyboard	*Mouse*
Chart	Chart
Add Legend	Add Legend

Adding a Legend to a Chart

1. Make the chart the active chart.

2. Choose Add Legend from Chart.   The legend box appears to the right of the chart, still selected.

3. Drag the legend where you want it.

 Note: After you add a legend to a chart, the command in Chart changes to Delete Legend. Choose this to get rid of the legend if you need to in the future.

Chart Add Overlay

The Chart Add Overlay command creates a combination chart. Use it, rather than the Combination command in Gallery, when you have formatting in the chart that you want to keep.

Keystrokes

Keyboard   *Mouse*

Chart   Chart

Add Overlay   Add Overlay

Example

Suppose that you had a chart showing many different series and you had given each series a color and a pattern to distinguish it. Then you decided that a Combination type chart would make things clearer. Rather than lose your formatting, you could choose Add Overlay from Chart instead of Combination from Gallery to create the new chart.

Adding an Overlay

1. Make the chart the active chart.   Your chart is not a Combination-type chart.

2. Choose Add Overlay from Chart.   Excel changes the chart into a combination chart.

Chart Attach Text

(*see also* Chart Add Arrow, Chart Add Legend)

The Chart Attach Text command creates text boxes on your chart. It places them in certain locations or attaches them to certain objects depending on what you specify in the dialog box.

Keystrokes

Keyboard

Chart

Attach Text

Chart Title, Value (Y)Axis, Category (X)Axis, Series and Data Point, Overlay Value (Y)Axis, or Overlay Category (X)Axis

Series Number and Point Number if Series and Data Point chosen

Enter

Mouse

Chart

Attach Text

Chart Title, Value (Y)Axis, Category (X)Axis, Series and Data Point, Overlay Value (Y)Axis, or Overlay Category (X)Axis

Series Number and Point Number if Series and Data Point chosen

OK

Example

Suppose that a chart you've created looks good, but you feel that some explanatory text needs to be added. Choose Attach Text from Chart and choose the Chart Title option and OK. A selected text box appears at the top of the screen. Type `Rainfall Progression`, for example, and that becomes the title of your chart. Now choose Attach Text from Chart again, and this time choose Series and Data Point. Type **1** in the Series Number box and **1** in the Point Number box and choose OK. On the screen the first data marker in the first series gets a text box displaying the value of the first data point in the first series: "10" here.

360 Chart Axes

 Attaching Text to a Chart

1. Make the chart that you want to attach text to the active chart.

2. Choose Attach Text from Chart.   Excel displays the Attach Text dialog box. Six options are displayed; some (like the overlay options) may not be available if they are not relevant.

3. Choose only one of the available options.   If you want to choose another option you can go back into the dialog box.

4. Choose OK.   Excel draws a text box on the chart.

> **Tip:** Use text boxes like these in conjunction with other additional objects on a chart for best effect. For example, use an arrow to explain what a text box refers to.

Chart Axes

The Chart Axes command removes or adds the x-, y- or z- (in 3-D charts) axes in your charts. This option is not available with Pie charts, either basic or 3-D, since Pie charts have no axes.

Use this option when your chart screen has too much clutter and the actual values or titles on the x-, y-, or z-axis are not as important. The trends in a Line chart can often be very obvious without needing a Value (Y) Axis, for example, if you have a legend or other explanatory material.

Keystrokes

Keyboard	*Mouse*
Chart	Chart
Axes	Axes
Category (X) Axis and/or Value (Y) Axis or in 3-D Category (X) Axis and/or Series (Y) Axis and/or Value (Z) Axis	Category (X) Axis and/or Value (Y) Axis or in 3-D Category (X) Axis and/or Series (Y) Axis and/or Value (Z) Axis
Enter	OK

Removing or Adding Axes Lines

1. Make the chart that you want to change the active chart.

2. Choose A<u>x</u>es from the <u>C</u>hart menu.
   Excel displays the Axes dialog box. By default all the boxes representing the two or three axes are checked, meaning that the axes are displayed.

3. Choose any option.
   If an option is checked, choosing it unchecks it and vice versa. Unchecked axes aren't displayed in the chart.

4. Press Enter or choose OK.

Chart Edit Series

Each chart divides its data into series within categories. You can use the <u>C</u>hart Edit <u>S</u>eries command to change the arguments in a series as an alternative to directly changing the series in the formula bar.

Use Edit Series to either create or edit a series. If you want to create a series, choose New Series in the Series box. If, after you have created or edited a series, you want to remain in the dialog box to work on another series, choose Define and then pick another series to work on.

Keystrokes

Keyboard	*Mouse*
<u>C</u>hart	<u>C</u>hart
Edit <u>S</u>eries	Edit <u>S</u>eries
S<u>e</u>ries	S<u>e</u>ries
<u>N</u>ame	<u>N</u>ame
<u>X</u> Labels	<u>X</u> Labels
<u>Y</u> Labels	<u>Y</u> Labels
<u>P</u>lot Order	<u>P</u>lot Order
<u>D</u>efine	<u>D</u>efine
D<u>e</u>lete	D<u>e</u>lete
Enter	OK

362 Chart Edit Series

Example

Suppose that you want to change the order of a series from 9 to 5. Choose Edit Series from Chart. Pick the series in the Series scroll box and its arguments appear in the other boxes: Name, X Labels, Y Values, and Plot Order. Choose Plot Order and enter 5 and then choose OK.

Editing a Data Series

1. Choose Edit Series from Chart. — Excel displays the Edit Series dialog box.

2. Choose your series in the Series box. — The Name, X Labels, Y Values, and Plot Order boxes display the information for this chart.

3. Change the relevant argument in any or all of the boxes. — The first three arguments can either be names in text or absolute references to a worksheet.

4. Choose Define to register your changes and remain in the dialog box to work on another series.

5. Choose Delete to delete the selected series.

6. Choose OK.

 Tip: You can leave the X Labels box empty after the first series in each category because Excel uses that series only to determine X Label names.

 Note: You can edit a series directly in the formula bar after selecting it on the chart.

Chart Gridlines

The Chart Gridlines command removes or adds gridlines to your chart. These can be major gridlines drawn from tick marks or data series labels, or minor gridlines drawn at intervals between the major gridlines.

Excel doesn't use major or minor gridlines with most chart types and subtypes. For the most part, they tend to clutter the screen. Line and Scatter charts are types of charts that can profitably use them to pinpoint some value or compare values.

Keystrokes

Keyboard

Chart

Gridlines

Major and/or Minor (for Category (X) Axis) and/or Major and/or Minor (for Value (Y) Axis

Enter

Mouse

Chart

Gridlines

Major and/or Minor (for Category (X) Axis) and/or Major and/or Minor (for Value (Y) Axis

OK

Example

The figure shows a Combination-type chart with major gridlines on the y-axis.

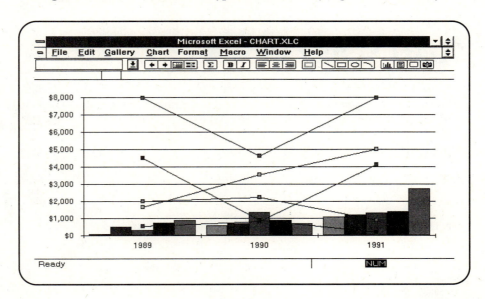

Inserting or Removing Gridlines

1. Make the chart the active chart.
2. Choose Gridlines from Chart.   Excel displays the Gridlines dialog box.
3. Check an option to add it to the chart; uncheck to remove it.
4. Choose OK.

Chart Select Chart

.The Chart Select Chart command selects everything in the chart window. Use it as an alternative to selecting the chart using the mouse or the keyboard.

Keystrokes

Keyboard	Mouse
Chart	Chart
Select Chart	Select Chart

Chart Select Plot Area

The Chart Select Plot Area command selects the area in which Excel plots data, including axes, markers, and series. Use this command as an alternative to selecting the plot area using the mouse or the keyboard.

Keystrokes

Keyboard	Mouse
Chart	Chart
Select Plot Area	Select Plot Area

CHECK.COMMAND

(*see* Macro Functions—Customizing)

CHOOSE( ) (*see also* Function, INDEX)

Syntax

CHOOSE(*index_num,value1,value2,...*)

Description

CHOOSE is a function that returns one of several values given to it. Index_num, the first value you give the function, specifies the position of the value that CHOOSE returns. If index_num is 3, the third value following index_num is returned. If index_num is 1, the value immediately following index_num is returned.

Note: You can use CHOOSE to return a range of cell addresses only if CHOOSE is within another function that uses the value that it returns.

The information required for function CHOOSE:

index_num is the index that CHOOSE uses to choose one value out of the list of values that you give it.

value1,value2,... is a list of values. Each value can be a number, text, logical value, cell reference, defined name, formula, or macro.

Note: If you are using CHOOSE in a macro, then value1,value2,... can be action-taking functions such as another macro or a formula.

Note: If index_num is an array, every value is returned. If index_num is an array and some of the values are action-taking values, then all the actions are performed.

Examples

If cell E1 contains "Total", then =CHOOSE(2,A1,E1,B2,5) returns "Total".

If cells G3 to H4 contain 1,2,3, and 4, then =SUM(CHOOSE (3,A1:C4,E1:F2,G3:H4)) returns 10. The CHOOSE function is evaluated first and returns G3:H4. Next, the formula =SUM(G3:H4) is evaluated to produce the answer 10.

Similarly, if cells G3 to H4 contain 1,2,3, and 4, then =SUM(G3:CHOOSE (3,A1,E1,H4)) returns 10. The CHOOSE function is evaluated first and returns H4. Next, the formula =SUM(G3:H4) is evaluated to produce the answer 10.

Formula	*Returns*
=CHOOSE(1,"First Place","Second Place","Third Place")	"First Place"
=CHOOSE(4,TRUE,"Fun","is",2,"guess")	2
=CHOOSE(2,A1,B2:C2,D1)	#VALUE!

CLEAN() *(see also CHAR, TRIM)*

Syntax

CLEAN(*text*)

Description

CLEAN is a function that returns text with nonprintable characters removed.

Tip: CLEAN is useful for converting text that was imported from another application. Another application may be able to print or use characters that Excel does not. For example, data files may contain some special codes at the beginning or end that contain information for the operating system of the computer. These codes may not be printable.

The information required for function CLEAN:

text is any single symbol or group of symbols.

Example

CHAR(5) is unprintable. Therefore, =CLEAN("ABC"&CHAR(5)) returns "ABC".

CLEAR

(*see* Macro Functions That Perform Edit Commands)

CLOSE

(*see* Macro Functions That Perform Control Commands)

CLOSE.ALL

(*see* Macro Functions That Perform File Commands)

CODE() (*see also* CHAR)

Syntax

CODE(*text*)

Description

CODE is a function that returns the numeric code for the first letter (or symbol) of the text string or character that you gave the function. In the character set for your computer, this numeric code is a numeric representation of the first character of the text you gave the function.

Different operating environments can have different character sets. The Macintosh has its own character set, as does the OS/2 operating system and the windows environment on a DOS operating system (which uses ANSI code). The number that is returned for a particular text letter is based on the computer environment in which you are working.

The information required for function CODE:

text is any single symbol or group of symbols.

Examples

Formula	*Cell Contains*	*Returns*
=CODE("A")		65
=CODE(D3)	Aluminum	65
=CODE(B2)	] (a result from =CHAR(93) function)	93

	A	B	C	D
1		FUNCTION CODE		
2	Letters or text		Has a Coresponding	
3	begining with a		Code Ranging from:	
4	character from:			
5		1 to 9	49 to	57
6		:;<=>?@	58 to	64
7		A to Z	65 to	90
8		[\]^_	91 to	96
9		a to z	97 to	122

The table of characters and their corresponding codes shown in the figure could be used to encrypt a private note that you don't want others to read accidentally. Instead of writing alphabetic letters and punctuation, use the numerical equivalent.

COLOR.PALETTE

(*see* Macro Functions That Perform Options Commands)

COLUMN() *(see also* Function, COLUMNS, ROW)

Syntax

COLUMN(*reference*)

Description

COLUMN is a function that returns the column number of the cell or cells addressed by *reference*.

The information required for function COLUMN:

reference is a cell address, range of cell addresses, or name that specifies either of these. If *reference* is omitted, it is assumed to be the column where the COLUMN function is entered. If *reference* is an array that spans several columns, then COLUMN returns a horizontal array of these column numbers.

 Note: *Reference* cannot be several groups of cell addresses.

Examples

Suppose that the name checkbook referred to the array J7:L78. Then the formula =COLUMN(checkbook) would return {9,10,11}, where 9, 10 and 11 are the column numbers for J, K, and L.

Formula	*Returns*
=COLUMN(D9)	4
=COLUMN(B1:E3)	{2,3,4,5}
=COLUMN(C6:G29)	{3,4,5,6,7}

COLUMN.WIDTH

(see **Macro Functions That Perform Format Commands***)*

COLUMNS()

(*see also* Function, COLUMN, ROWS)

Syntax

COLUMNS(*array*)

Description

COLUMNS is a function that returns the number of columns in the array of cells addressed by *array*.

The information required for function COLUMNS:

array is an array, an array formula, a cell address, a range of cell addresses, or a name that specifies one of these.

Examples

Suppose that the name checkbook referred to the array J7:L78. Then the formula =COLUMNS(checkbook) would return 3 since there are three columns, columns J, K, and L, in the array J7:L78.

Formula	Returns
=COLUMNS(D9)	1
=COLUMNS({6,0;1,9;8,3})	2
=COLUMNS(C6:G29)	5

COMBINATION

(*see* Macro Functions That Perform Gallery Commands)

CONSOLIDATE

(*see* Macro Functions That Perform Data Commands)

Constant Value

A *constant value* is any nonchanging date, numeric value, text, or time entered into a cell.

Note: If the date, numeric value, or time constant is not displayed properly after it is entered, use the Format Number command and select the desired format. If the text constant is not displayed properly after it is entered, use the Format Alignment command and select the desired alignment.

Tip: A date and time can be entered in a single cell if they are separated by one or more spaces. Excel will then separate them by two spaces. The date or the time may come first.

COPY

(*see* Macro Functions That Perform Edit Commands)

COPY.CHART

(*see* Macro Functions That Perform Edit Commands)

COPY.PICTURE

(*see* Macro Functions That Perform Edit Commands)

COS()

(*see also* **Function, SIN, TAN, ACOS, ACOSH, COSH, PI**)

Syntax

COS(*number*)

Description

COS is a function that returns the cosine of the given number, which represents the radian measure of an angle. Cosine is a standard trigonometric function based on the one-unit circle, $x^2 + y^2 = 1$. An angle with one side on the x-axis has a second side that intercepts a point (x,y) on the unit circle. The cosine of this angle is the x value of the (x,y) point on the unit circle.

The information required for function COS:

number is a number that represents an angle in radian units.

 Tip: Use the PI() function to convert from degrees to radians by multiplying by PI()/180. (30 degrees * PI()/180 = 0.5235 radians)

Examples

Formula	Returns
=COS(PI()/2)	0
=COS(PI())	1
=COS(0.5235)	0.8660

COSH()

(*see also* **Function, COS, SINH, ACOSH, ASINH, PI**)

Syntax

COSH(*number*)

Description

COSH is a function that returns the hyperbolic cosine of the given number. The hyperbolic cosine is a standard trigonometric function based on the unit hyperbola, $x^2 - y^2 = 1$, rather than the one-unit circle, $x^2 + y^2 = 1$. The formula for the hyperbolic cosine is

$$\text{COSH}(X) = \frac{e^X + e^{-X}}{2}$$

The information required for function COSH:

number is any number.

Examples

Formula	Returns
=COSH(0)	1
=COSH(PI( )/2)	2.5092
=COSH(PI( ))	11.5920

COUNT()

(*see also* Function, COUNTA, SUM, AVERAGE, DCOUNT, DCOUNTA)

Syntax

COUNT(*value1,value2,...*)

Description

COUNT is a function that returns the count of how many numeric values are in the list of value1,value2,....

Only the values that are numbers or that can be converted to numeric values are counted by the function COUNT. For an evaluation of whether a value can be converted to a numeric value, see the guidelines later in this section.

374   COUNT( )

The information required for function COUNT:

value1,value2,... where the values can be any type of data, but only numerical values are counted.

Tip: The numerical value 0 is a number and, therefore, is included when the function COUNT counts how many numbers there are. So, if you have turned off the display of zero values (in the Display dialog box under the Options menu), then you could be counting a zero value that you don't see in your display of the worksheet. In order to avoid the possible confusion associated with counting numerical values that are invisible with the current options, turn on the display of zero values for the areas where you use the COUNT function.

Note: Like other functions that use many items of information, COUNT is limited to accepting a maximum of 14 values: value1,value2,...,value14.

Here are the guidelines that COUNT uses for counting a value as a numeric value. A value is:

- Counted as a numeric value if it is typed directly into the list of values for the function and is one of the following:

    a logical value

    a number that is in text form

- Not counted as a numeric value if it is a cell address in the list of values for the function, where the addressed cell:

    is empty

    contains text

    contains a logical value

- Ignored, and an error value is returned by the function if:

    Text is in the list of values for the function.

    An error value is in a cell whose address is in the list of values for the function.

Examples

If you had graded a test and wanted to know how many students took the test, COUNT would be useful. For example, if cells B2 through B7 contained the test grades 99, 98, "withdrew", 95, 92, 100, 966, then the formula =COUNT(B2:B7) would return 5, because only five students actually took the test.

Here's an example to help you become familiar with the automatic conversions that take place. If cells C3 through C7 contain: 5, TRUE, "900", "ABC", 04/24/91, then the formula =COUNT(C3:C7,"2",9,FALSE) returns 6. In this example, the values that are typed directly into the list of values for the function are "2", 9, and FALSE. These three are counted as numeric values. The values that are in cell addresses and are counted as numeric values are 7, 12, 04/24/91. The other three values that reside in cell addresses, TRUE, "900", "ABC", have no effect on the result returned since they are not numbers and they are not typed directly into the list of values for the function. Hence, there is a total of six numeric values.

	Formula	Cell(s) Contain	Formula Returns
a)	=COUNT(–1,9,"2")		3
b)	=COUNT(19,FALSE)		2
c)	=COUNT(19,D2)	FALSE	1
d)	=COUNT(C4:C6)	6, empty cell, 2	2
e)	=COUNT(C2:C3)	09/02/91, 14.52	2

COUNTA()

(*see also* Function, COUNT, SUM, AVERAGE, DCOUNT, DCOUNTA)

Syntax

COUNTA(*value1,value2,...*)

Description

COUNTA is a function that returns the count of how many nonblank values are in the listings of values given to the function by you, the user.

The information required for function COUNTA:

value1,value2,... where the values can be any type of data, but only the nonblank values are counted.

Note: Like other functions that use many items of information, COUNTA is limited to accepting a maximum of 14 values: value1,value2,...,value14.

Note: Blank spaces, the numerical value 0, or an error message in a cell counts as a nonblank value. Any cell with this type of data is included in the count of nonblank values that COUNTA returns.

Examples

Formula	*Cell(s) Contain*	*Formula Returns*
=COUNTA(C4:C8)	"PLANTS","MULCH", "SPRINKLER","FERTILIZER", empty	4
=COUNTA(1,C1:C5, "SOMETHING")	2,#NUM!,"4",–8,FALSE	7

CREATE.NAMES

(*see* Macro Functions That Perform Formula Commands)

CREATE.OBJECT

(*see* Macro Functions That Perform Actions)

CUSTOM.REPEAT

(*see* Macro Functions—Customizing)

CUSTOM.UNDO

(*see* Macro Functions—Customizing)

CUT (*see* Macro Functions That Perform Edit Commands)

Data Consolidate

The Data Consolidate command uses 11 different functions, like SUM and AVERAGE, to combine data from different ranges of cells into one range. The cell ranges can be in different worksheets and the consolidation can be linked.

Keystrokes

Keyboard	*Mouse*
Data	Data
Consolidate	Consolidate
Alt+Function	Click on desired function in Function box.
Use up or down arrow key to select desired function.	
Top Row	Top Row
Left Column	Left Column
Reference	Reference
Add	Add
Create Links to Source Data	Create Links to Source Data

Example

Suppose that you have sales figures for the last six months of the previous two years entered in a worksheet, in cell ranges J23:J28 and M23:M28. You want to find out the top figure for each month over the two years. Select a range of cells to receive the data: O23:O28. Choose Consolidate from Data. Choose the MAX function. Enter the two cell ranges: in columns J and M. Choose OK. On the worksheet, Excel has consolidated the two columns of data into one, showing the greater of the month sales figures.

Consolidating Data

1. Select the range of cells to consolidate to.	The cells are highlighted.
2. Choose Co<u>n</u>solidate from <u>D</u>ata.	Excel displays the Consolidate dialog box.
3. Choose the function to use.	The function is highlighted.
4. Choose whether to take column (<u>T</u>op Row) and/or row (<u>L</u>eft Column) headings.	
5. Enter the first reference to consolidate from.	You can use the point method of selecting cells if you want.
6. Choose <u>A</u>dd to add this reference to the All References box.	The All References box lists this reference.
7. Add other references to consolidate from.	All References list this reference.
8. Choose OK.	

Data Delete

(*see also* **Data Form, Data Sort, Data Set Database, Data Set Criteria**)

The <u>D</u>ata <u>D</u>elete command deletes those records that match the criteria range. To use the Delete command, both the database and criteria ranges must already be defined. (See "Data Set Criteria" for information on setting criteria.)

Keystrokes

Keyboard	*Mouse*
<u>D</u>ata	<u>D</u>ata
<u>D</u>elete	<u>D</u>elete
Enter	OK

Example

Suppose you have a customer database and want to delete all records for customers located in Texas. Set the criteria to Texas for the State field. Choose Delete from Data. Choose OK for the warning message, and all records that meet the criterion are deleted permanently.

 Deleting Records in a Database

1. Enter the field value under the field Name in the criteria range.

2. Choose Delete from Data.   Excel displays a warning message saying: Matching records will be deleted permanently.

3. Press Enter or choose OK.   All records that meet the criteria are deleted.

 Note: You can't undo your delete through Undo in the Edit menu. Delete in the Form dialog box can be a safer option when deleting just one or a few records.

Data Extract

(*see also* Data Set Criteria, Data Set Extract)

The Data Extract command finds records in a database and then copies them to a specified area on the worksheet. The database and criteria must already be set up and defined. Optionally, you may set up and define an extract range.

Keystrokes

Keyboard	*Mouse*
Data	Data
Extract	Extract

The records that meet the criteria are copied to an area on the worksheet that you have selected (using the exact database field names) or that you previously defined with Set Extract.

Extracting Records

1. Enter a field value under the appropriate fieldname in the records. criteria range.

    The criteria range is now set up to extract only the appropriate

2. Select the cell(s) containing the fieldname(s) to indicate to Excel where the extracted data is to go.

    The cells are highlighted on the worksheet.

3. Choose Extract from Data.

    The records that meet the criteria are copied to the worksheet below the selected cell.

 Note: The steps shown here do not use an extract range.

Data Find

(*see also* **Data Set Database, Data Set Criteria**)

The Data Find command searches for and finds records when the database and criteria ranges are set up and defined. (See "Data Set Criteria" for information on setting criteria.) When a record exists that matches the criteria, the record is highlighted.

Keystrokes

Keyboard   *Mouse*

Data   Data

Find   Find

The search starts from the active record if the active cell is actually in the database. If the active cell is not in the database, the search starts at the first record. When a record is found, use the down and up arrow keys to find the next record or previous record in the database that matches the criteria. Press Alt-D and Alt-F to exit Find from the keyboard. Click outside the database on the worksheet to exit Find using the mouse.

Finding a Record, Searching for Another, and Exiting Find

1. Select a cell outside the database.	Find will then start at the beginning of the database.
2. Choose Find from Data.	Excel displays the top line of the database as the top line on the screen. If Find finds a record to match the criteria, it highlights the record.
3. Press the down arrow key to find the next record that matches the criteria.	Find highlights the next record down that matches the criteria.
4. Exit Find by choosing Exit Find from Data or clicking outside the database.	The worksheet is displayed as normal.

> **Tip:** If Find doesn't work, make sure your database and criteria ranges are set up properly.

Data Form

(see also **Data Find, Data Extract, Data Delete, Data Set Database, Data Set Criteria, Data Set Extract, Data Sort)**

Using the Data Form command, you can find records in a database and move between them, use your own criteria to select only certain records, and add, delete, and alter records. You must have a database defined before you can use Form.

Keystrokes

Keyboard	*Mouse*
Data	Data
Form	Form
New	New

384 Data Form

Keyboard	Mouse
Delete	Delete
Restore	Restore
Previous	Find Prev
Next	Find Next
Criteria	Criteria
Close	Close

Example

Suppose that you have a database set up with five fields: Name, Address, $ per hour, Hours, and Salary (which is the sum of $ per hour and hours). You want to add a new record. Bring up the Form dialog box and choose the New button (the figure shows the dialog box at this stage), fill in the fields: for example, Jennifer, Fairfield, 25, and 10 (the database automatically calculates the salary). Choose Close and the record is added to the database.

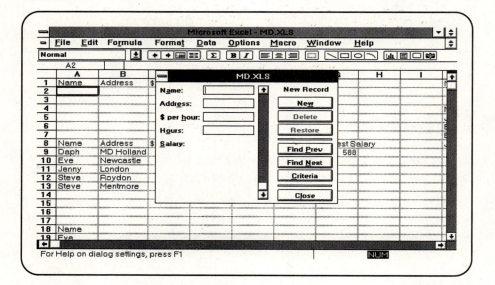

Adding a New Record to a Database Using Form

1. Choose Fo**r**m from the **D**ata menu. — The Form dialog box appears on screen.
2. Choose **N**ew. — The field values beside the field names go blank, as shown in the figure.
3. Enter the field values for the new record in the individual boxes. — Each field value is displayed beside its field name.
4. Choose **C**lose to add the new record and exit the dialog box. — The new record is displayed in the database on the worksheet.

 Note: Form is an alternative to working on the database directly in the worksheet. Beginners usually find it easier to use.

Data Parse

Sometimes when you import data into Excel, particularly from database files, the data may all go into a single column. Use the **D**ata **P**arse command to spread the data between different columns.

Keystrokes

Keyboard	*Mouse*
Data	**D**ata
Parse	**P**arse
Guess	**G**uess
Enter	OK

Example

Suppose that you imported a database report file from dBASE with headings and column data neatly arranged. On importation, all the data went into many rows but in the same column. You want to put each heading and its corresponding value in separate columns. Select all the data and choose Parse from Data. Choose Guess and Excel places square brackets where it thinks the data should be divided between cells (it takes the first row as a model). Add or delete brackets if you want; in this example you should have brackets around each heading title. Choose OK.

 Parsing a Column

1. Select all the cells with data in the column to parse.
   The data must all be in one column.

2. Choose Parse from Data.
   Excel displays the Parse dialog box with the first row of the column in the Parse Line box.

3. Choose Guess to let Excel enter the proposed dividing brackets to separate among cells.
   Excel enters square brackets.

4. Add or delete brackets if you want.
   Anything enclosed in brackets is put in a separate cell.

5. Choose Clear to start again.
   Excel removes the brackets.

6. Press Enter or choose OK to parse.

Data Series

Use the Data Series command when you want to enter dates and numbers that increment or decrease in a constant way in cells that are beside one another.

Keystrokes

Keyboard

Data

Series

Mouse

Data

Series

Data Series

Keyboard	*Mouse*
Row or Columns	Rows or Columns
Linear, Growth, or Date	Linear, Growth, or Date
If Date, Day, Weekday, Month, or Year	If Date, Day, Weekday, Month, or Year
Step Value	Step Value
Enter a number	Enter a number
Stop Value	Stop Value
Enter a number	Enter a number
Enter	OK

Example

Suppose that you want to enter a series of headings in a column for each of the 10 years of the 1980's, starting at December 1980. Enter **Dec-80** in the first cell; then select it and the following nine cells. Choose Series from Data. Then choose the Columns option, the Date option, and the Year option; leave Step Value at 1; and leave a blank at Stop Value. Choose OK and Excel fills in the headings, from Dec-80 to Dec-89.

Creating a Series

1. Enter the beginning value.
2. Select the cell containing the value together with the cells to contain the whole series.   This can be in a column or a row.
3. Choose Series from Data.
4. Choose either Rows or Columns.   Excel fills it in automatically depending on what you selected in step 2.
5. Choose Linear, Growth, or Date.   Linear increases arithmetically, Growth increases by multiplication, and Date relates to dates.
6. If you chose Date, choose between Day, Weekend, Month, and Year.

7. Enter the value to increase by at Step Value.

    If you chose Linear in step 5, it adds this value; if you chose Growth, it multiplies by this value.

8. Enter a ceiling value at Stop Value.

    This is optional.

Data Set Criteria

(*see also* **Data Find, Data Extract, Data Delete, Data Set Database**)

Use the Data Set Criteria command to define a set of database criteria entered in your worksheet. Define the criteria on the worksheet using this command as an alternative to setting criteria in the Form command.

Keystrokes

Keyboard	*Mouse*
Data Set Criteria	Data Set Criteria

 Creating a Criteria Range

1. Enter (either by typing or copying and pasting) the field names of your database into a blank row on the worksheet.

    The criteria range needs to have the same field names as the database.

2. Select all the field names and one blank row (at least) underneath each field name.

    The area selected will be the criteria range.

3. Choose Set Criteria from Data.

    This defines your criteria range. Choose Goto in Formula to see the name Criteria and to highlight the exact range when you need to.

4. On the worksheet, enter the criteria in the blank cells under the field names.

    When the cells remain blank, Find or Extract or Delete select all database records.

Data Set Database

(*see also* **Data Form**, **Data Find, Data Delete, Data Set Criteria, Data Set Extract, Data Sort**)

Use the Data Set Database command to define an area of your worksheet as a database. You must create and define your database to Excel before you can use the database options.

Keystrokes

Keyboard *Mouse*

Data Data

Set Database Set Database

Example

Suppose that you want to create a database of your friends and acquaintances. On any row of the worksheet, type **Name**, **Address**, **Telephone**, each in separate cells. On the next row down, type, for example, **Jennifer Blair** under Name, **Fairfield** under Address, and **(515) 473-9979** under Telephone. This is one record. On lower rows, enter as many records as you need to. Select everything you've entered including the field names. Choose Set Database from Data.

 Creating a Database

1. Enter the field names on a row of the worksheet, one field name per cell.

    These are the headings for your database and they define how many fields you can have in each record.

2. On the next row, under each field name, enter the field value for the first record. Each row contains one record.

3. On lower rows, enter as many records as you want to, using the same columns.

4. Select all cell entries.

    This selection is your database.

5. Choose Set Database from Data.

    The defined database range is expanded as you add records.

> **Tip:** Take care that any records added to the database afterwards are included in the database range. You can make certain by adding a record through Form or by inserting a new record in a middle row of the defined database range.

Data Set Extract

(*see also* Data Extract, Data Set Database, Data Set Criteria)

When using the Data Set Extract command, you can optionally define an extract range for your database to Excel with Set Extract. All extracted records that meet the criteria setup are then copied into the defined area.

Keystrokes

Keyboard	*Mouse*
Data	Data
Set Extract	Set Extract

Example

Suppose that you have a database with three fields containing a name, address, and telephone number and you want to extract the telephone numbers for people in the 515 area. This is already set up in the criteria range. Enter Name and Telephone on a blank line underneath the database, select the cells containing Name and Telephone, and choose Set Extract from Data. Then choose Extract to copy the records that meet the criteria to the extract range.

 Creating an Extract Range

1. Enter the field names you want information about in blank cells on one row of the worksheet.

   Use rows underneath the database to avoid overwriting any database records.

2. Select the entered field names.

   This is the extract range. Select blank rows underneath if you want a certain number of records only.

3. Choose Set Extract from Data.   The range is now defined to Excel as a name, Extract, visible through Goto in Formula.

 Note: You don't have to define an extract range to use extract. Alternatively, you can select the field names (step 2) and just choose Extract. Excel copies the records in the same way to this temporary extract range.

Data Sort

The Data Sort command sorts selected data on a database or worksheet to your specifications in either ascending or descending order, using one to three sort keys that refer to rows or columns.

Sort keys identify the order of sorting. For example, if you are sorting rows, the column of the first key is sorted first, then the column of the second key, and finally the column of the third key. The second key comes into play when there are entries in the column of the first key that are the same; the third key comes into play when there are entries in the column of the second key that are the same.

When you choose ascending order, Excel puts numbers first, then text, then logical values (anything that produces TRUE or FALSE), then error values (where a formula in a cell produces a nonsense value). With descending order, this is reversed. Blank cells always come last with either ascending or descending order.

Keystrokes

Keyboard

Use Shift and arrow keys to select range

Data Sort

Row or Columns

Alt-1

Ascending or Descending

Alt-2

Mouse

Select range

Data, Sort

Row or Columns

1st Key

Ascending or Descending

2nd Key

392 Data Sort

Keyboard	*Mouse*
<u>A</u>scending or <u>D</u>escending	<u>A</u>scending or <u>D</u>escending
Alt-3	3rd Key
<u>A</u>scending or <u>D</u>escending	<u>A</u>scending or <u>D</u>escending

Example

Suppose that an area on your worksheet has sales figures for each outlet in Iowa. You would like to sort the figures by area code to compare them. Select all relevant cells that include columns containing sales figures, outlet telephone numbers, number of salesmen, and the approximate population of the area. Omit the headings. Sort in ascending order using the area code as the key.

 Sorting a Range of Cells

1. Select the rows and columns to be sorted. If you're sorting by rows in a database, leave out the field names; if you're sorting by column, include the field names.

2. Choose <u>S</u>ort from the <u>D</u>ata menu.   You see the Sort dialog box.

3. Choose <u>R</u>ows if you're sorting the order of rows (records in a database, for example); choose <u>C</u>olumns if you're rearranging the order of columns.   The circle beside the Rows or Columns option goes black.

4. Type the 1st Key cell number.   This tells Excel which row or column you are sorting by.

5. Specify Ascending or Descending.   The circle beside the Ascending or Descending option goes black.

6. If needed, type the 2nd and 3rd Keys in the appropriate spaces, specifying Ascending or Descending in each case.

7. Choose OK.

Note: Though Sort is in the Data menu you can sort data that is not defined as a database also.

DATA.DELETE

(*see* **Macro Functions That Perform Data Commands**)

DATA.FIND

(*see* **Macro Functions That Perform Data Commands**)

DATA.FIND.NEXT

(*see* **Macro Functions That Perform Data Commands**)

DATA.FIND.PREV

(*see* **Macro Functions That Perform Data Commands**)

DATA.FORM

(*see* **Macro Functions That Perform Data Commands**)

DATA.SERIES

(*see* Macro Functions That Perform Data Commands)

Date (*see also* Data, Series; Serial Number; Time)

Date is a distinct data type used in Excel for specifying a calendar date. The actual value stored is a serial number. The dates can be entered in these formats: m/d/yy, d-mmm-yy, d-mmm, mmm-yy, m/d/yy h:mm, or a custom format.

Capitalization does not matter when you type in a date. After the date is successfully entered, Excel will display it in the format specified for that cell. The date must be typed in using the format specified in Windows Control Panel, International, Date Format, or one of the Excel standard date formats that contains *mmm*. Otherwise, Excel will assume that the date is just a character string or, worse, will interpret the characters as a different date. After the date is successfully entered, Excel will display it in the format specified for that cell.

Example

Dates can be used directly in formulas if enclosed in double quotation marks. The formula ="5/24/91"–"4/15/91" returns the answer of 39, the number of days between the two dates. Do *not* format the answer as a date to see the months/days/years between two dates, because Excel gives a misleading answer. See "Serial Number."

Inserting the Current Date into the Formula Bar

1. Put the text cursor in the formula bar.

   The text cursor in the formula bar flashes.

2. Press Ctrl-+.

   The current date appears in the formula bar.

Note: If Excel shows the date as a number between 1 and 65,380, the format for that cell is numeric. Choose a date format using the Forma**t** **N**umber command.

Caution: Do not type a space in front of a date such as 4/91. Excel will interpret the date as a character string.

Excel interprets a month name followed by one or two digits as month and year. For example, May 29 is 5/1/1929.

Tip: A date and time can be entered in a single cell if they are separated by one or more spaces. Excel will then separate them by two spaces. The date or the time may come first.

A series of dates may be entered automatically using the Data Series command.

If the date is off by four years, to correct it, choose Options Calculation and click on the 1904 Date System check box.

DATE()

(see also **DATEVALUE, DAY, MONTH, YEAR, TIMEVALUE, TODAY)**

Syntax

DATE(*year,month,day*)

Description

DATE is a function that returns a number which corresponds to the particular date: year, month, and day.

Note: Excel 3 for Windows uses a different numbering system (the 1900 Date System) for the DATE function than Excel for the Macintosh.

The information required for function DATE:

year is a number between 1900 and 2078. If you use two digits to specify a year, DATE uses the range of 1920 to 2019. To specify a date outside of this range, use all four digits.

month is a number representing the month of the year. If you specify a *month* that is greater than 12, then DATE adds a year for each extra 12 months. For example, if *month* is 14, one year is added to the year and 2 is used for the month.

day is the day of the month. If *day* is greater than the number of days in the month, then the extra days are added onto the next month. For example, DATE(89,6,34) is the same as DATE(89,7,4) because June has only 30 days.

 Tip: Use DATE to find dates that fall many days before or after a particular date.

Examples *(based on the 1900 Date System)*

Formula	Returns
=DATE(74,3,30)	27118
=DATE(74,3,31)	27119
=DATE(75,0,1)	27364
=DATE(74,12,1)	27364

DATEVALUE()

(see also **DATE, DAY, MONTH, YEAR, TIMEVALUE, TODAY**)

Syntax

DATEVALUE(*date_text*)

Description

DATEVALUE is a function that returns a number which corresponds to the particular date specified by date_text.

The information required for function DATEVALUE:

date_text is quoted text that represents a date between January 1, 1900, and December 31, 2078. If your date is not in this range, the error #VALUE! is returned. If the year portion of the date is left out of date_text, then DATEVALUE assumes that you want to use the current year.

Note: Excel 3 for Windows uses a different numbering system (the 1900 Date System) for the DATEVALUE function than Excel for the Macintosh. On the Macintosh, date_text can range from January 1, 1904, to December 31, 2078.

Tip: Use DATEVALUE to find dates that fall many days before or after a particular date.

Examples *(based on the 1900 Date System)*

Formula	Returns
=DATEVALUE("May 1, 1991")	33359
=DATEVALUE("4/18/92")	33712
=DATEVALUE("1-7-90")	32880
=DATEVALUE("6 Sep 85")	31296

DAVERAGE()

(*see also* **Function, AVERAGE, Dfunction, DCOUNT, DCOUNTA, DSUM**)

Syntax

DAVERAGE(*database,field,criteria*)

Description

DAVERAGE is a function that returns the average of all the values in the database that are in the column of the database which is headed by the value you gave for field and that match the criteria that you specified. (See "Dfunction" and "AVERAGE" for more information.)

Example

See "Dfunction."

DAY()

(*see also* **MONTH, YEAR, WEEKDAY, HOUR, MINUTE, SECOND, TODAY**)

Syntax

DAY(*serial_number*)

Description

DAY is a function that returns a number which represents the day of the month corresponding to the particular date specified by serial_number. The returned number ranges from 1 to 31 (the number of days in a month).

The information required for function DAY:

Serial_number is a number that represents a particular date in the range of January 1, 1900, to December 31, 2078. For more information on serial_number, see "NOW." Serial_number can also be given as text.

Note: Excel 3 for Windows uses a different numbering system (the 1900 Date System) for the DAY function than Excel for the Macintosh. On the Macintosh, date_text can range from January 1, 1904, to December 31, 2078.

Examples *(based on the 1900 Date System)*

The formula =DAY(32880) returns 7 because serial_number 32880 stands for the date January 7, 1990.

The formula =DAY(31296) returns 6 because serial_number 31296 stands for the date September 6, 1985.

Formula	Returns
=DAY("May 1, 1991")	1
=DAY("4/18/92")	18

DAYS360() *(see also DAY)*

Syntax

DAYS360(*start_date,end_date*)

Description

DAYS360 is a function that returns a number which represents the number of days between start_date and end_date, based on a 360-day year (a year with 12 months, each month containing exactly 30 days).

Tip: If your records are based on the 360-day year, use DAYS360 to compute bills to be paid or expected payments.

The information required for function DAYS360:

start_date and *end_date* are either serial numbers or text that represents a date. A *serial number* is a number that represents a particular date in the range of January 1, 1900, to December 31, 2078. For more information on serial_number, see "NOW."

Note: Excel 3 for Windows uses a different numbering system (the 1900 Date System) for the DAYS360 function than Excel for the Macintosh. On the Macintosh, date_text can range from January 1, 1904, to December 31, 2078.

Note: DAYS360 returns a negative number if end_date represents a date that occurs before start_date.

Examples *(based on the 1900 Date System)*

The formula =DAYS360(32880,32889) returns 9 because serial_number 32880 stands for the date January 7, 1990, and serial_number 32889 stands for the date January 16, 1990.

The formula =DAYS360(31296,31661) returns 360 because exactly a year separates the two dates, since serial_number 31296 stands for the date September 6, 1985, and serial_number 31661 stands for the date September 6, 1986. (Note that subtracting the two serial numbers yields 365, the number of days that actually exist between these dates.)

The formula =DAYS360("5-Aug-92",33848) returns 26. The serial_number 33848 stands for the date September 1, 1992, and DAYS360 calculates on the basis of a 30-day month. (Even the month of August, which has 31 days, is treated as a 30-day month by the function DAYS360.) Adding one day in September makes a total of 26.

Note: If you want to get the exact number of days between two dates, convert the dates to a numerical code using DATE or DATEVALUE; then subtract them.

Formula	*Returns*
=DAYS360("July 1, 1991","8/30/91")	59
=DAYS360("March 21, 1990","February 21, 1990")	–30

DCOUNT()

(*see also* Function, COUNT, Dfunction, DAVERAGE, DCOUNTA, DSUM)

Syntax

DCOUNT(*database, field, criteria*)

Description

DCOUNT is a function that returns the number of numerical values in all the values in the database that are in the column of the database which is headed by the value you gave for field and that match the criteria that you specified. (See "Dfunction" and "COUNT" for more information.)

Example

See "Dfunction."

DCOUNTA()

(*see also* Function, COUNTA, Dfunction, DAVERAGE, DCOUNT, DSUM)

Syntax

DCOUNTA(*database, field, criteria*)

Description

DCOUNTA is a function that returns the number of nonblank values in all the values in the database that are in the column of the database which is headed by the value you gave for field and that match the criteria that you specified. (See "Dfunction" and "COUNTA" for more information.)

Example

See "Dfunction."

DDB() *(see also* Functions, VDB, SLN, SYD*)*

Syntax

DDB(*cost,salvage,life,period,factor*)

Description

DDB is a function that returns the depreciation of an asset for a specific period, using the double-declining-balance method if you specify a factor of 2, or another method if you specify a factor other than 2.

The double-declining-balance method computes an accelerated rate of depreciation. As you choose larger factors, the depreciation for any one period increases. As you can see from this formula for DDB, depreciation is highest in the first period and decreases in later periods: DDB = ((cost − total depreciation from prior periods) * factor) / life

The information required for function DDB:

cost is a positive number that represents the initial cost of the asset.

salvage is a positive number that represents the value at the end of the depreciation, which is sometimes also referred to as the salvage value of the asset.

life is a positive number that represents the number of periods over which the asset depreciates, which is sometimes also referred to as the useful life of the asset.

period is a positive number that represents the interval of time for which DDB calculates the depreciation.

 Note: *period* must be in the same units as life.

factor is a positive number that represents the rate at which the balance declines. If factor is not included, it is assumed to be 2.

Example

Suppose you bought a printing press for your business for $100,000. It has a lifetime of 10 years, at which time the salvage value is $40,000. Examples of the depreciation of the printing press follow:

Depreciation for	Is Calculated by	Which Yields
The first year	=DDB(100000,40000,10,1)	$20,000.00
The first month	=DDB(100000,40000,10*12,1)	$1,666.67
The first week	=DDB(100000,40000,10*52,1,2)	$384.62
The first day	=DDB(100000,40000,10*365,1)	$54.79
The last year	=DDB(100000,40000,10,10)	$0.00
The fourth year	=DDB(100000,40000,10,4,2.5)	$2,187.50 (using a factor of 2.5)
The tenth month	=DDB(100000,40000,10*12,10,0.5)	$401.30 (using a factor of 0.5)

DEFINE.NAME

(*see* Macro Functions That Perform Formula Commands)

DEFINE.STYLE

(*see* Macro Functions That Perform Format Commands)

DELETE.ARROW

(*see* Macro Functions That Perform Chart Commands)

DELETE.BAR

(*see* Macro Functions— Customizing)

DELETE.COMMAND

(*see* Macro Functions—Customizing)

DELETE.FORMAT

(*see* Macro Functions That Perform Actions)

DELETE.MENU

(*see* Macro Functions—Customizing)

DELETE.NAME

(*see* Macro Functions That Perform Formula Commands)

DELETE.OVERLAY

(*see* Macro Functions That Perform Chart Commands)

DELETE.STYLE

(*see* Macro Functions That Perform Format Commands)

DEMOTE

(*see* Macro Functions That Perform Actions)

DEREF (*see* Macro Functions—Value Returning)

Dfunction (*see also* Function)

Syntax

Dfunction(database,field,criteria)

Description

The Dfunctions are the functions that operate on a database: DAVERAGE, DCOUNT, DCOUNTA, DGET, DMAX, DMIN, DPRODUCT, DSTDEV, DSTDEVP, DSUM, DVAR, DVARP. All Dfunctions perform a two-part operation. They choose rows of information in the database (or table) that fulfill the criteria specified by you, and they return a result from operating on one column of these chosen rows. You specify the one column that the function operates on when you give the field value for the function. You specify the specific operation (such as counting, averaging, summing, or multiplying) on the values by the function name DAVERAGE, DCOUNT, etc.

The information required for each Dfunction has the same structure. And the operations that each function performs is almost exactly the same as its counterpart nondatabase function, the function without the first letter *D*. For detailed information on each function, see individual related listings. For example, for more information on DAVERAGE, see the listing for AVERAGE. (The only exception to this is the DGET function, which is only for databases.)

 Note: In database terminology, the type of database that Excel uses is a flat database. One row in this type of database is a record, and the information in one column is a field.

> **Tip:** If there are no restrictions or matching criteria for a field, then leave the comparison cell underneath the field name blank.

The information required for each Dfunction:

database is one range of cell addresses.

field is one column in the database, specified by its field name (heading) or field number. The first column of the database is the first field, even if the database does not begin in column A.

criteria is the standard for evaluating whether a value should be included in the calculations of the function. Criteria does not have to include all the field names of the database, but must include at least one field name and one cell for specifying the values.

Examples

The example in Figure A is a good introduction to the Dfunctions. In =DCOUNT(A5:D15,"Bonus",A3:D4), cells A5 to D15 are the database, "Bonus" is the column of values that is counted, and cells A3 to D4 have the criteria. The criteria specifies that numbers in the Bonus field (the column headed by "Bonus") must be greater than zero. The rows of information from the database that do not match the criteria are the rows of information for Bruce Conners and Roger Madison. All other rows have a value greater than zero in the Bonus column. Due to the elimination of two rows of information, DCOUNT returns a count of 7 nonzero bonuses in the Bonus column rather than 9, the number that the function COUNT would return.

In the formula in Figure B, =DAVERAGE(A5:D15,"Hourly_Rate",A3:D4), cells A5 to D15 are the database, "Bonus" is the column of values that is counted, and cells A3 to D4 have the criteria. The 40 under "Hours/Wk" in the criteria area specifies that numbers in the Hours/Wk field (the column headed by "Hours/Wk") must be equal to 40. The rows of information from the database that match this criteria are the rows of information for Anne Barret, George Corley, and Linda Nabat. All other rows have a smaller number of Hours/Wk. The average of the numbers in the Hourly_Rate column for these three employees is $11.60, the amount that the function DAVERAGE returns. If you had used the AVERAGE function, all the values in the Hourly_Rate column would have been averaged.

> **Note:** In this example, the criteria specifies conditions on the Hours/Wk column, but the column that is averaged is the Hourly_Rate column. In the criteria you can specify criteria for any field or column of information.

Dfunction 407

In the example in Figure C, =DSUM(A5:E15,"Wage",A3:E4), the wages of permanent employees are totaled. An employee that is permanent has a status of Perm and a number of Hours/Wk greater than zero. Hence, the criteria specifies Perm in the Status column and >0 in the Hours/Wk column. DSUM returns the sum of the wages of all the employees that match this criteria. If you had used the SUM function, the total wages would have been $2,595.80 rather than $2,150.80.

Figure A

Microsoft Excel - DFUNCT1.XLS
D17: =DCOUNT(A5:D15,"Bonus",A3:D4)

	A	B	C	D
1			Salaries of BeeZBees Inc.	
2				
3	Name	Hourly_Rate	Hours/Wk	Bonus
4				>0
5	Name	Hourly_Rate	Hours/Wk	Bonus
6				
7	Anne Barret	$14.50	40	$300.00
8	Bobby Barner	$6.80	35	$500.00
9	Bruce Conners	$5.00	20	$0.00
10	George Corley	$7.80	40	$300.00
11	Jamie Falcon	$9.00	25	$200.00
12	Kathy Kolender	$11.50	30	$100.00
13	Roger Madison	$14.50	On Call	$0.00
14	John Monroe	$8.70	34	$450.00
15	Linda Nabat	$12.50	40	$100.00
16				
17			Number of Bonuses:	7

Figure B

Microsoft Excel - DFUNCT2.XLS
C17: =DAVERAGE(A5:D15,"Hourly_Rate",A3:D4)

	A	B	C	D
1			Salaries of BeeZBees Inc.	
2				
3	Name	Hourly_Rate	Hours/Wk	Bonus
4			40	
5	Name	Hourly_Rate	Hours/Wk	Bonus
6				
7	Anne Barret	$14.50	40	$300.00
8	Bobby Barner	$6.80	25	$500.00
9	Bruce Conners	$5.00	20	$0.00
10	George Corley	$7.80	40	$300.00
11	Jamie Falcon	$9.00	25	$200.00
12	Kathy Kolender	$11.50	30	$100.00
13	Roger Madison	$14.50	On Call	$0.00
14	John Monroe	$8.70	34	$450.00
15	Linda Nabat	$12.50	40	$100.00
16				
17	Average Full Time Hourly Rate:		$11.60	

Dfunction

 Note: In this example, the condition specified in the Status column of the criteria is a text string. Whatever is displayed in the criteria section is matched, be it text, numbers, or any other type of value.

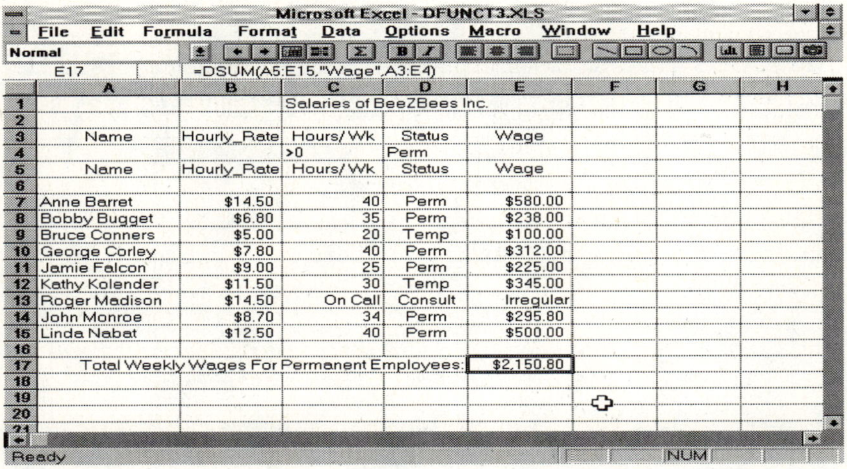

Figure C

In the example in Figure D, you see four sets of criteria for one database. Each of the first three criteria sets up the calculation of the largest and smallest quantity sold of one cookie. The last criteria area in the worksheet has nothing under Cookie, so that the quantities of every cookie are included. The formulas for the maximum and minimum quantity of cookies are as follows:

Cookie Type	Maximum	Minimum
Sandwich	=DMAX(A3:D12, "Quantity",G3:H4)	=DMIN(A3:D12,"Quantity",G3:H4)
Thin Mint	=DMAX(A3:D12, "Quantity",G5:H6)	=DMIN(A3:D12,"Quantity",G5:H6)
Shortbread	=DMAX(A3:D12, "Quantity",G7:H8)	=DMIN(A3:D12,"Quantity",G7:H8)
All Cookies	=DMAX(A3:D12, "Quantity",G9:H10)	=DMIN(A3:D12,"Quantity",G9:H10)

Note: In this example, the range of cells for criteria does not include all the fields of the database. Only two columns of information are evaluated in the above formulas, so only these two field names and comparison values are included in the range of cells for criteria.

Figure D

The example in Figure E gives you more experience with criteria and the use of field numbers rather than field names. The field number 4 is the field called "Coffee". You can use either the number or the name of a field in any formula. The formula =DCOUNTA(A4:D12,4,G8:J9) is the same as the formula =DCOUNTA(A4:D12,"Coffee",G8:J9). The formulas that are used to calculate the count of the "Yes" answers are:

Drink Soda   =DCOUNTA(A4:D12,2,G4:J5)

Drink Tea   =DCOUNTA(A4:D12,3,G6:J7)

Drink Coffee   =DCOUNTA(A4:D12,4,G8:J9)

Drink ALL Three   =DCOUNTA(A4:D12,4,G10:J11)

Note: A value is counted only if all the values in its row match the specified criteria.

Figure E

DGET( ) *(see also* Function, Dfunction*)*

Syntax

DGET(*database, field, criteria*)

Description

DGET is a function that gets one value from all the values in the database. DGET extracts the value that is in the column of the database which is headed by *field* and which satisfies the criteria that you specified. (See "Dfunction" for more information.)

Example

See "Dfunction."

DIALOG.BOX

(*see* Macro Functions—Customizing)

DIRECTORY

(*see* Macro Functions—Value Returning)

DISABLE.INPUT

(*see* Macro Functions—Customizing)

Display (*see also* Page Setup)

The Display feature in Excel controls the appearance of the spreadsheet on the screen.

Keystrokes

Keyboard	*Mouse*
Options	Options
Display	Display

Display Option	*Effect on Spreadsheet*
Automatic Page Breaks	Displays automatic page breaks that Excel inserts. Page breaks that are manually inserted are always displayed.
Formulas	Shows formulas contained in cells instead of their value
Gridlines	Displays gridlines between cells
Grid Line & Heading Color	Sets color for gridlines and headings

Display Option	*Effect on Spreadsheet*
Hide All	Prevents any graphic objects from being displayed
Outline Symbols	Displays outline symbols if spreadsheet contains an outline
Row & Column Headings	Displays lettered or numbered headings at the top of each column of cells and numbers at the left of each row of cells
Show All	Makes all graphic objects visible
Show Placeholders	Displays embedded charts and pictures as rectangles to speed up scrolling
Zero Values	If turned off, all cells whose value is zero are shown as blank. Cells specifically formatted to show zero values are not affected.

Note: To see values on a macro sheet, turn off Options, Display, Formulas.

Caution: Alignment has no effect when Options, Display, Formulas is turned on.

Tip: Changing values with Options Display affects the active spreadsheet only.

DISPLAY

(*see* Macro Functions That Perform Options Commands)

DMAX() *(see also* Function, MAX, Dfunction, DMIN)

Syntax

DMAX(*database, field, criteria*)

Description

DMAX is a function that returns the maximum value of all values in the database that are in the column of the database which is headed by the value you gave for field and that match the criteria that you specified. (See "Dfunction" and "MAX" for more information.)

Example

See "Dfunction."

DMIN() *(see also* Function, MIN, Dfunction, DMAX)

Syntax

DMIN(*database, field, criteria*)

Description

DMIN is a function that returns the minimum value of all values in the database that are in the column of the database which is headed by the value you gave for field and that match the criteria that you specified. (See "Dfunction" and "MIN" for more information.)

Example

See "Dfunction."

DOCUMENTS

(see Macro Functions—Value Returning)

DOLLAR( ) *(see also* FIXED, TEXT, VALUE)

Syntax

DOLLAR(*number,decimals*)

Description

DOLLAR is a function that returns the text form of *number* rounded off to the requested number of decimals, with a currency format. (This format is $#,##0.00, where # is an optional place holder for a number.)

The rounding rules for DOLLAR are the same as given in the function ROUND. DOLLAR employs the traditional rules of rounding: If the next smaller digit is five or more, then the digit is rounded up. If the next smaller digit is four or less, then the digit remains the same.

Numbers are rounded according to the following guidelines:

- If a decimal is less than 0, it is rounded to the left of the decimal point.
- If a decimal is 0, it is rounded to the nearest integer.
- If a decimal is greater than 0, it is rounded to the right of the decimal point.

Note: Excel also offers a command for formatting a number into currency format. The Number command on the Format menu leaves the number as a numerical value, whereas the DOLLAR function converts the number into text.

The information required for function DOLLAR:

number is any number.

decimals is a number that specifies how many digits of a number to round. If decimals has a fractional part, that fractional part is ignored. For example, =DOLLAR(0.12,–1.7) returns the same result as =DOLLAR(0.12,–1).

Examples

Formula	Returns
=DOLLAR(12345.6789,–3)	"$12,000"
=DOLLAR(–12345.6789,–1)	"($12,350)"

Formula	Returns
=DOLLAR(12345.6789,0)	"$12346"
=DOLLAR(-12345.6789,2)	"($12,345.68)"
=DOLLAR(12.123)	"$12.12"
=DOLLAR(-12.345)	"($12.35)"

 Note: The Microsoft Excel Function Reference manual says that numbers converted into text with the DOLLAR function can be used as numbers in formulas because Excel automatically converts them when it calculates. But the guidelines in the SUM function section of the manual illustrate that this is not true when text is referred to in a cell, not listed in the list of values for the function.

In formulas all text that is referenced by the formula (that is, not directly typed into the list of values for the function of the formula) is ignored by the formula. To convert text in a cell into a numerical value, use the VALUE function.

DPRODUCT()

(*see also* Function, PRODUCT, Dfunction, DSUM)

Syntax

DPRODUCT(*database, field, criteria*)

Description

DPRODUCT is a function that returns the product of all the values in the database that are in the column of the database which is headed by the value you gave for field and that match the criteria that you specified. (See "Dfunction" and "PRODUCT" for more information.)

Example

See "Dfunction."

DSTDEV()

(*see also* Function, STDEV, Dfunction, DSTDEVP)

Syntax

DSTDEV(*database,field,criteria*)

Description

DSTDEV is a function that returns the standard deviation (based on a sample) of all the values in the database that are in the column of the database which is headed by the value you gave for field and that match the criteria that you specified. (See "Dfunction" and "STDEV" for more information.)

Example

See "Dfunction."

DSTDEVP()

(*see also* Function, STDEVP, Dfunction, DSTDEV)

Syntax

DSTDEVP(*database,field,criteria*)

Description

DSTDEVP is a function that returns the standard deviation (based on the entire population) of all the values in the database that are in the column of the database which is headed by the value you gave for field and that match the criteria that you specified. (See "Dfunction" and "STDEVP" for more information.)

Example

See "Dfunction."

DSUM()

(*see also* Function, SUM, Dfunction, DAVERAGE, DCOUNT, DCOUNTA)

Syntax

DSUM(*database, field, criteria*)

Description

DSUM is a function that returns the sum of all the values in the database that are in the column of the database which is headed by the value you gave for field and that match the criteria that you specified. (See "Dfunction" and "SUM" for more information.)

Example

See "Dfunction."

DUPLICATE

(*see* Macro Functions That Perform Actions)

DVAR()

(*see also* Function, VAR, Dfunction, DVARP)

Syntax

DVAR(*database, field, criteria*)

Description

DVAR is a function that returns the variance (based on a sample) of all the values in the database that are in the column of the database which is headed by the value you gave for field and that match the criteria that you specified. (See "Dfunction" and "VAR" for more information.)

Example

See "Dfunction."

DVARP()

(*see also* Function, VARP, Dfunction, DVAR)

Syntax

DVARP(*database,field,criteria*)

Description

DVARP is a function that returns the variance (based on the entire population) of all the values in the database that are in the column of the database which is headed by the value you gave for field and that match the criteria that you specified. (See "Dfunction" and "VARP" for more information.)

Example

See "Dfunction."

E

ECHO (*see* Macro Functions—Customizing)

Edit Clear (*see also* Edit Delete)

Edit Clear is a command that removes all data from a cell or range, leaving a blank cell or range. Clearing a cell does not delete it; rather it erases data from the cell. It should be distinguished from Edit Delete, which deletes the cell entirely and adjusts other cells in the worksheet to close up the space. If you clear a cell that was referenced by another cell, its value will be zero.

Keystrokes

Keyboard	*Mouse*
Use arrow keys to select cell or Shift-arrow keys to select range.	Select cell or range.
Edit Clear or Del key	Edit, Clear
Select All, Formats, Formulas, or Notes.	Select All, Formats, Formulas, or Notes.
Enter	OK

 Clearing a Cell or Range

1. Select the cell or range.   The cell or range is highlighted.
2. Select Edit Clear.   The dialog box appears.

3. In the dialog box, select the attributes you want to clear: All, Formats, Formulas, or Notes.

   A black dot indicates that the option is selected.

4. Choose OK.

   The cell or range is cleared.

Edit Copy *(see also* Edit Fill Right, Down, Left, Up*)*

The Edit Copy command duplicates a selected cell or range of cells. It can be used to duplicate a cell or range of cells either on the same worksheet or on another one. All characteristics of the cell, including the contents, format, and any notes, are copied. If preferred, you can select which characteristics you want to copy by using Edit Paste Special.

Keystrokes

Keyboard

Use arrow keys to move to copy cell or to corner of copy range. Use Shift-arrow keys to extend range.

Ctrl-Ins

Use arrow keys to move to duplicate cell location or upper-left corner of duplicate range location.

Enter

Mouse

Move to copy cell or to corner of copy range. Drag to extend range.

Edit, Copy

Move to duplicate cell location or to upper-left corner of duplicate range location.

Edit, Paste

 Note: To copy to a different worksheet, switch to the other worksheet and select the new location after you press Ctrl-Ins or select Edit Copy from the menu.

Copying a Cell or Range of Cells

1. Move to the cell you want to copy. If you are copying a range of cells, move to one corner of the range and extend the active box area.

   The cell or range of cells will be highlighted.

2. Press Ctrl-Ins, or select Edit Copy from the menu.

   The cell or range of cells will be surrounded by the flashing, dotted line.

3. Move to the new location. If you are copying a range of cells, move to the upper-left corner of the range.

   The new location is highlighted.

4. Press Enter or select Edit Paste from the menu.

   The cell or range of cells will be copied to the new location.

You can copy the selected area to different locations as many times as you want. In this case, use Edit Paste instead of Enter in step 4. Then repeat steps 3 and 4 with the new location(s).

 Note: You can use Edit Copy to copy data in the formula bar. Select the characters you want to copy, select Edit Copy, press Enter, and move to the cell where you want to paste the characters. If you want to insert the copied characters, position the insertion point in the formula bar where you want to copy the characters. If you want to replace characters in the formula bar, select the characters you want to replace. Select Edit Paste.

 Caution: If you use Edit Copy over cells that are not empty, you will delete whatever is in those cells. Use Edit Insert if you want to insert cells rather than copy them.

Tip: When you use Edit Copy, relative references that were in the selected cells are adjusted to the new location. This could result in some unforeseen circumstances. Use absolute references if you want the references in the new cells to remain the same.

Edit Cut

The Edit Cut command selects a cell or range of cells for moving or inserting. It prepares you for the following commands: Edit Paste, Edit Paste Special, and Edit Insert.

Keystrokes

Keyboard

Use arrow keys to move to cell. (Use Shift-arrow keys to extend selected area.)

Shift-Del

Mouse

Select a cell, or drag mouse to extend selected area.

Edit, Cut

 Cutting a Cell or Range of Cells

1. Using the mouse or arrow keys, move to the cell you want to cut.

   The cell you want to cut is marked as the active cell.

2. If you are cutting a range of cells, move to one corner of the range and extend the active box area.

   The cells you want to cut are marked as the active cells.

3. Press Shift-Del, or select the Edit menu and then Cut.

   The area you want to cut is surrounded with a flashing, dotted line.

Note: You can cut more than one area of cells at a time. Using the mouse, hold down Ctrl when you select additional cells. On the keyboard, use Shift-F8 to go into Add mode (you will see Add at the bottom of the worksheet). You can then select another cell or range of cells. This process can be repeated as often as you wish.

Note: You can use Edit Cut to move data in the formula bar. Select the characters you want to move, select Edit Cut, and move to the cell where you want to paste the characters. If you want to insert copied characters in the formula bar, move the cursor to the position where you want to move the characters.

Edit Delete *(see also* Edit Clear*)*

Edit Delete is a command that removes a cell or range from the worksheet and moves other cells to close up the resulting space. It is the opposite of Edit Insert.

Keystrokes

Keyboard

Use arrow keys to select cell or Shift-arrow keys to select range.

Edit Delete

Shift Cells Left, Shift Cells Up, Entire Row, or Entire Column

Enter

Mouse

Select cell or range.

Edit, Delete

Shift Cells Left, Shift Cells Up Entire Row, or Entire Column

OK

Note: Using the keyboard, you can select an entire row or column by selecting the first cell in that row or column and pressing Shift-Spacebar to select the entire row or Ctrl-Spacebar to select the entire column.

Edit Fill Right, Down, Left, Up

(*See also* **Workgroups**)

The Edit Fill command copies formulas or data to adjacent cells in a column or row. This command selects the source and target in one step. It takes the first cell in the range and copies it to all the additional selected cells in the range.

Keystrokes

Keyboard

Use arrow keys to move to copy cell. Use Shift-arrow keys to extend selection.

Edit or Shift-Edit (Shift-Alt-E)

h

w

h

w

Mouse

Select copy cell. Drag to extend selection.

Edit or Shift-Edit

Fill Right

Fill Down

Fill Left

Fill Up

 Using Edit Fill

1. Select the cell you want to copy and extend the selection to the entire range to which you want to copy.

   The range is highlighted.

2. Select Edit to copy to the right or down; select Shift-Edit to copy to the left or up.

   If you select Edit, Exel lets you copy to the right or down; if you select Shift-Edit, Excel lets you copy to the left or up.

3. Select Fill Right, Fill Down, Fill Left, or Fill Up. Or type h, w, h, or w.

   The data is copied from the first to all adjacent selected cells in the direction you selected.

Edit Insert

The Edit Insert command inserts a cell or range of cells. The range of cells can be part of a column or row, or it can be an entire column or row.

If you do an Edit Copy or Edit Cut command, then when you select the Edit Insert command, it appears as an Edit Insert Paste command. The Edit Insert Paste command performs the same function as the Edit Insert command, with the addition of pasting the information that you had copied or cut into the cells that you insert.

Keystrokes

Keyboard

Use the arrow keys to highlight the cell or cells that you want to insert cells above or to the left of.

Edit Insert

Mouse

Highlight the cell or cells that you want to insert cells above or to the left of.

Edit, Insert

 Inserting Cells

1. Select or highlight the area of cell or cells where you want to insert cells.
2. Select Edit Insert.
3. Select your desired option from the dialog box.
4. Select OK or press Enter.

Inserted cells will be above or to the left of the cells you highlight in this step.

 Copying *and* Inserting Cells

1. Use the Edit Copy command to select the cell or range you want to copy.
2. Switch to another worksheet if you wish. Move to the upper-left corner of the area where you want to insert the copied cells.

The area you have chosen to insert is surrounded with the marquee.

The cell or range is highlighted.

3. Select Edit Insert Paste or press Ctrl-+.

   A dialog box is displayed.

4. Select the option you want in the dialog box, shifting cells down or to the right.

   Cells are shifted to the right or down, according to your selection, and the copied cell or range is inserted.

Edit Paste

The Edit Paste command is used to move a cell or range of cells on the worksheet or to another worksheet. It follows Edit Cut.

Keystrokes

Keyboard

Use the arrow keys to move to paste location, or switch to another worksheet.

If you are moving a range, move to upper-left corner of new location.

If the marquee (the dashed flashing border) is still around the cell(s) that you are going to copy or move, then either press Enter to paste the cells *once* or press Shift-Ins to paste the copied information repeatedly.

Mouse

Move to paste location, or switch to another worksheet.

If you are moving a range, move to upper-left corner of new location.

Edit, Paste

Note: When moving a range of cells, it is easiest to select the upper-left corner of the new location. If you select the whole area, it must be the same size and shape as the area you cut or Excel will not execute the move. The new location can overlap the cut area. The cells in their new location will still refer to the same cells as before they were moved.

Pasting a Cell or Range of Cells

1. The cell or cells to be moved or copied have already been cut using Edit Cut and are surrounded by the marquee.

2. Move to the new location, or the upper-left corner of the new range.   The new location is highlighted.

3. From the keyboard, press Enter or use Shift-Insert, or with the mouse, select Edit Paste.   The cell or cells are moved from the old location to the new location.

 Caution: If you Edit Paste over cells that are not empty, you will delete whatever is in those cells. If other formulas refer to the pasted-over location, they will show the error value #REF!. Use Edit Insert if you want to insert cells (see "Edit Insert") rather than paste over them.

 Using Paste Between Two Worksheets

1. Cut or copy the cell or range you want to move or copy.   The cell or range is surrounded by the marquee.

2. Switch to another worksheet. Move to the cell where you want to insert the cut or copied cell or range of cells.   The cell where you want to insert the cell or range is highlighted.

3. Use Ctrl-+ or select Edit Insert Paste.   The cell or range is inserted and other cells are moved down or to the right.

 Note: When using Ctrl-+, use the plus sign by the numeric keypad; otherwise, use Ctrl, Shift, and the plus sign on the regular keyboard.

Edit Paste Special

Edit Paste Special is a command that allows you to select the attributes you want to paste: formulas, values, formats, or notes. You may also combine formulas or values of the copied and pasted areas. Additionally, you may transpose rows and columns when copying. Finally, Edit Paste Special allows you to copy only the nonblank cells from the copied range of cells.

Edit Paste Special allows you to fine-tune the copying process by selecting which attribute of a cell or range you want to copy. If you copy formulas, the formulas and their resulting values will be copied without pasting over formats or notes. If you copy formats, only the formats will be copied, without pasting over the formulas or values. Copying values will result in omitting formulas, notes, and formats. Finally, you can copy just the notes attached to a cell without pasting over the formulas, values, or formats.

Keystrokes

To Copy Selected Attributes

Keyboard	Mouse
Options, Full Menus	Options, Full Menus
Edit Copy or Ctrl-Ins	Edit, Copy
Use Shift-arrow keys to select range.	Drag mouse to select range.
Edit, Paste Special	Edit, Paste Special
Formulas, Values, Formats, or Notes	Formulas, Values, Formats, or Notes
Enter	OK

To Combine Formulas and Values of the Copy and Paste Areas

Keyboard	Mouse
Options, Full Menus	Options, Full Menus
Use arrow keys to select cell or Shift-arrow keys to select range.	Select cell or range.
Edit Copy or Ctrl-Ins	Edit, Copy
Use Shift-arrow keys to select range.	Drag mouse to select range.
Edit, Paste Special	Edit, Paste Special

Edit Paste Special

Keyboard	Mouse
Fo<u>r</u>mulas or <u>V</u>alues	Fo<u>r</u>mulas or <u>V</u>alues
N<u>o</u>ne, A<u>d</u>d, <u>S</u>ubtract, <u>M</u>ultiply, or D<u>i</u>vide	N<u>o</u>ne, A<u>d</u>d, <u>S</u>ubtract, <u>M</u>ultiply, or D<u>i</u>vide
Enter	OK

Note: The divide operation divides the paste cell by the copied cell. The subtract operation subtracts the copied cell from the paste cell. If you chose to copy formulas, the formulas are retained and are enclosed in parentheses, connected by the chosen operation. If one cell contains a formula and one just a value, the formula is enclosed in parentheses and is combined with the value using the operation you selected. When values are combined, the original values are not retained. Only the resulting value is pasted.

Copying Selected Cell Attributes

1. If you are using short menus, switch to the full menus by choosing <u>O</u>ptions and then Full <u>M</u>enus.

   Full Menus will be operational.

2. Select the area you want to copy.

   The selected area will be highlighted.

3. Select <u>E</u>dit <u>C</u>opy or press Ctrl-Ins.

   The selected area will be surrounded by the marquee.

4. Choose the paste area.

   The paste area will be highlighted.

5. Select <u>E</u>dit Paste Special.

   A dialog box will appear.

6. Select the attribute you want to copy: Fo<u>r</u>mulas to paste only the contents of the area (without copying cell notes or the format); <u>V</u>alues to paste only the value shown in the cell or cells; Forma<u>t</u>s to paste only the formats; or <u>N</u>otes to copy only notes attached to the cell or cells.

   A black dot indicates that the option is selected.

7.	Select OK.	The attribute you select will be copied to the selected paste area.

 Combining Formulas and Values of the Copy and Paste Areas

1.	If you are using short menus, switch to the full menus by choosing Options and then Full Menus.	Full Menus will be operational.
2.	Select the area you want to copy.	The selected area will be highlighted.
3.	Select Edit Copy or press Ctrl-Ins.	The selected area will be surrounded by the marquee.
4.	Choose the paste area.	The paste area will be highlighted.
5.	Select Edit Paste Special.	A dialog box will appear.
6.	In the Paste section, select Formulas or Values if you want to copy only selected attributes.	A black dot indicates that the option is selected.
7.	In the Operation section, select the operation you want to use to combine the copy and paste cells: None, Add, Subtract, Multiply, or Divide.	A black dot indicates that the option is selected.
8.	Select OK.	The attribute you select will be copied and combined with the selected paste area using the operation you selected.

 Transposing Copied Rows and Columns

1.	If you are using short menus, switch to the full menus by choosing Options and then Full Menus.	Full Menus will be operationl.
2.	Select the area you want to copy.	The selected area will be highlighted.

3. Select Edit Copy or press Ctrl-Ins.   The selected area will be surrounded by the marquee.

4. Choose the paste area.   The paste area will be highlighted.

5. Select Edit Paste Special.   A dialog box will appear.

6. Select Transpose.   An *x* indicates that the option is selected.

7. Select OK.   The range you selected will be copied, with rows transposed into columns and vice versa.

>
> **Tip:** When selecting the paste area, select just the upper-left corner since the shape of the paste area will change and may be difficult to determine exactly.

 ## Copying Nonblank Cells

1. If you are using short menus, switch to the full menus by choosing Options and then Full Menus.   The Full Menus will be operational.

2. Select the area you want to copy.   The selected area will be highlighted.

3. Select Edit Copy or press Ctrl-Ins.   The selected area will be surrounded by the marquee.

4. Choose the paste area.   The paste area will be highlighted.

5. Select Edit Paste Special.   A dialog box will appear.

6. Select Skip Blanks.   An *x* indicates that the option is selected.

7. Select OK.   The range you selected will be copied, except for any blank cells in the copy area.

> **Note:** When you are copying only nonblank cells, nonblank cells in the paste area will not be pasted over if the corresponding cells in the copy area are blank.

Edit Redo (u) *(see also* Edit Undo*)*

Once you have undone an Edit command using Edit Undo, Edit Redo (u) allows you to redo that same command. Edit Redo (u) is the opposite of Edit Undo. Once you have undone a command, the menu automatically changes to read Redo instead of Undo.

Keystrokes

Keyboard

Alt-Backspace or Edit Redo(u)

Mouse

Edit, Redo(u)

Edit Undo

Edit Undo is a command that undoes any Edit command immediately after you have executed it. Edit Undo reverses or undoes the last Edit command. The menu will specify exactly which command you have executed and can therefore undo, for example, Undo Paste.

Keystrokes

Keyboard

Alt-Backspace or Edit Undo

Mouse

Edit, Undo

EDIT.COLOR

(see Macro Functions That Perform Options Commands*)*

EDIT.DELETE

(*see* Macro Functions That Perform Edit Commands)

EDIT.REPEAT

(*see* Macro Functions That Perform Edit Commands)

EDIT.SERIES

(*see* Macro Functions That Perform Chart Commands)

EDITION.OPTIONS

(*see* Macro Functions That Perform Actions)

ELSE (*see* Macro Functions—Control)

ELSE.IF (*see* Macro Functions—Control)

ENABLE.COMMAND

(*see* Macro Functions—Customizing)

END.IF (*see* Macro Functions—Control)

ERROR (*see* Macro Functions—Control)

Error Value

An *error value* is a type of value, an expression of information in a strictly defined, precise form. An error value is a value that indicates some error occurred in the cell where the error value resides. There are seven error values: #NAME?, #VALUE!, #DIV/0!, #NULL!, #N/A!, #NUM!, #REF!.

Error Value	Description	Situations That Would Create Error
#NAME?	Incorrect name	Some type of name is expected. A function name is expected and the name you gave is not one of the built-in functions or custom functions. Or a name that refers to a value is expected and the name you gave is not defined. (Make sure that you have quotation marks around text values.)
#VALUE!	Invalid value or values	One or more values that you entered into the cell or included in the list of values for the function in the cell are not the correct type or are not in the specified range of values for that particular value that goes into that particular function.
#DIV/0!	Division by 0	The formula you entered divides some number by 0. (This is mathematically undefined in the real number system.)
#NULL!	Null	This error rarely occurs. It indicates that the result of the entered value is void, has no effect, is null or nothing.

Error Value	Description	Situations That Would Create Error
#N/A!	Not applicable	You highlighted an area larger than was needed to display some result. The #N/A! is displayed in the extra cells that are not needed to display the result.
#NUM!	Number(s) out of range	A result cannot be calculated for a specific value or values given to the function. (Some of the matrix and statistical functions accept values as valid for which they sometimes cannot calculate an answer.)
#REF!	Invalid reference to cell address or range of cell addresses	The formula in the cell where the a #REF! error is has a reference to a cell that you deleted from the spreadsheet. (This occurs immediately after you use the delete command.) Or you copied a formula with relative references and the calculated references for the new location would be off the end of the spreadsheet (to the left of column A or above the first row).

The error value is one of six types of values: numbers, text, logical values, references, arrays, and error values. For more information about values in general and a summary of these other five types of values, see "Values."

Examples

If you entered =PRODUCT(2,cost) and you had not yet defined the name cost, then the error value #NAME? would appear, since there is no name called cost.

If you entered =LEN(25), then the error value #VALUE? would appear, since the function called LEN is expecting a text value inside the parentheses and you gave it a number.

If you entered =5/(2–2), then the error value #DIV/0! would appear, because 2–2 is 0 and 5/0 is division by 0, which is undefined.

EXACT() *(see also* LEN, SEARCH*)*

Syntax

EXACT(*text1,text2*)

Description

EXACT is a function that returns a logical value that specifies whether two text strings are exactly the same (TRUE) or not the same (FALSE). EXACT compares the text strings symbol by symbol. Differences in spacing, punctuation, and capital or lowercase letters yield a result of FALSE. Differences in formatting (such as alignment) are ignored.

Note: It makes no difference whether values for the function are typed directly into the list of values or are listed as cell addresses that contain text. The returned value is the same.

Tip: EXACT can check if a text string is an element in an array of text strings. All you need to do is to first highlight an area of cells that is the same size as the text array that you are checking. Enter the formula with the two arguments: the single text string and the array. Instead of pressing Enter, press these three keys at the same time: Ctrl, Shift, and Enter. (On the Macintosh, press only the Command and Enter keys.) For a formula that returns an array, the simultaneous pressing of these keys is equivalent to pressing Enter.

The information required for function EXACT:

text1 is any single symbol or group of symbols.

text2 is any single symbol or group of symbols.

Examples

Formulas That Return TRUE

=EXACT("a)","a)")

=EXACT("3000",3000)

Formulas That Return FALSE

=EXACT("a)","a]")

=EXACT("3,000",3000)

Formulas That Return TRUE	Formulas That Return FALSE
=EXACT("fast food","fast food")	=EXACT("fast food","Fast Food")
=EXACT("9.99",9.99)	=EXACT("$9.99",9.99)
=EXACT("anywhere ","anywhere ")	=EXACT("anywhere","any where")

The figure shows an example of using EXACT to check an array of text. In this example, EXACT checks if the text in cell D3 is in a list of text strings in cells F3 to I3.

[Figure: Microsoft Excel - EXACT.XLS spreadsheet showing cell F5 with formula {=EXACT(D3,F3:I3)}. Row 1: "Transaction Records". Row 3: "Type the transaction option:" in A3, "ADD" in D3, and ADD, DELETE, CHANGE, DISPLAY headers in F3:I3. Row 5: TRUE, FALSE, FALSE, FALSE in F5:I5.]

In the example in the figure, the user of the spreadsheet types an option in cell D3. EXACT checks the option in D3 against a list of text strings or options in cells F3 to I3. In this example, because the first option ADD was entered in cell D3, the value TRUE is the first element of the array returned by EXACT. The other three options do not match the user entered option (the text in cell D3), so the value FALSE is returned in the remaining three cells of the array returned by EXACT.

EXEC *(see Macro Functions—Control)*

EXECUTE *(see Macro Functions—Control)*

External Reference

An *external reference* is a type of link, reference, or connection to information in another worksheet. An external reference is a link between Excel documents, or a link between an Excel document and some other worksheet in another application (such as Lotus 1-2-3). You create an external reference by typing a linking formula.

To create a linking formula, in one cell of your worksheet, type an equal sign followed by the name of a worksheet document (other than the one you are currently using), an exclamation mark, and a reference in the named worksheet.

Example

Suppose cell D7 of the file called totals.xls has the value 400 in it. Create an external reference (or link) to this file by typing `=totals.xls!D7` in cell A1 of the current worksheet, Ltest. The value 400 appears in cell A1.

Now type `390` in cell D7 of the totals.xls worksheet and then switch to the Ltest worksheet. The value you just typed in the totals.xls worksheet, 390, appears automatically in cell A1 of the Ltest worksheet, where the external reference =totals.xls!D7 is typed.

EXP() (*see also* Function, LN, LOG)

Syntax

EXP(*number*)

Description

EXP is a function that returns *e* raised to the power of the given number.

The symbol *e* is a constant that stands for the number 2.71828182845904. EXP uses *e* as the base, *number* as the exponent, and returns the value e^{number}, which equals $2.71828182845904^{number}$. To raise any other base to a power, use the exponentiation operator ^.

The information required for function EXP:

number is a real number (an integer, fraction, etc.) that is to be used in the calculation as the power or exponent of e.

Note: EXP is the inverse of the natural logarithm, the LN(number) function.

 Note: The EXP function is useful in many growth calculation formulas that raise the number e to a power. For example, e is used in the monetary calculation of continuously accruing interest and in the calculation of population growth for various biological species.

Examples

Formula	Returns
=EXP(1)	2.718281828
=EXP(−1)	0.367879441
=EXP(4)	54.59815003
=SQRT(EXP(8))	54.59815000
=EXP(LN(5))	5

EXTRACT

(*see* **Macro Functions That Perform Data Commands**)

F

FACT() *(see also* Function, PRODUCT, DPRODUCT)

Syntax

FACT(*number*)

Description

FACT is a function that returns the factorial of the given number. Factorial is a standard mathematical function that gives the product of all the consecutive numbers from 1 up to the number on which the factorial is applied. The factorial of a number is usually written with an exclamation mark after the number on which the factorial function is to be applied. For example, the factorial of 7 looks like 7! and equals 7 * 6 * 5 * 4 * 3 * 2 * 1.

The information required for function FACT:

number is a nonnegative number.

Examples

Formula	Returns
=FACT(3)	6
=FACT(3.7)	6
=FACT(0)	1
=FACT(−5)	#NUM! (error message)
=FACT(7)	5040
=FACT(9)	362880

FALSE() *(see also* Function, TRUE*)*

Syntax

FALSE( )

Description

FALSE is a function that returns the logical value of FALSE.
The information required for function FALSE:

No information is required for function FALSE.

 Note: Using function FALSE( ) creates the same effect as using the logical value FALSE. Either can be typed directly into the worksheet or into a formula. Function FALSE is included in order to maintain compatibility with other spreadsheet programs.

Examples

Formula with FALSE Function	*Formula with FALSE Logical Value*	*Both Return the Logical Value*
=FALSE( )	FALSE	FALSE
=NOT(FALSE( ))	=NOT(FALSE)	TRUE

FCLOSE *(see* Macro Functions—Control*)*

File Close

Close is a command in the File menu that closes the current Excel file displayed in your workspace. Each time you use the Close command, it closes only one file, the file that was displayed in your workspace immediately before using the File Close command.

Keystrokes

Keyboard *Mouse*

File   File

Close   Close

Example

Suppose that myfile.xls is displayed in the workspace. If you saved the file after the last change you made to it, then to close it, you would simply select File and then Close.

 Closing a File

1. Select File from the main menu.   The File menu appears.

2. Select Close in the File menu.   If you made changes to the file currently displayed in the workspace, then a dialog box appears asking `Save changes in <name of your file>?` with three options for your response.

3. Choose Yes to save the file and then close it. Choose No to close the file without saving it. Choose Cancel to return to the display of the file in the workspace without saving or closing the file.   You return to your worksheet.

FILE.CLOSE

(*see* Macro Functions That Perform File Commands)

File Delete

File Delete is a command that allows you to delete any files in any directory. You can delete Excel files of any type: worksheets, charts, macros, or workspace files. When you delete a file with the File Delete command, the file is no longer available. You cannot open a deleted file in Excel and ,therefore, you cannot use a deleted file.

Keystrokes

Keyboard	Mouse
File	File
Delete	Delete

 Deleting a File

1. Select File from the main menu. — The File menu appears.
2. Select Delete in the File menu. — A dialog box opens that allows you to choose files to delete.
3. Select the name of the file you want to delete.
4. Select OK or press Enter. — A dialog box appears asking `Delete file '<file name>'?`.
5. Select the Yes box to delete the file or the "No" box if you do not want to delete the file.
6. Repeat steps 3, 4, and 5 to delete each file that you wish to delete.
7. Select the Close box in the Delete dialog box in order to return to your workspace.

FILE.DELETE

(*see* Macro Functions That Perform File Commands)

File Exit

File Exit is a command that allows you to exit Microsoft Excel. If there are any files with changes that haven't been saved, when you choose the File Exit command, Excel asks if you want to save these changes. If you choose not to save changed files, then you lose your changes permanently. Once you exit Microsoft Excel, you must restart Excel to use it.

Keystrokes

Keyboard   *Mouse*

File   File

Exit   Exit

 Exiting a File

1.	Select File in the main menu.	The File menu appears.
2.	Select Exit in the File menu.	If there are any files with changes that haven't been saved, Excel prompts you with a dialog box for each file.
3.	Select Yes to save the changes, No to lose the changes, or Cancel to cancel the process of exiting Excel.	Yes saves the file as revised, No closes the file in its last saved state, and Cancel returns you to the workspace as it was before you chose File Exit.

File Links

File Links is a command that allows you to open, change, or update links in the document that is currently displayed. The File Links command manages the files and information that are tied to the current worksheet through links. A *link* is a connection to information in another document. (See "External Reference" for an explanation and example of links.)

The File Links command allows you to:

- View a listing of the files that the current worksheet is linked to.

- View the types of links that exist in the current worksheet.

- Open a document that is linked to the current worksheet.
- Change the set of links to a document to refer to a different document.
- Update values that are gotten from links to other documents that are closed.

 Note: The Change option applies the new link name to *all* links that referred to the old file name.

File Links Update is useful when you change values in a file, save and close it, and then open a file that refers to the changed file without automatically updating all its links (since there may be some links that you don't want to update). In this case, you can selectively update some specific links to other files and not others using the File Links Update command.

Keystrokes

Keyboard   ***Mouse***

File   File

Links   Links

Example

Suppose that your active worksheet (currently displayed in the workspace) contained two links that were the following external references: sums89.xls!D7 and sums89.xls!F7. You created a new file called sums90.xls, which is an up-to-date version of the sums89.xls file. The information in the sums90 file is arranged in the exact same structure, and locates the exact same cells as the sums89 file. You want to change the links to refer to the new file in order to have the most current information in your active worksheet.

To change all the sums89.xls links to refer to the sums90 file, select File and then Links. Select sums89 in the Links box of the File Links dialog box. Select the Change box in the File Links dialog box. (A new dialog box headed "change links to SUMS89.XLS" replaces the File Links dialog box.) In the "change links to SUMS89.XLS" dialog box, select the sums90.xls file. Select the OK box or press Enter.

The result is the links in your active worksheet; sums89.xls!D7 and sums89.xls!F7 change to sums90.xls!D7 and sums90.xls!F7.

Using the File Links Command

1. Select File in the main menu.   The File menu appears.
2. Select Links in the File menu.   A dialog box appears with boxes that contain the types of links that are in the current worksheet, all the files that are linked to the current worksheet, open, change, and update options, and read-only choices. Individual instruction for these choices follows.

- To view the type of link of any of the files in the Links box, select the name of the link in the Links box and view its type in the Link Type box.

- To view all the types of links that exist in the document, select the down arrow of the Link Type box. A menu appears that displays all the types of links in the current worksheet.

- To open a document that your current file is linked to, select in the Links box of the File Links dialog box the name of the file that you want to open. Select the Open box.

- To redirect all the links going from a specific document to another document, select the file name that you want to change from the Links box in the File Links dialog box. Select the Change box in the File Links dialog box. In the Change Links to <old file name> dialog box, either select a file name from the listing of files or type a file name in the Copy from File box. Select the OK box or press Enter.

- To update links to a file that is closed, select in the Links box of the File Links dialog box the name of the closed file whose values you want to update from the current file and select the Update box.

 Note: If a file is currently open, the update option is not needed and not available. Therefore, it is displayed in a gray color.

File List

The *file list* is a numbered list of files under the File menu that you can use to open files. The file list is a shortcut means of opening files. If you want to open a file that is in the file list, which is positioned just above the Exit command in the File menu, then all you need to do is select that file.

Keystrokes

Keyboard

<u>F</u>ile

Type the number next to the name of the file in the File menu.

Mouse

<u>F</u>ile

Click on the name of the file in the File menu.

Example

Suppose that the file list in the File menu looks like this:

<u>1</u> Recipes.xls
<u>2</u> Deadlines.xlc
<u>3</u> Appointments.xls

To open the file called Appointments.xls, select <u>F</u>ile in the main menu. Then select <u>3</u> Appointments.xls in the File menu.

 Opening a File

1. Select <u>F</u>ile in the main menu.   The File menu appears.
2. Select the file's name in the File menu.   The file that you selected is opened and becomes the current active document.

File New

<u>N</u>ew is a command in the <u>F</u>ile menu that allows you to create a new document in the workspace. The new document can be one of three types: a worksheet, a chart, or a macro sheet.

When Excel is first started, a blank worksheet called *sheet1* is automatically created. Hence, you need to use the File New command only when you are already working in the program and wish to create a brand-new file.

Keystrokes

Keyboard   *Mouse*

File   File

New   New

Creating a New File

1. Select File in the main menu.   The File menu appears.
2. Select New in the File menu.   A dialog box with these three options appears: Worksheet, Chart, and Macro Sheet.
3. Select which type of document you want to create: a Worksheet, a Chart, or a Macro Sheet.
4. Select the OK box or press Enter.   You return to your worksheet.

File Open

Open is a command in the File menu that allows you to open any existing file that was previously created and saved in Excel or previously imported into Excel. By default, only files with the Excel suffixes are displayed in the File Open dialog box. But you can open any Excel document under any name, and you can import a file that wasn't created in Excel.

When you choose the File Open command, you can choose any available directory for the file you want to open and any file in the selected directory. If there are more directories or more files than can fit in the box that encloses these, then a scroll bar is displayed to the right of the box. To view directories or files that are not displayed, move the scroll bar up or down.

Note: A file remains open as long as you do not close the file or exit from Excel. If you open another file, the most recently opened file will appear in the workspace. To view or work in any hidden open file, use the Window command.

When you first use the File Open command, only files that have Excel suffixes are listed in the dialog box for the Open command. These suffixes are four in number, and each ending represents the type of document the file contains: *.xls* indicates that the file is a worksheet; *.xlm*, a macro sheet; *.xlc*, a chart; and *.xlw*, a workgroup. You may open other files by typing *.* and selecting the open button. When you do this, all the files in the current directory are displayed in the File Open dialog box.

Keystrokes

Keyboard	*Mouse*
File	File
Open	Open
Arrow keys to select file	Click on the file name

 Opening a File

1. Select File in the main menu. — The File menu appears.

2. Select Open in the File menu. — A dialog box with the following appears: the name of the current directory, a listing of the available directories, and a listing of all the names of the Excel files in the current directory.

3. If the current directory is not the directory where your file is located, then in the Directories box, select the directory of your file.

4. If the name of the file that you want to open is listed in the Files box of the Open dialog box, then highlight it. Otherwise, scroll the Files box until the name of the file that you want to open appears; then highlight it.

5. Select OK or press Enter. — You return to your worksheet.

File Page Setup

File Page Setup is a command that allows you to make changes to the setup of the printed page. With File Page Setup, you can add a header or footer; set the size of the left, right, top and/or bottom margins; and center the page horizontally or vertically. On a worksheet or macro sheet, you can include or not include the row and column headings and/or the gridlines in the workspace. On a chart, with the size box, you can change the size of the chart to the same size as the screen, retain the height-to-width ratio and fit the chart to the page, or change the height-to-width ratio and fit the chart to the full page. You can adjust the orientation of the page to portrait or landscape; choose the paper (letter, legal, ledger size, or custom paper size); and reduce, enlarge, or—on a worksheet or macro sheet—fit the entire document on one page.

When you select the File Page Setup command, a Page Setup dialog box appears with all the options named above. Once you choose your settings and select OK, the page settings remain as you set them until you reset them with the File Page Setup command or until you restart Excel.

 Note: These page settings that you specify do not affect the workspace. They change only the appearance of the document on the printed page.

Keystrokes

Keyboard   *Mouse*

File   File

Page Setup   Page Setup

Example

Suppose that you want to add the heading "November 1991 Sales Report" to every page of your document before printing it. To do this, select File and then Page Setup. Type **November 1991 Sales Report** in the header box. Select OK box or press Enter.

If you print your document or view it with the File Print Preview command, the heading "November 1991 Sales Report" appears at the top of every page.

Setting Up the Page Format

1. Select File in the main menu.

   The File menu appears.

2. Select Page Setup in the File menu.

   The Page Setup dialog box appears, allowing you to choose options described in steps 4 through 11.

3. If desired, type a header or footer in the header or footer box.

4. To set the size of the left, right, top, and/or bottom margins, type a number in their respective boxes.

5. To center the text on the page horizontally or vertically, turn on the horizontal or vertical check boxes, respectively.

6. To include either the workspace row and column headings or the gridlines in a printed worksheet or macro sheet page, turn on either of these check boxes. To not include either feature, turn off the respective check boxes.

7. To change the size of a chart, select the radio button beside the desired size (Screen Size, Fit to Page, or Full Page).

   When you turn on or select a circle automatically, any other circle that was previously selected is turned off.

8. Select either the Portrait or scape radio button in the Orientation box.

   Portrait orients your page Land-vertically, while Landscape orients it horizontally.

9. Choose the paper size by selecting the appropriate radio button for letter, legal, ledger, or custom paper size.

10. Reduce or enlarge the contents of the document by typing in a percentage to reduce or enlarge by.

One hundred is the actual size of the page. A number over one enlarges the document, and a number less than one hundred reduces the size of the text in the document.

11. To compress a worksheet or macro sheet so that it fits on one page, select the Fit To Page box.

Some options are not available with some printers.

12. Select OK or press Enter.

You return to your worksheet.

File Print

File Print is a command that allows you to print your document. Before printing, you can choose various options: the number of copies of the document that you want to print; which pages in the document you want to print; the quality of the printing—draft or not; on worksheets and macro sheets, whether to print the sheet, the notes in the sheet, or both of these; and whether to print the document on paper with a printer or to view the document in the Print Preview screen. (See "File Print Preview" for more information on the Print Preview screen.)

Keystrokes

Keyboard   *Mouse*

File   File

Print   Print

 Printing a Document

1. Select File in the main menu.

   The File menu appears.

2. Select Print in the File menu.

   The Print Setup dialog box appears, allowing you to choose any of the options described in steps 3 through 7.

3. To print more than one copy, set the number of copies of the document that you want to print by putting the number of copies you want in the Copies box.

   The desired number of copies will be printed and properly collated.

4. If you do not want to print the entire document, select the radio button to the left of From: and then type in the number of the first page that you want to print in the From box and the number of the last page that you want to print in the To box.

   These pages and all pages between them will be printed.

5. If you want draft quality, select the Draft Quality radio button.

6. On worksheets and macro sheets, to print the notes in the worksheet or macro sheet, or both the worksheet or macro sheet and the notes, select the corresponding radio button.

7. To view the document in the Print Preview screen before printing, select the Preview radio button. If Preview is on and you want to print the document immediately, deselect the Preview radio button.

8. Select OK or press Enter.

   Printing commences and a dialog box appears to update you on the status of the print job.

File Printer Setup

File Printer Setup is a command that allows you to select the specifications for your printer. When you installed Windows, you installed some printer specifications with the Printers program under Program Manager, Main, Control Panel. These installed printers are listed when you choose the File Printer Setup command.

With the File Printer Setup command, you can change the active printer or the global printer settings. You can view and/or change the graphics resolution, the type of printers available, the orientation, the paper feed, the text mode, the paper width, the paper height, whether printing can be done in color or not, margins, information about the active printer, and other letter-quality fonts.

Keystrokes

Keyboard   *Mouse*

File   File

Printe_r Setup   Printe_r Setup

 Setting Up the Printer

1. Select File in the main menu.   The File menu appears.

2. Select Printer Setup in the File menu.   The Printer dialog box appears.

3. If desired, change the active printer by selecting another printer.

4. If desired, view or change printer settings by selecting the Setup box and selecting any new options.   The Printer Driver dialog box appears.

5. Select OK or press Enter to keep any new settings, or select Cancel to return to the old settings.

6. Select OK or press Enter.   You return to your worksheet.

File Print Preview

File Print Preview is a command that allows you to preview on your monitor screen how your printed file would look if you printed it. When you choose File Print Preview, a screen appears with the Print Preview options along the top and the first page of the active file in very small print underneath these options.

You can look at the next or previous page of your document, zoom in or out for a close-up of part of the page or a view of the entire page on the screen, activate the File Print command, activate the File Page Setup command, change the margins for the page and/or the column margins on a worksheet or macro sheet, or exit the Print Preview screen. The Print Preview screen remains active until you choose the Print or Close options.

Keystrokes

Keyboard   *Mouse*

<u>F</u>ile   <u>F</u>ile

Print Pre<u>v</u>iew   Print Pre<u>v</u>iew

 Previewing a File Before Printing

1. Select <u>F</u>ile in the main menu.
   The File menu appears.

2. Select Print Pre<u>v</u>iew in the File menu.
   A screen appears with several Print Preview options along the top and the first page of the active file in very small print.

3. To look at the next or previous page of your document, select the <u>N</u>ext or <u>P</u>revious box in the top row of this screen.

4. To see a close-up of part of the page on the screen, select <u>Z</u>oom, or click on page.

5. To see the entire page on the screen, zoom out by *either* selecting the <u>Z</u>oom box or by clicking the mouse when the cursor takes the shape of a magnifying glass.
   When you zoom with the magnifying glass, the area where the magnifying glass was before zooming is the area of the page that is expanded.

6. If your pages are set up as you want them, select the Prin<u>t</u> box in the Print Preview screen.
   The Print Preview screen disappears, you return to your workspace document, and the Print dialog box appears. (See "File Print" for more information on the Print dialog box.)

7. If your pages are not set up as you want them, select the <u>S</u>etup box in the Print Preview screen.
   The Page Setup dialog box appears. (See "File Page Setup" for information on the Page Setup dialog box.)

8. To change columns or margins, select the associated guideline (a black dotted line) and move in either direction to shrink or expand the margin or columns as needed.

   The cursor moves the column or margin along with it.

9. If no guidelines are visible, select the Margins box.

   The Margins box acts as a toggle switch, turning the display of the margin and column guidelines on and off.

10. Select the Close box to exit the Print Preview screen.

    Your document reappears, as revised in the normal workspace.

FILES (*see* Macro Functions—Value Returning)

File Save (*see also* Save As)

File Save is a command that saves the active file. The active file is the only file that is currently displayed in your workspace and has a highlighted title bar (top bar). Each time you use the Save command, it saves the document in its current state in the workspace. When you save a document that has been saved previously, it is saved with the name that you gave it the last time that it was saved (which is listed in the title bar at the top of the worksheet). When you save a document, the previous version of the document that was in the file before you saved is lost (or can no longer be opened with the File Open command).

 Note: If more than one file is open at a time, the File Save command will not save all the open files. The File Save command saves only one file at a time—only the active file in the workspace.

Keystrokes

Keyboard *Mouse*

File File

Save Save

Saving a File

1. Select File in the main menu. — The File menu appears.

2. Select Save in the File menu. — If you have previously saved the current document, then at this point you return to your worksheet. If you have not previously saved the current document, then a dialog box appears allowing you to a) choose the directory that you want to save the file in and b) give a name to the document.

3. If the Save dialog box is open, to change the directory, click twice on the directory that you want to save the file in. — The directory that you selected becomes the current directory.

4. Type a name in the Save Worksheet As box, the Save Macro As box, or the Save Chart As box. — The name that you just typed is the name of your document. When the current directory is the same as the directory that you saved this file in, this name will be listed in the Files box for the File Open command.

5. Select the OK box or press Enter. — You return to your worksheet.

File Save As

File Save As is a command that allows you to save the active file in any directory with any name. The active file is the only file that is currently displayed in your workspace and has a highlighted title bar (top bar). Each time you use the Save As command, it saves only the current version of the file that was active before you selected the File Save As command.

When you use Save As, no changes are made to any files that were previously saved; only a new copy of the current document in the workspace is created with the new name that you specify. If you use the same name for your document that it had prior to your using the Save As command, then the Save As command performs the same operations as the Save command.

> **Note:** If more than one file is open at a time, the File Save As command will not save all the open files. The File Save As command saves only one file at a time—only the active file in the workspace.

Keystrokes

Keyboard   *Mouse*

<u>F</u>ile   <u>F</u>ile

Save <u>A</u>s   Save <u>A</u>s

Examples

Suppose that you created and saved a worksheet called Checkbook. You also made some changes to it that you want to save under a new name. (You want to keep the original file Checkbook without these changes, so that you can use it as a starting point for other worksheets that you want to create.)

To save your changes under a new file name called checks90 in the current directory and still keep the old file Checkbook, make sure that the file with the changes that you made is currently displayed in your workspace. Select <u>F</u>ile and then Save <u>A</u>s. Type **checks90** in the Save Worksheet As box. (Later when you want to open this file, choose this name from the Files box for the File Open command.) Select OK or press Enter. You now have a file called checkbook.xls and a file called checks90.xls.

 ### Saving a File

1. Select <u>F</u>ile in the main menu.   The File menu appears.

2. Select Save <u>A</u>s in the <u>F</u>ile menu.   A dialog box appears with a listing of the available directories and a box for naming the file.

3. If you wish to save the file in a directory other than the current directory, click twice on the directory that you want to save the file in.

4. Select the Options box to access any of the options described in steps 5 through 9.

5. To change the file format, click on the down arrow on the right side of the File Format box; then highlight the desired file format: Normal, Template, Excel 2.1, SYLK, Text, etc.

6. To create a backup file, turn on the Create Backup File box.

7. To require anyone who is trying to open the file to type a password before he opens the file, type a password in the Protection Password box.

    No one will be able to open the file in Excel without first typing the password that you specify in this box.

8. To require anyone opening the file to type a password in order be able to save the file, type a password in the Write Reservation Password box.

    No one will be able to save the file in Excel without first typing to the password that you specify in this box.

9. To specify read-only recommended, turn on the Read-only Recommended box.

    No one will be able to make any changes to the file.

10. Type a name in the Save Worksheet As box, the Save Macro As box, or the Save Chart As box.

    This name is the name of your document. When the current directory is the same as the directory that you saved this file in, this name will be listed in the Files box for the File Open command.

11. Select OK or press Enter.

    You return to your worksheet.

File Save Workspace

File Save Workspace is a command that allows you to save all the files in the workspace under one name. When you use the File Save Workspace command, *all* the Excel documents in the workspace—all worksheets, charts, and macro sheets—are saved with the name that you specify followed by *.xlw*. When you open a single workspace, *all* the files that you saved when you used the File Save Workspace command are opened.

Keystrokes

Keyboard   *Mouse*

<u>F</u>ile   <u>F</u>ile

Save <u>W</u>orkspace   Save <u>W</u>orkspace

 ### Saving a Workspace

1. Select <u>F</u>ile in the main menu.   The File menu appears.

2. Select Save <u>W</u>orkspace in the File menu.   A dialog box for the workspace appears.

3. If you wish to change the directory for the workspace, select the directory in which you want to save the workspace.

4. Type a name in the Save Workspace As box.   This name is the name of your workspace file. (Later, when you want to open all the files that are contained in the workspace, use the File Open command and specify this name.)

5. Select OK or press Enter.

6. If you opened a workspace and are saving it with the same name that it had when you opened it, a dialog box will appear asking whether you want to replace the existing workspace or not. Select OK to replace the earlier versions of the files in the workspace with the newest files, or Cancel to rename your workspace.   If you choose OK, you will overwrite the files with the current versions of the files. If you choose Cancel, you will return to the Save Workspace As box, where you can save the workspace under a different name.

7. In the dialog box that appears for each unsaved document, select Yes to save changes made to the document, No to lose the changes that have been made to the document, or Cancel to cancel the Save Workspace command. In each dialog box, choose one of these three options by selecting the Yes, No, or cancel boxes, respectively.

A dialog box appears for each document in the workspace with changes that have not been saved.

FILL.DOWN

(see Macro Functions That Perform Edit Commands)

FILL.LEFT

(see Macro Functions That Perform Edit Commands)

FILL.RIGHT

(see Macro Functions That Perform Edit Commands)

FILL.UP

(see Macro Functions That Perform Edit Commands)

FILL.WORKGROUP

(*see* Macro Functions That Perform Edit Commands)

FIND() (*see also* SEARCH, MID, LEN, EXACT)

Syntax

FIND(*find_text,within_text,start_at_num*)

Description

FIND is a function that returns a numerical index to within_text. This index tells you the beginning character of the first occurrence of find_text in within_text.

FIND begins its search into within_text at the character specified by start_at_num. FIND looks for the given value find_text from left to right. When FIND discovers an exact replica of the find_text string in within_text, then it returns the numerical position that indicates where the first occurrence of the find_text string of characters begins in the within_text string of characters.

FIND distinguishes between upper- and lowercase letters. FIND does not find a string in the within_text string if corresponding letters are of different cases.

FIND returns a #VALUE! error if:

- start_at_num is less than 1.

- start_at_num indicates a position beyond the end of within_text. (This occurs when start_at_num is larger than the length of within_text.)

- find_text is not in the within_text string of characters.

 Tip: The first and second conditions that create a #VALUE! error can be easily detected by checking the conditions: start_at_num < 1, and start_at_num > LEN(within_text), where *LEN* is built-in.

> **Note:** If you want to use wild-card characters or ignore the difference between upper- and lowercase letters when searching, then use the SEARCH function. The SEARCH function behaves in the same way as the FIND function except that it overlooks the case of letters and uses wild-card characters.

The information required for function FIND:

find_text is any single symbol or group of symbols. If text is typed directly into the list of values for the function, then it must be enclosed in quotation marks.

If *find_text* is an empty string, "", or a reference to an empty cell, then FIND returns start_at_num or the default value for start_at_num. (The default value when start_at_num is not specified is 1.) Wild-card characters in find_text are not allowed.

within_text is any single symbol or group of symbols.

start_at_num is a number that acts as an index in the within_text string of characters. If start_at_num is 1, then the search for find_text begins at the first character. If start_at_num is 8, then the search for find_text begins at the eighth character. If start_at_num is not included in the list of values for the function, then start_at_num is assumed to be 1 and the search for find_text begins at the first character.

Examples

=FIND("find me", "Look inside me for find me", 4)
    within_text = "Look inside me for find me"
    find_text = "find me"
    start_at_num = 4

In this example, the string to search is the within_text string, "Look inside me for find me". The text that the FIND function is looking for is the "find me" text string. The position that this search starts at is the start_at_num position, which, in this example, is the fourth character. The fourth character of the within_text string is "k". Searching from left to right, the first occurrence of "find me" starts at the 20th character of the within_text. FIND returns 20 for this example.

If everything about this example were the same, except that start_at_text was 21, then FIND would not find the "find me" string of characters! In this second example, FIND would return #VALUE!, even though the "find me" does exist in the within_text string.

Formula	Returns
=FIND("Super","SuperBowl Sunday")	1
=FIND("Super","SuperBowl Sunday",2)	#VALUE!
=FIND("S","SuperBowl Sunday",6)	11
=FIND("s","Superstructure",1)	6

FIXED() *(see also* DOLLAR, TEXT, VALUE*)*

Syntax

FIXED(*number,decimals*)

Description

FIXED is a function that returns the text form of *number* rounded off to the requested number of decimals, with a fixed format of decimals and commas. (This format is #,##0.00, where # is an optional place holder for a number.)

Rounding for FIXED uses the same procedure as the function ROUND. FIXED employs the traditional rules of rounding: If the next smaller digit is five or more, then the digit is rounded up. If the next smaller digit is four or less, then the digit remains the same.

Numbers are rounded according to the following guidelines:

- If a decimal is less than 0, it is rounded to the left of the decimal point.
- If a decimal is 0, it is rounded to the nearest integer.
- If a decimal is greater than 0, it is rounded to the right of the decimal point.

Note: Excel also offers a command for formatting a number into fixed format. The Number command on the Format menu leaves the number as a numerical value, whereas the FIXED function converts the number into text.

The information required for function FIXED:

number is any number.

decimals is a number that specifies how many digits of number to round. If decimals has a fractional part, that fractional part is ignored. For example, =FIXED(0.12,–1.7) returns the same result as =FIXED (0.12,–1).

Examples

Formula	Returns
=FIXED(12345.6789,–3)	"12,000"
=FIXED(–12345.6789,–1)	"–12,350"
=FIXED(12345.6789,0)	"12346"
=FIXED(–12345.6789,2)	"–12,345.68"
=FIXED(12.123)	"12.12"
=FIXED(–12.345)	"(12.35)"

Footer *(see also* Header)

The Footer feature specifies the footer, if any, to be printed at the bottom of each page.

The footer is always printed 1/2 inch above the bottom of the page and 3/4 inch from the sides of the page. The following codes can be combined and inserted in the footer box to format the footer. Each code applies to the characters that follow it.

Code	Result in Footer
&B	Bold characters
&C	Center alignment
&D	Current date
&F	Filename of spreadsheet
&I	Italic characters
&L	Left alignment
&N	Print total number of pages
&P	Page number
&P+number	Page numbers plus the base number
&P–number	Page numbers minus the base number

Code	Result in Footer
&R	Right alignment
&S	Strikethrough characters
&T	Current time
&U	Underline characters
&&	A single ampersand
&"fontname"	Change to specified font. Fontname must be inside double quotes.
&nn	Change to specified font size

 Caution: If the bottom margin is less than 1/2 inch, the footer will be printed on top of the spreadsheet data. If the error `Not Supported by the Current Printer` is displayed when the Page Setup dialog box is closed, an option has been selected that is not supported by the current printer. Turn off the options one at a time until the nonsupported option is found, or select another printer with the Printer Setup option that supports all the options selected.

Keystrokes

Keyboard	Mouse
File	File
Page Setup	Page Setup

Example

&"Modern"&12&LProfit && Loss Statement&CPage &P of &N&R&D: If this example is entered in the Footer box on the Page Setup dialog box, the footer will be printed at the bottom of the page in Modern font 12 points tall. *Profit & Loss Statement* will be printed at the left border, *Page 1 of 20* will be centered, and the current date will be printed at the right border.

FOPEN *(see* Macro Functions—Control)

FOR *(see* Macro Functions—Control)

FOR.CELL *(see* Macro Functions—Control)

Format 3-D View (for charts)

Use the Format 3-D View command in a chart window to alter perspective and rotation angles in a three-dimensional chart. This command gives you a virtually unlimited number of views for a 3-D chart.

Each option in this dialog box controls the angle of the view of the chart. As you change the various options, you can choose the Apply button to see the effect of your changes on this representation without exiting the dialog box. Choose the Default button, and the option numbers revert to the Excel defaults.

Elevation controls the height from which you view the chart in degrees. With Perspective, the greater the number, the more the chart "stretches back into the distance." 0 means no perspective. The Rotation number (range 0 to 360) gives the angle in degrees of the whole chart around the vertical axis. Right Angle Axes puts the axes at right angles and cancels out the Perspective option. Height % of Base: The range is from 5 to 500. 100 makes the height and width equal; 500 makes the height (including the walls) five times greater than the width.

Keystrokes

Keyboard	*Mouse*
Format	Format
3-D View	3-D View
Type a number in the Elevation, Rotation, Perspective, Right Angle Axes, and Height boxes. Some of these options may not be available with certain charts and sets of options.	Click on an arrowhead next to the Elevation, Rotation, Perspective, Right Angle Axes, and Height boxes to change the picture.
Apply	Apply
Default	Default
Enter	OK

Format 3-D View (for charts) 469

Example

Suppose that your chart is displayed as a 3-D Column chart, and you wish to rotate the chart around to better compare the different series. Choose 3-D View from Format and type **60**, replacing 30 in the Rotation box. Choose OK. The figure shows the before chart (on the left) and the after chart (on the right).

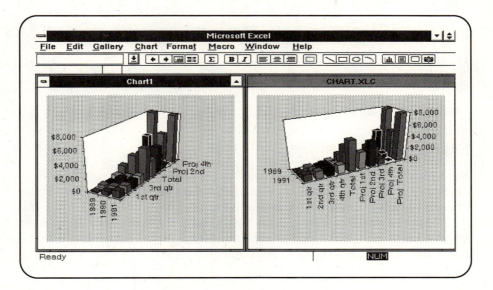

 Formatting a 3-D Chart

1. Make the chart the active chart.

2. Choose 3-D View from Format. Excel displays the Format 3-D dialog box.

3. Make your changes.

4. Choose Apply and move the whole dialog box to the side of the screen to see the effect on the chart.

5. Choose OK to exit.

Format Alignment

Alignment is a command under the Format menu that allows you to align the contents of the selected cells. There are five types of alignment that you can choose from: general, left, center, right, and fill. You can also choose to wrap text or not.

Keystrokes

Keyboard	*Mouse*
Format	Format
Alignment	Alignment

Examples

Suppose that you want to align some highlighted cells to display values in the center of the cell. To do this, select Format and then Alignment. Turn on the Center check box. Select OK or press Enter.

Suppose that you want to align highlighted cells to display values on the left side of the cell. Select the Format command and then Alignment. Turn on the Left check box. Select OK or press return.

 Aligning Values

1. Select the Format command.

2. Select Alignment.   The Alignment dialog box appears with these options: General, Left, Center, Right, Full. (For a detailed description of the Alignment dialog box, press the F1 key at this time, while the Alignment dialog box is visible. To exit Help, choose File Exit in the Help box.)

3. Select the options you want to set.

4. Choose OK or press Enter.

Format Border

<u>B</u>order is a command under the Forma<u>t</u> menu that allows you to add a border around the selected cell, each cell in a range of cells, the entire selected range of cells, or an object. You can choose to put a border on the left, right, top, or bottom of the cell, cells, or object that is selected. Or you can put a border as an outline around the cell, cells, or object that is selected. You can choose the color of the border out of 17 colors, and you have several options for the style of the border. You can shade the selected item or not.

Keystrokes

Keyboard	*Mouse*
Forma<u>t</u>	Forma<u>t</u>
<u>B</u>order	<u>B</u>order

Examples

Suppose that you want to put a green border around the outside of selected items and shade an entire selected region. Select Forma<u>t</u> and <u>B</u>order. In the Border dialog box, select the outline option in the box that is labeled Border. Select the color green in the Color pull-down menu. Turn on the Shade check box. Then choose OK or press Enter.

    Suppose that you want to put a thin red border underneath some selected items. To do this, select the Forma<u>t</u> command in the menu bar and then select <u>B</u>order. In the Border dialog box, select the bottom option in the box that is labeled Border. Select the thin line option in the Style box, and select the color red in the Color pull-down menu. Select OK or press Enter.

 Creating a Border

1. Select the Forma<u>t</u> command in the menu bar.

2. Select <u>B</u>order.   The Border dialog box appears with these options: Border, Style, Color, Shade. (For a detailed description of the <u>B</u>order dialog box, press the F1 key at this time, while the Border dialog box is visible. To exit Help, choose <u>F</u>ile E<u>x</u>it in the Help box.)

3. Select the options you want to set.

4. Select OK or press Enter.

Format Bring To Front

Bring To Front is a command under the Format menu that allows you to bring the selected object or objects to the front, on top of all other objects in the document. If this command appears in gray, it is not available. This command is available only when an object or objects (such as an embedded chart, a drawn object, or a copy of an embedded chart or drawn object) are selected. A selected object appears with an outline box around it (an outline box has square shaded boxes on its corners and midpoints).

Keystrokes

Keyboard   *Mouse*

Format   Format

Bring To Front   Bring to Front

Example

Suppose that you have created two embedded charts that you display side by side in two overlapping areas. The chart on the left, called *Reapers Inc*, is an overview of the entire company. The chart on the right, called *Colorado Division*, gives information for your particular branch of the Reapers Inc company. You want to be able either to look at the full detail of the chart on the left, Reapers Inc, or to look at the left side of the Reapers Inc chart along with the entire Colorado Division chart, the chart on the right.

To look at the entire Reapers Inc chart, select the Reapers Inc chart. Then select the Format command in the menu bar and Bring To Front. To look at the left side of the Reapers Inc chart and the entire Colorado Division chart, select the Colorado Division chart. Select Format and then Bring To Front.

Bringing an Object to the Front

1. Select the object or objects that you want to display on top of all other objects. (If you want to select more than one object, hold down the Shift key while you are selecting objects.)

2. Select the Format command in the menu bar.

3. Select the Bring To Front command under the Format options.

The object you selected is displayed on top.

Format Cell Protection

Cell Protection is a command under the Format menu that allows you to lock or hide cell(s) or objects. The lock and hide options come into effect only when document protection is turned on. The locked option prevents the entering of any values in a cell when document protection is turned on. The hidden option prevents formulas from being displayed in the formula bar when document protection is turned on.

The Cell Protection dialog box automatically comes up with the lock option chosen and the hide option not chosen.

Keystrokes

Keyboard   *Mouse*

Format   Format

Cell Protection   Cell Protection

Examples

Suppose that you want to protect and hide a group of cells. To do this, select the cells that you want to protect and hide. Select Format and Cell Protection. (The Cell Protection dialog box appears.) If the lock check box is on, leave it turned on. If the lock check box is turned off, turn it on. Turn on the hide check box. Select OK or press Enter.

Suppose you do not want to protect or hide a group of cells. Select the cells that you do not want to protect and hide. Select Format and Cell Protection. (The Cell Protection dialog box appears.) Turn off the lock check box. Turn off the hide check box. Select OK or press Enter.

 Protecting or Hiding

1. Select the cell(s) or object that you want to protect or hide.

2. Select the Format command in the menu bar.

3. Select Cell Protection.

    The Cell Protection dialog box appears with the lock and hide options. (For a detailed description of the Cell Protection dialog box, press the F1 key at this time, while the Cell Protection dialog box is visible. To exit Help, choose File Exit in the Help box.)

4. Leave the lock check box turned on if you want write protection when document protection is on. Turn off the lock check box to turn off write protection.

5. Turn on the hide check box to hide formulas when document protection is on; otherwise, turn it off.

6. Select OK or press Enter.

Format Column Width

Column Width is a command under the Format menu that allows you to change the column width of the column or columns that are selected. You can specify your own column width with a number, select the Standard Width option, or select a width of zero by choosing the Hide option. The Best Fit option gives a best-fit size to the column, which is as wide as the largest value in the column.

Keystrokes

Keyboard   *Mouse*

Forma<u>t</u>   Forma<u>t</u>

<u>C</u>olumn Width   <u>C</u>olumn Width

Examples

Suppose that you want to change the column width of the first column, which contains long labels, to 50. To do this, select Forma<u>t</u> and then <u>C</u>olumn Width. Type the number 50 in the small box labeled Column Width. Select OK or press Enter.

Suppose that you want to make standard width the columns selected by the cursor. To do this, select Forma<u>t</u> and <u>C</u>olumn Width. Turn on the Standard Width box. Select OK or press Enter.

Suppose that you want to hide the column where the cursor is. Select Forma<u>t</u> and then <u>C</u>olumn Width. Select the <u>H</u>ide box. Then select OK or press Enter.

Changing the Column Width

1. Select the Forma<u>t</u> command in the menu bar.

2. Select <u>C</u>olumn Width.   The Column Width dialog box appears with these options: <u>C</u>olumn Width, <u>S</u>tandard Width, <u>H</u>ide, <u>U</u>nhide, or <u>B</u>est Fit. (For a detailed description of the Column Width dialog box, press the F1 key at this time, while the Column Width dialog box is visible. To exit Help, choose <u>F</u>ile E<u>x</u>it in the Help box.)

3. Select the options you want to set.

4. Select OK or press Enter.

Format Font

Font is a command under the Format menu that allows you to change the font of the selected cells. Some options that you can choose from are font, size, style, and color. The size is the size for the particular selected font in points. You can choose a style of bold, italic, underline, or strikeout. There are 17 colors to choose from.

Note: On a monochrome monitor, the color options have no effect.

Keystrokes

Keyboard	Mouse
Format	Format
Font	Font

Example

Suppose that you want to make some highlighted or selected cells appear in Roman font with a red color in a size of 18 points. To do this, select Format and then Font. The Font dialog box appears with these boxes: font, size, style, color, printer fonts, and normal fonts. Select Roman in the Font box. Highlight or select Red in the Color pull-down menu. Highlight or select the number 18 in the Size box. Then choose OK or press Enter.

Changing a Font

1. Select the Format command in the menu bar.
2. Select Font.   The Font dialog box appears with these boxes: font, size, style, color, printer fonts, and normal fonts. (For a detailed description of the Font dialog box, press the F1 key at this time, while the Font dialog box is visible. To exit Help, choose File Exit in the Help box.)

3. Highlight or select the options you want to set.

4. Select OK or press Enter.

Format Group

Group is a command under the Format menu that allows you to group several selected objects together to create a single new object. When you group objects together with the Format Group command, this group of objects is treated as one object or one unit. After you select a group of objects (which have been combined into one object with the Format Group command), every change you make to this selection is made equally to all the objects in the group. If you move a grouped object, all the objects in the group move as a unit.

If this command appears in gray, then it is not available. If the Format Ungroup command appears where the Format Group command previously was, then the current selection is an object that was created with Format Group. This command is available only when objects (such as embedded charts, drawn objects, or groups of objects) are selected. A selected object or objects appear inside an outline box (an outline box has square shaded boxes on its corners and midpoints).

Keystrokes

Keyboard   *Mouse*

Format   Format

Group   Group

Example

Suppose that you have created a picture with several graphic objects in it. You want to move this picture as a unit, without changing the spacing between the different pieces in the picture. To do this, select all the graphic objects that are in your picture. (Hold down the Shift key while you are selecting these graphic objects.) Select the Format command in the menu bar and then Group.

Grouping Objects

1. Select the objects that you want to group together into one object. (To select more than one object, hold down the Shift key while you are selecting objects.)

2. Select the Forma_t command in the menu bar.

3. Select the Group command under the Forma_t options.   The objects you selected are grouped into one new object.

Format Justify

Justify is a command under the Forma_t menu that rearranges text so that it fills the selected range evenly. Before you select the Format Justify command, type text into the leftmost column of an area where you want your text to appear as a paragraph. When you have selected the area for your paragraph and chosen the Format Justify command, the text that you typed into the left column of this area will be arranged as a paragraph in this selected area.

 Note: The Format Justify command cannot be used on anything other than text.

Keystrokes

Keyboard   *Mouse*

Forma_t   Forma_t

Justify   Justify

Example

Suppose that you want to write a paragraph of information in your worksheet. You want to have the paragraph evenly spread over a certain area, and you want to be able to make changes to the paragraph without having to manually reformat single cells one at a time. To create this paragraph, and after every time that you make changes to the paragraph, justify the text with the Format Justify command: First, select the area where you want your paragraph to be distributed. (Make sure that your text is within the leftmost side of the selected area and that all other selected cells are blank.) Then select Format and Justify.

 Justifying Text

1. Select the area where you want your paragraph to be distributed. Make sure that your text is in the leftmost side of the selected area and that all other cells are blank.

2. Select the Format command in the menu bar.

3. Select Justify.   (For a detailed description of the Justify command, press the F1 key while the Justify command is highlighted. To exit Help, choose File Exit in the Help box.)

Format Legend (for charts)

Use the Format Legend command in a chart window to position the legend box in any of five standard positions: Bottom, Corner, Top, Right, and Left.

Keystrokes

Keyboard

Format

Legend

Bottom, Corner, Top, Right, or Left

Font or Text to access Format Font/Format Text commands

Enter

Mouse

Format

Legend

Bottom, Corner, Top, Right, or Left

Font or Text to access Format Font/Format Text commands

OK

Example

Suppose that your legend box is displayed in the default position to the right of the chart. You feel it could be more integrated in the whole chart display if it were displayed along the bottom of the chart. Choose Legend from Forma_t_, and then choose _B_ottom and OK.

 Moving a Legend

1. Make the chart the active chart.
2. Choose _L_egend from Forma_t_.   Excel displays the Legend dialog box.
3. Choose one of the options.
4. Choose OK.   Excel moves the legend to the new location.

Format Main Chart

Use the Forma_t_ _M_ain Chart command to apply special formatting options, such as the coloring and the amount of space between categories. Also, if you already applied custom formatting, changing the chart type through this command (rather than through the Gallery menu) retains the formatting. With Combination charts your choices apply only to the main chart; with noncombination charts your choices apply to the whole chart.

Different options are displayed and become available according to the type of chart, including 3-D charts. Chapter 13, "Advanced Charting," takes you through the available options. Or press the F1 key while the dialog box is on-screen for a brief explanation of each option.

Keystrokes

Keyboard	*Mouse*
Forma_t_	Forma_t_
_M_ain Chart	_M_ain Chart
Main Chart _T_ype and Data V_i_ew	Main Chart _T_ype and Data V_i_ew
Enter	OK

Example

Suppose that your Column chart contains only one data series. By default, Excel colors the markers the same color, but you want to see them in different colors. Choose Main Chart from Format. Check Vary by Category and choose OK.

 Formatting a Main Chart

1. Make the chart the active chart.
2. Choose Main Chart from the Format menu.   Excel displays the Main Chart dialog box, with different choices unavailable and available with different chart types.
3. Choose your available option(s).
4. Choose OK.   Excel reformats the chart to your specifications.

Format Move (for charts)

Use the Format Move command in a chart window to reposition arrows and legends.

Keystrokes

Keyboard

Format

Move

Left, Right, Up, or Down arrow keys

Mouse

Format

Move

Drag the mouse.

Example

Suppose that an arrow, created with the Add Arrow command in Chart, points to a data marker on your chart. You want to point it to another marker on the chart. Select the arrow by clicking on it. Choose Move from Format. Reposition the arrow.

Moving an Object

1. Select the object.

2. Choose Mo*v*e from Forma*t*. The mouse pointer automatically positions on the object.

3. Use the mouse or the arrow keys to move the object. Using the arrow keys, you can move vertically, horizontally, and to the left and right—always at right angles.

4. Click with the mouse button to fix the object.

Format Number

Number is a command under the Format menu that allows you to change the format of a number, date, or time in the active cell or cells. You can choose one of the standard formats or define one of your own.

When you format a number with the Format Number command, the number may be displayed to appear as a text value (as in the case of the format for a number with a dollar sign in the example below), but it is treated as a number in all formulas.

Keystrokes

Keyboard *Mouse*

Format Format

Number Number

Examples

Suppose that you want to format some numbers in your worksheet with the standard U.S. currency format. Highlight the numbers that you want to format, and select Format and then Number. The Number dialog box appears with a listing of several standard formats. Select "$#,##0.00_);($#,##0.00)". Then choose OK or press Enter.

Suppose that you want to format some numbers in your worksheet with a particular format that you want to create. In a range of cells, you want to be able to enter a two-digit number and a three-digit number with the word "to" between them. To do this, highlight the numbers that you want to format with your custom-designed format, and select Forma_t and then _Number. Type `"## to ###"` in the Format box of the Format Number dialog box. Choose OK or press Enter.

When you type five digits in one of these formatted cells (for example, 04321), these digits appear with the word "to" between them, (04 to 321). If you type seven digits in one of these formatted cells (for example, 7654321), then the extra digits appear on the left, (7654 to 321).

Formatting Numbers with a Standard Format

1. Select the Forma_t command.

2. Select _Number.   The Number dialog box appears. (For a description of the Number dialog box, press the F1 key at this time, while the Number dialog box is visible. To exit Help, choose _File E_xit in the Help box.)

3. Select the options you want to set.

4. Select OK or press Enter.

Formatting Numbers with a Custom-Designed Format

1. Select the Forma_t command.

2. Select _Number.   The Number dialog box appears. (For a description of the Number dialog box, press the F1 key at this time, while the Number dialog box is visible. To exit Help, choose _File E_xit in the Help box.)

3. In the Format box of the Format Number dialog box, type a single number symbol "#" to represent each one digit of the number in the formatted cell. Type *any* other symbols or letters you want to use in your custom format. One decimal point in your custom format will make the decimal point in any number entered into one of these formatted cells line up with the decimal point of the custom-designed format.

4. Select OK or press Enter.

 Note: When you enter a number into a cell that is formatted with this custom format, your custom format will appear with each # replaced by a number that you typed into the cell. The # symbol is replaced by digits, starting with the rightmost digit.

Format Object Placement

Object Placement is a command under the Forma<u>t</u> menu that allows you to choose how an object is attached to the cells underneath it. There are three options for attaching an object to the underlying cells: a) move and size the object with the underlying cells, b) move but don't size the object with the underlying cells, and c) neither move nor size the object with the underlying cells (free floating).

These three options are clearly demonstrated by the behavior of an object when you hide the column of cells underneath it. If you move and size the object with the underlying cells, the object is hidden when you hide the underlying cells. If you move but don't size the object with the underlying cells, the object is not hidden when you hide the underlying cells, but the object moves to the right. If you neither move nor size the object with the underlying cells (free floating), the object is not hidden when you hide the underlying cells, and the object remains in the same position as it was directly before you hid the column of cells. (With this last option, if the object was in the very center of the displayed worksheet, then it will remain in the center of the worksheet unless you move the entire worksheet with the scroll bar.)

If the Format Object Placement command appears in gray, then it is not available. This command is available only when an object or objects (such as an embedded chart, a drawn object, or a copy of an embedded chart or drawn object) are selected. A selected object appears with an outline box around it (an outline box has square shaded boxes on its corners and midpoints).

 Note: If some objects are attached with the first option, moving and sizing with cells, and others are not, then your objects may change position relative to each other when you make changes to cells in the worksheet.

Keystrokes

Keyboard	*Mouse*
Forma<u>t</u>	Forma<u>t</u>
Object P<u>l</u>acement	Object P<u>l</u>acement

Example

Suppose that you want to keep the size of an embedded chart *fixed* no matter what happens to the underlying cells, but you want the chart to move if you resize the underlying cells. To do this, select the embedded chart. Then select the Forma<u>t</u> command in the menu bar and select Object P<u>l</u>acement. (The Object Placement dialog box appears.) Select the circle next to the Move but Don't Size with Cells option. Select OK or press Enter.

 Placing an Object

1. Select the object or objects that you want to attach or not attach to underlying cells. (If you want to select more than one object, hold down the Shift key while you are selecting objects.)

2. Select the Forma<u>t</u> command in the menu bar.

3. Select the Object P̲lacement command under the Forma̲t options.

    The Object Placement dialog box appears with these options:
    a) Move and Size with Cells,
    b) Move but Don't Size with Cells, c) Don't Move or Size with Cells. (For a detailed description of the Object Placement dialog box, press the F1 key at this time, while the Object Placement dialog box is visible. To exit Help, choose F̲ile E̲x̲it in the Help box.)

4. Select one of these three options.

5. Select OK or press Enter.

Format Overlay (for charts)

Use the Forma̲t O̲verlay command to apply special formatting options, such as dropping lines from the data markers and specifying at which data series to start the overlay. This command is only available with Combination charts.

Different options are displayed and become available according to the type of chart. Chapter 13, "Advanced Charting," takes you through the available options. Or press the F1 key while the dialog box is on-screen for a brief explanation of each option.

Keystrokes

Keyboard

Forma̲t

O̲verlay

Main Chart T̲ype and Data V̲iew

Enter

Mouse

Forma̲t

O̲verlay

Main Chart T̲ype and Data V̲iew

OK

Example

Suppose that your chart is set up as a Combination chart with the overlay series drawn in line format. To emphasize the overlay markers, you want to draw lines from the markers to the horizontal axis. Choose Overlay from Format and check the Drop Lines option. Choose OK.

 Formatting an Overlay

1. Make the chart the active chart.
2. Choose Overlay from Format.   Excel displays the dialog box.
3. Choose your available option(s).
4. Choose OK.

Format Patterns

Patterns is a command under the Format menu that allows you to choose a pattern for shading the selected cell(s) or object and the foreground and background colors. You may choose between 14 patterns and 17 colors for the foreground and background of your selected cell(s) or object.

Keystrokes

Keyboard	*Mouse*
Format	Format
Patterns	Patterns

Example

Suppose that you want dotted shading with a foreground color of yellow and a background color of green for the selected items. To do this, select the Format command and then Patterns. (The Patterns dialog box appears.) In the Cell Shading box, select dotted shading in the Pattern pull-down menu, the color yellow in the Foreground pull-down menu, and the color green in the Background pull-down menu. Select OK or press Enter.

Changing the Pattern of Selected Items

1. Select the Forma<u>t</u> command in the menu bar.

2. Select the <u>P</u>atterns command.

   The Patterns dialog box appears with the patterns, foreground, and background options in the Cell Shading box. (For a detailed description of the Patterns dialog box, press the F1 key at this time, while the Patterns dialog box is visible. To exit Help, choose <u>F</u>ile E<u>x</u>it in the Help box.)

3. Select your patterns, foreground, and background options.

4. Select OK or press Enter.

Format Patterns (for charts)

Use the Forma<u>t</u> <u>P</u>atterns command in a chart window to change the appearance of borders and areas, legend boxes, data markers, 3-D walls and floors, tick marks, labels, gridlines, arrows, and text borders. The options available depend on what object you selected on the chart.

Keystrokes

Keyboard

Forma<u>t</u>

<u>P</u>atterns

If axis selected, <u>A</u>utomatic or
<u>S</u>tyle, <u>C</u>olor, and <u>W</u>eight under Axis

Mouse

Forma<u>t</u>

<u>P</u>atterns

If axis selected, <u>A</u>utomatic or
<u>S</u>tyle, <u>C</u>olor, and <u>W</u>eight under Axis

Format Patterns

Keyboard	*Mouse*
Under Tick Mark Type: M̲ajor and/or Mino̲r; and None, Inside, Outside, or Cross	Under Tick Mark Type: M̲ajor and/or Mino̲r; and None, Inside, Outside, or Cross
Under Tick Labels: N̲one, L̲ow, High, or Ne̲xt to Axis	Under Tick Labels: N̲one, L̲ow, High, or Ne̲xt to Axis
If anything other than an axis, under Border: A̲utomatic, N̲one, or S̲tyle and C̲olor and W̲eight	If anything other than an axis, under Border: A̲utomatic, N̲one, or S̲tyle and C̲olor and W̲eight
Under Area: A̲utomatic, Non̲e, or P̲atterns and F̲oreground and B̲ackground	Under Area: A̲utomatic, Non̲e, or P̲atterns and F̲oreground and B̲ackground
F̲ont or T̲ext to access Format Font/Format Text commands	F̲ont or T̲ext to access Format Font/Format Text commands
Enter	OK

Example

Suppose that you want to give the background area between the axes of your chart a color and pattern so that it looks good on a printout. Choose Select Plot Area from C̲hart; then choose P̲atterns from Forma̲t. In the Area options, choose Pattern and select the fourth pattern down, a grid type of pattern. Choose Foreground and the color red to give the grid lines a color and leave white as the Background color. Choose OK.

Choosing a Pattern

1. Select the chart area or object to change.

    Different options will be available according to what you select.

2. Choose P̲atterns from Forma̲t.

    Excel displays the Patterns dialog box.

3. For Border, Area, and Axis options, you can choose the A̲utomatic, selection, choose N̲one, or customize your own S̲tyle, C̲olor, and W̲eight.

    The Sample box in the lower right of the dialog box displays your custom selections.

4. If you selected an axis, choose Tick Mark Types and Tick Labels.

5. Choose OK.   Excel reformats your chart.

 Tip: Double-click on a chart item or object to quickly get to the Patterns dialog box.

Format Row Height

Row Height is a command under the Format menu that allows you to change the row height of the row or rows that are selected. You can specify your own row height with a number, select the Standard Height option, or select a height of zero by choosing the Hide option. The Standard Height option gives a best-fit size to the row height, which is as high as the tallest value in the column.

Keystrokes

Keyboard   *Mouse*

Format   Format

Row Height   Row Height

Examples

Suppose that you want to change to 30 the row height of the title row where the cursor is. To do this, select Format and then Row Height. Type the number 30 in the small box labeled `Row Height`. Select OK or press Enter.

Suppose that you want to make standard height the rows selected by the cursor. Select Format and Row Height. Turn on the Standard Height box. Select OK or press Enter.

Suppose that you want to hide the row where the cursor is. To do this, select Format and then Row Height. Select the Hide box. Then select OK or press Enter.

Changing the Row Height

1. Select the Format command in the menu bar.

2. Select Row Height. The Row Height dialog box appears with these options: Row Height, Standard Height, Hide, Unhide. (For a detailed description of the Row Height dialog box, press the F1 key at this time, while the Row Height dialog box is visible. To exit help, choose File Exit in the Help box.)

3. Select the options you want to set.

4. Select OK or press Enter.

Format Scale (for charts)

Use Scale from the Format menu in a chart window to set the positioning, the order, and the scale of tick marks and axes. The command is only available when an axis is selected.

Keystrokes

Keyboard	*Mouse*
Format	Format
Scale	Scale

See Chapter 13, "Advanced Charting," for a full discussion of the many options available with this command. Briefly, with a category axis (usually the x-axis) selected, you are telling Excel where you want the Value (usually the y) axis to cross. With a Value axis selected, you are telling Excel the minimum and maximum values to be displayed on the axis.

Example

With a standard Column chart the y-axis intersects with the x-axis to the left of the chart, before the first category. You want it to display toward the center to avoid giving the impression of a time progression along the x-axis. Select the x-axis, choose Scale from Format, and enter **3** at the Value (Y) Axis Crosses at Category Number option. Choose OK and the Y-axis moves to the center of the chart.

 ### Changing an Axis

1. Select the axis that you want to change.   The axis gets rectangles at each end to indicate selection.

2. Choose Scale from Format.   The Scale dialog box appears.

3. Choose your combination of options to rescale the axis or move it.

4. Choose OK.   Excel reformats the axis to your specifications.

Format Send To Back

Send To Back is a command under the Format menu that allows you to send the selected object or objects to the back, behind all other objects in the document. If this command appears in gray, it is not available. This command is available only when an object or objects (such as an embedded chart, a drawn object, or a copy of an embedded chart or drawn object) are selected. A selected object appears with an outline box around it (an outline box has square shaded boxes on its corners and midpoints).

Keystrokes

Keyboard	*Mouse*
Format	Format
Send To Back	Send To Back

Example

Suppose that you created a text box with the text box icon in the menu bar, and then put a graphic box around your text box. When you create a surrounding graphic box, the text box that you first created disappears behind the surrounding graphic box. To send the surrounding graphic box behind the now hidden text box, follow the procedure below for sending an object to the back: If the surrounding graphic box (which is hiding your text box) is not already selected, then select it. Select the Forma<u>t</u> command in the menu bar and then S<u>e</u>nd To Back.

 Sending an Object to the Back

1. Select the object or objects that you want to display behind all other objects.   (If you want to select more than one object, hold down the Shift key while you are selecting objects.)

2. Select the Forma<u>t</u> command in the menu bar.

3. Select the S<u>e</u>nd To Back command under the Forma<u>t</u> options.   The object you selected goes behind the other objects.

Format Size

Use the Forma<u>t</u> Si<u>z</u>e command in a chart window to change the size of an arrow. The size changes from the arrowhead end. Using the arrow keys can give you more control than dragging the mouse.

Keystrokes

Keyboard	*Mouse*
Forma<u>t</u>	Forma<u>t</u>
Si<u>z</u>e	Si<u>z</u>e
Left, Right, Up, or Down arrow keys	Drag the mouse.

Example

Suppose that an arrow points to a data marker on your chart. You wish to make it bigger so that the head is closer to the marker. Select the arrow by clicking on it. Choose Size from Format. Reposition the arrow.

 Sizing an Arrow

1. Select the arrow.
2. Choose Size from Format.
3. Use the mouse or the arrow keys to size the object.   The arrow keys change the small increments, which can give you more control than using the mouse.
4. Click with the mouse button to fix the object.

Format Style

Style is a command under the Format menu that allows you to apply a previously defined style to the selected cell(s), give a name to a style, or merge all the styles from another document into the active document. When you define a style, you can include in your style a specific format choice for any of the following: Number, Font, Alignment, Border, Pattern, or Protection.

Keystrokes

Keyboard	*Mouse*
Format	Format
Style	Style

Examples

Suppose that you want to apply the style called *currency* to the selected items. Select the Format command in the menu bar and then Style. The Style dialog box appears with a Style Name box and a Define box. Select the word currency in the Style Name pull-down box. Select OK or press Enter.

Suppose that you want to create a style called *title* and apply it to the selected items. This style includes a percent Number format; a script, bold font; and Locked Cell Protection. To do this, select Forma<u>t</u> and then <u>S</u>tyle. The <u>S</u>tyle dialog box appears with a Style Name box and a Define box. Select the <u>D</u>efine box. (The Style dialog box expands to include more options.) Type `title` in the Style Name box. (*Title* is automatically given the current style options.) In the Include box, turn on the Number, Font, and Protection check boxes. Turn off the Alignment, Border, and Pattern check boxes. In the Change box, select the Number box. (The Number dialog box option appears.) Set the Number format to #%. (For more information on the Number option, see "Format Number.") In the Change box, select the Font box. (The Font dialog box option appears.) Set the Font Name to Script, and the Font Style to Bold. (For more information on the Font option, see "Format Font.") In the Change box, select the Protection box. The Cell Protection dialog box option appears. Set Cell Protection to Locked. (For more information on the Cell Protection option, see "Format Cell Protection.") Select OK in the Styles dialog box or press Enter.

Applying a Previously Defined Style

1. Select the Forma<u>t</u> command in the menu bar.

2. Select <u>S</u>tyle.
   The Style dialog box appears with a Style Name pull-down box listing all the styles and an option to define a style. (For a detailed description of the Style dialog box, press the F1 key at this time, while the Style dialog box is visible. To exit Help, choose <u>F</u>ile E<u>x</u>it in the Help box.)

3. Select your choice of style in the Style Name pull-down box.

4. Select OK or press Enter.

Defining a New Style or Changing the Definition of a Style

1. Highlight or select the Forma<u>t</u> command in the menu bar.

2. Select Style. The Style dialog box appears with a Style Name pull-down box listing all the styles and an option to define a style. (For a detailed description of the Style dialog box, press the F1 key at this time, while the Style dialog box is visible. To exit Help, choose File Exit in the Help box.)

3. Select the Define box. The Style dialog box expands to include more options.

4. If, and only if, you are defining a *new* style, type a *new* name for your style in the Style Name box. This new name is automatically given the style options that are in the selected item(s).

5. In the Include box, turn on the check boxes for the options that you want to include, and turn off the check boxes for options that you do not want to include. The options are Number, Font, Alignment, Border, Pattern, and Protection. (For more information on these options, see "Format Number," "Format Font," "Format Alignment," "Format Border," "Format Patterns," or "Format Cell Protection.")

6. In the Change box, highlight or select the box that will allow you to change the current options to the ones that you want for this style: Number, Font, Alignment, Border, Pattern, or Protection. When you select any of these options, the dialog box for that option appears.

7. Select OK or press Enter.

Note: If you want to define and/or change more than style, you can use the Add box between styles without choosing the OK box each time you define and/or change a style. You can also delete a style with the Delete box.

Merging All the Styles from Another Document into the Active Document

1. Select the Forma**t** command in the menu bar.

2. Select **S**tyle.　　　　　　　The Style dialog box appears with a Style Name pull-down box listing all the styles and an option to define a style. (For a detailed description of the Style dialog box, press the F1 key at this time, while the Style dialog box is visible. To exit Help, choose **F**ile E**x**it in the Help box.)

3. Select the **D**efine box.　　　The Style dialog box expands to include more options.

4. Select the **M**erge box.　　　The Merge dialog box appears.

5. Select the name of the document whose styles you wish to include in your active document.

6. Select OK in the Merge dialog box or press Enter.

7. You return to the Style dialog box. Either return to your document by selecting OK or pressing Enter or use the Style dialog box to apply, change, or define a style.

 Note: If you have no new styles defined in other documents, no names of documents will appear in the Merge dialog box.

Format Text (for charts)

Use the Forma**t** **T**ext command in a chart window to define the orientation of a text box and the alignment of text within the box.

Keystrokes

Keyboard

Format

Text

For Text Alignment: Left, Center, or Right

For Vertical (alignment): Top, Center, or Bottom

For Orientation: N and then choose with an arrow key

Automatic to restore default text orientation

Mouse

Format

Text

For Text Alignment: Left, Center, or Right

For Vertical (alignment): Top, Center, or Bottom

For Orientation: Click on one choice of four

Automatic to restore default text orientation

Example

Suppose that you previously attached a text box using the series and data point option, and now you want to display the text in the box vertically, not horizontally. Select the text box, choose Text from Format, and choose the box under Orientation showing text vertically. Choose OK.

Changing Text Box Orientation

1. Select the text box to orient or align.

   White boxes show that the text box is selected.

2. Choose Text from Format.

3. Choose the alignment or orientation you want.

4. Choose OK.

   Excel reorients the text box on your chart.

Note: This option is only available when you select a text box that was originally created with the Attach Text command from Chart.

Format Ungroup

Ungroup is a command under the Format menu that allows you to ungroup or separate several selected objects that are currently grouped together as a single object. When you group objects together with Format Group, the group of objects is treated as one unit. After grouping some objects, you may decide to change some aspect of only one object in the group. The Format Ungroup command allows you to separate these objects again so that you can make changes to any object in the group.

The Format Ungroup command appears where the Format Group command previously was, when the current selection is an object that was created with the Format Group command. This command is available only when a single grouped object is selected. A selected group object appears with an outline box around it (an outline box has square shaded boxes on its corners and midpoints).

Keystrokes

Keyboard	*Mouse*
Format	Format
Ungroup	Ungroup

Example

Suppose that you have created a grouped object for a picture with several graphic objects in it. You want to shade only one object in this picture. To do this, you first need to Ungroup the picture: Select your picture (the grouped object) and then choose the Format command in the menu bar followed by Ungroup. Then shade the object.

 Ungrouping or Separating Objects

1. Select the grouped object that you want to separate into individual objects.

2. Select the Format command in the menu bar.

3. Select the Ungroup command under the Format options.   The objects are separated.

FORMAT.FONT

(*see* Macro Functions That Perform Format Commands)

FORMAT.LEGEND

(*see* Macro Functions That Perform Format Commands)

FORMAT.MAIN

(*see* Macro Functions That Perform Format Commands)

FORMAT.MOVE

(*see* Macro Functions That Perform Format Commands)

FORMAT.NUMBER

(*see* Macro Functions That Perform Format Commands)

FORMAT.OVERLAY

(*see* Macro Functions That Perform Format Commands)

FORMAT.SIZE

(*see* Macro Functions That Perform Format Commands)

FORMAT.TEXT

(*see* Macro Functions That Perform Format Commands)

FORMULA

(*see* Macro Functions That Perform Actions)

Formula Apply Names

Apply Names is a command under the Formula menu that allows you to replace a reference with the name that is given to that reference. Before you use Apply Names, you must define a name or names for the reference that you want to replace. See "Formula Define Name" or "Formula Create Names" to do this.

For example, if the name *Goals* was defined to refer to cell B2, using the Formula Apply Names command would cause the name *Goals* to replace the reference *B2* wherever it appeared in the worksheet.

 Note: The text "B2" will not be replaced by any name that refers to B2 since it is not a reference.

Keystrokes

Keyboard	*Mouse*
Formula	Formula
Apply Names	Apply Names

Example

Suppose that you want to replace all references to cell C4 with the name *AvgScore*, which is already defined as referring to cell C4. Select Fo_rmula and _Apply Names. The Apply Names dialog box with a listing of all the names that have been defined in the worksheet appears. Select AvgScore and then choose OK.

 Applying Names

1. Select the Fo_rmula command.

   The Formula menu appears.

2. Select _Apply Names.

   The Apply Names dialog box with a listing of all the names that have been defined in the worksheet appears. An Options box for more options and check boxes to choose to Ignore Relative/Absolute addressing or Use Row and Column Names also appears. (For a detailed description of Apply Names, press the F1 key at this time, while the Apply Names dialog box is visible. To exit Help, choose _File E_xit in the Help box.)

3. Select the names that you want to replace references. (Pressing the Shift key when highlighting will allow you to highlight as many names as you wish.)

4. Select OK.

   If a match was found, you return to your worksheet and every occurrence of the selected reference is replaced by the name you applied. If there was no reference in the worksheet for any of your selected names, a No Match message appears and you must select the OK box to return to your worksheet.

Formula Bar

The *formula bar* is the right side of the bar in the workspace that sits just above the worksheet and directly below the menu bar. The formula bar displays the current value for the active cell. Any new information that you enter into an active cell is immediately displayed on the right side of the formula bar.

The far left side of the bar that contains the formula bar displays the reference or location of the active cell. The middle of the bar that contains the formula bar is empty unless you enter a value into a cell. (When you enter a value into a cell, two boxes appear in the middle section of the formula bar. One of these boxes contains an *x* and the other contains a check mark.)

The formula bar gets its name from its role as the displayer of formulas. If you enter a formula into a cell and press Enter, the result of the formula appears in the cell, but the formula you typed remains displayed in the formula bar. If you move the cursor to a cell that contains a value which is a result of a formula, the formula bar displays the formula rather than the result of the formula.

> **Tip:** When you are entering a lengthy value into your spreadsheet, the entire value may not fit in its destination cell. Values that are in the process of being entered are displayed on the right side of the formula bar, which extends approximately 75% of the width of the workspace. Because there is more space in the formula bar for display input than in most cells, you may find it easier to look in the formula bar at new values that you are entering rather than in their destination cell.

Example

If you enter "=SUM(1,2)" into cell B1, when you press Enter, the result of this formula (3) is displayed in cell B1 and =SUM(1,2) remains in the formula bar.

Formula Create Names

Create Names is a command under the Formula menu that allows you to quickly create names for several values. If you have a list of values in a column/row with labels for these values in the adjoining column/row, you can make each label be defined as the name for each corresponding value by using the Formula Create Names command once.

Keystrokes

Keyboard   *Mouse*

Formula   Formula

Create Names   Create Names

Example

Suppose that you have two columns: the left column (A2:A6) has labels and the right column (B2:B6) has the values that correspond to these labels. You want the labels in the column under A to become the names for the values in column B.

Highlight cells A2 to B6. Select Formula and Create Names. The Create Names dialog box appears. Select the box next to the Left Column option since the labels are in the left column (column A is the left column in the selected area). Then select OK.

Note: After this example is executed, the value in cell B2 has the name that is in cell A2, the value in cell B3 has the name that is in cell A3, the value in cell B4 has the name that is in cell A4, and so on.

Creating Names

1. Select a row or column of values and an adjacent row or column of labels for those values.

2. Select the Formula command.   The Formula menu appears.

3. Select Create Names.   The Create Names dialog box with these options appears: Top Row, Right Column, Bottom Row, Left Column. (For a short description of the Create Names dialog box, press the F1 key at this time, while the Create Names dialog box is visible. To exit Help, choose File Exit in the Help box.)

4. Select the option that describes the column or row where the names are in the selected area.

5. Select OK or press Enter.

 Note: The workspace will appear unchanged after this command, but you can view the new names that you just created by using the Formula Paste Name command or the Formula Define Name command.

Formula Define Name

Define Name is a command under the Formula menu that allows you to define or redefine a name, delete a name from the list of names in the worksheet or macro sheet, or view the list of names in the worksheet or macro sheet. When you give a name to a value, you can use that name anywhere that you want to use the value. See "Name" for more information.

Keystrokes

Keyboard	*Mouse*
Formula	Formula
Define Name	Define Name

Examples

Suppose that you want to give the name *BaseballTeam* the range of cells $A$2:$B$3 and you want to delete the name *George* from your list of names.
    To add the name *BaseballTeam*, highlight the range of cells from A2 to B3. Select Formula and Define Name. (The Define Name dialog box appears.) Next, enter `BaseballTeam` in the Name box. Select the Add box.
    Since the Define Name dialog box is already open, to delete the name *George*, either select the name George in the Names in Sheet box or type `George` in the Name box. Select the Delete box and then choose OK.

Defining a Name

1. Select the value or range of values that you want to associate with one name.

2. Select the Fo<u>r</u>mula command.   The Formula menu appears.

3. Select <u>D</u>efine Name.   The Define Name dialog box appears.

4. Enter the name that you want to call the value in the <u>N</u>ame box of the Define Name dialog box.

5. Select either the <u>A</u>dd box in the Define Name dialog box or OK.   The name that you entered in the Name box appears in the Names in Sheet box.

6. Select OK.   The Define Names dialog box disappears and you return to your worksheet.

 Deleting a Name

1. Select the Fo<u>r</u>mula command.   The Formula menu appears.

2. Select <u>D</u>efine Name.   The Define Name dialog box appears.

3. In the Define Name dialog box, either select the name that you want to delete in the Names in <u>S</u>heet box or type the name that you want to delete in the <u>N</u>ame box.

4. Select the <u>D</u>elete box in the Define Name dialog box.   The name that you selected in the Names in Sheet box disappears from this box and is no longer defined in the worksheet.

5. Select OK.   The Define Name dialog box disappears and you return to your worksheet.

Defining a Constant Name or Redefining a Name

1. Select the Formula command.   The Formula menu appears.

2. Select Define Name.   The Define Name dialog box appears.

3. In the Define Name dialog box, either select the name that you want to redefine in the Names in Sheet box or type a new name to be defined (or an old name that you want to redefine) in the Name box and press Enter.   The value which that name refers to appears in the Refers To box.

4. Type in the value for the name (any reference, array, number, text, etc.) in the Refers To box of the Define Name dialog box.

5. Select OK.   The Define Name dialog box disappears and you return to your worksheet.

 Viewing the Names in the Sheet

1. Select the Formula command.   The Formula menu appears.

2. Select Define Name.   The Define Name dialog box appears. (For a detailed description of any of the options, press the F1 key at this time, while the Define Name dialog box is visible. To exit Help, choose File Exit in the Help box.)

3. View the names that are defined in the sheet by looking at the Names in Sheet box.   When you highlight a name, its value appears in the Refers To box.

4. Select the Close box.   The Define Name dialog box disappears and you return to your worksheet.

Formula Find *(see also* Formula Replace*)*

The Formula Find command searches for formulas, values, characters, or notes that you specify. It does not search for text.

You may use the two wild-card characters (? and *) in your search: ? replaces any one character. * replaces any number of characters. Since Excel interprets ? and * as wild cards, to locate one of these as a character, insert a tilde (~) before the wild-card character. To find B3*10, for example, type **B3~*10** in the Find What box.

Keystrokes

Keyboard

Use arrow keys to select one cell or range.

Formula Find or Shift-F5

In Find What box, type text.

Select options in Find What box.

Enter to search forward;
Shift-Enter to search backward

F7 to locate next match;
Shift-F7 to find previous match

Mouse

Select cell or range.

Formula, Find

In Find What box, type text.

Select options in Find What box.

OK to search forward;
Shift-OK to search backward

F7 to locate next match;
Shift-F7 to find previous match

 Using Formula Find

1. To search through the entire worksheet, select one cell at which you want Excel to start. Otherwise, select the range in which you want to search.

    The cell or range is highlighted.

2. Select Formula Find.

    The dialog box appears.

3. Type the characters you want to find in the Find What box.

    Excel will use the characters you type in its search.

4. Select the type of search: Formulas, Values, or Notes.

    Your selection is blackened.

5. Select W<u>h</u>ole if you want the search to find only cells that exactly match the Find What box. Select <u>P</u>art if you want the search to find all cells that include the characters in the Find What box.

   Your selection is blackened.

6. Select <u>R</u>ows to search horizontally or Co<u>l</u>umns to search vertically.

   Your selection is blackened.

7. Select <u>M</u>atch Case if you want the search to find only cells that exactly match the case (upper and lower) that you typed in the Find What box.

   Your selection is blackened.

8. Press Enter or choose OK to search forward. Press Shift-Enter (or Shift-OK) to search backward.

   Microsoft Excel highlights the first occurrence of the search.

9. Use F7 to move forward from occurrence to occurrence. Use to Shift-F7 move backward.

   Excel moves from occurrence to occurrence in the direction you specify.

> **Tip:** If you type an exclamation point (!) in the Find What box and choose the Formulas option, Microsoft Excel will locate cells that contain references to other worksheets.

Formula Goto

<u>G</u>oto is a command under the Fo<u>r</u>mula menu that allows you to go to the cell or cells in the worksheet that are specified by whatever name you select or reference that you specify.

Keystrokes

Keyboard   *Mouse*

Fo<u>r</u>mula   Fo<u>r</u>mula

<u>G</u>oto   <u>G</u>oto

Example

Suppose you want to move to the area in your worksheet called *NewPurchases*. Select Formula and Goto. Select NewPurchases; then choose OK or press Enter.

Going to a Named Cell or Cells

1. Select the Formula command.   The Formula menu appears.

2. Select the Goto command.   The Goto dialog box appears with options for specifying the name or reference that you want to go to. (For a detailed description of any of the options, press the F1 key at this time, while the Goto dialog box is visible. To exit Help, choose File Exit in the Help box.)

3. Select the name that you want to go to.

4. Select OK or press Enter.   You return to your worksheet with the area specified name selected and displayed in the active window.

Going to a Reference

1. Select the Formula command.

2. Select the Goto command.   The Goto dialog box appears with options for specifying the name or reference that you want to go to. (For a detailed description of any of the options, press the F1 key at this time, while the Goto dialog box is visible. To exit Help, choose File Exit in the Help box.)

3. Type the reference that you want to go to.

4. Select OK or press Enter.   You return to your worksheet with the area that you specified in the reference box highlighted and displayed in the active window.

 Tip: If you have a large area that you often need to highlight (for example a print area), give a name to the entire area and use the Goto command to highlight it.

Formula Note

Note is a command under the Formula menu that allows you to record notes for a particular cell or cells. The note does not appear in the worksheet, although you do have a note indicator symbol that appears in the upper-right corner of the cell when you create a note for that cell. You can view any note in any cell at any time.

Keystrokes

Keyboard	*Mouse*
Formula	Formula
Note	Note

Examples

Suppose that you want to keep a memo in one cell to remind yourself that your friend Patricia Wright gave you the information contained in that cell or cells. Place the cursor on the cell or cells that you want the note attached to. Then select Formula and Note. The Cell Note dialog box appears with a box for all the notes in the worksheet and a box for new notes. Type `Patricia Wright` in the Notes box and then select the OK box or press Enter.

Creating or Viewing Notes

1. Select the Formula command.   The Formula menu appears.

2. Select Note.   The Cell Note dialog box appears with a box containing all the notes in the worksheet, each preceded by a reference to the cell where the note is and a space for creating a new note for the current active cell. (For a detailed description of any of the options, press the F1 key at this time, while the Note dialog box is visible. To exit Help, choose File Exit in the Help box.)

3. To create a new note or change a note that already exists in the current cell, type your note in the Notes box and then select Add or OK.

4. To view a note in another cell, select the note in the Notes in Sheet box.   The entire note appears in the Notes box.

5. When you are finished, if you want to save the changes you have made, select OK or press Enter; otherwise, select the Close box.   You return to your worksheet.

 Note: If you want to add several notes for several different cells in the worksheet, use the Cell box to specify where the note is to be attached, the Notes box to type in the new note, and the Add box to record the note permanently as a "Note in Sheet."

Formula Paste Function

Paste Function is a command under the Formula menu that allows you to paste a built-in worksheet function into the current active cell of the worksheet. You can choose any worksheet function to paste into the active cell or cells. If the function you choose has arguments, you must include these values in the list of values for the function before you press Enter. For more information on any one of the functions listed in the Paste Function dialog box, you can 1) see the listing "Function" in this complete reference, 2) press the F1 key when the function name is selected, or 3) see the listing of the specific function (listed by name) in this reference.

Keystrokes

Keyboard   *Mouse*

Fo<u>r</u>mula   Fo<u>r</u>mula

Pas<u>t</u>e Function   Pas<u>t</u>e Function

Example

Suppose that you can't remember the exact name of a function that you want to use, or you aren't sure what functions are available. The Formula Paste Function command gives you both a listing of the functions and the ability to directly paste the function into the currently active cell.

To see the listing, select Fo<u>r</u>mula and Pas<u>t</u>e Function. The Paste Function dialog box appears with a list of all the built-in worksheet functions. Scroll through the list of functions until you reach the function that you want to paste into the active cell. Select the function that you want to paste and then choose OK.

 Pasting a Function

1. Select the Fo<u>r</u>mula command.
   The Formula menu appears.

2. Select Pas<u>t</u>e Function.
   The Paste Function dialog box with a list of all the built-in worksheet functions appears. (For a detailed description of any of the functions, press the F1 key at this time while the Paste Function dialog box is visible; then choose the Search option in the Help screen menu. To exit Help, choose <u>F</u>ile E<u>x</u>it in the Help box.)

3. Scroll to the function that you want to use.

4. Select the function that you want to paste.

5. Select OK. The Paste Function dialog box disappears, you return to your worksheet, and the formula appears in the formula bar.

Formula Paste Name

Paste Name is a command under the Formula menu that allows you to either paste an already defined name in the current active cell of the worksheet or paste the entire list of defined names into the active cell or cells. You can choose any defined name to paste into the active cell or cells.

Keystrokes

Keyboard   *Mouse*

Formula   Formula

Paste Name   Paste Name

Example

Suppose that you can't remember the exact name of a value. Move the cursor to an empty cell where you want the name to appear. Select Formula and Paste Name. The Paste Name dialog box appears with a list of all the names that you have defined in the worksheet. Scroll through the list of names until you reach the name that you want to paste into the active cell. Select the name that you want to paste and then choose OK.

 Pasting a Name

1. Select the Formula command. The Formula menu appears.

2. Select Paste Name. The Paste Name dialog box with these options appears: Paste Name and Paste List. (For a detailed description of either of the options, press the F1 key at this time, while the Paste Name dialog box is visible. To exit Help, choose File Exit in the Help box.)

3. Select the name you want to paste.

4. Select OK.　　　　　　　　　　　You return to your worksheet and an equal sign, followed by the name you chose to paste, appears in the formula bar.

 Pasting the Entire List of Names

1. Select the Formula command.　　The Formula menu appears.

2. Select Paste Name.　　　　　　The Paste Name dialog box with these options appears: Paste Name and Paste List.

3. Select the Paste List box.　　　The Paste Name dialog box disappears and you return to your worksheet.

Formula Reference

Reference is a command under the Formula menu that allows you to change any references in the formula bar from relative to absolute (for example, A1 to $A$1), from absolute to mixed absolute (for example, $A$1 to A$1), from mixed absolute to mixed relative (for example, A$1 to $A1), and from mixed relative to relative (for example, $A1 to A1). In order to use this command, the cursor must be in the formula bar. (When the cursor is in the formula bar, the two boxes with an *X* and a checkmark in them appear in the middle of the formula bar.)

Keystrokes

Keyboard	Mouse
Formula	Formula
Reference	Reference

Example

Suppose that you want to change all your relative references in the formula in cell D5 to absolute references. To do this, move the cursor to cell D5, and then move the cursor onto the formula bar. Select the Formula command and then Reference.

Changing Your References

1. Make sure that the cursor is on the formula bar.

   Two boxes appear in the formula bar. One has an *X* in it and the other has a checkmark.

2. Select the Formula command.

   The Formula menu appears.

3. Select Reference.

   The references in the formula bar change, according to the guidelines mentioned above.

Formula Replace *(see also* Formula Find*)*

The Formula Replace command searches for cell contents and replaces them with whatever characters you specify. Formula Replace does not search notes or the values produced by formulas. It searches and replaces only the contents of cells.

Keystrokes

Keyboard

Option, Full Menus

Use arrow keys to select cell or range.

Formula Replace

In Find What box, type text.

In Replace With box, type text.

Select options in Find What box.

Replace or Shift-Replace

Find Next or Shift-Find Next

Replace All

Esc

Mouse

Option, Full Menus

Select cell or range.

Formula, Replace

In Find What box, type text.

In Replace With box, type text.

Select options in Find What box.

Replace or Shift-Replace

Find Next or Shift-Find Next

Replace All

Close

Using Formula Replace

1. Select Options, Full Menus if you are using Short Menus.

   Full Menus are in effect.

2. To search through the entire worksheet, select one cell at which you want Excel to start. Otherwise, select the range in which you want to search.

   The cell or range is highlighted.

3. Select Formula Replace.

   The dialog box appears.

4. Type the characters you want to find and replace in the Find What box. In the Replace With box, type the characters that will replace what is in the Find What box.

   Excel will use the characters you type to search and replace characters in the cells.

5. Select Whole if you want the search to find only cells that exactly match the Find What box. Select Part if you want the search to find all cells that include the characters in the Find What box.

   Your selection is blackened.

6. Select Rows to search horizontally or Columns to search vertically.

   Your selection is blackened.

7. Select Match Case if you want the search to find only cells that exactly match the case (upper and lower) that you typed in the Find What box.

   Your selection is blackened.

8. Select Replace, Shift-Replace, Find Next, Shift-Find Next, or Replace All.

   If you selected Replace, the characters are replaced and the next occurrence is highlighted. If you selected Shift-Replace, the characters are replaced and the previous occurrence is highlighted. If you selected Find Next, the cell is left unchanged and the next occurrence is highlighted. If you selected Shift-Find Next, the cell is left unchanged and the previous occurrence is highlighted. If you selected Replace All, all occurrences in the worksheet or range are replaced.

9. Close to exit the dialog box.   You return to the worksheet.

Note: Selecting Close only closes the dialog box, retaining the changes you have made. If you need to undo the changes, use Edit Undo Replace.

Caution: Replace All replaces all occurrences in the entire worksheet of the characters you typed in the Find What box, even if you highlighted only one cell.

Formula Select Special

The Formula Select Special command selects cells that have specific characteristics. You can look for blank cells and cells with constants, formulas, or notes; compare cells in rows or columns; find dependents (cells that refer to other cells) or precedents (cells that are referred to by other cells); or find the last cell on the worksheet (lower-right corner), the current region, current array, or any graphic objects. You can also select visible cells so that any changes you make affect only visible cells.

If you select Blanks, Excel will highlight all blank cells. Choosing Constants will highlight all cells that are not formulas and do not start with an equal sign, that is, cells for which you have entered values directly. Within this option you can search for Numbers, Text, Logicals, or Errors. Formulas are the opposite of constants and you can specify the same four items within this choice: Numbers, Text, Logicals, or Errors. Selecting Notes will highlight all cells that have notes attached to them.

The active cell is the comparison cell. This is the cell that Microsoft Excel uses as the basis of comparison. Select Row Differences to search throughout selected cells in a row. Select Column Differences to search throughout selected cells in a column. The comparison is based on formulas, not the resulting values. Cells with comparable relative references are considered the same.

Keystrokes

Finding Cells with Blanks, Constants, Formulas, or Notes

Keyboard	Mouse
Options, Full Menus	Options, Full Menus
Use arrow keys to select cell or range.	Select cell or range
Formula Select Special	Formula, Select Special
Select options from the dialog box. (If you want more information on any option, press F1.)	Select options from the dialog box. (If you want more information on any option, press F1.)
Enter	OK

Note: You must have Full menus to use the Formula Select Special command.

Note: For the Notes option only, you can press Ctrl-? (the question mark requires the Shift key) from the worksheet without choosing Formula Select Special.

Note: Once the results of the search are highlighted, you can move from cell to cell using Tab (or Shift-Tab to move backward). If there is more than one contiguous area highlighted, you can move from one area to another area using Ctrl-Tab (or Shift-Ctrl-Tab to move backward).

Finding Row and Column Differences from a Comparison Cell

Keyboard	Mouse
Options, Full Menus	Options, Full Menus

520 Formula Select Special

Keyboard

Use arrow keys to select comparison cell. Use Shift plus arrow keys to extend to range (in the same row or column as comparison cell) you want to search.

Formula Select Special

Ctrl-\ or Shift-Control-¦

Enter

Mouse

Select cell you want to use as comparison. Drag mouse to extend to range (in the same row or column as the comparison cell) you want to search.

Formula, Select Special

Row or Column Differences

OK

Finding Dependents and Precedents

Keyboard

Options, Full Menus

Use arrow keys to select cell or range.

Formula Select Special

Precedents or Dependents

Direct Only or All Levels

Enter

Mouse

Options, Full Menus

Select cell or range.

Formula, Select Special

Precedents or Dependents

Direct Only or All Levels

OK

A set of keyboard equivalents may be activated directly from the worksheet without selecting Formula Select Special. These equivalents are:

Precedents-Direct Only	Ctrl-[
Precedents-All Levels	Ctrl-{ (requires Shift key)
Dependents-Direct Only	Ctrl-]
Dependents-All Levels	Shift-Ctrl-}

 Note: If you select more than one cell, Microsoft Excel will locate all cells that relate to any of the cells.

Finding the Last Cell on the Worksheet, Current Region, Current Array, or Graphic Objects

Keyboard

Options, Full Menus

Formula Select Special

Mouse

Options, Full Menus

Formula, Select Special

Keyboard

La<u>s</u>t Cell, Ctrl-*, Ctrl-/, or O<u>b</u>jects

Enter

Mouse

La<u>s</u>t Cell, Current Re<u>gi</u>on, Current Array, or O<u>b</u>jects

OK

Pasting Visible Cells

Keyboard

<u>O</u>ptions, <u>F</u>ull Menus

Use arrow keys to select cell or range.

F<u>o</u>rmula <u>S</u>elect Special

<u>V</u>isible Cells Only

<u>E</u>dit <u>C</u>opy

Use arrow keys to select paste cell or upper-left corner of range.

<u>E</u>dit <u>P</u>aste

Mouse

<u>O</u>ptions, <u>F</u>ull Menus

Select cell or range.

Click on visible cells button in Toolbar or choose F<u>o</u>rmula <u>S</u>elect Special.

Click on <u>V</u>isible Cells Only (if necessary).

<u>E</u>dit, <u>C</u>opy

Select paste cell or upper-left corner of range.

<u>E</u>dit, <u>P</u>aste

 Finding Cells with Blanks, Constants, Formulas, or Notes

1. If you are using Short Menus, select <u>O</u>ptions, <u>F</u>ull Menus.

   The Full Menus are activated.

2. Select a cell or range.

   The cell or range is highlighted. If you selected a cell, Excel will search the entire worksheet.

3. Choose F<u>o</u>rmula <u>S</u>elect Special.

   The dialog box appears.

4. Select Blan<u>k</u>s, <u>C</u>onstants, F<u>o</u>rmulas, or <u>N</u>otes.

   Your selection is blackened.

5. If you selected Constants or Formulas, unselect the suboptions you do not want to find. The suboptions are Numbers, Text, Logicals, and Errors.

   You will see an X next to each suboption for options which you want to search.

6. Press Enter or choose OK.

   Excel highlights the results of the search.

Finding Row and Column Differences from a Comparison Cell

1. If using Short Menus, select Options, Full Menus.

   The Full Menus will be operational.

2. Starting from the cell you want to use as the comparison cell, extend the selection to the other cells in the same row or column with which you want to compare the comparison cell.

   The full range will be highlighted, with the comparison cell in white and the rest in reverse.

3. Select Formula Select Special.

   The dialog box appears.

4. Choose Row Differences or Column Differences.

   Your selection is blackened.

5. Press Enter or choose OK.

   Any cells in the same row or column as the comparison cell that are different will be highlighted.

Finding Dependents and Precedents

1. If using Short Menus, select Options, Full Menus.

   The full menus are activated.

2. Select the cell or cells for which you want to find precedents or dependents.

   The cell or cells are highlighted.

3. Select Formula Select Special.

   The dialog box appears.

4. Select Precedents if you want to find cells on which the chosen cell or cells are based. Select Dependents to find cells that depend on the chosen cell or cells.

   Your selection is blackened.

5. Select Direct Only to search for precedents or dependents that are directly precedent or dependent on the chosen cell or cells. Select All Levels to search for precedents of precedents or dependents of dependents.

   Your selection is blackened.

6.	Press Enter or choose OK.	Excel will highlight all cells that are precedents or dependents according to your selections.

Finding the Last Cell on the Worksheet, Current Region, Current Array, or Graphic Objects

1.	If using Short Menus, use Options, Full Menus.	The Full Menus are activated.
2.	Select Formula Select Special.	The dialog box appears.
3.	Choose Last Cell, Current Region, Current Array, or Objects.	The option you selected is blackened.
4.	Press Enter or choose OK.	Excel highlights the last cell, current region, current array, or graphic objects, if any.

> **Note:** The *last cell* is the lower-right corner of the worksheet and determines the worksheet's size. The size of the worksheet affects the amount of memory or disk space that the worksheet takes up. The *current region* is a range containing the active cell that is bounded by blank rows, columns, and/or worksheet borders.

Pasting Visible Cells

1.	If using Short Menus, select Options, Full Menus.	The Full Menus are operational.
2.	Select the cell or range to copy.	The cell or range is highlighted.
3.	Choose Formula Select Special or the visible cells button on the Toolbar.	If you chose Formula Select Special, the dialog box appears. If you used the visible cells button on the Toolbar, it is highlighted.
4.	If you used Formula Select Special, choose Visible Cells Only.	Your choice is blackened.

5. Select Edit Copy.	The cell or range is surrounded by the marquee.
6. Select paste cell or range.	The paste cell or range is highlighted.
7. Select Edit Paste.	Only the visible cells are copied.

 Note: The Visible Cells Only option of Formula Select Special allows you to make changes in the worksheet that affect only visible cells.

Examples

In the example shown in Figure A, E5 is the comparison cell and you want to select Column Differences to compare E5 with E6-E8. The formula for E5 is =SUM(B5:D5). The result of finding column differences with the Formula Select Special command is shown in Figure B. In Figure B, cells E6 and E7 have relative references that are the same; that is, they also add the three cells to the left of them. Therefore, cells E6 and E7 are not highlighted. However, E8 adds the three cells above it, so it is highlighted as a difference.

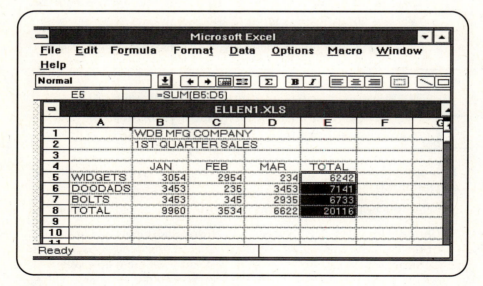

Figure A

In Figure C, the formula for cell E7 is =SUM(B7:D7). Therefore, cells B7,C7, and D7 are precedents for E7. The formula for E8 is =SUM(E5:E7). Therefore, E8 is a dependent of (is dependent on) E7.

Figure B

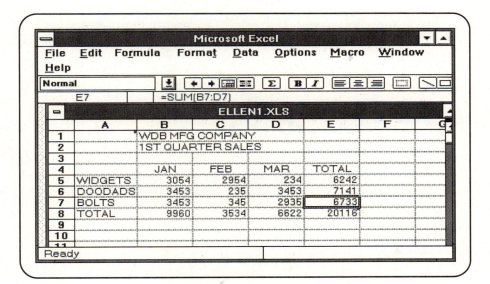

Figure C

Formula Show Active Cell

Show Active Cell is a command under the Formula menu that scrolls the worksheet so that the active cell is in the center of the display area.

Keystrokes

Keyboard   *Mouse*

Formula   Formula

Show Active Cell   Show Active Cell

Example

Suppose that you need to look at some values in the far end of your worksheet. You left the cursor in the area that you want to return to after you view the information you need to see. To return to the cursor, select the Formula command and then Show Active Cell.

 Showing the Active Cell

1. Select the Formula command.   The Formula menu appears.
2. Select Show Active Cell.   You return to your worksheet with the active cell displayed and the cursor on it.

Formula—Goal Seek

When you use the Goal Seek dialog box, you can specify a result and Excel will supply one of the inputs or values to get that result. In other words, Goal Seek varies a value in a cell until a formula reaches a specified value.

Keystrokes

Keyboard   *Mouse*

Formula   Formula

Goal Seek   Goal Seek

Keyboard	*Mouse*
Set Cell	Set Cell
To Value	To Value
By Changing	By Changing
Enter	OK

Example

Given overheads of $15,000, you want to know the revenues necessary to generate a $10,000 profit for the first quarter. Select cell G20, which contains the simple formula to calculate profits (revenues minus overheads). Choose Goal Seek from Formula. G20 appears in Set Cell. Type $10,000 in To Value, and enter the cell containing revenues (G16) in By Changing. Choose OK and Excel displays the result in G16.

 Goal Seeking

1. Select the cell that contains the formula you want to use.
   This is optional but saves time because you won't afterwards have to type in the cell.

2. Choose Goal Seek from Formula.
   Excel displays the Goal Seek dialog box.

3. Specify the formula cell in Set Cell.
   This is unnecessary if you followed step 1.

4. Type the desired result for the active cell in To Value.

5. In By Changing, enter the cell containing the value to change.

6. Choose OK.
   Excel displays a dialog box showing the calculations.

7. If you want, choose Pause to stop the calculating temporarily.

8. Choose Step to see the calculation after each iteration or Continue to let Excel continue as normal.

Formula—Solver

The Solver is a step beyond the Table command from Data and Goal Seek from Formula. Using it, you can involve several formulas, interlinked or otherwise, in what-if questions. You can also set conditions, or constraints, which must be met to arrive at a result, and you can customize the calculation by setting the maximum time, number of iterations, precision, etc.

The Solver dialog box contains these options:

Subject to the Constraints shows the conditions that must be met. Specify these using Add, Change, and Delete.

Use *Options* to specify the maximum time, number of iterations, and precision in the calculation.

Reset returns the box values you got when originally invoking this dialog box this time.

Solve starts the calculating.

Keystrokes

Keyboard	*Mouse*
Formula	Formula
Solver	Solver
Set Cell	Set Cell
Max, Min, or Value of	Max, Min, or Value of
Solve	Solve

Example

Solver5.xls in the Solverex subdirectory of Excel contains a good example of a set of interlinked formulas that could use Solver in problem solving and question posing. Open this worksheet, which shows the percentage return you get from different weightings of stocks in an investment portfolio. Choose Solver from Formula. Enter **E18**, the portfolio return in Set Cell, choose Max, and enter **E10:E14** in By Changing Cells. Set a constraint of making each percentage of stock held (E10:E14) greater than zero; in other words, which weighting (percentage) of each stock will result in maximizing portfolio return. Choose Solve. Solver finds that you should increase percentage held in stocks A and C.

Specifying a Calculation to Solver

1. Select the cell containing the formula that you want to use.

2. Choose Sol_v_er from Fo_r_mula.   Excel displays the Solver Parameters dialog box.

3. Specify the formula cell in S_e_t Cell.   This is not necessary if you followed step 1.

4. Choose between M_a_x, Mi_n_, and V_a_lue of.

5. In _B_y Changing Cells, specify the cells to change.   This basic problem is now set up.

6. _A_dd, _C_hange, or _D_elete a constraint if you wish.

7. Fine-tune your calculations with _O_ptions if you wish.   An example would be setting a maximum time to finish.

8. Choose _S_olve.   Excel calculates and displays the Solver dialog box at the end.

9. Choose between _K_eep Solver Solutions and Restore _O_riginal Values.   Solver has changed the worksheet (if it found a solution).

10. Choose OK.

FORMULA.ARRAY

(*see* Macro Functions That Perform Actions)

FORMULA.CONVERT

(*see* MacroFunctions That Perform Actions)

FORMULA.FILL

(*see* Macro Functions That Perform Actions)

FORMULA.FIND

(*see* Macro Functions That Perform Formula Commands)

FORMULA.FIND.NEXT

(*see* Macro Functions That Perform Formula Commands)

FORMULA.FIND.PREV

(*see* Macro Functions That Perform Formula Commands)

FORMULA.GOTO

(*see* Macro Functions That Perform Formula Commands)

FORMULA.REPLACE

(*see* Macro Functions That Perform Formula Commands)

FPOS (*see* Macro Functions—Control)

FREAD (*see* Macro Functions—Control)

FREADLN (*see* Macro Functions—Control)

FREEZE.PANES

(*see* Macro Functions That Perform Options Commands)

FSIZE (*see* Macro Functions—Control)

FULL (*see* Macro Functions That Perform Actions)

Function

Syntax

=FunctionName(*List_Of_Values_For_The_Function*)

Description

A function is a built-in operation that all Excel worksheets automatically perform on some specific information. A function is called *built-in* because all the instructions and operations to change information are included in your copy of Excel.

A function has three activities associated with it. First, the function has a specific operation that it performs on values. For example, the function called SUM adds numerical values together. But, second, before the function can perform an operation on values, it has to get the values from some place. With every function, a set of parentheses encloses all the values (or arguments) that the function uses when it operates. For example, when you enter the function SUM, you also enter a list of values that the function operates on. The last activity of a function is to display the result of the operation it performed on the values that you gave it. The function displays its result in the cell or cells where you entered the function.

All the information about a function is contained in the three parts of a function associated with the three activities of a function:

- A function's operation: The name of a function gives the specific operation of that function. To get a full description of all the activities of a particular function, look in this complete reference under the name of the function.

- The values that the function uses when it operates: These values are enclosed in parentheses following the function name and are 1) provided by you, the user, to the function and 2) used in the calculation of the result. There are several different types of values that a function can use:

A *number value* is a number; a cell address, formula, or function that yields a number; or a name that represents a number.

A *text value* is numbers in quotation marks or in text format; letters and/or nonnumeric symbols; a cell address, formula, or function that yields any of these; or a name that represents text. If text is typed directly into the list of values for the function, then it must be enclosed in quotation marks.

A *logical value* is TRUE; FALSE; a cell address, formula or function that yields TRUE or FALSE; or a name that represents a logical value.

An *array* is a cell address, constant array, or range of cell addresses. (See "Array.")

An *error* is a message that briefly indicates some error in the formula you entered. Explanations of the various errors follow:

Error	*Meaning*
#NAME?	Unrecognized function name or a defined name is expected
#VALUE!	A value or values given to the function are not of the right type.
#DIV/0!	Division by 0
#NULL!	No effect
#N/A!	Not applicable

Error	Meaning
#NUM!	A result cannot be calculated for a specific value or values given to the function. (See individual functions for any special restrictions on values.)
#REF!	Missing or inappropriate reference to a cell address or range of cell addresses.

- The function displays the result of its operation in the cell or cells where you entered the function. If the function returns a result that is a single value, the answer is displayed in a single cell. If the function returns a result that is an array of values, the result is displayed in a range of cells.

There are two major types of functions, *worksheet functions* and *macro functions*. Worksheet functions can be used anywhere; macro functions can be used only in macros. Functions can be pasted from the Paste Function dialog box under the Formula command or directly typed into a cell or cells. Worksheet functions are listed in the Paste Function dialog box of every worksheet and macro sheet. Macro functions are listed only in the Paste Function dialog box of every macro sheet. For a short summary of all worksheet functions, see "Worksheet Function." For a complete summary of macro functions, see the reference entries that begin with the words "Macro Functions."

Entering a Function

1. In the cell or cells where you want the result of the function to appear, paste the function from the Paste Function dialog box under the Formula menu, or type it directly into the cell.

Note: If you type the function directly into the cell, remember to start with an equal sign (=).

Note: If the function returns an array of values, make sure that you highlight an area large enough to display your entire result before you enter the function.

2. If you pasted the function from the Paste Function dialog box and a one-word description of each of the values in the List_Of_Values_For_The_Function appeared, delete these descriptions before you type in the actual value that you want the function to use.

3. If you typed the function directly into the cell, type the values you want the function to use inside the parentheses.

Note: You will skip step 3 for functions that have no arguments. For example, the function PI() does not take any arguments. It just returns the number pi: 3.14159265358979 wherever it is used.

4. If the function returns a single value, press Enter.

If the function returns an array of values, make sure that in step one you highlighted a large enough area to accommodate your result. (If you did not, delete what you have done and go back to step 1.) Next, hold down the Ctrl key; then hold down the Shift key; then press the Enter key. Once you have pressed the Enter key, you can take your fingers off the Ctrl and Shift keys.

Tip: Use the INDEX function to access array elements from an array result.

Examples

To enter an example of the SUM function with numbers in the list of values for the function, perform the following steps:

1. Place the cursor in cell A1.

2. To enter the formula, paste the SUM function from the Paste Function dialog box through the Formula menu.

   =SUM(number1,number2,...) appears in cell A1.

3. Delete the words number1,number2,... inside the parentheses.

4. Type 3,5,2 (the amounts to be added) inside the parentheses so that the function looks like =SUM(3,5,2).

5. Press Enter. The number 10, the sum of 3 + 5 + 2, appears in cell A1.

To enter an example of the PRODUCT function with numbers and cell addresses in the list of values for the function, perform these steps:

1. Enter the number **0.05** in cell B1.
2. Place the cursor in cell B3.
3. To enter the formula, type the function name with an equal sign in front: **=PRODUCT(**.
4. Skip step 2.
5. Type **300,B1** (a number and cell address) followed by the right parenthesis so that the function looks like =PRODUCT(300,B1).
6. Press Enter.

The number 15, the product of 300 times 0.05, appears in cell B3.

To enter an example of the AVERAGE function with a range of cell addresses in the list of values for the function, perform these steps:

1. Enter the numbers **93**, **85**, **95**, and **87** in cells B2, B3, B4, and B5.
2. Place the cursor in cell B7.
3. To enter the formula, paste the AVERAGE function from the Paste Function dialog box through the Formula menu.

   =AVERAGE(number1,number2,...) appears in cell B7.
4. Delete the words number1,number2,... inside the parentheses.
5. Type **B2:B5** (a range of cell addresses) inside the parentheses so that the function looks like =AVERAGE(B2:B5).
6. Press Enter.

The number 90 (the average of 93, 85, 95, and 87) appears in cell B7.

FV( )

(*see also* **Functions, Annuity Functions, IPMT, NPER, PMT, PPMT, PV, RATE**)

Syntax

FV(*rate,nper,pmt,pv,type*)

Description

FV is a function that returns the future value of an investment based on periodic constant payments and a constant interest rate.

Note: Use the same unit of measure for specifying rate and nper. If payments are monthly, then rate and nper should be based on one-month periods.

Note: In annuity functions, a negative number represents cash that you pay out and a positive number represents cash that you receive.

The information required for function FV (all of the following values are numbers; for more information, see "Annuity Functions"):

rate is the interest rate per period.

nper is the total number of payment periods in an annuity.

pmt is the payment made each period and does not change over the life of the annuity. (Usually pmt includes principal and interest but no other fees or taxes.)

pv is the present value or total lump-sum amount that a series of future payments is worth now, in the present.

type is 0 or 1, indicating when payments are due, as shown below.

If type Is	*Payments Are Due*
0 or not included	At the end of the period
1	At the beginning of the period

Examples

Suppose that you are looking into a special IRA account that requires an initial deposit of $1,000 and monthly deposits of $300 at the end of the month over a fixed two-year period, and does not allow withdrawals of any kind for the entire two years. The annual interest rate for this account is 10%. What is the future value of this account?

This question can be answered using the following formula: =FV(10%/12,12*2,−300,−1000,0). (The 300 and 1000 are negative because you pay these amounts.) In your account at the end of these two years, you would have $7,320.67, the amount that is returned by this formula.

Suppose that you are planning for the cost of your child's college education. Statistics estimate that you will need to save $120,000 for four years of college. At present you have a total of $20,000 in your savings. You plan on putting away an additional $3,500 at the beginning of each year. Your child will be in college in 10 years. The annual interest rate for your savings account is 10%. What is the future value of your money at the end of these next 10 years?

This question can be answered using the following formula: =FV(10%,10,−3500,−20000,1). This formula returns $113,233.90. You see from this that you must invest a little more than you had planned. So you estimate that the most you can invest in one year is $3,900. The new future value uses this formula: =FV(10%,10,−3900,−20000,1), which returns $120,246.40. This will be enough for four years of college.

FWRITE (see Macro Functions—Control)

FWRITELN (see Macro Functions—Control)

G

Gallery

All the commands in the Gallery menu, except Preferred and Set Preferred, change the chart type of your chart. Excel has six basic types, one combination type, and four 3-D types. Each type has up to eight subtypes. Below are these 11 types of charts in Excel (see Chapters 6 and 13 for figures that show examples of each chart type):

Gallery Area	Gallery Combination
Gallery Bar	Gallery 3-D Area
Gallery Column	Gallery 3-D Column
Gallery Line	Gallery 3-D Line
Gallery Pie	Gallery 3-D Pie
Gallery XY (Scatter)	

Keystrokes

Keyboard

Gallery

Area, Bar, Column, Line, Pie, XY (Scatter), Combination, 3-D Area, 3-D Column, 3-D Line, or 3-D Pie

Use the left or right arrow keys.

Next or Previous

Enter

Mouse

Gallery

Area, Bar, Column, Line, Pie, XY (Scatter), Combination, 3-D Area, 3-D Column, 3-D Line, or 3-D Pie

Box 1, Box 2, Box 3, Box 4, Box 5, Box 6, Box 7, or Box 8

Next or Previous

OK

Example

Suppose that you entered data in a worksheet that contains figures on output per manhour for your factories in three different countries: Ireland, Somalia, and Sudan. You create a chart that represents this data. Excel assigns it the default Column format, but you want to see it in a Pie chart with a three-dimensional effect. Choose 3-D Pie from Gallery; then choose the subtype you want and OK.

 Changing a Chart Type

1. Make the chart that you want to change the active chart.

2. Choose the chart type you want (11 are available) from the Gallery menu.   Excel displays the relevant chart type dialog box.

3. Choose the subtype you want.   Excel highlights the subtype box.

4. Choose OK.   Excel redraws the chart in the window to your specifications.

Gallery 3-D Area (see Gallery)

Gallery 3-D Column (see Gallery)

Gallery 3-D Line (see Gallery)

Gallery 3-D Pie (see Gallery)

Gallery Area (see Gallery)

Gallery Bar (*see* Gallery)

Gallery Column (*see* Gallery)

Gallery Combination (*see* Gallery)

Gallery Line (*see* Gallery)

Gallery Pie (*see* Gallery)

Gallery Preferred

(*see also* Gallery Set Preferred)

Use the Gallery Preferred command to revert to the default chart type. If you have already reset the default chart with the Set Preferred command, Preferred restores your custom-made default. If you have not used Set Preferred, Preferred restores the Excel default, the Column chart.

Keystrokes

Keyboard *Mouse*

Gallery   Gallery

Preferred   Preferred

Example

Suppose that you have played around with many different chart types and formatting options for a chart and you now feel that the screen is too fussy. Choose Preferred to get back the original Excel default or your own default (set with Set Preferred).

 Reverting to the Default Chart Type

1. Make the chart that you want to change the active chart.

2. Choose Preferred from the Gallery menu.

Excel redraws the chart.

Gallery Set Preferred

(*see also* **Gallery Preferred**)

If you find yourself using the same chart type and formatting a lot, you might want to make this the default chart type, in place of the Column type with its default formatting. Excel allows you to change your default using Gallery Set Preferred.

Keystrokes

Keyboard	*Mouse*
Gallery	Gallery
Set Preferred	Set Preferred

Example

For a series of charts that compare rainfall with crop yield in a particular area, you could set up a Combination chart with special fonts. Rainfall is displayed as a Line type, while crop yield is displayed as a Column type. You know that all other data relating to the same topic will be displayed similarly. Make this the default chart type by choosing Set Preferred from Gallery.

Creating a New Default Chart

1. Make the chart that you want to set as the default type the active chart.

2. Choose Set Preferred from the Gallery menu.

   This chart becomes the default chart type until you exit Excel.

 Note: This new chart only remains as the default until you exit Excel.

Gallery XY (Scatter) (see Gallery)

GALLERY.3D.AREA

(see Macro Functions That Perform Gallery Commands)

GALLERY.3D.COLUMN

(see Macro Functions That Perform Gallery Commands)

GALLERY.3D.LINE

(see Macro Functions That Perform Gallery Commands)

GALLERY.3D.PIE

(*see* **Macro Functions That Perform Gallery Commands**)

GALLERY.AREA

(*see* **Macro Functions That Perform Gallery Commands**)

GALLERY.BAR

(*see* **Macro Functions That Perform Gallery Commands**)

GALLERY.COLUMN

(*see* **Macro Functions That Perform Gallery Commands**)

GALLERY.LINE

(*see* **Macro Functions That Perform Gallery Commands**)

GALLERY.PIE

(*see* **Macro Functions That Perform Gallery Commands**)

GALLERY.SCATTER

(*see* Macro Functions That Perform Gallery Commands)

GET.BAR (*see* Macro Functions—Customizing)

GET.CELL (*see* Macro Functions—Value Returning)

GET.CHART.ITEM

(*see* Macro Functions—Value Returning)

GET.DEF (*see* Macro Functions—Value Returning)

GET.DOCUMENT

(*see* Macro Functions—Value Returning)

GET.FORMULA

(*see* Macro Functions—Value Returning)

GET.LINK.INFO

(*see* Macro Functions—Value Returning)

GET.NAME (*see* Macro Functions—Value Returning)

GET.NOTE (*see* Macro Functions—Value Returning)

GET.OBJECT

(*see* Macro Functions—Value Returning)

GET.WINDOW

(*see* Macro Functions—Value Returning)

GET.WORKSPACE

(*see* Macro Functions—Value Returning)

GOAL.SEEK

(*see* Macro Functions That Perform Formula Commands)

GOTO (*see* Macro Functions—Control)

GRIDLINES

(*see* Macro Functions That Perform Chart Commands)

GROUP

(*see* Macro Functions That Perform Format Commands)

GROWTH() (*see also* LOGEST, TREND, LINEST)

Syntax

GROWTH(*known_y's,known_x's,new_x's,const*)

Description

GROWTH is a function that returns new y values to an exponential curve that it calculates. GROWTH first fits an exponential curve to the known_y's and known_x's values given in the list of values for the function. GROWTH then uses the new_x's values to calculate corresponding y values on this exponential curve. GROWTH returns an array of these y values on this exponential curve.

The exponential curve, which is calculated from the known_y's and known_x's values, is sometimes called an *exponential regression.* GROWTH can project new y values on the exponential curve that are beyond the section of the curve outlined by the known x and y values. To do this, just specify values in the new_x's array that are outside the range of the known_x's array.

 Note: The LOGEST function listing gives information on how Microsoft Excel calculates the exponential curve used by GROWTH. To get the values that describe this exponential curve, use LOGEST on your known_y's and known_x's data.

The information required for function GROWTH:

known_y's is an array of y values that have an exponential relationship of the form y = b * m ^ x.

known_x's is an array of x values that correspond to the y values of the known_y's array. The known_x's and their corresponding known_y's satisfy an exponential relationship of the form y = b * m ^ x.

new_x's is an array of x values that GROWTH uses to calculate new y values on the exponential curve that is calculated from the known_y's and known_x's values.

Note: GROWTH returns the error #VALUE! if there are empty cells or text in the known_x's, known_y's, or new_x's array cells.

const is a logical value that specifies whether the constant b in the exponential curve y = b * m ^ x is forced to the value 1.

Given	Then
const is TRUE or const is omitted.	b is calculated as normal.
const is FALSE.	The m values are adjusted so that b is equal to one. (GROWTH uses the formula y = m ^ x.)

The arrays of known_y's, known_x's, and new_x's have particular forms, as shown in the following:

Form of known_y's

Given	Then
The array known_y's spans a single column.	Each column of known_x's is a separate variable.
The array known_y's spans a single row.	Each row of known_x's is a separate variable.
Any known_y's is less than or equal to 0.	The function returns #NUM! error value.

Form of known_x's

Given

The array known_x's is a single set of variables (the dependent variable y depends on only one factor).

The array known_x's contains more than one set of variables (the dependent variable y depends on more than one factor).

known_x's is not included.

Then

known_x's and known_y's can be ranges of any shape so long as the dimensions of these arrays are the same.

known_y's must be a vector or range with a height of one row or a width of one column.

known_x's is assumed to be the array {1,2,3,...}, which is equal in size to the known_y's array.

Form of new_x's

Given

known_y's is a single column.

known_y's is a single row.

new_x's is omitted.

known_x's and new_x's are omitted.

Then

known_x's and new_x's have the same number of columns.

known_x's and new_x's have the same number of rows.

new_x's is the same as known_x's.

new_x's is the same default value as known_x's.

Note: There must be one column or row of new_x's for each independent variable (same as known_x's).

GROWTH is a function that returns an array. The procedure for entering any function that returns an array is to highlight the target array area on the spreadsheet before typing in the formula; type in the formula; and then before pressing Enter, press Ctrl, Shift, and Enter all at the same time.

An array constant must have commas between the values for each row and semicolons between rows.

Examples

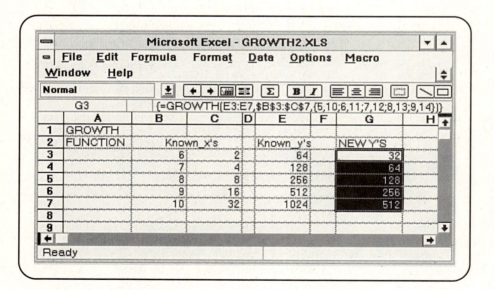

H

HALT (*see* Macro Functions—Control)

Header (*see also* Footer)

The Header feature specifies the header, if any, to be printed at the top of each page.

The header is always printed 1/2 inch from the top of the page and 3/4 inch from the sides of the page. The following codes can be combined and inserted in the header box to format the header. Each code applies to the characters that follow it.

Code	*Result in Header*
&B	Bold characters
&C	Center alignment
&D	Current date
&F	Filename of spreadsheet
&I	Italic characters
&L	Left alignment
&N	Print total number of pages
&P	Page number
&P+number	Page numbers plus the base number
&P–number	Page numbers minus the base number
&R	Right alignment
&S	Strikethrough characters
&T	Current time

Code	Result in Header
&U	Underline characters
&&	A single ampersand
&"fontname"	Change to specified font. Fontname must be inside double quotes.
&nn	Change to specified font size

 Caution: If the top margin is less than 1/2 inch, the header will be printed on top of the spreadsheet data. If the error `Not Supported by the Current Printer` is displayed when the Page Setup dialog box is closed, an option has been selected that is not supported by the current printer. Turn off the options one at a time until the nonsupported option is found, or select another printer with the Printer Setup option that supports all the options selected.

Keystrokes

Keyboard	Mouse
File	File
Page Setup	Page Setup

Example

&"Modern"&12&LProfit && Loss Statement&CPage&P of &N&R&D: If this example is entered in the Header box on the Page Setup dialog box, the header will be printed at the top of the page in Modern font 12 points tall. *Profit & Loss Statement* will be printed at the left border, *Page 1 of 20* will be centered, and the current date will be printed at the right border.

HELP *(see Macro Functions—Customizing)*

HIDE

(see Macro Functions That Perform Window Commands)

HIDE.OBJECT

(*see* Macro Functions That Perform Actions)

HLINE (*see* Macro Functions That Perform Actions)

HLOOKUP()

(*see also* Function, VLOOKUP, LOOKUP, MATCH, INDEX)

Syntax

HLOOKUP(*lookup_value,table_array,row_index_num*)

Description

HLOOKUP is a function that returns a value from the specified array which is in the column where the lookup_value was matched and in the row indicated by row_index_num. HLOOKUP looks in the first row of array for the lookup_value. When lookup_value is found, then HLOOKUP returns the value that is in the column which is headed by the value that was matched to lookup_value and the row which is in the position given by row_index_num.

HLOOKUP matches lookup_value with a value in the first row of array:

- If lookup_value is in the first row of array, HLOOKUP matches lookup_value with this value.

- If HLOOKUP can't find lookup_value in the first row of array, it matches with the next largest value in the first row of array that is less than or equal to lookup_value.

- If lookup_value is smaller than the smallest value in the first row of array, then no occurs and HLOOKUP returns the #N/A error.

 Note: HLOOKUP is similar to VLOOKUP. HLOOKUP looks in the first row for lookup_value, while VLOOKUP looks in the first column.

The information required for function HLOOKUP:

lookup_value is a value that HLOOKUP looks for in the first row of array.

table_array is a range of cells that contain numbers, text, or logical values.

Important: In order to ensure a correct answer, the values in the entire first row of table_array *must* be in ascending order: −1, 0, 1, 2, ..., A, ..., Z, FALSE, TRUE. (Upper- and lowercase letters are equivalent.) All other rows in table_array can be in any order.

row_index_num is the row number in table_array that specifies which row the returned value comes from. For example, if you specify a 3 for row_index_num, then the returned value will come from the third row. If row_index_num is less than 1, then HLOOKUP returns #VALUE! error. If row_index_num is larger than the number of rows in table_array, then HLOOKUP returns the #REF error value.

Note: row_index_num refers to the row number in table_array, not to the row numbers for the worksheet.

Tip: An easy way to ensure that the first column is in ascending order is to highlight the array; from the main menu select Data and then Sort; choose Row and Ascending; and press Enter.

Examples

Formula

=HLOOKUP(4,{1,2,3,4,5;"Monday", "Tuesday","Wednesday","Thursday", "Friday"},2)

=HLOOKUP(2.39,{1,2,3,4,5;"Monday", "Tuesday","Wednesday","Thursday", "Friday"},1)

=HLOOKUP(0.1,{1,2,3,4,5;"Monday", "Tuesday","Wednesday","Thursday", "Friday"},1)

Returns

"Thursday", the value that is in the second column where 2 matched 2, and in the second row

2, the value that is in the second column where 2.39 matched 2, and in the first row

#N/A

In the example in the figure, the value 120.47 is the result of the formula =HLOOKUP("Hz",B2:F14,12). This value is the result of fixing the column position by looking up "Hz" and the row position from the 12 in the formula. The position of the second column of array is fixed by matching "Hz" with "Heat". The position of the 12th row of the array (which contains the information for November) is fixed by the 12 in the formula. The value in the second column and 12th row is 120.47.

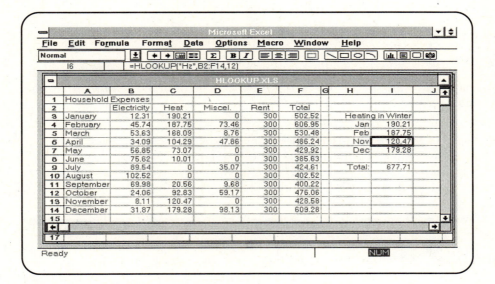

 Tip: In the example in the figure, the formula =HLOOKUP ("Hz",B2:F14,12) matches "Hz" with "Heat" since *Hz* alphabetically comes after the word *Heat*. If the formula =HLOOKUP("H",B2:F14,12) had been used, "H" would have matched "Electricity" since *H* comes before *Heat*. If you are looking for the last text item that begins with a particular letter, use that particular letter followed by the letter *z* as your lookup_value.

HOUR( )

(*see also* MINUTE, SECOND, DAY, MONTH, WEEKDAY, YEAR)

Syntax

HOUR(*serial_number*)

Description

HOUR is a function that returns the hour of the day corresponding to the particular time specified by serial_number. The returned number is a whole number that ranges from 0 (12:00 AM) to 23 (11:00 PM).

The information required for function HOUR:

Serial_number is a number that represents a particular time in the range of 12:00:00 AM to 11:59:59 PM. For more information on serial_number, see "TIME" and "NOW." Serial_number can also be given as text.

 Note: Excel 3 for Windows uses a different numbering system (the 1900 Date System) for dates than Excel for the Macintosh.

Examples

The formula =HOUR(0.413461) returns 9 because serial_number 0.413461 stands for the time 9:55:23 AM.

The formula =HOUR(32880.543576) returns 13 because serial_number 0.543576 stands for the time 1:02:45 PM or 13:02:45. (The 32880 portion of the serial number stands for the date January 7, 1990. The date is ignored.)

Formula	Returns
=HOUR("12:15:55 AM")	0
=HOUR("2:20:10 PM")	14

HPAGE (*see* Macro Functions That Perform Actions)

HSCROLL

(*see* Macro Functions That Perform Actions)

I–K

IF (*see* Macro Functions—Control)

IF( ) (both worksheet and macros)

(*see also* Function, AND, OR, NOT, TRUE, FALSE)

Syntax

IF(*logical_test,value_if_true,value_if_false*)

Description

The worksheet and macro form of the IF function returns either value_if_true or value_if_false (which are values that you specify). Which of these two values IF returns depends upon whether the logical_test that you specify yields a TRUE or FALSE result. If logical_test yields a TRUE value, then IF returns value_if_true. If logical_test yields a FALSE value, then IF returns value_if_false.

- For a more complex structure, value_if_true and/or value_if_false can be a maximum of seven levels of nested IF functions. One example in general form:

    =IF(t1,IF(t2,IF(t3,IF(t4,IF(t5,IF(t6,IF(t7,all_7_true,f7),f6),f5),f4),f3),f2),f1)

- The value_if_true or value_if_false of an IF function in a macro can be a GOTO function, another macro, or an action-taking function.

- IF returns the value of the evaluation of value_if_true and value_if_false. For example, =IF(TRUE,9/0,"false value") returns

#DIV/0! since 9/0 evaluates to the error #DIV/0!. A second example is where the logical_test selects a value_if_true or value_if_false that is an unsuccessful action-taking function (such as GOTO). In this case, IF returns the result of the logical_test, since the action could not successfully be taken.

- If any of the values supplied to the function IF are arrays, every element of the array is evaluated when Excel is calculating the IF statement. If some of the values given to IF are action-taking functions, all of the actions are taken. For example, if cell C2 contains "Worksheet" and cell C3 contains "Chart", the formula =IF({C2="Worksheet",C3="Chart"},new(1),new(2)) will create two new files, the first one a worksheet and the second one a chart.

- The latest version of Excel 3.0 compensates for extremely small errors made during computer calculations. Due to the limitations of a physical machine (with limited units of storage for values), simple arithmetic, such as subtracting two numbers, can create an extremely small difference between the actual result and the result that is calculated. For example, =0.9–0.8 yields a value that is 2.8E–17 smaller than 0.1. This "mistake" is so small that it doesn't appear unless you subtract 0.1 from a cell containing =0.9–0.8. When Excel performs a logical test, rounding occurs so that this small mistake doesn't give you a false result for expressions like 0.9–0.8=0.1 that involve computations with possible tiny computer errors.

The information required for function IF:

logical_test is any value or expression that can be reduced to TRUE or FALSE.

value_if_true is the value that is returned when logical_text reduces to TRUE. If value_if_true is not included, then IF returns TRUE.

value_if_false is the value that is returned when logical_text reduces to FALSE. If value_if_false is not included, then IF returns FALSE.

Examples

If Cell A5 Returns	Formula Is	Formula Returns
5	=IF(A5<10,"Too Young",A5)	"Too Young"
37	=IF(A5<10,"Too Young",A5)	37
Exempt	=IF(A5="Exempt","No Taxes",H39)	"No Taxes"

The IF function is useful for problems with ranges of values, where each range corresponds to one result. The following example demonstrates one of these uses:

Suppose that you have several test scores to which you want to assign a letter grade. Your system of grading is to assign an "A" to any score above 89, a "B" to a score between 89 and 80, a "C" to a score between 79 and 70, a "D" to a score between 69 and 60, and an "F" to a score below 60. If you gave the name *grade1* to your numerical score, then the following formula would return a letter grade for the number represented by grade1: =IF(grade1>89,"A",IF(grade1>79,"B",IF(grade1>69,"C",IF(grade1>59,"D","F")))). If grade1 referred to a cell containing the number 75, then this formula would return "C".

The example in the figure shows a row of IF formulas that avoid calculating negative taxes. (Taxes are 0 for no income.)

	A	B	C	D	E	F
1	INCOME STATEMENT					
2		1986	1987	1988	1989	1990
3	Sales	45677.00	66778.00	77888.00	88999.00	106798.80
4	Cost of Goods Sold	27406.20	40066.80	46732.80	53399.40	64079.28
5						
6	Gross Profit	18270.80	26711.20	31155.20	35599.60	42719.52
7						
8	Expenses	20554.65	26711.20	27260.80	31149.65	37379.58
9	Profit Before Taxes	-2283.85	0.00	3894.40	4449.95	5339.94
10	Taxes (@36%)	0.00	0.00	1401.98	1601.98	1922.38
11						
12	Profit After Tax	-2283.85	0.00	2492.42	2847.97	3417.56

Cell B10: =IF(B9<0,0,B9*0.36)

INDEX() (array form)

(*see also* Function, CHOOSE, LOOKUP, HLOOKUP, VLOOKUP, MATCH)

Syntax

INDEX(*array,row_num,column_num*)

Description

The array form of INDEX is a function that returns the contents of the cell located at by row_num and column_num. The array form of INDEX restricts

562 INDEX() (array form)

array to one continuous, unbroken area. INDEX locates the value it returns in the cell at the intersection of row_num and column_num in array, according to the following guidelines.

Condition	Value Returned
Both row_num and column_num are greater than or equal to 1.	INDEX returns the value in the cell at the intersection of row_num and column_num.
Either row_num or column_num is 0.	INDEX returns the entire row or column (the row or column that has a nonzero _num number).
Either row_num or column_num is not included, and array has more than one column and more than one row.	INDEX returns the entire row or column that was specified.

Note: If *array* is only one row or column, then only the dimension of the array that is greater than 1 needs to be specified. If you leave off row_num, then remember to include a comma for each omitted value, as done here: INDEX(array,,column_num).

The information required for function INDEX:

array is one cell address, one range of cells, or a name that refers to one cell address or one range of cells.

row_num is a number that specifies a row in *array*.

column_num is a number that specifies a column in *array*.

Examples

Formula	Returns
=INDEX({1,2,3;4,5,6},2,1)	4
=INDEX({1,2,3;4,5,6},2)	{4,5,6}
=INDEX({1,2,3;4,5,6},2,0)	{4,5,6}
=INDEX({1,2,3;4,5,6},0,2)	{2;5}

In the example in the figure, INDEX returns the entire third column of the array B3:H14.

INDEX() (reference form) 563

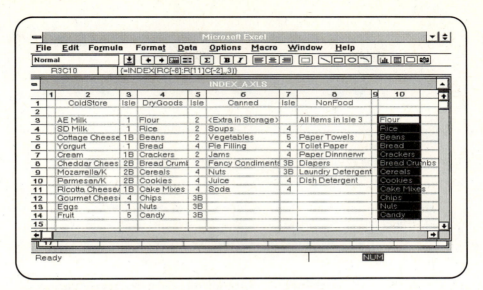

INDEX() (reference form)

(*see also* Function, CHOOSE, LOOKUP, HLOOKUP, VLOOKUP, MATCH)

Syntax

INDEX(*reference,row_num,column_num,area_num*)

Description

The reference form of INDEX is a function that returns the contents of the cell located at the intersection of row_num and column_num in the region of reference that is specified by area_num. The reference form of INDEX allows reference to be more than one area. INDEX uses the specified area_num to pick one of the areas in reference. INDEX then locates a value in the cell at the intersection of row_num and column_num in that chosen area.

> **Note:** The Microsoft Excel Function Reference manual says that the reference form of the INDEX function always returns a reference. But the figure in "Examples" and any examples you may care to try show that the INDEX function always returns the value at the location that you specify with reference, row_num, column_num, and area_num, not the reference of the cell.

The information required for function INDEX:

reference is one or more cell addresses, range of cell addresses, or names that refer to a cell address or range of cell addresses.

 Note: If the specified area in reference is only one row or column, then the row_num or column_num is optional. If you omit row_num or column_num, remember to include a comma for the omitted value, as done here: INDEX(reference,,column_num,2).

row_num is a number that specifies a row in the specified area of reference.

column_num is a number that specifies a column in the specified area of reference.

area_num is a number that selects one area from reference. For example, if area_num is 1 or not included, the first area is selected. If area_num is 3, the third area is selected.

Examples

Suppose that in the example in the figure you defined the name StoreMap to refer to four areas on your worksheet called ColdStore, DryGoods, Canned, and NonFood. In our example, these names refer to the following cell ranges.

Name	Cell Range
ColdStore	B3:C14
DryGoods	D3:E14
Canned	F4:G11
NonFood	H5:H10
StoreMap	A set of four areas: {ColdStore, DryGoods, Canned, NonFood}, which is the same as {B2:C20, D2:E35, F3:G11, H5:H10}

The following formulas return addresses on the basis of the above information, where StoreMap is four areas: B3:C14, D3:E14, F4:G11, and H4:H10, and each of these areas is named:

=INDEX(StoreMap,2,1,1) returns "SD Milk", the contents of B4. The first area in StoreMap is the ColdStore area, B3:C14. The first column and second row of the ColdStore area intersect cell B4.

INDEX() (reference form)

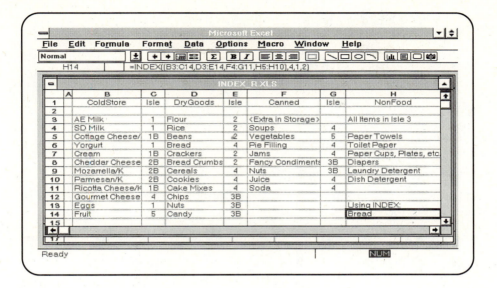

=INDEX(StoreMap,7,1,1) returns "Mozzarrella/K", the contents of B9. The first area in StoreMap is the ColdStore area, B3:C14. The first column and seventh row of the ColdStore area intersect cell B9.

=INDEX(StoreMap,6,2,3) returns "3B", the contents of G9. The third area in StoreMap is the Canned area, F4:G11. The second column and sixth row of the Canned area intersect cell G9.

=INDEX(StoreMap,6,,4) returns "Dish Detergent", the contents of cell H10. The fourth area in StoreMap is the NonFood area, H5:H10. The sixth row of the NonFood area intersects cell H10.

=INDEX(StoreMap,4,1,2) returns "Bread", the contents of D6. The second area in StoreMap is the DryGoods area, D3:E14. The cell in the first column and fourth row of the DryGoods area is D6.

=INDEX(StoreMap,6,4,3) returns #REF! because there is no fourth column in the third area of StoreMap, the Canned area that ranges from F4 to G11—two columns.

=INDEX(DryGoods,4,2) returns "4", the contents of E6. There is only one area in DryGoods, D2:E14, so there is no need to include a value for area_num. The cell in the second column and fourth row of the area specified by DryGoods is E6.

INDIRECT( )

(*see also* **Function, OFFSET, TEXTREF**)

Syntax

INDIRECT(*ref_text,a1*)

Description

INDIRECT is a function that returns the contents of a cell whose address is specified in the reference value ref_text.

> **Note:** The operation of INDIRECT is analogous to indirect addressing in the instruction set architecture of many computers.

The information required for function INDIRECT:

ref_text is a cell address that contains another cell address or a name that specifies a cell address.

> **Note:** If ref_text is not a valid cell address, then INDIRECT returns the error #REF!.

a1 is a logical value that specifies the reference style of ref_text.

If	Then
a1 is TRUE or not included	ref_text is in A1 reference style
a1 is FALSE	ref_text is in R1C1 reference style

Examples

If cell B7 contains D2 and cell D2 contains the number 9.32, then =INDIRECT(B7) returns 9.32.

If cell R3C4 contains R7C3 and cell R7C3 contains the word "Exempt", then =INDIRECT(R3C4,FALSE) returns "Exempt".

If cell B7 contains taxRate and the name tax refers to a cell that contains the number 0.08, then =INDIRECT(B7,TRUE) returns 0.08.

INFO( )

(*see also* Function, DIRECTORY, GET.DOCUMENT, GET.WORKSPACE)

Syntax

INFO(*type_num*)

Description

INFO is a function that returns information about the current operating environment.

The information required for function INFO:

type_num is text that specifies what type of text you want returned.

If type_num Is	Then INFO Returns
"directory"	Pathname of the current directory or folder
"memavail"	Amount of memory available in bytes
"numfile"	Number of active worksheets
"osversion"	Text specifying the current operating system version
"recalc"	Current recalculation mode, "Automatic" or "Manual"
"release"	Text specifying the version of Microsoft Excel
"system"	Name of operating environment: "Mac" = Macintosh "pcos2" = OS/2 "pcdos" = Windows
"totmem"	Total bytes of memory available, including memory already in use. (In Excel for the OS/2, this does not include virtual memory.)
"memused"	Amount of memory being used for data

Examples

If you have two Excel worksheet files open, then =INFO("numfile") returns 2. If you have two windows open and both are for the same spreadsheet file, then =INFO("numfile") returns 1.

INITIATE (see Macro Functions—Control)

INPUT (see Macro Functions—Control)

INSERT

(*see* Macro Functions That Perform Edit Commands)

INT( ) (*see also* Function, MOD, ROUND, TRUN)

Syntax

INT(*number*)

Description

INT is a function that returns the largest integer that is less than or equal to the given number. INT rounds down numbers. In this process, if the given number is positive, the fractional part of a number is discarded and only the integer part is returned. If the given number is negative, the next smaller integer is returned.

The information required for function INT:

number is any number.

Examples

Formula	Returns
=INT(54.99)	54
=INT(−9.2)	−10
=INT(4.12)	4
=SQRT(INT(9.3215))	3

IPMT( )

(*see also* Functions, Annuity Functions, FV, NPER, PMT, PPMT, PV, RATE)

Syntax

IPMT(*rate,per,nper,pv,fv,type*)

Description

IPMT is a function that returns interest payment for a given period of investment based on periodic constant payments and a constant interest rate.

> **Note:** Use the same unit of measure for specifying rate and nper. If payments are monthly, then rate and nper should be based on one-month periods.

> **Note:** In annuity functions, a negative number represents cash that you pay out and a positive number represents cash that you receive.

The information required for function IPMT (all of the following values are numbers; for more information, see "Annuity Functions"):

rate is the interest rate per period.

per is a number in the range of 1 to nper. per is the specific period for which you are requesting interest.

nper is the total number of payment periods in an annuity.

pv is the present value—the total amount that a series of future payments is worth now, in the present. As according to standard business practice, in the payment functions, interest calculations do not apply to pv.

fv is the future value or cash balance that you want to achieve after the last payment is made. If fv is not included, IPMT assumes that fv is 0. (For example, a loan has a future value of 0.)

type is 0 or 1, indicating when payments are due.

If type Is	Payments Are Due
0 or not included	At the end of the period
1	At the beginning of the period

Examples

The following formula returns the payment on the interest during the first month of a five-year $25,000 loan at 14% annual interest with payments at the end of each month: =IPMT(14%/12,1,12*5,25000). In the first month, you pay $291.67 of the interest (the amount that this formula returns). For this same loan, the payment on the interest of the 12th month, =IPMT(14%/12,12,12*5,25000), is $252.20 (the amount that this formula returns).

The following formula returns the payment on the interest during the last year of a 10-year $5,000 loan at 10% annual interest with payments at the end of each year: =IPMT(10%,10,10,5000,0,0). In the last year, you pay $73.98 of the interest (the amount that this formula returns).

The following formula returns the payment on the interest during the first month of a five-year $10,000 loan at 11% annual interest with payments at the beginning of each month: =IPMT(11%/12,1,12*5,10000,0,1). In the first month, you pay $0.00 of the interest (the amount that this formula returns). Payment on the interest during the second month of this same five-year $10,000 loan at 11% annual interest, according to the formula =IPMT(11%/12,2,12*5,10000,0,1), is $89.69.

Note: If you specify a type of 1 for payment in the first period, and a period or "per" of 1, then IPMT returns 0 in all cases (as you would expect).

IRR( ) *(see also* Functions, MIRR, NPV, RATE)

Syntax

IRR(*values,guess*)

Description

IRR is a function that returns the internal rate of return for an investment that is based on a series of periodic cash flows. The internal rate of return is the interest rate received for an investment consisting of payments (negative) and income (positive) that occur at regular intervals or periods of time.

IRR calculates the internal rate of return by repeated approximations, and therefore may have zero or more solutions. If, after 20 iterations, the results of IRR do not decrease to a difference of 0.0000001 between two successive approximations, then IRR returns #NUM! error.

> **Note:** IRR is related to the net present value function, NPV. IRR is the rate that makes NPV zero. For example, the formula =NPV(IRR(B2:B6,10%),B2:B6) returns 0 (provided that B2:B6 contains some appropriate information for IRR, as outlined in the values guidelines below).

The information required for function IRR:

values is an array or reference to an array of values that represent payments and income.

When entering values for the array values, there are guidelines and restrictions that you must follow:

- At least one positive value and one negative value must be in the values array.

- Make sure to enter your payment and income values in the correct sequence, since IRR uses the order of value1,value2,... when interpreting cash flows.

guess is your general approximation of what rate IRR will return. If guess is not included, then IRR assumes it is 10%. If IRR returns the #NUM! error, then try different guesses.

A function that requires numeric values, such as IRR, uses the following conversion rules:

- Converts a value to a numeric value if the value is typed directly into the list of values for the function and is one of the following:

    a logical value

    a number that is in text form

- Does not convert an argument to a numeric value if the argument is a cell address where the addressed cell:

    is empty

    contains text

    contains a logical value

- Returns an error if the argument is a cell address and the addressed cell has an error value in it.
- Returns the #VALUE! error if there is a text argument.

Examples

Suppose that you are looking into a special investment that costs $10,000 and pays $500 after the first year and twice as much as the previous year for the next four years after that. What is the internal rate of return on this investment? This question can be answered by entering the following numbers into cells B2 to B6: −10000, 500, 1000, 2000, 4000, 8000, then using the formula =IRR(B2:B6). Your internal rate of return for this investment is 11.29%, the value that this formula and the values return.

Suppose that you are looking into buying a business that costs $10,000 to start. You estimate that maintenance and repairs of the building and equipment for the business will cost approximately $200 after one and a half years of running the business, $500 after two and a half years, $650 after three and a half years, and $800 after four and a half years. You estimate that the business makes a profit of $0.00 at the end of the first year, $1,000 at the end of the second year, $2,400 at the end of the third year, and $7,000 at the end of the fourth year, and $10,000 at the end of the fifth year. What is the internal rate of return of your business after four years? After five years?

Note: Before using IRR, decide whether to calculate the IRR on the basis of the personal funds that you put into and get out of an investment, such as a business, or from the perspective of money coming into or going out of the investment or business.

For this example, let's calculate IRR based on the cash flow in and out of your personal funds. So money spent on repairs and maintenance is negative, and profit coming back to you is positive. To use the IRR function, the cash flows must be in the order that they occur. As you are organizing the values, enter them into your worksheet.

Cell address	Year	Cash Flow
B1	0	− 10000
B2	1	+ 0
B3	1.5	− 200
B4	2	1000

Cell address	Year	Cash Flow
B5	2.5	– 500
B6	3	2400
B7	3.5	– 650
B8	4	7000
B9	4.5	– 800
B10	5	10000

Using all the preceding information, after four years, the internal rate of return is calculated by =IRR(B1:B8), which returns –0.583%. IRR returned a negative value since you did not get back your entire investment in the business.

After five years, the internal rate of return is =IRR(B1:B10), which returns 8.71%.

Note: To calculate the internal rate of return on an annual basis, first calculate the length of the period between cash flows. In the example, every half year you are putting money into the business or getting money out of the business. So your rate for the five years of operation is approximately 8.71% * 2 or 17.41%.

IS Functions

(see also **ISBLANK, ISERR, ISERROR, ISLOGICAL, ISNA, ISNONTEXT, ISNUMBER, ISREF, ISTEXT)**

Syntax

ISBLANK(*value*)

ISERR(*value*)

ISERROR(*value*)

ISLOGICAL(*value*)

ISNA(*value*)

ISNONTEXT(*value*)

ISNUMBER(*value*)

ISREF(*value*)

ISTEXT(*value*)

Description

An IS function is a function that has a name beginning with the letters *IS* and returns TRUE or FALSE to signify whether the value given to it is of a specific type or not. The IS functions are ISBLANK, ISERR, ISERROR, ISLOGICAL, ISNA, ISNONTEXT, ISNUMBER, ISREF, ISTEXT. For details and examples on each specific function, see the separate listing for that function.

 Note: The Microsoft Excel Function Reference manual states that "if value is an array, then the IS functions test only the first element in the array." But as you can see from the example in the figure, this is not the case. The ISTEXT function used in the example returns TRUE if value is a text value. But in this example, ISTEXT returns FALSE even though the first cell of the array, cell B1, contains the text "text letters." In this example, every cell of the array contains text, yet the ISTEXT function returns FALSE. If the formula =ISTEXT(B3) is used instead of =ISTEXT(B3:C3), then the function returns TRUE.

Example

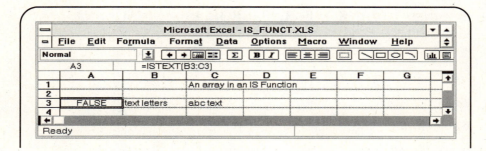

ISBLANK( )

(see also Function, ISERR, ISERROR, ISLOGICAL, ISNA, ISNONTEXT, ISNUMBER, ISREF, ISTEXT, GET.CELL, TYPE)

Syntax

ISBLANK(*value*)

Description

ISBLANK is a function that returns TRUE if *value* refers to a cell that is blank or empty. See "IS Functions" for more information on the use of ISBLANK.
The information required for function ISBLANK:

value is any reference to a cell.

> **Note:** If *value* is an array, ISBLANK returns FALSE even if every cell in the array is blank or empty.

Examples

If cell C6 contains no characters, not even a space, then =ISBLANK(C6) returns TRUE. If cell C6 contains any character (for example, 0), then =ISBLANK(C6) returns FALSE.

ISERR( )

(see also Function, ISBLANK, ISERROR, ISLOGICAL, ISNA, ISNONTEXT, ISNUMBER, ISREF, ISTEXT, GET.CELL, TYPE)

Syntax

ISERR(*value*)

Description

ISERR is a function that returns TRUE if *value* is or refers to an error value, excepting the #N/A error. These error values are #VALUE!, #REF!, #DIV/0!, #NUM!, #NAME? and #NULL!. See "IS Functions" for more information on the use of ISERR.

The information required for function ISERR:

value is any reference to a cell.

Note: If *value* is an array, ISERR returns TRUE even if none of the cells in the array have an error value in them.

Examples

If cell C6 contains any error value except #N/A (for example, #NAME?), then =ISERR(C6) returns TRUE. If cell C6 contains any characters or symbols that are not error values (for example, the text "error"), then =ISERR(C6) returns FALSE.

Formula	Returns
=ISERR(TRUE)	FALSE
=ISERR(#DIV/0!)	TRUE

ISERROR()

(see also **Function, ISBLANK, ISERR, ISLOGICAL, ISNA, ISNONTEXT, ISNUMBER, ISREF, ISTEXT, GET.CELL, TYPE)**

Syntax

ISERROR(*value*)

Description

ISERROR is a function that returns TRUE if *value* is or refers to any of the error values. These error values are #N/A, #VALUE!, #REF!, #DIV/0!, #NUM!, #NAME? and #NULL!. See "IS Functions" for more information on the use of ISERROR.

The information required for function ISERROR:

value is any reference to a cell.

Note: If *value* is an array, ISERROR returns TRUE even if none of the cells in the array have an error value in them.

Examples

If cell C6 contains an error value (for example, #VALUE!), then =ISERROR(C6) returns TRUE. If cell C6 contains any characters or symbols that are not error values (for example, the text "incorrect"), then =ISERROR(C6) returns FALSE.

Formula	Returns
=ISERROR(#N/A)	TRUE
=ISERROR(–99)	FALSE

ISLOGICAL()

(*see also* Function, ISBLANK, ISERR, ISERROR, ISNA, ISNONTEXT, ISNUMBER, ISREF, ISTEXT, GET.CELL, TYPE)

Syntax

ISLOGICAL(*value*)

Description

ISLOGICAL is a function that returns TRUE if *value* is or refers to a logical value. See "IS Functions" for more information on the use of ISLOGICAL.

The information required for function ISLOGICAL:

value is any reference to a cell.

Note: If *value* is an array, ISLOGICAL returns FALSE even if each cell in the array has a logical value in it.

Examples

If cell C6 contains any characters or symbols that are not logical values (for example, the text "true"), then =ISLOGICAL(C6) returns FALSE.

Formula	Returns
=ISLOGICAL(TRUE)	TRUE
=ISLOGICAL(1)	FALSE
=ISLOGICAL(FALSE)	TRUE

ISNA()

(*see also* Function, ISBLANK, ISERR, ISERROR, ISLOGICAL, ISNONTEXT, ISNUMBER, ISREF, ISTEXT, GET.CELL, TYPE)

Syntax

ISNA(*value*)

Description

ISNA is a function that returns TRUE if *value* is or refers to the #N/A error. If any other error values are used for value (#VALUE!, #REF!, #DIV/0!, #NUM!, #NAME? or #NULL!), then FALSE is the result. See "IS Functions" for more information on the use of ISNA.

The information required for function ISNA:

value is any reference to a cell.

 Note: If *value* is an array, ISNA returns TRUE even if none of the cells in the array have the error value #N/A in them.

Examples

If cell C6 contains any characters or symbols that are not the error value #N/A (for example, the text "N/A error"), then =ISNA(C6) returns FALSE.

Formula	Returns
=ISNA(#DIV/0!)	FALSE
=ISNA(#N/A)	TRUE

ISNONTEXT( )

(*see also* Function, ISBLANK, ISERR, ISERROR, ISLOGICAL, ISNA, ISNUMBER, ISREF, ISTEXT, GET.CELL, TYPE)

Syntax

ISNONTEXT(*value*)

Description

ISNONTEXT is a function that returns TRUE if *value* is or refers to a value that is not text. See "IS Functions" for more information on the use of ISNONTEXT.

The information required for function ISNONTEXT:

value is any reference to a cell.

Note: ISNONTEXT returns FALSE for all numbers in text format, wherever they are listed. (See "Examples.")

Note: If *value* is an array, ISNONTEXT returns FALSE even if all of the cells in the array have values that are not text.

Examples

If cell C6 contains any characters or symbols that are not text values (for example, the number 5), then =ISNONTEXT(C6) returns TRUE. If cell C6 contains the number "5" (which is text), then =ISNONTEXT(C6) returns FALSE.

Formula	Returns
=ISNONTEXT("Text 1")	FALSE
=ISNONTEXT(–4)	TRUE
=ISNONTEXT("9")	FALSE

ISNUMBER( )

(*see also* Function, ISNONTEXT, ISBLANK, ISERR, ISERROR, ISLOGICAL, ISNA, ISTEXT, ISREF, GET.CELL, TYPE)

Syntax

ISNUMBER(*value*)

Description

ISNUMBER is a function that returns TRUE if *value* is or refers to a number. See "IS Functions" for more information on the use of ISNUMBER.

The information required for function ISNUMBER:

value is any reference to a cell.

Note: ISNUMBER returns FALSE for all numbers in text format, wherever they are listed. (See "Examples.")

Note: If *value* is an array, ISNUMBER returns FALSE even if all of the cells in the array have values that are numbers.

Examples

If cell C6 contains any characters or symbols that are numerical values (for example, the number 5), then =ISNUMBER(C6) returns TRUE. If cell C6 contains the number "5" (which is text), then =ISNUMBER(C6) returns FALSE.

Formula	Returns
=ISNUMBER("Letters")	FALSE
=ISNUMBER(1000)	TRUE
=ISNUMBER("1000")	FALSE

ISREF( )

(*see also* Function, ISNONTEXT, ISBLANK, ISERR, ISERROR, ISLOGICAL, ISNA, ISNUMBER, ISTEXT, GET.CELL, TYPE)

Syntax

ISREF(*value*)

Description

ISREF is a function that returns TRUE if *value* is a cell address, an array of cells, a range of cells, or a name that refers to one of these. See "IS Functions" for more information on the use of ISREF.

The information required for function ISREF:

value is any reference to a cell.

Note: If you change the reference style, all references are converted to the new reference style and ISREF returns the same result as it did with the previous reference style.

Note: If *value* is an array, ISREF returns FALSE even if all of the cells in the array have values that are reference values.

Examples

If *tax* refers to a name that you defined with the Formula, Define Name dialog box, then the formula =ISREF(tax) returns TRUE since any name is a reference to a cell address or range of cell addresses.

Using the same reasoning, with the A1 style referencing, the formula =ISREF(C6) returns TRUE, since C6 is a reference to a cell.

If the spreadsheet is in A1 reference style, formula =ISREF(R returns an Error in Formula dialog box. If the spreadsheet is in R1C1 reference style, formula =ISREF(R returns TRUE.

The following examples assume that the spreadsheet is in A1 reference style (the style that is automatically set up on the spreadsheet):

Formula	Returns
=ISREF(D1)	TRUE
=ISREF("cell C1")	FALSE

ISTEXT( )

(*see also* Function, ISNONTEXT, ISBLANK, ISERR, ISERROR, ISLOGICAL, ISNA, ISNUMBER, ISREF, GET.CELL, TYPE)

Syntax

ISTEXT(*value*)

Description

ISTEXT is a function that returns TRUE if *value* is or refers to a text value. See "IS Functions" for more information on the use of ISTEXT.

The information required for function ISTEXT:

value is any reference to a cell.

Note: ISTEXT returns TRUE for all numbers in text format, wherever they are listed. (See "Examples.")

Note: If *value* is an array, ISTEXT returns FALSE even if all of the cells in the array have values that are text.

Examples

If cell C6 contains the number "5" (which is text), then =ISTEXT(C6) returns TRUE. If cell C6 contains any characters or symbols that are not text values (for example, the number 5), then =ISTEXT(C6) returns FALSE.

Formula	Returns
=ISTEXT("Text 1")	TRUE
=ISTEXT(-4)	FALSE
=ISTEXT("9")	TRUE

JUSTIFY

(*see* **Macro Functions That Perform Format Commands**)

L

LAST.ERROR

(*see* Macro Functions—Value Returning)

LEFT( )

(*see also* Function, RIGHT, MID, FIND, SEARCH)

Syntax

LEFT(*text,num_chars*)

Description

LEFT is a function that returns a copy of the leftmost characters of the argument *text*. LEFT starts copying the first character of *text* and copies characters until it has as many characters as num_chars specifies. It then returns this partial copy of the *text* argument.

 Tip: LEFT can be used with other functions like SEARCH to extract data.

The information required for function LEFT:

text is any single symbol or group of symbols. If the argument *text* is typed directly into the argument list, then it must be enclosed in quotation marks.

num_chars is the number of characters that LEFT will copy and return from *text*. If num_chars is not included, it is assumed to be one. If num_chars is larger than the length of *text*, then LEFT returns the entire argument called *text*.

 Note: #VALUE! error is returned if num_chars is less than 0.

Examples

Formula   *Returns*

=LEFT("Abbott and Costello",6)   "Abbott"

=LEFT("More Wrong than Right",4)   "More"

LEGEND

(*see* **Macro Functions That Perform Chart Commands**)

LEN() (*see also* EXACT, SEARCH)

Syntax

LEN(*text*)

Description

LEN is a function that returns how many characters there are in *text*.
The information required for function LEN:

No information is required for function LEN.

Examples

Formula	Returns
=LEN("ABCD")	4
=LEN("98765four0")	10

LINEST( ) *(see also* LOGEST, TREND, GROWTH*)*

Syntax

LINEST(*known_y's,known_x's,const,stats*)

Description

LINEST is a function that returns an array of values that describe a straight line which fits the known_y's and known_x's values given to the function. Using the "least squares" procedure, LINEST fits a straight line to the known_y's and known_x's values given in the list of values for the function. This straight line has the form y = m * x + b, where *m* and *x* are arrays. LINEST returns the description of this straight line in an array containing the b value and the array elements from m. The returned array delineates all the mi values of the m array in the straight line equation above: $\{m_n, m_{n-1}, ..., m_1, b\}$.

The array m consists of the calculated mi values that correspond to each xi set from the known_x's array. In the equation y = $m_1 * x_1 + m_2 * x_2 + ... + b$ (an expanded version of y = m * x + b), the y value represented in the known_y's array is the dependent variable, which is determined by the x value(s) or independent variables. In the list of values for the function, these x values are represented by the known_x's array values. The value b is a constant, and the m values are coefficients that correspond to the x values of the known_x's array. LINEST returns these values in reverse order: $\{m_n, m_{n-1}, ..., m_1, b\}$, where *n* is the number of values in the known_y's array.

If additional statistics are requested with stats, LINEST also returns the requested information:

$\{m_n, m_{n-1}, ..., m_1, b; se_n, se_{n-1}, ..., se_1, se_b; r^2, se_y; F, df; ss_{reg}, ss_{resid}\}$

The information required for function LINEST:

known_y's is an array of y values that have a linear relationship: y = m * x + b.

known_x's is an array of x values that correspond to the y values in the known_y's array. The known_x's and their corresponding known_y's satisfy a linear relationship: y = m * x + b.

> **Note:** LINEST returns the error #VALUE! if there are empty cells or text in the known_x's or known_y's array cells.

const is a logical value that specifies whether the constant b in the straight line y = m * x + b is forced to the value 1.

Given That const Is	Then
TRUE or omitted	b is calculated as normal.
FALSE	The m values are adjusted so that b is equal to zero. (LINEST uses the formula y = m * x.)

stats is a logical value that specifies whether to display additional statistics on the regression equation.

Given That stats Is	Linest Returns
TRUE	The values that describe the line and additional statistics: $\{m_n, m_{n-1}, ..., m_1, b;$ $se_n, se_{n-1}, ..., se_1, se_b;$ $r^2, se_y;$ $F, df;$ $ss_{reg}, ss_{resid}\}$
FALSE or omitted	Just the values that describe the line: $\{m_n, m_{n-1}, ..., m_1, b\}$

The arrays of known_y's and known_x's have particular forms, as shown in the following:

Form of known_y's

Given	Then
The array known_y's spans a single column.	Each column of known_x's is a separate variable.
The array known_y's spans a single row.	Each row of known_x's is a separate variable.

Form of known_x's

Given

The array known_x's is a single set of variables (the dependent variable y depends on only one factor).

The array known_x's contains more than one set of variables (the dependent variable y depends on more than one factor).

known_x's is not included.

Then

known_x's and known_y's can be ranges of any shape so long as the dimensions of these arrays are the same.

known_y's must be a vector or range with a height of one row or a width of one column.

known_x's is assumed to be the array {1,2,3,...}, which is equal in size to the known_y's array.

Description of Error Values

Statistic	Is
$se_1, se_2, ..., se_n, se_b$	standard error values for the coefficients $m_1, m_2, ..., m_n,$ and the constant b
r^2	the coefficient of determination, ranging from 0 to 1. 1 represents perfect correlation or a perfect fit of your data to a line/curve. 0 represents no correlation.
se_y	the standard error for y estimate
F	the F statistic, which measures whether the relationship between independent and dependent variable is by chance
df	the degrees of freedom
ss_{reg}	the regression sum of squares
ss_{resid}	the residual sum of squares

If the known_y's and known_x's data closely describe a straight line, the calculated line using LINEST will closely fit your data. If your data describes a relationship that is closer to an exponential curve, then LOGEST will fit your data better.

If the calculated regression curve does not fit your data closely, the y values that you calculate from the regression equation given by LINEST may not be valid. Check the error values given in the additional regression statistics section of the returned array and/or check that derived y values are in the range of the known_y's values.

590 LINEST( )

LINEST is a function that returns an array of one or five rows. The procedure for entering the LINEST function is to first highlight the target array area on the spreadsheet before typing in the formula. Make sure that you highlight an area large enough for the returned array. Next type in the formula, and press Ctrl, Shift, and Enter all at the same time.

Tip: To extract one value of the regression equation at a time from the array of regression equation values returned by LINEST, use the function INDEX.

Tip: An array constant must have commas between the values for each row and semicolons between rows.

Examples

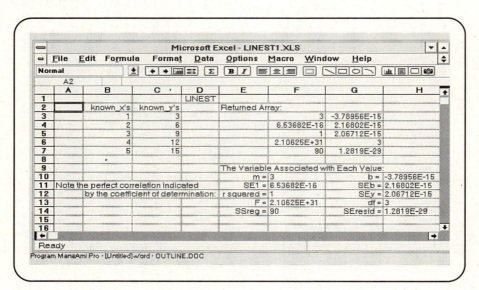

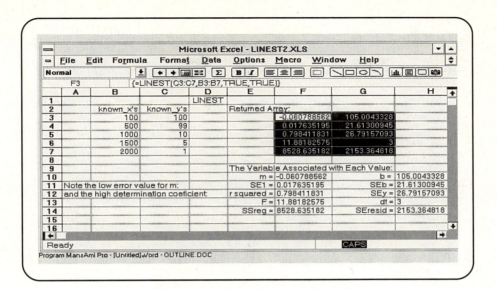

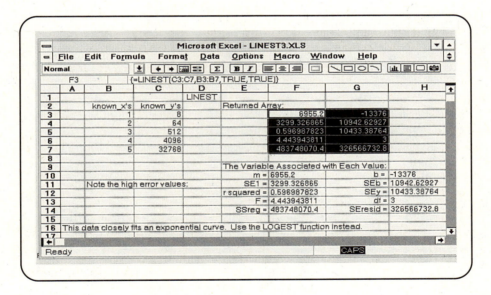

LINKS

(*see* Macro Functions That Perform File Commands)

LIST.NAMES

(*see* Macro Functions That Perform Formula Commands)

LN( ) (*see also* Function, EXP, LOG)

Syntax

LN(*number*)

Description

LN is a function that returns the natural logarithm of a number. *Ln* is an abbreviation for natural logarithm. The natural logarithm uses the number e (2.71828182845904) as its base. The natural logarithm function, LN(number), is the inverse of the EXP(number) function. For example, since $EXP(2) = e^2 = 2.718281828^2 = 7.3890561$, then $LN(7.3890561) = 2$. (See function EXP for a description of e.)

The information required for function LN:

number is a positive number for which you want a natural logarithm.

 Note: The LN function (the natural logarithm) is a specialization of LOG, the logarithm. $LN(x) = LOG(x,e) = LOG(x,EXP(1))$.

Examples

Formula	Returns
=LN(77)	4.3438054
=LN(0.367879441)	−1
=LN(EXP(2))	2

LOG( ) (see also Function, LOG10, LN, EXP)

Syntax

LOG(*number,base*)

Description

LOG is a function that returns the logarithm of *number* using the specified *base*. LOG is an abbreviation for logarithm. Taking the logarithm is the inverse of raising the given base number to a power. For example, since base 7 raised to the 2 power equals 49, the logarithm of 49 in base 7 is 2. (Since $7^2 = 49$, then LOG(49,7)=2.)

The logarithm is similar to the natural logarithm, with the exception that you can specify any base.

The information required for function LOG:

number is a positive number for which you want the logarithm.

base is a number used as the base in the calculation of the logarithm of *number*. If a number for base is not included in the list of values for LOG, then it is assumed to be 10.

Examples

Formula	Returns
=LOG(25,5)	2
=LOG(100)	2
=LOG(8,2)	3
=LOG(7^9,7)	9

LOG10( ) *(see also* Function, LOG, LN, EXP*)*

Syntax

LOG10(*number*)

Description

LOG10 is a function that returns the logarithm of the given number using base 10. LOG10 is a specialized version of the LOG function. The LOG10 function gives the logarithm base 10 of the argument *number*. LOG10 is the inverse of raising 10 to a power. For example, since 10 raised to the 2 power equals 100, LOG10(100), the base 10 logarithm of 100 is 2. (Since $10^2 = 100$, then LOG10(100)=2.)

The information required for function LOG10:

number is a positive number for which you want a base 10 logarithm.

> **Note:** The logarithm function LOG(x) can be used to replace the logarithm base 10 function LOG10( ): LOG10(x) = LOG(x,10) = LOG(x).

Examples

Formula	Returns
=LOG10(10)	1
=LOG10(0.10)	−1
=LOG10(10000000)	7

LOGEST( ) *(see also* LINEST, GROWTH, TREND*)*

Syntax

LOGEST(*known_y's,known_x's,const,stats*)

Description

LOGEST is a function that returns an array of values that describe an exponential curve which fits the known_y's and known_x's values given in the list of values for the function. This exponential curve has the form $y = b * m \char`\^ x$ where m and x are arrays. LOGEST returns the description of this exponential curve in an array containing the value b and the array elements from m. The returned array delineates all the mi values of the m array in the exponential curve equation above: $\{m_n, m_{n-1}, ..., m_1, b\}$.

The array m consists of the calculated mi values that correspond to each xi set from the known_x's array. In the equation $y = b * ((m_1 \char`\^ x_1) * (m_2 \char`\^ x_2) *...)$ (an expanded version of $y = b * m \char`\^ x$), the y value represented by the known_y's array is the dependent variable, which is determined by the x value(s) or independent variables. In the list of values for the function, these x values are represented by the known_x's array values. The value b is a constant, and the m values are bases that correspond to the x values of the known_x's array. LOGEST returns these values in reverse order: $\{m_n, m_{n-1}, ..., m_1, b\}$ where n is the number of values in the known_y's array.

If additional statistics are requested with stats, LOGEST also returns the requested information:

$$\{m_n, m_{n-1}, ..., m_1, b; se_n, se_{n-1}, ..., se_1, se_b; r^2, se_y; F, df; ss_{reg}, ss_{resid}\}$$

This exponential curve, calculated from the known_y's and known_x's arrays, is sometimes called an *exponential regression*.

The information required for function LOGEST:

known_y's is an array of y values that have an exponential relationship of the form $y = b * m \char`\^ x$.

known_x's is an array of x values that correspond to the y values given in the known_y's array. The known_x's and their corresponding known_y's satisfy an exponential relationship of the form $y = b * m \char`\^ x$.

Note: LOGEST returns the error #VALUE! if there are empty cells or text in the known_x's or known_y's array cells.

const is a logical value that specifies whether the constant b in the exponential curve $y = b * m \char`\^ x$ is forced to the value 1.

Given	Then
const is TRUE or const is omitted.	b is calculated as normal.
const is FALSE.	The m values are adjusted so that b is equal to one. (LOGEST uses the formula $y = m \char`\^ x$.)

stats is a logical value that specifies whether to display additional statistics on the regression equation.

 Note: See "LINEST" for a description of the additional regression statistics.

Given That stats Is	*LOGEST Returns*
TRUE	The values for the exponential curve and additional statistics: $\{m_n, m_{n-1}, \ldots, m_1, b;$ $se_n, se_{n-1}, \ldots, se_1, se_b;$ $r^2, se_y;$ $F, df;$ $ss_{reg}, ss_{resid}\}$
FALSE or omitted	Just the values for the exponential curve: $\{m_n, m_{n-1}, \ldots, m_1, b;\}$

The arrays of known_y's and known_x's have particular forms, as shown in the following:

Form of known_y's

Given	*Then*
The array known_y's spans a single column.	Each column of known_x's is a separate variable.
The array known_y's spans a single row.	Each row of known_x's is a separate variable.

Form of known_x's

Given	*Then*
The array known_x's is a single set of variables (the dependent variable y depends on only one factor).	known_x's and known_y's can be ranges of any shape so long as the dimensions of these arrays are the same.

The array known_x's contains more than one set of variables (the dependent variable y depends on more than one factor).

known_y's must be a vector or range with a height of one row or a width of one column.

Given

known_x's is not included.

Then

known_x's is assumed to be the array {1,2,3,...}, which is equal in size to the known_y's array.

If the known_y's and known_x's data closely describes an exponential curve, the calculated line using LOGEST will closely fit your data. If your data describes a relationship that is closer to a straight line, then the function LINEST will better fit your data to a line.

If the calculated regression curve does not fit your data closely, the y values that you calculate from the regression equation given by LOGEST may not be valid. Check the error values given in the additional regression statistics section of the returned array and/or check that derived y values are in the range of the known_y's values.

LOGEST is a function that returns an array of one or five rows. The procedure for entering LOGEST is to first highlight the area for the resultant array on the spreadsheet *before* typing in the formula. Make sure that you highlight an area large enough for the array to be returned. Next, type in the formula, and press Ctrl, Shift, and Enter all at the same time.

Tip: To extract one value of the regression equation at a time from the array of regression equation values returned by LOGEST, use the function INDEX.

Note: An array constant must have commas between the values for each row and semicolons between rows.

Examples

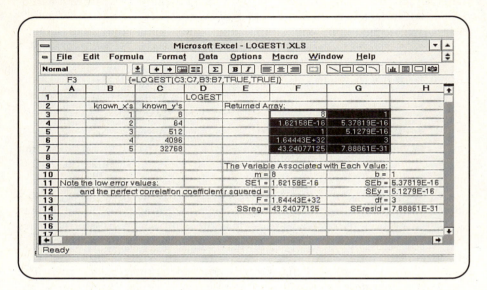

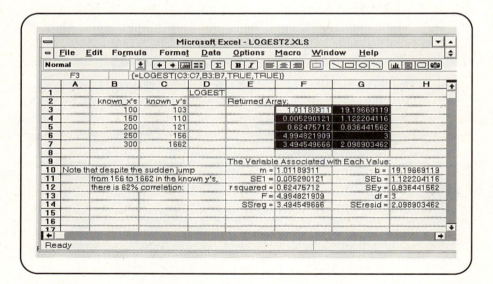

Logical Value

A *logical value* is a type of value, an expression of information in a carefully defined, precise form. There are two values that are logical values, TRUE and FALSE. You may type these values directly into the cell, or you may type an expression that represents TRUE or FALSE.

In an expression that represents TRUE (such as 2+2=4), after simplifying both sides of the equal sign, the final values on either side of the equal sign are equal. In an expression that represents FALSE (such as 5+5=3), after simplifying both sides of the equal sign, the final values on either side of the equal sign are not equal. A logical value can be represented by any expression that can be mathematically evaluated precisely to yield a logical value or either TRUE or FALSE.

Logical values are generally used when you want to single out specific values or ranges of values. You could use a logical value to test if another value is positive, for example, =C3>0. You could use a logical value to test if two values are equal, or if one is larger than the other.

A logical value is one of six types of values: numbers, text, logical values, references, arrays, and error values. For more information about values in general and a summary of these other five types of values, see "Values."

Whenever you see a request for a logical value, you can use a logical value or you can use a reference, formula, or name that represents or yields a logical value.

Syntax

TRUE

FALSE

value1*?*value2 (where *value1* and *value2* represent any value or formula that yields a single value, and *?* represents one of the relational operators: =, <, >, etc.)

Examples

A True Logical Value

TRUE

C3="level 3" and cell C3 contains the symbols: level 3

C3 > 0 and cell C3 contains 321.90

A False Logical Value

FALSE

"Three"=3

C3 < A1, where cell C3 contains 5 and cell A1 contains 2

LOOKUP( ) (array form)

(see also Function, HLOOKUP, VLOOKUP, INDEX)

Syntax

LOOKUP(*lookup_value,array*)

Description

The array form of LOOKUP is a function that returns a value from the first row or column of values in the specified array. The array form of LOOKUP looks in the first row or column of array for the lookup_value. When lookup_value is found according to the following guidelines, then LOOKUP returns the value in result_vector that corresponds to the found or matched value in lookup_vector. LOOKUP searches for lookup_value in:

- the first row of array, if array has more columns than rows (it is wider than it is tall) or has an equal number of rows and columns.

- the first column of array, if array has more rows than columns (it is taller than it is wide).

LOOKUP returns:

- If lookup_value is in the first row/column of array, LOOKUP returns the value from result_vector that corresponds to this matched cell.

- If LOOKUP can't find lookup_value in the first row/column of array, it matches with the next largest value in the first row/column of array that is less than or equal to lookup_value. LOOKUP returns the value from result_vector that corresponds to this matched cell.

- If lookup_value is smaller than the smallest value in the first row/column of array, LOOKUP returns the #N/A error.

Note: HLOOKUP and VLOOKUP also perform the operations that LOOKUP does. You may favor using HLOOKUP or VLOOKUP since they provide more options.

The information required for function LOOKUP:

lookup_value is a value that LOOKUP looks for in the lookup_vector.

array is a range of cells that contains numbers, text, or logical values. In order to ensure a correct answer, the values in array must be in ascending order: –1, 0, 1, 2, ..., A ,..., Z, FALSE, TRUE. (Upper- and lowercase letters are equivalent.)

Examples

Formula	*Returns*
=LOOKUP(2,{1,2,3,4,5;"Monday","Tuesday", "Wednesday", "Thursday","Friday"})	"Tuesday"
=LOOKUP(2.39,{1,2,3,4,5;"Monday","Tuesday", "Wednesday", "Thursday","Friday"})	"Tuesday"
=LOOKUP(5.1,{1,2,3,4,5;"Monday","Tuesday", "Wednesday","Thursday","Friday"})	"Friday"
=LOOKUP(0.1,{1,2,3,4,5;"Monday","Tuesday", "Wednesday","Thursday","Friday"})	#N/A
=LOOKUP("bake",{"A","Angel Food Cake";"C", "Coffee Cake";"D","Devils Food Cake"})	"Angel Food Cake"

LOOKUP() (vector form)

(*see also* Function, HLOOKUP, VLOOKUP, INDEX)

Syntax

LOOKUP(*lookup_value,lookup_vector,result_vector*)

Description

The vector form of LOOKUP is a function that returns a value from the row or column of values specified by result_vector. This form of LOOKUP looks in the row or column of lookup_vector for the lookup_value. When lookup_value is found according to the following guidelines, then LOOKUP returns the value in result_vector that corresponds to the found or matched value in lookup_vector:

- If lookup_value is in lookup_vector, LOOKUP returns the value from result_vector that corresponds to this matched cell.

- If LOOKUP can't find lookup_value in lookup_vector, it matches with the next largest value in lookup_vector that is less than or equal to lookup_value. LOOKUP returns the value from result_vector that corresponds to this matched cell.

- If lookup_value is smaller than the smallest value in lookup_vector, LOOKUP returns the #N/A error.

The information required for function LOOKUP:

lookup_value is a value that LOOKUP looks for in the lookup_vector.

lookup_vector is one row or column of numbers, text, or logical values. In order to ensure a correct answer, the values in lookup_vector must be in ascending order: −1, 0, 1, 2, ..., A, ..., Z, FALSE, TRUE. (Upper- and lowercase letters are equivalent.)

result_vector is one row or column of numbers, text, or logical values that is the same size as lookup_vector. LOOKUP returns the one value from this row or column that corresponds to lookup_value in lookup_vector.

Examples

Formula	*Returns*
=LOOKUP(3,{1,2,3,4,5},{"Monday","Tuesday","Wednesday","Thursday","Friday"})	"Wednesday"

Formula	Returns
=LOOKUP(2.71,{1,2,3,4,5},{"Monday", "Tuesday","Wednesday", "Thursday","Friday"})	"Wednesday"
=LOOKUP(6.9,{1,2,3,4,5},{"Monday", "Tuesday","Wednesday","Thursday","Friday"})	"Friday"
=LOOKUP(0,{1,2,3,4,5},{"Monday","Tuesday", "Wednesday","Thursday","Friday"})	#N/A
=LOOKUP("brownies",{"A";"C";"D"},{"Angel Food Cake";"Coffee Cake";"Devils Food Cake"})	"Angel Food Cake"

LOWER( ) *(see also* Function, UPPER, PROPER)

Syntax

LOWER(*text*)

Description

LOWER is a function that returns text with all lowercase letters.

Note: LOWER changes letters only. Characters that are not letters remain unchanged.

The information required for function LOWER:

text is any single symbol or group of symbols.

Examples

Formula	Returns
=LOWER("Twas Brilliago I saw...")	"twas brilliago i saw..."
=LOWER("ONE TIME ONLY")	"one time only"

Macro Functions That Perform Actions

Macro functions that perform actions allow you to use a nonactive macro function in a macro sheet to perform *any activity* in a sheet or chart that can be done by directly acting on a worksheet, a macro sheet, and/or a chart without accessing any menu.

The following action macro functions are specific macro functions *that you can use in a macro sheet*.

Name: A1.R1C1

Syntax: A1.R1C1(*logical*)

Description: Displays row and column headings and cell references in a) the R1C1 style if you specify a logical value of TRUE or b) the A1 style (the style that automatically comes up) if you specify a logical value of FALSE

Name: ACTIVATE

Syntax: ACTIVATE(*window_text,pane_num*)

Description: Activates either the window specified by the window_text value that you supply (if more than one window is open) or the pane specified by the pane_num value that you supply (if the window is split)

Arguments: *window_text* is the name of the window in text form. If there is more than one window for the document, the first window is activated. If window_text is not specified, then the active window remains active.

If pane_num Is	Then the Following Pane Is Activated
1	Top left
2	Top right

If pane_num Is	Then the Following Pane Is Activated
3	Bottom left
4	Bottom right

Name: ACTIVATE.NEXT

Syntax: ACTIVATE.NEXT()

Description: Activates the next window. ACTIVATE.PREV and ACTIVATE.NEXT are equivalent to pressing Ctrl-F6 or Ctrl-Shift-F6.

Name: ACTIVATE.PREV

Syntax: ACTIVATE.PREV()

Description: Activates the previous window. ACTIVATE.PREV and ACTIVATE.NEXT are equivalent to pressing Ctrl-F6 or Ctrl-Shift-F6.

Name: APP.ACTIVATE

Syntax: APP.ACTIVATE(*title_text,wait_logical*)

Description: Activates an application

Arguments: *title_text* is the name of an application as displayed in its title bar.

If *wait_logical* is TRUE, then Excel waits to be activated before activating the title_text application. If wait_logical is FALSE or not included, then Excel immediately activates the title_text application.

Name: BEEP

Syntax: BEEP(*tone_num*)

Description: Sounds one of four tones, specified by tone_num. (Most computers are not equipped to provide all 4 tones.)

Arguments: *tone_num* is a number from 1 to 4. If it is omitted, 1 is assumed.

Name: CANCEL.COPY

Syntax: CANCEL.COPY()

Description: Equivalent to pressing Esc in Windows

Name: CREATE.OBJECT

Syntax:
CREATE.OBJECT(*object_type,ref_1,x_offset1,y_offset1,ref_2, x_offset2, y_offset2*);
CREATE.OBJECT(*object_type,ref_1,x_offset1,y_offset1,ref_2, x_offset2, y_offset2,text*);
CREATE.OBJECT(*object_type,ref_1,x_offset1,y_offset1,ref_2, x_offset2,y_offset2, xy_series*)

Description: Draws an object on the worksheet or macro sheet and returns a value identifying the created object

Arguments:

If object_type Is	Then the Object Is
1	Line
2	Rectangle
3	Oval
4	Arc
5	Embedded chart
6	Text box
7	Button
8	Picture

ref_1 is a cell where the upper-left corner of the object is drawn.

x_offset1 is the distance, measured horizontally in points from the upper-left corner of ref_1 to the upper-left corner of the object. A point is 1/72 of an inch.

y_offset1 is the distance, measured vertically in points from the upper-left corner of ref_1 to the upper-left corner of the object.

ref_2 is a cell where the lower-right corner of the object is drawn.

x_offset2 is the distance, measured horizontally in points from the upper-left corner of ref_2 to the lower-right corner of the object.

y_offset2 is the distance, measured vertically in points from the upper-left corner of ref_2 to the lower-right corner of the object.

text specifies the text that appears in a text box or button.

xy_series applies to charts and corresponds to the First Row/Column Contains box.

If xy_series Is	Then Result Is
0	If selection is ambiguous, Excel displays a dialog box
1	First row/column is the data series
2	First row/column are the category (x) axis labels
3	First row/column are x values and created chart is an xy chart

Name: DELETE.FORMAT

Syntax: DELETE.FORMAT(*format_text*)

Description: Deletes a specified custom number format (equivalent to deleting a specified format with the Format Number command)

Arguments: *format_text* is the format in text form. #VALUE! is returned if the format is invalid (for example, a built-in format).

Notes: General format is given to values whose format was deleted with this function.

Name: DEMOTE

Syntax: DEMOTE(*rowcol*)

Description: Demotes the selected rows or columns in an outline

Arguments: If *rowcol* is 1 or not included, rows are demoted. If rowcol is 2, columns are demoted.

Name: DUPLICATE

Syntax: DUPLICATE( )

Description: Duplicates the selected object. #VALUE! is returned if the selection is not an object.

Name: EDITION.OPTIONS

Syntax:
EDITION.OPTIONS(*edition_type,edition_name,reference,option*);
EDITION.OPTIONS?(*edition_type,edition_name,reference*)

Description: Options are set or actions performed on the specified publisher or subscriber.

Arguments: If *edition_type* is 1, the type of edition is a publisher. If edition_type is 2, the type of edition is a subscriber.

edition_name is the name of the edition that you want to act on or change the options in.

reference gives the range occupied by the publisher or subscriber. Required if you have more than one publisher or subscriber.

If option for a Publisher Is	Then Action Is
1	Cancel the publisher
2	Send the edition now
3	Select the range or object published to the specified edition

If option for a Publisher Is	*Then Action Is*
4	Update the edition automatically when the file is saved
5	Update the edition on request only

If Option for a Subscriber Is	*Then Action Is*
1	Cancel the subscriber
2	Get the latest edition
3	Open the publisher document
4	Update automatically when new data is available
5	Update on request only

Name: FORMULA

Syntax: FORMULA(*formula_text,reference*)

Description: Enters a formula in the cell specified by *reference* or in the active cell

Arguments: *formula_text* is text, a number, a logical value, a cell address or range of cell addresses, a formula in text form, or a reference to a cell containing any of these.

If the active document is a worksheet, FORMULA is equivalent to entering formula_text in the cell specified by *reference*. If formula_text is text, a number, or a logical value, it is entered as a constant. If formula_text is a formula, it is entered just as you would enter it in the formula bar of a worksheet, only with quotation marks around it. References must be in R1C1 style. If the active document is a chart, using FORMULA is equivalent to entering a text label or a SERIES formula.

reference is either a reference to a cell in the active worksheet or an external reference to a worksheet. The value of *reference* specifies where the formula_text value is entered. On a chart, *reference* can be a text label or a series formula. It must be in R1C1 style.

Name: FORMULA.ARRAY

Syntax: FORMULA.ARRAY(*formula_text,reference*)

Description: Enters an array formula in the range specified by *reference*, or in the current selection

Arguments: *formula_text* is the text that you want in the array. For more information, see "FORMULA" above.

reference is either a reference to a cell in the active worksheet or an external reference to a named document. The value of *reference* specifies where the formula_text value is entered. It must be in R1C1 style.

Name: FORMULA.CONVERT

Syntax:
FORMULA.CONVERT(*formula_text,from_a1,to_a1,to_ref_type,rel_to_ref*)

Description: Changes the reference style and type of a formula between A1 and R1C1 and between relative and absolute

Arguments: *formula_text* is the formula in text form whose references you want to change.

If references are in A1 style, then *from_a1* should be TRUE. If references are in R1C1 style, then from_a1 should be FALSE.

If *to_a1* is TRUE, then references are returned in A1 style. If to_a1 is FALSE, then references are returned in R1C1 style.

If to_ref_type Is	Then Reference Type Returned Is
1	Absolute
2	Absolute row, relative column
3	Relative row, absolute column
4	Relative

rel_to_ref is an absolute reference that specifies what cell the relative references are relative to.

Name: FORMULA.FILL

Syntax: FORMULA.FILL(*formula_text,reference*)

Description: Enters a formula in the range specified by reference or in the current selection

Arguments: *formula_text* is the text that fills the selected range. See "FORMULA" above for more information.

reference specifies where the formula_text value is entered.

Name: FULL

Syntax: FULL(*logical*)

Description: Changes the active window from its normal size to its full size or from its full size to the previous size

Arguments: If you specify TRUE for *logical*, then FULL makes the window its full size. If you specify FALSE, then the window goes back to its previous size. If the value *logical* is not included, then the window is enlarged or restored to its previous size if it is already enlarged.

Name: HIDE.OBJECT

Syntax: HIDE.OBJECT(*object_id_text,hide*)

Description: Hides or displays the specified object

Arguments: *object_id_text* is the number or the name and number of the object, as text, as it appears in the reference area when the object is selected. If this value is omitted, all selected objects are operated on.

If *hide* is TRUE or not included, the object is hidden. If FALSE, it is displayed.

Name: HLINE

Syntax: HLINE(*num_columns*)

Description: Scrolls the active window by the specified number of columns. #VALUE! is returned if the active document is a chart.

Arguments: If *num_columns* is positive, then HLINE scrolls to the right the number of columns that is specified. If num_columns is negative, then HLINE scrolls to the left the specified number of columns.

Name: HPAGE

Syntax: HPAGE(*num_windows*)

Description: Scrolls the active window horizontally, one window at a time. One window is defined as the number of visible columns. If only three columns are visible in the window, then HPAGE scrolls only three columns at a time.

Arguments: If *num_windows* is positive, then HPAGE scrolls to the right. If num_windows is negative, HPAGE scrolls to the left.

Name: HSCROLL

Syntax: HSCROLL(*position,col_logical*)

Description: Scrolls the active document horizontally, by the column number or percentage that you give for the position value

Arguments: *position* is the position that you want to scroll to. The value of *position* can be an integer to represent a column number, or a fraction to represent the horizontal displacement of a column in the entire document. If you give it the value 1, then the document scrolls to the rightmost edge. If you give it a value of 0, the document scrolls to the leftmost edge.

If *col_logical* is TRUE, HSCROLL scrolls the document to the column given by *position*. If col_logical is FALSE or not included, HSCROLL scrolls the document to the horizontal position represented by the fractional value of *position*.

Name: PROMOTE

Syntax: PROMOTE(*rowcol*)

Description: Promotes the currently selected rows or columns in an outline

Arguments: If *rowcol* is 1 or not included, rows are promoted. If rowcol is 2, columns are promoted.

Name: SELECT

Syntax: Form 1, cells on a worksheet or macro sheet:
SELECT(*selection,active_cell*)

Form 2, worksheet and macro sheet objects:
SELECT(*object_id_text,replace*)

Form 3, chart items:
SELECT(*item_text,single_point*)

Description: Selects cells on either a worksheet or a macro sheet (form 1); worksheet and macro sheet objects (form 2); or chart items (form 3).

Arguments: Form 1: *selection* is the cell or range of cells that you want to select.

active_cell is the cell in the selection that you want to make the active cell. The required format for *selection* and *active_cell* is R1C1 style or a reference to the active worksheet such as !$B$4:$B$7 or !Expenses.

Form 2: *object_id_text* is the text form of either the number or the name and number of the object (as it would appear in the reference area when the object is selected). To give the name of more than one object, include parentheses and a space after each object:
SELECT("Line 3, Oval 2, Arc 1").

If *replace* is TRUE, then SELECT selects only the objects specified by object_id_text. If replace is FALSE, then SELECT selects any objects that were previously selected in addition to the specified objects.

Form 3:

If item_text Is	*Then Item Selected Is*
"Chart"	Entire chart
"Plot"	Plot area
"Legend"	Legend
"Axis 1"	Main chart value axis
"Axis 2"	Main chart category axis
"Axis 3"	Overlay chart value axis or 3-D series axis
"Axis 4"	Overlay chart category axis
"Title"	Chart title
"Text Axis 1"	Label for the main chart value axis
"Text Axis 2"	Label for the main chart category axis
"Text Axis 3"	Label for the main chart series axis
"Text n"	nth floating text item
"Arrow n"	nth arrow
"Gridline 1"	Major gridlines of value axis
"Gridline 2"	Minor gridlines of value axis
"Gridline 3"	Major gridlines of category axis
"Gridline 4"	Minor gridlines of category axis
"Gridline 5"	Major gridlines of series axis
"Gridline 6"	Minor gridlines of series axis
"Dropline 1"	Main chart droplines
"Dropline 2"	Overlay chart droplines
"HiLoline 1"	Main chart hi-lo lines
"HiLoline 2"	Overlay chart hi-lo lines
"Sn"	Entire series
"SnPm"	Data associated with point m in series n if single_point is TRUE

If item_text Is	Then Item Selected Is
"Text SnPm"	Text attached to point m of series n
"Text Sn"	Series title text of series n of an area chart
"Floor"	Base of a 3-D chart
"Walls"	Back of a 3-D chart

If *single_point* is TRUE, then SELECT selects a single point. If single_point is FALSE, then if there is only one series in the chart, SELECT selects a single point. Otherwise, SELECT selects the entire series.

Name: SELECT.END

Syntax: SELECT.END(*direction_num*)

Description: Selects the cell at the edge of the range in the direction specified by direction_num (equivalent in Windows to pressing Ctrl-Arrow key in one direction)

If direction_num Is	Then Direction Is
1	Left
2	Right
3	Up
4	Down

Name: SET.UPDATE.STATUS

Syntax: SET.UPDATE.STATUS(*link_text,status,type_of_link*)

Description: Sets the update status of a link to manual or automatic

Arguments: *link_text* is the pathname of the linked file whose status is updated.

If *status* is 1, then the update is automatic. If *status* is 2, then the update is manual.

If type_of_link Is	Then the Type of Link Document Is
1	Not available
2	DDE
3	Not available
4	Outgoing NewWave

Name: SHOW.DETAIL

Syntax: SHOW.DETAIL(*rowcol,rowcol_num,expand*)

Description: Expands or collapses detail according to the specified value of expand

Arguments: If *rowcol* is 1 or not included, rows are expanded or collapsed. If rowcol is 2, columns are expanded or collapsed.

rowcol_num is the number that specifies the summary row or summary column to expand or collapse. If in A1 mode, give the column as a number.

If *expand* is TRUE, detail is expanded. If FALSE, detail is collapsed. If not included, change occurs from current expanded detail to collapsed or from current collapsed detail to expanded.

Name: SHOW.LEVELS

Syntax: SHOW.LEVELS(*row_level,col_level*)

Description: Displays the number of row and column levels that you specify

Arguments: *row_level* is the number of row levels of an outline to display. If not included, no action is taken on rows.

col_level is the number of column levels of an outline to display. If not included, no action is taken on columns.

Name: SPLIT

Syntax: SPLIT(*col_split,row_split*)

Description: Splits a window (equivalent to the Split command on the Control menu or to dragging the split bar in the active window's scroll bar)

Arguments: *col_split* is the position where the window is to be split vertically, measured in columns from the left of the window.

row_split is the position where the window is to be split horizontally, measured in rows from the top of the window.

Name: TEXT.BOX

Syntax: TEXT.BOX(*add_text,object_id_text,start_num,num_chars*)

Description: Replaces the characters in the specified text box with the value of add_text that you give to the function

Arguments: *add_text* is the text that you want to add to the text box.

object_id_text is the name in text form of the text box that you want to add and/or replace text in, for example, "Text 1", "Text 4".

start_num is the starting position for the first character to be replaced. If it is 0, then no characters are replaced. If it is not included, then all characters are replaced.

num_chars is the number of characters to replace. If it is not included, then it is assumed to be 1.

Name: UNLOCKED.NEXT

Syntax: UNLOCKED.NEXT( )

Description: Moves to the next unlocked cell in a protected worksheet (equivalent to pressing Tab)

Name: UNLOCKED.PREV

Syntax: UNLOCKED.PREV( )

Description: Moves to the previous unlocked cell in a protected worksheet (equivalent to pressing Shift-Tab)

Name: VLINE

Syntax: VLINE(*num_rows*)

Description: Scrolls the active window by the specified number of rows. #VALUE1 is returned if the active document is a chart.

Arguments: If *num_rows* is positive, then VLINE scrolls down the number of rows that is specified. If num_rows is negative, then VLINE scrolls up the specified number of rows.

Name: VPAGE

Syntax: VPAGE(*num_windows*)

Description: Scrolls the active window vertically, one window at a time. A window is the number of visible rows.

Arguments: If *num_windows* is positive, then VPAGE scrolls down. If num_windows is negative, then VPAGE scrolls up.

Name: VSCROLL

Syntax: VSCROLL(*position,row_logical*)

Description: Scrolls the active document vertically, by the row number or percentage that you give for the position value

Arguments: *position* is the position that you want to scroll to. The value of *position* can be an integer to represent a row number, or a fraction to represent a particular vertical displacement of a row in the document. If you give *position* the value 0, then the document scrolls to the top edge. If you give *position* a value of 1, then the document scrolls to the bottom edge.

If *col_logical* is TRUE, VSCROLL scrolls the document to the row given by *position*. If col_logical is FALSE or not included, VSCROLL scrolls the document to the horizontal position represented by the fractional value of *position*.

Macro Functions That Perform Chart Commands

Macro functions that perform Chart commands perform the exact same operations as the Chart commands do in a worksheet or a chart. In a macro sheet you may want to use the commands that are normally available in any worksheet. The macro functions are designed to allow you to activate any *command, activity,* or *operation* in a worksheet by using a nonactive macro function in a macro sheet.

The following command-equivalent macro functions are specific macro functions *that you can use in a macro sheet*.

Name: ADD.ARROW

Syntax: ADD.ARROW( )

Command Equivalent: Chart Add Arrow

Description: Adds an arrow to the active chart

Notes: After you create an arrow with ADD.ARROW, the arrow remains selected.

Name: ADD.OVERLAY

Syntax: ADD.OVERLAY( )

Command Equivalent: Chart Add Overlay

Description: Adds an overlay to a 2-D chart. If the active chart already has an overlay, ADD.OVERLAY takes no action but returns TRUE.

Name: ATTACH.TEXT

Syntax:
ATTACH.TEXT(*attach_to_num,series_num,point_num*);
ATTACH.TEXT?(*attach_to_num,series_num,point_num*)

Command Equivalent: Chart Attach Text

Description: Attaches text to certain parts of the selected chart. Use ATTACH.TEXT with the FORMULA function.

Arguments: *attach_to_num* is a number which specifies what item on the chart to attach text to.

If attach_to_num Is	In 2-D, ATTACH.TEXT Attaches Text to	In 3-D, ATTACH.TEXT Attaches Text to
1	Chart title	Chart title
2	Value(y) axis	Value(z) axis
3	Category(x) axis	Series (y) axis
4	Series or data point	Category(x) axis
5	Overlay value (y) axis	Series or data point
6	Overlay category (x) axis	Does not apply

series_num is a number that specifies the series if attach_to_num requests a series or data point (that is, if attach_to_num is 4 on a 2-D chart or 5 on a 3-D chart). The macro is interrupted if attach_to_num specifies a series or data point and series_num is not included.

point_num is an optional value that specifies the number of the data point when series_num is specified.

Notes: Bold text is not automatic. You need to use FORMAT.FONT to make text bold.

Name: AXES

Syntax:
For 2-D charts:
AXES(*x_main,y_main,x_over,y_over*);
AXES?(*x_main,y_main,x_over,y_over*)
For 3-D charts:
AXES(*x_main,y_main,z_main*); AXES?(*x_main,y_main,z_main*)

Command Equivalent: Chart Axes

Description: Controls whether to display the axes on a chart or not. There are two forms, one for 2-D charts and one for 3-D charts.

Arguments: If any of the arguments are TRUE, Excel turns on the check box and displays the corresponding axis. If any of the arguments are FALSE, Excel turns off the check box and hides the corresponding axis:

x_main is a logical value that specifies whether the X-axis is to be displayed or hidden.

y_main is a logical value that specifies whether the Y-axis is to be displayed or hidden.

z_main is a logical value that specifies whether the Z-axis is to be displayed or hidden.

x_over is a logical value that specifies whether the X-axis on the overlay chart is to be displayed or hidden.

y_over is a logical value that specifies whether the Y-axis on the overlay chart is to be displayed or hidden.

Notes: If a 2-D chart has no overlay, the x_over and y_over are not included.

Name: CALCULATE.NOW

Syntax: CALCULATE.NOW( )

Command Equivalent: Chart Calculate Now

Description: Calculates all open documents. Use CALCULATE.NOW when calculation is set at manual.

Notes: The CALCULATE.NOW function is equivalent to *both* Chart Calculate Now and Options Calculate Now.

Name: DELETE.ARROW

Syntax: DELETE.ARROW( )

Command Equivalent: Chart Delete Arrow

Description: Deletes the selected arrow

Name: DELETE.OVERLAY

Syntax: DELETE.OVERLAY( )

Command Equivalent: Chart Delete Overlay

Description: Deletes an overlay from the active chart. If the chart has no overlay, no action is taken and DELETE.OVERLAY returns TRUE.

Name: EDIT.SERIES

Syntax:
EDIT.SERIES(*series_num,name_ref,xref,y_ref,z_ref,plot_order*);
EDIT.SERIES?(*series_num,name_ref,xref,y_ref,z_ref,plot_order*)

Command Equivalent: Chart Edit Series

Description: Creates or changes chart series by adding a new SERIES function or modifying an existing SERIES function in a chart

Arguments: *series_num* is the number of the series that you want to change. If 0 or not included, a new data series is created.

name_ref is the name of the data series as an external reference, a name defined as a single cell, or a name defined as text.

xref is an external reference to the name of the worksheet and the cells that contain either category labels for all charts except scatter charts or X-coordinate data for scatter charts.

y_ref is an external reference to the name of the worksheet and the cells that contain values for 2-D charts or Y-coordinate data for scatter charts. Required for 2-D but does not apply to 3-D.

z_ref is an external reference to the name of the worksheet and the cells that contain values for all 3-D charts. Required for 3-D but does not apply to 2-D.

plot_order is the number that specifies whether the data series is plotted first, second, and so on in the chart. Plot_order can be a maximum of 255. When it is omitted and you are creating a new series, then Excel plots the series last and gives it the correct plot_order.

Notes: xref, y_ref, and z_ref can be arrays or references to a multiple selection but not names that refer to a multiple selection.

Name: GRIDLINES

Syntax:
GRIDLINES(*x_major,x_minor,y_major,y_minor,z_major,z_minor*);
GRIDLINES?(*x_major,x_minor,y_major,y_minor,z_major,z_minor*)

Command Equivalent: Chart Gridlines

Description: Turns chart gridlines on or off, depending on specified values

Arguments: The arguments correspond to check boxes in the Chart Gridlines dialog box. TRUE corresponds to an on box and FALSE corresponds to an off box. If any value is not included, a FALSE value is assumed:

x_major and *x_minor* correspond to the Category (X) Axis:Major Gridlines check box and the Category (X) Axis:Minor Gridlines check box, respectively.

y_major and *y_minor* correspond to the Value (Y) Axis:Major Gridlines check box and the Value (Y) Axis:Minor Gridlines check box, respectively. On 3-D charts y_major and y_minor correspond to the Series (Y) Axis:Major Gridlines check box and the Series (Y) Axis:Minor Gridlines check box, respectively.

z_major and *z_minor* correspond to the Value (Z) Axis:Major Gridlines check box and the Value (Z) Axis:Minor Gridlines check box, respectively (3-D charts only).

Name: LEGEND

Syntax: LEGEND(*logical*)

Command Equivalent: Chart Add Legend or Chart Delete Legend

Description: Adds a legend or deletes a legend from a chart

Arguments: If *logical* is TRUE, then LEGEND is equivalent to Chart Add Legend. If logical is FALSE, then LEGEND is equivalent to Chart Delete Legend. If not included, no action is taken.

Name: SELECT.CHART

Syntax: SELECT.CHART( )

Command Equivalent: Chart Select

Description: Selects a single point if there is only one series in the chart or selects the entire series if there is more than one series in the chart

Notes: SELECT.CHART( ) is equivalent to SELECT("Chart"). This function is included for compatibility with earlier versions of Excel.

Name: SELECT.PLOT.AREA

Syntax: SELECT.PLOT.AREA( )

Command Equivalent: Chart Plot Area

Description: Selects the plot area of the active chart

Notes: SELECT.PLOT.AREA( ) is equivalent to SELECT("Plot"). This function is included for compatibility with earlier versions of Excel.

Macro Functions That Perform Control Commands

Macro functions that perform Control commands perform the exact same operations as the Control commands do in a worksheet or a chart. In a macro sheet you may want to use the commands that are normally available in any worksheet. The macro functions are designed to allow you to activate any *command, activity,* or *operation* in a worksheet by using a nonactive macro function in a macro sheet.

The following command-equivalent macro functions are specific macro functions *that you can use in a macro sheet*.

Name: APP.MAXIMIZE

Syntax: APP.MAXIMIZE( )

Command Equivalent: Control Maximize

Description: Maximizes the Excel window

Notes: This function is only for Excel for Windows or OS/2.

Name: APP.MINIMIZE

Syntax: APP.MINIMIZE( )

Command Equivalent: Control Minimize

Description: Minimizes the Excel window

Notes: This function is only for Excel for Windows or OS/2.

Name: APP.MOVE

Syntax: APP.MOVE(*x_num,y_num*); APP.MOVE?(*x_num,y_num*)

Command Equivalent: Control Move (for an application window)

Description: Moves the Excel window. APP.MOVE returns #VALUE! error if the window is already maximized.

Arguments: *x_num* gives the position of the horizontal edge of your Excel window, measured in points from the left edge of your Excel window.

y_num gives the position of the vertical edge of your Excel window, measured in points from the top edge of your Excel window.

Notes: This function is only for Excel for Windows or OS/2.

Name: APP.RESTORE

Syntax: APP.RESTORE( )

Command Equivalent: Control Restore

Description: Restores the Excel window to its previous size and location

Notes: This function is only for Excel for Windows or OS/2.

Name: APP.SIZE

Syntax: APP.SIZE(x_num,y_num); APP.SIZE?(x_num,y_num)

Command Equivalent: Control Size (application)

Description: Changes the size of the Excel window. APP.SIZE? doesn't display a dialog box, instead it is equivalent to dragging a window border with a mouse or pressing Alt-Spacebar-S.

Arguments: x_num gives the width of your Excel window, measured in points.

y_num gives the height of your Excel window, measured in points.

Notes: This function is only for Excel for Windows or OS/2.

Name: CLOSE

Syntax: CLOSE($save\_logical$)

Command Equivalent: Control Close

Description: Closes the active window

Arguments:

If save_logical Is	Then Excel
TRUE	Saves the file
FALSE	Does not save the file
Not included	If changes have been made, displays a dialog box asking if you want to save the file

Notes: Not in earlier versions, CLOSE now closes a macro sheet that it is in.

Name: MOVE

Syntax:
MOVE($x\_pos,y\_pos,window\_text$);
MOVE?($x\_pos,y\_pos,window\_text$)

Command Equivalent: Control Move or equivalent to moving a window by dragging its title bar

Description: Moves the upper-left corner of a window to a specified horizontal and vertical position. The dialog box form MOVE? is used only in Excel for Windows or OS/2.

Arguments: *x_pos* and *y_pos* specify the exact horizontal and vertical positions, respectively, measured in points. In Excel for Windows or OS/2, this measurement spans from the left edge of your workspace to the lower-left corner of your window.

window_text is the name of the window that you want to move. If it is not included, the active window is assumed.

Notes: MOVE does not change the size of the window or make a document active or inactive.

Name: SIZE

Syntax: SIZE(*width,height,window_text*)

Command Equivalent: Equivalent to Control Size in Windows and OS/2. Also equivalent to dragging the size box in all applications.

Description: Changes the size of a window by moving its lower-right corner so that the window has the width and height that you specify (see above). Size does not change the position of the upper-left corner of the window nor its active/inactive status.

Arguments: *width* specifies the width of the window in points.

height specifies the height of the window in points.

window_text is the window to be sized either as text in quotes or as a reference to a cell containing text. The active window is assumed if window_text is not included.

Notes: An error results if you try to resize a window that is at its maximum size.

Macro Functions That Perform Data Commands

Macro functions that perform Data commands perform the exact same operations as the Data commands do in a worksheet or a chart. In a macro sheet you may want to use the commands that are normally available in any worksheet. The macro functions are designed to allow you to activate any *command, activity,* or *operation* in a worksheet by using a nonactive macro function in a macro sheet.

The following command-equivalent macro functions are specific macro functions *that you can use in a macro sheet.*

Name: CONSOLIDATE

Syntax:
CONSOLIDATE(*source_refs,function_num,top_row,left_col,create_links*);
CONSOLIDATE?(*source_refs,function_num,top_row,left_col,create_links*)

Command Equivalent: Data Consolidate

Description: From multiple ranges on multiple worksheets, it consolidates data into a single range on a single worksheet.

Arguments: *source_refs* is external references in quotation marks to areas on other worksheets that contain data to be consolidated on the destination worksheet. Source_refs must include the full pathname and cell reference or named ranges.

function_num is a number that represents one of 11 functions that you can use to consolidate the data.

If *function_num* Is	Function Is
1	AVERAGE
2	COUNT
3	COUNTA
4	MAX
5	MIN
6	PRODUCT
7	STDEV
8	STDEVP
9	SUM
10	VAR
11	VARP

The following three values correspond to check boxes: *top_row* and *left_col* are TRUE or FALSE. If not included, FALSE is assumed. If both are not included, data is consolidated by position. *create_links* is TRUE or FALSE. If not included, FALSE is assumed.

Notes: Using CONSOLIDATE() with no values and no consolidation on the active worksheet results in an error. Using CONSOLIDATE() with no values and a consolidation on the active worksheet results in a reconsolidation used before.

Name: DATA.DELETE

Syntax: DATA.DELETE( ); DATA.DELETE?( )

Command Equivalent: Data Delete

Description: Deletes data that matches the current criteria for the current database. In the DATA.DELETE? form of the function, a warning message is displayed saying that matching records will be permanently deleted, do you approve or cancel? In the DATA.DELETE form of the function, matching records are deleted without a warning message.

Name: DATA.FIND

Syntax: DATA.FIND(*logical*)

Command Equivalent: Data Find

Description: Finds records in a database that match criteria in the criteria range

Arguments: If logical is TRUE, Excel executes the Data Find command. If logical is FALSE, Excel executes the Data Exit Find command.

Name: DATA.FIND.NEXT

Syntax: DATA.FIND.NEXT( )

Command Equivalent: Data Find

Description: Finds the next matching record in a database. It is equivalent to pressing the down arrow after the Data Find command is chosen.

Notes: If no matching record is found, FALSE is returned.

Name: DATA.FIND.PREV

Syntax: DATA.FIND.PREV( )

Command Equivalent: Data Find

Description: Finds the previous matching record in a database. It is equivalent to pressing the up arrow after the Data Find command is chosen.

Notes: If no matching record is found, FALSE is returned.

Name: DATA.FORM

Syntax: DATA.FORM( )

Command Equivalent: Data Form

Description: Displays the data form. If no database is defined on the active sheet, #VALUE! is returned.

Notes: Useful in creating custom data forms

Name: DATA.SERIES

Syntax: DATA.SERIES(*rowcol,type_num,date_num,step_value, stop_value*)

Command Equivalent: Data Series

Description: Useful in entering increasing or decreasing series of values (on a worksheet or macro sheet)

Arguments: If *rowcol* is 1, the series is entered in rows. If rowcol is 2, the series is entered in columns.

If *type_num* is 1, the type of series is Linear. If type_num is 2, the type of series is Growth. If type_num is 3, the type of series is Date.

date_num is used as follows if type_num is 3: If date_num is 1, the date unit is day. If date_num is 2, the date unit is weekday. If date_num is 3, the date unit is month. If date_num is 4, the date unit is year. If type_num is 3 and date_num is not included, then date_num is assumed to be 1.

step_value specifies the step for the series (numerically). If not included, it is assumed to be 1.

stop_value is the stop value for the series. If not included, then the function stops after the entire selected range is filled in.

Notes: Stop value must be equal to or higher than the value in the active cell of the selection.

Name: EXTRACT

Syntax: EXTRACT(*unique*); EXTRACT?(*unique*)

Command Equivalent: Data Extract

Description: Finds database records that match the criteria in the criteria section and copies them into a separate extract range

Arguments: *unique* corresponds to the Unique Records Only check box. If unique is TRUE, the check box is on and duplicate records are excluded from the extract list. If unique is FALSE or not included, the check box is off and duplicate records are included in the extract list.

Name: PARSE

Syntax: PARSE(*text*); PARSE?(*text*)

Command Equivalent: Data Parse

Description: Distributes the contents of a single column to fill several adjacent columns

Arguments: *text* is the line to be parsed in text form. It is a copy of the first nonblank cell in the selected column with square brackets as separators to indicate where to distribute (parse) text.

Name: SET.CRITERIA

Syntax: SET.CRITERIA()

Command Equivalent: Data Set Criteria

Description: Defines the name Criteria for the selected range on a worksheet or macro sheet

Notes: Used in conjunction with other database functions

Name: SET.DATABASE

Syntax: SET.DATABASE()

Command Equivalent: Data Set Database

Description: Gives the name Database to the selected range on a worksheet or macro sheet

Name: SET.EXTRACT

Syntax: SET.EXTRACT()

Command Equivalent: Data Set Extract

Description: Gives the name Extract to the selected range on the active sheet

Name: SORT

Syntax:
SORT(*sort_by,key1,order1,key2,order2,key3,order3*);
SORT?(*sort_by,key1,order1,key2,order2,key3,order3*)

Command Equivalent: Data Sort

Description: Sorts the rows or columns of the selection according to the contents in a key row or column in the selection

Arguments: *sort_by* is the number 1 or 2. If sort_by is 1, sorting occurs by rows. If sort_by is 2, sorting occurs by columns.

Each value, *key1, key2,* and *key3,* is a reference to the cell or cells that you want to use as the first, second, and third sort keys respectively. The sort key identifies which column to sort by when sorting rows or which row to sort by when sorting columns. The sort key can be specified with an R1C1-style reference or as an external reference to the active worksheet.

Each of *order1*, *order2*, and *order3* is the number 1 or the number 2. order1, order2, and order3 specify whether to sort the row or column containing key1, key2, and key3 respectively in ascending order (represented by 1) or descending order (represented by 2).

Notes: To sort more than three keys, sort more than once.

Name: TABLE

Syntax: TABLE(*row_ref,column_ref*)

Command Equivalent: Data Table

Description: Creates a table based on the input values and formulas you define on a worksheet

Arguments: *row_ref* and *column_ref* specify the single cell that is used as the row input and column input, respectively, of your table. row_ref and col_ref can be specified as an R1C1-style cell address or as an external reference to a single cell on the active worksheet. If either is an R1C1 reference, it is assumed to be relative to the active cell in the selection.

Notes: Useful for what-if types of analysis

Macro Functions That Perform Edit Commands

Macro functions that perform Edit commands perform the exact same operations as the Edit commands do in a worksheet or a chart. In a macro sheet you may want to use the commands that are normally available in any worksheet. The macro functions are designed to allow you to activate any *command, activity,* or *operation* in a worksheet by using a nonactive macro function in a macro sheet.

The following command-equivalent macro functions are specific macro functions *that you can use in a macro sheet*.

Name: CLEAR

Syntax:
CLEAR(*type_num*); CLEAR?(*type_num*)

Command Equivalent: Edit Clear

Description: Clears formulas, formats, notes, or all three from the active worksheet, macro sheet, or chart. The function is applied to the selected or highlighted area.

Arguments:

If type_num Is	On a Worksheet, Macro or an Entire Chart, CLEAR Clears
1	All
2	Formats (if a chart, clears the chart format or clears pictures)
3	Formulas (if a chart, clears all data series)
4	Notes

If type_num Is	On a Chart Where a Single Point or an Entire Data Series Is Selected, CLEAR Clears
1	Selected Series
2	Format in the selected point or series

Name: COPY

Syntax: COPY()

Command Equivalent: Edit Copy

Description: Defines the selection that will be copied when you use Paste or Paste Special

Name: COPY.CHART

Syntax: COPY.CHART(*size_num*)

Command Equivalent: Edit Copy Chart

Description: Copies a chart

Arguments: If *size_num* is 1, chart is copied as shown on screen. If size_num is 2, chart is copied as shown when printed.

Notes: Using COPY.PICTURE with no *appearance_num* value also copies a chart.

Name: COPY.PICTURE

Syntax: COPY.PICTURE(*appearance_num,size_num*)

Command Equivalent: Edit Picture

Description: Copies the selection to the clipboard as a graphic. Use COPY.PICTURE to make a duplicate image of the current selection in another program.

Arguments: If *appearance_num* is 1, picture is copied as closely as possible to what is shown on screen. If appearance_num is 2, picture is copied as if the selection were printed.

If *size_num* is 1, picture is copied the same size as the window of the chart on the screen. If size_num is 2, picture is copied as if the selection were printed.

Name: CUT

Syntax: CUT( )

Command Equivalent: Edit Cut

Description: Defines a selection that is moved when you use the PASTE function

Name: EDIT.DELETE

Syntax:
EDIT.DELETE(*shift_num*); EDIT.DELETE?(*shift_num*)

Command Equivalent: Edit Delete

Description: Removes selected cells from the worksheet and shifts other cells to close up the gap

Arguments: *shift_num* determines which way to shift cells after deletion or else to delete the entire row or column.

If shift_num Is	Then EDIT.DELETE
1	Shifts cells left
2	Shifts cells up
3	Deletes the entire row
4	Deletes the entire column
Not included and a horizontal range is selected	Shifts cells up
Not included and a vertical range is selected	Shifts cells left

Name: EDIT.REPEAT

Syntax: EDIT.REPEAT( )

Command Equivalent: Edit Repeat

Description: Repeats certain actions and commands as outlined by the Edit Repeat command

Name: FILL.DOWN

Syntax: FILL.DOWN( )

Command Equivalent: Edit Fill Down

Description: Copies the contents and formats of the cells in the top row of a selection into the rest of the rows in the selection

Name: FILL.LEFT

Syntax: FILL.LEFT( )

Command Equivalent: Edit Fill Left

Description: Copies the contents and formats of the cells in the right column of a selection into the rest of the rows in the selection

Notes: To view the Edit Fill Left and Edit Fill Up commands, press Shift while selecting the Edit menu.

Name: FILL.RIGHT

Syntax: FILL.RIGHT( )

Command Equivalent: Edit Fill Right

Description: Copies the contents and formats of the cells in the left column of a selection into the rest of the rows in the selection

Name: FILL.UP

Syntax: FILL.UP( )

Command Equivalent: Edit Fill Up

Description: Copies the contents and formats of the cells in the bottom row of a selection into the rest of the rows in the selection

Notes: To view the Edit Fill Left and Edit Fill Up commands, press Shift while selecting the Edit menu.

Name: FILL.WORKGROUP

Syntax:
FILL.WORKGROUP(*type_num*);
FILL.WORKGROUP?(*type_num*)

Command Equivalent: Edit Fill Workgroup

Description: Fills the contents of the active worksheet's selection to an area that is the same on all other worksheets in the workgroup

Arguments: *type_num* is a number that corresponds to the choices in the Edit Fill Workgroup dialog box: 1 = All information is filled into other worksheets. 2 = Formulas are filled. 3 = Formats are filled.

Name: INSERT

Syntax: INSERT(*shift_num*); INSERT?(*shift_num*)

Command Equivalent: Edit Insert

Description: INSERT shifts the selected cells to accommodate new cells on a worksheet. The new cells can be a blank cell, range of cells, or cells pasted from the clipboard. The size and shape of the inserted range of cells is the same as the current selection.

Arguments: If the selected range of cells is an entire row, then *shift_num* is optional.

If shift_num Is	*Then INSERT Shifts*
1	Cells right
2 or not included	Cells down
3	The entire row
4	The entire column

Name: PASTE

Syntax: PASTE( )

Command Equivalent: Edit Paste

Description: Pastes a selection or object that you cut or copied using the CUT or COPY function

Name: PASTE.LINK

Syntax: PASTE.LINK( )

Command Equivalent: Edit Paste Link

Description: Pastes copied data or objects and establishes a link with the source of the data or object. The source can be another worksheet or another application.

Name: PASTE.PICTURE

Syntax: PASTE.PICTURE( )

Command Equivalent: Edit Picture

Description: Pastes a picture of the Clipboard contents onto the worksheet at the active cell. Changes to the source data are not reflected in the picture, since this picture is not linked.

Name: PASTE.PICTURE.LINK

Syntax: PASTE.PICTURE.LINK( )

Command Equivalent: Edit Picture Link and equivalent to using the camera tool on the Toolbar

Description: Pastes a linked picture of the Clipboard contents onto the worksheet at the active cell. Changes to the source data are reflected in the picture, since this picture is linked.

Name: PASTE.SPECIAL

Syntax: Form 1—from a worksheet to a worksheet:
PASTE.SPECIAL(*paste_num,operation_num,skip_blanks,transpose*);
PASTE.SPECIAL?(*paste_num,operation_num,skip_blanks,transpose*)

Form 2—from a worksheet to a chart:
PASTE.SPECIAL(*rowcol,series,categories,replace*);
PASTE.SPECIAL?(*rowcol,series,categories,replace*)

Form 3—from a chart to a chart:
PASTE.SPECIAL(*paste_num*);
PASTE.SPECIAL?(*paste_num*)

Command Equivalent: Edit Paste Special

Description: Pastes specified components of a copy area into the current selection

Arguments: The information that goes into Form 1 of the PASTE.SPECIAL function:

If Paste_num Is	*PASTE.SPECIAL Pastes*
1	Everything
2	Formulas
3	Values
4	Formats
5	Notes

If operation_num Is	*PASTE.SPECIAL Operation When Pasting Is*
1	None
2	Add
3	Subtract
4	Multiply
5	Divide

skip_blanks corresponds to the Skip Blanks check box. If skip_blanks is TRUE, PASTE.SPECIAL skips blanks in the copy area when pasting. If skip_blanks is FALSE, PASTE.SPECIAL pastes normally.

Transpose corresponds to the Transpose check box. If transpose is TRUE, PASTE.SPECIAL transposes column and rows when pasting. If transpose is FALSE, PASTE.SPECIAL pastes normally.

The information that goes into Form 2 of the PASTE.SPECIAL function:

If rowcol Is	**PASTE.SPECIAL Pastes Values of a Data Series in a**
1	Row
2	Column

series, categories, and *replace* are logical values that correspond to the Series Names In First Column or Series Names In First Row, Categories In First Column or Categories In First Row, and Replace Existing Categories check boxes, respectively. In all cases, TRUE represents an on check box and FALSE represents an off check box. Whether the value represents a check box referring to "In First Row" or "In First Column" is determined by the rowcol value listed above.

If *series* is TRUE, then PASTE.SPECIAL uses the contents of the cell in the first column of each row (or the first row of each column) as the name of the data series in that row or column. If *series* is FALSE, then PASTE.SPECIAL uses the contents of the cell in the first column of each row (or the first row of each column) as the first data point of the data series.

If *categor*ies is TRUE, then PASTE.SPECIAL uses the contents of the first row (or column) of the selection as the categories for the chart. If *categories* is FALSE, then PASTE.SPECIAL uses the contents of the first row (or column) as the first data series in the chart.

If *replace* is TRUE, then PASTE.SPECIAL applies categories while replacing existing categories with information from the copied cell range. If replace is FALSE, then PASTE.SPECIAL applies new categories and does not replace old ones.

The information that goes into Form 3 of the PASTE.SPECIAL function:

If paste_num Is	**PASTE.SPECIAL Pastes**
1	Everything (formats and data series)
2	Formats only
3	Formulas (data series) only

Name: UNDO

Syntax: UNDO()

Command Equivalent: Edit Undo

Description: Reverses the same actions and commands as Edit Undo does

Macro Functions That Perform File Commands

Macro functions that perform File commands perform the exact same operations as the File commands do in a worksheet or a chart. In a macro sheet you may want to use the commands that are normally available in any worksheet. The macro functions are designed to allow you to activate any *command, activity,* or *operation* in a worksheet by using a nonactive macro function in a macro sheet.

The following command-equivalent macro functions are specific macro functions *that you can use in a macro sheet*.

Name: CHANGE.LINK

Syntax:
CHANGE.LINK(*old_text,new_text,type_of_link*);
CHANGE.LINK?(*old_text,new_text,type_of_link*)

Command Equivalent: File Links

Description: Changes a link from one supporting document to another

Arguments: *old_text* and *new_text* are path names. old_text is the active dependent document that you want to change and new_text is the new link.

type_of_link is 1 for a Microsoft Excel link or 2 for a DDE link.

Notes: The document whose links you are changing must be active when this function is calculating.

Name: CLOSE.ALL

Syntax: CLOSE.ALL()

Command Equivalent: File Close All

Description: Closes all unprotected and hidden windows. If changes have been made to any document, it displays a message asking if you want to save the file.

Name: FILE.CLOSE

Syntax: FILE.CLOSE(*save_logical*)

Command Equivalent: File Close

Description: Closes the entire active document

Arguments: If *save_logical* is TRUE, the file is saved. If save_logical is FALSE, the file is not saved. If save_logical is not included and you've made changes to the file, then a dialog box is displayed asking if you want to save the file.

Name: FILE.DELETE

Syntax:
FILE.DELETE(*file_text*);
FILE.DELETE?(*file_text*)

Command Equivalent: File Delete

Description: Deletes a file from the disk. The FILE.DELETE? version of the function allows the use of the asterisk (*) to represent any string of characters and the question mark (?) to represent a single character.

Arguments: *file_text* is the name of the file to delete.

Notes: Useful for deleting temporary files created in the macro. If file_text can't be found, FILE.DELETE displays a message that says that the file can't be deleted. If a file_text is open when you delete it, the file remains open even though it is deleted.

Name: LINKS

Syntax: LINKS(*document_text,type_num*)

Command Equivalent: File Links

Description: Returns a horizontal array of the names (in text form) of all worksheets that are referred to with external references in the specified document.

Arguments: *document_text* is the name of the document, including its pathname. The active document is used if document_text is not included. #N/A results if the document specified by document_text is not open or if the document contains no external references.

type_num specifies the type of linked documents to return.

If type_num Is	LINKS Returns
1 or not included	Microsoft Excel link
2	DDE link

If type_num Is	LINKS Returns
3	Reserved
4	Outgoing NewWave link
5	Publisher
6	Subscriber

Notes: The document names are always returned in alphabetical order. If type_num is 5 or 6, LINKS returns a two-row array where the first row contains the edition name and the second row contains the reference.

Name: NEW

Syntax:
NEW(*type_num,xy_series*);
NEW?(*type_num,xy_series*)

Command Equivalent: File New

Description: Creates a new Excel document or opens a template

Arguments: *type_num* is a number that specifies the type of the new Excel document that will be created.

If type_num Is	The New Document Created Is a
1	Worksheet
2	Chart
3	Macro sheet
4	International macro sheet
Quoted text	Template

xy_series specifies how data is arranged in a chart.

If xy_series Is	Result of NEW
0	Dialog box is displayed if selection is ambiguous.
1 or not included	First row/column is the first data series.
2	First row/column are the category (x) axis labels.
3	First row/column are the x-values; the created chart is a scatter chart.

Notes: To create new sheets from any template you cannot use NEW. Use the OPEN function.

Name: OPEN

Syntax:
OPEN(*file_text,update_links,read_only,format,prot_pwd, write_res_pwd,ignore_rorec,file_origin*);
OPEN?(*file_text,update_links,read_only,format,prot_pwd, write_res_pwd,ignore_rorec,file_origin*)

Command Equivalent: File Open

Description: Opens an existing file or workspace

Arguments: *file_text* is the name in text form of the file that you want to open. file_text can include a pathname and a drive. In the dialog box form, OPEN?, file_text can include wild-card characters: * to represent any sequence of characters and ? to represent any single character.

update_links specifies whether and how to update external and remote references.

If update_links Is	The Update Is
0	Neither external nor remote references
1	External references only
2	Remote references only
3 or not included	External and remote references

read_only corresponds to the Read Only check box in the File Links dialog box. If read_only is TRUE, changes cannot be saved even though the document can be modified. If read_only is FALSE or not included, changes to the document can be saved. Read_only applies only to documents in Excel, WKS, and SYLK.

If *format* is 1 or not included, values are separated by tabs. If format is 2, values are separated by commas.

prot_pwd is the password in text form that is required to unprotect a protected file. If not included and file_text requires a password, Excel displays the Password dialog box. Passwords are case-sensitive and are not recorded when you open a document and enter the password when the macro recorder is on.

write_res_pwd is the password in text form that is required when opening a read-only file with full write privileges. If not included and file_text requires a password, Excel displays the Password dialog box.

ignore_rorec controls whether the read-only message is displayed. If ignore_rorec is TRUE, the message is not displayed. If ignore_rorec is FALSE or not included, Excel displays the alert when opening a read_only recommended document.

file_origin is a number that states the origination of a text file.

If file_origin Is	Then Original Operating Environment for the File Is
1	Macintosh
2	Windows (ANSI)
3	DOS or OS/2 (PC-8)
Omitted	Current operating environment

Name: OPEN.LINKS

Command Equivalent: File Links

Syntax:
OPEN.LINKS(*document_text1,document_text2,...,read_only, type_of_link*);
OPEN.LINKS?(*document_text1,document_text2,...,read_only, type_of_link*)

Description: Opens documents that are linked to another document. Use LINKS in conjunction with OPEN.LINKS.

Arguments: *document_text1,document_text2,...* is a list of 1 to 12 names of supporting documents in text form, or arrays or references that contain text.

read_only corresponds to the Read Only check box in the File Links dialog box. If read_only is TRUE, changes cannot be saved even though the document can be modified. If read_only is FALSE or not included, changes to the document can be saved. Read_only applies only to documents in Excel, WKS, and SYLK.

type_of_link specifies what type of link you want to get information about.

If type_of_link Is	OPEN.LINKS Returns
1 or not included	Microsoft Excel link
2	DDE link
3	Reserved
4	Outgoing NewWave link
5 and 6	Publisher and subscriber

Name: PAGE.SETUP

Syntax: Form 1 for worksheets and macro sheets:

PAGE.SETUP(*head,foot,left,right,top,bot,heading,grid,h_center, v_center,orientation,paper_size,scaling*);
PAGE.SETUP?(*head,foot,left,right,top,bot,heading,grid,h_center, v_center,orientation,paper_size,scaling*)

Form 2 for charts:

PAGE.SETUP(*head,foot,left,right,top,bot,size,h_center,v_center, orientation,paper_size,scaling*);
PAGE.SETUP?(*head,foot,left,right,top,bot,size,h_center, v_center,orientation,paper_size,scaling*)

Command Equivalent: File Page Setup

Description: Controls the printed appearance of documents

Arguments: The following 10 values correspond to check boxes and text boxes in the File Page Setup dialog box. These values are logical values where TRUE corresponds to an on check box and FALSE corresponds to an off check box.

head, foot, left, right, and *top* all correspond to check boxes with the same name.

bot corresponds to the Bottom check box.

heading corresponds to the Row & Column Headings check box.

grid corresponds to the Gridlines check box.

h_center corresponds to the Center Horizontally check box.

v_center corresponds to the Center Vertically check box.

size determines how the chart is printed on the page within the margins.

If size Is	*Then Size to Print Chart Is*
1	Screen size
2	Fit to page
3	Full page

If *orientation* is 1, the direction in which your document is printed is portrait format. If orientation is 2, the direction in which your document is printed is landscape format.

If paper_size Is	Then Paper Type Is
1	Letter
2	Letter (small)
3	Tabloid
4	Ledger
5	Legal
6	Statement
7	Executive
8	A3
9	A4
10	A4 (small)
11	A5
12	B4
13	B5
14	Folio
15	Quarto
16	10x14
17	11x17
18	Note
19	ENV9
20	ENV10
21	ENV11
22	ENV12
23	ENV14
24	C sheet
25	D sheet
26	E sheet

scaling is a number or the value TRUE. PAGE.SETUP uses the scaling number as a percentage to increase or decrease the size of the document. To fit the print area on a single page, use TRUE. If your printer does not provide scaling, then the scaling value is ignored.

Name: PRINT

Syntax:
PRINT(*range_num,from,to,copies,draft,preview,print_what,color, feed*);
PRINT?(*range_num,from,to,copies,draft,preview,print_what,color, feed*)

Command Equivalent: File Print

Description: Prints the active document

Arguments:

If range_num1 Is	*Then the Following Pages Are Printed*
1	All pages
2	The pages specified by the arguments *from* and *to*

from is the page number of the first page to be printed. (Ignored if range_num is 2.)

to is the page number of the last page to be printed. (Ignored if range_num is 2.)

copies is the number of copies to be printed.

The following three logical values correspond to check boxes, where a value of TRUE corresponds to an on check box and a value of FALSE corresponds to an off check box:

draft corresponds to the Draft Quality check box.

preview corresponds to the Preview check box.

If print_what Is	*Then PRINT Prints*
1	Document only
2	Notes only
3	Document then notes

color corresponds to the Print Using Color check box.

If feed Is	*Then the Type of Paper Feed Is*
1	Continuous (paper cassette)
2	Cut sheet or manual (manual feed)

Name: PRINT.PREVIEW

Syntax: PRINT.PREVIEW( )

Command Equivalent: File Print Preview

Description: Displays on the screen a preview of the page and page breaks of the active document

Name: PRINTER.SETUP

Syntax: PRINTER.SETUP(*printer_text*)

Command Equivalent: File Printer Setup

Description: Identifies (or sets up the name of) the printer that you want to use

Arguments: *printer_text* is the name of the printer you will use. Enter it exactly as it would appear in the File Printer Setup dialog box.

Name: QUIT

Syntax: QUIT( )

Command Equivalent: Equivalent to File Exit in Excel for Windows

Description: Quits Excel and closes any open documents. If there are some documents with changes that haven't been saved, Excel displays a message asking if you want to save these documents.

Name: SAVE

Syntax: SAVE( )

Command Equivalent: File Save

Description: Saves the active document

Notes: Use SAVE.AS when you want to change the name of the file.

Name: SAVE.AS

Syntax:
SAVE.AS(*document_text,type_num,prot_pwd,backup,write_res_pwd, read_only_rec*);
SAVE.AS?(*document_text,type_num,prot_pwd,backup,write_res_pwd, read_only_rec*)

Command Equivalent: File Save As

Description: Saves a file with a new filename, file type, protection password, or write-reservation password. Useful for creating backups, templates, and add-in documents.

Arguments: *document_text* specifies the name of a document to save. You can include the full pathname.

type_num is a number from 1 to 26 that specifies the file format for saving. Documents that are worksheets use the type_num values 1-9, 12-14, 18, 25, and 26. Documents that are macro sheets use the type_num values 1-3, 6, 9, and 16-26. Documents that are charts use the type_num values 1, 16, and 17.

If type_num Is	Then File Format Is
1	Normal
2	SYLK
3	Text
4	WKS
5	WK1
6	CSV
7	DBF2
8	DBF3
9	DIF
10	Reserved
11	DBF4
12	Reserved
13	Reserved
14	Reserved
15	WK3
16	Microsoft Excel 2.x
17	Template
18	Add-in macro
19	Text (Macintosh)
20	Text (Windows)
21	Text (OS/2 or DOS)
22	CVS (Macintosh)
23	CVS (Windows)
24	CVS (OS/2 or DOS)
25	International macro
26	International add-in macro

prot_pwd is a password of 15 characters of text or less or a reference to a cell containing this type of value. If a file is saved with a password, the password must be entered again when opening the file in order to gain access.

If *backup* is TRUE, Excel creates a backup file. If it is FALSE, no backup is created. If it is not included, no changes in status occur.

write_res_pwd is a password that allows the user to write to a file. If a file was saved with a password that is not given when opening the file, then the file is opened as a read-only (that is, it cannot be saved before closing it).

If *read_only_rec* is TRUE, Excel saves the document as read only recommended. If it is FALSE, saving is done as normal. If it is not included, Excel uses the current settings (from previous saves).

Name: SAVE.WORKSPACE

Syntax:
SAVE.WORKSPACE(*name_text*);
SAVE.WORKSPACE?(*name_text*)

Command Equivalent: File Workspace

Description: Saves a workspace (including a list of the currently opened documents, their position and status, and various workspace and display settings). The preferred chart format is also saved with a workspace.

Arguments: *name_text* specifies the name of a workspace document to save. You can also include a driver and pathname specifier. If not included, it is assumed to be RESUME.XLW or the name of the last workspace document opened in the current session (if any were opened).

Name: UPDATE.LINK

Syntax: UPDATE.LINK(*link_text,type_of_link*)

Command Equivalent: File Links

Description: Updates a link to another document

Arguments: *link_text* is the full pathname as quoted text, of the link as displayed in the File Links dialog box. If it is not included, only links from the active document to other Excel documents are updated.

If type_of_link Is	Then the Type of Link Document to Update Is
1 or not included	Excel link
2	DDE link
3	Not available
4	Outgoing NewWave link

Macro Functions That Perform Format Commands

Macro functions that perform Format commands perform the exact same operations as the Format commands do in a worksheet or a chart. In a macro sheet you may want to use the commands that are normally available in any worksheet. The macro functions are designed to allow you to activate any *command, activity,* or *operation* in a worksheet by using a nonactive macro function in a macro sheet.

The following command-equivalent macro functions are specific macro functions *that you can use in a macro sheet*.

Name: ALIGNMENT

Syntax:
ALIGNMENT(*type_num,wrap*);
ALIGNMENT?(*type_num,wrap*)

Command Equivalent: Format Alignment

Description: Aligns the contents of the selected cells

Arguments: *type_num* is a number from 1 to 5 that specifies the type of alignment.

If type_num Is	Alignment Is
1	General
2	Left
3	Center
4	Right
5	Fill

wrap is a logical value that specifies whether to turn on the text wrap (TRUE) or turn off the text wrap (FALSE). If not included, FALSE is assumed.

Name: APPLY.STYLE

Syntax:
APPLY.STYLE(*style_text*); APPLY.STYLE?(*style_text*)

Command Equivalent: Format Style

Description: Applies a previously defined style to the current selection

Arguments: *style_text* is the name in quotation marks of a previously defined style. If style_text is not defined, APPLY.STYLE returns #VALUE!.

Name: BORDER

Syntax:
BORDER(*outline,left,right,top,bottom,shade,outline_color, left_color,right_color,top_color,bottom_color*);
BORDER?(*outline,left,right,top,bottom,shade,outline_color, left_color,right_color,top_color,bottom_color*)

Command Equivalent: Format Border

Description: Adds a border to the selected cell, range of cells, or object

Arguments: *outline, left, right, top,* and *bottom* are numbers from 0 to 7 specifying the following:

If Value Is	Then Line Style Is
0	No border
1	Thin line
2	Medium line
3	Dashed line
4	Dotted line
5	Thick line
6	Double line
7	Hairline

shade corresponds to the Shade box in the Format Border dialog box. A value of TRUE results in shading the selected area. A value of FALSE results in no shading.

outline_color, left_color, right_color, top_color, and *bottom_color* are specifications for the color of each respective part of the border. These arguments are numbers between 1 and 16 which correspond to colors in the Color box in the Format Border dialog box. Zero stands for automatic color.

Notes: For compatibility reasons, TRUE and FALSE create a single-line border (TRUE) or no border (FALSE) for outline, left, right, top, and bottom.

Name: BRING.TO.FRONT

Syntax: BRING.TO.FRONT()

Command Equivalent: Format Bring To Front

Description: Brings the selected object or objects in the front, on top of all other objects. BRING.TO.FRONT returns #VALUE! if the selected item is not an object(s).

Name: CELL.PROTECTION

Syntax:
CELL.PROTECTION(*locked,hidden*);
CELL.PROTECTION?(*locked,hidden*)

Command Equivalent: Format Cell Protection

Description: Gives you control of cell protection and display

Arguments: *locked* is a logical value that turns on the Locked check box if it is TRUE, or turns off the Locked check box if it is FALSE. If it is not included, it is assumed to be TRUE.

hidden is a logical value that turns on the Hidden check box if it is TRUE, or turns off the Hidden check box if it is FALSE. If it is not included, it is assumed to be FALSE.

Notes: Options activated with CELL.PROTECTION are activated only when the PROTECT.DOCUMENT function or equivalent command is chosen.

Name: COLUMN.WIDTH

Syntax: COLUMN.WIDTH(*width_num,reference,standard,type_num*)

Command Equivalent: Format Column Width

Description: Changes the width of the columns that are specified by *reference*

Arguments: *width_num* is how wide you want the column to be.

reference is the columns whose width you wish to change. If not included, the current selection is assumed. If included, it must be an external reference to the active worksheet or a quoted R1C1-style reference in text form that is relative to the active cell.

standard is TRUE to choose the standard width or FALSE to use width_num or type_num. If not included, a FALSE value for standard is assumed.

If type_num Is	COLUMN.WIDTH
1	Hides the column selection by setting the column width to 0
2	Unhides the column selection by setting the column width to the value set before the selection was hidden
3	Sets the column selection to a best-fit column width, which is the length of the longest data string in the column

Name: DEFINE.STYLE

Syntax: Form 1, equivalent to choosing the Define button in the Format Style dialog box:
DEFINE.STYLE(*style_text,number,font,alignment,border,pattern, protection*);
DEFINE.STYLE?(*style_text,number,font,alignment,border,pattern, protection*)

Form 2, using arguments from the FORMAT.NUMBER function:
DEFINE.STYLE(*style_text,attribute_num,format_text*)

Form 3, using arguments from the FORMAT.FONT function:
DEFINE.STYLE(*style_text,attribute_num,name_text,size_num,bold, italic,underline,strike,color,outline,shadow*)

Form 4, using arguments from the ALIGNMENT function:
DEFINE.STYLE(*style_text,attribute_num,type_num,wrap*)

Form 5, using arguments from the Border function:
DEFINE.STYLE(*style_text,attribute_num,left,right,top,bottom, left_color,right_color,top_color,bottom_color*)

Form 6, using arguments from the PATTERNS (cell form) function:
DEFINE.STYLE(*style_text,attribute_num,aauto,apattern,afore, aback*)

Form 7, using arguments from the CELL.PROTECTION function:
DEFINE.STYLE(*style_text,attribute_num,locked,hidden*)

Command Equivalent: Format Style

Description: Creates and changes cell styles. There are seven forms of this function.

Arguments: Form 1:

style_text is the name, in quotation marks, on which you are defining the style.

Each of the following values given to the function by you corresponds exactly to the check boxes for the Format Style command: *number, font, alignment, border, pattern,* and *protection.* If the value TRUE is given for one of these values, that style of formatting is used.

Forms 2 through 7:

style_text is the name, in quotation marks, on which you are defining the style.

If attribute_num Is	Then the Style Is Applied to
2	Number format
3	Font format
4	Alignment
5	Border
6	Pattern
7	Cell protection

Form 2:

A description of the value *format_text* is available below in "FORMAT.NUMBER."

Form 3:

A description of the values *name_text, size_num, bold, italic, underline, strike, color, outline,* and *shadow* is available below in "FORMAT.FONT."

Form 4:

A description of the values *type_num* and *wrap* is available above in "ALIGNMENT."

Form 5:

A description of the values *left, right, top, bottom, left_color, right_color, top_color,* and *bottom_color* is available above in "BORDER."

Form 6:

A description of the values *aauto, apattern, afore,* and *aback* is available below in "PATTERNS."

Form 7:

A description of the values *locked* and *hidden* is available above in "CELL.PROTECTION."

Name: DELETE.STYLE

Syntax: DELETE.STYLE(*style_text*)

Command Equivalent: Format Style

Description: Deletes a style from the active document and returns the selected cell as Normal style

Arguments: *style_text* is the name of the style to be deleted. If style_text does not exist, #VALUE! is returned and the macro interrupted.

Name: FORMAT.FONT

Syntax: Form 1:
FORMAT.FONT(*name_text,size_num,bold,italic,underline,strike, color,outline,shadow*);
FORMAT.FONT?(*name_text,size_num,bold,italic,underline,strike, color,outline,shadow*)

Form 2:
FORMAT.FONT(*name_text,size_num,bold,italic,underline,strike, color,outline,shadow,object_id_text,start_num,char_num*);
FORMAT.FONT?(*name_text,size_num,bold,italic,underline,strike, color,outline,shadow,object_id_text,start_num,char_num*)

Form 3:
FORMAT.FONT(*color,backgd,apply,name_text,size_num,bold,italic, underline,strike,outline,shadow*);
FORMAT.FONT?(*color,backgd,apply,name_text,size_num,bold,italic, underline,strike,outline,shadow*)

Command Equivalent: Format Font

Description: Formats fonts in cells with form 1, text boxes with form 2, and chart items with form 3

Arguments: *name_text* is the name of the font as listed in the Format Font dialog box.

size_num is the font size in points.

The values *bold, italic, underline, strike,* and *color* correspond to check boxes, where TRUE represents on and FALSE represents the check box turned off (except for the color box). The value color is a number from 0 to 16 that corresponds to the colors in the Format Font dialog box. (0 is automatic color and so on.) The values *outline* and *shadow* are ignored by Excel for Windows, because they are available only on the Macintosh. If one of these values is not included, that aspect of the font is not changed.

object_id_text identifies the text box that you want to format. Either the object number alone or the text identifier "Text 1", "Text 2", etc., can be used.

start_num is the first character to be formatted.

char_num is how many characters are to be formatted. If not included, all characters in the text box (starting from start_num) are formatted.

If *backgd* is 1, the background is automatic. If backgd is 2, the background is transparent. If backgd is 3, the background is white out.

apply is for the Apply To All check box, applicable to data labels only.

Name: FORMAT.LEGEND

Syntax:
FORMAT.LEGEND(*position_num*);
FORMAT.LEGEND?(*position_num*)

Command Equivalent: Format Legend

Description: Determines the position and orientation of the legend on a chart. It returns TRUE if a legend is selected, FALSE otherwise.

position_num specifies the position:

If position_num Is	Position of Legend Is
1	Bottom
2	Corner
3	Top
4	Right
5	Left

Name: FORMAT.MAIN

Syntax:
FORMAT.MAIN(*type_num,view,overlap,gap_width,vary,drop,hilo, angle,gap_depth,chart_depth*);
FORMAT.MAIN?(*type_num,view,overlap,gap_width,vary,drop,hilo, angle,gap_depth,chart_depth*)

Command Equivalent: Format Main Chart

Description: Formats a chart according to the values listed below, which you specify

Arguments:

If type_num Is	Type of Chart Is
1	Area
2	Bar
3	Column
4	Line
5	Pie
6	XY (scatter)
7	3-D area
8	3-D column
9	3-D line
10	3-D pie

view is a number from 1 to 4 that specifies one of the views in the Data View box.

For an Area Chart, If the Value for view Is	Then the View Is
1	Overlapped
2	Stacked
3	Stacked 100%

For a Bar Chart, If the Value for view Is	Then the View Is
1	Side by side
2	Stacked
3	Stacked 100%

For a Column Chart, If the Value for view Is	Then the View Is
1	Side by side
2	Stacked
3	Stacked 100%

For a Line Chart, If the Value for view Is	Then the View Is
1	Normal
2	Stacked
3	Stacked 100%

For a Pie Chart, If the Value for view Is	Then the View Is
1	Normal

For an XY (scatter) Chart, If the Value for view Is	Then the View Is
1	Normal

For a 3-D Area Chart, If the Value for view Is	Then the View Is
1	Stacked
2	Stacked 100%
3	3-D layout

For a 3-D Column Chart, If the Value for view Is	Then the View Is
1	Side by side
2	Stacked
3	Stacked 100%
4	3-D layout

For a 3-D Line Chart, If the Value for view Is	Then the View Is
1	3-D layout

For a 3-D Pie Chart, If the Value for view Is	Then the View Is
1	Normal

overlap is a number from –100 to 100 specifying the positioning of the bars or columns. It corresponds to the Overlap box.

If overlap is greater than zero, then overlap specifies the percentage of overlap you want. If overlap is less than zero, then bars or columns are separated by the maximum available distance. If not included or 0, bars or columns do not overlap.

gap_width is a number from 0 to 500 that specifies the space between bar or column clusters as a percentage of the width of the bar or column.

For the following three check boxes: TRUE is on, FALSE is off, and not included means does not change:

vary corresponds to the Vary by Categories check box.

drop corresponds to the Drop Lines check box.

hilo corresponds to the Hi-Lo Lines check box.

angle is a number from 0 to 360 that specifies the angle in degrees of the first pie slice if the chart is a pie chart. If not included, the default is 50.

gap_depth and *chart_depth* apply to 3-D charts only.

gap_depth is a number from 0 to 500 that specifies a depth of gap in front of and behind a bar, column, area, or line as a percentage of the depth of the bar, column, area, or line. The default is 50 for a 3-D layout or 0 if view is side-by-side, stacked, or stacked 100%.

chart_depth is a number from 20 to 2000 that specifies the visual depth of the chart as a percentage of the width. The default is 100.

Name: FORMAT.MOVE

Syntax:
FORMAT.MOVE(*x_offset,y_offset,reference*);
FORMAT.MOVE?(*x_offset,y_offset,reference*);
FORMAT.MOVE(*x_pos,y_pos*);
FORMAT.MOVE?(*x_pos,y_pos*)

Command Equivalent: Equivalent to moving an object with the mouse

Description: Moves the selected object to the specified position. TRUE is returned if successful; otherwise, FALSE is returned. The first form of this function moves chart items and the second moves worksheet objects.

Arguments: *x_offset* and *y_offset* specify the horizontal and vertical positions, respectively, measured in points from the upper-left corner of the object to the upper-left corner of the cell specified by reference. (A point is 1/72 of an inch.)

reference is a cell address or range of cells. If reference is a range of cells, then only the upper-left cell is used in the calculations. If reference is not included, cell A1 is used.

x_pos and *y_pos* specify the exact horizontal and vertical positions, respectively, measured in points from the base of the object to the lower-left corner of the window. (A point is 1/72 of an inch.)

Name: FORMAT.NUMBER

Syntax:
FORMAT.NUMBER(*format_text*); FORMAT.NUMBER?(*format_text*)

Command Equivalent: Format Number

Description: Formats numbers, dates, and times in the selected cells

Arguments: *format_text* is text in quotes that represents a standard format (such as "$#,##0.00").

Name: FORMAT.OVERLAY

Syntax:
FORMAT.OVERLAY(*type_num,view,overlap,width,vary, drop,hilo, angle,series_dist,series_num*);
FORMAT.OVERLAY?(*type_num,view,overlap,width,vary, drop,hilo, angle,series_dist,series_num*)

Command Equivalent: Format Overlay

Description: Formats the overlay chart according to the values that you give (listed below)

Arguments: *type_num* specifies the type of chart.

If type_num Is	Type of Chart Is
1	Area
2	Bar
3	Column
4	Line
5	Pie
6	XY (scatter)

view is a number from 1 to 4 that specifies one of the views in the Data View box.

For an Area Chart, If the Value for view Is	Then the View Is
1	Overlapped
2	Stacked
3	Stacked 100%

For a Bar Chart, If the Value for view Is	Then the View Is
1	Side by side
2	Stacked
3	Stacked 100%

For a Column Chart, If the Value for view Is	Then the View Is
1	Side by side
2	Stacked
3	Stacked 100%

For a Line Chart, If the Value for view Is	Then the View Is
1	Normal
2	Stacked
3	Stacked 100%

For a Pie Chart, If the Value for view Is	Then the View Is
1	Normal

For an XY (scatter) Chart, If the Value for view Is	Then the View Is
1	Normal

overlap is a number from −100 to 100 specifying the positioning of the bars or columns. It corresponds to the Overlap box.

If overlap is greater than zero, then overlap specifies the percentage of overlap you want. If overlap is less than zero, then bars or columns are separated by the maximum available distance. If not included or 0, bars or columns do not overlap.

width is a number from 0 to 500 that specifies the space between bar or column clusters as a percentage of the width of the bar or column. Width corresponds to the Gap Width box.

For the following three check boxes: TRUE is on, FALSE is off, not included means does not change.

vary corresponds to the Vary by Categories check box.

drop corresponds to the Drop Lines check box.

hilo corresponds to the Hi-Lo Lines check box.

angle is a number from 0 to 360 that specifies the angle in degrees of the first pie slice if the chart is a pie chart. If not included, the default is 50.

series_dist is the number 1 for automatic series distribution or 2 for manual series distribution. If not included, 1 is the assumed value for series_dist. If number 2 is specified, then series_num must be specified.

series_num is the number of the first series in the overlay chart, which corresponds to the First Overlay Series box.

Name: FORMAT.SIZE

Syntax:
FORMAT.SIZE(*width,height*);
FORMAT.SIZE?(*width,height*);
FORMAT.SIZE(*x_off,y_off,reference*);
FORMAT.SIZE?(*x_off,y_off,reference*)

Command Equivalent: Equivalent to sizing an object with a mouse

Description: Sizes the selected worksheet. Returns TRUE if successful; otherwise, returns FALSE

Arguments: *width* specifies the width of the selected chart object measured in points (1/72 of an inch).

height specifies the height of the selected chart object measured in points (1/72 of an inch).

x_off and *y_off* specify the width and height, respectively, of the selected chart object measured in points (1/72 of an inch) from the lower-right corner of the object to the upper-left corner of reference. If either is not included, it is assumed to be 0.

reference is a cell address or range of cells used as the base for the offset and for sizing. If reference is a range of cells, then only the upper-left cell is used in the calculations. If reference is not included, cell A1 is used.

Name: FORMAT.TEXT

Syntax:
FORMAT.TEXT(*x_align,y_align,orient_num,auto_text,auto_size, show_key,show_value*);
FORMAT.TEXT?(*x_align,y_align,orient_num,auto_text, auto_size, show_key,show_value*)

Command Equivalent: Format Text

Description: Formats the selected worksheet text box or any item on a chart

Arguments:

If x_align Is	*Then Horizontal Alignment Is*
1	Left
2	Center
3	Right

If y_align Is	*Then Vertical Alignment Is*
1	Top
2	Center
3	Bottom

If orient_num Is	*Then FORMAT.TEXT Arranges the Text*
0	Horizontally
1	Vertically
2	Upward
3	Downward

auto_text corresponds to the Automatic Text check box. If selected text was created with Chart Attach Text and later edited, if the auto_text value is TRUE, the original text is restored.

auto_size corresponds to the Automatic Size check box. If the border around selected text was changed, this option restores the border to automatic size (where the border automatically adjusts to fit around the text even if it was changed).

show_key corresponds to the Show Key check box.

show_value corresponds to the Show Value check box.

A summary of which values apply to each text item follows:

Value	Applies to
x_align,y_align,orient_num,auto_size	Worksheet text box
All values	Attached data label
x_align,y_align,orient_num,auto_size	Unattached data label
orient_num	Tickmark label

Name: GROUP

Syntax: GROUP()

Command Equivalent: Format Group

Description: Creates a single object from several selected objects and returns the object identifier of the group. If either no object is selected, only one object is selected, or a group is already selected, then GROUP returns the #VALUE! error and interrupts the macro.

Name: JUSTIFY

Syntax: JUSTIFY()

Command Equivalent: Format Justify

Description: Rearranges text so that it fills the range evenly

Name: MERGE.STYLES

Syntax: MERGE.STYLES(*document_text*)

Command Equivalent: Format Style, then Merge

Description: Merges all the styles from another document into the active document

Arguments: *document_text* is the name of the document from which the styles come.

Notes: If any of the styles from the document specified by document_text have the same name as styles in the active document, a dialog box appears asking if you want to replace the existing definitions of the styles with the "merged" definitions.

Name: OBJECT.PROTECTION

Syntax: OBJECT.PROTECTION(*locked,lock_text*)

Command Equivalent: Format Object Protection

Description: Changes the protection status of the selected object

Arguments: If *locked* is TRUE, OBJECT.PROTECTION locks the object. If locked is FALSE, OBJECT.PROTECTION unlocks the object.

lock_text applies only to an object that is a text box or a button. If lock_text is TRUE or not included, text cannot be changed. If lock_text is FALSE, text can be changed.

Notes: You cannot lock or unlock a single object with OBJECT.PROTECTION when document protection is turned on for objects.

Name: PATTERNS

Syntax: Form 1 for cells:
PATTERNS(*apattern,afore,aback*);
PATTERNS?(*apattern,afore,aback*)

Form 2 for lines (arrows) on worksheets:
PATTERNS(*lauto,lstyle,lcolor,lwt,hwidth,hlength,htype*);
PATTERNS?(*lauto,lstyle,lcolor,lwt,hwidth,hlength,htype*)

Form 3 for text boxes, rectangles, ovals, arcs, and pictures:
PATTERNS(*bauto,bstyle,bcolor,bwt,shadow,aauto,apattern,afore, aback,rounded*);
PATTERNS?(*bauto,bstyle,bcolor,bwt,shadow,aauto,apattern,afore, aback,rounded*)

Form 4 for chart plot areas, bars, columns, pie slices, and text labels:
PATTERNS(*bauto,bstyle,bcolor,bwt,shadow,aauto,apattern,afore, aback,invert,apply*);
PATTERNS?(*bauto,bstyle,bcolor,bwt,shadow,aauto,apattern,afore, aback,invert,apply*)

Form 5 for chart axes:
PATTERNS(*lauto,lstyle,lcolor,lwt,tmajor,tminor,tlabel*);
PATTERNS?(*lauto,lstyle,lcolor,lwt,tmajor,tminor,tlabel*)

Form 6 for chart gridlines,hi-lo lines, drop lines, lines on a picture line chart, and picture charts of bar, column, and 3-D column charts:
PATTERNS(*lauto,lstyle,lcolor,lwt,apply*);
PATTERNS?(*lauto,lstyle,lcolor,lwt,apply*)

Form 7 for chart data lines:
PATTERNS(*lauto,lstyle,lcolor,lwt,mauto,mstyle,mfore,mback,apply*);
PATTERNS?(*lauto,lstyle,lcolor,lwt,mauto,mstyle,mfore,mback,apply*)

Form 8 for picture chart markers:
PATTERNS(*type,picture_units,apply*);
PATTERNS?(*type,picture_units,apply*)

Command Equivalent: Format Patterns

Description: Changes the appearance of the selected cells, objects, or single chart item. There are separate forms. Cells on a worksheet or macro sheet are handled by form 1. Objects on a worksheet or macro sheet are handled by form 2 or 3. Chart items are handled by forms 4 through 8. Only form 2 can be used on a worksheet, macro sheet, or chart.

Arguments: The information that goes into these forms is in alphabetical order.

aauto specifies the area settings.

If aauto Is	*Then the Settings Are*
0	Set by the user (customized)
1	Automatic (set by Excel)
2	None

aback is a number from 1 to 16 that corresponds to the 16 area background colors in the Format Patterns dialog box.

afore is a number from 1 to 16 that corresponds to the 16 area foreground colors in the Format Patterns dialog box.

apattern is a number from 1 to 18 that corresponds to the 18 area patterns in the Format Patterns dialog box. If 0 and a cell are selected, no pattern is applied.

apply corresponds to the Apply To All check box. If TRUE, any formatting changes are applied to all items that are similar to the selected item on the chart. If FALSE, formatting changes are applied only to the selected item on the chart.

bauto is a number from 0 to 2 that specifies the border settings. For a list of what these values represent, see "aauto" above.

bcolor is a number from 1 to 16 that corresponds to the 16 border colors in the Format Patterns dialog box.

bstyle is a number from 1 to 8 that corresponds to the 8 border styles in the Format Patterns dialog box.

If bwt Is	*Then the Style Is*
1	Hairline
2	Thin
3	Medium
4	Thick

If hlength Is	*Then the Length of the Arrowhead Is*
1	Short
2	Medium
3	Long
If htype Is	*Then the Style of the Arrowhead Is*
1	No head
2	Open head
3	Closed
If hwidth Is	*Then the Width of the Arrowhead Is*
1	Narrow
2	Medium
3	Wide

invert corresponds to the Invert If Negative check box and applies only to data markers. If TRUE, PATTERNS inverts the pattern in the selected item if it corresponds to a negative number. If FALSE, PATTERNS removes the inverted pattern, if present, from the selected item that corresponds to a negative value.

lauto is a number from 0 to 2 that specifies the line settings. See "aauto" above for a list of what each number represents.

lcolor is a number from 1 to 16 that corresponds to the 16 line colors in the Format Patterns dialog box.

lstyle is a number from 1 to 16 that corresponds to the 8 line styles in the Format Patterns dialog box.

lwt is a number from 1 to 4 that corresponds to the four line weights in the Format Patterns dialog box. See "bwt" above for the listing of what each number represents.

mauto is a number from 0 to 2 that specifies the marker settings. See "aauto" above for a list of what each number represents.

mback is a number from 1 to 16 that corresponds to the 16 marker background colors in the Format Patterns dialog box.

mfore is a number from 1 to 16 that corresponds to the 16 marker foreground colors in the Format Patterns dialog box.

mstyle is a number from 1 to 9 that corresponds to the 9 marker styles in the Format Patterns dialog box.

picture_units is the number of units that you want each picture to represent in a scaled, stacked picture chart. Applies only to picture charts when type is 3.

rounded corresponds to the Round Corners check box and applies to text boxes and rectangles. If TRUE, PATTERNS rounds the corners on text boxes and rectangles. If FALSE, the corners are square. If the selection is an arc or an oval, then the value rounded is ignored.

shadow corresponds to the Shadow check box. If TRUE, PATTERNS adds a shadow to the selected item. If FALSE, PATTERNS removes any existing shadow on the selected item. If the selection is an arc, then the shadow value is ignored. Shadow also does not apply to area charts or bars in bar charts.

If tlabel Is	Then the Position of Tick Labels Is
1	None
2	Low
3	High
4	Next to axis

If tmajor/tminor Is	Then the Type of Major/Minor Tick Marks Is
1	None
2	Inside
3	Outside
4	Cross

If type Is	Then the Type of Pictures That Are Used in a Picture Chart Are
1	Stretched to reach a particular value
2	Stacked on top of each other to reach a particular value
3	Stacked on top of each other, and you specify the number of units each picture represents

Name: PLACEMENT

Syntax: PLACEMENT(*placement_type*)

Command Equivalent: Format Object Placement

Description: Determines how the selected object or objects are attached to the cells beneath them. (This attachment affects how the objects are moved or sized whenever you move or size the cells.)

Arguments: PLACEMENT returns #VALUE! if an object is not selected. If *placement_type* is not included, no changes occur to the current status. Otherwise:

If placement_type Is	Then the Selected Object Is
1	Moved and sized with cells
2	Moved but not sized with cells
3	Free-floating (i.e., not affected by moving and sizing cells)

Name: ROW.HEIGHT

Syntax:
ROW.HEIGHT(*height_num,reference,standard_height,type_num*);
ROW.HEIGHT?(*height_num,reference,standard_height,type_num*)

Command Equivalent: Format Row Height

Description: Changes the height of rows in a reference

Arguments: *height_num* specifies how high the rows are to be, in units of the font that correspond to the Normal cell style. Ignored if standard_height is TRUE.

reference is the specification for the rows whose height you wish to change. It must be either an external reference to the active worksheet or an R1C1 style reference that is in the form of either a name or text. If reference is a relative address, then it is relative in relation to the active cell. If it is not included, the current selection is the assumed value for reference.

If *standard_height* is TRUE, height_num is ignored and the row height is a standard height that may vary from row to row depending on the fonts used in each row. If standard_height is FALSE or not included, the row height is set by height_num.

type_num corresponds to the Hide or Unhide button in the Format Row Height dialog box or to setting the selection to a best-fit height:

If type_num Is	Then ROW.HEIGHT
1	Sets the row height to 0 in order to hide the selected row

If type_num Is	Then ROW.HEIGHT
2	Sets the row height to the value it was set to before selection was hidden (unhides the selected row)
3	Sets the row selection to best-fit height, varying from row to row depending on the font size and number of wrapped lines of text

Name: SCALE

Syntax: Form 1 (Use when the selection is the category (x) axis, 2-D chart):

SCALE(*cross,cat_labels,cat_marks,between,max,reverse*);
SCALE?(*cross,cat_labels,cat_marks,between,max,reverse*)

Form 2 (Use when the selection is the value (y) axis on a 2-D chart, or x or y (value) axis on an xy scatter chart):
SCALE(*min_num,max_num,major,minor,cross,logarithmic,reverse,max*);
SCALE?(*min_num,max_num,major,minor,cross,logarithmic,reverse,max*)

Form 3 (Use when the selection is the category (x) axis, 3-D chart):
SCALE(*cat_labels,cat_marks,reverse,between*);
SCALE?(*cat_labels,cat_marks,reverse,between*)

Form 4 (Use when the selection is the series (y) axis, 3-D chart):
SCALE(*series_labels,series_marks,reverse*);
SCALE?(*series_labels,series_marks,reverse*)

Form 5 (Use when the selection is the value (z) axis on a 3-D chart):
SCALE(*min_num,max_num,major,minor,cross,logarithmic,reverse,min*);
SCALE?(*min_num,max_num,major,minor,cross,logarithmic,reverse,min*)

Command Equivalent: Format Scale

Description: Changes the position, formatting, and scaling of the category axis, the value axis, or series axis. The form is determined by the selected axis. See the information below and the syntax given above to determine which form you should use.

Arguments: In all the following forms, logical values that correspond to check boxes (in the command form of the function) represent an "on check box" with a value of TRUE and an "off check box" with a value of FALSE.

Form 1, category (x) axis, 2-D chart:

cross is a number that corresponds to the Value (Y) Axis Crosses At Category box. Assumed to be 1 if not included. Ignored if max is TRUE.

cat_labels is a number that corresponds to the Number of Categories Between Tick Labels box. Assumed to be 1 if not included.

cat_marks is a number that corresponds to the Number of Categories Between Tick Marks box. Assumed to be 1 if not included.

between corresponds to the Value (Y) Axis Crosses Between Category box. (Applies only if cat_labels is not 1.)

max corresponds to the Value (Y) Axis Crosses At Maximum Category box. If TRUE, it overrides all values for cross.

reverse corresponds to the Categories In Reverse Order check box.

Forms 2 and 5, value (y) axis on a 2-D chart, or x or y (value) axis on an xy scatter chart, and value (z) axis on a 3-D chart:

min_num corresponds to the Minimum box and is the minimum value for the value axis.

max_num corresponds to the Maximum box and is the maximum value for the value axis.

major corresponds to the Major Unit box and is the major unit of measure.

minor corresponds to the Minor Unit box and is the minor unit of measure.

cross in form 2 corresponds to the Category (X) Axis Crosses At box for the value (y) axis of a 2-D chart or the Value (Y) Axis Crosses At box for the x-axis of an xy chart. In form 5 cross corresponds to the Floor (XY Plane) Crosses At box.

logarithmic corresponds to the Logarithmic Scale check box.

max corresponds to the Category/Value Axis Crosses At Maximum Value/Category box.

min (in form 5 only) corresponds to the Floor (XY Plane) Crosses At Minimum Value check box.

reverse corresponds to the Values/Categories In Reverse Order check box.

Form 3, category (x) axis, 3-D chart:

cat_labels is a number that corresponds to the Number Of Categories Between Tick Labels box. Assumed to be 1, if not included.

cat_marks is a number that corresponds to the Number Of Categories Between Tick Marks box. Assumed to be 1, if not included.

reverse corresponds to the Categories In Reverse Order check box.

between corresponds to the Value (Z) Axis Crosses Between Category box.

Form 4, series (y) axis, 3-D chart:

series_labels is a number that corresponds to the Number Of Series Between Tick Labels box. Assumed to be 1, if not included.

series_marks is a number that corresponds to the Number Of Series Between Tick Marks box. Assumed to be 1, if not included.

reverse corresponds to the Series In Reverse Order check box.

Name: SEND.TO.BACK

Syntax: SEND.TO.BACK( )

Command Equivalent: Format Send To Back

Description: Sends the selected object or objects to the back, behind other objects. #VALUE! is returned and the macro interrupted if the selected value is not an object or group of objects.

Name: UNGROUP

Syntax: UNGROUP( )

Command Equivalent: Format Ungroup

Description: Separates a grouped object into individual objects. #VALUE! is returned and the macro is interrupted if the selection is not a grouped object.

Notes: Useful for isolating one object in order to size, move, or format it.

Name: VIEW.3D

Syntax:
VIEW.3D(*elevation,perspective,rotation,axes,height%*);
VIEW.3D?(*elevation,perspective,rotation,axes,height%*)

Command Equivalent: Format 3-D View

Description: Adjusts the view of the active 3-D chart

Arguments: *elevation* is a number from −90 to 90 that corresponds to the Elevation box in the Format 3-D View dialog box. The value of elevation gives the viewing elevation of the chart, measured in degrees. 0 corresponds to a straight-on view of the chart. 90 corresponds to a "bird's eye" view of the chart from above. −90 corresponds to a view of the chart from below. If elevation is not included, it is assumed to be 25.

perspective is a number from 0 to 100 percent that corresponds to the Perspective box in the Format 3-D View dialog box. The value of perspective gives the perspective of the chart. The higher the perspective is, the closer the simulated view. If perspective is not included, it is assumed to be 30.

rotation is a number from 0 to 360 that corresponds to the Rotation box in the Format 3-D View dialog box. The value of rotation gives the rotation of the chart measured in degrees around the (z) axis. As you rotate the chart, the back and side walls are moved so that they do not block the view of the chart. If rotation is not included, it is assumed to be 30.

axes corresponds to the Right Angle Axes check box. If axes is TRUE, then the axes are fixed in the plane of the screen. If axes is FALSE, then the axes can rotate in the plane of the screen. If not included, then axes is assumed to be FALSE for a chart view that is a 3-D layout or TRUE for a chart view that is not a 3-D layout.

height% is a number from 5 to 500% that corresponds to the Height box in the Format 3-D View dialog box. The value of height% gives the height of the chart as a percentage of the length of the base. If not included, it is assumed to be 100.

Macro Functions That Perform Formula Commands

Macro functions that perform Formula commands perform the exact same operations as the Formula commands do in a worksheet or a chart. In a macro sheet you may want to use the commands that are normally available in any worksheet. The macro functions are designed to allow you to activate any *command, activity,* or *operation* in a worksheet by using a nonactive macro function in a macro sheet.

The following command-equivalent macro functions are specific macro functions *that you can use in a macro sheet.*

Name: APPLY.NAMES

Syntax:
APPLY.NAMES(*name_array,ignore,use_rowcol,omit_col,omit_row, order_num,append_last*);
APPLY.NAMES?(*name_array,ignore,use_rowcol,omit_col,omit_row, order_num,append_last*)

Command Equivalent: Formula Apply Names

Description: Replaces definitions with their respective names. APPLY.NAMES returns #VALUE! error if no names are defined.

Arguments: *name_array* is the array of name or names that are to be applied.

The following values are check boxes:

ignore corresponds to the Ignore Relative/Absolute check box.

use_rowcol corresponds to the Use Row And Column Names check box. If this value is FALSE, the next two check box values are ignored.

omit_col corresponds to the Omit Column Name IF Same Column check box.

omit_row corresponds to the Omit Row Name IF Same Column check box.

order_num determines which range name is listed first when a cell address is replaced by a row-oriented and a column-oriented range name. If order_num is 1, then the order of range names is row then column. If order_num is 2, then the order of range names is column then row.

append_last decides whether the names most recently defined are also replaced. If append_last is TRUE, then the definitions of the names in name_array and the definitions of the last names defined are replaced. If append_last is FALSE or not included, then only the definitions of the names in name_array are replaced.

Name: CREATE.NAMES

Syntax:
CREATE.NAMES(*top,left,bottom,right*);
CREATE.NAMES?(*top,left,bottom,right*)

Command Equivalent: Formula Create Names

Description: Creates names from text labels on a worksheet

Arguments: *Top, left, bottom,* and *right* correspond to the Top Row, Left Column, Bottom Row, Right Column check boxes respectively. If the value is TRUE, this corresponds to the check box being turned on. If the value is FALSE, this corresponds to the check box being turned off.

Notes: The label text used to create names is not included in the range to be named.

Name: DEFINE.NAME

Syntax:
DEFINE.NAME(*name_text,refers_to,macro_type,shortcut_text, hidden*);
DEFINE.NAME?(*name_text,refers_to,macro_type,shortcut_text, hidden*)

Command Equivalent: Formula Define Name

Description: Defines a name on an active worksheet or macro sheet

Arguments: *name_text* is the name in text form that refers to refers_to. Name_text must start with a letter and cannot include spaces or symbols or look like a reference.

refers_to is the value that is named. The value can be a number, text, a logical value, an external reference, the current selection, or a formula. If refers_to is an external reference, the name is defined to refer to these cells. If refers_to is not included, the name is defined to refer to the current selection. If refers_to is a formula, then the references must be in R1C1 style.

If the document in the active window is a function macro, then *macro_type* should be 1. If the document in the active window is a command macro, then macro_type should be 2. If the document in the active window is a not a macro (that is, name_text is not a macro), then macro_type should be 3 or not included.

shortcut_text is a single text letter that specifies the shortcut key that can be used for the macro.

If *hidden* is TRUE, the name is a hidden name. If hidden is FALSE or not included, the name is a normal name.

Notes: You can use DEFINE.NAME to hide names that you don't want the user to change.

Name: DELETE.NAME

Syntax: DELETE.NAME(*name_text*)

Command Equivalent: Formula Define Name

Description: Deletes the specified name

Arguments: *name_text* is the name that you want to delete in text form (with quotation marks).

Notes: Deleting a name that is used in a formula causes the formula to return an error.

Name: FORMULA.FIND

Syntax:
FORMULA.FIND(*text,in_num,at_num,by_num,dir_num, match_case*);
FORMULA.FIND?(*text,in_num,at_num,by_num,dir_num, match_case*)

Command Equivalent: Formula Find

Description: Selects the next or previous cell containing the specified text. Returns TRUE if found, FALSE otherwise.

Arguments: *text* is the text to be found and corresponds to the Formula What box.

If in_num Is	**FORMULA.FIND Searches for**
1	Formulas
2	Values
3	Notes

If at_num Is	**FORMULA.FIND Looks for**
1	A cell containing only the text value and no other characters
2	A cell containing the text value either by itself or as a part of a longer string of characters

If by_num Is	**FORMULA.FIND Searches by**
1	Rows
2	Columns

If dir_num Is	**FORMULA.FIND Searches for**
1 or not included	The next occurrence of text
2	The previous occurrence of text

match_case corresponds to the Match Case check box. TRUE results in matching characters exactly, including upper- and lowercase matching, and FALSE results in matching without considering the case.

Notes: In Excel for Windows or OS/2, the dialog box form of FORMULA.FIND is equivalent to pressing Shift-F5.

Name: FORMULA.FIND.NEXT

Syntax: FORMULA.FIND.NEXT()

Command Equivalent: Equivalent to pressing Shift-F7 in Excel for Windows or OS/2

Description: Finds the next cells on the worksheet. Returns TRUE if found, FALSE otherwise. See "FORMULA.FIND" above for more information.

Name: FORMULA.FIND.PREV

Syntax: FORMULA.FIND.PREV()

Command Equivalent: Equivalent to pressing Shift-F7 in Excel for Windows or OS/2

Description: Finds the next previous cells on the worksheet. Returns TRUE if found, FALSE otherwise. See "FORMULA.FIND" above for more information.

Name: FORMULA.GOTO

Syntax:
FORMULA.GOTO(*reference,corner*);
FORMULA.GOTO?(*reference,corner*)

Command Equivalent: Formula Goto command or pressing F5

Description: Scrolls through the worksheet and selects the area named by *reference*

Arguments: *reference* is the location of the selected area. reference is either a reference in R1C1 style or an external reference, or it can be omitted if the FORMULA.GOTO was previously performed. If omitted, *reference* is assumed to be the cells that were selected before the previous goto was performed. This last feature distinguishes function FORMULA.GOTO from SELECT.

corner is a logical value. If corner is TRUE, FORMULA.GOTO places *reference* in the upper-left corner of the active window; otherwise, scrolling occurs as normal.

Notes: When recording a macro, references entered into the Reference box of the Formula Goto menu command dialog box are recorded as text in R1C1 style. (This is also the format that the macro function FORMULA.GOTO uses.)

Name: FORMULA.REPLACE

Syntax:
FORMULA.REPLACE(*find_text,replace_text,look_at,look_by, active_cell,match_case*);
FORMULA.REPLACE?(*find_text,replace_text,look_at,look_by, active_cell,match_case*)

Command Equivalent: Formula Replace (full menus)

Description: Finds and replaces text in cells on a worksheet

Arguments: *find_text* is the text to be found. Wild-card characters are allowed. Use * to match any sequence of characters and ? to match a single character. To match "*" exactly, use ~*. To match "?" exactly, use ~?.

replace_text is the text that you want to replace with find_text.

If look_at Is	*FORMULA.REPLACE Looks for find_text*
1	As the only value in the cell
2	As part of the contents of the cell or the entire contents

If look_by Is	*FORMULA.REPLACE Looks for find_text by*
1	Rows (horizontally)
2	Columns (vertically)

If *active_cell* is TRUE, then find_text is replaced in the active cell only; otherwise, find_text is replaced in the entire selection, or in the entire document if the selection is a single cell.

match_case corresponds to the Match Case check box. TRUE results in matching characters exactly, including upper- and lowercase matching, and FALSE results in matching without considering the case.

Name: GOAL.SEEK

Syntax:
GOAL.SEEK(*target_cell,target_value,variable_cell*);
GOAL.SEEK?(*target_cell,target_value,variable_cell*)

Command Equivalent: Formula Goal Seek

Description: Calculates the necessary values that will achieve a specific goal. If goal is an amount returned by a formula, then GOAL.SEEK calculates the values that will return the amount that is your goal.

Arguments: *target_cell* corresponds to the Set Cell box and is a reference to the cell containing the formula used to calculate the values that yield the answer given by target_value. If target_cell does not contain a formula, then GOAL.SEEK returns an error.

target_value is the value that must be returned when the values in variable_cell are applied to the formula in target_cell.

variable_cell corresponds to the By Changing Cell box and is the single cell where the GOAL.SEEK function returns its answer, the values that cause the formula in target_cell to return the value given by the target_value.

Notes: GOAL.SEEK can be used for optimizations.

Name: LIST.NAMES

Syntax: LIST.NAMES( )

Command Equivalent: Formula Paste Name, then Paste List

Description: Lists 1) all unhidden names defined on your worksheet, 2) the cells to which the names refer, 3) whether a macro corresponding to a particular name is a command macro or a custom function, and 4) the shortcut key for each command macro. If the current selection is a single cell or four or more columns wide, these four types of information are returned in four columns, the first type in the first column and so on. If selection included fewer than four columns, then LIST.NAMES does not include the information that would have been pasted into missing columns. For the third type of information returned, 1 represents a custom function, 2 represents a command macro, and 0 represents anything else.

Notes: LIST.NAMES completely replaces the contents of cells that it pastes into.

Name: NOTE

Syntax:
NOTE(*add_text,cell_ref,start_char,num_char*);
NOTE?( )

Command Equivalent: Formula Note

Description: Creates a note or replaces characters in a note. NOTE returns the number of characters in the cell specified by cell_ref.

Arguments: *add_text* is up to 255 characters in quotes that you want to add to note. If you do not want to add text but just want to delete text, you can omit add_text.

cell_ref is the cell to which you want to add the note text. If not included, cell_ref is given the value of the active cell.

start_char is a number that is an index into the note and tells the character where add_text should be added.

num_char is the number of characters that you want to replace in note. (The characters from start_char to the number produced from adding start_char and num_char are replaced by add_text.)

Name: OUTLINE

Syntax:
OUTLINE(*auto_styles,row_dir,col_dir,create_apply*)

Command Equivalent: Formula Outline

Description: Creates an outline and defines settings for automatically creating outlines

Arguments: The following three values: *auto_styles, row_dir,* and *col_dir* are logical values that correspond to the Automatic Styles check box, the Summary Rows Below Detail check box, and the Summary Columns To Right Of Detail check box. For these three values, TRUE corresponds to turning on the check box, FALSE corresponds to turning off the check box, and not including a value corresponds to not changing the check box.

If *create_apply* is 1, OUTLINE creates an outline with the current settings. If create_apply is 2, OUTLINE applies outlining styles to the selection based on outline levels.

Name: SELECT.LAST.CELL

Syntax: SELECT.LAST.CELL( )

Command Equivalent: Formula Select Special, then Last Cell

Description: Selects the cell that is at the intersection of the last row and column which contains a formula, value, or format or which is referred to in a formula or name

Name: SELECT.SPECIAL

Syntax:
SELECT.SPECIAL(*type_num,value_type,levels*);
SELECT.SPECIAL?(*type_num,value_type,levels*)

Command Equivalent: Formula Select Special

Description: Selects groups of similar cells from one of several categories

Arguments: *type_num* is a number from 1 to 13 that corresponds to the options in the Formula Select Special dialog box.

If type_num Is	Then the Following Is Selected
1	Notes
2	Constants
3	Formulas

If type_num Is	Then the Following Is Selected
4	Blanks
5	Current region
6	Current array
7	Row differences
8	Column differences
9	Precedents
10	Dependents
11	Last cell
12	Visible cells only (outlining)
13	All objects

value_type is a number specifying which types of constants or formulas you want to select. It is applicable only when type_num is 2 or 3. To make value_type a number that represents more than one type, add the corresponding number for each type that you wish to select. (For example, a value_type that represents all types is 23, which is the sum of 1, 2, 4, and 16.)

If value_type Is	SELECT.SPECIAL Selects Constants or Formulas That Are
1	Numbers
2	Text
4	Logical values
16	Error values

levels is applicable only when type_num is 9 or 10, and is assumed to be 1 if not included.

If levels Is	SELECT.SPECIAL Selects Precedents and Dependents That Are
1	Direct only
2	All levels

Name: SHOW.ACTIVE.CELL

Syntax: SHOW.ACTIVE.CELL()

Command Equivalent: Formula Show Active Cell or Ctrl-Backspace in Excel for Windows

Description: Scrolls the active window so that the active cell becomes visible. #VALUE! is returned if the selected value is an object.

Notes: ISfunctions are useful for testing whether an error is returned (which means the selected item is an object).

Macro Functions That Perform Gallery Commands

Macro functions that perform Gallery commands perform the exact same operations as the Gallery commands do in a worksheet or chart. In a macro sheet you may want to use the commands that are normally available in any worksheet. The macro functions are designed to allow you to activate any *command, activity,* or *operation* in a worksheet by using a nonactive macro function in a macro sheet.

The following command-equivalent macro functions are specific macro functions *that you can use in a macro sheet*.

Name: COMBINATION

Syntax: COMBINATION(*type_num*)

Command Equivalent: Gallery Combination

Description: Changes the format of the active chart to the combination format that you select from the gallery

Arguments: *type_num* is the number that corresponds to the chart number in the Gallery Combination Box.

Name: GALLERY.3D.AREA

Syntax:
GALLERY.3D.AREA(*type_num*);
GALLERY.3D.AREA?(*type_num*)

Command Equivalent: Gallery 3-D Area

Description: Changes the active chart to a 3-D area chart

Arguments: *type_num* is the number of the format in the Gallery 3-D Area dialog box that you want to apply to the 3-D area chart.

Name: GALLERY.3D.COLUMN

Syntax:
GALLERY.3D.COLUMN(*type_num*);
GALLERY.3D.COLUMN?(*type_num*)

Command Equivalent: Gallery 3-D Column

Description: Changes the active chart to a 3-D column chart

Arguments: *type_num* is the number of the format in the Gallery 3-D Area dialog box that you want to apply to the 3-D column chart.

Name: GALLERY.3D.LINE

Syntax:
GALLERY.3D.LINE(*type_num*); GALLERY.3D.LINE?(*type_num*)

Command Equivalent: Gallery 3-D Line

Description: Changes the active chart to a 3-D line chart

Arguments: *type_num* is the number of the format in the Gallery 3-D Area dialog box that you want to apply to the 3-D line chart

Name: GALLERY.3D.PIE

Syntax:
GALLERY.3D.PIE(*type_num*); GALLERY.3D.PIE?(*type_num*)

Command Equivalent: Gallery 3-D Pie

Description: Changes the active chart to a 3-D pie chart

Arguments: *type_num* is the number of the format in the Gallery 3-D Area dialog box that you want to apply to the 3-D pie chart.

Name: GALLERY.AREA

Syntax:
GALLERY.AREA(*type_num,delete_overlay*);
GALLERY.AREA?(*type_num,delete_overlay*)

Command Equivalent: Gallery Area

Description: Changes the format of the active chart to an area chart

Arguments: *type_num* is the number of the format in the Gallery Area dialog box that you want to apply to the area chart.

If *delete_overlay* is TRUE, Excel deletes the overlay chart (if present) and applies the new format to the main chart. If delete_overlay is FALSE or not included, Excel applies the new format to the active chart.

Name: GALLERY.BAR

Syntax:
GALLERY.BAR(*type_num,delete_overlay*);
GALLERY.BAR?(*type_num,delete_overlay*)

Command Equivalent: Gallery Bar

Description: Changes the format of the active chart to a bar chart

Arguments: *type_num* is the number of the format in the Gallery Area dialog box that you want to apply to the bar chart.

If *delete_overlay* is TRUE, Excel deletes the overlay chart (if present) and applies the new format to the main chart. If delete_overlay is FALSE or not included, Excel applies the new format to the active chart.

Name: GALLERY.COLUMN

Syntax:
GALLERY.COLUMN(*type_num,delete_overlay*);
GALLERY.COLUMN?(*type_num,delete_overlay*)

Command Equivalent: Gallery Column

Description: Changes the format of the active chart to a column chart

Arguments: *type_num* is the number of the format in the Gallery Area dialog box that you want to apply to the area chart.

If *delete_overlay* is TRUE, Excel deletes the column chart (if present) and applies the new format to the main chart. If delete_overlay is FALSE or not included, Excel applies the new format to the active chart.

Name: GALLERY.LINE

Syntax:
GALLERY.LINE(*type_num,delete_overlay*);
GALLERY.LINE?(*type_num,delete_overlay*)

Command Equivalent: Gallery Line

Description: Changes the format of the active chart to a line chart

Arguments: *type_num* is the number of the format in the Gallery Area dialog box that you want to apply to the line chart.

If *delete_overlay* is TRUE, Excel deletes the overlay chart (if present) and applies the new format to the main chart. If delete_overlay is FALSE or not included, Excel applies the new format to the active chart.

Name: GALLERY.PIE

Syntax:
GALLERY.PIE(*type_num,delete_overlay*);
GALLERY.PIE?(*type_num,delete_overlay*)

Command Equivalent: Gallery Pie

Description: Changes the format of the active chart to a pie chart

Arguments: *type_num* is the number of the format in the Gallery Area dialog box that you want to apply to the pie chart.

If *delete_overlay* is TRUE, Excel deletes the overlay chart (if present) and applies the new format to the main chart. If delete_overlay is FALSE or not included, Excel applies the new format to the active chart.

Name: GALLERY.SCATTER

Syntax:
GALLERY.SCATTER(*type_num,delete_overlay*);
GALLERY.SCATTER?(*type_num,delete_overlay*)

Command Equivalent: Gallery XY (Scatter)

Description: Changes the format of the active chart to an xy scatter chart

Arguments: *type_num* is the number of the format in the Gallery Area dialog box that you want to apply to the xy chart.

If *delete_overlay* is TRUE, Excel deletes the overlay chart (if present) and applies the new format to the main chart. If delete_overlay is FALSE or not included, Excel applies the new format to the active chart.

Name: PREFERRED

Syntax: PREFERRED()

Command Equivalent: Gallery Preferred

Description: Changes the format of the active chart to the format currently defined by the SET.PREFERRED macro function or the Gallery Set Preferred command

Name: SET.PREFERRED

Syntax: SET.PREFERRED()

Command Equivalent: Gallery Set Preferred

Description: Changes the default format for creating a new chart or formatting a chart (with either the Gallery Preferred command or the function PREFERRED) to the format of the active chart

Macro Functions That Perform Macro Commands

Macro functions that perform Macro commands perform the exact same operations as the Macro commands do in a worksheet or chart. In a macro sheet you may want to use the commands that are normally available in any worksheet. The macro functions are designed to allow you to specify any *command, activity,* or *operation* in a worksheet in the form of a non-active function.

The following command-equivalent macro functions are specific macro functions *that you can use in a macro sheet*.

Name: ASSIGN.TO.OBJECT

Syntax:
ASSIGN.TO.OBJECT(*macro_ref*);
ASSIGN.TO.OBJECT?(*macro_ref*)

Command Equivalent: Macro Assign to Object

Description: Assigns a macro to be run when an object is clicked with the mouse. ASSIGN.TO.OBJECT returns #VALUE! and interrupts the macro if no object is selected.

Notes: To change the assignment of macro to object, select the object and use ASSIGN.TO.OBJECT again.

Name: RUN

Syntax: RUN(*reference,step*); RUN?(*reference,step*)

Command Equivalent: Macro Run

Description: Runs a macro

Arguments: *reference* is the macro that you want to run, or number 1 or 2, which represent Auto_Open or Auto_Close macros on the active macro sheet. If the macro sheet containing the macro is not the active document, *reference* can be an external reference to the name of the macro. If *reference* is a range of cells, then RUN begins with the macro function in the upper-left cell of *reference*. If *reference* is 1, Excel runs all Auto_Open macros on the active macro sheet. If *reference* is 2, Excel runs all Auto_Close macros on the active macro sheet. If not included, the function in the active cell of the macro is executed and execution continues down that column.

If *step* is TRUE, Excel runs the macro in single-step mode. If FALSE or not included, the macro is run normally.

Macro Functions That Perform Options Commands

Macro functions that perform Options commands perform the exact same operations as the Options commands do in a worksheet or chart. In a macro sheet you may want to use the commands that are normally available in any worksheet. The macro functions are designed to allow you to activate any *command, activity,* or *operation* in a worksheet by using a nonactive macro function in a macro sheet.

The following command-equivalent macro functions are specific macro functions *that you can use in a macro sheet*.

Name: CALCULATE.DOCUMENT

Syntax: CALCULATE.DOCUMENT( )

Command Equivalent: Options Calculate Document

Description: Calculates the active document

Name: CALCULATE.NOW

Syntax: CALCULATE.NOW( )

Command Equivalent: Options Calculate Now

Description: Calculates all open documents. Use CALCULATE.NOW when calculation is set at manual.

Notes: The CALCULATE.NOW function is equivalent to *both* Chart Calculate Now and Options Calculate Now.

Name: CALCULATION

Syntax:
CALCULATION(*type_num,iter,max_num,max_change,update,precision, date_1904,calc_save,save_values*);
CALCULATION?(*type_num,iter,max_num,max_change,update,precision, date_1904,calc_save,save_values*)

Command Equivalent: Options Calculation

Description: Controls when and how formulas are calculated in the open documents

Arguments: The following values correspond to values in the check boxes:

type_num is a number from 1 to 3 that specifies the type of calculation: 1 is automatic, 2 is automatic except tables, 3 is manual.

iter is a value for the Iteration check box. If not included, it is assumed to be FALSE.

max_num is the maximum number of iterations. If not included, it is assumed to be 100.

max_change is the maximum change of each iteration. If not included, it is assumed to be 0.0001.

update is the value for the Update Remote References check box. If not included, it is assumed to be TRUE.

precision is the Precision As Displayed check box. If not included, it is assumed to be FALSE.

date_1904 is the 1904 Date System check box. If not included, it is assumed to be FALSE in Excel for Windows and OS/2.

calc_save is equivalent to the Recalculate Before Save check box. If calc_save is FALSE, the document is not recalculated before saving (in manual mode). If not included, it is assumed to be TRUE.

save_values is the value for the Save External Link Values check box. If not included, it is assumed to be TRUE.

Notes: See worksheet function "NOW" for more information on date_1904.

Name: COLOR.PALETTE

Syntax:
COLOR.PALETTE(*file_text*);
COLOR.PALETTE?(*file_text*)

Command Equivalent: Options Color Palette

Description: Copies a color palette from an open document to the active document

Arguments: *file_text* is a quoted text string that specifies the name of the document that you want to copy color from. If the document named file_text is not open, #VALUE! results and the macro is interrupted.

Name: DISPLAY

Syntax:
DISPLAY(*formulas,gridlines,headings,zeros,color_num,reserved, outline,page_breaks,object_num*);
DISPLAY?(*formulas,gridlines,headings,zeros,color_num,reserved, outline,page_breaks,object_num*);
DISPLAY(*cell,formula,value,format,protection,names,precedents, dependents,note*)

Command Equivalent: Options Display

Description: Form 1 controls the display on the screen of formulas, gridlines, row and column headings, zeros, and other values displayed on the screen. Form 2 controls which commands on the Info window are to be used.

Arguments: The values *formulas, gridlines, headings, zeros, color_num, outline,* and *page_breaks* correspond to check boxes. All the values except color_num are logical values where TRUE represents an on check box and the value FALSE represents an off check box. Color_num is a number from 0 to 16 that represents the gridline and heading colors in the Options Display dialog box. If a value is not included, then the following defaults apply to the values that are not included: the default for formulas is FALSE on worksheets and TRUE on macro sheets, the default for gridlines is TRUE, the default for headings is TRUE, the default for zeros is TRUE, the default for color_num is 0 for automatic color, the default for outline is TRUE, and the default for page_breaks is FALSE.

reserved is reserved for international versions of Excel.

object_num corresponds to the options in the Object box. If object_num is 1 or not included, the Show All option is chosen. If object_num is 2, the Show Placeholders option is chosen. If object_num is 3, the Hide option is chosen.

Form 2: All the values correspond to commands with the same name on the Info menu. All the values except precedents and dependents are logical values where TRUE represents a display of the info item and the value FALSE represents no display of the item. Omission represents no change to the item.

precedents is a number that states which precedents to list. *dependents* is a number that states which dependents to list. If precedents or dependents is 0, then none are listed. If precedents or dependents is 1, then only the direct precedents or dependents are listed. If precedents or dependents is 2, then all levels are listed.

Name: EDIT.COLOR

Syntax:
EDIT.COLOR(*color_num,red_value,green_value,blue_value*);
EDIT.COLOR?(*color_num,red_value,green_value,blue_value*)

Command Equivalent: Options Color Palette

Description: Defines the color for one of the 16 color palette boxes

Arguments: *color_num* is one of the colors from the 16 color palette boxes.

red_value,green_value,blue_value are numbers that specify how much red, green, and blue value are in each color.

Name: FREEZE.PANES

Syntax: FREEZE.PANES(*logical*)

Command Equivalent: Options Freeze Panes and Unfreeze Panes (full menus)

Description: Freeze or unfreeze panes that were formerly split by a previous execution of the SPLIT function. Returns #VALUE! if no panes are set or if the active window is not a worksheet or a macro sheet.

Arguments: If *logical* is TRUE, the function is equivalent to the Options Freeze Panes command. If logical is FALSE, the function is equivalent to the Options Unfreeze Panes command.

Name: PRECISION

Syntax: PRECISION(*logical*)

Command Equivalent: Options Calculation

Description: Controls the storage space of values.

Arguments: *logical* corresponds to the Precision As Displayed check box. If logical is TRUE, values are stored exactly as they are displayed. If logical is FALSE, values are stored with a full 15 digits of accuracy.

Notes: The Precision As Displayed check box and its corresponding logical value do not affect numbers in General format. Function PRECISION may permanently alter your data with its limitations on storage.

Name: PROTECT.DOCUMENT

Syntax:
PROTECT.DOCUMENT(*contents,windows,password,objects*);
PROTECT.DOCUMENT?(*contents,windows,password,objects*)

Command Equivalent: Options Protect Document, Options Unprotect Document, Chart Protect Document, or Chart Unprotect Document, depending upon what type of document is active

Description: Adds or removes protection from the active worksheet, macro sheet, or chart

Arguments: The following three logical values correspond to check boxes, where a value of TRUE corresponds to an on check box and a value of FALSE corresponds to an off check box:

contents corresponds to the Cells check box. If TRUE or not included, then the entire active document is protected (in the case of a worksheet, the cells are protected). If FALSE and the given password is correct, then protection is removed from the entire active document.

windows corresponds to the Windows check box. If TRUE, then windows cannot be moved or sized. If FALSE and the given password is correct, then windows are free to be moved or sized after this function is applied.

objects corresponds to the Objects check box and applies only to worksheets and macro sheets. If TRUE, then all locked objects on worksheets or macro sheets are locked or protected. If FALSE, then all locked objects on worksheets or macro sheets are neither locked nor protected.

password is a password in text form. If password is not included, then anyone will be able to unprotect the document without a password; and when you try to unprotect a protected document, the function displays the normal Password dialog box. Regarding macros, passwords are not recorded when you run the macro recorder. And if password is specified, the Password dialog box is still displayed when you run the macro. Re-enter it to verify it.

Notes: If all three logical values (contents, windows, and objects) are FALSE, then PROTECT.DOCUMENT carries out the Unprotect Document command. The following commands can be used on unprotected (unlocked) cells in a worksheet: Edit Copy, Edit Paste, Edit Fill Right, Edit Fill Down, Formula Paste Name, and Formula Paste Function.

Name: REMOVE.PAGE.BREAK

Syntax: REMOVE.PAGE.BREAK( )

Command Equivalent: Options Remove Page Break

Description: Removes manual page breaks that you set with SET.PAGE.BREAK function or its equivalent command. No action occurs if the active cell is not to the right of or below the manual page break.

Notes: REMOVE.PAGE.BREAK does not remove automatic page breaks.

Name: SET.PAGE.BREAK

Syntax: SET.PAGE.BREAK( )

Command Equivalent: Options Set Page Break (full menus)

Description: Sets manual page breaks for a printed worksheet. Overrides automatic page breaks and changes later page breaks.

Name: SET.PRINT.AREA

Syntax: SET.PRINT.AREA( )

Command Equivalent: Options Set Print Area

Description: Sets up or defines the area to be printed. Use the function PRINT or the File Print command to print the selection.

Notes: If you set a print area that is a multiple selection, the areas are printed in the same order that they were selected.

Name: SET.PRINT.TITLES

Syntax: SET.PRINT.TITLES( )

Command Equivalent: Options Set Print Titles (full menus)

Description: Sets up or defines the current selection as the titles in the document that will be printed

Notes: The selection must consist of entire rows or columns.

Name: SHORT.MENUS

Syntax: SHORT.MENUS(*logical*)

Command Equivalent: Options Short Menus or Options Full Menu; Chart Short Menus or Chart Full Menu

Description: Sets up the active document with short or full menus

Arguments: If *logical* is TRUE or not included, then short menus are displayed. If logical is FALSE, then full menus are displayed.

Name: STANDARD.FONT

Syntax:
STANDARD.FONT(*font_text,size_num,bold,italic,underline,strike, color,outline,shadow*)

Command Equivalent: Options Standard Font

Description: Sets the attributes of the standard font (or Normal style) for the active worksheet or macro sheet. For more information on defining and applying styles, see the DEFINE.STYLE and APPLY.STYLE functions under "Macro Functions That Perform Format Commands." In the same section FORMAT.FONT has information on font_text, size_num, bold, italic, underline, strike, color, outline, and shadow. (font_text is the same as name_text.)

Notes: STANDARD.FONT is equivalent to using the DEFINE.STYLE and APPLY.STYLE functions. STANDARD.FONT is included for compatibility with earlier versions of Excel.

Name: WORKSPACE

Syntax:
WORKSPACE(*fixed,decimals,r1c1,scroll,status,formula, menu_key, remote,entermove,underlines,tools,notes,nav_keys, menu_key_action*);
WORKSPACE?(*fixed,decimals,r1c1,scroll,status,formula, menu_key,remote,entermove,underlines,tools,notes,nav_keys, menu_key_action*)

Command Equivalent: Options Workspace

Description: Changes the workspace settings for a document

Arguments: All of the following values: fixed, r1c1, scroll, status, formula, remote, entermove, tools, notes, and nav_keys, are logical values that correspond to check boxes. An "on" check box is represented by TRUE, and an "off" check box is represented by FALSE.

fixed corresponds to the Fixed Decimal check box.

decimals is a number that specifies the number of decimal places. It is ignored if fixed is FALSE or not included.

r1c1 corresponds to the R1C1 check box.

scroll corresponds to the Scroll Bars check box.

status corresponds to the Status Bar check box.

formula corresponds to the Formula Bar check box.

menu_key is a text value that corresponds to the Alternate Menu Or Help Key box. The value of menu_key is your choice of an alternate key that can be used to access the menu.

remote corresponds to the Ignore Remote Requests check box.

entermove corresponds to the Move Selection After Enter/Return check box.

underlines is available only for Excel on the Macintosh.

tools corresponds to the Tool Bar check box.

notes corresponds to the Note Indicator check box.

nav_keys corresponds to the Alternate Navigation Keys check box.

menu_key_action specifies whether to use Excel menus or Lotus 1-2-3 Help.

If menu_key_action Is	Then the Alternate Menu or Help Key Activates
1 or not included	Microsoft Excel menus
2	Lotus 1-2-3 Help

Macro Functions That Perform Window Commands

Macro functions that perform Window commands perform the exact same operations as the Window commands do in a worksheet or chart. In a macro sheet you may want to use the commands that are normally available in any worksheet. The macro functions are designed to allow you to activate any *command, activity,* or *operation* in a worksheet by using a nonactive macro function in a macro sheet.

The following command-equivalent macro functions are specific macro functions *that you can use in a macro sheet*.

Name: ARRANGE.ALL

Syntax: ARRANGE.ALL( )

Command Equivalent: Window Arrange All

Description: Rearranges and opens windows so that all windows are displayed at the same time

Name: HIDE

Syntax: HIDE( )

Command Equivalent: Window Hide

Description: Hides the active window

Notes: HIDE can be used to speed up your macro.

Name: NEW.WINDOW

Syntax: NEW.WINDOW( )

Command Equivalent: Window New Window

Description: Creates a new window for the active worksheet or macro sheet. An error results if the active document is a chart or a window that is part of a workgroup.

Notes: You can use MOVE, SIZE, and ARRANGE.ALL to position the new window.

Name: SHOW.CLIPBOARD

Syntax: SHOW.CLIPBOARD( )

Command Equivalent: In Excel for Windows, equivalent to running the Clipboard application from the Control menu. In OS/2, equivalent to Window Show Clipboard command.

Description: Displays the contents of the Clipboard in a new window

Notes: The Clipboard must already be on the desktop if you want to display its contents in a new window. If not available, run SHOW.CLIPBOARD twice. To close the Clipboard, use CLOSE.

Name: SHOW.INFO

Syntax: SHOW.INFO(*logical*)

Command Equivalent: Window Show Info

Description: Controls the display of the info window

Arguments: If *logical* is TRUE, the info window is activated. If logical is FALSE and the info window is the current window, then the document linked to the info window is activated.

Notes: Before using SHOW.INFO, use ACTIVATE and SELECT or FORMULA.GOTO to select the cell or range that you want information about.

Name: UNHIDE

Syntax: UNHIDE(*window_text*)

Command Equivalent: Window Unhide

Description: Displays hidden windows

Arguments: *window_text* is the name of the window to display (or unhide).

Notes: #VALUE! is returned and the macro is interrupted if window_text is not the name of an open document. Windows of add-in documents cannot be hidden.

Name: WORKGROUP

Syntax: WORKGROUP(*name_array*)

Command Equivalent: Window Workgroup

Description: Creates a workgroup

Arguments: *name_array* is a text list of open, unhidden worksheets and macro sheets that you want to collect into a workgroup. (Charts cannot be included.) If name_array is not included, then the most recently created workgroup is recreated. If name_array is not included and there is no recently created workgroup in the current session, then all open, unhidden worksheets are created as a workgroup.

Notes: #VALUE! is returned and the macro interrupted if none of the documents in name_array is found or if any of the documents in name_array is a chart.

Macro Functions—Control

Control macro functions control the flow of execution of macros and the flow of data and information between and among macros and documents. Control macro functions do not perform actions. They direct which cell of the macro formulas Excel goes to when executing the macro.

Name: ARGUMENT

Syntax:
ARGUMENT(*name_text,data_type_num*);
ARGUMENT(*name_text,data_type_num,reference*)

Description: Describes the arguments used in a custom function (a type of macro) or subroutine. (The *arguments* of a function are the values that the user of the function supplies to the function. For example, name_text and data_type_num are arguments of this function, ARGUMENT.) A custom function or subroutine must contain at least one ARGUMENT function for each argument or required value in a macro function.

Arguments: You specify the name of the argument with the *name_text* value and the type of value with *data_type_num*. data_type_num is 1 for number, 2 for text, 4 for a logical value, 8 for a reference, 16 for an error, and 64 for an array. For values that are a type which is a combination of these values, add together all the corresponding numbers that represent each of these types to get the final number for data_type_num. (For example, if a value can be either a number or text, then data_type_num is 3.)

Name: BREAK

Syntax: BREAK()

Description: Interrupts a FOR-NEXT, a FOR.CELL-NEXT, or a WHILE-NEXT loop. The execution of the function BREAK causes the macro to stop executing the loop and proceed to execute the statement that follows the NEXT statement at the end of the current loop.

Name: ELSE

Syntax: ELSE()

Description: In conjunction with the functions IF (the for-macro-sheets-only form of IF), ELSE.IF, and END.IF, ELSE controls which functions are executed in a macro. If the results of all preceding groups of IF and ELSE.IF statements are FALSE, then the formulas between the ELSE function and the END.IF function are executed. ELSE must be in a cell by itself.

Name: ELSE.IF

Syntax: ELSE.IF(*logical_test*)

Description: In conjunction with the functions IF (the for-macro-sheets-only form), ELSE, and END.IF, ELSE.IF controls which functions are executed in a macro. If the results of all preceding groups of IF and ELSE.IF statements are FALSE, then the ELSE.IF function is executed.

Arguments: If *logical_test* is TRUE, then the functions grouped with that END.IF (the functions between that ELSE.IF and the next ELSE.IF, ELSE, or END.IF function) are executed. If logical_test is FALSE, then the sequence of execution goes to the next ELSE.IF, ELSE, or END.IF function. ELSE.IF must be in a cell by itself.

Name: END.IF

Syntax: END.IF( )

Description: END.IF is used in conjunction with the functions IF (the for-macro-sheets-only form of IF), ELSE.IF, and ELSE. END.IF marks the ending of the block of functions that are grouped with the preceding IF function.

Name: ERROR

Syntax: ERROR(*enable_logical,macro_ref*)

Description: Stipulates what action is taken if an error is encountered when a macro is running.

Arguments: If *enable_logical* is FALSE or 0, all errors are ignored. If enable_logical is TRUE or 1, then *macro_ref* is run if it is included, or normal checking occurs if macro_ref is not included. If enable_logical is 2, then macro_ref is run if it is included, or normal checking occurs if macro_ref is not included, and if the Cancel button is chosen in an alert message, then FALSE is returned and the macro is not interrupted.

Name: EXEC

Syntax: EXEC(*program_text,window_num*)

Description: Starts the program named by the text given in *program_text*. If *window_num* is 1, then the window containing the program that is run appears at normal size. A window_num of 2 or an omission of this value minimizes the window size. A window_num of 3 maximizes the window size.

Name: EXECUTE

Syntax: EXECUTE(*channel_num,execute_text*)

Description: Executes or carries out commands in another program

Arguments: A previously run INITIATE function returns the numerical value *channel_num*.

Execute_text is text in quotes that represents commands that you want to carry out. An error value of #VALUE! refers to an invalid channel_num, #REF! refusal of the request, #N/A that the program you are accessing is busy, and #DIV/0! that you pressed Esc after waiting for a response.

Name: FCLOSE

Syntax: FCLOSE(*file_num*)

Description: Closes the file_specified by *file_num*. The FOPEN function returns a file_num value.

Name: FOPEN

Syntax: FOPEN(*file_text,access_num*)

Description: Opens the file named by the text value *file_text* and returns a number that represents that file. FOPEN does not load the file into memory and display it. Instead, FOPEN returns a number that is used in other functions to represent that open file. If the *access_num* value is 1, the file is opened for reading and writing. If the access_num value is 2, the file is opened for reading only. If the access_num value is 3, a new file is opened for reading and writing.

Name: FOR

Syntax: FOR(*counter_text,start_num,end_num,step_num*)

Description: Starts a FOR-NEXT loop

Arguments: The *counter_text* text value is the name of the variable that keeps the current count. The loop starts at the number specified by *start_num* and ends at the number specified by *end_num*. Each time through the loop, the number given for *step_num* is added to the current count kept track of in the name given by counter_text. If step_num is not included, 1 is assumed.

Name: FOR.CELL

Syntax: FOR.CELL(*ref_name,area_ref,skip_blanks*)

Description: Starts a FOR.CELL-NEXT loop, where the instructions between FOR.CELL and NEXT are repeated over a range of cells, one cell at a time

Arguments: *ref_name* is the cell currently being operated on. *area_ref* is the area of cells that the loop operates on. And a value of TRUE for *skip_blanks* results in skipping blank cells in area_ref. FALSE or omission results in not skipping blank cells.

Name: FPOS

Syntax: FPOS(*file_num,position_num*)

Description: Sets the position of a file for other functions such as FREAD and FWRITE

Arguments: The numerical value *file_num* is the ID number of the open file opened by FOPEN.

position_num, the position in the file, is specified in character units. Position_num can range from 1 for the first character to the size of the file as given by the FSIZE function.

Name: FREAD

Syntax: FREAD(*file_num,num_chars*)

Description: From the current position in the file, FREAD reads *num_chars* number of characters from the file specified by *file_num.* (The numerical value file_num is the ID number of the open file opened by FOPEN.)

Name: FREADLN

Syntax: FREADLN(*file_num*)

Description: FREAD reads from the current position in the file specified by *file_num* to the end of the file specified by file_num. (The numerical value file_num is the ID number of the open file opened by FOPEN.)

Name: FSIZE

Syntax: FSIZE(*file_num*)

Description: Returns the number of characters in a file (which is the same as the position of the last character in the file)

Arguments: The numerical value *file_num* is the ID number of the open file opened by FOPEN.

Name: FWRITE

Syntax: FWRITE(*file_num,text*)

Description: From the current position in the file, FWRITE writes the *text* value into the file specified by *file_num.* (The numerical value file_num is the ID number of the open file opened by FOPEN.)

Name: FWRITELN

Syntax: FWRITELN(*file_num,text*)

Description: From the current position in the file, FWRITE writes the *text* value, followed by a carriage return and line feed, into the file specified by *file_num*. (The numerical value file_num is the ID number of the open file opened by FOPEN.)

Name: GOTO

Syntax: GOTO(*reference*)

Description: Makes the upper-left cell of *reference* the next function to be executed. The value *reference* can be an external reference.

Name: HALT

Syntax: HALT(*cancel_close*)

Description: Stops all macros from running

Arguments: If *cancel_close* is TRUE, then the macro is stopped and the closing of documents is prevented. If cancel_close is FALSE, then the macro is stopped and the closing of documents is allowed. If cancel_close is in a macro that does not have Auto_close, then the macro only stops.

Name: IF

Syntax: IF(*logical_test*)

Description: IF (for macro-sheets-only form) may be used in conjunction with the functions ELSE, ELSE.IF, and END.IF. IF controls which functions are executed in a macro.

Arguments: If *logical_test* is TRUE, then the functions between the IF function and the next ELSE.IF, ELSE, or END.IF function are executed. If logical_test is FALSE, then the sequence of execution goes to the next ELSE.IF, ELSE, or END.IF function. IF must be in a cell by itself.

Name: INITIATE

Syntax: INITIATE(*app_text,topic_text*)

Description: Opens a DDE channel to an application and returns the number of that open channel. See "EXECUTE" above and "SEND.KEYS" below.

Arguments: The DDE name of the application is *app_text*, and *topic_text* is the description of something that you are accessing.

Name: INPUT

Syntax: INPUT(*message_text,type_num,title_text,default,x_pos,y_pos*)

Description: Displays a dialog box. The dialog box is in the position specified by *x_pos* and *y_pos*. It has the title that is specified by *title_text* and contains the words inside the dialog box which are specified in *message_text*. The type of value that can be inputted is specified by *type_num*. And *default* is the value that is automatically given if the user does not input a value.

Type_num is a number that represents a type. The values 0, 1, 2, 4, 8, 16, and 64 represent respectively a formula, a number, text, a logical value, a reference, an error, and an array. If a value can be more than one type, then add the corresponding numbers for those types.

Name: NEXT

Syntax: NEXT( )

Description: Marks the end of a FOR-NEXT, FOR.CELL-NEXT, or WHILE-NEXT loop. Once the loop is finished executing, the macro continues immediately after the NEXT() function.

Name: ON.DATA

Syntax: ON.DATA(*document_text,macro_text*)

Description: Starts the macro specified by *macro_text* when data is sent to the document named in *document_text* or data is received from the document specified by document_text

Name: ON.KEY

Syntax: ON.KEY(*key_text,macro_text*)

Description: Runs the macro specified by *macro_text* when the key or key combination specified by *key_text* is pressed. (Key combinations can be created with Alt, Ctr, and/or Shift.)

Name: ON.RECALC

Syntax: ON.RECALC(*sheet_text,macro_text*)

Description: Runs the macro specified by *macro_text* when the sheet named by *sheet_text* is recalculated. Only one ON.RECALC function per each recalculation is allowed.

Name: ON.TIME

Syntax: ON.TIME(*time,macro_text,tolerance,insert_logical*)

Description: Runs the macro specified by *macro_text* at the time specified by *time*. *Time* is a serial number that specifies the date and time. (See worksheet function "DATE" and related functions.) If Excel is not in the needed mode when the time value comes up, then the *tolerance* value specifies the time to stop waiting. Not including *tolerance* makes it such that the macro_text macro runs as soon as possible after the specified time. If *insert_logical* is TRUE, macro_text runs at *time*. If it is FALSE and macro_text macro is not set to run, then ON.TIME returns the error #VALUE!.

Name: ON.WINDOW

Syntax: ON.WINDOW(*window_text,macro_text*)

Description: Runs the macro specified by *macro_text* when the window named by *window_text* is activated

Name: POKE

Syntax: POKE(*channel_num,item_text,data_ref*)

Description: Sends the data specified by the *data_ref* reference (cell(s) or document) to another application, which is specified by *channel_num*. (The numerical value channel_num is returned by the INITIATE function.) The value *item_text* specifies the application that you are accessing with channel_num. An error value of #VALUE! refers to an invalid channel_num, #REF! refusal of the request, and #DIV/0! that you pressed Esc after waiting for a response.

Name: REGISTER

Syntax:
REGISTER(*module_text,procedure_text,type_text,function_text, argument_text*)

Description: REGISTER 1) makes accessible to Excel the procedure specified by *procedure_text* in the dynamic link library or resource code that is specified by *module_text* and 2) returns the number that identifies the code so that it can be used by CALL and UNREGISTER. The value *type_text* specifies the data types of the return value and values specified in *argument_text*. You can specify the name and arguments of the function you are registering. The values *function_text* and *argument_text* are the names in text form of the function and arguments (or values that go into the function). For more information, see the Microsoft Excel Function Reference manual, Appendix A, "Using the CALL and REGISTER Functions."

Name: REQUEST

Syntax: REQUEST(*channel_num,item_text*)

Description: Requests from the application that is specified by the *channel_num* value, an array of a specific type of information that is specified by the *item_text* code. (The numerical value *channel_num* is returned by the INITIATE function.) An error value of #VALUE! refers to an invalid channel_num, #REF! refusal of the request, #N/A that the program you are accessing is busy, and #DIV/0! that you pressed Esc after waiting for a response.

Name: RESTART

Syntax: RESTART(*level_num*)

Description: Restarts macro calls by eliminating *level_num* number of RETURN statements from the stack. (When one macro calls another macro, the RETURN statement at the end of the second macro returns control to the macro that called it.) If level_num is not included, then the next RETURN that is encountered will halt macro execution.

Name: RESULT

Syntax: RESULT(*type_num*)

Description: Sets the type of data that a custom function or subrouting returns

Arguments: A value of 1, 2, 4, 8, 16, and 64 for *type_num* represents, respectively, a number, text, a logical value, a reference, an error, and an array. If the result value is more than one type, then add the corresponding numbers for all the types it is.

Name: RETURN

Syntax: RETURN(*value*)

Description: Ends the currently running macro and returns any value that is included with the function. If no value is included, then it just ends the currently running macro. Command macros run by the user do not return values. Control is returned to the caller: the calling macro, the calling formula, or the calling user.

Name: SEND.KEYS

Syntax: SEND.KEYS(*key_text,wait_logical*)

Description: Sends keystrokes to the active document in the same manner as if they were typed on the keyboard

Arguments: *key_text* is the key or key combination that is sent to another application.

If *wait_logical* is TRUE, Excel waits for the keys to be processed before returning control to the macro; otherwise, it does not wait.

Name: SET.NAME

Syntax: SET.NAME(*name_text,value*)

Description: Defines the *name_text* name on a macro sheet to refer to the value called *value*. If *value* is not included, then name_text is deleted.

Name: SET.VALUE

Syntax: SET VALUE(*reference,values*)

Description: Changes the value of the cell or cells that are specified by *reference* to the value or values that are specified by *values*. This change occurs without changing any formulas entered in the cells.

Name: STEP

Syntax: STEP( )

Description: Changes the normal flow of macro execution to the step mode of execution where the macro runs one cell at a time. In this mode, a dialog box displays the current cell in the macro and the formula that is about to be calculated, and allows you to control the flow: taking one step at a time or continuous, without single-stepping.

Name: TERMINATE

Syntax: TERMINATE(*channel_num*)

Description: Closes the DDE channel specified by *channel_num*, which was previously opened with the INITIATE function

Name: UNREGISTER

Syntax: UNREGISTER(*register_number*)

Description: Removes the dynamic link library or code resource represented by *register_number*, the value returned from the REGISTER function. The UNREGISTER function frees memory after you are finished using the specified resources.

Name: VOLATILE

Syntax: VOLATILE( )

Description: Specifies that a custom function is volatile or recalculated every time a calculation occurs on the worksheet

Name: WAIT

Syntax: WAIT(*serial_number*)

Description: Pauses the macro until the time specified by *serial_number*. See the worksheet function "NOW" for more information.

Name: WHILE

Syntax: WHILE(*logical_test*)

Description: Executes the statements between the WHILE function and the corresponding NEXT function that comes after it, until the value of *logical_test* is FALSE

Macro Functions—Customizing

Customizing macro functions allows you to add or remove custom-designed and built-in menu bars, menus, commands, help information, and dialog boxes on your worksheet, macro sheet, or chart.

Name: ADD.BAR

Syntax: ADD.BAR(*bar_num*)

Description: Creates a new menu bar and returns the bar ID number or restores an old menu bar

Arguments: *bar_num* is the number of a built-in menu bar that you want to restore.

Notes: A new menu bar is created but not displayed with ADD.BAR. See "SHOW.BAR" below.

Name: ADD.COMMAND

Syntax: ADD.COMMAND(*bar_num,menu,command_ref,position*)

Description: Adds a command to a menu or restores a deleted built-in command to its original menu

Arguments: *bar_num* is the number of the menu bar that you want to add a command to.

menu is the menu to which you want to add the new command.

command_ref is a reference to an area on the macro sheet that describes the new command or commands.

position is the placement of the new command.

If bar_num Is	*Then Built-in Menu Bar Is a*
1	Worksheet or macro sheet menu bar (full menus)
2	Chart menu bar (full menus)
3	Null menu bar — no active document

If bar_num Is	Then Built-in Menu Bar Is a
4	Info menu bar
5	Worksheet or macro sheet menu bar (short menus)
6	Chart menu bar (short menu)

Name: ADD.MENU

Syntax: ADD.MENU(*bar_num,menu_ref,position*)

Description: Adds a menu to a menu bar or restores built-in menus

Arguments: *bar_num* is the number of the menu bar that you want to add a menu to.

menu_ref is a reference to an area on the macro sheet that describes the new menu or name of the deleted built-in menu that you want to restore.

position is the placement of the new menu. Menus are numbered from left to right starting with 1. See "ADD.COMMAND" above for a list of values for bar_num.

Name: ALERT

Syntax: ALERT(*message_text,type_num*)

Description: Displays a dialog box and message and waits for you to choose a button

Arguments: *message_text* is the message surrounded by quotes that is displayed in the dialog box.

type_num specifies the type of dialog box to display. A type_num of 1 stands for a dialog box with OK and Cancel buttons. A type_num of 2 or 3 stands for a dialog box with an OK button. A type_num of 2 has a different icon at the left than a type_num of 3.

Name: CALL

Syntax: Form 1, used with a register:
CALL(*register_ref,argument1,...*)

Form 2, used alone:
CALL(*module_text,procedure_text,type_text,argument1,...*)

Description: Calls a procedure in a dynamic link library or code resource. Use cautiously. If it is used incorrectly, CALL can accidentally cause errors in the systems operation.

Arguments: *register_ref* is returned by a previously executed REGISTER function. For more information, see the REGISTER function and Appendix A, "Using the CALL and REGISTER Functions" in the Microsoft Excel Function Reference manual.

argument1,... are arguments that the procedure accepts.

The second form uses the arguments to the REGISTER function and simultaneously calls and registers a code resource. See function "REGISTER" for a description of module_text, procedure_text, and type_text arguments.

Name: CANCEL.KEY

Syntax: CANCEL.KEY(*enable,macro_ref*)

Description: Does not allow a macro to be interrupted or specifies a macro to run when the current macro is interrupted

Arguments: The logical value *enable* specifies whether a macro can be interrupted by the Esc key (TRUE) or not (FALSE). If *enable* is TRUE and *macro_ref* is included, then the macro that is specified by macro_ref (by name or as a cell reference) is executed when Esc is pressed.

Name: CHECK.COMMAND

Syntax: CHECK.COMMAND(*bar_num,menu,command,check*)

Description: Adds (chooses a command) or removes (unchooses) a check mark from a command name on a menu. The command you add or remove is specified by the value of command, which is in the menu that is specified by the value of *menu*. And the specified menu is in the bar_num menu bar.

Arguments: *bar_num* is a number. But *menu* and *command* can be either the number that represents the desired menu or command or the name of the menu or command.

Check is a logical value that specifies TRUE for adding the check mark and command and FALSE for removing the check mark and command.

Name: CUSTOM.REPEAT

Syntax: CUSTOM.REPEAT(*macro_text,repeat_text,record_text*)

Description: Creates an Edit Repeat command for custom commands and allows the macro recorder to record custom commands

Arguments: The text for the Edit Repeat command is *repeat_text*. When the Edit Repeat command is run, the macro referenced by *macro_text* is run. And *record_text* is the formula that is recorded. Similar to CUSTOM.UNDO.

Name: CUSTOM.UNDO

Syntax: CUSTOM.UNDO(*macro_text,undo_text*)

Description: Creates an Edit Undo command for custom commands

Arguments: The text for the Edit Undo command is *undo_text*. When the Edit Undo command is run, the macro referenced by *macro_text* is run.

Name: DELETE.BAR

Syntax: DELETE.BAR(*bar_num*)

Description: Deletes the custom bar specified by bar_num

bar_num is a number that specifies which menu bar.

Name: DELETE.COMMAND

Syntax: DELETE.COMMAND(*bar_num,menu,command*)

Description: Deletes the command specified by the value of *command*, which is in the *bar_num* menu bar and in the menu that is specified by the value of menu

Arguments: *bar_num* is a number. But *menu* and *command* can be either the number that represents the desired menu or command or the name of the menu or command.

Name: DELETE.MENU

Syntax: DELETE.MENU(*bar_num,menu*)

Description: Deletes the menu that is in the bar_num menu bar and is specified by the value of menu that you give the function

Arguments: *bar_num* is a number. But *menu* and *command* can be either the number that represents the desired menu or the name of the menu.

Name: DIALOG.BOX

Syntax: DIALOG.BOX(*dialog_ref*)

Description: Displays the dialog box that you describe in the *dialog_ref* range of cells in your macro sheet or worksheet. This definition must be a table that is at least seven columns wide and two rows high.

Columns one through seven describe, respectively, the item number, horizontal position, vertical position, item width, item height, text, and initial value or result. The first row describes the size, position type, and name of the dialog box. The remaining rows of dialog_ref describe the items in the rows of the dialog box.

The remaining rows of this table contain numbers 1 through 22, which respectively represent dialog box items: default OK button, cancel button, OK button, default cancel button, static text, text edit box, integer edit box, number edit box, formula edit box, reference edit box, option button group, option button, check box, group box, list box, linked list box, icons, linked file list box, linked drive and directory box, directory text box, drop-down list box, and drop-down combination edit/list box.

Name: DISABLE.INPUT

Syntax: DISABLE.INPUT(*logical*)

Description: Blocks or unblocks all input from the keyboard and mouse to Excel (except for input to visible dialog boxes)

Arguments: If *logical* is TRUE, then DISABLE.INPUT blocks all input from the keyboard and mouse to Excel. If it is FALSE, input is unblocked or enabled.

Name: ECHO

Syntax: ECHO(*logical*)

Description: Controls screen updating when a macro is run

Arguments: If *logical* is TRUE, then screen updating is turned on. If *logical* is FALSE, then screen updating is turned off. If *logical* is not included, then screen updating is switched from off to on or from on to off.

Name: ENABLE.COMMAND

Syntax: ENABLE.COMMAND(*bar_num,menu,command,enable*)

Description: Enables (allows the use of) a command or disables (disallows the use of) a command on a menu. The command you enable or disable is specified by the value of *command*, which is in the bar_num menu bar and in the menu that is specified by the value of *menu*.

Arguments: *bar_num* is a number. But *menu* and *command* can be either the number that represents the desired menu or command or the name of the menu or command. Enable is a logical value that specifies TRUE for enabling the command and FALSE for disabling the command.

Name: GET.BAR

Syntax: GET.BAR( ); GET.BAR(*bar_num,menu,command*)

Description: The first form, which has no values to specify, returns the number of the active menu bar. The second form returns the name or position number of the command specified by the value of *command,* which is in the menu that is specified by the value of *menu,* which is in the menu bar specified by bar_num.

Arguments: *bar_num* is a number. But *menu* and *command* can be either the number that represents the desired menu or command or the name of the menu or command.

Name: HELP

Syntax: HELP(*file_text!topic_num*)

Description: Starts the Help command and displays the custom Help topic specified by file_text!topic_num

Arguments: *file_text!topic_num* is quoted text that gives the name of a text file (text_file) followed by an !, followed by the number of the topic in this text file.

Name: MESSAGE

Syntax: MESSAGE(*logical,text*)

Description: Displays and removes messages in the message area of the status bar

Arguments: If *logical* is TRUE, then messages are displayed in the status bar. If *logical* is FALSE, then messages are removed and the status bar returns to normal.

text is the message that you want to display.

Name: RENAME.COMMAND

Syntax: RENAME.COMMAND(*bar_num,menu,command,name_text*)

Description: Changes the name of a menu or the name of a built-in or custom menu command. *command* specifies the command that you want to rename. This command is in the menu that is specified by the value of *menu,* which is in the menu bar specified by bar_num. If the value of *command* is 0, then the menu is renamed rather than the command.

Arguments: *bar_num* is a number. But *menu* and *command* can be either the number that represents the desired menu or command or the name of the menu or command.

name_text is the new name for the command or menu.

Name: SHOW.BAR

Syntax: SHOW.BAR(*bar_num*)

Description: Displays the menu bar that is specified by bar_num

Arguments: *bar_num* is the number that the ADD.BAR function returns when it adds a menu bar. (SHOW.BAR is used after ADD.BAR, since ADD.BAR does not display the menu bar that it adds.) See function "ADD.BAR" above for a full listing of what each value of bar_num represents.

Macro Functions—Value Returning

Value-returning macro functions return a value or manipulate information in your spreadsheet. Value-returning macro functions do not perform any actions. They give you information about various aspects of your Excel documents.

Name: ABSREF

Syntax: ABSREF(*ref_text,reference*)

Description: Returns the absolute reference of the cells specified by *reference* that are offset by the value specified by *ref_text*. The ref_text value must be an R1C1-style relative reference in text form, for example, "R[1]C[1]".

Name: ACTIVE.CELL

Syntax: ACTIVE.CELL( )

Description: Returns the address or reference of the active cell (or the cell where the cursor is) in the selection as an external reference. #N/A results if an object or chart is selected.

Name: CALLER

Syntax: CALLER( )

Description: CALLER returns information about the cell or range of cells that called the custom function that is currently running. CALLER is used in combination with other functions and only inside a custom function or an Auto_Open or Auto_Close macro. If the custom function is entered in a single cell, then CALLER returns the address of that cell. If the custom function is part of an array formula that is entered in a range of cells, then CALLER returns the address of that range of cells. If CALLER is in a macro that was called by an Auto_Open or Auto_Close macro, then it returns the name of the sheet that called the

Auto_Open or Auto_Close macro. If CALLER is in a macro that was called by an assigned-to-object macro, it returns the object identifier. #REF! is returned when the currently running macro is a command macro called or started by the user.

Name: DEREF

Syntax: DEREF(*reference*)

Description: Returns the value/values of the cell/cells in the specified reference. *reference* must be an absolute reference if it refers to an active sheet.

Name: DIRECTORY

Syntax: DIRECTORY(*path_text*)

Description: Sets the current drive and directory or folder to the specified *path_text*. If included, the value path_text must be in quotes. If it is not included, the name of the current directory or folder is returned in text form.

Name: DOCUMENTS

Syntax: DOCUMENTS(*type_num*)

Description: Returns a horizontal array of the names of all open documents in alphabetical order and in quoted text form

Arguments: If *type_num* is 1 or not included, the names of all open documents, except add-in documents, are returned. If type_num is 2, only the names of all add-in documents are returned. If type_num is 3, the names of all open documents are returned.

Name: FILES

Syntax: FILES(*directory_text*)

Description: Returns a horizontal array of the names of all files in the directory or folder that is specified by *directory_text*. Wild-card characters * and ? can be used in directory_text.

Name: GET.CELL

Syntax: GET.CELL(*type_num,reference*)

Description: Returns information about the formatting, location, or contents of the cell in the upper-left corner of the first area in the specified value *reference* or in the current selection. The type of information that is returned is specified by *type_num*, a numerical value that can range from 1 to 40. For information about the 40 different types of information that type_num can specify, see the Microsoft Excel Function Reference manual.

Name: GET.CHART.ITEM

Syntax: GET.CHART.ITEM(*x_y_index,point_index,item_text*)

Description: Returns the position of a point on a chart item

Arguments: If x_y_index is 1, GET.CHART.ITEM returns the horizontal position of the point. If x_y_index is 2, it returns the vertical position of the point. The point whose position is returned is specified by *point_index*. The *item_text* value is a code that specifies which item on the chart to select. If the selected item is anything other than a line, then point_index specifies a point that is in the upper, middle, or lower position and to the left or right. Arrows are divided into 1 for the shaft and 2 for the head. A pie is divided into outermost, counter clockwise or clockwise, midpoints, and center points. If point_index is not included, 1 is assumed. For information about point_text, see the Microsoft Excel Function Reference manual.

Name: GET.DEF

Syntax: GET.DEF(*def_text,document_text,type_num*)

Description: Returns the name (in text form) of the specified *def_text* reference (in text form). In order to allow def_text to be in another document, the document that def_text is in is specified by *document_text*. If *type_num* is 1 or not included, then only normal names are returned. If type_num is 2, only hidden names are returned. If type_num is 3, then all names are returned.

Name: GET.DOCUMENT

Syntax: GET.DOCUMENT(*type_num,name_text*)

Description: Returns information about the open document named by *name_text*. If name_text is not included, then the active document is assumed. The type of information that is returned is specified by *type_num*. For information about the 48 different types of information that type_num can specify, see the Microsoft Excel Function Reference manual.

Name: GET.FORMULA

Syntax: GET.FORMULA(*reference*)

Description: As it would appear in the formula bar, GET.FORMULA returns the text form of the contents of the cell that is specified by the value *reference*.

Name: GET.LINK.INFO

Syntax: GET.LINK.INFO(*link_text,type_num,type_of_link,reference*)

Description: Returns the type of information specified by *type_num* about the link that is specified by *link_text*. The value link_text is the pathname of the link as viewed in the File Links dialog box. If the value type_num is 1, then 1 is returned when the link is set to automatic; 2 is returned otherwise. type_num of 2 applies only to Excel on the Macintosh. The value *reference* specifies the range in R1C1 reference-style of the publisher or subscriber that you want information about.

If type_of_link Is	Then GET.LINK.INFO Returns Information about
1	Not applicable
2	DDE links
3	Not applicable
4	Outgoing NewWave links
5	Publisher links
6	Subscriber links

Name: GET.NAME

Syntax: GET.NAME(*name_text*)

Description: Returns the definition of the specified value *name_text* as it would appear in the Refers To box of the Formula Define Name dialog box

Name: GET.NOTE

Syntax: GET.NOTE(*cell_ref,start_char,num_char*)

Description: Returns some characters from the note attached to the cell that is specified by *cell_ref*. The numerical values *start_num* and *num_char* are indices into the requested note. The characters between the position of start_num and the position of start_num plus num_char are returned.

Name: GET.OBJECT

Syntax: GET.OBJECT(*type_num,object_id_text,start_num,count_num*)

Description: Returns the specific information requested by *type_num* about the object that is specified by *object_id_text*. For information about the 40 different types of information that type_num can specify, see the Microsoft Excel Function Reference manual. The value object_id_text can be the number alone or the name and number of the object that you want information about. If the object that you want information about is a text box, the value *start_num* gives the first character in the text box specified by object_id_text, and *count_num* is the number or characters after start_num. If these character count values are not included, then values of 1 and 255 for start_num and count_num are assumed.

Name: GET.WINDOW

Syntax: GET.WINDOW(*type_num,window_text*)

Description: Returns the specific information requested by *type_num* about the window that is specified by *window_text*. For information about the 22 different types of information that type_num can specify, see the Microsoft Excel Function Reference manual. The active window is assumed if window_text is not included.

Name: GET.WORKSPACE

Syntax: GET.WORKSPACE(*type_num*)

Description: Returns the specific information requested by *type_num* about the workspace. For information about the 40 different types of information that type_num can specify, see the Microsoft Excel Function Reference manual.

Name: LAST.ERROR

Syntax: LAST.ERROR( )

Description: Returns the address of the cell where the last macro sheet error occurred. #N/A! is returned if no error has occurred.

Name: NAMES

Syntax: NAMES(*document_text,type_num*)

Description: Returns a horizontal text array of all the names that are defined in the document that is specified by the *document_text* value. If *type_num* is 1 or not included, then only normal names are returned. If type_num is 2, then only hidden names are returned. If type_num is 3, then all names are returned.

Name: REFTEXT

Syntax: REFTEXT(*reference,a1*)

Description: Returns the absolute reference text form of the specified *reference* value (an address to a cell or range of cells). To revert back into reference form, the REFTEXT function converts a reference in text form to an absolute reference. If a1 is TRUE, then REFTEXT returns an A1-style reference; otherwise, REFTEXT returns an R1C1-style reference.

Name: RELREF

Syntax: RELREF(*reference,rel_to_ref*)

Description: Returns a relative reference for the upper-left cell of the specified value *rel_to_ref*, which is relative to the specified value *reference*. The returned reference is an R1C1-style reference in text form.

Name: SELECTION

Syntax: SELECTION( )

Description: Returns the reference or object identifier of the selection as an external reference. Picture n is returned for an imported or linked graphic, a chart picture, a worksheet range, or a linked worksheet range. Chart n is returned for a linked chart. And the remaining objects (button, rectangle, etc.) return the name of the object followed by its identifying number n.

Name: TEXTREF

Syntax: TEXTREF(*text,a1*)

Description: Returns the absolute reference of the specified *text* value which is a reference (an address to a cell or range of cells). (The TEXTREF function converts from relative or absolute reference form to absolute reference text form.) If a1 is TRUE, then text is in A1-style; otherwise, text is in R1C1-style.

Name: WINDOWS

Syntax: WINDOWS(*type_num*)

Description: Returns the names of all open windows, including hidden windows, that are of the specified *type_num*. If type_num is 1 or not included, the names of all open windows, except those containing add-in documents, are returned. If type_num is 2, only the names of windows containing add-in documents are returned. If type_num is 3, the names of all open windows are returned.

Macro Assign to Object

The Assign to Object command in the Macro menu links a selected drawn object on a worksheet or macro sheet (often a macro button) with a macro. After the linking, the macro can be invoked by clicking on the object.

Keystrokes

Keyboard   *Mouse*

Macro   Macro

Assign to Object   Assign to Object

Assign Macro or Reference   Assign Macro or Reference

Enter   OK

Example

Suppose that you want to make a worksheet easy to use by staff who don't know computers very well. You create a series of macros that display custom dialog boxes to input data. Afterwards you decide to link them to macro buttons on the worksheet with button titles explaining their purpose. Create a button and when the Assign to Object dialog box comes on screen, choose the macro to link the button with. Choose OK to finish.

Assigning a Macro to an Object

1. Select the object to link with the macro.

2. Choose Assign to Object from Macro.
   If you created a macro button, this step is bypassed. Excel displays the Assign to Object dialog box.

3. Select the macro to link to in the Assign Macro box or type the macro reference in Reference.

4. Choose OK.
   Afterwards you can invoke the macro by clicking on the object.

Tip: To change the text in an object or button, you need to select it first. To avoid invoking the macro while doing this, press Ctrl as you click on it or use the object selection tool in the Toolbar. Then click on any word to change it.

Macro Record

The Record command in the Macro menu creates a macro. When you choose the command, Excel prompts you for a name and key (so that you can invoke it afterwards without using the menu). You then perform the steps that you want recorded. Afterwards choose Stop Recorder from the same position on the Macro menu.

Keystrokes

Keyboard	Mouse
Macro	Macro
Record	Record
Name	Name
Key	Key
Enter	OK
Stop Recorder	Stop Recorder

Example

Suppose that you have a worksheet that you use repeatedly to enter temporary information, and you decide that a macro that cleared certain cells would be useful. Choose Record from Macro, name the macro *Clear*, and give it the key combination Ctrl-C. Select the range of cells on the worksheet, press the Delete key, and then press Enter. Choose Stop Recorder from Macro to stop recording.

 Creating a Macro

1. Choose Record from Macro.
   Excel displays the Run dialog box, prompting you for a name and a key.

2. Accept the default name and key or enter one or both.

3. Choose OK to start recording.

4. Perform the operations on the worksheet that you want to record in a macro.

5. Choose Stop Recorder from Macro.
   Your macro is recorded.

> **Note:** After you choose Record, the same command reads Stop Recorder. Choose Stop Recorder after you finish recording and the command changes back to Record.

Macro Relative Record

When the Relative Record command displays in the Macro menu, then any cells cited in macro instructions are absolute references and vice versa. Absolute referencing means that, regardless of where the active cell is before you run the macro, the instructions always work on the same cells. With relative referencing, the instructions start from the active cell and perform further instructions relative to that cell.

Keystrokes

Keyboard   *Mouse*

Macro   Macro

Relative Record   Relative Record

Absolute   Absolute Record

Example

By default, Excel records in absolute mode. Often you will want to record a macro you can use anywhere on the worksheet. For example, suppose that you want a macro to reverse the position of adjacent columns. Choose Relative Record from Macro first and then record the macro. In the future, the macro will run from wherever you position the active cell.

 Recording in Relative and Absolute Modes

1. Choose Relative Record from Macro.

   Excel changes the command display to read Absolute Record. While this is so, all recording is done in relative mode.

2. Record any macros you need in relative mode.

3. Choose Absolute Record from Macro to change back to absolute mode.

 Tip: It's possible to change back and forth between relative and absolute modes even while you're recording a macro.

Macro Run

Use the Run command in the Macro menu to invoke a macro. Only macros that belong to macro sheets that are actually open will be available to run. The alternative to using Run is to press Ctrl and the assigned macro key.

Keystrokes

Keyboard	*Mouse*
Macro	Macro
Run	Run
Step (optional)	Step (optional)
Enter	OK

Example

Suppose that you have a macro called *Erin* in the Bright macro sheet and you want to run this macro. Choose Run from Macro and, assuming the macro sheet is open, the macro is displayed as Bright!Erin in the Run box in the dialog box. Select this macro. Choose Step if you want the macro to pause after every instruction. Choose OK to start it.

Running a Macro

1. Choose <u>R</u>un from the <u>M</u>acro menu.

   Excel displays the Run dialog box.

2. In the Run box, choose the macro that you want to run.

   Only macros on macro sheets that are actually open are available.

3. Choose <u>S</u>tep if you want the macro to pause after every instruction.

4. Choose OK to start the macro running.

> ▶ **Tip:** Use the Run option when you are unsure of the keystroke required to invoke the macro or if you don't know whether the macro sheet is open or not.

Macro Set Recorder

Use Se<u>t</u> Recorder in the <u>M</u>acro menu to indicate to Excel exactly where to place the macro instructions on the macro sheet.

Keystrokes

Keyboard	*Mouse*
<u>M</u>acro	<u>M</u>acro
Se<u>t</u> Recorder	Se<u>t</u> Recorder

Example

Suppose that you've already recorded a macro on a macro sheet and added explanatory notes in the column beside it. Now you want to record another macro and place it underneath the first macro in the same column. Select a blank cell underneath the first macro on the macro sheet. Choose Se<u>t</u> Recorder from the <u>M</u>acro menu. Now record your macro.

Defining a Macro Recorder Range

1. Select a cell or range of cells on the macro sheet where you want Excel to place the macro.

   If you select a range, the first cell should be blank.

2. Choose Set Recorder from Macro.

   This defines the recorder range to Excel.

3. Go to the worksheet and record your macro instructions.

 Note: When no recorder range is defined, Excel places a new macro in the first column of the macro sheet that is completely empty.

Macro Start Recorder

When you're in the middle of recording a macro on the worksheet using the Record command, you may wish to perform some worksheet steps that you don't want to record. In that case, choose Stop Recorder. When you want to continue recording, choose Start Recorder. (Choosing Record at this stage would indicate to Excel that you wanted to record a second macro.)

Keystrokes

Keyboard	*Mouse*
Macro	Macro
Record	Record
Stop Recorder	Stop Recorder
Start Recorder	Start Recorder
Stop Recorder	Stop Recorder

Example

Suppose that you want to record a macro that clears an area of a worksheet and then inserts a row of headings. Choose Macro and then Record, select the area, and clear it. At this stage, you notice that this particular worksheet has data in cells that you would like to clear but you don't want to record clearing them, because other worksheets won't have this data. Choose Stop Recorder, clear the cells, choose Start Recorder, and insert your headlines. Choose Stop Recorder when the macro is complete.

 ### Restarting the Recording of a Macro

1. Choose Record from the Macro menu and specify the name of the macro.

2. Perform the steps that you want to record.

3. If there are some instructions that you don't want to record, choose Stop Recorder.

4. Perform the commands that you don't want to be recorded.

5. Choose Start Recorder to restart recording the macro instructions.

6. Choose Stop Recorder when you're finished.

Your macro is recorded.

Macro Stop Recorder

(*see* Macro Record and Macro Start Recorder)

MATCH()

(*see also* Function, HLOOKUP, VLOOKUP, LOOKUP, INDEX)

Syntax

MATCH(*lookup_value,lookup_array,match_type*)

Description

MATCH is a function that returns the position of an element in the specified lookup_array. MATCH looks for lookup_value in the one row or column of values specified by lookup_array. When lookup_value is found according to the following guidelines, then MATCH returns the position of the found or matched value in lookup_array.

    MATCH looks for lookup_value in one of three different ways, depending on what you specify for match_type. The three possible modes of looking for lookup_value follow.

match_type Is	Method of Matching lookup_value with a Value in lookup_array	Necessary Sorted Order of lookup_array
1 or not included	MATCH matches lookup_value with the next largest value in lookup_array that is less than or equal to lookup_value. (If lookup_value is smaller than the smallest value in lookup_array, MATCH returns the #N/A error.)	lookup_array *must* be in ascending order: –1, 0, 1, 2, ..., A, ..., Z, FALSE, TRUE. (Upper- and lower-case letters are equivalent.)
0	MATCH finds the first value that is exactly equal to lookup_value. (If there is no value equal to lookup_value, then MATCH returns the #N/A error.)	lookup_array can be in any order.

MATCH ()

match_type Is	Method of Matching lookup_value with a Value in lookup_array	Necessary Sorted Order of lookup_array
–1	MATCH matches lookup_value with the next smallest value in lookup_array that is greater than or equal to lookup_value. (If lookup_value is greater than the greatest value in lookup_array, MATCH returns the #N/A error.)	lookup_array *must* be in descending order: TRUE, FALSE, Z, ..., B, A, ..., 2, 1, 0, –1, –2, ..., etc. (Upper- and lowercase letters are equivalent.)

 Note: Functions LOOKUP, HLOOKUP, and VLOOKUP all find a value in an array. Function MATCH finds a position.

You can use MATCH with VLOOKUP or HLOOKUP functions when you don't know anything about the position of the value you are looking for. First, find the row or column with MATCH; then use that row or column number in VLOOKUP or HLOOKUP to find the value.

The information required for function MATCH:

lookup_value is a value that MATCH looks for in the *lookup_array*.

lookup_array is one row or column of cells that contain numbers, text, or logical values.

match_type is 1, 0 or –1. Match_type sets the mode of search for lookup_value.

Examples

Formula	Returns
=MATCH(2.39,{1,2,3,4,5},1)	2
=MATCH(2.39,{5,4,3,2,1},–1)	3
=MATCH(2,{5,2,4,1,3},0)	2
=MATCH(2.39,{5,4,3,2,1},0)	#N/A
=MATCH("Rz",{"Cream";"Red";"White"},1)	2
=MATCH("z",{"Cream";"Red";"White"})	3

The example in the figure uses both MATCH and HLOOKUP. Since you know that you want a name from your table, you can use function HLOOKUP with the lookup_value of "name". This gives you the column position of the information you want. You can find the row where a person has Level O Access by using MATCH. The formula =MATCH("oz",B3:B8,1) finds the row where a person has an Access Level of O. To find the value that is the name of a person who has an access level of O, use the formula =VLOOKUP ("oz",B3:D8,MATCH("oz",B3:B8,1)). With MATCH and VLOOKUP or HLOOKUP, you can do two lookups in one formula.

MAX( ) *(see also* Function, DMAX, MIN*)*

Syntax

MAX(*number1,number2,...*)

Description

MAX is a function that returns the largest number of those in the list of values given to the function.

The information required for function MAX:

MAX()

number1,number2,... where each of these values can be a real number, cell address, formula, or function that yields a real number. Each argument must be separated from other values by a comma. MAX takes up to 14 elements: number1,number2,...,number14.

MAX follows the same guidelines as other functions when automatically converting values to numerical values and including them in its calculations. MAX:

- Includes the value in the consideration of the largest or maximum number if it is typed directly into the list of values for the function and is one of the following:

    a logical value

    a number that is in text form

- Does not include the value in the consideration of the largest or maximum number if it is a cell address in the list of values for the function, where the addressed cell:

    is empty

    contains text

    contains a logical value

- Returns:

    An Error in Formula message dialog box when there are more than 14 elements or text in the list of values for the function.

    An error value when it is given a value that is a cell address with an error value in it.

Examples

Formula	Cell Contains	Returns
=MAX(C4,–2,98,99,39)	59	99
=MAX(C4:C6,TRUE,"120")	56,,119	120
=MAX(–1,D2)	FALSE	–1
=MAX(C2:C3)	1/12/90, 9999	32885 (date 1/12/90 converts to number 32885)

MDETERM()

(*see also* Function, MMULT, MINVERSE, TRANSPOSE)

Syntax

MDETERM(*array*)

Description

MDETERM is a function that returns the matrix determinant of an array. MDETERM uses the standard mathematical method of calculating the matrix determinant. Mathematical applications of the matrix determinant most often use the determinant for solving a system of equations that have several variables.

MDETERM requires that the number of columns in the array equal the number of rows. (In mathematical terminology, the calculation of a solution of simultaneous equations with a matrix determinant necessitates that the total number of different variables in all the equations equal the total number of equations in the system.)

For a three-by-three array, the matrix determinant is calculated:

$$C_1R_1 * (C_2R_2 * C_3R_3 - C_2R_3 * C_3R_2)$$
$$+ C_1R_2 * (C_2R_3 * C_3R_1 - C_2R_1 * C_3R_3)$$
$$+ C_1R_3 * (C_2R_1 * C_3R_2 - C_2R_2 * C_3R_1)$$

where C_iR_j stands for the entry in the ith column and the jth row of the matrix or array.

Note: For all matrix functions, a matrix is represented by an array or range of cell addresses.

The information required for function MDETERM:

array is a cell address, constant array, or range of cell addresses that contain real numbers; or a formula or function that yields an array of real numbers. This array contains numbers but no text or empty cells. The array must be a square array, with the number of columns being equal to the number of rows.

Note: #VALUE! is returned if text or empty cells are present in any array or the number of columns doesn't equal the number of rows.

Examples

Formula	*Returns*
=MDETERM({4,3;1,2})	5
=MDETERM({1,–2,0;3,5,6;2,1,4})	14
=MDETERM({9,8,7;6,5,4;3,2,1})	0
=MDETERM(A1:C2)	#VALUE! (error message: # columns does not equal # rows.)

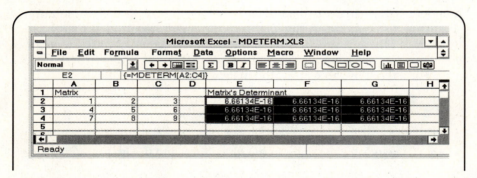

The figure is an example of how small computer errors can occur when calculating the matrix determinant. According to the formula for calculating a matrix determinant, the solution should be zero:

$$1 * (5 * 9 - 8 * 6)$$
$$+ 4 * (8 * 3 - 2 * 9)$$
$$+ 7 * (2 * 6 - 5 * 3)$$
$$= (45 - 48) + 4 * (24 - 18) + 7 * (12 - 15)$$
$$= -3 + 4 * 6 + 7 * -3$$
$$= -3 + 24 + -21$$
$$= 0$$

Note: In the figure, the answer calculated by the spreadsheet is 6.66E–16, yet the calculated answer is 0. This difference is due to the 16-digit accuracy of the MDETERM function. This difference of a factor of E–16 (or $1/10^{16}$) generally should not significantly affect the results. This small error in accuracy happens irregularly, as can be noted when you try the third example under "Examples" where the result is zero for the matrix (array) {9,8,7;6,5,4;3,2,1}.

MEDIAN( )

(*see also* Function, AVERAGE, DAVERAGE, COUNT, COUNTA, SUM)

Syntax

MEDIAN(*number1,number2,...*)

Description

MEDIAN is a function that returns the median of some unsorted numerical values that it is given. The median of several numbers is the number that is in the middle of the *sorted* list of numbers. Half the numbers in the list are smaller than the median, and half the numbers are larger than the median.

Note: If there is an even number of numbers, then MEDIAN returns the average of the two numbers that fall in the middle of the list. Also, cells containing the value zero are included in the calculation of the median.

The information required for function MEDIAN:

number1,number2,... where each of these values can be a real number, cell address, formula, or function that yields a real number. Each argument must be separated from other values by a comma. MEDIAN takes up to 14 elements: number1,number2,...,number14.

MEDIAN follows the same guidelines as other functions when converting numerical values and including them in its calculations. MEDIAN:

- Includes the value in the calculation of the median if it is typed directly into the list of values for the function and is one of the following:

    a logical value

    a number that is in text form

- Does not include the value in the calculation of the median if it is a cell address in the list of values for the function, where the addressed cell:

    is empty

    contains text

    contains a logical value

- Returns:

    An Error in Formula message dialog box when there are more than 14 elements or text in the list of values for the function.

    An error value when it has an argument that is a cell address with an error value in it.

Examples

Formula	Cell Contains	Returns
=MEDIAN(1,2,3,4,5)		3
=MEDIAN(7,6,5,4,D2)	FALSE	5.5 (FALSE is ignored)
=MEDIAN(C2:C4)	1/1/00,	9999 (date 1/1/00 converts to number 36526)

Menu, Menu Bar

The *menu* is a list of commands that are available in Excel. The *menu bar* contains the names of categories of commands. The command types that appear in the menu bar are File, Edit, Formula, Format, Data, Options, Macro, Window, and Help. If you highlight one of these command categories, a list of all the commands that fall under that command category appears directly under the highlighted command.

Command Category	Description of Category's Commands
File	Open, close, save, or print documents
Edit	Copy, move, or clear the current selection
Formula	Change formulas; create, define, and use names; and select cells
Format	Change the appearance of cells
Data	Perform database operation or rearrange data
Options	Change display, print, or calculation settings
Macro	Record or run a macro
Window	Rearrange window or activate specified window
Help	Get help

The commands that are available through the menu give you the ability to manipulate the information on your spreadsheet. The menu in the menu bar is your key to the main computation capabilities of Excel.

> **Tip:** If the command in a menu that you want to choose is gray (to signify that menu option is not available), then look at the status bar. If the word Enter is in the status bar, then the menu option is not available because you are in the midst of entering a value into the spreadsheet. Save changes by either pressing Enter or selecting the check box in the middle of the formula bar, or select the box in the formula bar with the x in it to cancel any changes to the active cell listed on the left side of the formula bar.

Example

If you highlight the word File in the menu bar, a box with the following commands drops down: New..., Open..., Close, Links..., Save, Save As..., Save Workspace..., Delete..., Print Preview, Page Setup..., Print..., Printer Setup..., File List, Exit. The ellipsis (...) after a command means that a dialog box with several options for that command will appear when it is selected.

MERGE.STYLES

(*see* **Macro Functions That Perform Format Commands**)

MESSAGE (*see* **Macro Functions—Customizing**)

MID( )

(*see also* **Function, FIND, SEARCH, LEFT, RIGHT**)

Syntax

MID(*text,start_num,num_chars*)

Description

MID is a function that returns characters from the value *text* in the list of values for the function. MID starts copying characters at the position indexed by start_num and copies as many characters as num_chars specifies.

> **Tip:** MID can be used with other functions like FIND to extract data starting from or ending in a specific character or string of characters. For instance, you can use MID and SEARCH together to extract a social security number: When cell C3 contains Alexander Abrovanich #123-56-8900, =mid(C3,find("#",C3,1),10) returns #123-56-8900.

The information required for function MID:

text is any single symbol or group of symbols. If *text* is typed directly into the argument list, then it must be enclosed in quotation marks.

start_at_num is a number that acts as an index into the within_text string of characters. If start_at_num is 1, then the MID function begins copying from the first character of text. If start_at_num is 8, then the MID function begins copying from the eighth character of text.

If start_at_num is not included in the argument list, then start_at_num is assumed to be 1 and the search for find_text begins at the first character.

num_chars is the number of characters that MID will copy and return from the text string of characters.

Note: #VALUE! error is returned if a) start_at_num is less than 1 (one cannot start before the beginning of text); b) num_chars is less than 0 (one cannot copy backwards or "uncopy" text).

Examples

In the example =MID("copy me",5, 3), the 5 indicates that copying starts at the blank space character " ". Three characters are copied, so the letters *m* and *e* are also copied. The returned result is " me".

Formula	*Returns*
=MID("Interest Rates",1,5)	"Inter"
=MID("Financial",3,4)	"nanc"
=MID(in,2,2)	#NAME!
=MID("rest",4,–3)	#VALUE!
=MID("forest",0,2)	#VALUE!

MIN( ) *(see also* Function, MAX, DMIN)

Syntax

MIN(*number1,number2,...*)

MIN ()

Description

MIN is a function that returns the smallest number of those in the values given to MIN by you, the user.

The information required for function MIN:

number1,number2,... where each of these values can be a real number, cell address, formula, or function that yields a real number. Each argument must be separated from other values by a comma. MIN takes up to 14 elements: number1,number2,...,number14.

MIN follows the same guidelines as other functions when including numerical values in its calculations. MIN:

- Includes the value in the calculation of the smallest number if it is typed directly into the list of values for the function and is one of the following:

    a logical value

    a number that is in text form

- Does not include the value in the calculation of the smallest number if it is a cell address in the list of values for the function, where the addressed cell:

    is empty

    contains text

    contains a logical value

- Returns:

    An Error in Formula message dialog box when there are more than 14 elements or text in the list of values for the function.

    An error value when it has an argument that is a cell address with an error value in it.

Examples

Formula	Cell Contains	Returns
=MIN(−2,9,C4,−9,0)	−10	−10
=MIN(TRUE,C4:C6,"10")	56,,119	1 (TRUE is converted to 1)
=MIN(7,D2)	FALSE	7
=MIN(C2:C3)	1/1/00, 9999	9999 (date 1/1/00 converts to number 36526)

MINUTE( )

(*see also* HOUR, SECOND, DAY, MONTH, WEEKDAY, YEAR)

Syntax

MINUTE(*serial_number*)

Description

MINUTE is a function that returns the minutes in the hour corresponding to the particular time specified by serial_number. The returned number is a whole number that ranges from 0 to 59.

The information required for function MINUTE:

serial_number is a number that represents a particular time in the range of 12:00:00 AM to 11:59:59 PM. For more information on serial_number, see "TIME" and "NOW." Serial_number can also be given as text.

 Note: Excel 3 for Windows uses a different numbering system (the 1900 Date System) for dates than Excel for the Macintosh.

Examples

The formula =MINUTE(0.413461) returns 55 because serial_number 0.413461 stands for the time 9:55:23 AM.

The formula =MINUTE(32880.543576) returns 2 because serial_number 0.543576 stands for the time 1:02:45 PM. (The 32880 portion of the serial number stands for the date January 7, 1990. The date is ignored.)

Formula	Returns
=MINUTE("12:15:55 AM")	15
=MINUTE("2:20:10 PM")	20

MINVERSE( )

(*see also* Function, MDETERM, MMULT, TRANSPOSE)

Syntax

MINVERSE(*array*)

Description

MINVERSE is a function that returns the inverse matrix for a matrix (which is represented by an array). Calculation of the inverse matrix is a standard mathematical procedure, which is illustrated in Figure A. Like the inverse of other mathematical operations, a matrix times its inverse is equal to the identity matrix. (The *identity matrix* is an array filled with zeros in all the entries except the diagonal, which contain ones.) Similar to the matrix determinant, applications of the inverse matrix most often involve solving a system of equations with several variables.

Calculation of the inverse matrix proceeds with the formula shown in Figure A.

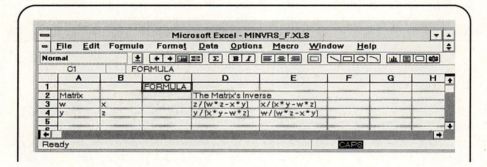

Figure A

 Note: MINVERSE requires that the number of columns in the array equal the number of rows. (This is because the method of calculation of a solution of simultaneous equations involving the use of an inverse matrix necessitates that the total number of different variables in all the equations equal the total number of equations in the system.)

For all matrix functions, a matrix is represented by an array or range of cell addresses.

Some inverse matrices that cannot be calculated return the error message #NUM! in all array entries. For example, you cannot calculate the inverse for a matrix when the formula for the inverse has a denominator (or determinant) of zero. In the formula in Figure A, if w * z – x * y is zero, then the denominator of each entry is zero.

The information required for function MINVERSE:

array is a cell address, constant array, or range of cell addresses that contain real numbers; or a formula or function that yields an array of real numbers. This array contains numbers but no text or empty cells. The array must be a square array, with the number of columns being equal to the number of rows.

Note: #VALUE! is returned if text or empty cells are present in any array or the number of columns doesn't equal the number of rows.

Examples

Formula	Returns
=MINVERSE({4,3;2,1})	{–.5,1.5;1,–2}
=MINVERSE({1,2,1;5,5,2})	{–0.5, 0, 0.5; –0.5, 1, –1.5; 2.5, –2, 2.5}
=MINVERSE({9,8,7;6,5,4;3,2,1})	{#NUM!,#NUM!,#NUM!;#NUM!, #NUM!,#NUM!;#NUM!,#NUM!, #NUM!}
=MINVERSE(A1:C2)	#VALUE! (error message: # columns does not equal # rows.)

Note: The answer calculated by the spreadsheet in the example in Figure B is an array with values that are extremely large. But you cannot calculate the inverse matrix for the array {1,2,3;4,5,6;7,8,9}, because the formula has some zero denominators. This discrepancy between the actual result and the calculated result is due to the 16-digit accuracy of the MINVERSE function. This small error in accuracy happens irregularly, as can be noted by the result in the third example under "Examples," where the result of the matrix (array) {9,8,7;6,5,4;3,2,1}, which has some zero denominators, is the error value #NUM! in all array entries.

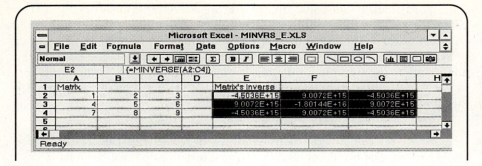

Figure B

> **Tip:** In order to avoid the use of an incorrect inverse matrix as shown in Figure B, you could enter an IF statement to check for an almost zero determinant. This is effective because the denominators in the formula for the inverse matrix are the positive or negative determinant of the matrix or array for which the inverse is being calculated. See "MDETERM" for the calculation of the determinant of the array {1,2,3;4,5,6;7,8,9}.

MIRR() *(see also* Functions, IRR, NPV, RATE*)*

Syntax

MIRR(*values,finance_rate,reinvest_rate*)

Description

MIRR is a function that returns the modified internal rate of return for an investment that is based on a series of periodic cash flows. The modified internal rate of return includes the payments (negative) and income (positive) of the investment and the interest received on the reinvestment of cash.

The following formula, which Excel uses to calculate MIRR, uses *n* to represent the number of values in the array values, *value[positive]* to represent the positive values in the array values, *value[negative]* to represent the negative values in the array values, *rrate* to represent reinvest_rate, and *frate* to represent finance_rate.:

$$\text{MIRR} = \left(\frac{-\text{NPV (rrate,values[positive])} * (1 + \text{rrate})^n}{\text{NPV (frate,values[negative])} * (1 + \text{frate})} \right)^{\frac{1}{n-1}} - 1$$

The information required for function MIRR:

values is an array or reference to an array of values that represent payments and income. The numbers in the values array represent payments (negative) and income (positive) that occur at regular periods of time.

When entering values, there are guidelines you must follow:

- At least one positive value and one negative value must be in the values array. MIRR returns the #DIV/0! error if there are no positive values or there are no negative values.

- Make sure to enter your payment and income values in the correct sequence, since MIRR uses the order of value1,value2,... when interpreting cash flows.

finance_rate is the interest rate that you pay on money used in the cash flows (the interest rate on the negative values in the array values).

reinvest_rate is the interest rate that you receive on cash flows as you reinvest them (the interest rate on the positive values in the array values).

A function that requires numeric values, such as MIRR, uses the following conversion rules:

- Converts a value to a numeric value if the argument is typed directly into the list of values for the function and is one of the following:

    logical value

    a number that is in text form

- Does not convert an argument to a numeric value if the argument is a cell address where the addressed cell:

    is empty

    contains text

    contains a logical value

- Returns an error, if the argument is a cell address and the addressed cell has an error value in it.

- Returns the #VALUE! error if there is a text argument.

Examples

Suppose that you started a business with a $25,000 loan at 10% interest. Suppose that you made a profit of $10 after the first year, $500 after the second year, $1,500 after the third year, $5,000 after the fourth year, and $21,000 after the fifth year, and you reinvested your profits at a rate of 11%. The modified internal rate of return for your business is the result of the following formula, where cells C1 to C6 contain –25000,10,500,1500,5000, and 21000: =MIRR(C1:C6,10%,11%). Your modified internal rate of return, which includes the reinvestment of your profit, is 3.08%, the value that this formula returns.

Suppose that you took out a $60,000 loan at 12% to start your own restaurant. The restaurant made no profit in the first year, made a profit of $30 at the end of the second year, $4,000 at the end of the third year, $12,000 at the end of the fourth year, and $37,000 at the end of the fifth year, and $85,000 at the end of the sixth year. What is the internal rate of return of your business after four years? After six years?

Enter the above values (–60000, 0, 30, 4000, 12000, 37000, 85000) into cells B1 to B7. After four years, the internal rate of return is calculated by =MIRR(B1:B5,12%,9%), which returns –27.7%. MIRR returned a negative value since you did not get back your entire investment in the restaurant.

After six years, the internal rate of return is =MIRR(B1:B7,12%,9%), which returns 15.82%.

MMULT( )

(*see also* **Function, MDETERM, MINVERSE, TRANSPOSE**)

Syntax

MMULT(*array1,array2*)

Description

MMULT is a function that returns the product of two matrices or arrays. MMULT multiplies two matrices using standard mathematical matrix multiplication procedures. The formula for calculating the product requires that the number of columns in the first matrix be equal to the number of rows in the second matrix.

Let *n* represent the number of columns in the first matrix and the number of rows in the second matrix. To calculate one element of the product matrix, which is in the ith row and jth column of the resultant matrix, multiply the elements in the ith row of the first matrix times corresponding elements in the jth column of the second matrix, and sum these products:

$$\text{result}_{ij} = a_{i1} * b_{1j} + a_{i2} * b_{2j} + \ldots + a_{in} * b_{nj}$$

This formula demonstrates why the first array, array1, must have the same number of columns as there are rows in the second array, array2.

Note: For all matrix functions, a matrix is represented by an array or range of cell addresses.

Note: MMULT is a function that returns an array. The procedure for entering any function that returns an array is to highlight the target array area on the spreadsheet before typing in the formula; type in the formula; and then before pressing the Enter key, press the Ctrl, Shift, and Enter keys all at the same time.

The information required for function MMULT:

array1,array2 where these two arrays can be a cell address, constant array, or range of cell addresses that contain real numbers; or a formula or function that yields an array of real numbers. Both arrays contain numbers but no text or empty cells. The number of columns in the first array must be the same as the number of rows in the second array.

Note: #VALUE! is returned if text or empty cells are present in any array or the number of columns in the first array doesn't match the number of rows in the second array.

Examples

Formula	*Returns*
=MMULT({2;1},{1,2,3,4})	{2,4,6,8;1,2,3,4}
=MMULT({2,1;0,1},{1,2,3;4,5,6})	{6,9,12;4,5,6}
=MMULT({1,2,3;4,5,6},{2,1;0,1})	#VALUE! (error message)
=MMULT(A1:B3,C1:D3)	#VALUE! (error message)

In the example in the figure, according to the formula for matrix multiplication: 1) elements in one row of the first matrix are multiplied with elements in corresponding positions of one column in the second matrix, 2) these product pairs for this one row and one column are then added together, and 3) the result is placed in one position in the resultant array.

Array1   Array2   Resultant Array
Row 1 * Column 1:   2 * 3 + 5 * 4 + 1 * 5 = 31 = entry in Row 1, Column 1
Row 1 * Column 2:   2 * 6 + 5 * 2 + 1 * 1 = 23 = entry in Row 1, Column 2
Row 2 * Column 1:   3 * 3 + 0 * 4 + 2 * 5 = 19 = entry in Row 2, Column 1
Row 2 * Column 2:   3 * 6 + 0 * 2 + 2 * 1 = 20 = entry in Row 2, Column 2

MOD() *(see also* Function, INT, MOD, ROUND*)*

Syntax

MOD(*number,divisor*)

Description

MOD is a function that returns the remainder after dividing *number* by *divisor*. The remainder is given the same sign as the divisor. *MOD* is an abbreviation for modulus. MOD returns the integer that is left over when dividing. For example, since 7 divided by 2 equals 3 with a remainder of 1, 7 mod 2 = 1.

The information required for function MOD:

number is any number. MOD gets a remainder from *number* by dividing *number* by *divisor*.

divisor is a number that divides *number*.

Examples

Formula	Returns
=MOD(5,2.5)	0
=MOD(5,2)	1
=MOD(–10,4)	2
=MOD(4,0)	#DIV/0! (error message)
=MOD(7,–2)	–1

MONTH( )

(see also DAY, YEAR, WEEKDAY, HOUR, MINUTE, SECOND, TODAY)

Syntax

MONTH(*serial_number*)

Description

MONTH is a function that returns a number which represents the month of the year corresponding to the particular date specified by serial_number. The returned number ranges from 1 to 12 (the number of months in a year).

The information required for function MONTH:

Serial_number is a number that represents a particular date in the range of January 1, 1900, to December 31, 2078. For more information on serial_number, see "NOW." Serial_number can also be given as text.

Tip: To display the numerical month returned by the MONTH function in text form (January, February, ...), use the Format Number command and type in the custom format mmmm or mmm in the format box.

Note: Excel 3 for Windows uses a different numbering system (the 1900 Date System) for the MONTH function than Excel for the Macintosh. On the Macintosh, date_text can range from January 1, 1904, to December 31, 2078.

Examples *(based on the 1900 Date System)*

The formula =MONTH(32880) returns 1 because serial_number 32880 stands for the date 1/7/90 (January 7, 1990).
    The formula =MONTH(31296) returns 9 because serial_number 31296 stands for the date 9/6/85 (September 6, 1985).

Formula	*Returns*
=MONTH("May 1, 1991")	5
=MONTH("4/18/92")	4

Mouse *(see also* **Keyboard***)*

A mouse can be a graphics tablet, a light pen, a mouse, a touch pad, a touch screen, or a track ball, all devices used to move the pointer on the screen.

 Selecting with a Mouse

1. Select a cell by clicking on the cell desired.   The cell is highlighted.

2. Select a range of cells by dragging from one corner to the opposite corner of the cells desired, or by clicking one corner of the range, holding down Shift, and clicking the opposite corner.

   The cells are highlighted.

3. Select an entire column or row by clicking on the column or row heading label.

   The column is highlighted.

4. Select the current array by pressing Ctrl-Shift-double-click on any cell in the array.

   The entire array is selected.

5. Select the entire worksheet by clicking the button to the left of the column A heading and above the row 1 heading.

   The entire worksheet is selected.

6. Select multiple columns or rows by dragging through column or row heading labels.

   All columns/rows are selected.

7. Select multiple areas in the worksheet by holding down Ctrl while dragging through the desired areas.

   All areas are selected.

Mouse Term	*Procedure*
Click	Point to an object and press and release the mouse button without moving the mouse.
Double-click	Point to an object and click twice quickly without moving the mouse.
Drag	Point to an object, press and hold the mouse button, move the mouse, and release the mouse button.
Point	Place the mouse cursor so that the tip of the pointer is on the desired object.

> **Tip:** Select a graphic object by pointing to the border of the object and clicking the mouse. Handles will appear if the object was selected. Hold down the Shift key and continue to select objects if desired. Only the mouse can select buttons and tools on the Toolbar or move, select, and size graphic objects on the worksheet.

MOVE

(*see* **Macro Functions That Perform Control Commands**)

Multiple Selection

A *multiple selection* is the selection of one or more areas on the spreadsheet. One area is a group of contiguous cells, an unbroken region, or a range of cells.

There are three ways that you can create and use a multiple selection. You can create a constant multiple selection with a pair of parentheses around all the areas that are included in your multiple selection (see the following "Syntax" and "Examples"). You can define a name, which refers to a constant multiple selection. You can also create a multiple selection by pressing the Ctrl key as you highlight various sections of the worksheet with the mouse or arrow keys.

To create a multiple selection, hold down the Ctrl key; then select areas on the spreadsheet. The first area you select will be the first element of your multiple selection. The second area you select will be the second element of your multiple selection, and so on. Keep holding down the Ctrl key until all areas have been selected.

Syntax

A reference to a multiple selection: (*range1,range2,...*)

Examples

Some examples of a multiple selection with one single area are a column (C1:C5), a row (A3:F3), a group of cells (A3:F5), or a single cell (G2). An example of a multiple selection with many areas is a combination of all these single areas: (C1:C5, A3:F3, A3:F5, G2).

Multiple Selection	*Number of Areas*
(D2:D5, A2)	2
(C1:C5,G2:G3, A6:F8,B2:B59)	4
(B1,C2:D9,D5)	3
(G1:G4,W3:W6,E2:E3)	3

N–O

N() (*see also* Function, T, GET.CELL)

Syntax

N(*value*)

Description

N is a function that returns the number that *value* converts to.
The information required for function N:

value is any value that you want to convert to a number.

If value Is	N Returns
A number	The number
A date in one of the standard formats (see function "CELL" for a listing)	The code number for that date (see "NOW" for more information)
TRUE	1
Anything other than above	0

Examples

If cell E1 contains 4, then =N(E1) returns 4. If cell E1 contains "4", then =N(E1) returns 0. If cell E1 contains "words", then =N(E1) returns 0. If cell E1 contains TRUE, then =N(E1) returns 1.

NA() *(see also* Function, ISNA*)*

Syntax

NA( )

Description

NA is a function that returns the error value #N/A. *#N/A* stands for "does not apply."

Note: Typing #N/A directly into a cell has the same effect as using the NA( ) function.

Note: Functions that return an array, return #N/A in selected cells that they cannot fill with information.

Tip: You can use #N/A or NA( ) to mark cells that should remain empty in your calculations.

The information required for function NA:

No information is required for function NA.

Examples

The formula =NA( ) returns #N/A.

NAMES *(see* Macro Functions—Value Returning*)*

NEW

(*see* Macro Functions That Perform File Commands)

NEW.WINDOW

(*see* Macro Functions That Perform Window Commands)

NEXT (*see* Macro Functions—Control)

NOT() (*see also* Function, AND, OR)

Syntax

NOT(*logical*)

Description

NOT is a function that returns the opposite of the given argument. NOT returns FALSE if the given logical is true and returns TRUE if the given logical is false.
The information required for function NOT:

logical is TRUE, FALSE, or some expression that evaluates to TRUE or FALSE.

If you give the function NOT a value that is not a logical value, it will convert the value as follows:

Type of Value	Converted to
0 or an empty cell	FALSE
Numerical values not equal to 0	TRUE
Text (including numbers in text form)	#VALUE! (error message)
An error message in a cell	The error message

Examples

Formula	Cell C1 Contains	Returns
=NOT(2+2=5)		TRUE
=NOT(C1)	"abc"	#VALUE!
=NOT(C1 = 0)	4	FALSE

Note *(see also* Text*)*

A *note* is text attached to a cell that can be displayed in a Cell Note window.

Keystrokes

Keyboard	*Mouse*
Select cell to attach note to.	Select cell to attach note to.
Fo**r**mula	Fo**r**mula
Note	**N**ote

 Viewing all the Notes in a Spreadsheet

1. Choose **W**indow and **S**how Info. — The Info window appears.

2. Choose **W**indow and **A**rrange All. — Your screen now shows both the Info window and the worksheet.

3. Make the worksheet active. — The border on the worksheet changes.

4. Choose Fo**r**mula, Select Special, **N**otes, and OK. — All cells with notes are selected.

5. Press Tab repeatedly. — You see notes one at a time.

> **Note:** To display a small red dot in the upper-right corner of each cell that contains a note, use Options, Workspace, Note Indicator. To display a note attached to a cell, double-click on the cell, or use Formula, Note. To delete a note, select the cell; then choose Edit, Clear, and Notes. To print notes with or without the spreadsheet, use File, Print, Both, or Notes.

NOTE

(*see* Macro Functions That Perform Formula Commands)

NOW()

(*see also* YEAR, MONTH, DAY, WEEKDAY, HOUR, MINUTE, SECOND, TODAY)

Syntax

NOW()

Description

NOW is a function that returns a number which corresponds to the current date and time. The whole number portion of the returned number represents the current date, and the fractional portion to the right of the decimal represents the time.

The information required for function NOW:

No information is required for function NOW.

Excel 3 for Windows uses a different numbering system for the various date functions than Excel for the Macintosh:

1900 Date System: Microsoft Excel for Windows and OS/2 uses dates starting from January 1, 1900, to December 31, 2078. Excel 3 for Windows assigns these dates to correspond to numbers starting from 1 for January 1, 1900, and ending in 65,380 for December 31, 2078.

1904 Date System: Microsoft Excel for the Macintosh uses dates starting from January 1, 1904, to December 31, 2078. Excel for the Macintosh assigns these dates to correspond to numbers starting with 0 for January 1, 1904, and ending in 63,918 for December 31, 2078.

The Date System is automatically changed when you open a document that was created in another system. The check box for the 1904 Date System is automatically turned on when you open a document that was created in Excel on a Macintosh computer. In the Windows version of Excel, the date system can be changed by checking the 1904 Date System check box in the dialog box for Options and Calculation.

Examples *(based on the 1900 Date System)*

If your computer clock says that today's date is April 18, 1992, and today's time is 9:55:23 AM, then NOW() returns 33712.413461. 33712 comes from the current date and 0.413461 corresponds to the current time.

Say that 15 minutes later you recalculate your NOW function. Because the current time at this point is 10:10:23, the NOW() function returns 33712.423877.

NPER( )

(see also **Functions, Annuity Functions, FV, IPMT, PMT, PPMT, PV, RATE)**

Syntax

NPER(*rate,pmt,pv,fv,type*)

Description

NPER is a function that returns the number of periods of an investment based on periodic constant payments and a constant interest rate. For more information, see "Annuity Functions."

Note: Make sure that you use the same unit of measure for specifying rate as is specified by the period of the payments. If payments are monthly, then rate should be based on one-month periods.

Note: In annuity functions, a negative number represents cash that you pay out and a positive number represents cash that you receive.

Note: If you get a negative number for nper, check that your payment, pv, and fv values have the correct sign.

The information required for function NPER (all of the following values are numbers; for more information, see "Annuity Functions"):

rate is the interest rate per period.

pmt is the payment made each period and does not change over the life of the annuity. (Usually pmt includes principal and interest but no other fees or taxes.)

pv is the present value or total lump-sum amount that a series of future payments is worth now, in the present.

fv is the future value or cash balance that you want to achieve after the last balance is made. If fv is not included, NPER assumes that fv is 0. (For example, a loan has a future value of 0.)

type is 0 or 1, indicating when payments are due, as shown below.

If type Is	Payments Are Due
0 or not included	At the end of the period
1	At the beginning of the period

Examples

Suppose that you loaned $1,000 to a friend at an annual interest rate of 7%. Your friend will pay you back $100 at the end of each month. How many payments should your friend give you? Use the following formula: =NPER(7%,100,–1000). (The 1000 is negative since you loan or pay out this money to your friend.) 17.79481 is returned by this formula. The first 17 payments you receive are $100. The last payment could be estimated at $79.48, or you could use the future value function to calculate the exact amount left over. The formula =FV(7%,17,100,–1000) returns the exact amount of the last payment, $74.79.
=NPER(10%/12,–500,10000) returns 21.969, almost exactly 22 periods. =NPER(14%/12,–200,2500,1) returns 13.420. =NPER(9.99%,1000,–10000) returns 72.546.

=NPER(10%,1000,–10000) returns #NUM! because it is not possible to pay this debt by paying $1,000 per period. Since the interest on $10,000 is $1,000, each payment would be paying the interest of the loan only. The principal would never decrease and the loan would never end.

=NPER(7%/12,–1500,–2000,40000) returns 23.526.

NPV( ) *(see also* Functions, PV, FV, IRR)

Syntax

NPV(*rate,value1,value2,...*)

Description

NPV is a function that returns the net present value of an investment that is based on a series of periodic cash flows and a discount rate. The net present value is the present value (today) of a series of future payments (negative) and income (positive).

The formula that NPV uses is NPV = (value1/(1 + rate)^1) + (value2/(1 + rate)^2) + ... + (valuen/(1 + rate)^n), where n is the number of values in the list of values (value1,value2,...) given to the NPV function.

- The NPV function starts its calculations with the date that begins one period before the date of value1 cash flow and ends with the last cash flow in the list. Future cash flows are the basis of NPV's calculations. If your first cash flow is a value that occurs "in the present," at the beginning of the first period, then the first value must be added to the NPV result, not included in the values.

- NPV is similar to the present value function, PV. The main difference between these two functions is that PV allows cash flow to be due at the beginning or end of a period. But NPV allows cash flows to vary, as opposed to cash flows for PV, which must be constant. For more information on annuities, see "Annuity Functions."

- NPV is also similar to the internal rate of return function, IRR. IRR is the rate that makes NPV zero for the values you give both functions. The formula NPV(IRR(values),values), where *values* is the same series of numbers in both functions, always returns 0.

The information required for function NPV:

rate is the rate of discount over the length of one period.

value1,value2,... are 1 to 13 values that represent payments and income.

When entering values, there are guidelines that you must follow:

- Make sure that value1,value2,... are spaced equally in time.

- Make sure to enter your payment and income values in the correct sequence, since NPV uses the order of value1,value2,... when interpreting cash flows.

- The nonnumeric values of value1,value2,... that are text and/or logic values are sometimes converted to numeric values, sometimes ignored, and sometimes cause errors.

A function that requires numeric values, such as NPV, uses the following conversion rules:

- Converts a value to a numeric value if the value is typed directly into the list of values for the function and is one of the following:

    a logical value

    a number that is in text form

- Does not convert an argument to a numeric value if the argument is a cell address where the addressed cell:

    is empty

    contains text

    contains a logical value

- Returns an error if the argument is a cell address and the addressed cell has an error value in it.

- Returns the #VALUE! error if there is a text argument.

Example

Suppose that you are looking into a special investment that pays $500 after the first year and twice as much as the previous year for the next four years after that. Assuming an annual discount rate of 8.5%, what is the most that you should pay for this investment? This question can be answered using the formula =NPV(8.5%,500,1000,2000,4000,8000). This formula returns $11,082.76. If the above investment costs less than $11,082.76, then it is a good investment.

Suppose you are looking into buying a business that costs $20,000 to start. You estimate that maintenance and repairs of the building and equipment for the business will cost approximately $200 after one and a half years of running the business, $500 after two and a half years, $650 after three and a half years, and $800 after four and a half years. You estimate that the business makes a profit of $0.00 after the first year, $1,000 after the second year, $2,400 after the third year, $7,000 after the fourth year, and $10,000 after the fifth year. Assuming an annual discount rate of 10%, what is the net present value of your business after five years?

 Note: Before using NPV, decide whether to calculate the NPV on the basis of the personal funds that you put into and get out of an investment, such as a business, or from the perspective of money coming into or going out of the investment or business.

For this example, let's calculate NPV based on the cash flow in and out of your personal funds. So money spent on repairs and maintenance is negative, and profit coming back to you is positive. To use the NPV function, first calculate the length of the period between cash flows. Every half year you are putting money into the business or getting money out of the business. So your interest rate is 10%/2 or 5% every six months. Secondly, the cash flows must be in the order that they occur (parentheses means a negative value).

Year	Cash Flow
1	+0
1.5	($200)
2	$1,000
2.5	($500)
3	$2,400
3.5	($650)
4	$7,000
4.5	($800)
5	$10,000

Note that the initial investment occurs at the beginning of the first period, so it is not included in the list of values given to NPV. Instead, the intial investment will be added on to the result of NPV. Using all the above information, we have the formula =NPV(5%,+0,–200,1000,–500,2400, –650,7000,–800, 10000) + –20000, which returns –7454.11. The net present value based on five years of operation is still negative. Based on your estimates, you will not get back all the money that you invested in your business in the first five years of operation. But a present value of only $7,454.11 is lacking.

Number

Number is a type of value, an expression of information in a defined, precise form. Number is a number, a quantifying value. It is the type of information that is used in mathematical formulas. Examples of the types of information that would be number values are a date, an age or weight, and an amount of money.

If any character in a cell is a letter or nonnumeric symbol, then the entire value in that cell is a text value, not a number. For example, 12$ and 12B are text values.

On the other hand, sometimes a value that contains a symbol can be a number. For example, if you type $12 into a cell, 12 appears in the formula bar and $12.00 appears in the cell. The $12 that you typed is a number.

Number is one of six types of values: numbers, text, logical values, references, arrays, and error values. For more information about values in general and a summary of these other five types of values, see "Values."

Whenever you see a request for a number value, you can use a number or you can use a reference, formula, or name that represents a number.

Syntax

Number is represented by numeric symbols: the digits 0, 1, 2, 3, 4, 5, 6, 7, 8, and 9; the decimal point (.) and the negative sign (–);and date symbols that include the above plus a slash (/).

Examples

0, 9999765, –423, 56.234, 4/10/81, 1:01:45, 28Feb76

OBJECT.PROTECTION

(*see* Macro Functions That Perform Format Commands)

OFFSET()

(*see also* Function, ABSREF, REFTEXT, RELREF, SELECT, SELECTION)

Syntax

OFFSET(*reference,rows,cols,height,width*)

Description

OFFSET is a function that returns a cell address which is specified by the information that you give OFFSET. The returned reference is calculated from a three-step process. First, Excel adds the number given by *rows* to the row number of *reference*. Second, Excel adds or moves the column of *reference* to the left or right as many columns as given by *columns*. In the third step, if *height* and *width* are 1, then the reference calculated from steps one and two is returned. If *height* and *width* are greater than 1, then an array reference is returned. The calculated reference from steps one and two is used as the upper-left corner of the array reference. The lower-right corner of the array reference is the cell address that is *height* columns away from the top of the array and *width* rows away from the leftmost cell of the array.

Note: If OFFSET returns a single cell address reference value to a cell, rather than to another formula, then the contents of the cell address that OFFSET returns will appear in the cell, not the actual cell address.

Note: In earlier versions of Excel, OFFSET was only a macro function.

The information required for function OFFSET:

reference is the base cell address that is added to when calculating the new cell address or range of cell addresses that the function returns.

Note: OFFSET returns #VALUE! if *reference* is a name that refers to more than one area on the spreadsheet.

rows is the number of rows added to *reference* to calculate the resultant cell address.

cols is the number of columns added to *reference* to calculate the resultant cell address. (Addition is from left to right, increasing the column number or alphabetic symbol that represents the column.)

Note: If *rows* or *cols* creates a resulting cell address that is off the edge of the worksheet (according to the limits for an Excel worksheet), then OFFSET returns the error #REF!.

height is the number of rows in the range of cell addresses that OFFSET returns. To calculate the end of the range of cell addresses, *height* is added to the row number in the first calculated cell address. If *height* is not included, it is assumed to be the same as the number of rows in *reference*.

width is the number of columns in the range of cell addresses that OFFSET returns. To calculate the end of the range of cell addresses, *width* is added to the column specified in the first calculated cell address. If *width* is not included, it is assumed to be the same as the number of columns in *reference*.

Examples

Formula	*Returns*
=OFFSET(B2,3,0,1,1)	Contents of B5
=OFFSET(offset(B2,3,0,1,1),3,0,1,1)	Contents of B8
=OFFSET(B2,−1,4,5,1)	F1:G6
=OFFSET(C2:D8,3,2,1,1)	E5
=OFFSET(C2:D8,−3,2,1,1)	#REF!

Note: If OFFSET returns a reference that is a single cell *and* the value returned by OFFSET is displayed in a cell, then the contents of that reference are displayed rather than the reference.

ON.DATA *(see* Macro Functions—Control*)*

ON.KEY *(see* Macro Functions—Control*)*

ON.RECALC *(see* Macro Functions—Control*)*

ON.TIME *(see* Macro Functions—Control*)*

ON.WINDOW *(see* Macro Functions—Control*)*

OPEN

(see Macro Functions That Perform File Commands*)*

OPEN.LINKS

(see Macro Functions That Perform File Commands*)*

Options—Calculate Now

When you've switched off automatic calculating through the Calculation command, choose Calculate Now from Options when you want Excel to update formula calculations.

Use this command in conjunction with Calculation when your worksheet has a lot of formulas that take time to calculate.

Keystrokes

Keyboard   *Mouse*

Options   Options

Calculate Now   Calculate Now

 Setting and Using Manual Calculation

1. Choose Calculation from Options.   Excel displays the Calculation dialog box.

2. Select the Manual option and choose OK.

3. Choose Calculate Now from Options when you want Excel to recalculate.   This recalculates the values in *all* the open documents.

4. Hold down Shift before accessing the Options menu and choose Calculate Document.   The command name changes when you hold Shift before choosing Options. This recalculates only the active document.

 Tip: Make the formula bar active by selecting a formula cell; then choose Calculate Now to see the result of the formula. You can also select part of a formula and see the result of just that part.

Options—Calculation

The Calculation dialog box controls how and when formulas are calculated in a document. The following are the options in the Calculation dialog box:

Calculation options: Choose between Automatic, Automatic except Tables, and Manual. The default is Automatic. If you use Manual, Excel only calculates when you choose the Calculate Now command. With Manual on, you can specify whether to recalculate before Save or not.

Iteration options: When goalseeking, you can limit the Maximum [number of] Iterations and stop when all values change by less than what you specify at Maximum Change.

Sheet options: Update Remote References applies to formulas that have references to other applications. When off, these formulas just use the last value received.

Precision as Displayed: Calculates numbers according to the number of digits displayed, instead of the default 15 digits.

1904 Date System: In the default date system, 1 is 1/1/1900. Check this option to change it to 1/2/1904 (as in Excel for the Macintosh).

Save External Link Values: Checking this option saves copies of values contained in a linked document. Unchecking this can reduce the disk space needed.

Keystrokes

Keyboard	*Mouse*
Options	Options
Calculation	Calculation
Enter	OK

Example

A worksheet with many formulas takes a long time to calculate every time you enter a new figure. Choose Calculation from Options, and then select Manual and OK. Excel waits for you to choose Calculate Now before recalculating formulas.

Setting Calculation Options

1. Choose Calculation from Options.

   Excel displays the Calculation dialog box.

2. Make your choices, the main one being either Automatic or Manual.

3. Choose OK.

Options—Color Palette

Use the Color Palette command in Options to customize one or more of the 16 basic colors and to copy color palettes between Excel documents.

Keystrokes

Keyboard	*Mouse*
Options	Options
Color Palette	Color Palette
Edit	Edit
Enter	OK

Example

Suppose that you decide that one of the greens in the basic color scheme, the second one down in the right column of the Color Palette dialog box, is too dark. Choose Color Palette from Options and select the color and then the Edit button. In the Edit dialog box, there is an arrowhead on the right of the screen beside a colored column going from dark to light. Drag the arrowhead up with the mouse and the color gets lighter. Choose OK. Back in the Color Palette, the color has changed to the new color as has every object in the worksheet with that color. Choose OK.

Creating a New Color

1. Choose Color Pal<u>e</u>tte from <u>O</u>ptions.

    Excel displays the Color Palette dialog box.

2. Choose the color you want to change.

    Excel has 12 basic colors.

3. Choose <u>E</u>dit.

    Excel displays the Edit dialog box.

4. Drag the arrowhead beside the color column on the right to lighten or darken the color.

    The ColorSolid box reflects the change.

5. Choose OK to leave the Edit dialog box.

    The Color Palette box reappears.

6. Choose OK to return to the worksheet.

 Note: If you have customized a color palette in a worksheet, you can transfer the palette to another document through the Color Palette dialog box. Choose Copy Colors From and select one of the documents in the list. Its colors are transferred to the current document.

 Note: As you drag the arrowhead in the Edit dialog box, the numbers in the <u>H</u>ue, <u>S</u>at (saturation), and <u>L</u>um (luminosity) box and the <u>R</u>ed, <u>G</u>reen, and <u>B</u>lue box change. You can also change these numbers directly. They divide naturally into two groups of three—Red, Green, and Blue being the second group. You should change the numbers one set at a time.

Options—Display

The options shown in the Display dialog box control how cells and objects are displayed on the screen and also the coloring of gridlines and headings.

Keystrokes

Keyboard	*Mouse*
Options	Options
Display	Display
Enter	OK

The full list of Cell options is Formulas, Gridlines, Row & Column Headings, Zero Values, Outline Symbols, and Automatic Page Breaks. By default all are checked except Formulas. Uncheck them to stop them from displaying.

In Objects you choose between Show All, Show Placeholders, and Hide All, meaning a choice between showing all objects, displaying selected pictures and charts as gray rectangles (all other objects displayed normally), and hiding all objects.

Use the drop-down scroll bar to choose a Gridlines & Heading Color.

Example

Suppose that you have many formulas entered in a very complicated worksheet, and you want to check that all of them are entered properly. Choose Display from Options, check the Formulas option, and choose OK. On the worksheet, the formulas are displayed in each cell rather than the values, plus the width of each column has doubled to accommodate long formulas.

 Changing Your Worksheet Display

1. Choose Display from Options. — Excel displays the Display dialog box.

2. Choose your options. — A checked option will be displayed; an unchecked option won't be displayed.

3. Choose OK to return to the worksheet.

 Note: The settings you make apply only to the active worksheet.

Tip: You can change between the three Object options by pressing Ctrl-6. Also, you can get rid of the Toolbar by pressing Ctrl-7 and can bring it back the same way. Ctrl-' switches back and forth between displaying and not displaying formulas.

Options—Freeze Panes

Splitting a window gives you two or more views of the same document. When combined with Freeze Panes in the Options menu, the split window can freeze the display of certain rows or columns. So a title row at the top, for instance, could be made to display at all times.

Keystrokes

Keyboard

Options

Freeze Panes

Mouse

Options

Freeze Panes

Example

Suppose that you are examining a complex set of figures showing the rankings of salesmen. The salesmen's names appear along the right of the worksheet with dates along the top. You want to permanently display this right column and top row as you look through the document. Use the Document Control menu or the mouse to split the screen twice so that the right column and top row show in the split windows as separate panes. Now choose Freeze Panes from Options, and the panes freeze as they are.

 Freezing Panes in a Split Window

1. Split the window into panes so that the row(s) and/or column(s) you want to freeze are displayed.

   To split a window, press Alt-+ and then T (or just choose Split from the Document Control menu), and place the cross where you want the split. Alternatively, place the mouse pointer on the thick line above the vertical scroll bar arrowhead and drag.

2. Choose Freeze Panes from Options.

The double lines separating the split panes disappear and the menu command changes to Unfreeze Panes.

 Note: If you want to split the window in a different way, you have to unfreeze the panes by choosing Unfreeze Panes.

Options—Full Menus

(*see* Options—Short Menus)

Options—Protect Document

Using the Protect Document command from Options, you can prevent three things from happening: the locked cells being changed, the window from being manipulated through the Close command in Control, and locked objects from being selected, moved, resized, or reformatted.

Keystrokes

Keyboard

Cell/Object Protection

Locked

Protect Document

Cells and/or Window and/or Objects

Password

Enter

Mouse

Cell/Object Protection

Locked

Protect Document

Cells and/or Window and/or Objects

Password

OK

Example

Suppose that you have several complex customized formulas in a worksheet that is used by many people frequently. You want to display the values produced by the formulas but not the formulas themselves (so that no one can tamper with them). Select the cells, choose Cell Protection from Format, and confirm that the Locked option is checked (if not, check it). Choose Protect Document from Options, make sure Cells is checked, and choose OK.

 Protecting Your Document

1. Select either the objects or the cells that you want to protect and make sure they are locked in Object Protection or Cell Protection in Format. (When locking objects and cells, this is an essential first step. By default, the Locked option is checked in the command.)

   The cell or object is now locked.

2. Choose Protect Document from Options.

   Excel displays the dialog box.

3. Choose to protect the Cells, Windows, or Objects by checking the option.

4. Enter a Password if you wish.

5. Choose OK.

   The menu command changes to Unprotect Document.

 Note: Protected windows don't display the Control menu or the Maximize button. You can close a protected window with Close from File as usual.

 Note: When you lock objects with the Move and Size with Cells options of Object Placement from the Format menu on (as is the case by default), then objects *do* move when surrounding cells are moved.

Options—Set Page Break

Excel divides a large document into pages whose sizes depend on the margin settings in Page Setup (in the File menu). You can manually set page breaks with the Set Page Break command in the Options menu.

Keystrokes

Keyboard

Options

Set Page Break

Mouse

Options

Set Page Break

Example

Suppose that you have a worksheet that tabulates soccer results for a league during the season. Each week you enter the goals scored, the scorers, and other details. You want each week to be printed separately. Select the cell in the first row and column of the results for each week, and choose Set Page Break from Options. The page break (which appears as a broken line on the screen) is set along the left and top side of the selected cell.

Inserting a Page Break

1. Select the cell at which you want to insert the page break.

   The page break will be inserted along the top of this cell with the left margin of the page along the left side of the cell.

2. Choose Set Page Break from Options.

   Excel displays a broken line on the worksheet.

Note: You can distinguish a manual from an automatic page break in a document by the broken lines: the strokes are closer together with a manual break. This may not be apparent with an EGA system.

> **Tip:** You can remove page breaks individually or globally. To remove a page break individually, select the same cell you set it at—the cell whose left and top sides coincide with the left and top margins of the page—and then choose Remove Page Break from Options.
>
> To remove all manual page breaks, select the whole worksheet (by clicking on the blank cell in the upper left of the worksheet, to the left of A), and choose Remove Page Break from Options.

Options—Set Print Area

With the Set Print Area command, you can limit what you print to a set range or ranges of cells. Excel names this range or ranges Print_Area, accessible through the Goto command.

Keystrokes

Keyboard

Options

Set Print Area

Mouse

Options

Set Print Area

Example

The Print command in Excel allows you to print single pages on your worksheet, but Set Print Area is a further refining of this selection process. Say you had a worksheet with sales figures and their breakdown for every week of the year. But for the printout, you want only the monthly totals. Make a multiple selection of the cells containing these figures, choose Set Print Area, and then print as normal.

Setting a Print Area

1. Select those cells you want to print (this can be a multiple selection).

   The cell range is highlighted on the worksheet.

2. Choose Set Print Area from Options.

   Excel now displays a new name in the Goto command dialog box: Print_Area.

3. Print as normal.

   Only the selected area(s) print.

Note: To remove this special print area (and the name Print_Area), select the whole worksheet (by clicking on the blank cell in the upper left of the worksheet, to the left of A), and choose Remove Print Area from Options.

Options—Set Print Titles

With the Set Print Titles command from the Options menu, you can specify a row(s) or column(s) on your worksheet that you would like to use as titles in printing. Excel then prints these titles on every page.

Keystrokes

Keyboard

Options

Set Print Titles

Mouse

Options

Set Print Titles

Example

Suppose that you have a worksheet listing stocks in hand for every day through the year. Only the top of the worksheet has the names of the individual items of stock, and since the list goes on for several worksheet pages, you would like to print these title names on every page. Select the row that contains the title names and choose Set Print Titles from Options.

 Setting Print Titles

1. Select the row(s) or column(s) that contain the titles.

   If you select more than one row or column, then the rows or columns must be adjacent.

2. Choose Set Print Titles from Options.

   Excel now displays a new name in the Goto command dialog box: Print_Titles.

3. Print as normal.

   Excel uses these titles on every page.

Note: If you specify rows, Excel prints them at the top of every page. If you specify columns, Excel prints them on the left of every page.

Note: To remove print titles (and the name Print_Title), select the whole worksheet (by clicking on the blank cell in the upper left of the worksheet, to the left of A) and choose Remove Print Titles from Options.

Options—Short Menus

Choose the Short Menus command in Options to display the minimum commands necessary to run Excel. With Short Menus, the menus appear less cluttered because many of the commands are out of sight. Working in this mode, you can learn the basics faster because your attention is not diverted to the more advanced commands. When in Short Menus mode, the same command changes and displays as Full Menus.

Keystrokes

Keyboard

Options

Short Menus

Mouse

Options

Short Menus

Options—Workspace

Use the options in the dialog box displayed by the Workspace command from Options to control settings in your defined workspace. You can choose from the following options in the Workspace dialog box:

Fixed Decimal Places: The number here (default of 2) determines the number of decimal places in constants. You can override this on the worksheet by typing a decimal point as you enter a number.

Display: Check any option to display or accept it—Status Bar, Tool Bar, Scroll Bars, Formula Bar, Note Indicator. The R1C1 style is an alternative to referencing rows and columns with the A1 style (R meaning rows and C meaning columns).

Alternate Menu or Help Key: Use these options to show or change the key you use to activate the menu bar or Help. Then choose between Microsoft Excel Menus and Lotus 1-2-3 Help. If you choose the former, typing the key brings up the Excel menu bar. If you choose the latter, typing the key brings up Lotus Help.

Alternate Navigation Keys: Check this for a shortcut set of keystrokes for working on the spreadsheet. For example, Ctrl-left arrow moves left one page; Ctrl-right arrow moves right one page. Press **F1** to see the full list of keystrokes (with the dialog box on screen).

Ignore Remote Requests: Check this to get Excel to ignore requests made by other applications.

Move Selection after Enter: Check this to have Excel automatically move the active cell down one row after a formula or value is entered in a cell.

Keystrokes

Keyboard	*Mouse*
Options	Options
Workspace	Workspace
Enter	OK

Example

Suppose that you tend to make a lot of notes in your cells, and now you want Excel to display exactly which cells contain notes. Choose Workspace from Options. Check Note Indicator and choose OK. On the worksheet, a red dot appears in the upper-right corner of each cell containing a note.

Customizing Settings in a Workspace

1. Choose Workspace from Options. — Excel displays the Workspace dialog box.
2. Choose your options. — Options are divided into four parts: the Fixed Decimal option, the Display options, the Alternate Menu options, and miscellaneous options on the bottom.
3. Choose OK to accept and exit.

OR() (*see also* Function, AND, NOT, TRUE, FALSE)

Syntax

OR(*logical1,logical2,...*)

Description

OR is a function that returns FALSE if all the logical values that are given to AND are false. But if one or more of the logical values is true, it returns TRUE.
   The information required for function OR:

   logical1,logical2,... are the logical values TRUE or FALSE, or expressions that are TRUE or FALSE.

   Here are the rules for nonlogical values:

Type of Value	Converted to
None of the logical1,logical2,... values is a logical value	#VALUE! (error message)

Type of Value	Converted to
Cell address where the cell is empty or contains text	No effect on the calculations
An error message in a cell	The error message
0 in the list of values for the function	FALSE
Numerical values not equal to 0 in the list of values for the function	TRUE

Examples

Formula	Returns
=OR(FALSE,0)	FALSE
=OR(TRUE,TRUE,FALSE,2+2=10)	TRUE
=OR("s"="s",2+2=4)	TRUE

OUTLINE

(*see* Macro Functions That Perform Formula Commands)

P–Q

PAGE.SETUP

(*see* Macro Functions That Perform File Commands)

PARSE

(*see* Macro Functions That Perform Data Commands)

PASTE

(*see* Macro Functions That Perform Edit Commands)

PASTE.LINK

(*see* Macro Functions That Perform Edit Commands)

PASTE.PICTURE

(*see* Macro Functions That Perform Edit Commands)

PASTE.PICTURE.LINK

(*see* Macro Functions That Perform Edit Commands)

PASTE.SPECIAL

(*see* Macro Functions That Perform Edit Commands)

PATTERNS

(*see* Macro Functions That Perform Format Commands)

PI( )

(*see also* Function, COS, SIN, TAN)

Syntax

PI( )

Description

PI is a function that returns the value of the mathematical constant pi to fifteen digits of accuracy, the number 3.14159265358979.

    The information required for function PI:

        No information is required for function PI.

Examples

Formula	*Returns*
=PI( )	3.141592654
=PI( )/3	1.047197551
=PI( )*2	6.283185307

PLACEMENT

(*see* **Macro Functions That Perform Format Commands**)

PMT()

(*see also* **Functions, Annuity Functions, FV, IPMT, NPER, PPMT, PV, RATE**)

Syntax

PMT(*rate,nper,pv,fv,type*)

Description

PMT is a function that returns the periodic payment for an annuity based on periodic constant payments and a constant interest rate. For more information, see "Annuity Functions."

> **Note:** Use the same unit of measure for specifying rate and nper. If payments are monthly, then rate and nper should be based on one-month periods.

> **Note:** In annuity functions, a negative number represents cash that you pay out and a positive number represents cash that you receive.

The information required for function PMT (all of the following values are numbers; for more information, see "Annuity Functions"):

rate is the interest rate per period.

nper is the total number of payment periods in an annuity.

pv is the present value—the total amount that a series of future payments is worth now, in the present. As according to standard business practice, in the payment functions, interest calculations do not apply to pv.

fv is the future value or cash balance that you want to achieve after the last balance is made. If fv is not included, PMT assumes that fv is 0. (For example, a loan has a future value of 0.)

type is 0 or 1, indicating when payments are due, as shown below.

If type Is	*Payments Are Due*
0 or not included	At the end of the period
1	At the beginning of the period

Examples

Suppose that you are looking into a $10,000 loan. You want to pay off the loan by making monthly payments at the beginning of each month in a five-year period. The annual interest rate for the loan is 11%. To calculate how much you should pay each month, use the following formula: =PMT(11%/12, 12*5,10000,0,1). Your monthly payment is the value that this formula returns, –215.45. (Note that the amount returned is negative. The negative sign indicates that you will have $215.45 *less* money after this payment.)

Suppose that you are planning for the cost of your child's college education. Statistics estimate that you will need to save $120,000 for four years of college. Your child will be in college in 16 years. You want to know how much you should save at the end of each month. The annual interest rate for the savings accounts where the money will be is 10%. You can calculate how much to save each month using the following formula: =PMT(10%/12, 10*12,0,120000,0). This formula returns –$255.08. If you save $255.08 per month for the next sixteen years, then you will have $120,000, enough to pay for four years of college for one child.

Suppose that you loaned $5,000 to a friend at an annual interest rate of 7%. Your friend will pay you back with payments at the end of each year for five years. How much should your friend pay you each year? Use the following formula: =PMT(7%,5,–5000). (The 5000 is negative since you loan or pay out this money to your friend.) $1,219.45 is returned by this formula. (The amount is positive because this is how much you receive.)

POKE (*see* Macro Functions—Control)

PPMT( )

(*see also* Functions, Annuity Functions, FV, IPMT, NPER, PMT, PV, RATE)

Syntax

PPMT(*rate,per,nper,pv,fv,type*)

Description

PPMT is a function that returns the payment on the principal during one period which you specify, for an investment that is based on periodic constant payments and a constant interest rate. For more information, see "Annuity Functions."

Note: Use the same unit of measure for specifying rate and nper. If payments are monthly, then rate and nper should be based on one-month periods.

Note: In annuity functions, a negative number represents cash that you pay out and a positive number represents cash that you receive.

The information required for function PPMT (all of the following values are numbers; for more information, see "Annuity Functions"):

rate is the interest rate per period.

per is a number in the range of 1 to nper. per is the specific period for which you are requesting interest.

nper is the total number of payment periods in an annuity.

pv is the present value—the total amount that a series of future payments is worth now, in the present. As according to standard business practice, in the payment functions, interest calculations do not apply to pv.

fv is the future value or cash balance that you want to achieve after the last balance is made. If fv is not included, PPMT assumes that fv is 0. (For example, a loan has a future value of 0.)

type is 0 or 1, indicating when payments are due, as shown below.

If type Is	*Payments Are Due*
0 or not included	At the end of the period
1	At the beginning of the period

Examples

The following formula returns the payment on the principal during the first month of a five-year $25,000 loan at 14% annual interest with payments at the end of each month: =PPMT(14%/12,1,12*5,25000). In the first month, you pay $290.04 of the principal (the amount that this formula returns). For this same loan, the payment on the principal of the 12th month, =PPMT(14%/12,12, 12*5,25000), is $329.51 (the amount that this formula returns).

The following formula returns the payment on the principal during the last year of a 10-year $5,000 loan at 10% annual interest with payments at the end of each year: =PPMT(10%,10,10,5000,0,0). In the last year, you pay $739.75 of the principal (the amount that this formula returns).

The following formula returns the payment on the principal during the first month of a five-year $10,000 loan at 11% annual interest with payments at the beginning of each month: =PPMT(11%/12,1,12*5,10000,0,1). In the first month, you pay $215.45 of the principal (the amount that this formula returns). Note that this is the same as the total monthly payment that you calculate with this formula =PMT(11%/12,1,12*5,10000,0,1). Payment on the principal during the second month of this same five-year $10,000 loan at 11% annual interest, according to the formula =PPMT(11%/12,2,12*5,10000,0,1), is $125.76.

Note: A type of 1, for payment that occurs in the beginning of the period, and a per of 1, for the interest paid in the first period, returns a value for the function PPMT that is the same as the total payment per period calculated by PMT.

PRECISION

(*see* Macro Functions That Perform Options Commands)

PREFERRED

(*see* Macro Functions That Perform Gallery Commands)

PRINT

(*see* Macro Functions That Perform File Commands)

PRINT.PREVIEW

(*see* Macro Functions That Perform File Commands)

PRINTER.SETUP

(*see* Macro Functions That Perform File Commands)

PRODUCT( )

(*see also* Function, FACT, SUMPRODUCT, SUM)

Syntax

PRODUCT(*number1,number2,...*)

Description

PRODUCT is a function that returns the product of all the given numbers. PRODUCT multiplies all the numbers that are given to it in the list of values for the function. You can give the function PRODUCT up to 14 numbers, cell addresses, ranges of cell addresses, functions, or formulas returning a number. The last example under "Examples" demonstrates what happens if you specify more than 14 elements.

The information required for function PRODUCT:

number1,number2,... where *each* of these numbers is any number or reference to a number (such as a cell address or a function that returns a number). Each number must be separated from other numbers by a comma.

Nonnumeric values, such as text and logic values, are sometimes converted to numeric values, sometimes ignored, and sometimes cause errors. A function, such as PRODUCT, that requires numeric values:

- Converts a value to a numeric value if the value is typed directly into the list of values for the function and is one of the following:

    a logical value

    a number that is in text form

- Does not convert a value to a numeric value if the value is a cell address in the list of values for the function, where the addressed cell:

    is empty

    contains text

    contains a logical value

- Returns an error if the list of values for the function contains a cell address and the addressed cell has an error value in it.

- Displays the #VALUES error if there is text in the list of values for the function.

Examples

Formula	Cell(s) Contain	Formula Returns
=PRODUCT(1,2,3)		6
=PRODUCT(–2,3)		–6

Formula	Cell(s) Contain	Formula Returns
=PRODUCT(B1:F4)	ALL cells contain 2	1024
=PRODUCT(6–1,B1:F4)	ALL cells contain 2	5120
=PRODUCT(C3)	TRUE	0
=PRODUCT(C3,C4)	"letters","6"	0
=PRODUCT(C4)		0
=PRODUCT(7,TRUE,"1,000")		7000

Here are some examples that illustrate the automatic conversion rules for nonnumeric values:

According to the rules, if a value is in a cell, the value is included in the calculations only if it is a number. If cells C3 through C6 contain the values FALSE,5,"3","letters", then the formula =PRODUCT(C3:C6) returns a 5. This is because the only value that is a number is the number 5. The remaining values from the cell addresses, which are text or logical values, are ignored. (The "3" is a text value because it is in quotation marks.)

Let's modify that formula to include some values that are typed directly into the list of values for the function. Cells C3 through C6 contain the values FALSE,5,"3","letters", and the formula is =PRODUCT(C3:C6,FALSE). This new formula now returns 0 because FALSE is converted to a number since it is typed directly into the list of values for the function. FALSE converts to 0, so 5 * 0 = 0.

Now let's change the first formula we used, =PRODUCT(C3:C6), to include some numbers in text form that are typed directly into the list of values for the function. Cells C3 through C6 still contain the values FALSE,5,"3","letters", and the new formula is =PRODUCT(C3:C6,"4"). This new formula now returns 20, because the number 5 from the cell addresses and the number 4 converted from the text value 4 in the list of values for the function are both used to calculate the product. (Once again, the "3" was not converted to a number and used since it is a text value in a cell.)

Let's modify the first formula we used to include some different text values that are typed directly into the list of values for the function. Cells C3 through C6 still contain the values FALSE,5,"3","letters", and the formula is =PRODUCT(C3:C6,"abc"). This new formula now returns the error value #VALUES!. Text values are not allowed because the function PRODUCT requests numeric values.

Our last example illustrates the limit of giving 14 elements to a function. In the following formula this limit is exceeded: =PRODUCT(B1,B2,B3,B4,B5,B6,B7,B8,B9,B10,B11,B12,B13,B14,B15). After you enter this formula, a dialog box saying Error in Formula appears. On the other hand, the formula =PRODUCT(B1:B15) would return a value and would not display the Error in Formula dialog box.

PROMOTE

(*see* Macro Functions That Perform Actions)

PROPER( ) (*see also* LOWER, UPPER)

Syntax

PROPER(*text*)

Description

PROPER is a function that returns text with the first letter of each word capitalized and all other letters lowercase.

Note: PROPER changes letters only. Characters that are not letters are unchanged. If the first character of a word in text is not a letter, then the first letter that follows it is capitalized.

The information required for function PROPER:

text is any group of symbols that is either enclosed in one pair of quotation marks or entered in a cell.

Examples

Formula	*Returns*
=PROPER("THE TITLE OF TODAY'S TALK")	"The Title Of Today's Talk"
=PROPER("62 n. bakers street")	"62 N. Bakers Street"

PROPER is useful for capitalizing the first letter of names, as shown in the figure.

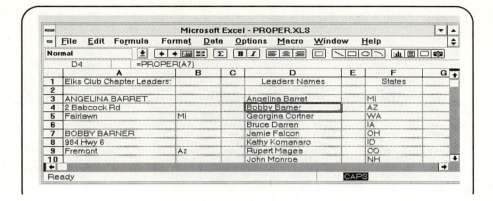

PROTECT.DOCUMENT

(*see* **Macro Functions That Perform Options Commands**)

PV()

(*see also* **Functions, Annuity Functions, FV, IPMT, NPER, PMT, PPMT, RATE**)

Syntax

PV(*rate,nper,pmt,fv,type*)

Description

PV is a function that returns the present value of an investment. The present value is the total amount that a series of future payments is worth now, in the present.

 Note: Use the same unit of measure for specifying rate and nper. If payments are monthly, then rate and nper should be based on one-month periods.

The information required for function PV (all of the following values are numbers; for more information, see "Annuity Functions"):

rate is the interest rate per period.

nper is the total number of payment periods in an annuity.

pmt is the payment made each period and does not change over the life of the annuity. (Usually pmt includes principal and interest but no other fees or taxes.)

fv is the future value or cash balance that you want to achieve after the last payment is made. If fv is not included, PV assumes that fv is 0. (For example, a loan has a future value of 0.)

type is 0 or 1, indicating when payments are due, as shown below.

If type Is	Payments Are Due
0 or not included	At the end of the period
1	At the beginning of the period

Examples

Suppose that you are looking into a car loan. The car costs $10,000. Your monthly payments of $200 are due at the beginning of each month and continue for a five-year period. If you finance the car, you pay an annual interest rate of 8.5%. Would you be better off paying cash or financing the car?

This question can be answered using the following formula: =PV (8.5%/12,12*5,-200,0,1). This formula returns $9817.29, which is $182.71 less than the cost of the car in cash. Therefore, it would be less expensive to finance the car.

Q+E Functions

Using the special functions listed in this section, you can access and manipulate the Q+E menu commands through an Excel macro sheet. These special functions work from inside the EXECUTE function.

For example, suppose that you want to find a name in a query data window and then print the entire contents of the query window in letter quality. This brief macro in Excel performs the task:

chan=INITIATE("QE",Query1), where Query1 is the query window name

name=REQUEST(chan,"R10C12"), which places the name in R10C12 into the variable "name"

=EXECUTE(chan,"[PRINT(1,FALSE)]"), which prints one copy of the data in the query window in good quality print

=TERMINATE(chan)

 Accessing Q+E Menu Commands Through a Macro

1. Use the Initiate function, for example, chan=INITIATE("QE", Query1).   The channel to Q&E is opened.

2. Use the special Q+E functions listed in this section inside the Execute function, for example, =EXECUTE(chan,"[PRINT (1,FALSE)]").   Your instructions are sent to Q&E.

3. Use the Terminate function, for example, =TERMINATE(chan).   The channel to Q&E is closed.

The EXECUTE function uses many other functions to access the Q+E menu. A full list of these functions follows. Most of them are direct equivalents to Q+E menu commands; those that are not are specified.

Name: ACTIVATE

Syntax: ACTIVATE(*windowname_text*)

Q+E Menu Equivalent: No equivalent

Description: Activates a query or Define window

Arguments: *Windowname_text* is the name of the window to activate.

Notes: ACTIVATE is only used on channels initiated with the System topic.

Name: ADD.AFTER

Syntax: ADD.AFTER(*field_values*)

Q+E Menu Equivalent: Define Edit Add After

Description: Adds a new field definition after a selected field, or a new field if no field is selected

Arguments: *Field_values* redefines or defines the field.

Name: ADD.BEFORE

Syntax: ADD.BEFORE(*field_values*)

Q+E Menu Equivalent: Define Edit Add Before

Description: Adds a new field definition before a selected field, or a new field if no field is selected

Arguments: *Field_values* redefines or defines the field.

Name: ADD.CONDITION

Syntax:
ADD.CONDITION(*logical_op,relational_op,value,case_sensitive*)

Q+E Menu Equivalent: Select Add Condition

Description: Adds a selection condition for records

Arguments: *logical_op* must be 1 standing for AND; or 2 standing for OR.

relational_op must be a number from 1 to 8 as designated below:

The Number	Stands for
1	=
2	!=
3	<
4	<=
5	>
6	>=
7	LIKE
8	NOT LIKE

Value gives the value for the condition.

case_sensitive can be TRUE or FALSE signifying that you want the condition to be case-sensitive or not.

Name: ADD.RECORD

Syntax: ADD.RECORD?( )

Q+E Menu Equivalent: Edit Add Record

Description: Displays the form for adding a new record

Name: ALLOW.EDIT

Syntax: ALLOW.EDIT(*enable*)

Q+E Menu Equivalent: Allow Editing in Edit

Description: You can't edit unless this is selected first.

Arguments: *Enable* is a logical: TRUE means editing is allowed; FALSE means it is not.

Name: ARRANGE.ALL

Syntax: ARRANGE.ALL( )

Q+E Menu Equivalent: Window Arrange All

Description: Rearranges windows

Name: CLOSE

Syntax: CLOSE( )

Q+E Menu Equivalent: File Close

Description: Closes the active window

Notes: CLOSE( ) terminates the channel if you are not using the System topic.

Name: CLOSE.INDEX

Syntax: CLOSE.INDEX(*index_file*)

Q+E Menu Equivalent: File Close Index

Description: Closes a dBASE file named *index_file*

Arguments: *Index_file* is the file to be closed.

Name: COLUMN.WIDTH

Syntax: COLUMN.WIDTH(*width,default_width*)

Q+E Menu Equivalent: Layout Column Width

Description: Changes the width of a column

Arguments: *Width* is the new width in numbers.

default_width is a logical where TRUE sets the column to the default width and FALSE sets the column to the width value.

Name: COMMAND

Syntax: COMMAND(*op_num,exec_string*).

Q+E Menu Equivalent: No equivalent

Description: Sends a string of execute commands to Q+E

Arguments: *op_num* is a number from 1 to 3. 1 means Q+E saves the exec_string to a buffer but does not execute it. 2 means exec_string is concatenated (added) to the buffer. 3 concatenates exec_string to the buffer and the buffer command is executed.

Exec_string is the execute command

Notes: You cannot include this command in a query file.

Use COMMAND to send a command in smaller pieces when, as in Excel, a macro language has a limit on the size of character variables.

Name: COPY

Syntax: COPY( )

Q+E Menu Equivalent: Edit Copy

Description: Copies whatever is selected to the clipboard

Name: COPY.SPECIAL

Syntax: COPY.SPECIAL(*colhdr,rec_num, formula,data*)

Q+E Menu Equivalent: Edit Copy Special

Description: Copies selected data to the clipboard according to specifications in arguments

Arguments: *Colhdr* is a logical. If TRUE, column headings are copied; if FALSE, they are not.

Rec_num is a logical. If TRUE, records number are copied; if FALSE, they are not.

Formula is a number, either 1 or 2. When the data is linked, use 1 to specify a query name formula type; use 2 to specify an SQL Select statement.

Data is a number from 1 to 3 specifying what is copied. 1 copies all data; 2 copies selected data; 3 copies SQL Select statement text.

Name: CUT

Syntax: CUT( )

Q+E Menu Equivalent: Edit Cut

Description: Removes selected data and places it into the clipboard

Name: DEFINE

Syntax: DEFINE(*name,source,charset_num*)

Q+E Menu Equivalent: File Define

Description: Opens the define window

Arguments: *Name* is the file you want to open in the define window. If it is blank, then the define window is blank.

Source is the database system.

Charset_num is 1 or 2. When the source is dBASEFile, 1 specifies the ANSI character set to store data; 2 specifies IBM PC.

Name: DEFINE.COLUMN

Syntax:
DEFINE.COLUMN(*heading_text,expression_text,add,dest_num*)

Q+E Menu Equivalent: Layout Define Column

Description: Adds a column or changes an existing selected column

Arguments: *heading_text* gives the new column heading if desired. When it is blank, Q+E takes expression_text.

expression_text defines the new values.

add is a logical. If TRUE, a new column is added together with other changes like a new heading and new values; if FALSE, only the heading and values changes are made.

Dest_num specifies a column number for a new column.

Name: DEFINE.FIELD

Syntax: DEFINE.FIELD(*data_type,parm_1,parm_2*)

Q+E Menu Equivalent: Layout Define Field

Description: Changes the field specifications of selected fields

Arguments: *data_type* is a number from 1 to 5 that varies according to whether the source is a text file or an Excel file. It specifies the kind of data in the column. With text files, 1 means a character; 2 means a numeric; and 3 means a date. With Excel files, 1 means a character; 2 means a floating point; 3 means an integer; 4 means a date; and 5 means a logical.

parm_1 is a number specifying the maximum width or the format in the columns. With text files, when data_type is 1 or 2, parm_1 is the maximum number of characters or digits; when data_type is 3, parm_1 specifies the format of the dates (see the Define Field dialog box). With Excel files, when data_type is 1, parm_1 is the maximum number of characters in the column.

parm_2 is the number of digits to the right of the decimal point. Data_type must be 2 and the source must be a text file for this to be relevant.

Name: DEFINE.INDEX

Syntax:
DEFINE.INDEX(*index_file,tag,expression,unique,desc,op_num*)

Q+E Menu Equivalent: File Define Index

Description: Creates, changes, or deletes a dBASE index file

Arguments: *index_file* is the name of the file.

tag is the name of the tag if the file is a dBASE IV(.mdx) file.

expression creates or rebuilds the index.

unique is a logical. If TRUE, the index will be unique; if FALSE, it will not.

desc is a logical. If TRUE, the index is sorted in descending order; if FALSE, it is not.

op_num is a number. If 1, the index is created or rebuilt; if 2, the index is deleted.

Name: DELETE

Syntax: DELETE(*name,source*)

Q+E Menu Equivalent: File Delete (in the Define dialog box)

Description: Deletes a database file

Arguments: *Name* is the database file.

Source is the database system.

Name: DELETE.FIELDS

Syntax: DELETE.FIELDS( )

Q+E Menu Equivalent: Delete Fields in Edit in Define window

Description: Deletes selected fields

Name: DELETE.RECORDS

Syntax: DELETE.RECORDS( )

Q+E Menu Equivalent: Edit Delete Records

Description: Deletes the selected records

Name: DISTINCT

Syntax: DISTINCT(*enable*)

Q+E Menu Equivalent: Distinct in Select

Description: Hides duplicate rows for SQL Server, Oracle, and Extended Edition Data Manager

Arguments: *Enable* is a logical. If TRUE, only unique rows appear; if FALSE, all rows are displayed.

Name: ECHO

Syntax: ECHO(*enable*)

Q+E Menu Equivalent: No equivalent

Description: Dictates whether the screen is updated after a command is executed

Arguments: *enable* is a logical. If TRUE, Q+E updates the screen after each command. If FALSE, the screen is redrawn when the DDE channel is terminated. TRUE is the default situation unless otherwise specified.

Name: EXIT

Syntax: EXIT( )

Q+E Menu Equivalent: File Exit

Description: Closes all windows and quits Q+E

Name: FETCH

Syntax: FETCH(*dest_app,dest_topic,dest_item,qe_item*)

Q+E Menu Equivalent: No equivalent

Description: Sends data to other applications

Arguments: *dest_app* is the destination application.

dest_topic is the destination file or document.

dest_item is a destination area on the worksheet or file.

qe_item specifies what Q+E data is sent.

Notes: FETCH cannot be used with Microsoft Word or included in query files. Also, if the destination application is Excel, the destination area is specified in RC (row and column).

Name: FETCH.ADVISE

Syntax: FETCH.ADVISE(*dest_app,dest_topic,dest_item,qe_item*)

Q+E Menu Equivalent: No equivalent

Description: Works the same as FETCH, but when the data sent in qe_item changes before FETCH.UNADVISE or CLOSE are executed, Q+E sends the data again with this command.

Name: FETCH.UNADVISE

Syntax: FETCH.UNADVISE(*dest_app,dest_topic,dest_item,qe_item*)

Q+E Menu Equivalent: No equivalent

Description: Cancels the previous FETCH.ADVISE so that qe_item data changes no longer are re-sent. Use the same arguments.

Name: FIND

Syntax: FIND(*string_text*)

Q+E Menu Equivalent: Search Find

Description: Finds and selects specified data

Arguments: *String_text* contains the characters to be found. Not case-sensitive.

Name: FIND.NEXT

Syntax: FIND.NEXT( )

Q+E Menu Equivalent: Search Find Next

Description: Finds and selects next occurrence of Find command string

Name: FIND.PREVIOUS

Syntax: FIND.PREVIOUS( )

Q+E Menu Equivalent: Search Find Previous

Description: Finds and selects last occurrence of Find command string

Name: FONT

Syntax:
FONT(*font_name, size_num, bold, italic, underline, strike, set_default*)

Q+E Menu Equivalent: Layout Font

Description: Reformats text

Arguments: *Font_name* is the font.

size_num is the type size.

bold, italic, underline, strike, and *set_default* are logicals. When TRUE, they are on.

Name: FORM?

Syntax: FORM?( )

Q+E Menu Equivalent: Edit Form

Description: Displays the selected record in a dialog box

Notes: Form? is not available through DDE.

Name: FORM.SETUP

Syntax: FORM.SETUP(*max_col,max_flds_per_col,max_fld_width*)

Q+E Menu Equivalent: Exit Form Setup

Description: Customizes the Form dialog box

Arguments: *max_col* is the maximum columns in the dialog box.

max_flds_per_col is the maximum fields per column.

max_fld_width is the maximum characters in each field.

Name: GOTO.RECORD

Syntax: GOTO.RECORD(*rec_num*)

Q+E Menu Equivalent: Search Goto

Description: Finds record number specified and selects the first field

ARGUMENTS: *Rec_num* is the record number.

Name: JOIN

Syntax: JOIN( )

Q+E Menu Equivalent: Select Join

Description: Joins the data in the top two query windows

Name: KEYS

Syntax: KEYS(*keys*)

Q+E Menu Equivalent: No equivalent

Description: Sends keystrokes to be executed

Arguments: *keys* can be one or more keystrokes including text and numbers. You could, for instance, tab to the next field and specify a change there.

Notes: Put Tab, Left, Right, Up, and Down in braces {}, for example, {Tab}.

Name: LOGOFF

Syntax: LOGOFF(*dbname*)

Q+E Menu Equivalent: File Logoff

Description: Logs off the specified database system

Arguments: *dbname* specifies the system.

Name: LOGON

Syntax: LOGON(*dbname*)

Q+E Menu Equivalent: File Logon

Description: Displays the Logon dialog box

Arguments: *dbname* specifies the system.

Name: MOVE.COLUMN

Syntax: MOVE.COLUMN(*dest_num*)

Q+E Menu Equivalent: Layout Move Column

Description: Moves a selected column

Arguments: *Dest_num* is the number representing the position of the column.

Name: ONLY.SHOW.TOTALS

Syntax: ONLY.SHOW.TOTALS(*enable*)

Q+E Menu Equivalent: Layout Only Show Totals

Description: Hides totals

Arguments: *Enable* is a logical. If TRUE, only total values are displayed; if FALSE, records and totals are displayed.

Name: OPEN

Syntax: dBASE:
OPEN(*spec_text,source,use_colhdr,charset_num,sql_num,set_default*)

TextFile:
OPEN(*spec_text,source,use_colhdr,charset_num,file_type,delim_text, hdr_line,set_default*)

ExcelFile:
OPEN(*spec_text,source,use_colhdr,scan_lines,guess_type,set_default*)

SQL Server, Oracle, Extended Edition: OPEN(*spec_text,source*)

Q+E Menu Equivalent: File Open

Description: Opens and displays a file

Arguments: *spec_text* is the name of the file to open.

source specifies the database system.

use_colhdr is a logical. If TRUE, the file column headings are used as field names. If FALSE, the underlying database field names are used.

charset_num is a number, 1 or 2. If 1, the ANSI character set is used; if 2, the IBM PC set is used.

sql_num is 1 or 2. If 1, ANSI SQL is used; if 2, dBASE IV SQL is used.

file_type is 1 or 2. If 1, text file contains character-delimited fields; if 2, text file contains fixed-length values.

delim_text specifies the delimiter character when file_type is 1. If it's Tab, enter "Tab".

hdr_line is a logical. If TRUE, Q+E uses the values in the first line for column headings. If FALSE, Field_1, Field_2, etc., are used.

set_default is a logical. If TRUE, the arguments will be used in the future as defaults; if FALSE, they will not. This applies only to dBASE, text, and Excel files.

scan_lines is the number of lines Q+E should scan to guess the width for each column.

guess_type is a logical. If TRUE, Q+E guesses the data types; if FALSE, all columns become character types.

Notes: This command can only be used on a System topic channel.

Name: OPEN.INDEX

Syntax: OPEN.INDEX(*index_file,use*)

Q+E Menu Equivalent: File Open Index

Description: Opens a dBASE index file

Arguments: *index_file* is the name of the file.

use is a logical. Used with dBASE III(.ndx), if TRUE, the index is used to sort; if FALSE, it is opened and maintained but not used to sort.

Name: OUTER.JOIN

Syntax: OUTER.JOIN( )

Q+E Menu Equivalent: Select Outer Join

Description: Joins the data in the top two query windows

Notes: This command can only be used with a System topic channel.

Name: PAGE.SETUP

Syntax:
PAGE.SETUP(*title_text,Lmargin_num,Rmargin_num,Tmargin_num, Bmargin_num,headings,rec_num,page_num,date,time*)

Q+E Menu Equivalent: File Page Setup

Description: Sets page formatting options

Arguments: *title_text* displays centered on the first line of each page.

Lmargin_num determines the left margin.

Rmargin_num determines the right margin.

Tmargin_num determines the top margin.

Bmargin_num determines the bottom margin.

headings, rec_num, page_num, date, and *time* are logicals. If TRUE, they turn the option on.

Name: PARSE.LINE

Syntax: PARSE.LINE(*string_text*)

Q+E Menu Equivalent: Layout Parse Line

Description: Specifies the parsing for a fixed-format text file

Arguments: *string_text* shows the byte offset and length of each field in each line contained in brackets.

Name: PASTE

Syntax: PASTE(*field_values*)

Q+E Menu Equivalent: Edit Paste

Description: Pastes from the clipboard or from the field_values argument

Arguments: *Field_values,* when used, overrides the clipboard.

Name: PASTE.APPEND

Syntax: PASTE.APPEND(*field_values*)

Q+E Menu Equivalent: Edit Paste Append

Description: Adds new records and field definitions

Arguments: *field_values,* when used, overrides the clipboard.

Name: PRINT

Syntax: PRINT(*copies_num,draft*)

Q+E Menu Equivalent: File Print

Description: Prints

Arguments: *Copies_num* is the number of copies.

Draft is a logical. If TRUE, prints in draft mode.

Name: QUERY.NOW

Syntax: QUERY.NOW( )

Q+E Menu Equivalent: Select Query Now

Description: Executes the SQL Select statement and displays the result

Name: REMOVE.COLUMN

Syntax: REMOVE.COLUMN( )

Q+E Menu Equivalent: Layout Remove Column

Description: Removes selected columns

Name: SAVE

Syntax: SAVE( )

Q+E Menu Equivalent: File Save

Description: Saves the current query definition

Name: SAVE AS

Syntax: dBASE:
SAVE.AS(*name,dest_text,use_colhdr,type,charset_num*)

Text files:
SAVE.AS(*name,dest_text,use_colhdr,type,charset_num,delimiter,hdr_line*)

Excel, SQL Server, Oracle, Extended Edition:
SAVE.AS(*name,dest_text,use_colhdr*)

Define Windows: SAVE.AS(*name,type,pack,charset_num*)

Q+E Menu Equivalent: File Save As

Description: Saves according to specifications

Arguments: *name* is the name for the file.

dest_text is the database system.

use_colhdr is a logical. If TRUE, the column headings are used as field names. If FALSE, the underlying database field names are used.

type is a number from 1 to 3. With dBASE files, 1 means dBASE II; 2 means dBASE III; and 3 means dBASE IV. With text files, 1 means character delimited; 2 means fixed format.

charset_num is 1 or 2. If 1, ANSI is used; if 2, IBM PC is used.

delimiter is the delimiter character and is relevant when type is 1 with text files.

hdr_line is a logical. If TRUE, the first line contains field names.

pack is a logical. If TRUE, the file is packed; if FALSE, it is not. This applies only to dBASE files.

Name: SAVE.LABELS.AS

Syntax: SAVE.LABELS.AS(*name,def_text,lines_between,start_col1,start_col2,start_col3, start_col4,charset_num*)

Q+E Menu Equivalent: File Save As (using the Mailing Labels destination)

Description: Saves in a mailing label format

Arguments: *name* gives the file name, with .Lab as the extension.

def_text describes the fields on each line. Use the plus sign (+) to put values together; use a semicolon (;) to separate lines.

lines_between is the number of vertical lines between each column.

start_col1, start_col2, etc., are numbers corresponding to the starting column positions of the labels.

charset_num is 1 or 2. If 1, ANSI is used; if 2, IBM PC is used.

Name: SAVE.QUERY.AS

Syntax: SAVE.QUERY.AS(*name*)

Q+E Menu Equivalent: File Save As (when the destination is QueryFile)

Description: Saves to a query (.qef) file

Arguments: *name* is the file name.

Name: SAVE.TEXT.AS

Syntax: SAVE.TEXT.AS(*name,width,lines,charset_num*)

Q+E Menu Equivalent: File Save As (when the destination is PrintToFile)

Description: Saves to a file formatted as text

Arguments: *name* is the name with extension .txt added.

width is the maximum number of characters on each line.

lines is the maximum number of lines per page.

charset_num is 1 or 2. If 1, ANSI is used; if 2, IBM PC is used.

Name: SELECT.AREA

Syntax: SELECT.AREA(*rowcol_text*)

Q+E Menu Equivalent: No equivalent

Description: Selects rows and columns

Arguments: *rowcol_text* specifies the rows and columns in the format RnCm:RxCy.

Name: SELECT.COLUMN

Syntax: SELECT.COLUMN(*col_expr_text*)

Q+E Menu Equivalent: No equivalent

Description: Selects a column based on its column expression

Arguments: *col_expr_text* is the column expression.

Name: SELECT.DELETED.RECORDS

Syntax: SELECT.DELETED.RECORDS(*enable*)

Q+E Menu Equivalent: Select Deleted Records

Description: Displays dBASE records marked for deletion or redisplays dBASE records not marked for deletion

Arguments: *enable* is a logical. If TRUE, displays dBASE records marked for deletion; if FALSE, displays dBASE records not marked for deletion.

Name: SELECT.RESET

Syntax: SELECT.RESET( )

Q+E Menu Equivalent: Select Reset Conditions

Description: Displays all records by removing selection conditions

Name: SORT.ASCENDING

Syntax: SORT.ASCENDING( )

Q+E Menu Equivalent: Sort Ascending

Description: Sorts the records in ascending order based on the selected column

Name: SORT DESCENDING

Syntax: SORT.DESCENDING( )

Q+E Menu Equivalent: Sort Descending

Description: Sorts the records in descending order based on the selected column

Name: SORT.RESET

Syntax: SORT.RESET( )

Q+E Menu Equivalent: Reset Sort

Description: Unsorts sorted records

Notes: If a dBASE file is saved after sorting, it cannot be unsorted.

Name: SQL.QUERY

Syntax: SQL.QUERY(*stmt_text*)

Q+E Menu Equivalent: Select SQL Query

Description: Replaces the current Select statement with a new one contained in stmt_text

Name: TOTALS

Syntax: TOTALS(*min,max,count,avg,sum*)

Q+E Menu Equivalent: Layout Totals

Description: Adds or removes totals

Arguments: All arguments are logicals. If TRUE, they display the minimum, the maximum, the count, the average, and the sum of the values.

Notes: *avg* and *sum* are good only for numeric fields.

Name: UNDO

Syntax: UNDO( )

Q+E Menu Equivalent: Edit Undo

Description: Undoes the last command executed if this is possible

Name: UPDATE.ALL

Syntax: UPDATE.ALL(*newval_text*)

Q+E Menu Equivalent: Edit Update All

Description: Changes all selected fields to the same value

Arguments: *Newval_text* is the new value.

Name: USE.INDEX

Syntax: USE.INDEX(*index_file*)

Q+E Menu Equivalent: File Use Index

Description: Sorts dBASE file records using the index

Arguments: *Index_file* is the index file name without an extension.

QUIT

(see **Macro Functions That Perform File Commands)**

R

RAND( ) *(see also* Function, INT, ROUND)

Syntax

RAND( )

Description

RAND is a function that returns a random number from 0 up to, but not including, 1. RAND picks a number from a list of random numbers. A new random number is picked every time you tell the worksheet to recalculate.

You can use RAND to create ranges of random numbers or fixed random numbers:

- For the range 0 up to num, excluding num, use INT(num * RAND( )), where num is the largest random number that you want to generate.

- For numbers between numbers low# and high# and including low# and high# numbers, use INT((1 + high# − low#) * RAND( )) + low#.

- To create a constant random number in a cell, which does not change when the worksheet recalculates:

    1. Type =RAND( ) in the formula bar.

    2. From the Options menu or via keystrokes, choose to calculate now. (After you do this, you see a random number appear in the cell.)

    3. Press the Enter key to make this number fixed.

The information required for function RAND:

No information is required for function RAND.

Examples

Formula

=RAND() * 10

=INT(RAND() * 10)

=ROUND(RAND() * 63,0) + 12

Returns

A random number that is greater than or equal to 0 and less than 10.

A random integer that is greater than or equal to 0 and less than 10.

A random integer that is greater than or equal to 12 and less than 75.

RATE()

(*see also* Functions, Annuity Functions, FV, IPMT, NPER, PMT, PPMT, PV)

Syntax

RATE(*nper,pmt,pv,fv,type,guess*)

Description

RATE is a function that returns the interest rate per period for an annuity. RATE is calculated by repeated approximations and therefore may have zero or more solutions. If, after 20 iterations, the results of RATE do not decrease to a difference of 0.0000001 between two successive approximations, then RATE returns #NUM! error. For more information, see "Annuity Functions."

Note: Make sure that you use the same unit of measurement for specifying nper as is specified by the period of the payments. If payments are monthly, then nper should be based on one-month periods (for example, five years of monthly payments is a total of 5 * 12 payments).

Note: In annuity functions, a negative number represents cash that you pay out and a positive number represents cash that you receive.

The information required for function RATE (all of the following values are numbers; for more information, see "Annuity Functions"):

nper is the total number of payment periods in an annuity.

pmt is the payment made each period and does not change over the life of the annuity. (Usually pmt includes principal and interest but no other fees or taxes.)

pv is the present value or total lump-sum amount that a series of future payments is worth now, in the present.

fv is the future value or cash balance that you want to achieve after the last payment is made. If fv is not included, RATE assumes that fv is 0. (For example, a loan has a future value of 0.)

type is 0 or 1, indicating when payments are due, as shown below.

If type Is	*Payments Are Due*
0 or not included	At the end of the period
1	At the beginning of the period

guess is your general approximation of what the rate will be. If guess is not included, then RATE assumes that it is 10%. If RATE returns the #NUM! error, then try different guesses. Try a number between 0 and 1 (0% and 100%).

Note: Unless you are extremely far away from the correct value, the guess that you start out with makes little difference in your answer.

Examples

Suppose that you are considering buying a bond that gives you payments of $5,000 each at the end of each year for 10 years. The cost of this bond is $25,000. The formula =RATE(10,5000,−25000,,0,10%) tells you that the interest rate for this bond is 0.150984 or approximately 15.1%, the number that is returned by the formula.

Suppose you are considering a special offer to buy a new sofa for only 10 payments of $125.98, due at the beginning of each month. The cash price of this sofa is $1,200. What interest rate are you paying if you buy the sofa with these timed payments? This question can be answered by this formula: =RATE(10,−125.98,1200,,1,5%), which returns 0.010976. This is the *monthly* interest rate since nper specifies a one-month period. The annual interest rate is 0.010976 * 12, which equals 0.131712 or approximately 13%.

References

A *reference* is a type of value, an expression of information in a structured and precise form. A reference is a cell address, a range of cell addresses, or name. A cell address is a reference that gives the location of a value. A range of cell addresses is a reference that gives the location of an array of values.

A *cell address* is a representation of the row and column that a cell is in. For example, the cell address of the upper-left corner of the spreadsheet is A1 because the leftmost column is column A, as you can see in the bar across the top of the spreadsheet, and the top row is 1, as you can see in the row labels along the side of the spreadsheet.

A *range of cell addresses* is the rectangular area of the spreadsheet that stretches from the first cell in the range down and to the right, across all rows and columns that are between the first and the second cell addresses. For example, the range of cell addresses B3:C5 includes all the following cells: B3, B4, B5, C3, C4, C5.

References can be either of two styles, A1-style or R1C1-style. The style that appears automatically is the A1-style, in which one or more letters are followed by a number. The letters represent the column position, and the number represents the row position. In the R1C1-style, the number that follows the *R* represents the row position, and the number that follows the *C* represents the column. To display and use R1C1-style references in your workspace, see the Options Workspace command.

References can be either of two types, relative or absolute. An *absolute reference* always refers to the same cell, no matter what you do with that cell. But a *relative reference* is an offset from some base reference value. Many of the things you can do to a cell containing a relative reference change the relative reference.

With A1-style references, when you copy a relative reference value to another cell, the offset amount that you move the contents of the cell is added onto the new relative reference in the new cell. For example, if you copy an A1-style relative reference in a cell to a new cell that is two rows below its previous location, then the new cell has a new value for that relative reference, which is two rows greater than the old reference value. Copying a cell containing B3 to a new location two rows below it would change the relative reference B3 to B5. The behavior of R1C1-style is a mirror image of the A1-style references.

Since there are two positions that each reference specifies, the column position and the row position, you may make only one of these positions relative and the other absolute or unchanging. See "Syntax" and "Examples" below for guidelines on structuring absolute and relative references.

A reference is one of six types of values: numbers, text, logical values, references, arrays, and error values. For more information about values in general and a summary of these other five types of values, see "Values."

Note: If a reference is used in a formula in a place where the type of value requested or expected is not a reference type, Excel uses the value or values that are referred to by the reference. For example, typing =C3 into cell A2 and pressing Enter results in the copying of the contents of cell C3 into cell A2. As long as =C3 is in cell A2, whenever the contents of cell C3 change, the contents of cell A2 also change to match cell C3. Likewise, the formula =SUM(C2:C4) adds all the values that are contained in cells C2, C3, and C4.

Syntax

In the following chart, (letter) represents one or more letters of the alphabet (which give the column location for the reference) and # represents a number.

For a Single Cell:

	A1-style References	R1C1-style References
Relative	(letter)#	R[#]C[#]
Absolute Row Relative Column	(letter)$#	R#C[#]
Relative Row Absolute Column	$(letter)#	R[#]C#
Absolute	$(letter)$#	R#C#

For a Range of Cell Addresses:

CellAddress1:CellAddress2, where *CellAddress#* follows the guidelines above.

Examples

Cell Addresses:

	A1-style Reference	Equivalent R1C1-style Reference
Relative	A6	R[6]C[1]
Relative Row Absolute Column	$A6	R[6]C1
Absolute Row Relative Column	A$6	R6C[1]

	A1-style Reference	Equivalent R1C1-style Reference
Absolute	$A$6	R6C1
Relative	D2	R2C4
Relative Row Absolute Column	$D2	R[2]C4
Absolute Row Relative Column	D$2	R2C[4]
Absolute	$D$2	R2C4

Range of Cell Addresses:

(See above for examples of relative and absolute addresses)

A1-style Reference	Equivalent R1C1-style Reference
Z3:Z7	R[3]C[26]:R[7]C[26]
K2:N4	R[2]C[11]:R[4]C[14]
D4:M4	R[4]C[4]:R[4]C[13]

REFTEXT (*see* Macro Functions—Value Returning)

REGISTER (*see* Macro Functions—Control)

Relative Reference

(*see also* Absolute Reference)

A *relative reference* (as distinct from an *absolute reference*) is a means of referring to cells in a worksheet in a way that locates the cell in relation to the active cell. To distinguish relative references in Excel, you do *not* put dollar signs before row and column references: A2, for example, as distinct from $A$2.

Example

Suppose that you have a formula in D5: =SUM($D$2:$D$4). This is an absolute reference. Copy the formula to cell F5 and the formula remains the same: =SUM($D$2:$D$4). Now change the formula in D5 to =SUM(D2:D4). It is now a relative reference. Copy the formula to F5 and it changes to =SUM(F2:F4) because its location has changed.

Changing a Cell Reference from Absolute to Relative

1. Make the cell containing the cell reference the active cell. — The cell reference appears in the formula bar.
2. Delete the dollar sign ($) before each row and column reference. — The cell reference appears in the formula bar.

> **Tip:** You can combine relative and absolute references in a single cell reference. For instance, $B3 will always refer to column B wherever you copy a formula with that cell reference, but the row reference will change.

RELREF (*see* Macro Functions—Value Returning)

Remote Reference

Remote reference is a reference to a document in another application, for example, Microsoft Word. The reference can be to a single cell, a cell range, a value, or a field. You create a remote reference by typing the correct syntax in a cell. When Excel accepts it after you press Enter, the link is created.

Example

=WinWord|'c:\business\Report.doc'!LINK3. First, you specify the application, WinWord here, meaning Microsoft Word for Windows. Then you specify the document name and location, after a | separator. Here it's c:\business\report.doc. Then you type an exclamation mark. Finally, you specify a cell, range, value, or field of data—here Link3.

REMOVE.PAGE.BREAK

(*see* Macro Functions That Perform Options Commands)

RENAME.COMMAND

(*see* Macro Functions—Customizing)

REPLACE( )

(*see also* Function, FORMULA.REPLACE, SUBSTITUTE, MID, SEARCH, TRIM)

Syntax

REPLACE(*old_text,start_num,num_chars,new_text*)

Description

REPLACE is a function that returns old_text with some characters *replaced* by new_text. A copy of old_text is made from the first character up to but not including the start_num position in old_text. Next, REPLACE adds the new_text characters to the end of this partial copy of old_text. Last, the rightmost portion of old_text from the position start_num+num_chars to the end of old_text is added to this copy.

The information required for function REPLACE:

old_text is any single symbol or group of symbols. If text is typed directly into the argument list, then it must be enclosed in quotation marks.

start_num is a number that acts as an index into the old_text string of characters. If start_num is 1, then the REPLACE function removes characters from old_text starting at the first character. If start_num is 5, then the REPLACE function removes characters from old_text starting at the fifth character of old_text.

If start_num is not included in the argument list, then start_num is assumed to be 1.

num_chars is the number of characters that REPLACE removes from old_text.

If *num_chars* is larger than the length of old_text or the sum of start_num, and num_chars indicates a position beyond the end of old_text, then REPLACE removes all the text that follows from the position given by start_num.

 Note: #VALUE! error is returned if num_chars is less than 0.

new_text is any single symbol or group of symbols, or a cell address, formula, or function that yields text. If text is typed directly into the argument list, then it must be enclosed in quotation marks.

In the result returned by REPLACE, new_text replaces the characters between the position indicated by start_num and (start_num + num_chars) in old_text.

Examples

Here is an example: =REPLACE("I kick it",4,3,"new"). The letter *i* in "kick" is in position 4. This letter and the two letters that follow it, *c* and *k*, are removed from old_text "I kick it" (for a total of three letters removed). The new_text "new" is put in their place. The returned result is "I knew it".

Formula	Returns
=REPLACE("Confidential #23-7135",14,8,"number")	"Confidential number"
=REPLACE("Can do some things",8,4,"many")	"Can do many things"

REPT()

Formula	Returns
=REPLACE("Can do some things",8,81,"many")	"Can do many"
=REPLACE("rest",4,–3,"test")	#VALUE!

REPT() *(see also* LOWER, PROPER*)*

Syntax

REPT(*text,number_times*)

Description

REPT is a function that returns *text* (any string of characters) as many times as requested by *number_times*.

> **Note:** The result returned by REPT cannot be longer than 255 characters.

The information required for function REPT:

text is any group of symbols that is either enclosed in one pair of quotation marks or entered in a cell.

number_times is a positive number less than 256. If number_times is 0, then REPT returns empty text, "". If number_times is not a whole number, then the fractional part is dropped (truncated).

Examples

Formula	Returns
=REPT("%",5)	"%%%%%"
=REPT("*",7.8)	"*******"

REPT is useful for creating borders or total lines, as shown in the figure.

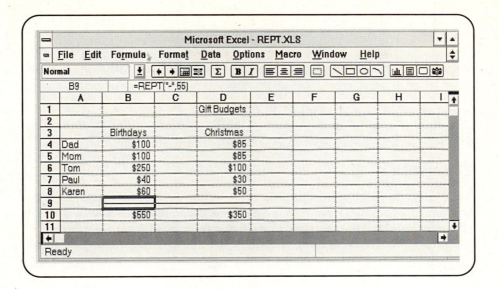

REQUEST (*see* Macro Functions—Control)

RESTART (*see* Macro Functions—Control)

RESULT (*see* Macro Functions—Control)

RETURN (*see* Macro Functions—Control)

RIGHT()

(*see also* Function, LEFT, MID, FIND, SEARCH)

Syntax

RIGHT(*text,num_chars*)

Description

RIGHT is a function that returns a copy of the rightmost characters of the argument *text*. RIGHT starts copying from the right side of *text* (the last character in *text*) and continues to copy one more character to the left until it has as many characters as num_chars specifies. It then returns this copy of *text*.

> **Tip:** RIGHT can be used with other functions like SEARCH to extract data.

The information required for function RIGHT:

text is any text value. If text is typed directly into the argument list, then it must be enclosed in quotation marks.

num_chars is the number of characters that RIGHT will copy and return from the text string of characters. If num_chars is not included, it is assumed to be one. If num_chars is larger than the length of text, then RIGHT returns the entire text.

> **Note:** #VALUE! error is returned if num_chars is less than 0.

Examples

Formula	*Returns*
=RIGHT("Marie Curie",5)	"Curie"
=RIGHT("1, 2, 3, What is this four?",8)	"is four?"

ROUND() *(see also* Function, INT, TRUNC, MOD)

Syntax

ROUND(*number,num_digits*)

Description

ROUND is a function that returns the given number rounded off to the specified number of digits, num_digits. Traditional rules of rounding are used. If the next smaller digit is five or more, then the digit is rounded up. If the next smaller digit is four or less, then the digit remains the same.

ROUND rounds numbers according to the following guidelines:

- If num_digits is less than 0, it rounds to the left of the decimal point.
- If num_digits is 0, it rounds to the nearest integer.
- If num_digits is greater than 0, it rounds to the right of the decimal point.

The information required for function ROUND:

number is a real number (an integer, fraction, etc.).

num_digits is a real number, cell address, formula, or function that yields a real number. Num_digits specifies how many digits to round off in the argument number. If num_digits has a fractional part, it is ignored. (See the last two examples under "Examples.")

Examples

Formula	Returns
=ROUND(12345.6789,−3)	12000
=ROUND(12345.6789,−1)	12350
=ROUND(12345.6789,0)	12346
=ROUND(12345.6789,2)	12345.68
=ROUND(−12345.6789,2)	−12345.68
=ROUND(12345.6789,1)	12345.7
=ROUND(12345.6789,1.7)	12345.7
=ROUND(12345.6789,−1.8)	12350

ROW() *(see also* Function, ROWS, COLUMN*)*

Syntax

ROW(*reference*)

Description

ROW is a function that returns the row number of the cell or cells addressed by *reference*.

The information required for function ROW:

reference is a cell address, range of cell addresses, or name that specifies either of these. If *reference* is omitted, it is assumed to be the row where the ROW function is entered. If reference is an array that spans several rows, then ROW returns a vertical array of these row numbers.

 Note: *Reference* cannot be several groups of cell addresses.

Examples

Suppose that the name checkbook referred to the array J7:L79. Then the formula =ROW(checkbook) would return {7,8,9}, where 7, 8, and 9 are the row numbers.

Formula	*Returns*
=ROW(D9)	9
=ROW(B1:E3)	{1,2,3}
=ROW(C6:G9)	{6,7,8,9}

ROW.HEIGHT

(see Macro Functions That Perform Format Commands*)*

ROWS( ) *(see also* Function, ROW, COLUMNS*)*

Syntax

ROWS(*array*)

Description

ROWS is a function that returns the number of rows in the array of cells addressed by *array*.

The information required for function ROWS:

array is an array, an array formula, a cell address, a range of cell addresses, or a name that specifies one of these.

Examples

Suppose that the name checkbook referred to the array J7:L78. Then the formula =ROWS(checkbook) would return 72 since there are 72 rows in the array J7:L78.

Formula	*Returns*
=ROWS(D9)	1
=ROWS({6,0;1,9;8,3})	3
=ROWS(C6:G29)	24

RUN

(see Macro Functions That Perform Macro Commands*)*

S

SAVE

(*see* Macro Functions That Perform File Commands)

SAVE.AS

(*see* Macro Functions That Perform File Commands)

SAVE.WORKSPACE

(*see* Macro Functions That Perform File Commands)

SCALE

(*see* Macro Functions That Perform Format Commands)

SEARCH( )

(*see also* FIND, MID, LEN, EXACT)

Syntax

SEARCH(*find_text,within_text,start_at_num*)

Description

SEARCH is a function that returns a numerical index to within_text. This index tells you the beginning character of the first occurrence of find_text in the within_text string of characters.

SEARCH begins its search into within_text at the character specified by start_at_num. SEARCH looks for the given value find_text from left to right. When SEARCH discovers an exact replica of the find_text string in within_text, then it returns the numerical position that indicates where the first occurrence of the find_text string of characters begins in the within_text string of characters.

SEARCH ignores differences between upper- and lowercase letters. An uppercase *S* or a lowercase *s* in the find_text string of characters matches an *s* of any case in the within_text string of characters.

SEARCH returns a #VALUE! error if:

- start_at_num is less than 1.

- start_at_num indicates a position beyond the end of within_text. (This occurs when start_at_num is larger than the length of within_text.)

- find_text is not in the within_text string of characters.

Tip: The first and second conditions that create a #VALUE! error can be easily detected by checking the conditions: start_at_num < 1 and start_at_num > LEN(within_text), where *LEN* is a built-in.

Note: Use the FIND function to distinguish between upper- and lowercase characters in the searching process.

The information required for function SEARCH:

find_text is any single symbol or group of symbols, or a cell address, formula, or function that yields text. If text is typed directly into the list of values for the function, then it must be enclosed in quotation marks.

If *find_text* is an empty string, " ", or a reference to an empty cell, then SEARCH returns start_at_num or the default value for start_at_num. (The default value when start_at_num is not specified is 1.) You can use these wild-card characters in find_text: ? matches a single character, and * matches any sequence of characters.

within_text is any single symbol or group of symbols, or a cell address, formula, or function that yields text. If text is typed directly into the list of values for the function, then it must be enclosed in quotation marks.

start_at_num is a number that acts as an index in the within_text string of characters. If start_at_num is 1, then the search for find_text begins at the first character. If start_at_num is 8, then the search for find_text begins at the eighth character. If start_at_num is not included in the list of values for the function, then start_at_num is assumed to be 1 and the search for find_text begins at the first character.

Examples

=SEARCH("find me", "Look inside me for find me", 4)
       within_text = "Look inside me for find me"
       find_text = "find me"
       start_at_num = 4

In this example, the string to search is the within_text string, "Look inside me for find me". The text that the SEARCH function is looking for is the "find me" text string. The position that this search starts at is the start_at_num position, which, in this example, is the fourth character. The fourth character of the within_text string is, "k". Searching from left to right, the first occurrence of "find me" starts at the 20th character of the within_text. SEARCH returns 20 for this example.

If everything about this example were the same, except that start_at_text was 21, then SEARCH would not find the "find me" string of characters! In this second example, SEARCH would return #VALUE! even though the "find me" does exist in the within_text string.

Formula	*Returns*
=SEARCH("in","Interest Rates")	1
=SEARCH("n","Financial interest",4)	5
=SEARCH("n","Financial interest",2)	3
=SEARCH("n","Financial interest",9)	12
=SEARCH("f","Financial interest",2)	#VALUE!
=SEARCH("I*d","Common Ideas",1)	8

SECOND()

(see also HOUR, MINUTE, DAY, MONTH, WEEKDAY, YEAR)

Syntax

SECOND(*serial_number*)

Description

SECOND is a function that returns the seconds of time in the particular time specified by serial_number. The returned number is a whole number that ranges from 0 to 59.

The information required for function SECOND:

Serial_number is a number that represents a particular time in the range of 12:00:00 AM to 11:59:59 PM. For more information on serial_number, see "TIME" and "NOW." Serial_number can also be given as text.

Note: Excel 3 for Windows uses a different numbering system (the 1900 Date System) for dates than Excel for the Macintosh.

Examples

The formula =SECOND(0.413461) returns 23 because serial_number 0.413461 stands for the time 9:55:23 AM.

The formula =SECOND(32880.543576) returns 45 because serial_number 0.543576 stands for the time 1:02:45 PM. (The 32880 portion of the serial number stands for the date January 7, 1990. The date is ignored.)

Formula	Returns
=SECOND("12:15:55 AM")	55
=SECOND("2:20:10 PM")	10

SELECT *(see* Macro Functions That Perform Actions)

SELECT.CHART

(*see* Macro Functions That Perform Chart Commands)

SELECT.END

(*see* Macro Functions That Perform Actions)

SELECT.LAST.CELL

(*see* Macro Functions That Perform Formula Commands)

SELECT.PLOT.AREA

(*see* Macro Functions That Perform Chart Commands)

SELECT.SPECIAL

(*see* Macro Functions That Perform Formula Commands)

SELECTION

(*see* Macro Functions—Value Returning)

SEND.KEYS (*see* Macro Functions—Control)

SEND.TO.BACK

(*see* Macro Functions That Perform Format Commands)

Serial Number (*see also* Date, Time)

Serial number is the decimal number that Excel uses to store dates and times. Dates are stored as the integer part of the number and times are stored as the fraction part of the number.

The date is stored as the number of days since the base date. The range of dates possible is 1/1/1900–12/31/2078, which corresponds to the numbers 1–65380. The time is stored as a fraction of 24 hours. The range of times possible is 12:00 am–11:59:59 pm, which corresponds to the fractions 0.0–0.999988425925926. For example, 6/21/91 12:00 pm is stored as 33410.5.

Note: To see the value of the serial number used to store a particular date or time, select the cell and choose Forma<u>t</u>, <u>N</u>umber, and General.

Note: Excel can use one of two base dates. 1/1/1900 is the default for Excel under Windows or OS/2. 1/2/1904 is the default for Excel for the Apple Macintosh.

Caution: If the date is off by four years, use the following commands to correct it: <u>O</u>ptions, <u>C</u>alculation, and click on the 1904 Date System check box.

SET.CRITERIA

(*see* Macro Functions That Perform Data Commands)

SET.DATABASE

(*see* Macro Functions That Perform Data Commands)

SET.EXTRACT

(*see* Macro Functions That Perform Data Commands)

SET.NAME (*see* Macro Functions—Control)

SET.PAGE.BREAK

(*see* Macro Functions That Perform Options Commands)

SET.PREFERRED

(*see* Macro Functions That Perform Gallery Commands)

SET.PRINT.AREA

(*see* Macro Functions That Perform Options Commands)

SET.PRINT.TITLES

(*see* Macro Functions That Perform Options Commands)

SET.UPDATE.STATUS

(*see* Macro Functions That Perform Actions)

SET.VALUE (*see* Macro Functions—Control)

SHORT.MENUS

(*see* Macro Functions That Perform Options Commands)

SHOW.ACTIVE.CELL

(*see* Macro Functions That Perform Formula Commands)

SHOW.BAR (*see* Macro Functions—Customizing)

SHOW.CLIPBOARD

(*see* macro functions That Perform Window Commands)

SHOW.DETAIL

(*see* Macro Functions That Perform Actions)

SHOW.INFO

(*see* Macro Functions That Perform Window Commands)

SHOW.LEVELS

(*see* Macro Functions That Perform Actions)

SIGN() (*see also* Function, ABS)

Syntax

SIGN(*number*)

Description

SIGN is a function that returns the sign of the given number.

The sign function returns −1, 0, or 1 according to the following conditions:

Condition	Returns
number > 0	1
number = 0	0
number < 0	−1

The information required for function SIGN:

number is any number.

Examples

Formula	Returns
=SIGN(3)	1
=SIGN(-5)	-1
=SIGN(0)	0
=SQRT(SIGN(29))	1

SIN()

(see also **Function, COS, TAN, ASIN, ACOSH, SINH, PI)**

Syntax

SIN(*number*)

Description

SIN is a function that returns the sine of the given number, which represents the radian measure of an angle. Sine is a standard trigonometric function based on the one-unit circle, $x^2 + y^2 = 1$. An angle with one side on the x-axis has a second side that intercepts a point (x,y) on the unit circle. The sine of this angle is the y value of the (x,y) point on the unit circle.

The information required for function SIN:

number is a real number that is an angle in radian units.

 Note: Use the PI function to convert from degrees to radians by multiplying by PI()/180. (30 degrees * PI()/180 = 0.5235 radians)

Examples

Formula	Returns
=SIN(PI()/2)	1
=SIN(PI())	0
=SIN(0.7854)	0.7071

SINH()

(*see also* Function, COS, COSH, ACOSH, ASINH, PI)

Syntax

SINH(*number*)

Description

SINH is a function that returns the hyperbolic sine of the given number. The hyperbolic sine is a standard trigonometric function based on the unit hyperbola, $x^2 - y^2 = 1$, rather than the one-unit circle, $x^2 + y^2 = 1$. The formula for the hyperbolic sine is

$$\text{SINH}(X) = \frac{e^x - e^{-x}}{2}$$

Note: This function is useful in the probability distribution equation for an expected result in an empirical experiment where time is the varying factor.

The information required for function SINH:

number is any number.

Examples

Formula	Returns
=SINH(0)	0
=SINH(PI()/2)	2.3013
=SINH(PI())	11.549

SIZE

(*see* Macro Functions That Perform Control Commands)

SLN() (*see also* Functions, DDB, SYD, VDB)

Syntax

SLN(*cost,salvage,life*)

Description

SLN is a function that returns the straight-line depreciation of an asset for a single period.

The information required for function SLN:

cost is the initial cost of the asset.

salvage is the value at the end of the depreciation, which is sometimes also referred to as the salvage value of the asset.

life is the number of periods over which the asset depreciates, which is sometimes also referred to as the useful life of the asset.

Examples

Suppose that you bought a car for $15,000. It has a useful life of seven years and a salvage rate (or resell value) of $3,900. The depreciation allowance for each year is =SLN(15000,3900,7), which returns $1,585.71.

Solver Functions

As mentioned in Chapter 14, "Analyzing, Calculating, and Using Solver," the Solver can be manipulated through macros with functions that Excel provides. The functions are straight equivalents of the commands and options in the Solver dialog boxes. The following 10 listings describe each of these functions.

Name: SOLVER.OK

Syntax: SOLVER.OK(*setcell,maxminval,valueof,bychanging*)

Solver Equivalent: Options in the Solver Parameters dialog box

Description: Specifies Set Cell and By Changing Cells options in the Solver Parameters dialog box, which is available through Solver in the Formula menu

Arguments: *setcell* corresponds to the Set Cell option and is optional. If used, it must be a cell reference in the active worksheet. *maxminval* corresponds to Max, Min, and Value Of. Use 1 to maximize, 2 to minimize, and 3 to specify that you want a value. *valueof* specifies the number when *maxminval* is 3. *bychanging* corresponds to By Changing and refers to cell(s) on the active worksheet.

Name: SOLVER.SOLVE

Syntax: SOLVER.SOLVE(*userfinish,showref*)

Solver Equivalent: Solve in the Solver Parameters dialog box

Description: Starts the Solver application

Arguments: *userfinish* is optional. If it's omitted or FALSE, Solver displays the Finish dialog box. If it's TRUE, the SOLVER.SOLVE function returns an integer value listed below in "Notes." *showref* is optional and is relevant when the Step Through Iterations box is checked in the Solver Options dialog box. You can do this manually or through the SOLVER.OPTIONS function. *showref* is a macro invoked when you want to regain control whenever Solver finds a new intermediate solution value.

Notes: Do not call the SOLVER.SOLVE function from a subroutine macro, because it returns Excel to Ready before resuming the menu. SOLVER.SOLVE returns the following values:

0   Solver found a solution
1   Solver has converged on the current solution
2   Solver can't improve on the current solution
3   Maximum time or number of iterations is reached
4   The values do not converge
5   Solver could not find a feasible solution
6   Solver stopped at the user's request
7   The linearity condition is not satisfied
8   Solver encountered an error value

Name: SOLVER.RESET

Syntax: SOLVER.RESET( )

Solver Equivalent: Reset in the Solver Parameters dialog box

Description: Wipes out all cell references and constraints in the dialog box and also restores the Options dialog box settings to the defaults

Notes: SOLVER.RESET is performed automatically when you use the SOLVER.LOAD function.

Name: SOLVER.FINISH; SOLVER.FINISH?

Syntax: *keepfinal,reportarray*; *keepfinal,reportarray*

Solver Equivalent: Solver.Finish dialog box

Description: You must call this if you entered TRUE in *userfinish* in SOLVER.SOLVE. Use the ? form to actually display the Finish dialog box with your arguments as defaults.

Arguments: *keepfinal* is optional. If it's 1 or omitted, the final solution values are kept in the adjustable cells. If it's 2, they are discarded and the former values restored. *reportarray* is optional and can be used to create reports. Use {1} for the Answer report; {2} for the Limit report; {1,2} for both.

Name: SOLVER.ADD

Syntax: SOLVER.ADD(*cellref,relation,formula*)

Solver Equivalent: Add button in Solver Parameters dialog box

Description: Adds a constraint to the current problem. If the constraint already exists, the function returns 4 and does nothing.

Arguments: *cellref* is the left side of the constraint and must be a cell reference. *relation* is the operator: 1 for <=, 2 for =, 3 for >=. *formula* is the constraint and can be a number, a formula (as text), or a cell reference.

Name: SOLVER.CHANGE

Syntax: SOLVER.CHANGE(*cellref,relation,formula*)

Solver Equivalent: Change in Solver Parameters dialog box

Description: Changes the right side (only) of an existing constraint. Change the left side and the operator by deleting the constraint and adding it again.

Arguments: *cellref* is the left side of the constraint and must be a cell reference. *relation* is the operator: 1 for <=, 2 for =, 3 for >=. *formula* is the constraint and can be a number, a formula (as text), or a cell reference.

Name: SOLVER.DELETE

Syntax: SOLVER.DELETE (*cellref,relation,formula*)

Solver Equivalent: Delete in Solver Parameters dialog box

Description: Deletes a constraint

Arguments: *cellref* is the left side of the constraint and must be a cell reference. *relation* is the operator: 1 for <=, 2 for =, 3 for >=.

formula is the constraint and can be a number, a formula (as text), or a cell reference.

Name: SOLVER.OPTIONS

Syntax: SOLVER.OPTIONS(*maxtime, iterations, precision, assumelinear, stepthru, estimates, derivatives, search*)

Solver Equivalent: Solver Options dialog box

Description: Specifies options in the Solver Options dialog box. The function returns the argument number when it's an invalid type and a 0 when the options are accepted.

Arguments: *assumelinear* must be TRUE or FALSE where TRUE means the Assume Linear Model check box is on. *stepthru* must be TRUE or FALSE where TRUE means the Step Through Iterations check box is on. Put 1 in *estimates* for Tangent, 2 for Quadratic. Put 1 in *derivatives* for Forward, 2 for Central. Put 1 in *search* for Quasi-Newton, 2 for Conjugate.

Name: SOLVER.LOAD

Syntax: SOLVER.LOAD(*loadarea*)

Solver Equivalent: Load Model button in Solver Options dialog box

Description: Loads a problem for Solver

Arguments: *loadarea* is a cell reference on the active worksheet that previously took the problem set up in Solver Parameters dialog box

Name: SOLVER.SAVE

Syntax: SOLVER.SAVE(*savearea*)

Solver Equivalent: Save Model button in Solver Options dialog box

Description: Saves the current problem to an area specified on the worksheet

Arguments: *savearea* is an area on the worksheet that should be large enough to contain the problem.

SORT

(*see* Macro Functions That Perform Data Commands)

SPLIT (*see* Macro Functions That Perform Actions)

SQRT()

Syntax

SQRT(*number*)

Description

SQRT is a function that returns the positive square root of the given number. The information required for function SQRT:

> *number* is any positive number. If you give SQRT a negative number, SQRT returns the error value #NUM!.

Examples

Formula	*Returns*
=SQRT(9)	3
=SQRT(–9)	#NUM!

STANDARD.FONT

(*see* Macro Functions That Perform Options Commands)

Status Bar

The *status bar* is the bar that stretches along the very bottom of the workspace window of your spreadsheet. It displays the current status of the workspace. Whenever you begin a new activity, such as entering a value or highlighting a command, the status bar displays a few words that describe the process taking place in the workspace.

When you start up Excel, the status bar displays the word Ready. (When you start up Excel, the status bar is automatically made active.) If you highlight a menu option in the menu bar, the status bar gives a short description of the command or commands that the menu offers. If you enter a value from the keyboard, the word Enter appears in the status bar.

The status bar is a useful guide when you are learning about Excel. If you are uncertain what command you need, then highlight each command in the menu bar and view its description in the status bar. If you are interrupted while working on your spreadsheet, the status bar and the formula bar can give you an indication of what you were about to do. If you are uncertain why a menu command is not available, then the information in the status bar can tell you whether you are in the midst of some process that must be finished before you can continue with other commands. The status bar provides useful information about the state of the workspace. For instance, the following example illustrates how the status bar can be used to tell you what your next options are.

Example

If you highlight the word Format in the menu bar, the status bar at the bottom of the workspace displays the words Change appearance of selection. The status or state of the workspace at this time is the first stage of processing Format menu commands. Therefore, the status bar summarizes what the Format menu commands do.

STDEV( )

(*see also* Function, DSTDEV, STDEVP, VAR, VARP)

Syntax

STDEV(*number1,number2,...*)

Description

STDEV is a function that returns an estimate of the standard deviation for a population based on a sample given in the list of values for the function.

Standard deviation is a statistical calculation that measures how far values deviate from the mean or average of the set of values. In statistics terminology, standard deviation is the square root of the variance. STDEV is equivalent to the square root of function VAR. The formula =STDEV(C1:C9) is equivalent to =SQRT(VAR(C1:C9)).

STDEV()

Standard deviation is calculated on the "nonbiased" method, using "n – 1" times n in the denominator:

$$\sqrt{\frac{n \Sigma x^2 - (\Sigma x)^2}{n(n-1)}}$$

As indicated by this formula, STDEV calculates on the basis that the values it is given are only a sample of the population. If you have the entire population to use in calculating the standard deviation, use the STDEVP function.

The information required for function STDEV:

number1,number2,... where each of these values can be a number, cell address, formula, or function that yields a number. These values represent a sample of the population.

Note: Values in the sample that are expressed as text, logical values, or empty cells cause errors.

Note: STDEV takes up to 14 elements in the list of values for the function: number1,number2,...,number14. (See "SUM" for an example of this limit.)

Examples

Suppose that keys produced for a computer keyboard are collected from the production line of the factory at random intervals. The size of the top of each key is a critical factor in determining whether it is used or discarded. You measure the length in centimeters of the top of each key in this sample and enter these measurements into cells B3:B11 of your Excel spreadsheet. You enter the STDEV formula and get the result 0.01589. In summary: Cells B3:B9 contain 1.38, 1.38, 1.37, 1.39, 1.35, 1.39, 1.36. The formula =STDEV(B3:B9) returns 0.01589.

Formula	*Returns*
=STDEV(1,2,3,4,5)	1.581139

STDEVP()

(*see also* Function, DSTDEVP, STDEV, VAR, VARP)

Syntax

STDEVP(*number1,number2,...*)

Description

STDEVP is a function that returns the standard deviation for a population when the entire population is put into the list of values for the function.

Standard deviation is a statistical calculation that measures how far values deviate from the mean or average of the set of values. In statistics terminology, standard deviation is the square root of variance. STDEVP is equivalent to the square root of function VARP. The formula =STDEVP(C1:C9) is equivalent to =SQRT(VARP(C1:C9)).

Standard deviation is calculated on the "biased" method; "n" times n is used in the denominator:

$$\sqrt{\frac{n \Sigma x^2 - (\Sigma x)^2}{n^2}}$$

842 STDEVP()

As indicated by this formula, STDEVP calculates on the basis that its values are the entire population. If you have only a sample of the entire population to use in calculating the standard deviation, use the STDEV function.

The information required for function STDEVP:

number1,number2,... where each of these values can be a number, cell address, formula, or function that yields a number. These values represent the entire population of data.

Note: Values in the population that are expressed as text, logical values, or empty cells cause errors.

Note: STDEVP takes up to 14 elements in the list of values for the function: number1,number2,...,number14. (See "SUM" for an example of this limit.)

Examples

Suppose that during a fixed time period *all* the keys produced for a computer keyboard are collected from the production line of a factory. The size of the top of each key is a critical factor in determining whether it is used or discarded. You measure the length in centimeters of the top of each key in this sample and enter these measurements into cells B3:B11 of your Excel spreadsheet. You enter the STDEV formula and get the result 0.01589. In summary: Cells B3:B9 contain 1.38, 1.38, 1.37, 1.39, 1.35, 1.39, 1.36. The formula =STDEV(B3:B9) returns 0.013997.

Formula	**Returns**
=STDEVP(1,2,3,4,5)	1.414214

STEP (*see* Macro Functions—Control)

SUBSTITUTE()

(*see also* Function, REPLACE, TRIM)

Syntax

SUBSTITUTE(*text,old_text,new_text,instance_num*)

Description

SUBSTITUTE is a function that returns a copy of the argument *text* with the instance or occurrence of old_text that is specified by instance_num removed and new_text put in its place.

The SUBSTITUTE function copies the argument *text* and looks for occurrences of old_text in the *text* argument. When it finds the instance_num occurrence of old_text, then it removes that occurrence of old_text and puts new_text in the position where old_text was removed. SUBSTITUTE is different from REPLACE in that there is no reference to positions in the text string.

> **Note:** If *text* is an array of text elements, then SUBSTITUTE will perform the operation described above on each element of the text array, and return an array. (See "Examples.")

The information required for function SUBSTITUTE:

text and *old_text* are text values. If *text* is typed directly into the argument list, then it must be enclosed in quotation marks. *Text can also be an array of text elements.*

new_text is any single symbol or group of symbols. If *text* is typed directly into the argument list, then it must be enclosed in quotation marks. In the result returned by SUBSTITUTE, *new_text* replaces *old_text* in *text*.

instance_num is a number giving the occurrence of old_text that is to be replaced. If instance_num is 1, then the first occurrence of old_text in *text* is replaced with new_text. If instance_num is 3, then the third occurrence of old_text in *text* is replaced with new_text.

If instance_num is not included, then every occurrence of old_text is replaced by new_text. If instance_num is less than zero, then #VALUE! is returned.

Examples

Formula	*Returns*
=SUBSTITUTE("Stars","St","C",1)	"Cars"
=SUBSTITUTE("less pest","e","a",3)	"less pest"
=SUBSTITUTE("Abracadabra","a","*")	"Abr*c*d*br*"
=SUBSTITUTE("not positive","n","g",0)	#VALUE!

In the figure, the first occurrence of the number symbol "#" in all the cells from B4 to B8 is replaced by two blank spaces. In this example, SUBSTITUTE operates on an array and returns an array.

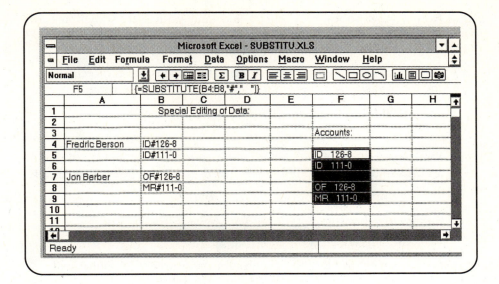

SUM()

(*see also* Function, AVG, COUNT, COUNTA, PRODUCT, SUMPRODUCT)

Syntax

SUM(*number1,number2,...*)

Description

SUM is a function that returns the sum of all the numbers given in the list of values for the function.

The information required for function SUM:

number1,number2,... where each of these numbers is a number. Each number must be separated from other numbers by a comma.

 Note: You can give the SUM function up to 14 elements, that is, a maximum total of 14 cell addresses, cell address ranges, numbers, and formulas returning a number. (See the figure for an example of the possible number of elements that can be given to a function.)

Nonnumeric values, such as text and logic values, are sometimes converted to numeric values, sometimes ignored, and sometimes cause errors. A function, such as SUM, that requires numeric values:

- Converts a value to a numeric value if the value is typed directly into the list of values for the function and is one of the following:

    a logical value

    a number that is in text form

- Does not convert a value to a numeric value if the value is a cell address in the list of values for the function, where the addressed cell:

    is empty

    contains text

    contains a logical value

- Returns an error if the list of values for the function contains a cell address and the addressed cell has an error value in it.
- Returns the #VALUES! error if there is text in the list of values for the function.

Examples

The SUM function is useful for displaying summary information such as that shown in the figure. In the figure all the values in the 1986–90 column are the result of using the SUM function.

	A	B	C	D	E	F	G	H
1	INCOME STATEMENT	1986	1987	1988	1989	1990		1986-90
2								
3	Sales	45,677.00	66,778.00	77,888.00	88,999.00	106,798.80		386,140.80
4	Cost of Goods Sold	27,406.20	40,066.80	46,732.80	53,399.40	64,079.28		231,684.48
5								
6	Gross Profit	18,270.80	26,711.20	31,155.20	35,599.60	42,719.52		154,456.32
7								
8	Expenses	20,554.65	26,711.20	27,260.80	31,149.65	37,379.58		143,055.88
9	Profit Before Taxes	-2,283.85	0.00	3,894.40	4,449.95	5,339.94		11,400.44
10	Taxes (@36%)	0.00	0.00	1,401.98	1,601.98	1,922.38		4,926.34
11								
12	Profit After Tax	-2,283.85	0.00	2,492.42	2,847.97	3,417.56		6,474.10
13								

Formula	Cell(s) Contain	Formula Returns
=SUM(2,4)		6
=SUM(−2,3)		1
=SUM(B1:F4)	All cells contain 2	20
=SUM(B1:F4,5 * 3)	All cells contain 2	35
=SUM(C3)	TRUE	0
=SUM(C3,C4)	"letters","6"	0
=SUM(C4)		0
=SUM(1000,FALSE,"1,000")		2000

Here are some examples that illustrate the automatic conversion rules for nonnumeric values:

According to the rules, if a value is in a cell, the value is included in the calculations only if it is a number. If cells C3 through C6 contain the values TRUE,5,"7","letters", then the formula =SUM(C3:C6) returns a 5. This is because the only value that is a number is the number 5. The remaining values from the cell addresses, which are text or logical values, are ignored. (The "7" is a text value since it is in quotation marks.)

Let's modify that formula to include some values that are typed directly into the list of values for the function. Cells C3 through C6 contain the values TRUE,5,"7","letters", and the formula is =SUM(C3:C6,TRUE). This new formula now returns 6 because TRUE is converted to a number since it is typed directly into the list of values for the function. TRUE converts to 1, so 5 + 1 = 6.

Now let's change the first formula we used, =SUM(C3:C6), to include some numbers in text form that are typed directly into the list of values for the function. Cells C3 through C6 still contain the values TRUE,5,"7","letters", and the new formula is =SUM(C3:C6,"20"). This new formula now returns 25, because the number 5 from the cell addresses and the number 20 converted from the text value "20" in the list of values for the function are both used to calculate the sum. (Once again, the "7" was not converted to a number and used because it is a text value in a cell.)

Let's modify the first formula we used to include some different text values that are typed directly into the list of values for the function. Cells C3 through C6 still contain the values TRUE,5,"7","letters", and the formula is =SUM(C3:C6,"text letters"). This new formula now returns the #VALUES! error. Text values are not allowed because the function SUM requests numeric values.

Our last example illustrates the limit of giving 14 values to a function. In the following formula this limit is exceeded: =SUM(E1,E2,E3,E4,E5,E6,E7,E8,E9,E10,E11,E12,E13,E14,E15). After you enter this formula, a dialog box saying Error in Formula appears; whereas, the formula =SUM(E1:E15) would return a value. It would not display the Error in Formula dialog box.

SUMPRODUCT()

(see also **Function, MMULT, PRODUCT, SUM)**

Syntax

SUMPRODUCT(*array1,array2,...*)

Description

SUMPRODUCT is a function that returns the sum of product pairs from two matrices. The product pairs come from multiplying elements in corresponding positions in each matrix. These product pairs are then added together to produce one number.

The function SUM can replace the function SUMPRODUCT: SUMPRODUCT(array1,array2,array3,array4,array5) is equivalent to SUM(array1 * array2 * array3 * array4 * array5).

Note: For all matrix functions, a matrix is represented by an array or range of cell addresses. All matrices (or arrays) must be the same size. The #VALUE! error message is the result if matrices have different sizes.

Note: SUMPRODUCT is a function that returns an array. The procedure for entering any function that returns an array is to highlight the target array area on the spreadsheet before typing in the formula; type in the formula; and then before pressing the Enter key, press the Ctrl, Shift, and Enter keys all at the same time.

The information required for function SUMPRODUCT:

array1,array2,... where each of these values can be an array or range of cell addresses that contain real numbers; or a formula or function that yields an array of real numbers. You can specify 2 to 14 arrays (array1,array2,...,array14) in the list of values for the function SUMPRODUCT.

SUMPRODUCT uses the number zero for any nonnumeric array entries in any array.

Example

In the figure, corresponding elements are multiplied together and then added:

```
Products in Row 1:  2 * 7 , 5 * 4 , 1 * 2
Products in Row 2: + 3 * 4 , 0 * 9 , 4 * 2
Sum of product pairs in Row 1= 14 + 20 + 2      = 36
Sum of product pairs in Row 2= 12 + 0 + 8       = 20
Sum of product pairs from both rows             = 56
```

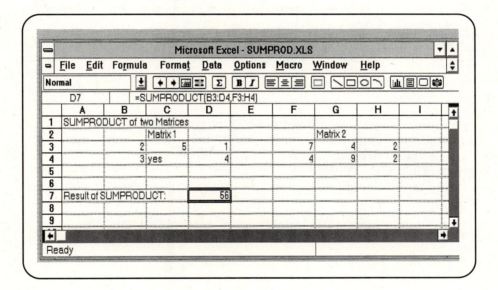

SYD() *(see also* Functions, DDB, SLN, VDB)

Syntax

SYD(*cost,salvage,life,per*)

Description

SYD is a function that returns the sum-of-years' digits depreciation of an asset for a specified period.

The information required for function SYD:

cost is the intial cost of the asset.

salvage is the value at the end of the depreciation, which is sometimes also referred to as the salvage value of the asset.

life is the number of periods over which the asset depreciates, which is sometimes also referred to as the useful life of the asset.

per is the period or interval of time for which SYD calculates the depreciation.

 Note: The value *per* must be in the same units as *life*.

Examples

Suppose that you bought a car for $15,000. It has a useful life of seven years and a salvage rate (or resell value) of $3,900.

The yearly depreciation for the first year is =SYD(15000,3900,7,1), which returns $2,775.00.

The yearly depreciation for the fifth year is =SYD(15000,3900,7,5), which returns $1,189.29.

The yearly depreciation for the seventh year is =SYD(15000,3900,7,7), which returns $396.43.

T

T() *(see also* Function, N, VALUE, CELL*)*

Syntax

T(*value*)

Description

T is a function that returns the text value you give it or "" if the value you give it is not text.

The information required for function T:

value is anything you want to use as text only.

Examples

If cell H4 contains 21, then =T(H4) returns "". If cell H4 contains "15", then =T(H4) returns "15". If cell H4 contains "words", then =T(H4) returns "words". If cell H4 contains TRUE, then =T(H4) returns "". If cell H4 contains "TRUE", then =T(H4) returns "TRUE".

Table *(see also* Lookup Table*)*

A *table* is a range of cells containing one or two series of input values, one or more formulas, and a series of results. The input values are substituted into the formulas to produce the results. A table is often used to see how substituting different values in a formula will affect the results of the formula.

One-input table with column input: The series of input values are placed in a column, and the formula is placed in the cell one row above and one column to the right of the first input value. Excel will substitute the column input values into the cell whose address is specified in Column Input Cell. Use that cell address in the formula. Additional formulas may be placed in cells to the right of the first formula. The series of results for each formula are displayed in the column or columns to the right of the input values, underneath each formula.

One-input table with row input: The series of input values are placed in a row, and the formula is placed in the cell one row below and one column to the left of the first input value. Excel will substitute the row input values into the cell whose address is specified in Row Input Cell. Use that cell address in the formula. Additional formulas may be placed in cells below the first formula. The series of results for each formula are displayed in the row or rows below the input values, to the right of each formula.

Two-input table: The formula is placed in the upper-left-corner cell of the table. Excel will substitute the column input values into the cell whose address is specified in Column Input Cell. Excel will substitute the row input values into the cell whose address is specified in Row Input Cell. Use these cell addresses in the formula. The series of column input values are placed in the cells below the formula. The series of row input values are placed in the cells to the right of the formula. The results are displayed in the cells at the column and row intersections of each of the input values.

Keystrokes

Select a rectangular area of cells containing the formulas, the input values, and the cells for the results. Do not select any additional cells outside this area.

Keyboard	*Mouse*
Data	Data
Table	Table
Row Input Cell and/or Column Input Cell	Row Input Cell and/or Column Input Cell

Note: To speed up recalculation of the spreadsheet, turn off the recalculation of Tables by using Options, Calculation, Automatic Except Tables.

Tables can be imported and exported from Excel. To recalculate a table after importing, the table must be defined as a table again. To redefine the table, use Data Table.

After adding or deleting input values or formulas use Data Table to redefine the table.

Caution: Tables cannot be used on macro spreadsheets.

Tip: To select an entire table, select any result cell in the table and use Formula, Select Special, Current Array.
If the input values are evenly spaced (for example, 10, 20, 30), use Data Series to speed up the input process.

TABLE

(*see* Macro Functions That Perform Data Commands)

TAN()

(*see also* Function, SIN, TAN, ATAN, ATANH, TANH, PI)

Syntax

TAN(*number*)

Description

TAN is a function that returns the tangent of the given number, which represents the radian measure of an angle. Tangent is a standard trigonometric function. The formula for tangent is

$$TAN(X) = \frac{SIN(X)}{COS(X)}$$

The information required for function TAN:

number is any number that represents an angle in radian units.

Tip: If your angle is in degrees, you can use the PI function to convert from degrees to radians by multiplying by PI()/180. (30 degrees * PI()/180 = 0.5235 radians)

Examples

Formula	Returns
=TAN(PI())	0
=TAN(PI()/4)	1
=TAN(1.0471)	1.7320

TANH()

(*see also* Function, ATANH, TAN, COSH, SINH, PI)

Syntax

TANH(*number*)

Description

TANH is a function that returns the hyperbolic tangent of the given number. The hyperbolic tangent is a standard trigonometric function based on the unit hyperbola, $x^2 - y^2 = 1$, rather than the one-unit circle, $x^2 + y^2 = 1$. The formula for the hyperbolic tangent is

$$\text{TANH}(X) = \frac{\text{SINH}(X)}{\text{COSH}(X)}$$

The information required for function TANH:

number is any number.

Examples

Formula	Returns
=TANH(0)	0
=TANH(PI()/2)	0.9172
=TANH(PI())	0.9963
=TANH(2*PI())	0.9999

TERMINATE (*see* Macro Functions—Control)

Text

Text is a type of value, an expression of information in a defined, precise form. The text value is any piece of information that you could communicate with the English language. Text values are used for descriptions, notes, labels, or names and addresses of people. In short, text is any string of characters that is not a defined name and is not one of the other types of values (that is, not a number, logical value, reference, array, or error value). (See "Name" for information on defined names.)

Text is one of six types of values: numbers, text, logical values, references, arrays, and error values. For more information about values in general and a summary of these other five types of values, see "Values."

Whenever you see a request for text, you can use a text value or you can use a reference, formula, or name that represents text.

Syntax

Text is any combination of letters, symbols (not including the digits 0, 1, 2, 3, 4, 5, 6, 7, 8, and 9), digits that come after a letter or symbol that is not a digit, and numbers specially formatted as text.

Text is also any string of characters enclosed in quotation marks.

Examples

"Miscellaneous", "28Feb76", "56.234", "Food", "4/10/81", "1:01:45", "0", "–423"

Typed directly into a cell: Miscellaneous, February, Food, SS#123-45-6789, or F45Base

TEXT() (*see also* Function, DOLLAR, FIXED, VALUE)

Syntax

TEXT(*value,format_text*)

TEXT()

Description

TEXT is a function that returns the *text* form of the argument *number* in the format specified by the argument format_text. This format can be any one of the formats listed in the dialog box for the Number option under the Format option on the main menu. Function TEXT rounds *number* when *number* has decimal places and the chosen format does not.

The information required for function TEXT:

value is any number.

format_text is almost any one of the formats listed in the dialog box for the Number option under the Format main menu option. Two exceptions that cannot be used are the "general" format and the use of asterisks (*) in any format. When entering a format that is listed in the Format Number dialog box, make sure to type it in exactly as you see it appear in the dialog box, *with quotation marks* around it. There are a few additional formats that you can use for format_text. See the examples below and "Format Number" for more information.

 Note: The difference between the Format Number command in the main menu and the TEXT function is that Format Number leaves *value* as a numerical value whereas the TEXT function converts the value into text.

Examples

Formula	Returns
TEXT(7.298,"$0.00")	"$7.30"
TEXT(3002,"#,##0.00")	"3,002.00"
TEXT(16.74,"$#,##0.00")	"$16.74"
TEXT(0.0825,"0.00%")	"8.25%"
TEXT(33502,"m-d-yy")	"9-21-91"
TEXT(33502,"m/d/yy")	"9/21/91"
TEXT(33502,"mmmm dd, yyyy")	"September 21, 1991"

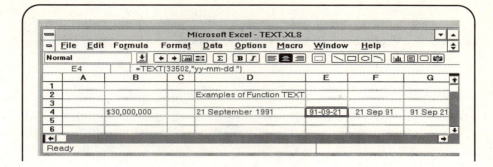

 Tip: The format for the date (yy-mm-dd) in the above example, where the year is first, followed by the numerical month and then the day, is a format that allows you to sort dates properly without needing to refer to any individual part of the date. The biggest change in the date is listed first, followed by the next biggest increase in time, and so on.

TEXT.BOX

(*see* Macro Functions That Perform Actions)

TEXTREF (*see* Macro Functions—Value Returning)

Time (*see also* Date, Serial Number)

Time is a distinct data type used in Excel for specifying a time of day. The actual value stored is a serial number. The formats are h:mm AM/PM, h:mm:ss AM/PM, h:mm, h:mm:ss, h:mm m/d/yy, or a custom format.

Capitalization does not matter when typing in a time. After the time is successfully entered, Excel will display it in the format specified for that cell. If the time is typed in without AM or PM, Excel interprets it as 24-hour clock time (military time).

Example

Times can be used directly in formulas if enclosed in double quotation marks. The formula ="4:33 pm"−"12:28 pm" gives the answer of 0.170139. Format the cell containing this formula as a time to see the answer in hours:minutes:seconds between the two times. See "Serial Number."

 Inserting the Current Time into the Formula Bar

1. Put the text cursor in the formula bar. The text cursor flashes in the formula bar.
2. Press Ctrl-+. The current time appears in the formula bar.

 Note: If Excel displays the time as a decimal fraction between 0 and 1, the format for that cell is numeric. Choose a time format using the Forma**t** **N**umber command.

 Caution: Do not type a space in front of a time. Excel will interpret the time as a character string.

 Tip: The AM or PM must be separated from the time by one or more spaces. Excel will then separate them by one space.
    A time and date can be entered in a single cell if they are separated by one or more spaces. Excel will then separate them by two spaces. The time or the date may come first.

TIME()

(*see also* TIMEVALUE, HOUR, MINUTE, SECOND, NOW)

Syntax

TIME(*hour,minute,second*)

Description

TIME is a function that returns a number which corresponds to the particular time specified by hour,minute,second. The numbers that TIME returns range from 0 to 0.99999999.

The information required for function TIME:

hour,minute,second are three numbers that represent a time between 12 AM (12:00:00) and just before midnight, 11:59:59 PM. If the time you specify is not in this range, the error #VALUE! is returned.

hour is the hour of the day, a number between 0 and 23.

minute is the minute of the day, a number between 0 and 59.

second is the second of the day, a number between 0 and 59.

 Tip: Use TIME to find times that fall hundreds of minutes before or after a particular time.

Examples

Formula	Returns
=TIME(13,02,45)	0.543576
=TIME(9,55,23)	0.413461
=TIME(12,00,00)	0.5
=TIME(23,59,59)	0.999988426

TIMEVALUE()

(*see also* TIME, HOUR, MINUTE, SECOND, NOW)

Syntax

TIMEVALUE(*time_text*)

Description

TIMEVALUE is a function that returns a number which corresponds to the particular time specified by time_text. The numbers that TIMEVALUE returns range from 0 to 0.99999999.

The information required for function TIMEVALUE:

time_text is quoted text that represents a time between 12 AM (12:00:00) and just before midnight, 11:59:59 PM. If your time is not in this range, the error #VALUE! is returned. If you give date information along with a time in time_text, then the date information is ignored.

Tip: Use TIMEVALUE to find times that fall hundreds of minutes before or after a particular time.

Examples

Formula	Returns
=TIMEVALUE("1:02:45 PM")	0.543576
=TIMEVALUE("9:55:23 AM")	0.413461
=TIMEVALUE("12:00 PM")	0.5
=TIMEVALUE("11:59:59 PM")	0.999988426

TODAY() *(see also* DATE, DAY, NOW)

Syntax

TODAY()

Description

TODAY is a function that returns a number which corresponds to today's date. Today's date is taken from the clock of your computer.

The information required for function TODAY:

No information is required for function TODAY.

> **Note:** Excel 3 for Windows uses a different numbering system (the 1900 Date System) for the various date functions than Excel for the Macintosh.

Example *(based on the 1900 Date System)*

If your computer clock says that today's date is April 18, 1992, then TODAY() returns 33712, the number that corresponds to that date.

TRANSPOSE()

(see also Function, MDETERM, MMinverse, MMULT)

Syntax

TRANSPOSE(*array*)

Description

TRANSPOSE is a function that returns the given array with the organization of rows and columns interchanged. TRANSPOSE reverses the vertical and horizontal positioning of the given array by making the first row of the given array the first column of the resultant array, the second row of the given array the second column of the resultant array, and so on.

> **Tip:** TRANSPOSE is often used in macros and on a worksheet to reorient an array returned from a function. A function that returns a horizontal array of information can be converted automatically to a vertical array by using TRANSPOSE.

> **Note:** TRANSPOSE is a function that returns an array with dimensions that are the reverse of the given array. If the given array has two rows and four columns, the resultant array will have four rows and two columns. Before entering the TRANSPOSE function, highlight an area for the resultant array that is the size of the resultant transposed array (an area with the same number of rows as the given array has columns and the same number of columns as the given array has rows). Type in the formula, and before pressing the Enter key, press the Ctrl, Shift, and Enter keys all at the same time.

The information required for function TRANSPOSE:

array is a cell address, constant array, or range of cell addresses that contain anything; or a formula or function that yields an array.

Examples

Formula	*Returns*
=TRANSPOSE({6,5,4;3,2,1})	{6,3;5,2;4,1}
=TRANSPOSE({"first",3;#DIV/0!,1})	{"first",#DIV/0!;3,1}

TREND() *(see also* **TREND, LINEST, LOGEST***)*

Syntax

TREND(*known_y's, known_x's, new_x's, const*)

Description

TREND is a function that returns an array of new y values that are on a straight line described by the x and y values that it was given. Using the "least squares" method, TREND first fits a straight line to the known_y's and known_x's. Then TREND uses the new_x's values from the list of values for the function to calculate corresponding y values on this straight line. TREND returns an array of these y values.

TREND can project new y values on the straight line that are beyond the section of the curve outlined by the known x and y values. Just give values in the new_x's array that are outside the range of the known_x's array.

The information required for function TREND:

known_y's is an array of y values that have an exponential relationship of the form y = b * m^x.

known_x's is an array of x values that correspond to the y values given in the known_y's array. The known_x's and their corresponding known_y's satisfy an exponential relationship of the form y = b * m^x.

new_x's is an array of x values that TREND uses to calculate new y values on the straight line that is calculated from the known_y's and known_x's values.

Note: TREND returns the error #VALUE! if there are empty cells or text in the known_x's, known_y's, or new_x's array cells.

const is a logical value that specifies whether the constant b in the straight line y = b * m^x is forced to the value 1.

Given	Then
const is TRUE or const is omitted	b is calculated as normal
const is FALSE	The m values are adjusted so that b is equal to 0. (TREND uses the formula y = m * x.)

The arrays of known_y's, known_x's, and new_x's have particular forms, as shown in the following:

Form of known_y's

Given

The array known_y's spans a single column.

The array known_y's spans a single row.

Then

Each column of known_x's is a separate variable.

Each row of known_x's is a separate variable.

Form of known_x's

Given

The array known_x's is a single set of variables (the dependent variable y depends on only one factor).

The array known_x's contains more than one set of variables (the dependent variable y depends on more than one factor).

known_x's is not included.

Then

known_x's and known_y's can be ranges of any shape so long as the dimensions of these arrays are the same.

known_y's must be a vector or range with a height of one row or a width of one column.

known_x's is assumed to be the array {1,2,3,...}, which is equal in size to the known_y's array.

Form of new_x's

Given

known_y's is a single column.

known_y's is a single row.

new_x's is omitted.

known_x's and new_x's are omitted.

Then

known_x's and new_x's have the same number of columns.

known_x's and new_x's have the same number of rows.

new_x's is the same as known_x's.

new_x's is the same default value as known_x's.

Note: There must be one column or row of new_x's for each independent variable (same requirement as known_x's).

The LINEST function listing gives information on how Microsoft Excel calculates the line used by TREND. To get the values that describe this line, use LINEST on your known_y's and known_x's data.

TREND is a function that returns an array. The procedure for entering any function that returns an array is to highlight the target array area on the spreadsheet before typing in the formula; type in the formula; and then before pressing Enter, press Ctrl, Shift, and Enter all at the same time.

An array constant must have commas between the values for each row and semicolons between rows.

Examples

	A	B	C	D	E
		E3		{=TREND(C3:C14,B3:B14,B3:B18)}	
1	TREND				
2		known_x's	known_y's		New y's
3		80	0.9		0.610256
4		81	1.7		1.550816
5		82	2.5		2.491375
6		83	3.2		3.431935
7		84	4		4.372494
8		85	4.9		5.313054
9		86	6		6.253613
10		87	7.7		7.194172
11		88	8.4		8.134732
12		89	9.4		9.075291
13		90	10		10.01585
14		91	10.7		10.95641
15		92	11.6		11.89697
16		93			12.83753
17		94			13.77809
18		95			14.71865

	A	B	C	D	E	F	G
		G3			{=TREND(E3:E7,$B$3:$C$7,{5,10;6,11;7,12;8,13;9,14})}		
1	TREND						
2	FUNCTION	Known_x's			Known_y's		NEW Y'S
3		6	2		31.8		26.5
4		7	4		37.1		31.8
5		8	8		42.4		37.1
6		9	8		47.7		42.4
7		10	10		53		47.7

TRIM( )

(see also CLEAN, MID, REPLACE, SUBSTITUTE*)*

Syntax

TRIM(*text*)

Description

TRIM is a function that returns text with one space between each word. TRIM leaves only one space between words and removes all other spaces.

> **Tip:** TRIM is useful for transforming text with unusual spacing from other applications.

The information required for function TRIM:

text is any group of symbols that is either enclosed in one pair of quotation marks or entered in a cell.

Examples

Formula	*Returns*
=TRIM("The space bar is easy to press")	"The space bar is easy to press"
=TRIM(" Out")	"Out"

TRUE( ) *(see also* Function, FALSE*)*

Syntax

TRUE( )

Description

TRUE is a function that returns the logical value of TRUE.

The information required for function TRUE:

No information is required for function TRUE.

> **Note:** Using function TRUE( ) creates the same effect as using the logical value TRUE. Either can be typed directly into the worksheet or into a formula. Function TRUE is included in order to maintain compatibility with other spreadsheet programs.

Examples

Formula with TRUE Function	*Using the TRUE Logical Value*	*Both Return a Logical Value*
=TRUE( )	TRUE	TRUE
=NOT(TRUE( ))	=NOT(TRUE)	FALSE

TRUNC( ) (see also Function, INT, MOD, ROUND)

Syntax

TRUNC(*number,num_digits*)

Description

TRUNC is a function that returns the given number without excess fractional digits. TRUNC returns only the integer part and a number of digits from the fractional part, which is specified by the number of digits, num_digits. TRUNC truncates or discards the fractional part of the given number that follows after the specified number of digits in the fractional part.

The information required for function TRUNC:

number is any number.

num_digits is a number. If num_digits is not an integer, it is truncated. If num_digits is not included in the formula, a default of no digits, 0 num_digits, is assumed. (See the first of the following examples.)

Examples

Formula	Returns
=TRUNC(12.3456789)	12
=TRUNC(–0.123456,2)	– 0.12
=TRUNC(–0.123456,5)	– 0.12345
=TRUNC(1.99999,0)	1

TYPE()

(see also **Function, GET.CELL, IS Functions: ISNONTEXT, ISBLANK, ISERR, ISERROR, ISLOGICAL, ISNA, ISNUMBER, ISTEXT, ISREF)**

Syntax

TYPE(*value*)

Description

TYPE is a function that returns the type of information that you give it.

If the Information That You Give TYPE Is	Then TYPE Returns
A number	1
Text	2
A logical value	4
An error	16

> **Note:** Function TYPE does not always return an 8 for a formula, or 64 for an array, contrary to the Microsoft Excel Reference manual.

The information required for function TYPE:

value is any value: a number, text, a logical value, a formula, an array, or an error.

Examples

Since 7/0 produces the error #DIV/0!, the formula =TYPE(7/0) returns 16 (the number that indicates an error value).

Formula	*Returns*
=TYPE("69 West Broadway")	2
=TYPE(45)	1
=TYPE(D3:F5)	64

U–V

UNDO

(*see* Macro Functions That Perform Edit Commands)

UNGROUP

(*see* Macro Functions That Perform Format Commands)

UNHIDE

(*see* Macro Functions That Perform Window Commands)

UNLOCKED.NEXT

(*see* Macro Functions That Perform Actions)

UNLOCKED.PREV

(*see* Macro Functions That Perform Actions)

UNREGISTER

(*see* Macro Functions—Control)

UPDATE.LINK

(*see* Macro Functions That Perform File Commands)

UPPER()

(*see also* LOWER, PROPER)

Syntax

UPPER(*text*)

Description

UPPER is a function that returns text with all uppercase letters.

> **Note:** UPPER changes letters only. Characters that are not letters are unchanged.

The information required for function UPPER:

text is any group of symbols that is either enclosed in one pair of quotation marks or entered in a cell.

Examples

Formula	Returns
=UPPER("143 Hwy 34")	"143 HWY 34"
=UPPER("Now")	"NOW"

Upper is useful for capitalizing abbreviations, as shown in the figure.

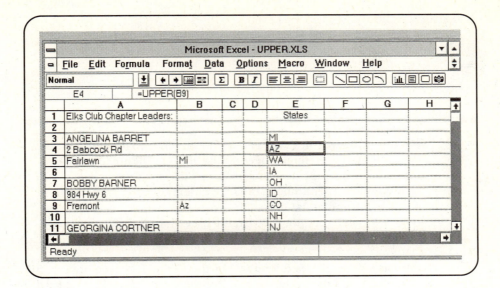

VALUE()

(*see also* TEXT, FIXED, DOLLAR)

Syntax

VALUE(*text*)

Description

VALUE is a function that returns the numerical form of text. VALUE can convert text that is directly typed into the list of values for the function or in a cell.

The information required for function VALUE:

text is any single symbol or group of symbols that is in a format which Excel is familiar with. The constant number, date, and time formats, which Excel creates, are all acceptable formats for text.

Examples

Formula	Returns
=VALUE("8%")	0.08
=VALUE("1,234,567")	1000000

=VALUE("$12,000")   12000

=VALUE("($1,000)")   −1000

=VALUE("07/07/67")   24660

=VALUE("01:07:23")   0.046793981

Note: The Microsoft Excel Function Reference manual mentions that you do not generally need to use the VALUE function. When numerical values are necessary, text in Microsoft Excel is automatically converted to numbers. But the guidelines in the SUM function section of the manual illustrate that this is not true when text is referred to in a cell, not listed in the list of values for the function.

In formulas, all text that is referenced by the formula (that is, not directly typed into the list of values for the function of the formula) is ignored by the formula. If you need to use the DOLLAR or FIXED function, then in numerical calculations you must remember to reconvert these values to numbers with the VALUE function.

Tip: If your currency and fixed decimal values are used solely as numbers, then use the fixed decimal formats listed under the Format Number command. These commands create the same effect as the functions DOLLAR and FIXED, except that the numbers remain numbers.

Values

Values are expressions of factual information. The information that you type into a cell in your worksheet or macro sheet is a value. The pieces of information that you give to a function are values. The information that worksheet functions and many macro functions return are values. Values are all the discrete items of information; the facts, figures, and formulas that represent your ideas.

There are six different types of values that categorize the information that you communicate in a spreadsheet. These six types of values are numbers, text, logical values, references, arrays, and error values. A short summary of each type follows. See the individual listing of any type for more information.

Number: The value called number is a number, a quantifying value. This type of information is used in mathematical formulas.

Text: The value called text is what you might call a description, note, or label. Anything you would communicate with the English language alone is text.

Logical value: There are two values that are logical values, TRUE and FALSE. You can type these values directly into the cell, exactly as printed here, or you can type an expression that represents TRUE or FALSE.

Reference: A reference is a cell address or a range of cell addresses. A cell address is a reference that gives the location of a value. A range of cell addresses is a reference that gives the location of an array of values.

Array: An array is a constant array, a value in a cell, or several values in a range of cells. A constant array is a list of values enclosed in curly braces. For more information see "Syntax" below.

Error value: An error value is a value that indicates some error occurred in the cell where the error value resides. There are seven error values.

Error Value	*Brief Explanation*
#NAME?	Incorrect name
#VALUE!	Invalid value or values
#DIV/0!	Division by 0
#NULL!	Null
#N/A!	Not applicable
#NUM!	Number(s) out of range
#REF!	Invalid reference to a cell address or range of cell addresses

Whenever you need one particular type of value, you can use that value as described above, or you can use a reference, formula, or name that represents or yields that particular type of value.

Syntax

Number: Numbers are represented by numeric symbols: the digits 0, 1, 2, 3, 4, 5, 6, 7, 8, and 9; the decimal point (.); and the negative sign (–).

Text: Text is any combination of letters, symbols (not including the digits 0, 1, 2, 3, 4, 5, 6, 7, 8, and 9), digits that come after a letter or symbol that is not a digit, and numbers specially formatted as text. Text is also any string of characters enclosed in quotation marks. (See "Number" for a description of numeric symbols.)

Logical value: TRUE or FALSE.

value1?value2 (where *value1* and *value2* is any value or formula that yields a single value, and *?* is one of the relational operators: =, <, >, etc.)

Reference (a cell address): In the following, the symbol "@" represents one or more letters of the alphabet (which give the column location for the reference) and # represents a number.

	A1-style Reference	*R1C1-style Reference*
Relative	@#	R[#]C[#]
Absolute Row Relative Column	@$#	R#C[#]
Relative Row Absolute Column	$@#	R[#]C#
Absolute	$@$#	R#C#

Reference (a range of cell addresses): *CellAddress1:CellAddress2*, where *CellAddress#* follows the guidelines above.

Array: An array is a list of values either in cell(s) or in a constant array. A constant array is a list of values enclosed in curly braces where the values are separated by commas between values in the different columns and by semicolons between the list of values in different rows: {value_R1C1,value_R1C2,...;value_R2C1,value_R2C2,...}.

Error values (exactly as listed here): #NAME?, #VALUE!, #DIV/0!, #NULL!, #N/A!, #NUM!, #REF!.

Examples

Examples of numbers: 4, 10000000, 12.0045, 12/30/92, 12:23, 30Jan90

Examples of text as it appears in a formula: "Lydia McCollum", "30Jan90", "12.2", "Sales".

Examples of text as it appears in a cell in a worksheet: Lydia McCollum, January, or Sales, B54.

Examples of logical values: TRUE, FALSE, 5=3, C3="Joe Namath", B2<1, A2>A1.

Examples of references (cell address):

A1-style Reference	*Equivalent R1C1-style Reference*
A3	R3C1
D4	R4C4
K2	R2C11

E100   R100C5

GP45   R45C198

Examples of references (range of cell addresses):

A1-style Reference	*Equivalent R1C1-style Reference*
A1:A2	R1C1:R2C1
D4:F4	R4C4:R4C6
K2:M8	R2C11:R8C13

Examples of arrays: {1,2,3,4,5,6,7;"Mon","Tue","Wed","Thur","Fri","Sat","Sun"}, E3:F5, and G2.

Example of an error value: If you entered =ADD(2,3), the error value #NAME? would appear since there is no function called ADD.

VAR()

(see also **Function, VARP, DVAR, STDEV, STDEVP)**

Syntax

VAR(*number1,number2,...*)

Description

VAR is a function that returns an estimate of the variance for a population based on a sample, which is given in the list of values for the function. *Variance* is a statistical calculation that measures deviations from the mean or average of a set of values. Variance is the square of standard deviation.

Variance calculated by VAR uses the formula:

$$\frac{n \sum x^2 - (\sum x)^2}{n(n-1)}$$

As indicated by this formula, VAR calculates on the basis that the list of values for the function is only a sample of the population. If you have the entire population to use for calculating the variance, use the VARP function.

The information required for function VAR:

number1,number2,... where each of these values can be a number, cell address, formula, or function that yields a number. These values represent a sample of the population.

Note: Values in the population that are expressed as text, logical values, or empty cells cause errors.

Note: VAR takes up to 14 elements in the list of values for the function: number1,number2,...,number14. (See "SUM" for an example of this limit.)

Examples

Suppose that keys produced for a computer keyboard are collected from the production line of the factory at random intervals. The size of the top of each key is a critical factor in determining whether it is used or discarded. The length in centimeters of the top of each key in this sample is measured and entered into cells B3:B11 of your Excel spreadsheet. The VAR formula is also entered. In summary: Cells B3:B9 contain .38, 1.38, 1.37, 1.39, 1.35, 1.39, 1.36. The formula =VAR(B3:B9) returns 0.000229.

Formula	Returns
=VAR(1,2,3,4,5)	2.5

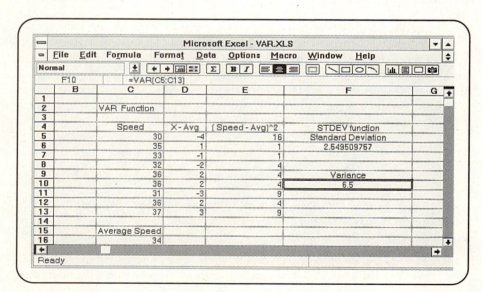

VARP()

(*see also* Function, VAR, DVARP, STDEV, STDEVP)

Syntax

VARP(*number1,number2,...*)

Description

VARP is a function that returns the variance for a population provided that the entire population is in the list of values for the function. *Variance* is a statistical calculation that measures deviations from the mean or average of a set of values. Variance is the square of standard deviation.

Variance calculated by VARP uses the formula:

$$\frac{n \sum x^2 - (\sum x)^2}{n^2}$$

As indicated by this formula, VARP calculates on the basis that the list of values given to the function is the entire population of data. If you have only a sample of the entire population to use in calculating the variance, use the VAR function.

The information required for function VARP:

number1,number2,... where each of these values can be a number, cell address, formula, or function that yields a number. These values represent the entire population of data.

Note: Values in the population that are expressed as text, logical values, or empty cells cause errors.

Note: VAR takes up to 14 elements in the list of values for the function: number1,number2,...,number14. (See "SUM" for an example of this limit.)

Examples

Suppose that during a fixed time period *all* the keys produced for a computer keyboard are collected from the production line of a factory. Since *all* the keys were collected during the fixed time period, we use the formula for variance for an entire population, VARP. The size of the top of each key is a critical factor in determining whether it is used or discarded. The length in centimeters of the top of each key in this sample is measured and entered into cells B3:B11 of your Excel spreadsheet. The VARP formula is also entered. In summary: Cells B3:B9 contain 1.38, 1.38, 1.37, 1.39, 1.35, 1.39, 1.36. The formula =VARP(B3:B9) returns 0.000196.

Formula	Returns
=VARP(1,2,3,4,5)	2

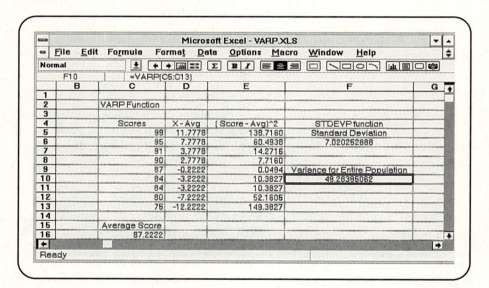

VDB () *(see also* Functions, DDB, SLN, SYD)

Syntax

VDB(*cost,salvage,life,start_ period,end_ period,factor,no_switch*)

Description

VDB is a function that returns the depreciation of an asset for any specified full or partial period, using the double-declining-balance method if you specify a factor of 2, or another method if you specify a factor other than 2. VDB stands for *variable double-declining balance*. See "DDB" for more information.

The information required for function VDB:

cost is a positive number that represents the initial cost of the asset.

salvage is a positive number that represents the value at the end of the depreciation, which is sometimes also referred to as the salvage value of the asset.

life is a positive number that represents the number of periods over which the asset depreciates, which is sometimes also referred to as the useful life of the asset.

start_period is a positive number that represents the beginning of the period for which VDB calculates the depreciation.

end_period is a positive number that represents the end of the period for which VDB calculates the depreciation.

Note: start_period and end_period must be in the same units as life.

factor is a positive number that represents the rate at which the balance declines. If factor is not included, it is assumed to be 2.

no_switch is a logical value that specifies whether to switch to straight-line depreciation when depreciation is greater than the calculated declining balance.

If no_switch Is	*VDB Calculation of Depreciation*
TRUE	does *not* switch to a straight-line depreciation calculation, even when depreciation is greater than the calculated declining balance.
FALSE or not included	switches to a straight-line depreciation calculation when depreciation is greater than the calculated declining balance.

Examples

Suppose that you bought some machinery for your business at $100,000. It has a lifetime of 10 years, at which time the salvage value is $40,000. Examples of the depreciation of the machinery follow:

Depreciation for	Is Calculated by	Which Yields
First year	=VDB(100000, 40000,10,0,1)	$20,000.00
First month	=VDB(100000, 40000,10*12,0,1,2)	$1,666.67
The second year to the third year	=VDB(100000, 40000,10,2,3)	$12,800.00
The second month to the end of the first year	=VDB(100000, 40000,10*12,2, 12,2.5)	$18,202.06 (using a factor of 2.5)
Last month	=VDB(100000, 40000,10*12,119, 120,0.5)	$500.00 (using a factor of 0.5)

VIEW.3D

(*see* **Macro Functions That Perform Format Commands**)

VLINE

(*see* **Macro Functions That Perform Actions**)

VLOOKUP()

(*see also* **Function, HLOOKUP, LOOKUP, INDEX**)

Syntax

VLOOKUP(*lookup_value,table_array,column_index_num*)

Description

VLOOKUP is a function that returns a value from the specified array, which is in the row where lookup_value was matched and in the column indicated by column_index_num. VLOOKUP looks in the first column of array for the lookup_value. When lookup_value is found, then VLOOKUP returns the value that is in the row which is headed by the value that was matched to lookup_value and the column which is in the position given by column_index_num.

VLOOKUP matches lookup_value with a value in the first column of array:

- If lookup_value is in the first column of array, VLOOKUP matches lookup_value with this value.

- If VLOOKUP can't find lookup_value in the first column of array, it matches with the next largest value in the first column of array that is less than or equal to lookup_value.

- If lookup_value is smaller than the smallest value in the first column of array, then no match occurs and VLOOKUP returns the #N/A error.

Note: VLOOKUP is similar to HLOOKUP. VLOOKUP looks in the first column for lookup_value, while HLOOKUP looks in the first row.

The information required for function VLOOKUP:

lookup_value is a value that VLOOKUP looks for in the first column of array.

table_array is a range of cells that contain numbers, text, or logical values.

Important: In order to ensure a correct answer, the values in the entire first column of table_array *must* be in ascending order: –1, 0, 1, 2, ..., A, ..., Z, FALSE, TRUE. (Upper- and lowercase letters are equivalent.) All other columns in table_array can be in any order.

column_index_num is the column number in table_array that specifies which column the returned value will come from. For example, if you give a 2 for column_index_num, the returned value will come from the second column. If column_index_num is less than 1, the #VALUE! error results. If it is greater than the number of columns in table_array, then the #REF error is the returned value.

> **Tip:** An easy way to ensure that the first column is in ascending order is to highlight the array; from the main menu select Data and then Sort; choose Column and Ascending; and press Enter.

Examples

Formula	*Returns*
=VLOOKUP("bake", {"A","Angel Food Cake"; "C","Coffee cake";"D", "Devils Food Cake"}, 2)	"Angel Food Cake"
=VLOOKUP(4,{1,"Monday";2, "Tuesday";3,"Wednesday";4, "Thursday";5,"Friday"},2)	"Thursday", the value that is in the second row where 2 matched 2, and in the second column
=VLOOKUP(2.39, {1,"Monday";2,"Tuesday";3, "Wednesday";4,"Thursday";5,"Friday"},1)	2, the value in the second row where 2.39 matched 2, and in the first column
=VLOOKUP(0,{1,"M";2, "T";3,"A";4,TRUE;5,"F"},2)	#N/A

An example in the figure is the text value Oscar Felix, which is the result of the formula displayed in the formula bar: =VLOOKUP("oz",B3:D8,3). This value is the result of fixing the row position by looking up "oz", and the column position by the 3 in the formula. The position of the fourth row of the array is fixed by matching "oz" with OP597. The third column is fixed by the 3 in the formula. The value in the fourth row and third column is Oscar Felix.

> **Tip:** In the example in the figure, the formula =VLOOKUP("oz",B3:D8,3) matches "oz" with OP597 since *oz* alphabetically comes after *OP* (ignoring the case as VLOOKUP does). If the formula =VLOOKUP("O",B3:D8,3) had been used, "O" would have matched MM325 since "O" comes before "OP". If you are looking for the last text item that begins with a particular letter, use that particular letter followed by the letter *z* as your lookup_value.

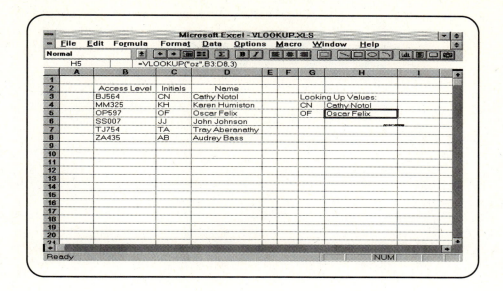

VOLATILE (*see* Macro Functions—Control)

VPAGE (*see* Macro Functions That Perform Actions)

VSCROLL

(*see* Macro Functions That Perform Actions)

W–Z

WAIT (*see* Macro Functions— Control)

WEEKDAY( )

(*see also* DAY, MONTH, YEAR, HOUR, MINUTE, SECOND, TODAY)

Syntax

WEEKDAY(*serial_number*)

Description

WEEKDAY is a function that returns a number which represents the day of the week corresponding to the particular date specified by serial_number. The returned number ranges from 1 (Sunday) to 7 (Saturday).

The information required for function WEEKDAY:

Serial_number is a number that represents a particular date in the range of January 1, 1900, to December 31, 2078. For more information on serial_number, see "NOW." Serial_number can also be given as text.

 Tip: To display the numerical day returned by the WEEKDAY function in text form (Saturday, Sunday, Monday, ...), use the Format Number command and type in the custom format dddd in the format box.

Note: Excel 3 for Windows uses a different numbering system (the 1900 Date System) for the WEEKDAY function than Excel for the Macintosh. On the Macintosh, date_text can range from January 1, 1904, to December 31, 2078.

Examples *(based on the 1900 Date System)*

The formula =WEEKDAY(33364) returns 2 or Monday. The serial_number 33364 stands for the date May 6, 1991, which is a Monday.

The formula =WEEKDAY(33712) returns 7, or Saturday. The serial_number 33712 stands for the date April 18, 1992, which is a Saturday.

Formula	Returns
=WEEKDAY("October 31, 1991")	5 (or Thursday)
=WEEKDAY("December 25, 1991")	4 (or Wednesday)

WHILE *(see* Macro Functions—Control)

Window Arrange All

The Arrange All command in Window displays and arranges all the open documents at the same time. This includes chart windows, macro sheet windows, and info windows (see "Window Show Info"). The windows appear tiled, with the active window in color (or highlighted, on a monochrome monitor).

Keystrokes

Keyboard	*Mouse*
Window	Window
Arrange All	Arrange All

Example

Suppose that you are linking three documents using the Consolidate command in Data. During the linkup, you want to use the point method of referencing cells in the documents. Choose Arrange All from Window and Excel displays the three documents on the screen simultaneously.

 Displaying All Open Documents

1. Make sure that all the documents you want to display are open.

2. Choose Arrange All from Window. Excel displays all the documents.

 Note: Documents that are hidden don't display.

 Tip: When an uneven number of documents are open, the active document always gets more display room after Arrange All.

Window Hide

The Hide command hides the active window. You can use Unhide to bring the window back into view.

Keystrokes

Keyboard   *Mouse*

Window   Window

Hide   Hide

Example

Hide can be useful when you want to make use of data or macros on certain sheets, but you don't need to access the sheets directly. You could open a macro sheet and then hide it with Hide from Window. Choose Arrange All and the macro sheet won't be displayed, though the macros can be accessed.

Hiding a Window

1. Make the window that you want to hide the active window.
2. Choose Hide from the Window menu.   The window disappears from view and does not appear in the list of windows open in the Window menu.

Note: Use Unhide to bring a window back into display.

Window New Window

The New Window command in the Window menu opens up a separate window containing the same document currently on display. Make a change to one document and both change. You can use this command to look at different sections of the same document at one time. As many windows on the same document can be open as you like.

Keystrokes

Keyboard

Window

New Window

Mouse

Window

New Window

Example

Suppose that you have a worksheet containing many interlinked calculations, all of which build up to a final result containing the net profit for a period. You are interested in seeing how the net profit changes as you make changes to an earlier section of the calculation figures. Open a new window through New Window and display in this new window the net profit while entering figures in the first window.

Opening a New Window

1. Make the document that you want to view the active document.

2. Choose New Window from Window.

    Excel opens another window containing the same document and makes this the active document.

3. Using the scroll bars, display the section of the document that you want to view in the new window.

    You can use Arrange All to see both windows at once.

Window Show Info

The Show Info command opens a window displaying information on the active cell in the active document. A special menu option, Info, goes with the info window. When chosen (checked), the commands in this menu—Cell, Formula, Value, etc.—display the relevant information about the cell.

Keystrokes

Keyboard

Window

Show Info

Info

Cell, Formula, Value, Format, Protection, Names, Precedents, Dependents, or Note

Mouse

Window

Show Info

Info

Cell, Formula, Value, Format, Protection, Names, Precedents, Dependents, or Note

Example

Show Info can be the quickest way to find information on a cell (see the figure). Other than the straightforward cell number, formula, and value, you can see the formatting, the protection, any worksheet names containing the cell, any precedents (cells upon which the cell is dependent), any dependents, and any notes associated with this cell.

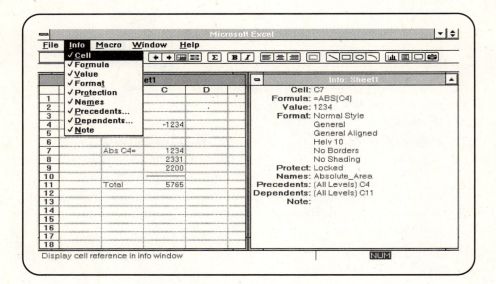

 Creating an Info Window

1. Select the cell about which you want to display information.

2. Choose Show Info from Window.

   Excel displays the info window. Only Cell, Formula, and Note display by default.

3. Choose any other information that you want to display from the Info menu.

 Note: Even though the info window does not display in the Window menu, it remains open after you go back to the worksheet window unless you close it yourself. Arrange All displays it as a normal window.

> **Tip:** You can change the cell about which you want to display information without choosing Show Info again (if the info window is already open). Just select a different cell and the new information is displayed in the info window.

Window Unhide

After a window is hidden using Hide, you can redisplay the window using Unhide.

Keystrokes

Keyboard	*Mouse*
Window	Window
Unhide	Unhide
Arrow key to select document	Hold the Shift key and click on a document
Spacebar	OK
Enter	

Example

Suppose that you previously hid a macro sheet and now you want to use it to insert another new macro. Choose Unhide from Window. Select the macro sheet in the displayed box and choose OK.

 Unhiding a Window

1. Choose Unhide from Window.	Excel displays a dialog box listing the hidden windows.
2. Select the window to unhide.	You can only select one at a time.
3. Choose OK.	The window is displayed.

Window Workgroup

The Workgroup command in Window groups worksheets and macro sheets together so that any change made to the active sheet also changes all other sheets in the group.

Keystrokes

Keyboard	*Mouse*
Window	Window
Workgroup	Workgroup
Ctrl-arrow key	Hold Shift while clicking on the sheet name
Spacebar	OK
Enter	

Example

The Workgroup command is very useful when you have an identical series of changes or additions to make to a number of worksheets or macro sheets. Suppose that you tabulate the performance of investment traders through a series of formulas that calculate basic figures. Each trader gets his or her own sheet. Create as many new worksheets as there are traders. Choose Workgroup to group them together. Enter the formulas in the active sheet, and they appear in all other sheets as well.

 Creating a Workgroup

1. Make one of the sheets the active sheet.

   You do the entries and changes on this sheet.

2. Choose Workgroup from Window.

   Excel displays a list of open worksheets and macro sheets.

3. Highlight all the sheets to include in the workgroup.

   These can be macro sheets and worksheets.

4. Choose OK.

   All sheets included get [Workgroup] added in the title bar.

Note: The workgroup remains until you close the active sheet or make another sheet the active sheet.

WINDOWS (*see* Macro Functions—Value Returning)

WORKGROUP

(*see* Macro Functions That Perform Window Commands)

Worksheet Functions

A *worksheet function* is a built-in operation that all Excel worksheets automatically perform on some specific information. Worksheet functions are one of two major types of functions: worksheet and macro. Worksheet functions can be used in either a worksheet or a macro sheet. They can be pasted from the Paste Function dialog box through the Formula command or directly typed into a cell or cells.

There are 11 different types of worksheet functions. All the worksheet functions, listed in their categories, follow.

Database Function	Function Returns
DAVERAGE	The average of selected database entries
DCOUNT	A number that is the count of how many numbers there are in the selected database entries
DCOUNTA	A number that is the count of how many values there are in the selected database entries
DGET	A single record from the selected database entries that matches criteria that you specify
DMAX	The largest of all the selected database entries
DMIN	The smallest of all the selected database entries

Database Function	Function Returns
DPRODUCT	The product or result from multiplying the numbers in the selected database entries
DSTDEV	Standard deviation based on a sample of values in the selected database entries
DSTDEVP	Standard deviation based on values in the selected database entries, which represent the *entire* population
DSUM	The sum of the numbers in the selected database entries
DVAR	Variance based on a sample of values in the selected database entries
DVARP	Variance based on values in the selected database entries, which represent the *entire* population

Date and Time Function	Function Returns
DATE	A code in number form for a date that you give it
DATEVALUE	A code in number form for a date that you give it
DAY	A day of the month in number form for a date that you give it
DAYS360	The number of days between two dates based on 30-day months
HOUR	An hour of the day in number form for a time that you give it
MINUTE	The minute in the hour in number form for a time that you give it
MONTH	A month in the year in number form for a date that you give it
NOW	A code in number form for the current time and date
SECOND	The seconds in the hour for a time that you give it
TIME	A code in number form for the time you give it
TIMEVALUE	A code in number form for the time you give it

TODAY	A code in number form for today's date
WEEKDAY	The day of the week in number form for a date that you give it
1YEAR	The year of a date that you give it
Financial Function	***Function Returns***
DDB	The depreciation of an asset for a specific period, using the double-declining-balance method
FV	The future value of an investment
IPMT	The interest payment for an investment period
IRR	The internal rate of return for an investment, not including finance cost or reinvestment gains
MIRR	The internal rate of return, when it is positive and when negative cash flows are financed at different rates
NPER	The number of payments for an investment
NPV	The net present value of an investment based on varying or constant cash flows
PMT	The periodic total payment for an investment
PPMT	The payment on an investment for a defined period
PV	The present value of an investment
RATE	The interest rate of an investment on a per period basis
SLN	The straight line depreciation of an asset
SYD	The sum-of-years'-digits depreciation of an asset for a specified period
VDB	The depreciation of an asset for a specified or partial period, using a declining-balance method
Information Function	***Function Returns***
ADDRESS	A cell address in text form as specified by information you give it
AREAS	The number of areas in the reference value that you give it

Information Function	Function Returns
CELL	Information about the formatting, location, or contents of a cell
COLUMN	The column number of cell address(es) that you give it
COLUMNS	The number of columns in a range of cell addresses that you give it
INDIRECT	The value that is in the cell which is addressed by the reference value that is in the cell whose address you give to the function
INFO	Information about the current operating environment
ISBLANK	TRUE if the value you give to the function is blank
ISERR	TRUE if any of the values you give to the function are any of the error values except #N/A
ISERROR	TRUE if any of the values you give to the function are any of the error values
ISLOGICAL	TRUE if the value you give to the function is a logical value
ISNA	TRUE if the value you give to the function is a #N/A error value
ISNONTEXT	TRUE if the value you give to the function is not a text value
ISNUMBER	TRUE if the value you give to the function is a number
ISREF	TRUE if the value you give to the function is a reference to a value
ISTEXT	TRUE if the value you give to the function is a text value
N	The numerical form of a value that you give to a function
NA	The error value #N/A
OFFSET	An offset in reference form from a reference that you give the function

ROW	The row number of cell address(es) that you give it
ROWS	The number of rows in a range of cell addresses that you give it
T	The text form of values you give it
TYPE	A number that specifies which type of value its argument is (a number, text, array, or error value, etc.)
Logical Function	*Function Returns*
AND	True if all the values you give it are true
FALSE	FALSE
IF	One of two values that you specify. Which value is returned depends on the test condition that you give the function. (It performs the same function as it does in the English language.)
NOT	The opposite of the value that you give it
OR	False if all the values you give it are false
TRUE	TRUE
Lookup Function	*Function Returns*
CHOOSE	A value from a list of values
HLOOKUP	A value in an array whose position is specified by the two values you give: 1) a lookup for the top row of the array and 2) a specified row number
INDEX (2 INDEX functions)	A value from an array that is at a position specified by you
LOOKUP (2 LOOKUP functions)	A value in an array or reference
MATCH	A value in an array or reference
VLOOKUP	A value in an array whose position is specified by the two values you give: 1) a lookup for the first column of the array and 2) a specified column number

Mathematical Function	Function Returns
ABS	The positive value of a number that you give it
EXP	The mathematical number e raised to a power that you give it
FACT	The factorial of a number that you give it
INT	The next smallest integer to a number that you give it
LN	The natural log of a number that you give it
LOG	The logarithm of a number that you give it
LOG10	The logarithm base 10 of a number that you give it
MOD	The remainder after division with two numbers that you specify
PI	The number π
PRODUCT	The product or result from multiplying numbers that you give it
RAND	A random number between 0 and 1
ROUND	The number that you give it rounded off
SIGN	The sign of a number that you give it
SQRT	The square root of a number that you give it
SUM	The sum of numbers that you give it
TRUNC	The integer portion of a number that you give it

Matrix Function	Function Returns
MDETERM	The matrix determinant of an array that you give it
MINVERSE	The inverse matrix of a matrix or array that you give to it
MMULT	The matrix product of two arrays
SUMPRODUCT	The sum of the product of corresponding pairs of elements from two arrays
TRANSPOSE	The reverse or transpose of an array

Statistical Function	Function Returns
AVERAGE	The average of some numbers that you give it
COUNT	A number that is the count of how many numbers there are in the list of values that you give it
COUNTA	A number that is the count of how many values there are in the list of values, cell addresses, and other references that you give it
GROWTH	Values along an exponential curve $y = b * m \wedge x$
LINEST	Values that describe a linear trend: $y = m_1 x_1 + m_2 x_2 + ... + b$ or $y = m * x + b$
LOGEST	Values that describe an exponential trend: $y = b * (m_1 \wedge x_1 * m_2 \wedge x_2 * ...)$ or $y = b * m \wedge x$
MAX	The largest of all the values that you give it
MEDIAN	The median of all the values that you give it
MIN	The smallest of all the values that you give it
STDEV	Standard deviation based on a sample of values that you give it
STDEVP	Standard deviation based on values that you give it that represent the *entire* population
TREND	Values along a linear trend $y = m * x + b$
VAR	Variance based on a sample of values that you give it
VARP	Variance based on values that you give it that represent the *entire* population

Text Function	Function Returns
CHAR	The character that corresponds to a numerical code that you give the function
CLEAN	The text that you give the function without control characters
CODE	The numerical code that corresponds to a character that you give the function
DOLLAR	The text format of a number with dollar formatting

Statistical Function	Function Returns
EXACT	True if two values that you give it are identical
FIND	A number that represents the position of some text within another piece of text (both of which are specified by you)
FIXED	The text format of a number with fixed decimal formatting
LEFT	Leftmost characters from a text value
LEN	The length of text that you give it
LOWER	The text that you give it, in all lowercase letters
MID	Some characters from some text that you give to MID
PROPER	The text that you give to PROPER with the first letter of each word capitalized and all the other letters lowercased
REPLACE	Text that you give to REPLACE with some specified old text characters replaced by specified new text
REPT	Text that you give it repeated as many times as you request
RIGHT	Rightmost characters from a text value
SEARCH	A number that represents the position of some text within another piece of text, both of which are specified by you (SEARCH is not case-sensitive.)
SUBSTITUTE	Text that you give to SUBSTITUTE with some part of it replaced by some new text
TEXT	The text format of a number with any valid formatting that you specify
TRIM	Text that you give it without multiple blank spaces
UPPER	Text that you give it all in uppercase letters
VALUE	The numerical form of the text value (a number in text format) that you give the function

Trigonometric Function	Function Returns
ACOS	The arccosine or inverse cosine of a number that you give to the function
ACOSH	The inverse hyperbolic cosine of a number that you give to the function
ASIN	The arcsine or inverse sine of a number that you give to the function
ASINH	The inverse hyperbolic sine of a number that you give to the function
ATAN	The arctangent or inverse tangent of a number that you give to the function
ATAN2	The arctangent of x and y coordinates that you give to the function
ATANH	The inverse hyperbolic tangent of a number that you give to the function
COS	The cosine of a number that you give to the function
COSH	The hyperbolic cosine of a number that you give to the function
SIN	The sine of a number that you give to the function
SINH	The hyperbolic sine of a number that you give to the function
TAN	The tangent of a number that you give to the function
TANH	The hyperbolic tangent of a number that you give to the function

WORKSPACE

(*see* Macro Functions That Perform Options Commands)

YEAR( )

(see also DAY, MONTH, WEEKDAY, HOUR, MINUTE, SECOND, TODAY)

Syntax

YEAR(*serial_number*)

Description

YEAR is a function that returns a number which represents the year corresponding to the particular date specified by serial_number. The returned number ranges from 1900 to 2078 (the range of years that Excel is equipped to handle in the date functions).

The information required for function YEAR:

Serial_number is a number that represents a particular date in the range of January 1, 1900, to December 31, 2078. For more information on serial_number, see "NOW." Serial_number can also be given as text.

Note: Excel 3 for Windows uses a different numbering system (the 1900 Date System) for the YEAR function than Excel for the Macintosh. On the Macintosh, date_text can range from January 1, 1904, to December 31, 2078.

Examples *(based on the 1900 Date System)*

The formula =YEAR(32880) returns 1990 because serial_number 32880 stands for the date January 7, 1990.

The formula =YEAR(31296) returns 1985 because serial_number 31296 stands for the date September 6, 1985.

Formula	Returns
=YEAR("May 1, 2001")	2001
=YEAR("4/18/92")	1992

Installing Microsoft Excel for Windows

As you probably know, Microsoft Excel 3 only runs in conjunction with Microsoft Windows. Therefore, Windows needs to be installed on your hard drive before you can attempt to install Excel. If you haven't already installed Windows, you should do so before proceeding.

Hardware Requirements

The following are the minimum hardware requirements for Excel:

- IBM PC/AT or compatible
- At least 2.5 megabytes of free disk space
- A graphics card compatible with Microsoft Windows version 3.0 or later, such as IBM VGA, IBM EGA, or Hercules Graphics
- 1 megabyte of random-access memory
- DOS version 3.1 or later
- Microsoft Windows 3.0 or later
- Mouse and printer are optional

Copying Your Source Disks

Copy the Excel disks to another set of disks before you install. Then keep the originals in a safe place and use the copies because disks are easily damaged. Also, if there is a virus on your hard drive, it could be transferred to the floppy disks in the installation process, making them unusable. Working off copied disks instead of originals is a good safeguard against these and other potential mishaps.

To copy your source disks, follow these steps:

1. Label the target disks (that is, the disks to be copied onto) with something like "Excel Working Copies." Label them "Setup," "Library," and "Help."

2. At the DOS prompt, type **Diskcopy** followed by the floppy disk drive letter typed twice: for example, Diskcopy A: A:.

   DOS sends a message to the screen: Insert SOURCE diskette in drive A:, followed by Press any key when ready....

3. Put the original Excel Setup disk in the floppy disk drive and press any keyboard character.

   After a short time, you see another message: Insert TARGET diskette in drive A:, again followed by Press any key when ready....

4. Insert the target disk into the floppy disk drive and press a keyboard character.

   DOS then copies files onto this disk. You may be prompted to change source and target disks several times because of the large number of files involved. When all the files are copied to the target disk, you will see this message: Copy another diskette (Y/N).

5. Press Y to indicate yes and repeat the above steps to copy the remaining Excel disks.

6. When you see Copy another diskette (Y/N) after all files on the three disks have been copied, answer N.

   Now use the working copies to install Excel.

Installing Excel

Follow these steps to install Excel:

1. Insert the Setup disk into drive A:.

2. Launch Windows if it is not already started.

3. Choose Run from File.
4. Type **A:Setup** and press Enter.

   Setup displays a dialog box.
5. Enter your name and organization.
6. Choose Continue.
7. Enter the drive and directory to install Excel.
8. Choose Continue.

   Setup displays all the options to be installed on the following screen. Uncheck any options you do not want installed. The disk space required and the disk space currently available are displayed at the bottom of the dialog box. Obviously, if the disk space required is greater than that available, you need to turn off some options to continue at this stage.

   A window at the bottom of the screen supplies information about the options.
9. When you've decided which options to install and which not to install, check or uncheck them respectively.
10. Choose Setup to commence the installation.
11. Replace the disk in the disk drive when prompted.

Keyboard and Function-Key Shortcuts

Keyboard shortcuts using the Ctrl and Alt keys allow you to bypass menus to implement menu commands directly and in some cases to implement the command *and* choose a dialog box option (such as Ctrl-! to choose Format Number and the format #,##0.00 from the dialog box). In some cases, these key combinations provide shortcuts for which there is no command equivalent.

Function-key shortcuts also allow you to bypass the menus altogether (as opposed to using the keyboard to move through menus quickly). For example, instead of clicking on the Help menu with the mouse or pressing Alt-H to open the Help menu, you can press F1.

Keyboard Shortcuts with the Ctrl and Alt Keys

Command	Key Combination
Chart Navigation (for moving through items on chart and/or moving between classes of items on chart)	Arrow keys
Format Border (Outline)	Ctrl-&
Format Border (remove all borders)	Ctrl-_ (underlining key)

Command	Key Combination
Format Column Width (Hide)	Ctrl-0 (zero)
Format Column Width (Unhide)	Ctrl-Shift-0 (zero)
Format Font (normal font)	Ctrl-1
Format Font Bold (toggle between bold and plain)	Ctrl-2
Format Font Italic (toggle between italic and plain)	Ctrl-3
Format Font Underline (toggle between underline and plain)	Ctrl-4
Format Font Strikeout (toggle between applying/removing strikeout)	Ctrl-5
Format Number (General format)	Ctrl-~
Format Number (#,##0.00 format)	Ctrl-!
Format Number (h;mm AM/PM format)	Ctrl-@
Format Number (d-mmm-yy format)	Ctrl-#
Format Number [($#,##0.00_);($#,##0.00) format]	Ctrl-$
Format Number (0% format)	Ctrl-%
Format Number (0.00E+00 format)	Ctrl-^
Format Row Height (Hide)	Ctrl-9
Format Row Height (Unhide)	Ctrl-Shift-9
Formula Bar: text wrapping while working in formula bar	Alt-Enter
Formula Select Special (Notes)	Ctrl-?
Formula Select Special (Current Region)	Ctrl-*

Command	Key Combination
Formula Select Special (Current Array)	Ctrl-/
Formula Select Special (Row Differences)	Ctrl-\
Formula Select Special (Column Differences)	Ctrl-|
Formula Select Special (Precedents: Direct Only)	Ctrl-[
Formula Select Special (Precedents: All Levels)	Ctrl-{
Formula Select Special (Dependents: Direct Only)	Ctrl-]
Formula Select Special (Dependents: All Levels)	Ctrl-}
Formula Select Special (Visible Cells Only)	Alt-;
Object (when object is selected, selects all objects on sheet)	Ctrl-Shift-Spacebar
Options Calculate Now	Ctrl-=
Options Display (Formulas: toggle between formulas/values)	Ctrl-' (Single left quotation mark)
Options Display (Outline Symbols: toggles between displaying/hiding outline symbols)	Ctrl-8
Options Display (Objects: switches among displaying objects, displaying placeholders for objects, and hiding all objects)	Ctrl-6
Options Workspace (Toolbar: toggle between displaying/hiding Toolbar)	Ctrl-7
Outline: demote a row or column	Alt-Shift-Right Arrow
Outline: promote a row or column	Alt-Shift-Left Arrow

Command	Key Combination
Toolbar: auto-sum button	Alt-=
Toolbar: select visible cells only button	Alt-;
Toolbar: Style Box	Alt-' (Single right quotation mark)
Selects entire worksheet	Ctrl-Shift-Spacebar

Shortcuts with the Function Keys

Command	Function Key
Help	F1
Context-sensitive help	Shift-F1
File New (Chart option)	Alt-F1
File New (Worksheet option)	Alt-Shift-F1
File New (Macro sheet option)	Alt-Ctrl-F1
Activate formula bar (Edit mode)	F2
Formula Note	Shift-F2
Window Show Info	Ctrl-F2
File Save As	Alt-F2
File Save	Alt-Shift-F2
File Open	Alt-Ctrl-F2
File Print	Alt-Ctrl-Shift-F2
Formula Paste Name	F3
Formula Paste Function	Shift-F3
Formula Define Name	Ctrl-F3
Formula Create Name	Ctrl-Shift-F3
Formula Reference	F4
Control Close (active document window)	Ctrl-F4

Command	Function Key
Control Close (application window)	Alt-F4
Formula Goto	F5
Formula Find (find cell containing specific contents)	Shift-F5
Control Restore (active document window)	Ctrl-F5
Next pane	F6
Previous pane	Shift-F6
Next document window	Ctrl-F6
Previous document window	Ctrl-Shift-F6
Formula Find (find next cell)	F7
Formula Find (find previous cell)	Shift-F7
Control Move (active document window)	Ctrl-F7
Turns Extend on or off (changes to Extend when already in Add)	F8
Turns on Add	Shift-F8
Control Size (active document window)	Ctrl-F8
Options Calculate Now	F9
Options Calculate Document	Shift-F9
Activate menu bar	F10
Control Maximize (active document window)	Ctrl-F10
File New (Chart option)	F11
File New (Worksheet option)	Shift-F11
File New (Macro sheet option)	Ctrl-F11
File Save As	F12
File Save	Shift-F12
File Open	Ctrl-F12
File Print	Ctrl-Shift-F12

Index

Symbols

, (comma) reference operator, 112
% (percentage) arithmetic operator, 111
! (exclamation mark), 59
(...) ellipsis, 10
( ) (space) reference operator, 112
* (multiplication) arithmetic operator, 35, 111
+ (addition) arithmetic operator, 35, 111
– (subtraction) arithmetic operator, 35, 111
/ (division) arithmetic operator, 35, 111
: (colon) reference operator, 112
= (equal to) comparison operator, 69
> (greater than) comparison operator, 69
>= (greater than or equal to) comparison operator, 69
< (less than) comparison operator, 69
<= (less than or equal to) comparison operator, 69
<> (not equal to) comparison operator, 69
^ (exponentiation) arithmetic operator, 35, 111
{ } (braces) in formulas, 258
1-2-3 files, consolidating data, 133
3-D charts, 225, 679-680, 468-469
 area, 228
 formatting, 229-230
 line, 228
 multi-category, 226-227
 pie, 229
 viewing, 669

A

A1.R1C1 macro function, 605
ABS( ) function, 327
absolute cell references, 61, 70
absolute references, 328, 708, 810
 changing to relative references, 813
absolute value, 327
ABSREF macro function, 708
accessing databases, 308-311
ACOS( ) function, 329
ACOSH( ) function, 329-330

ACTIVATE macro function, 605
ACTIVATE Q+E function, 789
ACTIVATE.NEXT macro function, 606
ACTIVATE.PREV macro function, 606
active cell, 27-28
ACTIVE.CELL macro function, 172, 708
Add Constraint dialog box, 273-274
Add player button, 182
add-in macros, 179, 193-195
ADD.AFTER Q+E function, 789
ADD.ARROW macro function, 617
ADD.BAR macro function, 173, 261-263, 702
ADD.BEFORE Q+E function, 789
ADD.COMMAND macro function, 195, 702-703
ADD.CONDITION Q+E function, 790
ADD.MENU macro function, 195, 197-198, 703
ADD.OVERLAY macro function, 617
ADD.RECORD Q+E function, 790
adding
    columns, 292-294
    records, 162-163
ADDRESS( ) function, 331-332
addresses, 26, 332
adjusting data markers, 242
ALERT macro function, 703
Alignment button, 41
Alignment command, 333-334
ALIGNMENT macro function, 647
ALLOW.EDIT Q+E function, 790
AND logic, 156
AND( ) function, 335
annuities, 779
annuity functions, 336-337
ANSI (American National Standards Institute) character set, 311
Answer report, 273

APP.ACTIVATE macro function, 606
APP.MAXIMIZE macro function, 622
APP.MINIMIZE macro function, 622
APP.MOVE macro function, 622
APP.RESTORE macro function, 622
APP.SIZE macro function, 623
application window, 14, 26
applications, activating, 606
APPLY.NAMES macro function, 670-671
APPLY.STYLE macro function, 648
arcs
    borders, 210
    fills, 210-211
    tools, 202-203
Arc tool, 42
arccosine, 329
area charts, 87-88, 228, 680
AREAS( ) function, 339-340
ARGUMENT macro function, 693
arguments, 114, 531
    describing, 693
    field, 164
arithmetic formulas, 109-110
arithmetic operators, 110
ARRANGE.ALL macro function, 691
ARRANGE.ALL Q+E function, 791
arrays, 341, 370, 532, 821, 862
    constant, 340
    formulas, 258
        constants in, 260-261
        editing, 259-260
        selecting, 259-260
        single-output, 259
    functions, 261
    horizontal positioning, 861-862
    matrix determinant, 725
    numeric, 340
    ranges, 260
    text, 340
    vertical positioning, 861-862
    x values, 864
    y values, 864

arrows, 211-212, 243, 356-357
    deleting, 619
    in charts, 617
    moving, 253, 481
    sizing, 253, 493-494
ascending sort order, 71
ASIN( ) function, 341
ASINH( ) function, 342
assets, depreciation, 402
    double-declining, 880
    straight-line, 834
    sum-of-years' digits, 850
Assign to Object dialog box, 171
Assign to Object macro command, 713-714
ASSIGN.TO.OBJECT macro function, 683
ATAN( ) function, 343
ATAN2( ) function, 343-344
ATANH( ) function, 344-345
ATTACH.TEXT macro function, 617
Auto-Sum button, 40
Automatic Except Tables option, 122
AVERAGE( ) function, 345-347
axes, 243, 360-361
    category, 248-249
    right angles, 230
    scaling, 248-249, 491-492, 667-669
    series, 248-249
    value, 248-249
    x-axis, 75
    y-axis, 75
AXES macro function, 618-619

B

backwards search, 158
bar charts, 88-89, 681
BEEP macro function, 606
Bold button, 41
Border command, 157
BORDER macro function, 648-649
borders, 202, 209-210, 246, 349-350, 471, 648
boxes
    style, 39
    text, 44, 66
branching, 172, 175
BREAK macro function, 693
Breakpoint dialog box, 181
Breakpoint Output dialog box, 180
breakpoints, 179
Bring to Front command, 214
BRING.TO.FRONT macro function, 649
built-in commands, changing, 196
built-in functions, 531
Button tool, 45
buttons, 45
    Add player, 182
    Alignment, 41
    Auto-Sum, 40
    Bold, 41
    command, 67
    Exit, 182
    Italic, 41
    macro, 170-171
    options, 275-276
    outline, 39
    reformatting, 209
    Toolbar, 39

C

Calculate Now option, 761
CALCULATE.DOCUMENT macro function, 684
CALCULATE.NOW macro function, 619, 684
calculation
    automatic, 122
    cells, 255-257
    constraints, 269
    documents, 619, 684
    formulas, 261-263, 684, 762

interest rates, 753-754, 809
iteration, 263
manual, 122, 761
matrices, 738-739
options, 763
pi, 778
repeated, 263
saving without, 124
updating, 761
values, displayed, 123-124
Calculation command, 122-123
Calculation dialog box, 123, 264
CALCULATION macro function, 684-685
Calculation option, 762-763
CALL macro function, 703
CALLER macro function, 708
Camera tool, 45
CANCEL.COPY macro function, 606
CANCEL.KEY macro function, 704
cancelling commands, 11
capitalization of text, 786
categories, 75, 224
    transferring, 131
Category (X) Axis Labels option, 81
category axis, 248-249
Cell Protection dialog box, 149
cell references
    absolute, 61, 70
    in formulas, 110
    in macro functions, 173-174
    relative, 173
cell referencing operators, 110
CELL( ) function, 352-354
CELL.PROTECTION macro function, 649
cells
    active, 27-28
    addresses, 26, 332, 810-812
    aligning contents, 470
    attributes, copying, 429
    blank, 519-521
    borders, 349-350, 471
    calculating, 255-257
    clearing, 419
    contents
        aligning, 647
        copying, 632
    copying, 420-422
    deleting, 423
    detaching objects from, 206
    displaying, 764-766
    dividing, 429
    editing, 30
    empty, 78
    fonts, formatting, 652-653
    formats, copying, 632
    formatting, 32
    formulas, entering, 609
    groups, 105, 677-678
    increasing by constant amount, 256
    inserting, 425-426
    linking to chart text, 251-252
    maximum digits, 31
    moving, 422-423, 426-427
    multiple selection, 104-105, 744
    multiplying by constant amount, 256
    nonblank, copying, 431
    notes, 750
    objects, 666
    protecting, 473-474, 649, 767-768
    ranges, 27
    removing, 631
    shifting, 631
    value, changing, 701
    visible, 521
CHANGE.LINK macro function, 636
CHAR( ) function, 355-356
characters
    deleting, 30
    non-printable, 366
Chart Add Arrow command, 356-357

Chart Add Legend command,
    357-358
Chart Add Overlay command, 358
Chart Attach Text command,
    359-360
Chart Axes command, 360-361
chart data, 73
Chart Edit Series command, 361-362
Chart Gridlines command, 363-364
Chart option, 74
Chart Select Chart command, 364
Chart Select Plot Area command,
    364
chart text, linking to cells, 251-252
Chart tool, 44, 77
Chart window, 79
charts, 73, 219
    3-D, 225-230, 468-469, 669,
        679-680
    area, 87-88, 680
    as separate documents, 78, 83
    bar, 88, 681
    closing, 85
    column, 89, 681
    combination, 231-232, 358, 679
    copying, 630
    creating, 44
    customizing, 86, 242, 249-250
    data
        configuring, 79
        markers, 74
        series, 75
    default, 541-543
    default format, 249-250
    embedded, 77-78, 84
        deleting, 85-86
        drawing on, 216
        saving, 85
    line, 89-90, 681
    linked to worksheets, 84
    main, 231-234
    menu bar, 74
    moving, 81-82

    new, 76
    overlay, 231-234, 617
        formatting, 657-659
        deleting, 619
    pie, 90-91, 682
    preferred, 682
    printing, 86
    resizing, 81-82
    scaling, 75-76
    scatter, 82, 92, 682
    selecting parts, 224-225
    separate documents, 84
    series, changing, 620
    text in, 244
CHECK.COMMAND macro function,
    195, 704
CHOOSE( ) function, 365-366
circles
    perfect, 202
    quarter, 202-203
circular references, 263
clauses, 294
CLEAN( ) function, 366-367
CLEAR macro function, 629-630
Clipboard
    copying to, 630, 792
    displaying contents, 692
    formats, 125
    importing with, 124
    pasting to, 800
CLOSE macro function, 623
CLOSE Q+E functions, 791
CLOSE.ALL macro function, 636
CLOSE.INDEX Q+E function, 791
closing active windows, 791
CODE( ) function, 367-368
codes, headers and footers, 100-101
Color Palette option, 763-764
color palettes
    copying, 685, 763-764
    defining color, 686
COLOR.PALETTE macro function,
    685

colors
- customizing, 763-764
- defining, 686
- gridlines, 764-766
- headings, 764-766

column charts, 89-90, 681
COLUMN( ) function, 369
COLUMNS( ) function, 370
COLUMN.WIDTH macro function, 649-650
COLUMN.WIDTH Q+E function, 791
columns, 26, 223
- adding, 793
- changing, 793
- computed
  - adding, 292-294
  - displaying, 292
- demoting, 142
- headings, 291
- moving, 798
- promoting, 142
- removing, 801
- selecting, 803
- sorting, 69, 628
  - muliple, 288
- totals, 292-294
- width, 31, 60, 291-292, 474-475, 649, 791

combination charts, 231-232, 358, 679
COMBINATION macro function, 679
command buttons, 67
- Criteria, 67-68
- Delete, 67
- Demote, 140
- Find Next, 68
- Find Prev, 67
- New, 67
- Restore, 67
- Setup, 101
- Zoom, 101

command macros, 57

COMMAND Q+E function, 791
command table, 196-197
commands
- adding to menu, 702
- Alignment, 333-334
- Border, 157
- Bring to Front, 214
- built-in, changing, 196
- Calculation, 122-123
- cancelling, 11
- categories, 729
- Chart Add Arrow, 356-357
- Chart Add Legend, 357-358
- Chart Add Overlay, 358
- Chart Attach Text, 359-360
- Chart Axes, 360-361
- Chart Edit Series, 361-362
- Chart Gridlines, 363-364
- Chart Select Chart, 364
- Chart Select Plot Area, 364
- choosing, 9
- customizing, 195-197
- Data Consolidate, 379
- Data Delete, 380-381
- Data Extract, 381-382
- Data Find, 382-383
- Data Form, 383-385
- Data Parse, 385-386
- Data Series, 386-388
- Data Set Criteria, 388
- Data Set Database, 389-390
- Data Set Extract, 390-391
- Data Sort, 391-393
- Define Field, 292
- Delete, 5, 163
- Display, 179
- Edit Clear, 419
- Edit Copy, 420-422
- Edit Cut, 422-423
- Edit Delete, 423
- Edit Fill, 424
- Edit Insert, 425-426
- Edit Paste, 426-427

Edit Paste Link, 145
Edit Paste Special, 145, 428-432
Edit Redo, 432
Edit Series, 239-241
Edit Undo, 432
executing, 695
File Close, 442-443
File Delete, 444
File Exit, 445
File Links, 445-447
File New, 448-449
File Open, 125, 449-450
File Page Setup, 451-453
File Print, 453-454
File Print Preview, 455-457
File Printer Setup, 454-455
File Save, 457-458
File Save As, 458-460
File Save Workspace, 460-461
Find, 158
Fonts, 247
Form Setup, 302
Format 3-D View, 468-469
Format Alignment, 470
Format Border, 471
Format Bring To Front, 472-473
Format Cell Protection, 473-474
Format Column Width, 474-475
Format Font, 476
Format Group, 477
Format Justify, 478-479
Format Legend, 479-480
Format Main Chart, 480-481
Format Move, 481
Format Number, 482-484
Format Object Placement, 484-485
Format Overlay, 486
Format Patterns, 487-489
Format Row Height, 490
Format Scale, 491-492
Format Send To Back, 492-493
Format Size, 493-494

Format Style, 494-497
Format Text, 497-498
Format Ungroup, 499
Formula, 179
Formula Apply Names, 501-502
Formula Create Names, 503-505
Formula Define Name, 505-507
Formula Find, 508-509
Formula Goto, 509-511
Formula Note, 511-512
Formula Outline, 144
Formula Paste Function, 512-513
Formula Paste Name, 514-515
Formula Reference, 515
Formula Replace, 516-518
Formula Select Special, 518-525
gallery, 539
Gallery Preferred, 541-542
Gallery Set Preferred, 542-543
Goto, 159
Group Box, 184
Insert, 163
keyboard shortcuts, 10, 909-913
Legend, 249
macro
   Assign to Object, 713-714
   Record, 715-716
   Relative Record, 716-717
   Run, 717-718
   Set Recorder, 718-719
   Start Recorder, 719-720
Move, 253
New, 54
Object Protection, 207
Open, 53
Page Setup, 98
Paste Function, 38, 164, 172
Patterns, 208
Print, 103-104
Print Preview, 101
Printer Setup, 95
Q+E, accessing through Excel, 318-319

Record, 169
repeating, 11, 631
Replace, 163
Run, 97, 176
Save, 47
Save As, 47-50
Scale, 248-249
selecting, 4-5
Send to Back, 214
Series, 255-257
Show Active Cell, 526
Size, 253
Solver, 269
Sort, 69
Table, 264
Text, 247
Undo, 10
undoing, 804
Window Arrange All, 888-889
Window Arrange Workgroup, 135
Window Hide, 889-890
Window New Window, 890-891
Window Show Info, 891-893
Window Unhide, 893
Window Workgroup, 894-895
with Shift Key, 10
Workgroups, 137-139
comments, macro, 176
comparison criteria, 68, 154-156
comparison operators, 68, 110-112
Compute SQL clause, 295
computed criteria, 154-156
computed field value, 66
computed fields, 68
Configure option, 98
configuring
  data, charts, 79
  printers, 98
Consolidate dialog box, 130
CONSOLIDATE macro function, 625
Consolidate option, 130

consolidating data, 130-132
  from 1-2-3 files, 133
constants
  arrays, 340
  in array formulas, 260-261
  values, 371
constraints, solver, 273-275
context-sensitive help, 18
Control menu, 8, 14
Control Panel option, 97
coordinates, x and y, 185
Copies option, 86
COPY macro function, 630
COPY Q+E function, 792
Copy Special dialog box, 305
COPY.CHART function, 630
COPY.PICTURE macro function, 630
COPY.SPECIAL Q+E function, 792
copying
  charts, 630
  color palettes, 763-764
  objects, 212-213
  records, 381-382
  source disks, 906
  to clipboard, 630, 792
COS( ) function, 372
COSH( ) function, 372-373
COUNT( ) function, 373-375
COUNTA( ) function, 375-376
Create Backup File option, 52
CREATE.NAMES macro function, 671
CREATE.OBJECT macro function, 606-607
criteria, 67
  comparison, 68, 154-156
  computed, 154-156
  ranges, 153-155, 388
    clearing, 156
    placing in worksheets, 157-158
Criteria command button, 67-68
Criteria screen, 69

curves, exponential, 547
custom function, 194
custom function macros, 57
CUSTOM.REPEAT macro functions, 704
CUSTOM.UNDO macro function, 705
customizing
    commands, 195-197
    help, 198-199
    menus, 197-198
    workspace settings, 774
CUT macro function, 631
CUT Q+E function, 792
cutting
    in macro sheets, 60
    objects, 212-213

D

data
    adding to workgroup, 136
    charts, 73, 234-236
    consolidating, 625
        from 1-2-3 files, 133
    deleting, 626
    entering, 29-30
    highlighting, 77
    joining, 797-799
    pasting, 125
    plotting, 219
    sorting, 391-393
Data Consolidate command, 379
data consolidation, 130-133
Data Delete command, 380-381
Data Extract command, 381-382
Data Find command, 382-383
Data Form command, 383-385
Data Form dialog box, 65
data markers, 74
    adjustments, 242
    pictures, 250-252
    related, 75
Data Parse command, 385-386

data series, 80
    deleting, 241-242
    groups, 75
    overlapping, 233
Data Series command, 386-388
Data Set Criteria command, 388
Data Set Database command, 389-390
Data Set Extract command, 390-391
Data Sort command, 391-393
data table, 264
DATA.DELETE macro function, 172, 625
DATA.FIND macro function, 626
DATA.FIND.NEXT macro function, 626
DATA.FIND.PREV macro function, 626
DATA.FORM macro function, 626
DATA.SERIES macro function, 627
database functions, 165-166, 895-896
databases
    accessing directly from Excel, 308-311
    creating, 64-65
    defining, 64, 389-390
    dialog boxes, customized, 192-193
    editing definitions, 304
    external
        accessing, 309-310
        extracting fields, 312
        extracting records, 312-313
        setting data, 317
        system files, 310
    extracting from, 288
    fields, 64
        defining, 302
        editing, 163
    files
        defining, 302-304
        deleting, 794
        joining, 284-285

flat, 405
forms, 301-302
functions, 164-166
joined, 301
Q+E files, 299
querying, 288
records, 63
    adding, 300
    deleting, 300
    editing, 300
    extracting, 160-162
    inserting, 67
searching, 158-159
sorting, 69-72
dates, 904
    entering, 32
    formatting, 32, 657, 857-858
    increasing, 256
    month, 741
    serial number, 828
date and time functions, 896-897
date series, 256
DATE( ) function, 395-396
DATEVALUE( ) function, 396
DAVERAGE( ) function, 398
DAY( ) function, 398-399
DAYS360( ) function, 399-400
DB.EXTRACT function, 315
DB.GET.DATABASE( ) function, 316
DB.LOGON( ) function, 317
DB.PASTE.FIELDNAMES( ) function, 317
DB.SET.DATABASE( ) function, 317
DB.SQL.QUERY( ) function, 318
dBASE files, 799
DBASEFile, 281
DCOUNT( ) function, 401
DCOUNTA( ) function, 401
DDB( ) function, 402
DDE (dynamic data exchange), 127, 130, 166, 697
debug points, 180
debugging macros, 176, 179-181

Define Column dialog box, 292
Define Field command, 292
Define Name dialog box, 161, 170
DEFINE Q+E function, 792
define windows, 303
DEFINE.COLUMN Q+E function, 793
DEFINE.FIELD Q+E function, 793
DEFINE.INDEX Q+E function, 793
DEFINE.NAME macro function, 672
DEFINE.STYLE macro function, 650-652
defined terms, 19
Delete command, 5, 163
Delete command button, 67
DELETE Q+E function, 794
DELETE.ARROW macro function, 619
DELETE.BAR macro function, 198, 705
DELETE.COMMAND macro function, 195, 705
DELETE.FIELD Q+E function, 794
DELETE.FORMAT macro function, 608
DELETE.MENU( ) function, 197
DELETE.NAME macro function, 672
DELETE.OVERLAY macro function, 619
DELETE.RECORDS Q+E function, 794
DELETE.STYLE macro function, 652
deleting
    arrows, 619
    cells, 423
    charts, embedded, 85-86
    data, external files, 314
    data series, 241-242
    fields, 794
    files, 444
    names, 672
    notes, 751
    objects, 212-213

overlays, 619
ranges, 423
records, 162-163, 794
Demote command button, 140
DEMOTE macro function, 608
dependents, 520
depreciation, 402
    double-declining, 402, 880
    straight-line, 834
    sum-of-years' digits, 850
DEREF macro function, 709
descending sort order, 71
destination files, 284
Dfunctions, 405-410
DGET( ) function, 410
dialog boxes, 11-13
    1-2-3 Help, 22
    Add Constraint, 273-274
    Assign to Object, 171
    Breakpoint, 181
    Breakpoint Output, 180
    Calculation, 123, 264
    Cell Protection, 149
    Consolidate, 130
    contents, 185-187
    Copy Special, 305
    customized, 182, 192-193
    Data Form, 65
    Define Column, 292
    Define Name, 161, 170
    definitions, 189
    Display, 31
    displaying, 703, 705
    Fill Workgroup, 136
    First Column Contains, 79
    First Row Contains, 79
    Font, 290
    Form, 66-68
    Format Number, 33
    Forms, 302
    From, 797
    Goal Seek, 262
    Goal Seeker, 526-527
    in macros, 190-192
    Logon, 798
    Macro Record, 58
    Main Chart, 233
    Object Placement, 207
    Open, 53, 126, 282
    Options, 52, 146
    Outline, 140, 144
    Page Setup, 98, 101
    Password Confirmation, 147
    Paste Fieldnames, 312
    Paste Function, 38, 113
    Paste Special, 223
    Patterns, 209
    placing in macro sheets, 187-190
    Print, 86, 101-103
    Printer Setup, 96
    Protect Document, 150
    Run, 60, 176
    Save As, 298
    Save Worksheet As, 47-48
    Select, 205
    Select Workgroup, 134
    selecting, 188
    Series, 256
    Set External Database, 310
    Single Step, 176
    Solver, 272-273, 528
    Solver Options, 275
    Solver Parameters, 269-272
    Sort, 70-71
    Table, 265
    Text, 54
    Totals, 293
    Unhide, 119
    Workspace, 120, 773-774
dialog editor, 182-185
Dialog.Box function, 190
DIALOG.BOX macro function, 705
directories, 49, 179, 269, 709
DIRECTORY macro function, 709
DISABLE.INPUT macro function, 706

disks
　protecting, 146-148
　source, copying, 906
　space, 907
display, 411, 686
Display command, 179
Display dialog box, 31
DISPLAY macro function, 685-686
Display option, 764-766
displaying
　columns, 292
　formulas, 503
　records, 803
　values, 178-179
　windows, hidden, 692
DISTINCT Q+E function, 794
DMAX( ) function, 413
DMIN( ) function, 413
document window, 14, 26
documents
　calculating, 684
　closing, 16, 637
　printing, 643
　protecting, 148, 207
　read-only, 147-148
DOCUMENTS macro function, 709
DOLLAR( ) function, 414
dollars, 31
Don't Move or Size with Cells option, 206
DOS, starting Excel, 25
double-declining depreciation, 402, 880
DPRODUCT( ) function, 415
drawing
　arcs, 42
　lines, 42
　on embedded charts, 216
　ovals, 42
　rectangles, 42
　shapes, 43, 201
drawing tools, 203
DSTDEV( ) function, 416

DSTDEVP( ) function, 416
DSUM( ) function, 417
DUPLICATE macro function, 608
DVAR( ) function, 417-418
DVARP( ) function, 418
dynamic data exchange (DDE), 127, 130, 166

E

ECHO macro function, 706
ECHO Q+E function, 795
Edit Clear command, 419
Edit Copy command, 420-422
Edit Cut command, 422-423
Edit Delete command, 423
Edit Fill command, 424
Edit Insert command, 425-426
Edit menu, 6
Edit mode, 30
Edit Paste command, 426-427
Edit Paste Link command, 145
Edit Paste Special command, 145, 428-432
Edit Redo command, 432
Edit Series command, 239-241
Edit Undo command, 432
EDIT.COLOR macro function, 686
EDIT.DELETE macro function, 631
EDIT.REPEAT macro function, 631
EDIT.SERIES macro function, 619-620
editing
　cells, 30
　definitions, databases, 304
　fields, 301
　macros, 172
　records, 162-163, 791
　SQLs, 296-297
　tables, 268-269
　workgroups, 137
EDITION.OPTIONS macro function, 608-609

Index 927

elements, position, 721
elevation, 230
ellipsis (...), 5, 10
ELSE macro function, 173, 693-694
ELSE.IF macro function, 694
embedded charts, 77-78, 84
    drawing on, 216
    saving, 85
ENABLE.COMMAND macro function, 195, 197, 706
END.IF macro function, 694
ERROR macro function, 694
error messages, 532
error values, 434-435, 875
errors
    linking, 308
    macro, 694
EXACT( ) function, 436
Excel window, 24
ExcelFile, 281
exclamation mark (!), 59
EXEC macro function, 694
EXECUTE macro function, 695
Exit button, 182
EXIT Q+E function, 795
EXP( ) function, 438-439
exponential curve, 547
exponential regression, 547
external databases, accessing, 309-310
external references, 438
EXTRACT macro function, 627
Extract option, 160
extracting
    from databases, 288
    ranges, 160
    records, 160-161

F

FALSE( ) function, 442
FCLOSE macro function, 695
FETCH Q+E functions, 795

FETCH.ADVISE Q+E function, 795
FETCH.UNADVISE Q+E function, 795
fields, 64
    arguments, 164
    computed, 68
    database, defining, 302
    definition, 789-790
    deleting, 794
    editing, 163, 301
    extracting, external database, 312
    moving between, 66, 286
    names, 66, 154
        pasting, 312, 317
    searching for, 287-288
    selecting, 286-287
    specifications, 793
    values, 64-66
        altering, 66
        blank, 67
        computed, 66
        restoring, 67
    zooming, 287
File Close command, 442-443
File Delete command, 444
File Exit command, 445
File Format options, 51-52
File Links command, 445-447
File menu, 47
File New command, 448-449
File Open command, 125, 449-450
File Page Setup command, 451-453
File Print command, 453-454
File Print Preview command, 455-457
File Printer Setup command, 454-455
File Save As command, 458-460
File Save command, 457-458
File Save Workspace command, 460-461
FILE.CLOSE macro function, 637
FILE.DELETE macro function, 637

files
   active, saving, 457-458
   closing, 442-443, 695
   database
      defining, 302
      deleting, 794
      joining, 284-285
   dBASE, 794, 799
   deleting, 444
      from disk, 637
   extensions
      .xlc (chart), 83
      .xlm (macros), 83
      .xls (worksheet), 49, 83
   external, 314
   formats, importing, 127
   formatting, 50
   importing, 126
   list, 448
   opening, with options button, 310-311
   protecting, 145-146
      read-only, 147
   Q+E, 281-283
      saving, 298-300
   query, 802
   source, 284
   system, external database, 310
FILES macro function, 709
Fill Workgroup dialog box, 136
FILL.DOWN macro function, 172, 632
FILL.LEFT macro function, 632
FILL.RIGHT macro function, 632
FILL.UP macro function, 632
FILL.WORKGROUP macro function, 632
financial functions, 897
Find command, 158
Find Next command button, 68
Find option, 158-159
Find Prev command button, 67
FIND Q+E function, 796

FIND( ) function, 463-464
FIND.NEXT Q+E function, 796
FIND.PREVIOUS Q+E function, 796
First Column Contains dialog box, 79
First Row Contains dialog box, 79
FIXED( ) function, 465-466
Font dialog box, 290
FONT Q+E function, 796
fonts, 32, 247, 476, 796
   bold, 41
   formatting, 290, 652-653
   italic, 41
   standard, 689
Fonts command, 247
footers, 466-467
   codes, 100-101
FOPEN macro function, 695
FOR macro function, 695
FOR.CELL macro function, 695
Form dialog box, 66-68, 797
Form option, 65
Form Setup command, 302
FORM.SETUP Q+E function, 797
FORM? Q+E function, 796
Format 3-D View command, 468-469
Format Alignment command, 470
Format Border command, 471
Format Bring To Front command, 472-473
Format Cell Protection command, 473-474
Format Column Width command, 474-475
Format Font command, 476
Format Group command, 477
Format Justify command, 478-479
Format Legend command, 479-480
Format Main Chart command, 480-481
Format Move command, 481
Format Number command, 482-484
Format Number dialog box, 33

Format Object Placement command, 484-485
Format Overlay command, 486
Format Patterns command, 487-489
Format Row Height command, 490
Format Scale command, 491-492
Format Send To Back command, 492-493
Format Size command, 493-494
Format Style command, 494-497
Format Text command, 497-498
Format Ungroup command, 499
FORMAT.FONT macro function, 652-653
FORMAT.LEGEND macro function, 653
FORMAT.MAIN macro function, 653-656
FORMAT.MOVE macro function, 656-657
FORMAT.NUMBER macro function, 657
FORMAT.OVERLAY macro function, 657-659
FORMAT.SIZE macro function, 659
FORMAT.TEXT macro function, 660
formats
    cell, copying, 632
    clearing, 629
    Clipboard, 125
    date and time, 32
formatting, 32-34, 244-245, 291-292, 486
    3-D charts, 229-230
    dates, 657
    files, 50
    font, 290
    fonts, in cells, 652-653
    main charts, 232-234
    numbers, 482-484, 657
    objects, graphic, 208-209
    options, 50
    overlay charts, 232-234, 657-659
    pages, 799
    patterns, 245-247
    symbols, 34
    times, 657, 857-858
forms, database, 301-302
Forms dialog box, 302
Formula Apply Names command, 501-502
formula bar, 27, 503
Formula command, 179
Formula Create Names command, 503-505
Formula Define Name command, 505-507
Formula Find command, 508-509
Formula Goto command, 509-511
FORMULA macro function, 609
Formula Note command, 511-512
Formula Outline command, 144
Formula Paste Function command, 512-513
Formula Paste Name command, 514-515
Formula Reference command, 515
Formula Replace command, 516-518
Formula Select Special command, 518-525
FORMULA( ) macro sheet function, 172
FORMULA.ARRAY macro function, 609-610
FORMULA.CONVERT macro function, 610
FORMULA.FILL macro function, 610
FORMULA.FIND macro function, 673
FORMULA.FIND.NEXT macro function, 673
FORMULA.FIND.PREV macro function, 674
FORMULA.GOTO macro function, 674

FORMULA.REPLACE macro function, 674-675
formulas, 35
   { } (braces), 258
   arithmetic, 109-110
   arrays, 258
      editing, 259-260
      constants, 260-261
      selecting, 259-260
   built-in, 37
   calculating, 261-263, 762
   calculation, 684
   cell references, 110
   clearing, 629
   copying, 424
   displaying, 503
   entering in cells, 609
   operators, 110
      − (subtraction), 35
      * (multiplication), 35
      + (addition), 35
      / (division), 35
      ^ (exponentiation), 35
   searching for, 508-509
   series, 236-239
Formulas option, 31
FPOS macro function, 696
fractional digits, truncating, 867-868
FREAD macro function, 696
FREADLN macro function, 696
Freeze Panes option, 766-767
FREEZE.PANES macro function, 687
From SQL clause, 295
FSIZE macro function, 696
FULL macro function, 610-611
full menus, 9, 689
function keys
   command shortcuts, 912-913
   keyboard shortcuts, 8
functions, 37, 113-115, 531-535
   ABSREF, 708
   ABS( ), 327
   ACOS( ), 329

ACOSH( ), 329-330
ACTIVATE, 605, 789
ACTIVATE.NEXT, 606
ACTIVATE.PREV, 606
ACTIVE.CELL, 172, 708
ADD.ARROW, 617
ADD.AFTER, 789
ADD.BAR, 173, 198, 702
ADD.BEFORE, 789
ADD.COMMAND, 195, 702-703
ADD.CONDITION, 790
ADD.MENU, 195, 197-198, 703
ADD.OVERLAY, 617
ADD.RECORD, 790
ADDRESS( ), 331-332
AND( ), 335
annuity, 336-337
ALERT, 703
ALIGNMENT, 647
ALLOW.EDIT, 790
APP.ACTIVATE, 606
APP.MAXIMIZE, 622
APP.MINIMIZE, 622
APP.MOVE, 622
APP.RESTORE, 622
APP.SIZE, 623
APPLY.NAMES, 670-671
APPLY.STYLE, 648
AREAS( ), 339-340
argument, 531
ARGUMENT, 693
ARRANGE.ALL, 691, 791
array, 261
ASIN( ), 341
ASINH( ), 342
ASSIGN.TO.OBJECT, 683
ATAN( ), 343
ATAN2( ), 343-344
ATANH( ), 344-345
ATTACH.TEXT, 617
AVERAGE( ), 345-347
AXES, 618-619
BEEP, 606

BORDER, 648-649
BREAK, 693
BRING.TO.FRONT, 649
built-in, 531
CALCULATE.DOCUMENT, 684
CALCULATE.NOW, 619, 684
CALL, 703
CALLER, 708
CANCEL.COPY, 606
CANCEL.KEY, 704
CELL( ), 352-354
CELL.PROTECTION, 649
CHANGE.LINK, 636
CHAR( ), 355-356
CHECK.COMMAND, 195, 704
CHOOSE( ), 365-366
CLEAN( ), 366-367
CLEAR, 629-630
CLOSE, 623, 791
CLOSE.ALL, 636
CLOSE.INDEX, 791
CODE( ), 367-368
COLOR.PALETTE, 685
COLUMN( ), 369
COLUMNS( ), 370
COLUMN.WIDTH, 649-650, 791
COMBINATION, 679
COMMAND, 791
CONSOLIDATE, 625
COPY, 630, 792
COPY.CHART, 630
COPY.PICTURE, 630
COPY.SPECIAL, 792
COS( ), 372
COSH( ), 372-373
COUNT( ), 373-375
COUNTA( ), 375-376
CREATE.NAMES, 671
CREATE.OBJECT, 606-607
custom, 194
CUSTOM.REPEAT, 704
CUSTOM.UNDO, 705
CUT, 631

database, 164-166, 895-896
date and time, 896-897
DATA.DELETE, 172, 625
DATA.FIND, 626
DATA.FIND.NEXT, 626
DATA.FIND.PREV, 626
DATA.FORM, 626
DATA.SERIES, 627
DATE( ), 395-396
DATEVALUE( ), 396
DAVERAGE( ), 398
DAY( ), 398-399
DAYS360( ), 399-400
DB.EXTRACT, 315
DB.GET.DATABASE( ), 316
DB.LOGON( ), 317
DB.PASTE.FIELDNAMES( ), 317
DB.SET.DATABASE( ), 317
DB.SQL.QUERY( ), 318
DCOUNT( ), 401
DCOUNTA( ), 401
DDB( ), 402
DEFINE, 792
DEFINE.COLUMN, 793
DEFINE.FIELD, 793
DEFINE.INDEX, 793
DEFINE.NAME, 672
DEFINE.STYLE, 650-652
DELETE, 794
DELETE.ARROW, 619
DELETE.BAR( ), 198, 705
DELETE.COMMAND, 195, 705
DELETE.FIELD, 794
DELETE.FORMAT, 608
DELETE.MENU( ), 197
DELETE.NAME, 672
DELETE.OVERLAY, 619
DELETE.RECORDS, 794
DELETE.STYLE, 652
DEMOTE, 608
DEREF, 709
Dfunction, 405-410
DGET( ), 410

Dialog.Box, 190
DIALOG.BOX, 705
DIRECTORY, 709
DISABLE.INPUT, 706
DISPLAY, 685-686
DISTINCT, 794
DMAX( ), 413
DMIN( ), 413
DOCUMENTS, 709
DOLLAR( ), 414
DPRODUCT( ), 415
DSTDEV( ), 416
DSTDEVP( ), 416
DSUM( ), 417
DVAR( ), 417-418
DVARP( ), 418
ECHO, 706, 795
EDIT.COLOR, 686
EDIT.DELETE, 631
EDIT.REPEAT, 631
EDIT.SERIES, 619-620
EDITION.OPTIONS, 608-609
ELSE, 173, 693-694
ELSE.IF, 694
ENABLE.COMMAND, 195, 197, 706
END.IF, 694
ERROR, 694
EXACT( ), 436
EXEC, 694
EXECUTE, 695
EXIT, 795
EXP( ), 438-439
EXTRACT, 627
FALSE( ), 442
FCLOSE, 695
FETCH, 795
FETCH.ADVISE, 795
FETCH.UNADVISE, 795
FILE.CLOSE, 637
FILE.DELETE, 637
FILES, 709
FILL.DOWN, 172, 632

FILL.LEFT, 632
FILL.RIGHT, 632
FILL.UP, 632
FILL.WORKGROUP, 632
financial, 897
FIND( ), 463-464, 796
FIND.NEXT, 796
FIND.PREVIOUS, 796
FIXED( ), 465-466
FONT, 796
FOPEN, 695
FOR, 695
FOR.CELL, 695
FORM?, 796
FORMAT.FONT, 652-653
FORMAT.LEGEND, 653
FORMAT.MAIN, 653-656
FORMAT.MOVE, 656-657
FORMAT.NUMBER, 657
FORMAT.OVERLAY, 657-659
FORMAT.SIZE, 659
FORMAT.TEXT, 660
FORM.SETUP, 797
FORMULA, 172, 609
FORMULA.ARRAY, 609-610
FORMULA.CONVERT, 610
FORMULA.FILL, 610
FORMULA.FIND, 673
FORMULA.FIND.NEXT, 673
FORMULA.FIND.PREV, 674
FORMULA.GOTO, 674
FORMULA.REPLACE, 674-675
FPOS, 696
FREAD, 696
FREADLN, 696
FREEZE.PANES, 687
FSIZE, 696
FULL, 610-611
FV( ), 535-537
FWRITE, 696
FWRITELN, 697
GALLERY.3D.AREA, 679
GALLERY.3D.COLUMN, 679

Index

GALLERY.3D.LINE, 680
GALLERY.3D.PIE, 680
GALLERY.AREA, 680
GALLERY.BAR, 680-681
GALLERY.COLUMN, 681
GALLERY.LINE, 681
GALLERY.SCATTER, 682
GET.BAR, 197, 706
GET.CELL, 709
GET.CHART.ITEM, 710
GET.DEF, 710
GET.DOCUMENT, 710
GET.FORMULA, 710
GET.LINK.INFO, 710
GET.NAME, 711
GET.NOTE, 711
GET.OBJECT, 711
GET.WINDOW, 712
GET.WORKSPACE, 712
GOAL.SEEK, 675-676
GOTO, 697
GOTO.RECORD, 797
GRIDLINES, 620
GROUP, 661
GROWTH( ), 547-549
HALT, 697
HELP, 707
HIDE, 691
HIDE.OBJECT, 611
HLINE, 611
HLOOKUP, 269, 553-555
HOUR( ), 556
HPAGE, 611
HSCROLL, 611-612
IF, 173, 559-561, 697
INDEX, 534, 561-565
INDIRECT( ), 566
INFO( ), 567
information, 897-899
INITIATE, 697
INPUT, 175, 697
INSERT, 633
INT( ), 568

IPMT( ), 569-570
IRR( ), 570-573
IS, 574
ISBLANK( ), 575
ISERR( ), 575-576
ISERROR, 576-577
ISLOGICAL( ), 577
ISNA( ), 578
ISNONTEXT, 579
ISNUMBER( ), 580
ISREF( ), 581
ISTEXT( ), 582
JOIN, 797
JUSTIFY, 661
KEYS, 797
LAST.ERROR, 172, 712
LEGEND, 621
LEFT( ), 585-586
LEN( ), 586-587
LINKS, 637-638
LINEST( ), 587-590
LIST.NAMES, 676
LN( ), 592-593
LOG( ), 593
LOG10( ), 594
LOGEST( ), 594-597
logical, 899
LOGOFF, 797
LOGON, 797
LOOKUP, 269, 600-602
lookup, 899
LOWER( ), 603
MATCH( ), 721-723
mathematical, 900
matrix, 900
MAX( ), 723-724
MDETERM( ), 725-727
MEDIAN( ), 727-728
MERGE.STYLES, 661
MESSAGE, 707
MID( ), 730-731
MIN( ), 731-732
MINUTE( ), 733

MINVERSE( ), 734-736
MIRR( ), 736-738
MMULT( ), 738-740
MOD( ), 740-741
MONTH( ), 741-742
MOVE, 623-624
MOVE.COLUMN, 798
N( ), 747
NA( ), 748
NAMES, 712
NEW, 638
NEW.WINDOW, 691
NEXT, 698
NOT( ), 749-750
NOTE, 676
Note, 750-751
NOW( ), 751-752
NPER( ), 752-754
NPV( ), 754-756
OBJECT.PROTECTION, 661-662
OFFSET( ), 758-759
ON.DATA, 698
ON.KEY, 698
ONLY.SHOW.TOTALS, 798
ON.RECALC, 698
ON.TIME, 698
ON.WINDOW, 699
OPEN, 639-640, 798
OPEN.INDEX, 799
OPEN.LINKS, 640
operations, 532
OR( ), 774-775
OUTER.JOIN( ), 799
OUTLINE, 677
PAGE.SETUP, 641-642, 799
PARSE, 627, 800
Paste, 37
PASTE, 633, 800
PASTE.APPEND, 800
PASTE.LINK, 633
PASTE.PICTURE, 633
PASTE.PICTURE.LINK, 633
PASTE.SPECIAL, 634-635

pasting, 114, 512-513
PATTERNS, 662-665
PI( ), 778
PLACEMENT, 665-666
POKE, 699
PMT( ), 779-780
PPMT( ), 781-782
PRECISION, 687
PREFERRED, 682
PRINT, 643, 800
PRINT.PREVIEW, 644
PRINTER.SETUP, 644
PRODUCT( ), 784-785
PROMOTE, 612
PROPER( ), 786
PROTECT.DOCUMENT, 687-688
PV( ), 787-788
Q+E, 788-789
QUERY.NOW, 800
QUIT, 644
RAND( ), 807-808
RATE( ), 808-809
REFTEXT, 712
REGISTER, 699
RELREF, 713
REMOVE.COLUMN, 801
REMOVE.PAGE.BREAK, 688
RENAME.COMMAND, 173, 195, 197, 707
REPLACE( ), 814-815
REPT( ), 816
REQUEST, 699
RESTART, 700
RESULT, 700
RETURN, 700
RIGHT( ), 818
ROUND( ), 819
ROW( ), 820
ROW.HEIGHT, 666
ROWS( ), 821
RUN, 683
Run macro, 193
SAVE, 644, 801

SAVE.AS, 644-646, 801
SAVE.LABELS.AS, 802
SAVE.QUERY.AS, 802
SAVE.TEXT.AS, 802
SAVE.WORKSPACE, 646
SCALE, 667-669
SEARCH( ), 824-825
SECOND( ), 826
SELECT, 172, 612-614
SELECT.CHART, 621
SELECT.COLUMNS, 803
SELECT.DELETED.RECORDS, 803
SELECT.END, 614
SELECT.LAST.CELL, 677
SELECT.PLOT.AREA, 621
SELECT.SPECIAL, 677-678
SELECT.RESET, 803
SELECTION, 713
SEND.KEYS, 700
SEND.TO.BACK, 669
SET.CRITERIA, 628
SET.DATABASE, 628
SET.EXTRACT, 628
SET.NAME, 700
SET.PAGE.BREAK, 688
SET.PREFERRED, 682
SET.PRINT.AREA, 689
SET.PRINT.TITLES, 689
SET.UPDATE.STATUS, 614
SET.VALUE, 701
SHORT.MENUS, 689
SHOW.ACTIVE.CELL, 678-679
SHOW.BAR( ), 198, 707
SHOW.CLIPBOARD, 692
SHOW.DETAIL, 615
SHOW.INFO, 692
SHOW.LEVELS, 615
SIGN( ), 831
SIN( ), 832
SINH( ), 833
SIZE, 624
SLN( ), 834

SOLVER.ADD, 836
SOLVER.CHANGE, 836
SOLVER.DELETE, 836
SOLVER.FINISH, 835
SOLVER.LOAD, 837
SOLVER.OK, 834
SOLVER.OPTIONS, 837
SOLVER.RESET, 835
SOLVER.SAVE, 837
SOLVER.SOLVE, 835
SORT, 628-629
SORT.ASCENDING, 803
SORT.DESCENDING, 803
SORT.RESET, 804
SPLIT, 615
SQL.QUERY, 804
SQRT( ), 838
STANDARD.FONT, 689
statistical, 901
STDEV( ), 839-840
STDEVP( ), 841-842
STEP, 701
Step, 178
SUBSTITUTE, 843-844
SUM, 37, 40, 113, 845-847
SUMPRODUCT( ), 848-849
SYD( ), 849-850
T( ), 851
TABLE, 629
TAN( ), 853-854
TANH( ), 854
TERMINATE, 701
text, 901-902
TEXT( ), 856-857
TEXT.BOX, 615
TEXTREF, 713
TIME( ), 859
TIMEVALUE( ), 860
TODAY( ), 861
TOTALS, 804
TRANPOSE( ), 861-862
TREND( ), 862-865
trigonometric, 903

TRIM( ), 865-866
troubleshooting, 115
TRUE( ), 866-867
TRUNC( ), 867-868
TYPE( ), 868-869
UNDO, 636, 804
UNGROUP, 669
UNHIDE, 692
UNLOCKED.NEXT, 616
UNLOCKED.PREV, 616
UNREGISTER, 701
UPDATE.ALL, 804
UPDATE.LINK, 646-647
UPPER( ), 872
USE.INDEX, 804
VALUE( ), 873-874
values, 532
VAR( ), 877-878
VARP( ), 879-880
VDB( ), 880-881
VIEW.3D, 669-670
VLINE, 616
VLOOKUP, 269, 882-884
VOLATILE, 701
VPAGE, 616
VSCROLL, 616-617
WAIT, 701
WEEKDAY( ), 887-888
WHILE, 173, 701
WINDOWS, 713
WORKGROUP, 692-693
worksheet, 533, 895
WORKSPACE, 690
YEAR( ), 904
FV( ) function, 535-537
FWRITE macro function, 696
FWRITELN macro function, 697

G

gallery command, 539
Gallery menu, 86-87
Gallery option, 74
Gallery Preferred command, 541-542
Gallery Set Preferred command, 542-543
GALLERY.3D.AREA macro function, 679
GALLERY.3D.COLUMN macro function, 679
GALLERY.3D.LINE macro function, 680
GALLERY.3D.PIE macro function, 680
GALLERY.AREA macro function, 680
GALLERY.BAR macro function, 680-681
GALLERY.COLUMN macro function, 681
GALLERY.LINE macro function, 681
GALLERY.PIE macro function, 681
GALLERY.SCATTER macro function, 682
GET.BAR macro function, 197, 706
GET.CELL macro function, 709
GET.CHART.ITEM macro function, 710
GET.DEF macro function, 710
GET.DOCUMENT macro function, 710
GET.FORMULA macro function, 710
GET.LINK.INFO macro functions, 710
GET.NAME macro function, 711
GET.NOTE macro function, 711
GET.OBJECT macro function, 711
GET.WINDOW macro function, 712
GET.WORKSPACE macro function, 712
Goal Seek dialog box, 262, 526-527
goal seeking, 261-263, 527
GOAL.SEEK macro function, 675-676
Goto command (see Formula Goto), 159, 509-511

GOTO macro function, 697
GOTO.RECORD Q+E function, 797
graphics objects, 204
gridlines, 243, 363-364, 620, 764-766
GRIDLINES macro function, 620
Group Box command, 184
GROUP macro function, 661
grouped objects, 215-216
groups, 477, 499
    cells, 677-678
growth series, 256
GROWTH( ) function, 547-549

H

HALT macro function, 697
headers, 551-552
    codes, 100-101
headings
    colors, 764-766
    column, 291
help, 20-21
    context-sensitive, 18
    customizing, 198-199
    Lotus 1-2-3, 21-22
    navigating, 19-20
    starting, 18-19
HELP macro function, 707
Help screen, 18
Hidden option, 149
HIDE macro function, 691
HIDE.OBJECT macro function, 611
hiding
    rows, 794
    totals, 798
    windows, 691, 890
HLINE macro function, 611
HLOOKUP function, 269, 553-555
HOUR( ) function, 556
HPAGE macro function, 611
HSCROLL macro function, 611-612
hyperbolic sine, 833
hyperbolic tangent, 854

I

identity matrix, 734-736
IF function, 173, 559-561, 697
importing, 124
    File Open command, 125
    files, 126
    formats
        Clipboard, 125
        file, 127
    with Clipboard, 124
increasing cells by constant amount, 256
INDEX function, 534, 561-565
INDIRECT( ) function, 566
info windows, 692
INFO( ) function, 567
information functions, 897-899
INITIATE macro function, 697
input, blocking, 706
INPUT function, 175, 697
Insert command, 163
INSERT macro function, 633
installing
    Excel, 906-907
        on network, 151
    printers, 97
    Q+E, 280
INT( ) function, 568
integers, 31
interest rates, 753-754, 809
intersection, axes, 76
inverse matrix, 734-736
investments, 752
    future value, 536
    net present value, 754-755
    present value, 787
    return rate, 736-738
IPMT( ) function, 569-570
IRR( ) function, 570-573
IS function, 574
ISBLANK( ) function, 575
ISERR( ) function, 575-576

ISERROR function, 576-577
ISLOGICAL( ) function, 577
ISNA( ) function, 578
ISNONTEXT function, 579
ISNUMBER( ) function, 580
ISREF( ) function, 581
ISTEXT( ) function, 582
Italic button, 41
iteration, 263

J

JOIN Q+E function, 797
jump terms, 19
justification, 333, 478-479
JUSTIFY macro function, 661

K

key combinations, macro, 59
keyboard, 3
    command shortcuts, 10, 909-913
    input, blocking, 706
    navigating help, 19
    scrolling, 29
    selecting commands, 4-5
    shortcuts
        with Alt and Ctrl keys, 7
        with function keys, 8
    starting Excel, 24
KEYS Q+E function, 797
keystrokes, repeating, 59

L

Label Definition scroll box, 299
labels
    creating names from, 671
    mailing, 802
LAST.ERROR macro function, 172, 712
layered objects, 214-215
Left Column option, 131
LEFT( ) function, 585-586
Legend command, 249
LEGEND macro function, 621
legends, 76, 92, 243, 249, 357-358, 479-480, 621
    moving, 253, 481
    orientation, 653
    sizing, 253
LEN( ) function, 586-587
Library subdirectory, 179
Like operator, 289
Limit report, 273
line chart, 89-91
line charts, 681
    3-D, 228
Line tool, 42, 203
linear series, 256
lines
    arrowheads, 211-212
    positioning, 202
LINEST( ) function, 587-590
linking
    chart text to cells, 251-252
    DDE (dynamic data exchange), 166
    dynamic data exchange (DDE), 127
    errors, 308
    Q+E
        to other applications, 305-307
    worksheets, 127-128
    worksheets and charts, 84
links, 445-447, 711, 636
    update status, 614
    updating, 646
LINKS macro function, 637-638
LIST.NAMES macro function, 676
listing names, 676
LN( ) function, 592-593
Locked option, 149, 207-208
locking objects, 207-208
LOG( ) function, 593
LOG10( ) function, 594

logarithms, 592-593
LOGEST( ) function, 594-597
logging off, 797
logic, OR, 156-157
logical
    functions, 899
    values, 532, 599-600
LOGOFF Q+E function, 797
Logon dialog box, 798
LOGON Q+E function, 797
LOOKUP function, 269, 600-602
lookup functions, 899
lookup table, 269
loops, 172
    FOR-NEXT, 695
    interrupting, 693
    marking end, 698
    starting, 695
Lotus 1-2-3
    Excel command equivalents, 21
    help, 21-22
Lotus 1-2-3 Help dialog box, 22
LOWER( ) function, 603

M

macro buttons, 170-171
macro commands
    Assign to Object, 713-714
    looping, 172
    Record, 715-716
    Relative Record, 716-717
    Run, 717-718
    Set Recorder, 718-719
    Start Recorder, 719-720
macro functions, 315, 533, 605
    A1.R1C1, 605
    ABSREF, 708
    ACTIVATE, 605
    ACTIVATE.NEXT, 606
    ACTIVATE.PREV, 606
    ACTIVE.CELL, 708
    ADD.ARROW, 617

ADD.BAR, 702
ADD.COMMAND, 702-703
ADD.MENU, 703
ADD.OVERLAY, 617
ALERT, 703
ALIGNMENT, 647
APP.ACTIVATE, 606
APP.MAXIMIZE, 622
APP.MINIMIZE, 622
APP.MOVE, 622
APP.RESTORE, 622
APP.SIZE, 623
APPLY.NAMES, 670-671
APPLY.STYLE, 648
ARGUMENT, 693
ARRANGE.ALL, 691
ASSIGN.TO.OBJECT, 683
ATTACH.TEXT, 617
AXES, 618-619
BEEP, 606
BORDER, 648-649
BREAK, 693
BRING.TO.FRONT, 649
CALCULATE.DOCUMENT, 684
CALCULATE.NOW, 619, 684
CALCULATION, 684-685
CALL, 703
CALLER, 708
CANCEL.COPY, 606
CANCEL.KEY, 704
CELL.PROTECTION, 649
CHANGE.LINK, 636
CHECK.COMMAND, 704
CLEAR, 629-630
CLOSE, 623
CLOSE.ALL, 636
COLOR.PALETTE, 685
COLUMN.WIDTH, 649-650
COMBINATION, 679
CONSOLIDATE, 625
COPY, 630
COPY.CHART, 630
COPY.PICTURE, 630

CREATE.NAMES, 671
CREATE.OBJECT, 606-607
CUSTOM.REPEAT, 704
CUSTOM.UNDO, 705
CUT, 631
DATA.DELETE, 625
DATA.FIND, 626
DATA.FIND.NEXT, 626
DATA.FIND.PREV, 626
DATA.FORM, 626
DATA.SERIES, 627
DEFINE.NAME, 672
DEFINE.STYLE, 650-652
DELETE.ARROW, 619
DELETE.BAR, 705
DELETE.COMMAND, 705
DELETE.FORMAT, 608
DELETE.NAME, 672
DELETE.OVERLAY, 619
DELETE.STYLE, 652
DEMOTE, 608
DEREF, 709
DIALOG.BOX, 705
DIRECTORY, 709
DISABLE.INPUT, 706
DISPLAY, 685-686
DOCUMENTS, 709
DUPLICATE, 608
ECHO, 706
EDIT.COLOR, 686
EDIT.DELETE, 631
EDIT.REPEAT, 631
EDIT.SERIES, 619-620
EDITION.OPTIONS, 608-609
ELSE, 693-694
ELSE.IF, 694
ENABLE.COMMAND, 706
END.IF, 694
ERROR, 694
EXEC, 694
EXECUTE, 695
EXTRACT, 627
FCLOSE, 695

FILE.CLOSE, 637
FILE.DELETE, 637
FILES, 709
FILL.DOWN, 632
FILL.LEFT, 632
FILL.RIGHT, 632
FILL.UP, 632
FILL.WORKGROUP, 632
FOPEN, 695
FOR, 695
FOR.CELL, 695
FORMAT.FONT, 652-653
FORMAT.LEGEND, 653
FORMAT.MAIN, 653-656
FORMAT.MOVE, 656-657
FORMAT.NUMBER, 657
FORMAT.OVERLAY, 657-659
FORMAT.SIZE, 659
FORMAT.TEXT, 660
FORMULA, 609
FORMULA.ARRAY, 609-610
FORMULA.CONVERT, 610
FORMULA.FILL, 610
FORMULA.FIND, 673
FORMULA.FIND.NEXT, 673
FORMULA.FIND.PREV, 674
FORMULA.GOTO, 674
FORMULA.REPLACE, 674-675
FPOS, 696
FREAD, 696
FREADLN, 696
FREEZE.PANES, 687
FSIZE, 696
FULL, 610-611
FWRITE, 696
FWRITELN, 697
GALLERY.3D.AREA, 679
GALLERY.3D.COLUMN, 679
GALLERY.3D.LINE, 680
GALLERY.3D.PIE, 680
GALLERY.AREA, 680
GALLERY.BAR, 680-681
GALLERY.COLUMN, 681

Index 941

GALLERY.LINE, 681
GALLERY.PIE, 681
GALLERY.SCATTER, 682
GET.BAR, 706
GET.CELL, 709
GET.CHART.ITEM, 710
GET.DEF, 710
GET.DOCUMENT, 710
GET.FORMULA, 710
GET.LINK.INFO, 710
GET.NAME, 711
GET.NOTE, 711
GET.OBJECT, 711
GET.WINDOW, 712
GET.WORKSPACE, 712
GOAL.SEEK, 675-676
GOTO, 697
GRIDLINES, 620
GROUP, 661
HALT, 697
HELP, 707
HIDE, 691
HIDE.OBJECT, 611
HLINE, 611
HPAGE, 611
HSCROLL, 611-612
IF, 697
INITIATE, 697
INPUT, 697
INSERT, 633
JUSTIFY, 661
LAST.ERROR, 712
LEGEND, 621
LINKS, 637-638
LIST.NAMES, 676
MERGE.STYLES, 661
MESSAGE, 707
MOVE, 623-624
NAMES, 712
NEW, 638
NEW.WINDOW, 691
NEXT, 698
NOTE, 676

OBJECT.PROTECTION, 661-662
ON.DATA, 698
ON.KEY, 698
ON.RECALC, 698
ON.TIME, 698
ON.WINDOW, 699
OPEN, 639-640
OPEN.LINKS, 640
OUTLINE, 677
PAGE.SETUP, 641-642
PARSE, 627
PASTE, 633
PASTE.LINK, 633
PASTE.PICTURE, 633
PASTE.PICTURE.LINK, 633
PASTE.SPECIAL, 634-635
PATTERNS, 662-665
PLACEMENT, 665-666
POKE, 699
PRECISION, 687
PREFERRED, 682
PRINT, 643
PRINT.PREVIEW, 644
PRINTER.SETUP, 644
PROMOTE, 612
PROTECT.DOCUMENT, 687-688
QUIT, 644
REFTEXT, 712
REGISTER, 699
RELREF, 713
REMOVE.PAGE.BREAK, 688
RENAME.COMMAND, 707
REQUEST, 699
RESTART, 700
RESULT, 700
RETURN, 700
ROW.HEIGHT, 666
RUN, 683
SAVE, 644
SAVE.AS, 644-646
SAVE.WORKSPACE, 646
SCALE, 667-669
SELECT, 612-614

SELECT.CHART, 621
SELECT.END, 614
SELECT.LAST.CELL, 677
SELECT.PLOT.AREA, 621
SELECT.SPECIAL, 677-678
SELECTION, 713
SEND.KEYS, 700
SEND.TO.BACK, 669
SET.CRITERIA, 628
SET.DATABASE, 628
SET.EXTRACT, 628
SET.NAME, 700
SET.PAGE.BREAK, 688
SET.PREFERRED, 682
SET.PRINT.AREA, 689
SET.PRINT.TITLES, 689
SET.UPDATE.STATUS, 614
SET.VALUE, 701
SHORT.MENUS, 689
SHOW.ACTIVE.CELL, 678-679
SHOW.BAR, 707
SHOW.CLIPBOARD, 692
SHOW.DETAIL, 615
SHOW.INFO, 692
SHOW.LEVELS, 615
SIZE, 624
SORT, 628-629
SPLIT, 615
STANDARD.FONT, 689
STEP, 701
TABLE, 629
TERMINATE, 701
TEXT.BOX, 615
TEXTREF, 713
UNDO, 636
UNGROUP, 669
UNHIDE, 692
UNLOCKED.NEXT, 616
UNLOCKED.PREV, 616
UNREGISTER, 701
UPDATE.LINK, 646-647
VIEW.3D, 669-670
VLINE, 616

VOLATILE, 701
VPAGE, 616
VSCROLL, 616-617
WAIT, 701
WHILE, 701
WINDOWS, 713
WORKGROUP, 692-693
WORKSPACE, 690
Macro Record dialog box, 58
macro sheets, 60-61, 167-168
   adding macros, 169-170
   altering instructions, 61
   function, 172-173
   placing dialog boxes, 187-190
macros, 59-61, 308
   (!) exclamation mark, 59
   activating, 170
   add-in, 179, 193-195
   adding to macro sheets, 169-170
   branching, 175
   breaking up performance, 176-177
   breakpoints, 179
   command, 57
   comments, 176
   custom function, 57
   debugging, 176, 179-181
   dialog boxes in, 190-192
   editing, 172
   errors during run, 694
   evaluating, 176-178
   functions, 174-176
      cell references, 173-174
   in Solver, 277-278
   interrupting, 178
   invoking, 171
   key combinations, 59
   linking with objects, 713-714
   linking with shapes, 45
   naming, 170
   pausing, 701
   recording, 57-59, 167-169, 715-716

Index 943

starting, 719-720
setting, 718
running, 59-60, 717-718, 683
automatically, 193-194
sheets, 167-169
stopping, 697
testing, 176
tracepoints, 179
values, displaying, 178-179
with mouse, 683
mailing labels, 299-300
Mailing Labels option, 299
main chart, 231-234
manual calculation, 761
margins, 101-103
markers
adjustments, 242
data, 74-75
pictures, 250-252
MATCH( ) function, 721-723
mathematical functions, 900
matrices
calculating, 738-739
identity, 734-736
inverse, 734-736
matrix functions, 900
MAX( ) function, 723-724
MDETERM( ) function, 725-727
MEDIAN( ) function, 727-728
menu bar, 9, 74, 728-729
menu bars
creating, 702
customizing, 195, 198
displaying, 708
menus, adding, 703
menu tables, 197
menus, 8, 728-729
adding to menu bars, 703
commands, adding, 702
Control, 8, 14
customizing, 195-198
Edit, 6
File, 47

full, 9, 689
Gallery, 86-87
names, changing, 707
Paste Function, 114
short, 9, 689
Window, 15, 119
MERGE.STYLES macro function, 661
MESSAGE macro function, 707
messages
displaying, 707
removing, 707
MID( ) function, 730-731
MIN( ) function, 731-732
MINUTE( ) function, 733
minutes, 733
MINVERSE( ) function, 734-736
MIRR( ) functions, 736-738
MMULT( ) function, 738-740
MOD( ) function, 740-741
modes
Edit, 30
Point, 36-37
MONTH( ) function, 741-742
mouse, 3
input, blocking, 706
manipulating windows, 16-17
navigating help, 19
pointer
question mark, 19
shapes, 6-7
selecting commands, 4-5, 742-744
starting Excel, 23-24
with macros, 683
Move and Size with Cells option, 206
Move command, 253
MOVE macro function, 623-624
MOVE.COLUMN Q+E function, 798
moving
active cell, 28
arrows, 253, 481
cells, 426-427

columns, 798
graphic objects, 205
in worksheet, 29
legends, 253, 481
objects, 656
ranges, 426-427
Multiplan, Excel command equivalent, 22
Multiple Selection tool, 213
multiple selections, 105, 744
multiplying cells by constant amount, 256

N

N( ) function, 747
NA( ) function, 748
names
creating from labels, 671
defining, 672
deleting, 672
field, 66
listing, 676
macro, 170
series, 223
NAMES macro function, 712
negative values, 31
net present value, investments, 754-755
networks, 150-151
New command, 54
New command button, 67
NEW macro function, 638
NEW.WINDOW macro function, 691
NEXT macro function, 698
non-printable characters, 366
Not Like operator, 289
NOT( ) function, 749-750
Note function, 750-751
NOTE macro function, 676
notes, 511-512, 676, 750
clearing, 629
deleting, 751
displaying, 751
printing, 751
viewing, 750-751
NOW( ) function, 751-752
NPER( ) function, 752-754
NPV ( ) function, 754-756
#NULL, 308
number values, 532
numbers, 757
dollars, 31
entering, 31
formatting, 414, 482-484, 608, 657
incrementing, 386-388
integers, 31
negative, 31
percentages, 31
rounding, 414, 465, 819
serial, 828
sine, 832
square root, 838
numeric arrays, 340
numeric values, 373-375

O

Object Placement dialog box, 207
Object Protection command, 207
OBJECT.PROTECTION macro function, 661-662
objects, 202
adding to charts, 243-245
attachment to cells, 666
bring to front, 649
bringing to front, 472-473
copying, 212-213
cutting, 212-213
deleting, 212-213
detaching from cells, 206
displaying, 764-766
filling, 210
graphic
formatting, 208-209
locking, 207-208
moving, 205

Index 945

resizing, 206
selecting, 204
sizing, 205
grouped, 215-216, 477, 499
layered, 214-215
linking with macros, 713-714
moving, 656
multiple, 204, 212-213, 661
on cell borders, 202
pasting, 212-213
placing, 484-485
protecting, 149, 767-768
selecting, 44
selecting all, 204
send to back, 669
sending to back, 492-493
OFFSET( ) function, 758-759
ON.DATA macro function, 698
ON.KEY macro function, 698
ON.RECALC macro function, 698
ON.TIME macro function, 698
ON.WINDOW macro function, 699
one-input tables, 264-266, 851-852
one-to-many relationship, 285
one-to-one relationship, 285
ONLY.SHOW.TOTALS Q+E
    function, 798
Open command, 53
Open dialog box, 53, 126, 282
OPEN macro function, 639-640
OPEN Q+E function, 798
OPEN.INDEX Q+E function, 799
OPEN.LINKS macro function, 640
opening files, 448, 695, 798-799
operators
    – (subtraction), 35, 111
    * (multiplication), 35, 111
    + (application), 35
    + (addition), 111
    / (division), 35, 111
    ^ (exponentiation), 35, 111
    % (percentage), 111
    < (less than), 69

<= (less than or equal to), 69
<> (not equal to), 69
= (equal to), 69
> (greater than), 69
>= (greater than or equal to),
    69
cell referencing, 110
    in formulas, 110
Like, 289
Not Like, 289
reference
    , (comma), 112
    (space), 112
    : (colon), 112
text, 110-111
options, 608
    area chart, 88
    Automatic Except Tables, 122
    bar charts, 89
    Calculate Now, 761
    Calculation, 762-763
    Category (X) Axis Labels, 81
    Chart, 74
    Color Palette, 763-764
    column chart, 90
    Configure, 98
    Consolidate, 130
    Control Panel, 97
    Copies, 86
    Create Backup File, 52
    Display, 764-766
    Don't Move or Size with Cells,
        206
    Extract, 160
    File Format, 51-52
    Find, 158-159
    Form, 65
    formatting, 50
    Formulas, 31
    Freeze Panes, 766-767
    Gallery, 74
    Hidden, 149
    Left Column, 131

line chart, 91
Locked, 149, 207-208
Mailing Labels, 299
Move and Size with Cells, 206
Outline dialog box, 144
Page Setup, 99-100
Paste Arguments, 114
Paste Special, 222
pie chart, 91
printing, 97
Protect Document, 767-768
Protection Password, 52
QueryFile, 299
Read-only recommended, 52
Rounded Corners, 209
Run, 59-60
scatter chart, 92
Set Extract, 160
Set Page Break, 769-770
Set Print Area, 770-771
Set Print Titles, 771-772
Shadow, 209
Short Menus, 772-774
Size, 99
Solver, 275-276
Source, 281
Top Row, 131
window, 24
Workspace dialog box, 121-122
Write Reservation Password, 52
X-values, 81
XY-Chart, 81
options button, 275-276, 310-311
Options dialog box, 52, 146
OR logic, 156
OR( ) function, 774-775
Order SQL clause, 295
orientation, 95
OS/2, starting Excel, 26
OUTER.JOIN( ) Q+E functions, 799
outline buttons, 39
Outline dialog box, 140, 144
OUTLINE macro function, 677

outlines, 39, 139-144, 677
  clearing, 145
  collapsing, 142
outlining tools, 141-142
Oval tool, 42, 203
overlay chart, 231-234
overlays
  deleting, 619
  formatting, 657-659
  in 2-D charts, 617

P

page breaks
  inserting, 769
  removing, 688, 770
  setting manual, 688
Page Setup command, 98
Page Setup dialog box, 98, 101
Page Setup options, 99-100
PAGE.SETUP macro function,
  641-642
PAGE.SETUP Q+E function, 799
PARSE macro function, 627
PARSE.LINE Q+E function, 800
parsing, 385-386, 800
Password Confirmation dialog box,
  147
passwords, 145-148
Paste Arguments option, 114
Paste Fieldnames dialog box, 312
Paste function, 37
Paste Function command, 38, 164,
  172
Paste Function dialog box, 38, 113
Paste Function menu, 114
PASTE macro function, 633
PASTE Q+E function, 800
Paste Special dialog box, 223
Paste Special option, 222
PASTE.APPEND Q+E function, 800
PASTE.LINK macro function, 633
PASTE.PICTURE macro function,
  633

PASTE.PICTURE.LINK macro
   function, 633
PASTE.SPECIAL macro function,
   634-635
pasting
   data, 125
   fieldnames, 312
   functions, 114, 512-513
   in macro sheets, 60
   objects, 212-213
   to Clipboard, 800
patterns, 214, 663-665
   fill, 210-211
   formatting, 245-247, 487-489
Patterns command, 208
Patterns dialog box, 209
PATTERNS macro function, 662-665
percentages, 31
PI( ) functions, 778
pie charts, 90-91, 229, 682
PLACEMENT macro function,
   665-666
plotting, 219-222
   area, 364, 621
   controlling, 222-224
   multiple selections, 225
PMT( ) function, 779-780
Point mode, 36-37
pointers
   dragging, 5
   mouse
      question mark, 19
      shapes, 6-7
positioning lines, 202
POKE macro function, 699
PPMT( ) function, 781-782
precedents, 520
PRECISION macro function, 687
PREFERRED macro function, 682
Presentation Manager, 26
previewing, 455-457, 644
print area, 104
Print command, 103-104

Print dialog box, 86, 101-103
PRINT macro function, 643
Print Preview command, 101
PRINT Q+E function, 800
PRINT.PREVIEW macro function,
   644
Printer Setup command, 95
Printer Setup dialog box, 96
PRINTER.SETUP macro functions,
   644
printers
   choosing, 95
   configuring, 98
   drivers, 96
   identifying, 644
   installing, 97
   settings, 95
   specifications, 454-455
printing, 103-104, 453-454, 641-643,
   800
   charts, 86
   margins, 101-103
   multiple copies, 104
   notes, 751
   options, 97
   pages, 104
   preview, 101-103
   previewing, 455-457, 644
   print area, 689
   reports, 272-273
   sections, 104-105
   titles, 689
   titles, specifying, 771-772
PRODUCT( ) function, 784-785
PROMOTE macro function, 612
PROPER( ) function, 786
Protect Document dialog box, 150
Protect Document option, 767-768
PROTECT.DOCUMENT macro
   function, 687-688
protecting, 661, 687
   cells, 473-474, 767-768
   disks, 146-148

documents, 148, 150, 207
graphic objects, 149
objects, 767-768
windows, 767-768
worksheets, 768
Protection Password option, 52
PV( ) function, 787-788

Q

Q+E (Query and Editing), 166, 279
   files, 281-283
   functions, 788-789
      ACTIVATE, 789
      ADD.AFTER, 789
      ADD.BEFORE, 789
      ADD.CONDITION, 790
      ADD.RECORD, 790
      ALLOW.EDIT, 790
      ARRANGE.ALL, 791
      CLOSE, 791
      CLOSE.INDEX, 791
      COLUMN.WIDTH, 791
      COMMAND, 791
      COPY, 792
      COPY.SPECIAL, 792
      CUT, 792
      DEFINE, 792
      DEFINE.COLUMN, 793
      DEFINE.FIELD, 793
      DEFINE.INDEX, 793
      DELETE, 794
      DELETE.FIELD, 794
      DELETE.RECORDS, 794
      DISTINCT, 794
      ECHO, 795
      EXIT, 795
      FETCH, 795
      FETCH.ADVISE, 795
      FETCH.UNADVISE, 795
      FIND, 796
      FIND.NEXT, 796
      FIND.PREVIOUS, 796
      FONT, 796
      FORM.SETUP, 797
      FORM?, 796
      GOTO.RECORD, 797
      JOIN, 797
      KEYS, 797
      LOGOFF, 797
      LOGON, 797
      MOVE.COLUMN, 798
      ONLY.SHOW.TOTALS, 798
      OPEN, 798
      OPEN.INDEX, 799
      OUTER.JOIN( ), 799
      PAGE.SETUP, 799
      PARSE.LINE, 800
      PASTE, 800
      PASTE.APPEND, 800
      PRINT, 800
      QUERY.NOW, 800
      REMOVE.COLUMN, 801
      SAVE, 801
      SAVE.AS, 801
      SAVE.LABELS.AS, 802
      SAVE.QUERY.AS, 802
      SAVE.TEXT.AS, 802
      SELECT.AREA, 803
      SELECT.COLUMNS, 803
      SELECT.DELETED.RECORDS, 803
      SELECT.RESET, 803
      SORT.ASCENDING, 803
      SORT.DESCENDING, 803
      SORT.RESET, 804
      SQL.QUERY, 804
      TOTALS, 804
      UNDO, 804
      UPDATE.ALL, 804
      USE.INDEX, 804
   installing, 280
   linking to Excel with SQL statement, 307-308
   linking to other applications, 305-307

menu commands, 296
    accessing through Excel, 318-319
    starting, 281-283
queries, 801
QUERY.NOW Q+E function, 800
QueryFile, 281
QueryFile option, 299
querying databases, 288
QUIT macro function, 644

R

RAND( ) function, 807-808
range of cell addresses, 810-812
ranges, 27
    clearing, 419
    copying, 420-422
    criteria, 153-158, 388
    database, 154
    deleting, 423
    extract, 160
    inserting, 425-426
    moving, 422-423, 426-427
    outlining, 139
    text, filling evenly, 661
RATE( ) function, 808-809
rates, 753
read-only documents, 147-148
Read-only recommended option, 52
Record command, 169
Record macro command, 715-716
Record Number indicator, 67
records, 63, 68
    adding, 162-163, 300, 385, 790, 800
    conditions, 790
    copying, 381-382
    deleting, 67, 162-163, 300, 794
        multiple, 153
    displaying, 68, 803
    duplicating, 302
    editing, 162-163, 300, 791
        SQL, 314-315

extracting, 160-162, 390-391
    external database, 312-313
    SQL, 314-315
inserting new, 67
matching, 68
moving between, 66, 383-385
previous, 67
searching, 158-159, 287-288, 382-383
selecting, 288-290
sorting, 163, 288
    ascending order, 803
    desending order, 804
    unsorting, 804
Rectangle tool, 42, 203
references, 810-811, 820
    absolute, 328, 708, 810
    cell, 173-174
    changing, 515
    changing from absolute to relative, 813
    circular, 263
    external, 438
    names, 501-502
    relative, 810-813
    remote, 813-814
REFTEXT macro function, 712
REGISTER macro function, 699
relative cell referencing, 173
Relative Record macro command, 716-717
relative references, 810-813
RELREF macro function, 713
remote references, 813-814
REMOVE.COLUMN Q+E function, 801
REMOVE.PAGE.BREAK macro function, 688
removing page breaks, 770
RENAME.COMMAND macro function, 173, 195, 197, 707
repeating command, 11
Replace command, 163

REPLACE( ) function, 814-815
reports
    Answer, 273
    Limit, 273
    printing, 272-273
REPT( ) function, 816
REQUEST macro function, 699
resizing
    object, 206
    windows, 20
RESTART macro function, 700
Restore command button, 67
RESULT macro function, 700
RETURN macro function, 700
RIGHT( ) function, 818
rotation angles, 229
ROUND( ) function, 819
Rounded Corners option, 209
rounding numbers, 819
ROW( ) function, 820
ROW.HEIGHT macro function, 666
rows, 26, 223
    blank, 65
    demoting, 142
    height, 490, 666
    hiding, 794
    inserting, 163
    promoting, 142
    selecting, 803
    sorting, 69-70, 628
ROWS( ) function, 821
Run command, 97, 176
Run dialog box, 60, 176
Run macro command, 717-718
RUN macro function, 193, 683
Run option, 59-60
running macros, 193-194
"running marquee" highlight, 77

S

Save As command, 47-50
Save As dialog box, 298
Save command, 47

SAVE macro function, 644
SAVE Q+E function, 801
Save Worksheet As dialog box, 47-48
SAVE.AS macro function, 644-646
SAVE.AS Q+E function, 801
SAVE.LABELS.AS Q+E function, 802
SAVE.QUERY.AS Q+E function, 802
SAVE.TEXT.AS Q+E function, 802
SAVE.WORKSPACE macro function, 646
saving
    charts as separate documents, 84
    embedded charts, 85
    files, 457-458
        Q+E, 298-300
    linked worksheets, 129
    query definitions, 801
    to query files, 802
    without calculating, 124
Scale command, 248-249
SCALE macro function, 667-669
scaling, 75-76, 248-249, 491-492, 667-669
scatter charts, 92, 82, 682
screens
    Help, 18
    updating, 706, 795
scroll bars, 66, 158
scrolling, 526, 674
    windows, 611, 616
    with keyboard, 29
SEARCH( ) function, 824-825
searching
    backwards, 158
    for fields, 287-288
    for formulas, 508-509
    for records, 158-159, 287-288, 382-383
SECOND( ) function, 826
seconds (time), 826
Select dialog box, 205
SELECT function, 172, 612-614
Select SQL clause, 295

Select Workgroup dialog box, 134
SELECT.AREA Q+E function, 803
SELECT.CHART macro function, 621
SELECT.COLUMNS Q+E function, 803
SELECT.DELETED.RECORDS Q+E function, 803
SELECT.END macro function, 614
SELECT.LAST.CELL macro function, 677
SELECT.PLOT.AREA macro function, 621
SELECT.RESET Q+E function, 803
SELECT.SPECIAL macro function, 677-678
selecting
    columns, 803
    dialog boxes, 188
    fields, 286-287
    parts of chart, 224-225
    records, 288-290
    rows, 803
SELECTION macro function, 713
Selection tool, 44
Send to Back command, 214
SEND.KEYS macro function, 700
SEND.TO.BACK macro function, 669
serial number, 828
series, 386-388
    adding to, 234, 239-241
    axis, 248-249
    chart, 620
    data, 75, 80
    date, 256
    deleting, 234, 239-242
    distribution, 233-234
    editing, 234, 239-241
    formula, 236-239
    growth, 256
    linear, 256
    multiple, 257
    names, 223
    overlapping, 233
Series command, 255-257
Series dialog box, 256
Set External Database dialog box, 310
Set Extract option, 160
Set Page Break option, 769-770
Set Print Area option, 770-771
Set Print Titles option, 771-772
Set Recorder macro command, 718-719
SET.CRITERIA macro function, 628
SET.DATABASE macro function, 628
SET.EXTRACT macro function, 628
SET.NAME macro function, 700
SET.PAGE.BREAK macro function, 688
SET.PREFERRED macro function, 682
SET.PRINT.AREA macro function, 689
SET.PRINT.TITLES macro function, 689
SET.UPDATE.STATUS macro function, 614
SET.VALUE macro function, 701
Setup command button, 101
Shadow option, 209
shapes
    drawing, 201
    exact, 202
    linking with macros, 45
Shift Key commands, 10
short menus, 9, 689
Short Menus option, 772-774
SHORT.MENUS macro function, 689
shortcuts, keyboard
    with Alt and Ctrl keys, 7
    with function keys, 8
Show Active Cell command, 526
Show Info window, 295
SHOW.ACTIVE.CELL macro function, 678-679
SHOW.BAR function, 198, 707

SHOW.CLIPBOARD macro function, 692
SHOW.DETAIL macro function, 615
SHOW.INFO macro function, 692
SHOW.LEVELS macro function, 615
SIGN( ) function, 831
SIN( ) function, 832
sine, 832-833
Single Step dialog box, 176
single-output array formulas, 259
SINH( ) function, 833
Size command, 253
SIZE macro function, 624
Size option, 99
sizing
    arrows, 253, 493-494
    graphic objects, 205
    legends, 253
SLN( ) function, 834
Solver, 269-272, 528-529
    constraints, 273-275
    options, 275-276
    resetting, 835
    saving problems, 276-277
    starting, 270
    with macros, 277-278
Solver command, 269
Solver dialog box, 272-273, 528
Solver functions
    SOLVER.ADD, 836
    SOLVER.CHANGE, 836
    SOLVER.DELETE, 836
    SOLVER.FINISH, 835
    SOLVER.LOAD, 837
    SOLVER.OK, 834
    SOLVER.OPTIONS, 837
    SOLVER.RESET, 835
    SOLVER.SAVE, 837
    SOLVER.SOLVE, 835
Solver Options dialog box, 275
Solver Parameters dialog box, 269-272
Solverex subdirectory, 269

Sort command, 69
Sort dialog box, 70-71
sort keys, 70-71
SORT macro function, 628-629
SORT.ASCENDING Q+E function, 803
SORT.DESCENDING Q+E functions, 803
SORT.RESET Q+E function, 804
sorting
    columns, 628
    data, 391-393
    databases, 69-72
    multiple columns, 288
    order, 71
    records, 163, 288, 803-804
    rows, 70, 628
sound, 606
source files, 284
Source option, 281
SPLIT macro function, 615
splitting windows, 615
SQL (Structed Query Languange), 294-297
    clauses, 295-296
    editing, 296-297
    editing records, 314-315
    extracting records, 314-315
    opening a query window, 297
    scroll box, 295
    Server, 294
    statements, 294-296
        clauses, 294
        to link Excel and Q+E, 307-308
SQL.QUERY Q+E function, 804
SQRT( ) function, 838
square root, 838
squares, 202-203
STANDARD.FONT macro function, 689
Start Recorder macro commands, 719-720

starting Excel
  from DOS, 25
  under OS/2, 26
  with a mouse, 23-24
  with keyboard, 24
statements, SQL, 294-296
statistical functions, 901
status bar, 27, 838-839
STDEV( ) function, 839-840
STDEVP( ) function, 841-842
Step function, 178
STEP macro function, 701
straight-line depreciation, 834
Structured Query Language (SQL), 294-297
styles, 39, 494-497, 648, 651
  deleting, 652
  merging, 661
subdirectories, 49
  Library, 179
  Solverex, 269
SUBSTITUTE function, 843-844
SUM function, 37, 40, 113, 845-847
sum-of-years' digits depreciation, 850
SUMPRODUCT( ) function, 848-849
SYD( ) function, 849-850
symbols
  clearing, 145
  formatting, 34

T

T( ) function, 851
Table command, 264
Table dialog box, 265
TABLE macro function, 629
tables, 851
  creating, 629
  data, 264
  editing, 268-269
  lookup, 269
  one-input, 264-266, 851-852
  selecting, 853
  two-input, 264, 266-268, 852
  what-if analysis, 264
TAN( ) function, 853-854
tangent, 853-854
TANH( ) function, 854
TERMINATE macro function, 701
testing macros, 176
text, 247
  alignment, 41-43, 333-334, 497-498
  arrays, 340
  attaching to chart, 618
  boxes, 44, 66, 359-360
    formatting, 660
  capitalization, 786
  converting imported, 366
  entering, 31
  functions, 901-902
  justified, 478-479
  operators, 110-111
  rearranging, 661
  reformatting, 796
  replacing, 675
  spacing, 866
  too long, 31
  uppercase, 872
  values, 532, 757, 855
Text Box tool, 44
Text command, 247
Text dialog box, 54
TEXT( ) function, 856-857
TEXT.BOX macro function, 615
TextFile, 281
TEXTREF macro function, 713
tick marks, 76, 247
time, 556, 904
  entering, 32
  formatting, 32, 657, 857-858
  increasing, 256
  inserting into formula bars, 858
  minutes, 733
  seconds, 826
TIME( ) function, 859

TIMEVALUE( ) function, 860
title bar, 26
titles
    printing, 689, 771-772
    short, 220
    transferring, 131
TODAY( ) function, 861
Tool bar, 3, 38, 77
tools
    Arc, 42, 203
    Button, 45
    Camera, 45
    Chart, 44, 77
    drawing, 203
    Line, 42, 203
    Multiple Selection, 213
    outlining, 141-142
    Oval, 42, 203
    Rectangle, 42, 203
    Selection, 44
    Text Box, 44
    Toolbar, 39
Top Row option, 131
totals
    adding, 804
    hiding, 798
    removing, 804
Totals dialog box, 293
TOTALS Q+E function, 804
tracepoints, 179
transferring
    categories, 131
    titles, 131
TRANSPOSE( ) function, 861-862
TREND( ) function, 862-865
trigonometric functions, 903
TRIM( ) function, 865-866
troubleshooting functions, 115
TRUE( ) function, 866-867
TRUNC( ) function, 867-868
two-input table, 264-268, 852
TYPE( ) function, 868-869
typface, *see* font

U

underlining, 185
Undo command, 10
UNDO macro function, 636
UNDO Q+E function, 804
undoing commands, 10-11, 804
UNGROUP macro function, 669
Unhide dialog box, 119
UNHIDE macro function, 692
UNLOCKED.NEXT macro function, 616
UNLOCKED.PREV macro function, 616
UNREGISTER macro function, 701
UPDATE.ALL Q+E function, 804
UPDATE.LINK macro function, 646-647
UPPER( ) function, 872
uppercase text, 872
USE.INDEX Q+E functions, 804

V

value axis, 248-249
VALUE( ) function, 873-874
values, 874-877
    absolute, 327
    average, 345
    averaging, 398
    cell, changing, 701
    computed field, 66
    constant, 371
    displayed calculation, 123-124
    displaying, 178-179
    error, 434-435, 875
    field, 64-65
        altering, 66
        blank, 67
        restoring, 67
    function, 532
    investments, 536
        present, 787

limits, 273
logical, 532, 599-600
median, 727
naming, 503-505
negative, 31
nonblank, 401
numbers, 532, 757
numeric, 373-375
storage space, 687
text, 532, 855
VAR( ) function, 877-878
VARP( ) function, 879-880
VDB( ) function, 880-881
VIEW.3D macro function, 669-670
viewing notes, 750-751
VLINE macro function, 616
VLOOKUP function, 269, 882-884
VOLATILE macro function, 701
VPAGE macro function, 616
VSCROLL macro function, 616-617

W

WAIT macro function, 701
WEEKDAY( ) function, 887-888
what-if analysis in tables, 264
Where SQL clause, 295
WHILE macro function, 701
WHILE( ) macro sheet function, 173
wildcards, 53, 68
Window Arrange All command, 888-889
Window Arrange Workgroup command, 135
Window Hide command, 889-890
Window menu, 15, 119
Window New Window command, 890-891
window option, 24
Window Show Info command, 891-893
Window Unhide command, 893

Window Workgroup command, 894-895
windows, 13
    activating, 606
    active, closing, 623, 791
    application, 14, 26
    arranging, 888
    Chart, 79
    closing, 795
    creating, 691
    define, 303
        activating, 789
        opening, 792
    document, 14, 26
    Excel, 24
    freezing panes, 687, 766-767
    hidden, 692
    hiding, 691, 890
    info, 692
    manipulating with mouse, 16-17
    maximizing, 622
    minimizing, 622
    moving, 622
    protecting, 767-768
    query
        activating, 789
        opening, 297
    rearranging, 691, 791
    resizing, 20
    scrolling, 611, 616
    Show Info, 295
    sizing, 611, 624
    split, 615
    unhiding, 893
WINDOWS macro function, 713
WORKGROUP macro function, 692-693
workgroups, 134-136, 894-895
    adding documents, 136
    commands, 137-139
    copying contents, 136
    creating, 692
    editing, 137
    entering data, 136

worksheets, 26
    changing display, 765-766
    charts, embedded, 78
    functions, 533, 895
    linked to charts, 84
    linking, 127-129
    moving around in, 29
    protecting, 768
    range, criteria, 157-158
    saving, 47-49
workspace, 117-120
    opening, 639
    saving, 646
    settings, 690
    settings, controlling, 773-774
Workspace dialog box, 120-122, 773-774
WORKSPACE macro function, 690
Write Reservation Password option, 52

X–Y–Z

x coordinate, 185
x-axis, 75-76, 360-361
X-values option, 81
.xlc (chart) file extension, 83
.xlm (macros) file extension, 83
.xls (worksheet) file extension, 49, 83
XY-Chart option, 81

y coordinate, 185
y-axis, 75-76, 360-361
YEAR( ) function, 904

Zoom command button, 101
zooming fields, 287

Sams—Covering The Latest In Computer And Technical Topics!

Audio

Advanced Digital Audio	$39.95
Audio Systems Design and Installation	$59.95
Compact Disc Troubleshooting and Repair	$24.95
Handbook for Sound Engineers: The New Audio Cyclopedia, 2nd Ed.	$99.95
How to Design & Build Loudspeaker & Listening Enclosures	$39.95
Introduction to Professional Recording Techniques	$29.95
The MIDI Manual	$24.95
Modern Recording Techniques, 3rd Ed.	$29.95
OP-AMP Circuits and Principles	$19.95
Principles of Digital Audio, 2nd Ed.	$29.95
Sound Recording Handbook	$49.95
Sound System Engineering, 2nd Ed.	$49.95

Electricity/Electronics

Active-Filter Cookbook	$24.95
Basic Electricity and DC Circuits	$29.95
CMOS Cookbook, 2nd Ed.	$24.95
Electrical Wiring	$19.95
Electricity 1-7, Revised 2nd Ed.	$49.95
Electronics 1-7, Revised 2nd Ed.	$49.95
How to Read Schematics, 4th Ed.	$19.95
IC Op-Amp Cookbook, 3rd Ed.	$24.95
IC Timer Cookbook, 2nd Ed.	$24.95
RF Circuit Design	$24.95
Transformers and Motors	$29.95
TTL Cookbook	$24.95
Understanding Digital Troubleshooting, 3rd Ed.	$24.95
Understanding Solid State Electronics, 5th Ed.	$24.95

Games

Master SimCity/SimEarth	$19.95
Master Ultima	$16.95

Hardware/Technical

First Book of Modem Communications	$16.95
First Book of PS/1	$16.95
Hard Disk Power with the Jamsa Disk Utilities	$39.95
IBM PC Advanced Troubleshooting & Repair	$24.95
IBM Personal Computer Troubleshooting & Repair	$24.95
Microcomputer Troubleshooting & Repair	$24.95
Understanding Fiber Optics	$24.95

IBM: Business

10 Minute Guide to PC Tools 7	$ 9.95
10 Minute Guide to Q&A 4	$ 9.95
First Book of Microsoft Works for the PC	$16.95
First Book of Norton Utilities 6	$16.95
First Book of PC Tools 7	$16.95
First Book of Personal Computing, 2nd Ed.	$16.95

IBM: Database

10 Minute Guide to Harvard Graphics 2.3	$ 9.95
Best Book of AutoCAD	$34.95
dBASE III Plus Programmer's Reference Guide	$24.95
dBASE IV Version 1.1 for the First-Time User	$24.95
Everyman's Database Primer Featuring dBASE IV Version 1.1	$24.95
First Book of Paradox 3.5	$16.95
First Book of PowerPoint for Windows	$16.95
Harvard Graphics 2.3 In Business	$29.95

IBM: Graphics/Desktop Publishing

10 Minute Guide to Lotus 1-2-3	$ 9.95
Best Book of Harvard Graphics	$24.95
First Book of Harvard Graphics 2.3	$16.95
First Book of PC Paintbrush	$16.95
First Book of PFS: First Publisher	$16.95

IBM: Spreadsheets/Financial

Best Book of Lotus 1-2-3 Release 3.1	$27.95
First Book of Excel 3 for Windows	$16.95
First Book of Lotus 1-2-3 Release 2.3	$16.95
First Book of Quattro Pro 3	$16.95
First Book of Quicken In Business	$16.95
Lotus 1-2-3 Release 2.3 In Business	$29.95
Lotus 1-2-3: Step-by-Step	$24.95
Quattro Pro In Business	$29.95

IBM: Word Processing

Best Book of Microsoft Word 5	$24.95
Best Book of Microsoft Word for Windows	$24.95
Best Book of WordPerfect 5.1	$26.95
First Book of Microsoft Word 5.5	$16.95
First Book of WordPerfect 5.1	$16.95
WordPerfect 5.1: Step-by-Step	$24.95

Macintosh/Apple

First Book of Excel 3 for the Mac	$16.95
First Book of the Mac	$16.95

Operating Systems/Networking

10 Minute Guide to Windows 3	$ 9.95
Best Book of DESQview	$24.95
Best Book of Microsoft Windows 3	$24.95
Best Book of MS-DOS 5	$24.95
Business Guide to Local Area Networks	$24.95
DOS Batch File Power with the Jamsa Disk Utilities	$39.95
Exploring the UNIX System, 2nd Ed.	$29.95
First Book of DeskMate	$16.95
First Book of Microsoft Windows 3	$16.95
First Book of MS-DOS 5	$16.95
First Book of UNIX	$16.95
Interfacing to the IBM Personal Computer, 2nd Ed.	$24.95
The Waite Group's Discovering MS-DOS, 2nd Edition	$19.95
The Waite Group's MS-DOS Bible, 4th Ed.	$29.95
The Waite Group's MS-DOS Developer's Guide, 2nd Ed.	$29.95
The Waite Group's Tricks of the UNIX Masters	$29.95
The Waite Group's Understanding MS-DOS, 2nd Ed.	$19.95
The Waite Group's UNIX Primer Plus, 2nd Ed.	$29.95
The Waite Group's UNIX System V Bible	$29.95
Understanding Local Area Networks, 2nd Ed.	$24.95
UNIX Applications Programming: Mastering the Shell	$29.95
UNIX Networking	$29.95
UNIX Shell Programming, Revised Ed.	$29.95
UNIX: Step-by-Step	$29.95
UNIX System Administration	$29.95
UNIX System Security	$34.95
UNIX Text Processing	$29.95

Professional/Reference

Data Communications, Networks, and Systems	$39.95
Handbook of Electronics Tables and Formulas, 6th Ed.	$24.95
ISDN, DECnet, and SNA Communications	$49.95
Modern Dictionary of Electronics, 6th Ed.	$39.95
Reference Data for Engineers: Radio, Electronics, Computer, and Communications, 7th Ed.	$99.95

Programming

Advanced C: Tips and Techniques	$29.95
C Programmer's Guide to NetBIOS	$29.95
C Programmer's Guide to Serial Communications	$29.95
Commodore 64 Programmer's Reference Guide	$24.95
Developing Windows Applications with Microsoft SDK	$29.95
DOS Batch File Power	$39.95
Graphical User Interfaces with Turbo C++	$29.95
Learning C++	$39.95
Mastering Turbo Assembler	$29.95
Mastering Turbo Pascal, 4th Ed.	$29.95
Microsoft Macro Assembly Language Programming	$29.95
Microsoft QuickBASIC Programmer's Reference	$29.95
Programming in ANSI C	$29.95
Programming in C, Revised Ed.	$29.95
The Waite Group's BASIC Programming Primer, 2nd Ed.	$24.95
The Waite Group's C Programming Using Turbo C++	$29.95
The Waite Group's C: Step-by-Step	$29.95
The Waite Group's GW-BASIC Primer Plus	$24.95
The Waite Group's Microsoft C Bible, 2nd Ed.	$29.95
The Waite Group's Microsoft C Programming for the PC, 2nd Ed.	$29.95
The Waite Group's New C Primer Plus	$29.95
The Waite Group's Turbo Assembler Bible	$29.95
The Waite Group's Turbo C Bible	$29.95
The Waite Group's Turbo C Programming for the PC, Revised Ed.	$29.95
The Waite Group's Turbo C++Bible	$29.95
X Window System Programming	$29.95

Radio/Video

Camcorder Survival Guide	$ 14.95
Radio Handbook, 23rd Ed.	$39.95
Radio Operator's License Q&A Manual, 11th Ed.	$24.95
Understanding Fiber Optics	$24.95
Understanding Telephone Electronics, 3rd Ed.	$24.95
VCR Troubleshooting & Repair Guide	$19.95
Video Scrambling & Descrambling for Satellite & Cable TV	$24.95

For More Information, See Your Local Retailer Or Call Toll Free
1-800-428-5331

All prices are subject to change without notice. Non-U.S. prices may be higher. Printed in the U.S.A.

Count On Sams For All Your Spreadsheet Needs

The First Book of Excel 3 for Windows
Christopher Van Buren
320 pages, 7 3/8 x 9 1/4, $16.95 USA
0-672-27359-4

The First Book of Quattro Pro 3
Patrick Burns
300 pages, 7 3/8 x 9 1/4, $16.95 USA
0-672-27367-5

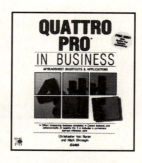

Quattro Pro In Business
Chris Van Buren
400 pages, 7 3/8 x 9 1/4, $29.95 USA
0-672-22793-2

SAMS

See your local retailer or call 1-800-428-5331.